This monumental compendium of cosmopolitical provocations and decolonial insights does more than just correct the misreadings that have threatened recently to engulf and mystify Fanon's work. These exhilarating essays and commentaries put his incendiary contribution back where it belongs: in the insurgent speculations and reconstructive efforts of creative thinkers struggling to transform the imperiled predicament of our planet. —**Paul Gilroy,** founding Director of the Sarah Parker Remond Centre for the Study of Race and Racism at University College London

This is a wonderful book. It succeeds in extracting Fanon's thought (the *Wretched/Damned of the Earth* in particular) from the realms of academia, Cultural Studies and Afropessimism and to locate it squarely where it originally belonged: within the domain of political practice, outside of which it makes very little sense. In academic reading, one remains a prisoner of the limits of the text itself; in a political reading, the text becomes a vehicle for addressing the problems raised by active militancy. Gibson has succeeded in bringing together an international array of brilliant contributors who all prove to be eloquent witnesses to the continued relevance of Fanonian concepts—such as the Manichean character of (neo)colonialism and racism, the corrupt nature of the so-called 'national bourgeoisie' and the continued relevance of 'national consciousness'—in the contemporary expanded reproduction of racial capitalism on a world scale. What is particularly fascinating is the way in which intense studies of Fanon's writings within the United States carceral system and South African informal settlements among other locations have enabled the production of political thought that takes Fanonian dialectical categories beyond their original subjective context, into concrete political practices combining the necessary experiences of particular struggles with conceptions of universal freedom. This is a militant work for militant readers. —**Michael Neocosmos,** Emeritus Professor in Humanities, Rhodes University, South Africa.

There is not one time, not one aspect of the world's experience, that does not give credence to Fanon's precepts. Our collective human history has taught us that the human is bound to face attempts to crush her or his integrity, to condemn them to despicable exploitation, treacherous oppression. It is in the very nature of that experience that we have learned how Fanon shall never die. For his precepts and action remain always universally relevant. This is also what Fanon Today affirms. The book is fundamentally relevant and useful. It reminds us that in the face of exploitation and repression, the human and the humanist will always find ways to combat those. Dense and eclectic, strategically thought out and organized, critically stimulating, this book is as incisive as it is compelling. —**Hanétha Véte-Congolo,** President of the Caribbean Philosophical Association

In this collective labor of love of the here and the now, voices of the damned—that pathologized, incarcerated, and evicted majority of the world's population—rise! From Algeria to Brazil, Ireland to Kenya, Palestine to Portugal, South Africa to Trinidad and beyond, they are breathing life into and actively humanizing our precious and oh-so-fragile earth. Meeting brutal structural violence with the courageous construction of democratizing institutions that nurture mental health, well-being, and solidarity, Fanonian praxis emerges in each chapter. Evincing a thoughtful agency that questions everything, the volume forges new relations spanning generations and locales. Through it, sixty years since the publication of *Les damnés de la terre*, Fanon's insights reach out to us, beckoning us to carry on the tireless work of building a world of the "we." —**Jane Anna Gordon**, author of *Statelessness and Contemporary Enslavement*

Coming out of the pandemic, the greatest challenge is how we express our anger, how we make it a *digna rabia*, a "dignified rage", as the Zapatistas say. Fanon must be part of the answer. This magnificent collection of essays helps us to focus our minds on that challenge, to direct our anger to the task of making a different world. An important book, an exciting book. —**John Holloway**, author of *We are the Crisis of Capital: A John Holloway Reader*

*Fanon Today: Reason and Revolt of the Wretched of the Earth*, edited and cordinated by Nigel C Gibson, gives the opportunity to several intellectuals and activists with different backgrounds from Brazil to Algeria, from Pakistan to South Africa, to tell how the struggle against injustice and racism inscribe itself into the continuity of the Fanonian visionary legacy. Not to be missed! —**Hassane Mezine**, Photographer, Film Director of *Fanon hier, aujourd'hui*

This is an indispensable book. It brings together many among the overlooked communities for whom Fanon actually wrote—the dispossessed, the downtrodden, the organic voices rising from the depths of misery on the verge of despair. What better way to commemorate the six decades since the publication of Les damnés de la terre than to remind readers of that great work that the people in solidarity with whom its ideas were generated not only speak but also write? Read and learn from these voices as, in those proverbial revolutionary words, the struggle continues. —**Lewis R. Gordon**, author of *Freedom, Justice, and Decolonization*

In Fanon Today, Nigel Gibson brings to life the Fanonian project of exploring the implications of radical theory in contemporary sites of struggles. This groundbreaking book commemorates the 60th anniversary of the Wretched of the Earth by exploring its significance in the work of intellectuals and organizers active in radical social movements. Fanon Today is a timely book about the turbulent present and its connections to the long history of racial capitalism. It is a landmark addition to the field of Fanonian studies and an absolutely necessary reading for anyone interested in decolonial thought and social movements. —**Yasser Munif**, author, *The Syrian Revolution: Between the Politics of Life and the Geopolitics of Death*

*Fanon Today* does not just bring Fanon into the immediate present, it also restores Fanon as a thinker of praxis, of organisation and struggle. There are a growing number of attempts to retrieve Fanon's thought from its immediate historical context and put it to work in the present. But there are very few that show much interest in the fact that most of Fanon's work was produced and grounded within struggle, within popular struggle. In keeping with Fanon's own internationalism his thought is brought into struggles in Palestine, Pakistan, Ireland, South Africa, Kenya, the prisons in the United States and more. The worldliness of the work gathered here speaks, implicitly but lucidly, to the spirit of a thinker who was, always, in motion towards the world. Edited by Nigel Gibson, a leading Fanon scholar, including work by a group of exciting younger thinkers, and graced by a contribution from Ato Sekyi-Otu, also one of the best Fanon scholars, and a singular philosophical presence in the examination of the contemporary African condition, the book has real intellectual heft. It is essential reading for anyone who aims to engage Fanon as a comrade in struggle rather than solely as an interlocutor in more isolated and abstracted forms of academic theorizing.
— **Richard Pithouse**, Editor, *New Frame* and author of *Being Human After 1492*

# FANON TODAY

## Reason and Revolt of the wretched of the earth

Edited by
Nigel C. Gibson

**Daraja Press**

Published by
Daraja Press
https://darajapress.com
2021

ISBN 9781990263019

Cover design: Kate McDonnell
Image of Fanon: Anastasya Eliseeva

Library and Archives Canada Cataloguing in Publication

Title: Fanon today : revolt and reason of the wretched of the Earth / Nigel C. Gibson.
Names: Gibson, Nigel C., editor.
Description: Includes bibliographical references.
Identifiers: Canadiana (print) 20210134313 | Canadiana (ebook) 20210138998 | ISBN
    9781990263019 (softcover) | ISBN 9781990263026 (ebook)
Subjects: LCSH: Fanon, Frantz, 1925-1961—Influence. | LCSH: Fanon, Frantz, 1925-
    1961—Political and social views. | LCSH: Imperialism. | LCSH: Decolonization. |
    LCSH: Postcolonialism.
Classification: LCC JC273.F36 F36 2021 | DDC 325/.3—dc23

# CONTENTS

# INTRODUCTION: THE RISING OF THE DAMNED

NIGEL C. GIBSON

Fanon's title *Les damnés de la terre* resonates with the opening lines of Eugéne Pottier's song *The Internationale*, written after the defeat of the Paris Commune in 1871: *Debout! Les damnés de la terre* (*Arise! the damned of the earth*). The *damnés de la terre* of Paris and their Commune (Pottier was elected to the Council of the Commune) were the harbingers of a new society. Fanon's title also connects with the Haitian communist negritude poet and novelist Jacques Roumain, who writes of the rising of *les damnés de la terre* in the conclusion to the poem *Sale nègre*, included in his 1945 collection *Bois-d'Ebène* (*Ebony Wood*). At the end of the poem, Roumain invokes the rising of *les damnés de la terre*, who ...

> have learned the language
> of the Internationale
> for we will have chosen our day...
>
> And here we are arisen
> All the damned of the earth
> all the upholders of justice
> marching to attack your barracks
> your banks
> like a forest of funeral torches
> to be done
> once
>   and
>     for
>       all
> with this world

Fanon had read Roumain's novel *Gouverneurs de la rosée*, about peasant life and solidarity, and quoted Roumain in *Black Skin, White Masks*. Fanon's first reference to the poem comes at the end of an article he wrote for *El Moudjahid* that was published in January 1958, *In the Caribbean, birth of a nation* (Fanon, 2017: 583-590). Fanon quotes from the beginning of the poem that 'we won't accept it anymore'.

The damned of the earth in Roumain's poem are the majority of the world's population: working people struggling to survive, hemmed in by seemingly normalized structures, discourses of domination, and everyday racial, gender, and class violence. The objects of this cascading violence are those who are constantly pathologized and incarcerated, as well as those who refuse and resist and have 'learned the language of the Internationale'.

In the conclusion to *Les damnés de la terre*, Fanon writes to his comrades, reflecting his concern about the creation of a society based on new and real human relations. He asks his comrades to flee from Europe's 'motionless movement' and to instead consider 'the future of humanity', the question of cerebral reality and the cerebral mass of all humanity, whose connections must be increased, whose channels must be diversified and whose messages must be rehumanized. He adds that this is not just about humanizing the world: 'We must invent and we must make discoveries. For Europe, for ourselves, and for humanity, comrades, we must turn over a new skin, [and] we must work out new concepts'[1] (1968: 203, 313, 316, translation altered).

There is something refreshing in Fanon's imperatives that speak to us as we face the multiple crises in this sixtieth year of Fanon's *Les damnés de la terre* and as we work with those struggling not only to survive, but to be free. It is this dialectic—of the movements from practice reaching for a new society and the 'fluctuating movement which... [the people] are giving shape to'—which is a form of theory with which we must engage. In the careful and painstaking work of praxis, a future can be seen in the present, where 'our perceptions and our lives are transfused with light' (1968: 227). It is these moments that I hope this book can help elucidate and promote.

Fanon died sixty years ago at the age of thirty-six. Almost sixty years later, the eighty-three-year-old President of Algeria Abdelaziz Bouteflika was forced to resign following mass demonstrations across the nation. Sixty years earlier, Bouteflika was part of the National Liberation Front (FLN) group leading the Malian Front on the Algerian southern border. This might well have been the second time he met Fanon, during Fanon's reconnaissance mission in the fall of 1960. (The first time was when he helped an injured Fanon in 1959.) In addition, according to Claudine Chaulet, who worked with the FLN in Tunis, "Boutefika was one of the many ... scribe/typists of *The Wretched of the Earth* (Cherki, 2006: 152). This is one connection across generations, but it is not one at all that indicates the continued resonance of Fanon's writings today. While Fanon in 2021 is having a remarkable afterlife in academic disciplines, one focus of this book is on the thinking and conversations with Fanon especially among activist and militant intellectuals both within and also connected to movements for social change. This was certainly Fanon's intention for writing *Les damnés de la terre* in 1961.

---

1. '*Camarades, il faut faire peau neuve*' (Fanon, 2011: 676) is not translated as 'new skin' in either English translation (see Paris, 2017). I am using the earlier Constance Farrington translation of *Les damnés de la terre* because it is still the one widely available, and in many ways preferable. One drawback of the translation, as well as its dated language, is that she translates *le colon* as 'settler' and *le colonisé* as 'native' rather than as colonizer and colonized. For a discussion of the Farrington and Philcox translations see Gibson, 2007.

# Translations

Fanon and Alioune Diop, the founder of the journal and publishing house *Présence Africaine*, had agreed by late 1960 that *Présence Africaine* would publish an English translation of *Les damnés de la terre*. This first English translation, by the Irish woman and sympathizer of the Algerian revolution Constance Farrington, was titled *The Damned*. It was published by *Présence Africaine* in 1963. Fanon and Diop had made the agreement with the understanding that the book would be accessible to African activists and intellectuals in the newly independent, former Anglophone colonies, such as Ghana, Kenya,[2] and the White-ruled Southern Rhodesia and South Africa (see Batchelor, 2017: 49-51). There is little evidence that it was widely distributed, and soon Grove Press in New York owned the English-language rights.

In a letter to Grove Press, Constance Farrington thought the book should be titled *The Rising of the Damned*, which, for her, would have an immediate anti-imperialist resonance (See Batchelor, 2017: 49). But Grove took no notice and in 1965 they reprinted the *Présence Africaine* English edition (containing the same paginations and French quotation marks) with a new cover and new title, *The Wretched of the Earth*. The first British edition, with the Farrington translation, was also published in 1965. In 1961, Editora Ulisseia published a Portuguese translation, *Os Condenados da Terra*; and in 1963, *Fondo de Cultura Económica* published a Spanish translation, *Los condenados de la tierra*, both of which refer to *les damnés*. Both of these translations were important to Fanon's work becoming known in Latin America. In 1968, Grove Press repaginated the book in the first Black Cat edition, and it was this edition, with its orange and black cover, that was republished 19 times over a ten-year period, selling over a million copies. By 1968, the popularity of these translations meant that *Les damnés de la terre* was available beyond Francophone Africa. But it is the later Grove Press editions in the United States that help drive the internationalization of Fanon's thought and the explicit political use of his writings within the context of the Black revolutionary struggle in the US.

Fanon had no doubt about the revolutionary character of the Black dimension in the US. While he lamented the situation in the Antilles, he remarks in *Black Skin, White Masks* that 'Black Americans are living a different drama'. In *The Wretched of the Earth*, Fanon, perhaps referring to Robert Williams, writes of Black radicals in the US arming themselves (1968: 39).

By the late 1960s, *The Wretched of the Earth* had become a 'bible' of the revolutionary movements and Fanon's writings became influential as the struggle moved from civil rights to Black Power in the US and took on a global dimension. By the 1970s, it was recognized for its global vision and revolutionary humanism (Turner and Alan, 1986) and was being read by Irish revolutionaries

---

2. Batchelor notes that Ngugi wa Th'iongo first became familiar with Fanon while reading the *Présence Africaine* edition (see 2017, 51).

interned in Long Kesh, as well as Black Consciousness intellectuals in South Africa. But by the 1980s, with 'Third Worldism' giving way to neoliberalism and structural adjustment, interest in Fanon's *Les damnés de la terre* declined. New academic engagements with Fanon in emergent fields such as postcolonial studies in the 1990s elevated Fanon's *Black Skin, White Masks* as a key text while *The Wretched of the Earth* became less studied and often dismissed as outdated. At the same time, Fanon, whose texts had been marginal in the academy, moved from the street to the seminar room. Over the past twenty years, this has helped herald new studies of Fanon and new translations of his work. Perhaps more importantly, it has helped herald the possibility of new connections between a new generation of readers and their grassroots struggles. Sixty years after its publication, Fanon's *Les damnés de la terre* is again being considered a handbook for social change as the famous American edition of *The Wretched of the Earth* declared it to be, 'the handbook for the Black revolution that is changing the shape of the world' (quoted in Bhabha, 2004: xvi).[3]

## Why Fanon, Why Now?

> It is always easier to recognize a new stage of revolt than a new stage of cognition, especially when the movement from practice is first striving to rid itself of what William Blake, in the age of revolutions ... had called 'mind-forged manacles'.
> —Lou Turner and John Alan, *Frantz Fanon, Soweto & American Black Thought*

Why has the *Wretched of the Earth* become the handbook for the revolution? Quite simply, as Flavio Zenun Almada argues here, 'because our conditions have not improved since Fanon's time and in some cases have worsened'. Resistance, and sometimes mass revolutionary movements, thus continue to emerge.

Sixty years after Fanon's *The Wretched of the Earth*, these revolts and resistances—local and global, often seemingly new and unique in their ways and locales—find a resonance with Fanon, the revolutionary humanist. The fearless and remarkable organizing in Sudan (2018), Algeria (2019), Chile (2019), Hong Kong (2014-2020), and the global movements for Black Lives (2020-21) are just some examples. And yet, despite their massive size, prolonged existence, and occasional success (such as in Algeria and Sudan), the movements sometimes fade, burn out, or accept limited promised reforms. They are often also the subject of enormous state-sanctioned violence and mass arrests.

The opening to the last decade's hope, and then dismay, was the Arab Spring, which began in Tunisia and deepened in Egypt with the overthrow of Mubarak in 2011. In many ways, the movements echoed what Fanon argues to be the

---

3. This re-emergence is not completely new. Almost thirty years ago, in a quite different moment after the end of apartheid rule in South Africa in 1994 and a high point of neoliberal optimism, Stuart Hall declared that it had become the 'Bible of decolonization'.

strengths and weaknesses of spontaneity: first, as massive outpourings that out-flank the political elites and experience a thrilling sense of power; and then, as the elites change course—allowing elections and abandoning political leaders in some cases—they regain the upper hand. In Egypt, the military played a control-ling role: first as so-called neutrals above politics, and then as a counter-revolu-tionary force, using the moment of popular discontent with the newly elected government to mount a military coup. Struggles did continue but with a tremen-dous cost in terms of human life, military-police-state violence and mass incar-ceration. In Tunisia, ten years after President Ben Ali's removal, the movements are stilled but not defeated. There have been victories, compromises, and also threats of regression alongside the rise of armed Islamist groups. The political system is weakened by corrupt political practices which, alongside structural economic crisis, continue to mean pauperization for the majority. While Tunisia is considered by some the 'lone success story' of the Arab Spring, the Arab Win-ter and the politics of death reached its apogee in Syria, where reaction to the Syrian revolution by the Assad regime meant the systematic murder, imprison-ment, and forcible uprooting of millions of people.

In Syria, it was a new generation of revolutionaries who emerged to support the children who had been arrested and tortured after they had painted the slo-gan 'The people want to topple the regime' in Daraa, on Syria's southern bor-der with Jordan, in 2011. The peaceful revolution that spread across the country was countered by an increasingly violent response from the regime, where the destruction of a living movement for human liberation required necropolitics on an industrial scale. In the context of the 'War on Terror', the Assad regime unleashed a systematic 'cleansing' as a politics of divide and rule, dismissing the revolutionaries as terrorists while releasing thousands of radical Islamists from security prisons to encourage the undermining of the revolution from the inside. In Syria today, mass imprisonment and torture are normalized and brutality is taken to its logical conclusion. Indeed, for many years after the Arab Spring, other regimes in North Africa and West Asia used Egypt and Syria as warnings to activists to tone down demands.

In Egypt and Syria we see two types of nationalism: the authoritarian state with the ethnicized nationalism of the Baath Party in Syria alongside El-Sisi's military-political regime in Egypt on one hand, and the dynamic cultural praxis of popular nationalism on the other. The former's focus, from its beginnings—as it was across the region—was rooted in seizing and maintaining state power and was akin to many nation-state building projects criticized by Fanon. It took the form of an authoritarian, one-party, military rule. Both regimes operate through a politics of death, including imprisonment of activists and journalists, extraju-dicial killings, forced disappearances, and sexual violence. In Syria, the politics of death meant targeted chemical attacks and urbicide with carefully calculated uses of technology (like targeting hospitals and bakeries), indiscriminate bomb-ing, and chemical attacks (see Munif, 2020). After a decade, Assad has regained control over most of the country, with the aid of Hezbollah fighters and Russian bombers.

What S'bu Zikode calls the politics of blood is seen globally from South Africa to Brazil, and from Palestine to Portugal: a permanent state of emergency, as Walter Benjamin puts it, which 'is also a "state of emergence".' (quoted in Bhabha, 1999: 183). The movements discussed in this book are often politics outside of, or at a distance from, the state. Their interest is not in taking over state power, but in encouraging new forms of horizontal and democratic organization, which, however fleeting and messy, are part of a movement from practice that recognizes the importance of thinking, of reaching for the future, and of attempting to get rid of 'mind-forged manacles' (quoted in Turner and Alan, 1999: p. 68) of unfreedom. What we might call the living politics that emerged, mindful of the internal contradictions, compromises, and opportunism—often justified by desperate situations—is one focus of this book.

Struggles are stilled and struggles continue, and at the same time, reckonings with Fanon's *The Wretched of the Earth* haunt us. In the final chapter of the book, Fanon wonders whether 'these notes on psychiatry will be found ill-timed and singularly out of place in such a book' (1968: 249). If that was the case then, it is certainly not the case today, where ideas of generational trauma and post-traumatic stress, as well as the social-economic character of mental health, are no longer considered marginal but ongoing. This recognition is a good thing, but how can one read Fanon's words—that one need only study a 'single day under a colonial regime ... to appreciate the scope and depth of the wounds inflicted on the colonized'—without thinking of the present reality as a 'breeding ground for mental disorders' (1968: 182-183)?

## Pandemic

The COVID-19 pandemic has not stopped freedom struggles. Indeed, it is commonplace to hear how the pandemic has not only shone a light on structural inequalities but has also exacerbated them. As Ato Sekyi-Otu puts it here, 'the pandemic has made inequalities and the geography of class injustice a demonstrable, incontrovertible fact' confirmed by 'the visible social organization of opulence and destitution', and by government lockdowns and isolation configured for the one percent. Over a year into the pandemic, the situation has not changed as the intersections of race and class become expressed as two societies in the United States, with Black and Brown people dying at three times the rate of Whites, and poor people dying at four times the rate. The problem is not only one of co-morbidities but also one of what doctors at Martin Luther King Hospital in Los Angeles call the 'medical desert', where people live with chronic shortages of primary care and other health services.[4] In Brazil, the situation is also acute along race and class lines as Deivison Fausto writes here of what he calls the genocide of Black people in Brazil.

---

4. See, for example, the story in the *New York Times*, https://www.nytimes.com/2021/02/08/us/covid-los-angeles.html

The talk of co-morbidities has quickly moved from the ontogenic to the socio-genic, from the ontology of the poor and the sociology of public health to structural racism and inequality. Fanon was among the first revolutionary writers to focus on mental trauma arising from colonialism, racism, and their legacies. The intimate connections Fanon drew between health and politics, from his early essay on 'The "North African Syndrome"' to the last chapter of *The Wretched of the Earth* on 'Colonial War and Mental Disorders', continue to highlight the practical and theoretical usefulness of Fanon's psychiatric praxis for those working in and thinking about health and healing in dehumanized situations. A psychiatrist by training, Fanon did not give up on his concerns about the traumatic and devastating psychological effects of colonialism, racism, and war on mental health after he resigned from Blida-Joinville Psychiatric Hospital in Algeria in 1956. However, still aware of these factors as well as the new context created by the revolutionary struggle, Fanon remained optimistic about the creation of a dis-alienated society. And to those subjugated to constant dehumanization, the work to address the demoralization and 'inferiority complexes' buried deep within them remains as crucial as it did in Fanon's time. In 2018, Richard Horton, the editor of global health journal *The Lancet,* titled a 'comment' as 'Frantz Fanon and the origins of global health' before later retitling it 'Frantz Fanon's Manifestos'. And the present reality is not far from Fanon's Manichean projection, seen clearly in manifest ways during this pandemic and expressed throughout this book, that 'what parcels out the world is to begin with the fact of belonging to or not belonging to a given race' (1968: 40).[5]

It is welcome that Fanon is receiving mainstream recognition. The publication of articles and new books on Fanon and mental health as well as the publication of an English translation of his psychiatric papers (Fanon, 2018) have helped open up his work into fields of mental health where it had often been marginalized, ignored, or dismissed.

This volume was originally conceived before the COVID-19 pandemic. The commemorative deadline, sixty years since the publication of *The Wretched of the Earth* and the death of its author, meant the time for its publication was set. The subtitle *Reason and Revolt of the Wretched of the Earth* refers both to Fanon's book and to the reason and maturity of contemporary revolts. The title could as well be 'the revolt and reason of the wretched of the earth' since, for Fanon, it is the mass movements themselves that creates a radical mutation in consciousness (Fanon, 1965). But Fanon also insists on the reason of revolt, including those 'attempts drowned in rivers of blood', in his demand to 'sanction all revolts' (1968: 207). This indicates how the dialectic of reason and revolt needs to be underscored and deepened in practice.

---

5. On the political economy of the COVID-19 vaccine see Achal Prabhala, Arjun Jayadev and Dean Baker, 'Want Vaccines Fast? Suspend Intellectual Property Rights', https://www.nytimes.com/2020/12/07/opinion/covid-vaccines-patents.html. On 'vaccine apartheid', see 'Wealthy Nations Block Effort to Waive Vaccine Patent Rights' https://www.democracynow.org/2021/3/11/rich_countries_block_vaccine_patent_waiver

All the chapters were written during the COVID-19 pandemic as well as during the global anti-police violence movement for Black Lives. Just a few months after the March 2020 COVID-19 lockdown in Nigeria, more people had been killed by the police than by COVID-19 in the country. Furthermore, multiple police murders had already occurred in Kenya (15 people), South Africa (12 people), and Uganda (6 people). Compiled during the time of loss and the brilliant clarity of the George Floyd moment across the world,[6] Fanon's words from *Black Skin, White Masks* became immediately concrete: 'they revolted [q]uite simply ... because it became impossible for them to breathe, in more than one sense of the word' (2008: 201). George Floyd's last words and Fanon's words reemerged on social media and movement posters.[7] The global revolt was not only an expression of the will to survive against the daily threat of death and the violence of police racism; it was also what Fanon called a 'combat breathing' (1965: 65), a breathing felt and seen in the global character and the depth of the struggle that has put American civilization on trial.

*Fanon Today: The Reason and Revolt of The Wretched of the Earth* is by no means exhaustive: it is rather something fragmentary, reflecting the moment. Given the lockdowns, repression, imprisonment, and ill-health, some authors had to drop out. There is one chapter that could not be completed that I want to mention here, which was on the anti-racist movement in France. France still promotes itself as non-racial and its politicians still insist that the police aren't racists.[8] This is the France almost seventy years after Fanon's 'The "North African Syndrome"' and *Black Skin, White Masks*, where Black and Brown people, Africans and Arabs, are routinely targeted for identity checks, subjected to arbitrary arrest, police violence, and death, and where Fanon is being 'rediscovered' in activist circles and his concepts are being actively engaged in practical ways.[9]

From the outset, *Fanon Today: The Reason and Revolt of The Wretched of the Earth* was conceived as a collection of contemporary activist engagements with Fanon's work. It did not eschew the academic but wanted academics to come down from their intellectual towers and engage with these movements. In this sense, the volume is just one iteration of an ongoing project to reflect and engage with Fanonian practices and I hope it will encourage others.[10]

---

6. With protests taking place in over 60 countries around the world.
7. According to the *New York Times*, more than 40 people have been recorded being killed by police after warning, 'I can't breathe'. 'Three Words. 70 Cases. The Tragic History of "I Can't Breathe"', by Mike Baker, Jennifer Valentino-DeVries, Manny Fernandez and Michael LaForgia. See https://www.nytimes.com/interactive/2020/06/28/us/i-cant-breathe-police-arrest.html Critical of legislation to reform the police (The George Floyd Justice in Policing Act passed in the US House of Representatives in March 2021), the Movement for Black Lives argues that there can be no justice in 'a system born of White supremacy and slave patrols' and has been advocating for the BREATHE act to re-imagine public safety based on investment in communities.
8. Of course, France is not alone. But where Britain's declaration of non-racialism is pragmatic (see David Olusoga, 'The poisonously patronising Sewell report is historically illiterate', https://www.theguardian.com/commentisfree/2021/apr/02/sewell-race-report-historical-young-people-britain), France's denialism is embedded in its philosophic universalism.
9. See, for example, the engagement with Fanon in Lilian Thuram's *La Pensée Blanche* (Paris: Mémoire D'Encrier, 2020). After reading *Black Skin, White Masks* Thuram gave a copy of that book to all the Black players on the world cup team and reflects today that he should have given a copy to the White players as well.
10. Lou Turner and Helen A. Neville's *Frantz Fanon's Psychotherapeutic Approaches to Clinically Work: Practicing Internationally with Marginalized Communities* is one such work, not only because it engages Fanon's 'psychopathol-

The focus of this book is the here and now. The chapters all begin from specific places and experiences, which also have global ramifications. The driving force of each is what I call Fanonian practices or, perhaps better, Fanonian praxis.[11] The work is not primarily intended to make discursive interventions into disciplinary fields but, as I have said, to engage with activists and intellectuals who are working toward radical social change. The sharing of these reflections is part of the work to humanize the world, and one question discussed throughout is, 'How can we connect with Fanon, the revolutionary, and develop new beginnings in action and in thought?'

Fanon was always a thinker who looked to enable the individual to reflect on thoughtful action. Sixty years after his death, what are the resonances and practical usages of Fanon by movements from below? In addition, I hope the collection, as a whole, can be educational in the vein of James Saki Sayles' remarkable *Meditations on Frantz Fanon's Wretched of the Earth* (2010). To that end, we have tried to make the book widely available to activist and radical circles through Daraja Press, which encourages distribution among grassroots movements at minimal cost. Familiarity with Fanon's writing is not necessary; rather, the connection with Fanon comes from the reader's own lived experiences.

## The Chapters

*Fanon Today: The Reason and Revolt of The Wretched of the Earth* has three parts. Each begins with a blacked-out-poem by Leah Kindler based on Fanon's *The Wretched of the Earth*.

## Part I: Fanonian Militants

The first section, 'Fanonian Militants', connects militant struggles globally—from Trinidad to England and from Kenya and South Africa to the United States—by telling part of the continuing story of grassroots resistance, thought, and organization through Fanonian perspectives of grassroot activists.

The book opens with Flavio Zenun Almada's 'The Particular Lived Experience of the Black in Portugal', specifically from the Lisbon 'ghetto' Cova da Moura, where the experience of Portuguese racism, police violence, torture, and the murder of Black youth drew him to Fanon. Analyzing this current situation

---

ogy of colonization/decolonization' with 'his dialectics of revolution' but also because of its emphasis on action and praxis: Fanon's clinical and psychotherapeutic practices, the uses of Fanon in clinical work, training clinicians and serving 'underserved communities of color around the world' (2020: 1).

11. In my book, *Fanonian Practices in South Africa: From Steve Biko to Abahlali baseMjondolo*, I gave three examples of Fanonian practice. First, Steve Biko's intellectual engagement with Fanon, which would result in the development of the Black Consciousness Movement and the beginning of the end of apartheid; second, a critique of post-apartheid South Africa using Fanon's concepts; and third, the emergence and thinking of new movements, like the shack dweller movement, Abahlali baseMjondolo. For me, the idea of Fanonian praxis is not at all limited to South Africa, but rather, the emphasis was on the praxis of engaging and using Fanon in different Fanonian locations, not simply geographically but also specifically from the perspective of the majority of the world.

through Fanon, he concludes that he lives in a city of *de facto apartheid* that Fanon describes in *The Wretched of the Earth*. In addition, Zenun Almada recounts how he first found Fanon and how reading *Black Skin, White Masks* gave him a deep understanding of his experience as a Black man living in racist Portugal. He suggests reading groups should be set up in every corner of the world, 'above all in the shanties, favelas, hoods, ghettos, *palanques*, *musseques* and barrios' where people will quickly identify with Fanon's words. 'Fanon wrote about them even without knowing them', he says. The new generation of readers now, he argues, has made Fanon's work more fundamental for the 21st Century, especially to those who 'dare to struggle' for a 'new humanity'.

Zenun Almada's personal reflections of finding Fanon in Cova da Moura in the 21st Century is echoed by Gene Reid, a Black worker in Los Angeles (L.A.), who has been studying Fanon since 1975. 'Black Mind in Motion' focuses on Black consciousness and the importance of the clarity of ideas in action to the transformation of reality. He gives two examples: first, Colin Kaepernick's 'act of defiance' realized as a 'new Black reality' as people across sports take a knee before games; and second, his experience of the gang truce in Watts as part of the 1992 L.A. rebellion. It was an event that scared the cops because it reflected a new power in the hands of the people in the community. The police did everything they could to break the truce. Fanon's *Black Skin, White Masks* spoke to him when he found it in 1975 and Fanon's *Wretched of the Earth* helped him understand his own experiences as a young man in the South after his grandfather compromised 'the revolutionary act of a Black being voted into political office in the newly integrated South' by working within the system.

Los Angeles, of course, has been the scene of important urban revolts and it should not be forgotten that the uprising in 1992 began in response to the acquittal of the police officers who had beaten Rodney King (which had been caught on videotape just as the murder of George Floyd was recorded by a teenager, Darnella Frazier). California was also the vanguard of the new incarceration scheme in the wake of the 1960s revolts and the increasing criminalization of Black youth connected to 'the war on drugs', which evolved into the judicial policy of 'three strikes you're out'. As Ruth Gilmore (2007) argues, the state's building of new prisons was connected to deindustrialization and surplus finance capital in the 1970s as well as the subsequent demand to produce 'criminals' to fill massive new prisons.

The revolutionary perspective from inside the prison sets the stage for Toussaint Losier's 'Setting Afoot a New People': Prison Intellectuals, New Afrikan Communism and the Making of *Meditations on Frantz Fanon's Wretched of the Earth*' which engages Sanyika Shakur and his learning of Fanon in the incarcerated 'university.' Shakur came across Fanon through James Yaki Sayles' important and essential piece of work on Fanon, *Meditations on Frantz Fanon's Wretched of the Earth*, written over many years from within the Illinois prison system in the form of a reading and study guide. In his introduction, Sayles says he had to read the book four times before he began to get an outline of the argument and suggests a careful reading which academics, who might claim to know Fanon, should also undertake. He then quotes Fanon's warning about 'wily intellectuals':

the 'same know-all, smart, wily intellectuals' who reproduce 'the manners and forms of thought picked up during their association with the colonialist bourgeoisie' (quoted in Sayles, 2010: 146-7). Sayles began circulating the first of what would become several pamphlets, *The 'Setting Afoot' of a New People*, in the early 2000s and his teachings have made unique contributions to the study of Fanon.

In 2011, Sanyika Shakur circulated two essays hinting at the continued influence of Fanon's *The Wretched of the Earth* and Sayles' *Meditations* among New Afrikan communists. Like Gene Reid, Losier underlines the importance that Sayles places on consciousness in his reading of Fanon, which he argues is more than 'guns and grenades' but rather the need to 'push people to question everything' as the 'key to it all'. The idea of the 'new Afrikan', concludes Losier, is more than skin color; rather, in Fanonian terms, it is to 'foster a new humanity'.

Connected with Fanon's discussions of a Manichean colonial world as discussed in the chapter by Zenun Almada, Wangui Kimari, an activist from Mathare Social Justice Centre in Nairobi, details the work of mothers whose children have been killed by the police within Nairobi's compartmentalized colonial geographies. In 'Looking for Justice in a Compartmentalized World: Mothers and Police Killings in Kenya', she discusses their experiences within these spaces of hunger and violence and, above all, their work to end the alienation and indifference to oppression they face on a daily basis. Theirs are efforts to make evident colonial violence in a postcolonial world, even as colonialism is regarded as past, and they simultaneously demand justice for the killings of their children. As part of their ungovernable activism, their 'rational revolts' demand recognition, equality, and justice while seeking to undo the violent dichotomies of their colonial worlds. Certainly, 'penetrat[ing] inside this compartmentalization', as Fanon puts it, can 'bring to light some of its key aspects' and also 'the backbone on which the decolonized society' can be built (see Fanon, 2004: 3).

In 'From "Caliban" to "Cockroaches": The Construction of Profane Space, Wretched Others, and Political Agency in a Postcolonial "Ghetto",' Johannah-Rae Reyes and Levi Gahman draw on their work as activists and engaged researchers connected with community members from Morvant, Trinidad. They employ the concepts of profane space and anticolonial explicatory insights offered in *The Wretched of the Earth* to provide an analysis of state-sanctioned violence in Trinidad. In doing so, they share with readers the rationality of revolt from Morvant. Here, they reiterate Ato Sekyi-Otu's (1996: 10) call from twenty-five years ago that 'the time has indeed come to remember Fanon' by casting light upon structural violence and taking seriously both the political agency and critical thought of people who reside in the 'hot spot' (i.e. high crime) community of Morvant. Reyes and Gahman focus on one such event in late June 2020, when three unarmed Afro-Caribbean men were gunned down by the police, spurring mass protests nationwide—during which another Afro-Caribbean woman, who was speaking out against police brutality, was shot and killed by the police. The killings, they argue, laid bare both the persistent coloniality of the Westminster-modeled Government of Trinidad and Tobago and the ways in which race, class, and space in Trinidad are inextricably linked to state violence and alienation.

S'bu Zikode's 'The Power of Abahlali and Our Living Politic[12] Has Been Built with Our Blood' was first given as a talk at American University in Washington in February 2021. It articulates with earlier discussions in this section about state violence and murders and engages many Fanonian concepts, giving voice to the rationality of revolt and the form of grassroots democratic organization in the context of the continuity of the colonial idea found in the post-apartheid ANC government in South Africa, as well as in universities and NGOs, that poor African people cannot think for themselves. Zikode speaks of the birth of Abahlali baseMjondolo as a response to the 'betrayal' by local ANC leaders as land promised was sold off. As brutal and unlawful evictions continue to terrorize communities, the price for land, for decent housing and the right to the city, is paid in blood. Zikode gives an important example of Fanon's idea of a living culture focusing on women's participation in the movement. Noting that while in the village women have a strategic power to influence or voice their opinion through male partners or neighbors, in Abahlali, where the majority of members are women and meetings are often run by women, male leaders are chosen by women and they know that they are accountable to women. 'This example shows', he argues, 'how our movement draws on our culture and history, sometimes advancing it quite radically, to build a movement, a movement that has survived for 15 years despite very serious repression'. The existence and growth of Abahlali (which is now the largest social movement in South Africa) in the context of ongoing repression underscores, Zikode argues, how 'the question of land, the question of the right to the cities and the question of building a participatory democracy were never resolved' because 'we were never allowed to participate in decision-making'. Zikode concludes by discussing Fanon's quote that 'Each generation must discover its mission, fulfill it or betray it'. In the face of all kinds of threats, humanity has to rise. And as Abahlali has emerged facing severe repression by the ANC who have become 'new oppressors', it has discovered its mission and, Zikode adds, 'we are in a process to fulfill it or betray it'. The scars and sacrifices that many comrades in Abahlali have borne are the scars and the sacrifices not only of Abahlali 'but to the struggle to humankind all over the world whose mouths are shut, who cannot say or express what they want to say'.

In 'Fanon and Palestine: The Struggle for Justice as the Core of Mental Health', psychiatrists Samah Jabr and Elizabeth Berger discuss the relevance of Fanon's work to mental health and wellbeing in occupied Palestine and also the importance of international solidarity initiatives as crucial elements of 'action in history'. The authors review the social/psychological conditions of the present moment. They discuss how emerging theory and practice within mental health reflect Fanon's contributions regarding Palestinian life under colonialism,[13] clin-

---

12. Editor's note, S'bu Zikode has always used the term politic, not politics, as it reflects a way of speaking in a form of English and feels closer to the Zulu term.
13. See, for example, Stephen Sheehi and Lara Sheehi, 'The settlers' town is a strongly built town: Fanon in Palestine', *Applied Psychoanalytic Studies*, May 2020.

ical problems encountered, the utility and lack of utility of prevailing psychiatric diagnoses and therapeutic interventions, and the nature of recovery as an aspect of social renewal and transformation. Akin to Fanon's case studies in the final chapter of *The Wretched of the Earth*, they begin their chapter with three vignettes and commentaries, which underscore and recognize the role of the occupation in individual patients' pathologies. The occupation is the 'framework within which psychological experience in Palestine takes place and often the engine driving psychological distress'.

In 'Reading the Term "White Syrian" through Fanon: An Anti-Colorist Feminist Critique', Razan Ghazzawi, an '"insider' blogger-activist' and queer feminist organizer in Syria, writes of their own experiences in the Syrian uprising, emphasizing the importance of words, terms, and feelings. Some new words that emerged within the uprising turned out to mobilize silence. Ghazzawi's focus is on the use of the term 'White Syrian', which became increasingly deployed among activists and refugee communities in exile. Initially, it was used to build bridges with Black people's struggles by renaming and framing the communities as 'Black Syrians', who were surviving different forms of oppression in the liberated areas, and calling those who live and benefit from the Assad state 'White Syrians'. Focusing on the intellectually uncritical and Manichean theorization of 'good' and 'bad', Ghazzawi highlights how the term White Syrian became quickly transformed and used to discipline, shame, and bully nonconforming revolutionary voices in the uprising, including those who demanded a different form of protest. In discussions with feminists and activists, Ghazzawi shows how words were used to discredit anti-militarist views, thereby closing down discussion of what self-determination for Syria would look like. Written from within the revolutionary movement and drawing from Fanon's work, Ghazawi considers the important questions of how language can be fixed by binary constructions, becoming a dead weight that silences people and ideas.

Annette Rimmer uncovers similar potent political forces in 'Voice of the Revolution: Radio and Women's Empowerment'. Using Fanon's 'This is the Voice of Algeria' from *A Dying Colonialism*, Rimmer explores the stories of a group of women who train as community radio producers and presenters at Shout FM, an urban community station in Northern England exploring the potential of feminist radio pedagogy and activism to break women's silence and enable their transformation into *privileged actors*. In their narratives, the women come to voice their own intersectional identities and challenge preconceived notions of womanhood, pornification, racial stereotyping, and objectification. The process of feminist radio pedagogy—problematizing, learning together and building relationships—raises consciousness and confidence to assert their own self-determination.

## Part II: Still Fanon

What David Pavón-Cuéllar's refers to as the stillness of Fanon has a double meaning. Fanon is still with us, and Fanon's analysis that bourgeois society is ossified and 'stills' human development into motionlessness and immobility still characterizes the postcolony.[14] It is the story of revolution and the whip of counter-revolution. Pavón-Cuéllar's concern is those who are still not liberated by what he calls 'imaginary decolonization'. They are still here in situations not very different from those Fanon talked about. The ruling elites know that those 'who take a stand against this living death are in a way a revolutionary'. They are both increasingly desperate and increasingly sophisticated. In her earlier chapter, Razan Ghazzawi calls Syria a 'military-carceral-paranoid' state, and this is not unique to Syria since one can see its form emerging across the world in response to mass movements. The goal is to destroy solidarity by creating a fragmented population through the internalization of fear of surveillance and detention and through a culture of distrust and self-censorship. In Syria, this stilling was successful for almost thirty years after the 1982 Hama massacre.

Yet, revolt occurs seemingly out of nowhere, breaking out from a long period of quiescence and often sparked by basic needs. For example, the massive *El Estallido Social* demonstrations in Santiago, Chile (2019-2020), the largest ever in the nation's history, started in reaction to a subway fare increase and quickly demanded the resignation of the president. The revolts in Lebanon in 2019-2021 (the 'October 17 Revolution') began in response to increased taxes on gasoline and quickly became a systemic critique of corruption and sectarianism, demanding the resignation of the government. While the cycle of these revolts globally is often repressive, the shutting down of means of communication, the crushing, killing, and incarceration of activists to immobilize movements and silence their leaders, and the threat of their re-emergence haunts the leaders.

This part begins with Ayyaz Mallick's reading of the immediacy of Fanon's analysis of the national bourgeoisie to contemporary Pakistan and is one that brings light to issues that have hounded the postcolonial world since Fanon. In 'Pakistan: The Immediacy of Frantz Fanon', Mallick asks how does this inept, senile and unproductive bourgeois caste holds power, and how we can begin to understand the seeming stillness and quietness in one postcolony when revolts and rebellions of the poor are proliferating in others.

In his chapter, Ato Sekyi-Otu asks why it is all quiet in the Ghanaian non-settler postcolony. Ghana, unlike South Africa[15] and neighboring Nigeria, has seen no collective outrage against inequality and police violence. Where is the popular outrage, and indeed memory, when—on a street corner in Cape Coast, close to Cape Coast Castle—Africans were sold and exported to the Americas, and the police beat a young man to a pulp who was supposedly guilty of breaking

---

14. The stillness 'weighs upon everyone with a 20,000 lb, force, do you feel it?' Marx asked in an 1856 speech at an anniversary of the *People's Paper*. And this is exactly the point. A feeling of trappedness and pointlessness. A feeling that we cannot win and forgetting that moment and time when all seemed possible. Thus we shout with Rosa Luxemburg, 'Order reigns in Berlin, you lackeys ... I was, I am, I shall be!' Luxemburg, 'Order Reigns in Berlin', January 14, 1919.

15. Abahlali baseMjondolo notes that the police in South Africa kill someone every twenty hours, a rate of close to two and a half times per capita as the police in the United States. They call this 'permanent slow Marikana', adding, 'yet there is no mass movement here against police violence'. ('The State Continues to Murder with Impunity', March 15, 2021 Abahlali baseMjondolo press statement http://abahlali.org/node/17235/).

COVID-19 restrictions? Confronted by this 'speechless void', Sekyi-Otu wonders whether 'the discursive conditions of insurgent politics' needs 'rethinking'. Faithful to Fanon's commitment to the 'practice of democratic enlightenment, we must hold onto the idea that a nascent emancipatory politics "gives proof of its rationality to itself",' Sekyi-Otu concludes. The challenge for a radical politics, he adds, is to attend to the cries of human suffering and hear the 'agonized pantings' of all those who cannot breathe.

Similarly, David Pavón-Cuéllar's 'The Still Wretched of the Earth: A Critique of Imaginary Decolonization' suggests that Fanon is still relevant because the wretched of the earth are still here. Fanon still speaks to the people of the 'Third World' and taking Fanon seriously, Pavón-Cuéllar argues, forces us to denounce how the independence of former colonies has merely concealed colonial violence, making it surreptitious, and thus contributes to the continuation of colonialism by other means. Indeed, this stillness and motionlessness is normalized. There seems to be nothing that can be done. This is reproduced in the institutionalized dehumanization reflected in the 'psychological services' and the global mental health industry, where pharmacology and the numbering of diagnoses for the Diagnostic and Statistical Manual of Mental Disorders reflects the negation of subjectivity and the objectification of the human. The objectivity of race and class is at most a statistical calculation which can be managed through coercion and consent. While the focus on corporate institutional racism, which has arrived since the global movement for Black Lives after George Floyd's murder by police, is welcome, the management of institutional racism through countless corporate statements and promotions of 'diversity trainings' and seminars is wholly superficial. Institutional racism is a much more sophisticated and resistant system. Miraj Desai wonders, in 'Of Signs, Symptoms, and Stereotypes: Fanon, Institutional Racism, and Institutional Subjectivity', whether institutions have become subjects to themselves with a haunting consciousness and subjectivity expressed through their reproduction. By socio-diagnosing institutional racism in the fields of health care, medicine, psychiatry, and psychology, Desai hopes to bring greater focus to what he calls institutional syndromes, with their overdetermining, alienating, and objectifying processes. This process of becoming-a-caricature, he argues, can have devastating consequences for individual 'mental health', and for life as internalized racism is repressed within social and institutional structures.

In 'Fanon, Movement and Self-Movement', Nigel C. Gibson emphasizes Fanon as a thinker of movement and self-movement. Biographically, we can track Fanon's short life in a series of critical-reflective movements. And in each of his books, his work as a clinical practitioner and political revolutionary can be viewed with an emphasis on the lack of movement and self-movement. The idea of self-movement takes Gibson into a discussion of Fanon's 'slightly stretching Marxism', in dialogue with Marx and Lenin. Here Gibson turns to David Marriott's discussion of C.L.R. James and Fanon in *Whither Fanon* (Marriott, 2018). Working with the idea of self-movement, Gibson discusses the questions of spontaneity and organization, the centrality of the rationality of revolt, and Fanon's raising the question of a 'lack of ideology' as a major problem at the end of his life as ways of thinking about Fanonian practices in the 21st century.

## Part III: Fanonian Practices

The third part, Fanonian practices, has two sections. Fanon is a man of the world and a revolutionary humanist who continues to be 'claimed' across the world, and thus is at home across the globe. The first section, 'Fanonian Homes', connects Fanon, Fanonian practices and debates to specific contexts, beginning with Fanon's first home in the US and his contemporary homes in Argentina and the North of Ireland, and then moves back to the new revolts in his chosen first home, Algeria. Fanon's home in South Africa has been well-established ever since Biko connected to Fanon through the US Black Power movements and developed the Black Consciousness Movement. Here, that connection continues through a discussion of Fanon with members of Abahlali baseMjondolo as they reflect on the meanings of *The Wretched of the Earth* for their movement. The second section shifts back to Fanonian practices, with three chapters on Fanon in Brazil heralding the new and important engagements with Fanon among intellectuals and activists.

## Fanonian Homes

In 'When Black Liberation Mattered: Frantz Fanon in the Theory and Practice of Pan-Africanism in the Black Power Era, 1965-1975', Lou Turner and Kurtis Kelley consider the revolutionary implications of Fanon's thought as a new generation of Black radical theorists and activists discovered him in the late 1960s and 1970s at a historic moment not unlike the contemporary one. In doing so, they demonstrate why Black radical America became Fanon's first home, not only as a revolutionary icon but also as a philosopher of revolution. It was a time when Black Liberation mattered, they argue, and Fanon's concepts from *The Wretched of the Earth* became important to ongoing discussions. In the face of enormous state repression the revolutionary movement was not realized, the moment faded, and new divides emerged between Black masses and Black leaders who were increasingly drawn away from mass activity. Now, as then, the US is Fanon's largest audience globally, and the question underlying the recreation of Fanonian dialectics of liberation in the US today is whether Black Liberation can matter again?

Alejandro De Oto's 'Fanon, Postcolonial Criticism and Theory: Notes in Latin American Contexts' begins where Turner and Kelley's chapter leaves off in the mid 1970s. But here, considering the Latin American, and specifically Argentine, context, Fanon remained a potent echo in terms such as 'revolution in the Third World' and the 'anticolonial struggle'. But what was the cost, or at least confusion, of the performative effect of his writing, asks De Oto, and how did it influence the ways Fanon's writings fell into oblivion in the academic arena? While Turner and Kelley highlight the importance of Fanon to Black liberation thought in the US in the 1970s, the 'Latin American emancipation theories' of the time never 'reached an articulation with processes of racialization that [Fanon's] writing suggested'. De Oto argues that it was the space opened up by the criticism of modernity by postcolonial criticism and 'the decolonial turn' within the academy that reintroduced, or indeed made possible, Fanon in Latin America. In other words, it was the new Fanon discussed by Homi Bhabha and other post-structuralist theorists in the 1980s that helped question and decenter social theory, bringing out what had been ignored by earlier engagements. By bringing race into focus, which De Oto calls the 'outstanding problem in Fanon's writing', as well as the 'processes of racialization' which are 'inscribed in most social relations in the region', Fanon has made a 'real' return to Latin America.

Feargal Mac Ionnrachtaigh's 'Promoting Sedition: The Irish Language revival in the North of Ireland—Power, Resistance and Decolonisation' draws on interviews with Irish language activists and his own activist work and engagements with Fanon. Born in 1981, the year of the hunger strike and the demand to re-establish political status, Mac Ionnrachtaigh situates himself as a product of the anticolonial struggle and reinforces the centrality of language revival in the North of Ireland to decolonization. Mac Ionnrachtaigh provides a rich history of struggle against British colonization, which ostracized the Irish language and normalized English as the lingua franca. Britain's first colony, Ireland, became a blueprint for a global practice of language colonization and the struggle for national liberation became intimately connected with the struggle for the Irish language. In his retelling, Mac Ionnrachtaigh re-inscribes Fanon's discussion of the three-stage struggle of national culture, paying special attention to the pitfalls of independence while emphasizing the idea of decolonization as an ongoing process. His discussion turns on two major periods. First, he discusses the Irish language movement from the time of the Easter rebellion of 1916 until the Anglo-Irish treaty and the counter-revolution of 1922, when the Free State took over the colonial administrative system and Anglicized Catholicism became the dominant identity divorced from wider socioeconomic issues such as land and rights. And second, he discusses the Irish language revival movement in the 1970s in the North of Ireland, connected to both the education of political prisoners in Long Kesh, 'inspired through the writings of Pearse, Freire, and Fanon', and to language activists' commitment to community revival and the promotion of self-respect in a community that had internalized colonial objectification. The structural limitation of the Good Friday Agreement (1998) can also be understood through a Fanonian lens as it gave initiative back to the colonial state in exchange for limited access to state power. The result was a period of stagnation, regression and division in the context of neoliberal promises and structural crisis. While language activists remained committed at a local level, Mac Ionnrachtaigh concludes by discussing the failure of the political state to protect Irish rights or deliver on its agreements, which catapulted the Irish language struggle back to the center stage of politics after 2016 with the emergence of the grassroots, autonomous *An Dream Dearg* movement.

In 'Generals to the Dustbin, Algeria Will Be Independent: The New Algerian Revolution as a Fanonian Moment', Hamza Hamouchene wonders whether Fanon is just another anticolonial figure from the past, irrelevant for our times, or whether we can learn something from him. While Fanon declared revolutionary Algeria to be his home, he became absent from Algerian political thought soon after his death. Hamouchene wonders what Fanon would say about contemporary Algeria and the new Algerian revolution and uses Fanon to discuss the bankruptcy of the postcolonial ruling elites and the rationality of revolt in the new Algerian revolution. Algerians who had been dazed and fearful for decades took to the street, took over public spaces, and began to make history. Chanting 'Generals to the dustbin', they also recovered their revolutionary credentials, evoking anticolonial veterans and historical figures who fought for freedom sixty years ago with their chants. This new generation is attempting to imagine a very different future.

Fanon has had a home in South Africa since Steve Biko and his comrades read his work and developed Black Consciousness during the apartheid period. After the first fully franchised election which elected the African National Congress (who remain in power), Fanon's critique in *The Wretched of the Earth* has been played out almost by rote. Apartheid might have formally ended, and there are no more pass books, but the exclusion of poor Black people from the cities continues. By 2005 a new generation of activists, disgusted with the betrayal and broken promises, created the shack dweller movement Abahlali baseMjondolo and developed what they call a living politic; they have found connections with Fanon. The roundtable discussion with Abahlali baseMjondolo and the editor took place at their Durban office on March 1, 2020. The discussion was based on a selection of quotes from Fanon's *The Wretched of the Earth*.

Since this meeting, Abahlali have continued to occupy land in Durban, where they are growing vegetables, and have built a political school at the democratically managed occupied land of eKhanana. The school is named the Frantz Fanon Political School where 'Khenana residents regularly gather at their Frantz Fanon School ... built by the residents for lectures on Fanon's philosophy, 'broken down into simple English', or to listen to lectures on social issues and communal living' (Erasmus, 2021).

Abahlali members meet outside the Frantz Fanon Political School. Photo by Nomfundo Xolo, February 21, 2021

Despite the moratorium on evictions during the COVID-19 pandemic, eKhenana was attacked by the local anti-land invasion unit and private security companies. Abahlali baseMjondolo won a court order and the eviction was declared illegal. The violence of evictions is not forgotten and communal buildings and structures are named after activists who have been killed. The Frantz Fanon Political School is located inside the Thuli Ndlovu Community Hall, named after an activist murdered in her home in 2014.

## Fanonian Practices in Brazil

In 'The Influence of Frantz Fanon's Thought on Black Female Intellectual Production In Brazil', Rosemere Ferreira da Silva discusses the work of Neusa Santos Souza and Lélia Gonzalez as essential to the re-emergence of Fanon's thought in contemporary Brazil. Both Souza and Gonzalez, starting with and including dialogical experiences in the Black Movement in Rio de Janeiro and in academia, built bridges between them, raising questions that became essential to understanding the construction of Black identities in Brazil. Both emphasized the importance of emotional life and emotional health in a society where there were few or no practicing Black psychoanalysts. And both were attentive to the relevance of ethno-racial questions, adding a critical voice on the place of the Black in Brazilian society. Now considered ahead of their time, their intellectual trajectories converge decisively in the interpretation of race, gender and class as a fundamental condition for Black existence in Brazil.

In 'The *Wretched* by COVID-19 and the Colonial Faces of Black Genocide in Brazil" Deivison Faustino discusses the contributions of *The Wretched of the Earth* to the comprehension of social and economic relations in societies structured by colonization, specifically the historic and sociological aspects that elucidate the colonial form of the 'entification of capitalism' in Brazil. Proposing a Fanonian analysis of the underlying dialectical relations between capitalism, colonialism, and racism in the current Brazilian political and sanitary juncture, he takes the notion of colonial violence from *The Wretched of the Earth* as a reference to problematize Brazilian responses to the COVID-19 pandemic and the Black genocide from COVID-19 in Brazil.

In 'Territorializing Existence as Resistance: A Fanonian Reading of the Munduruku and the Riverside Peoples Collective Self-Determination Processes in Amazonia', Léa Tosold, a researcher and activist member of autonomous grassroots organizations, proposes a Fanonian reading of the configuration of the Munduruku and the riverside peoples remarkable processes of resistance to the construction of dams in Tapajós, the last major free flowing river in Amazonia, between 2013 and 2015. Their existence is resistance, Tosold argues, as she describes the Munduruku people's actions in Brazil. For Tosold Fanon's work enables us to apprehend the potential of certain modes of collective self-determination in order to strengthen resistance and meaningfully contribute to the establishment of preconditions for structural transformation in contexts ruled by structural violence. The Fanonian framing helps us hear how the Munduruku struggle in Amazonia opened up in new languages the struggle for liberation from a racist, sexist, ecologically destructive society.

## Acknowledgments

*Fanon Today: Reason and Revolt of The Wretched of the Earth* marks the continuing relevance of Fanon's *Wretched of the Earth* for militants and activists and their continuous struggles to humanize the world. Here, Fanon is put to use, engaging new voices in the 'risings' of *les damnés*, the wretched of the earth, from around the world. This book is for them as they discover their mission. Given the state repression in a number of countries, I want to acknowledge those imprisoned who were forced to drop out of this project and others, given the pandemic, who couldn't make it in the end. It was a labor of love by all. And in addition, like any international and multilingual work, the issue of translation has been vital and I wish to thank all those who were involved in this massive task.

In conjunction with this book, readers might also consult Hassan Mezine's wonderful film, *Fanon, Yesterday and Today,* which includes some of the authors here. I thank Emerson College for giving me a course release to aid the completion of the book and Jaye Glenn and Jordan Reanier for their proofreading skills. As well as the authors, I'd like to thank Frieda Afary, Roberto Beneduce, Lundy Braun, Irene Calis, Mwelela Cele, Yashir Darolshafa, James Fabris, Jane Gordon,

Lewis R. Gordon, Michelle Gubbay, Anne Harley, Kate Josephson, Ronald Judy, Wabbie Long, Firoze Manji, Louis Mazza, Shogonya Mnyonge, Yasser Munif, Michael Neocosmos, Richard Pithouse, Jennifer Ryzenga, Greg Thomas, and John Trimbur, with whom discussions and debates continue to enliven differences.

## Bibliography

Batchelor, K. 2017. 'The Translation of *Les damnés de la terre* into English: Exploring Irish Connections.' In *Translating Frantz Fanon Across Continents and Languages*, edited by Kathryn Batchelor and Sue-Ann Harding. New York: Routledge.

Bhabha, H. K. 1999. 'Remembering Fanon: Self, Psyche, and the Colonial Condition.' In *Rethinking Fanon: The Continuing Dialogue*, edited by Nigel C. Gibson, 179–196. Amherst: Humanity Books.

Cherki A. 2006. *Frantz Fanon: A Portrait*, Ithaca: Cornell University Press.

Davids, M. F. 2011. *Internal Racism: A Psychoanalytic Approach to Race and Difference*. London: Red Globe/MacMillan.

Erasmus, D. 2021. 'The Gospel According to Abahlali baseMjondolo: Land Occupiers' Group Starts "Socialist" Commune in eThekwini.' *Daily Maverick*, https://www.dailymaverick.co.za/article/2021-04-18-the-gospel-according-to-abahlali-basemjondolo-land-occupiers-group-starts-socialist-commune-in-ethekwini/.

Fanon, F. 1963. *The Damned*. Translated by Constance Farrington. Paris: Présence Africaine.

Fanon, F. 1965. A Dying Colonialism New York: Monthly Review.

_____. 1968. *The Wretched of the Earth*. Translated by Constance Farrington. New York: Grove Press.

_____. 2004. *The Wretched of the Earth*. Translated by Richard Philcox. New York: Grove Press.

_____. 2008. *Black Skin, White Masks*. Translated by Richard Philcox. New York: Grove Press.

_____. 2011. *Oeuvres*. Paris: La Découverte.

_____. 2018. *Alienation and Freedom*, edited by Jean Khalfa and Robert J. C. Young. London: Bloomsbury.

Fink, S. 2021. 'Dying of Covid in a "Separate and Unequal" L.A. Hospital,' https://www.nytimes.com/2021/02/08/us/covid-los-angeles.html.

Gibson, N. 2007. 'Relative Opacity: A New Translation of Fanon's *Wretched of the Earth*: Mission Betrayed or Fulfilled?' *Social Identities* 13 (1, January): 69–95.

Gilmore, R. 2007. *Golden Gulag*, Berkeley CA: University of California Press.

Horton, R. 2018. 'Frantz Fanon and the Origins of Global Health.' *The Lancet*, https://www.thelancet.com/journals/lancet/article/PIIS0140-6736(18)32041-5/fulltext.

Marriott, D. 2018. Whither Fanon? Studies in the Blackness of Being, Stanford CA: Stanford University Press

Mukherjee, S. 2021. 'Why Does The Pandemic Seem To Be Hitting Some Countries Harder Than Others,' https://www.newyorker.com/magazine/2021/03/01/why-does-the-pandemic-seem-to-be-hitting-some-countries-harder-than-others.

Munif, Y. 2020. *The Syrian Revolution: Between the Politics of Life and the Geopolitics of Death.* London: Pluto Press.

Oxfam. 2020. 'The Inequality Virus,' https://oxfamilibrary.openrepository.com/bitstream/handle/10546/621149/bp-the-inequality-virus-250121-en.pdf.

Paris, W. 2017. 'The Skin of the World: A Brief Exploration of Fanon's Erotic Humanism,' https://philosophycommons.typepad.com/disability_and_disadvanta/2017/10/the-skin-of-the-world-a-brief-exploration-of-fanons-erotic-humanism.html.

Sayles, J. Y. 2010. *Meditations on Frantz Fanon's Wretched of the Earth,* Montreal: Kersplebedeb

Sekyi-Otu, A. 1996. *Fanon's Dialectic of Experience,* Cambridge MA: Harvard University Press.

Senghor, L. S. 1948. *Anthologie de la nouvelle poésie nègre et malgache de langue française,* Paris: PUF.

Turner, L. and Alan, J. 1986 *Frantz Fanon, Soweto and American Black Thought Expanded Edition,* Detroit MI: News and Letters

Turner, L., and Helen, A. N. 2020. *Frantz Fanon's Psychotherapeutic Approaches to Clinical Work: Practicing Internationally with Marginalized Communities.* New York: Routledge.

# PART I:
## FANONIAN MILITANTS

the

bloated

countries

of        former colonial

position

struggle

to

form

nation's

their independence                     is

bare

intolerable.

today, the issue which blocks the horizon, is the need for a redistribution of wealth.

time            for the world,
to choose between
capitalist      and      socialist

liberation

must not            define itself in relation to values which preceded it.

We know
the capitalist way
exploitation.

'Blacked-out-poem' by Leah Kindler based on Fanon's *The Wretched of the Earth*.

# THE PARTICULAR LIVED EXPERIENCE OF THE BLACK IN PORTUGAL

Flavio Zenun Almada

This year will mark the sixtieth anniversary of the death of the Third World revolutionary philosopher and psychiatrist Frantz Fanon. He passed at only thirty-six years old, but had had a huge intellectual production, leaving us works that still inform our contemporary politics. It is for this reason that I aim to present a humble opinion about the relevance of Frantz Fanon's works. Focused on his first book *Peau noire et Masques Blancs* (1952), what follows is based on the concrete experience of my youth. The text is divided into two parts. I start by presenting a reflection about the social context in which I first came across his works, using his theoretical formulations in order to provide readers with a wider understanding of my background.

The second part constitutes a narrative of some of the events that led me to engage with his work. I begin by focusing on the concept of the compartmentalized world presented by Fanon in *Les Damnés de La Terre* to describe the peripheral area of Lisbon, where I grew up. I know there may be a risk of being called anachronistic, since Fanon elaborated the concept of compartmentalized world (Fanon, 1961: 38) about the Third World African classical colonial city sixty years ago. The dialectic and historical movement needs to be taken into consideration since he did not analyze the social stratum of European colonial metropolis. Even so, I want to take a risk by saying that the Manichean world and its antagonistic structure of violence is incessant for all descendants of former Portuguese African colonies presently living in Lisbon.

The history of African peoples in Portugal can be traced through the centuries before the Transatlantic Slavery. The most obvious example is the long presence of African moors on the Iberian Peninsula. This process never stopped in the context of Transatlantic Slavery and colonization of African territories. From the time when Africans peoples were reduced to 'an object among other objects' (Fanon, 2008: 89) to the neocolonial 21st century, African people in Portugal have been subjected to total violence. Yes, we know that Portuguese official narrative loves to chant its white narcissistic mantra: — 'mirror, mirror on the wall, who is a better colonialist than me?' In short, so-called European modernity was built on African cadavers. It should be said that the European modernity *intelligentsia* also invented, unilaterally, 'la figure de *le nègre*' as antagonistic to the human, namely the White man and Africa as the land of the abject ape. However, I do not want to waste time judging the past, but rather prepare the future for the present.

Contemporaneous realities of the places where we live and where we resist speaking for ourselves and are kinds of neocolonial urban spaces where the majority of its inhabitants—who are Black Africans (with or without national citizenship) living as second class citizens in poor housing, high and chronic unemployment—lack access to quality education, high and disproportional levels of imprisonment of young Black men, police terrorism and others forms of premature accumulations of Black bodies. The urban design of Lisbon is compartmentalized; it has a White center, which is considered a place of civility and 'progress' and Black or Blackened peripheries which are marked as places of incivility and stagnation. The most paradigmatic case is Cova da Moura, located in Amadora municipality, where I am writing from now. Its own residents built it. Its history cannot be dissociated from Portuguese colonial violence. It began before the 1960s with the implementation of compulsory labor in African colonized territories and the importation of African workers, the majority being Cape Verdeans, to toil on construction of Lisbon's subways and the 25 de Abril Bridge (initially named the Salazar Bridge) during colonial and fascist regime of Salazar. These workers were replacements for the loss of the local White labour force who sought higher wages in central Europe.

This dynamic would be propelled after the April 25th revolution by the accession to European Union in 1986 and the subsequent European funds for the construction of new infrastructure. The majority of our people were offered unskilled jobs, such as cleaning services and construction manifesting, a latent racialization and hierarchization of social roles in labor context. Our African elders tell us stories of when they used to sleep in containers on the actual construction sites and how they improvised housing because White landlords would deny renting houses to Black Africans who were called 'nigger terrorists' during the African struggle for independence. Another story narrated by our elders tells of the times when groups of White mobs burned down their houses, much like the White supremacist Ku Klux Khan in the southern United States.

Our elders created groups to defend themselves and their families. It is worth mentioning that Portuguese legislation at the time forbade any access to public financial resources to immigrants. Furthermore, access to public housing was also denied to all migrants, including Africans until 2000. In my opinion, Cova da Moura categorizes as the twenty first century 'negro village, the medina, the reservation, is a place of ill fame, peopled by men of evil repute' (Fanon, 1961: 39). Since its construction its condition has not changed a lot, despite the active work of its residents to improve its infrastructure and resistance against demolition and gentrification. It is continuing to be, with little significant change, 'a hungry town, starved of bread, of meat... is a crouching village, a town on its knees, a town wallowing in the mire. It is a town of niggers' (Fanon, 1961: 39). The government can keep its word but realities speak eloquently for themselves. On this side of the city, the 'economic reality, inequality, and the immense difference of ways of life never come to mask the human realities' (Fanon, 1961: 40). The U.S. based newspaper *Portuguese Times* (October 25) had already written in 1990 'in Cova da Moura three thousand Cape Verdeans live or rather they survive in the condition of the wretched of the earth'.

Another matter that draws attention is the spatial configuration of Cova da Moura, which is surrounded by roads that isolate it from surrounding spaces.

On the southeast, long fences were built separating the area from the buildings around it. Overhead wires, electricity cables and masts surround the neighborhood. In addition, it is worth mentioning that we are under systematic police siege including near Damaia Train Station (Estação da Damaia) which is next to it. The ruthless selective arresting and searching of Black youth force us to redefine our body strategy (looking, moving and talking) in order to avoid being 'stopped and searched'. One strategy is for no more than two to walk together. But this does not guarantee safety because moving out the neighborhood and entering into the city center is a constant struggle to overcome fear and break visible and invisible barriers. So, the first questions that a Black youth will ask themselves is, 'are they [police teams] at the train station or are they sieging the "Bairro".' Yet it is worth mentioning that the Amadora municipality, where Cova Moura is located, with its large Black population has surveillance cameras covering the entire territory. In short, these visible and invisible barriers make me dare to mention that we live in compartmentalized city, a city of *de facto apartheid*.

Another barrier to be confronted is the representation of Cova da Moura in the Portuguese social imagination. It is not so much a representation but a case of an authentic disfiguration that advises that 'people of good heart'[1] should avoid visiting (enter the location here, as a reminder)because it is a place , according to them, where 'even the police do not enter', a place full of 'thugs', drug dealers, and delinquent juveniles, ready to jump on White people. In this use of 'bestial' language we find endless descriptions of what Fanon called the 'colonial vocabulary' (Fanon, 1961: 43). 'Uprooted youth that are neither studying nor working', 'huge crowds sitting on the street corners', 'Black gangs', 'single mothers with many children', the 'stinking zones', 'the zones of crime', of what they call 'Negro island' 'the Bronx' or 'the little African village'.

Cova da Moura is disfigured in social imagination as a place where one should not go, and where Black youth are presented as a corrosive element to 'Portuguese values' or 'our cultural soup'. If the media and right-wing politicians say , 'kill them', social scientists come with their 'objectivity', emulating the racist discourse with a 'scientific glaze', saying euphemistically to 'bury them'. It is almost tantamount to saying that Africans have 'shanty maps' in their protoplasm. The fabulation of dangers zone, inhabited by 'dangerous species' (Zenun Almada, 2020). If you pick up a taxi for instance and mention the name Cova da Moura as your intended destination you will be very lucky if a taxi driver takes you there – this is of course if you are a White person because if you Black, you will not even have a chance to speak; your mere physical appearance will ensure that the cab does not stop.

Likewise, if you call the emergency services for an ambulance there is a high risk that they will not appear and if they appear, it will be after hours of delay guided by police escort. Like other migrants, Blacks and impoverished 'barrios'

---

1. I should say that 'people of good heart' was recently translated by Chega, a right-wing criminal political party as 'Portuguese of good heart'. The 'Portuguese of good heart', according to these racist and fascist the people are non-white adding that 'the darker one is, less a 'Portuguese of good heart'.

the State Criminal Polices classifies Cova da Moura as Sensitive Urban Zones (ZUZ) (Zenun Almada, 2020). This means that such zones are patrolled like a militarized zone. It is worth noting that the presence of 'ethnic minorities' and 'black people' is taken as the criteria for such classification[2]. This classification of the 'space of incivility' and 'permanent tension' confirms that center of power which views the Cova da Moura and others Black neighborhoods as the classical colonial administrator used to see 'indigenous' spaces of residence in the colonies. So, the *hoods* are treated as internal colonies where we see 'the policeman and the soldier who are the official, instituted go-betweens, the spokesmen of the [oppressor] and his rule of oppression' (Fanon, 1961: 38).

Police terrorism is a daily occurrence, and in many instances their violent action results in death. To highlight a few examples of this widespread police violence since entering the new millennium, there should be included the police killing of Ângelo Semedo, a 16-year-old young Black man and the 27-year-old Celé. The latter was shot 54 times by the police. They did the same to Carlos Alves, another black man in 2018. In 2003 they killed another Black brother who was 20 at the time. In the following year police kidnapped and tortured 16-year-old José Carlos Vicente which resulted in his death. In 2010, the extent of police militarization was on full display when the Portuguese State introduced several armored vehicles into the neighborhood , with the excuse that they were for the protection of a NATO Conference that was being held in Lisbon. We in the Black community, however, knew that in reality their introduction was to intensify the policing of Black neighborhoods and we came out on the streets to demonstrate against NATO. Consequently a few days later our suspicions were confirmed from the mouth of a police officer and his *dogs*. From their new 'Ferrari', which is what we called their armoured vehicle, he shouted out: 'look, what we have now for your thugs'. The following week, there was another typical assault on another Black neighborhood called Casal da Mira, located in Amadora.

The epidemic nature of the violence and its individual impact upon Black people has received reflection and criticism by artists. In particular, there has been a burgeoning Hip-Hop movement where the sons and daughters of people of African descent sing in the Cape-Verdean language, known as *Kriolu*. These artists have been the most critical intellectual voices of Portugal's structural anti-Blackness. Furthermore, it can be said that the great catalyst and organizing dynamic of Black resistance movement against this state violence have been members of the Hip-Hop community. There is not one single rap album or mix-tape that I know from the Black peripheries of Lisbon that does not mention and criticize this epidemic state violence. Growing up in what we called the *ghetto* forced us to reflect upon the question of violence, especially the horizontal violence that, in its racist definition, is known as 'Black on Black violence'. There is a question that has been on my mind for years: 'Why is it that sometimes one does

---

2. See 2006 National Directive of Police of Public Security.

not even begin to understand the cause of horizontal violence'. I say this because I observed a lot of situations of horizontal violence that resulted in the death of our friends for no apparent reason. Sometimes it seems ridiculous, starting from mere eye contact and resulting in bullets or 'chinada'[3]. I remember that related to some of these tragic incidents the commentaries : 'you know they are violent' which some Black people mimicked 'you know Blacks are dumb, we kill each other for no reason!' Of course, we always answer: 'just because you are dumb does not mean that our people are dumb'.

It was Fanon who came to me with his insight in *Les Damnés de La Terre*:

> In the colonial world, the emotional sensitivity of the native is kept on the surface of his skin like an open sore which flinches from the caustic agent; and the psyche shrinks back, obliterates itself and finds outlet in muscular demonstrations which have caused certain very wise men to say that the native is a hysterical type. (Fanon, 1961: 56)

This is very important because it forced me to pay more attention to the body movement of our youth inside the community. This was due to many pressures (economic, physical, and psychological) against our people, and above all, the presence of militarized police teams that generate an atmosphere of fear and consequently tension inside the community. Even the body image of children shows these tensions. In our case, we used to move out of our neighborhood to another as far away as possible to avoid the police— but for what?— just to arrive at the conclusion that what differs from our neighborhood was urban design and the architecture of housing. It was not because we were involved in crime but rather that our collective experience teaches us that our presence would be taken by police as violence in and of itself, which may result in violent confrontation. When noticing the presence of police teams, mothers go out to look for their sons and call them to come back home. The entire community atmosphere changes and with it people's glances, walk, body movement, gestures and the rhythm of spoken words. All this makes us think that we are not protected, and we must do whatever we have to do to survive. Also, the evidence observed in several neighborhoods and confirmed by brothers and sisters is the fact that 'while ... the policeman has the right the livelong day to strike and to insult ... and to make him crawl to them, you will see the colonized reaching for his knife at the slightest hostile or aggressive glance cast on him by another native; for the last resort of the native is to defend his personality vis-a-vis his brother' (Fanon, 1963: 54). Here Fanon here gives us a clue about horizontal violence and to avoid internalizing the pathological nature which is sold by the 'constellation of postulates' that has taught some of us to claim, irrationally, that 'Black people do not know how to behave'. I am still reflecting upon this excerpt and I will continue until this world as we know it is brought to an end.

---

3. It *is a street terminology, used in Lisbon to describe a conflict that involves cutting someone with knife*

In addition, I would like to add that there was another set of circumstances that led me to be introduced to Fanon's work around 2005. I must confess that at the time I feared that I would not see past the age of 25, as many of my childhood friends from the Black African peripheral communities of Lisbon did not. As a member of a hip-hop community, we used to escape Lisbon's peripheral areas in search of jobs, festivals, shows, clubs and other such things. The center of Lisbon, particularly Bairro Alto, is the place where people go to enjoy nightlife because of the many clubs and bars that attract tourists. It is also a meeting place for young Black and poor youth from various neighborhoods of Lisbon and also a focal point where hip-hop battles would take place. We were always there participating in these hip-hop battles. And, not infrequently, the police would appear, perhaps on three or more occasions in one night to harass us since, in Lisbon, four Black youth at night is considered by the police as a 'gang of criminals' that must be chased, beaten, and then charged for aggression against police officers. At times, for no apparent reason, they didn't hesitate to shoot at us.

At the same time, Black brothers had to fight right wing mobs who would attack them and this constituted another form of policing. I remember on May 25, 2005 we went to Queluz to celebrate African liberation day with friends when the Public Security Police (PSP) suddenly appeared at the festival and started shooting at the crowd, the majority of whom were African people attending the concert. We all ran to Queluz train station to get home to Cova da Moura. The situation became very tense on the train. Me and my brothers stayed near the train door, watching everything until we arrived at our station. We joked with each other about the situation and of course we cursed the racist police. The next month, on June 10th—a day that used to be celebrated in Portugal as *The Day of Race* and of Portuguese communities (Dia da Raça e das Comunidades Portuguesas)—television channels, including the State television (RTP) and many newspapers were stating that 'yesterday approximately 500 young people's created panic in Carcavelos Beach when, at 3 pm, they attacked and robbed the beach goers, according to police' (Mendes, 2005). The image was of a group of young Black people running with police on their back. We knew that it was not true because our uncles and seniors told us that they suffered the same thing in 1996.

Regardless, we spoke with our friends with Cape Verdean origins who were from another neighborhood and had been there. They told us that it was a lie and explained to us what happened; they formed a group of dancers, from different regions, to compete 'Kuduro' and suddenly the police showed up and began to shoot in the air. They started running as could be seen in the image. They did not need to say much more because we knew that the very presence of Blackness is sufficient to trigger violence, but that Black truth is unheard because Blackness is seen as evil and/or a problem in White civil society. The presence of Black youth at the beach was also seen as a contestation for space. The police repression shows who has the right to occupy certain spaces.

A few days later, we were taken into custody by surprise, because a national channel TVI, broadcasted our faces from the train incident, associating us with what became known as 'Arrastão de Carcavelos' (Dragnet of Carcavelos). They began to circulate those images through the media over the following days. This infuriated us and we wanted to sue the TVI channel, but all the lawyers we contacted told us that they did not want to 'start a war with the media'. We mocked them, saying sarcastically: 'It is just because we do not have millions, if we had millions, you would even sell your soul'. Later the National Front, a Nazi group, organized a demonstration against 'immigrants' in Lisbon. In this situation it is obvious that the migrants became a euphemism for Blackness and nationalism for Whiteness. So we went there as a counter-protest. Again, the police persecuted and harassed us until we returned to our neighborhoods. Weeks later, evidence came to light confirming that the so-called 'Arrastão' was a myth. We always knew that our innocence would not save us because we knew that structural innocence is not a position that Blackness can occupy in a culture that has an '*imago* of the Black which is responsible for every possible conflictual situation' (see Fanon, 2008: 146).

These particular 'bestializations' of Black youth in public spaces intensified the curfews around Black/African migrant's bodies and neighborhoods. The question is who is the public? So, when those military police attacked us, which was unfortunately not an usual occurrence, we would say: 'Hmmm, White power sent their dogs to pacify us, to show to Whites that the Black city is "under control".' It is worth adding that all these examples fit a surveillance of Black people which is conducted by the state's apparatus of violence. Policing Black people's 'presence' is what even ordinary White citizens do as well as what Black people, who have internalized the myth of the Black's pathological nature, do. From our point of view , all this gratuitous violence against us (Black people in Portugal) is not dependent on any kind of transgression but rather because Portuguese culture has an '*imago* of the Black which is responsible for every possible conflictual situation' (Fanon, 2008: 146). It is always 'my Black friend', the 'Black teacher', the 'Black lawyer', the 'Black family', the 'Black writer', and so on. In some areas of the country where a few Black individuals live, you find out that they are known as 'the Black' (preto) in a pejorative way and treated as property by possessive pronouns. And it must be said that 'When they like me, they tell me my color has nothing to do with it. When they hate me, they add that it's not because of my color' (Fanon, 2008: 96).

Fanon helped me become aware of the fact that our positionality applied not only to the impoverished or those without a college degree. It is a collective experience, even for those brothers and sisters who have a PhD and a fat wallet (of course I am not on the side of any bourgeois blood suckers). So, Fanon is perfectly right, in my opinion, to write that 'against all the arguments I have just cited, I come back to one fact: Wherever they go, 'the Black remains a Black' (Fanon, 2008: 150). Yet, as he puts it, 'I tell you I was walled in: neither my refined manners nor my literary knowledge nor my understanding of the quantum theory could find favor' (Fanon, 2008: 97). This is important because some intellectuals want to put the grammar of suffering of other racially oppressed peoples in the same category as the suffering of Black people and it's not, despite that we are all being discriminated against by White supremacist colonial, capitalist and imperialist system. It is funny that the answer of most Black youth is similar as that given by Fanon, after demonstrating his solidarity with the persecution of Jews:

> *manu ka mesti ku ben flanu ma tudu kuza ki nu ta passa é igual a di otus djentis ki també ta perseguidu pamodi kes djentis lá sima ka abri boka, si ka investigadu nem ka ta sabedu. Na nós kasu ta odjadu pele. A és inda és podi sukundi, mas nós nu ta konsigui muda de pele*[4]

As Fanon puts it, 'The Jew is not liked as soon as he has been detected. But with me things take on a new face. I'm not given a second chance. I am overdetermined from the outside. I am a slave not to the 'idea' others have of me, but to my appearance' (Fanon, 2008: 95). It is obvious that they are not disputing in a suffering Olympics league and by no means do they say that we must isolate ourselves. The brother added 'we do not need to commit any crime; we just need to appear because the system sees our presence as crime'.

Another fact that proves this culture has an *imago* of the Black it is that for immigration officers, the Black and the illegal immigrant are equivalent, policed by state and individuals. The conclusion about policing Blackness is a deadly combination of capitalism and intrinsic anti-Blackness since, as Fanon puts it, 'it belongs in a characteristic whole: that of the shameless exploitation of one group of men by another' (Fanon, 1980: 37-38). This means that policing Blackness gives continual profits to the world's military and surveillance industries while also continuing to employ White people in what they called assimilation, or in the neocolonial vocabulary, integration.

We could include on this list of profiteers academics, politicians, lawyers, NGOs and so on. Therefore, we began to organize meetings and exchange experiences of anti-Black racism. We focused on the following issues: Forms of state policing Blackness, especially special forces curfews in our African neighborhoods; the disproportionate incarceration of Black youth in Portuguese prisons; racist and anti-Black narratives in the history books and social communication; policing and persecution of racialized immigrants by immigration services; housing policies and the demolition of African neighborhoods; racialization of social roles resulting from structural 'delirious Manichaeism' (Fanon, 2008: 160), which posits Blackness as degraded, animalized and a bestialized humanity; the racial state project, especially the laws that blocked the access to Portuguese citizenship to more than a generation of Black people born in Portugal (Zenun Almada, 2020)[5]; and immigration laws.

Our observations and experiences showed us that the economic, symbolic, and psychological violence against our peoples is normalized by a strong, structural, anti-black apparatus of Portuguese society and that it is difficult to destroy

---

4. Bro, there is no need to persuade us that our suffering is identical to those other peoples that are also persecuted against because these peoples have white skin, and if they do not open their mouth, they will not even be noticed. In our case the first thing that is seen is skin color. They can even pass unnoticed. Could we change the color of our skin?
5. I am referring to the March 10, 1981 law of nationality that still blocked descendants of migrants born in Portugal, from having full citizenship.

this 'normal'. Why? Because Portugal 'lusotropicalist' ideology is alive. It was invented by Brazilian sociologist Gilberto Freire and it was adopted by the colonial and fascist Portuguese state with a clear objective in managing Indigenous and African peoples during colonialism. In short, this fairy tales says that 'we', Portuguese, 'we' are 'non-racist because we mixed with every people and culture'. It is a glorification of colonial raping of African and Indigenous women, of enslaving Africans and plundering African and indigenous lands. So, to whomever they refer when they say 'we'; we know this 'we' is a violent word.

Days later, I had the same conversation that I have mentioned before with my friend Vitor who used to visit his family in our neighborhood while he was attending the university on the north side of Portugal. We spoke about anti-Blackness emulation and alienation in our communities. He told me: —*Man, you must read Frantz Fanon! I am sure that you would love it!* I did not know who Frantz Fanon was. But I could vaguely remember that Fanon was acclaimed in *Revolutionary Suicide* by Huey P. Newton, the former Minister of Defense of Black Panther Party for Self Defense. But, anyway, *Who is Frantz Fanon? Why must I read his books?* He did not say much more and both of us went on with our struggles. I tried to follow his recommendation, but it was difficult because I could not find any of his books at the bookstores.

Surprisingly, months later, Vitor brought me *Peau noire et Masques Blancs*. It was in this way that I found Frantz Fanon: not in academia but on the street corner of the 'ghetto' of Lisbon. In fact, I must say that when we started to speak about his work, we were attacked by many people, including from some 'leftists' , that we were promoting an 'anti-White' pamphleteering, an 'obsession with race' and other epithets. Some of them were stinking of fear. But after a few minutes of conversation with them, it became abundantly clear that most of these critics had never read Fanon's works and others had just read the preface of *Les Damnés de La Terre* by Jean Paul Sartre. On this latter issue, after reading Fanon I came to understand that the 'leftist' attack was an anti-Black unconscious response which White people try to impose on us Blacks. A 'whiter' liberal reading of Fanon instead of a structural Manichean delirium and political economy of anti-Blackness of this world. They were seeking to avoid confronting their own anti-Blackness.

By opening *Peau noire, masques blancs,* I was confronted with a very complex book full of psychological and philosophical terminologies anecdotes, culturally idiomatic expressions, metaphors, street language mobilizations, and a combination of several scientific areas to reveal the deepest complexity of Manichean world as a structurally violent *modus* of depersonalization and alienation. Its first pages provoked me. Its first lines: 'Don't expect to see any explosion today. It's too early...or too late' (Fanon, 2008: xi). But the explosion started earlier with Aimé Césaire's quotation: '*I am talking about millions of men whom they have knowingly instilled with fear and a complex of inferiority, whom they have infused with despair and trained to tremble, to kneel and behave like flunkeys*' (Fanon, 2008: xi). The explosions kept following with a series of questions and declarations: What does a man want? What does the Black man want? (2008: xi). These are questions that continue to be raised today, particularly among us. Why? Simply, because our conditions have not improved since Fanon's time and in some cases have worsened. One just needs to see the systematic terror that consumes Black life in every corner of the world, and to see the way Black lives are treated as superfluous, as waste, whose deaths, torture, public execution, and sexual violation do not cause any commotion. This demands that we ask: why? Fanon comes straight to the truth saying, 'at the risk of arousing the resentment of my colored brothers, I will say that the Black is not a man' (Fanon, 2008: xi). This means that we are treated as not human or as a bestialized humanity and Black life is struggling to be seen as human among other humans, but when dealing with the world , he or she finds himself or herself 'an object among other objects' (Fanon, 2008: 89).

Then, Fanon invites us to follow him into deep hell to 'zone of nonbeing, an extraordinarily sterile and arid region, an incline stripped bare of every essential from which a genuine new departure can emerge' (Fanon, 2008: xii). By the zone of nonbeing, I understand Fanon to be saying that Black people are not recognized as entirely human beings by the global racial capitalist/colonial and imperialist structure of White supremacy. Moreover, even the invention of category of 'human' was a product of Transatlantic Slavery. It then became a category that was imposed on colonialism in Africa and elsewhere. The history of liberal democracy from its beginning until now, has been the history of racial terror that stinks of the blood of African, and Indigenous peoples, who were reduced to condition of slavery and colonial subjugation through total violence. The liberal rhetoric of the word human, without euphemism and hypocrisy, means White bourgeois man. To go to the deepest hell is to become conscious that the biologization of bodies of Black peoples is infernal since it does not let our Black body abandon an essentialist fabulation (re) created by slavery and (neo) colonial disfiguration. Painfully, it is to discover that to live in a zone of nonbeing is to be dead and alive at the same time because power structures see us as 'nothingness' or just as 'dark flesh'. This gave me a clue to understand why most Black people, when facing anti-Black violence, scream 'we are human' and also so called 'allies' say , 'Black people are human'. Why does one have to say such an affirmation: simply because unconsciously there is an understanding that Black people live in the condition of the 'zone of nonbeing' because there has always been a question-mark, since the very beginning of European Enlightenment, about the full humanity of the African. That question mark is the doorway into a zone of nonbeing, and it is the key to the door which keeps us 'overdetermined from without', by the walls, barriers, and fences of that zone enclosing us.

I could relate to what Fanon was writing because of my own personal experience and the collective experiences of my community. All those experiences contributed to seeing that Fanon's theory came from praxis. His text made me reflect on my own experience, particularly the chapter L'expérience Vécue du Noir. When I read 'in the train I was given not one but two, three places' it sounds like if Fanon was there with us on the train. Because it was the frequency of experiencing this kind of behavior that gave rise to a sensation that it was not a human being that was entering but some kind of 'beast'. Fanon explained it very well, 'The white gaze, the only valid one, is already dissecting me. I am fixed. Once their microtomes are sharpened, the Whites objectively cut sections of my reality. I have been betrayed. I sense, I see in this white gaze that it's the arrival not of a new man, but of a new type of man, a new species. A Negro, in fact!' (Fanon, 2008: 95). This description is very familiar to many Black people that pick-up Lisbon train lines, especially the Sintra line to Cova da Moura, which is referred to as the 'jungle' because of the presence of many Black people. That chapter in the book made me remember catching the train or bus to go into the center of Lisbon and the feelings of tension, fear, and rage, in the air and those gestures of fear: White ladies shaking and hiding their things, mobiles phones, and bags; White men moving from theirs seats, running like a devil; the dirty commentaries about color, odors, the complaints, anecdotes and shock with our presence:

> —Look at those niggers '*pretos*' coming in!
> —Do not look at them. You know they are crazy!

The dirty commentaries follow quietly:

> —'this country is lost because we now have this kind of people who come here to rob, sell drugs and do other crimes', said a white man to another who bowed his head when I looked into his eyes.

The unconfessed racist sentiments show his face through gestures, looks and body language as we got on the bus or train. And you ask yourself: why people are fearing you given that it is the very first time that they have ever seen you? After reading Fanon, I came to the conclusion that they think they 'know you' because Portuguese society has a fixed concept of 'Black' and for these reasons I could relate to the passage in the book that says the 'The Black ... is a 'phobogenic' object, provoking anxiety' (Fanon, 2018: 129). Yes, there are many, many times when we enter these spaces it becomes heavy with anxiety. Sometimes some antiblack racists try to position themselves to stop our bodies from entering. Obviously, we would reject this way of policing Blackness and would say, 'get the fuck out of the way because I am coming in'.

One conclusion that I took from reading Fanon is that the surveillance and patrolling Black bodies gave a kind of stabilization of the White imagination and psyche because the Black body is treated as 'an excess' in order for the state and for civil society to define its Whiteness. The Kriolu MC Celso Lopes, known by his stage name Kromo di Ghetto, summarized the experience of Black youth in Portugal as follows: 'it is like the Black in Portugal is extra[6]. This passage of his rap song was describing and narrating that in Portugal the presence of Blacks in public space is seen as a threat and the individual and institutional acts try to confine the 'Black' and remove their presence from the imagination of the nation . It is for that reason that there are a lot of narratives of Black people in Portugal that have what we call an 'antiblack excavation of origins'. To give a reader

6. *Pretu na tuga sta amais'.*

a clue I will transcribe the following conversation between a White Portuguese and Black Person that happened on a train.

— Where are you from in Africa?

— I am a Black person in Portugal!

— Portugal?

— Yes, I was born and raised in Lisbon!

— I mean ...I know Africa very well!

— I do not know Africa, I never been there yet.

— So, where are your parents from in Africa?

— They are from Portugal. And are you from North Africa?

— Hell no, do you not see, that I am a pure Portuguese?

— You mean, White and Portuguese are synonymous? Take it easy because I am African in Europe with Portuguese citizenship.

— So, you are Portuguese?

— What does it mean to be Portuguese? I will never sing the Portuguese anthem.

— Why?

— By the way, which part of Africa do you know, since it is a huge continent, not a country?

— We cannot even say anything to you (vocës) folks anymore!

— What do you mean by 'we' and 'you' if I am the only one speaking with you?

The question about 'we' is fundamental since they never included Black people because it is assumed that in order to, he/she escape his/her 'jungle' must *become* Portuguese (White).

As another member of Hip-Hop Kriolu Tuka says 'two Black people in the city is too much for them'. This means that Black people are seen in Portugal as bodies that occupy too much space and do not fit. It is through the negation of the Black that so-called Portuguese (White) identity defines itself. In *Peau noire, Masques Blancs*, Frantz Fanon reminds us that 'For not only must the black man be black; he must be black in relation to the white man. Some people will argue that the situation has a double meaning. Not at all. The black man has no ontological resistance in the eyes of the white man' (Fanon, 2008: 90). The specificity of the grammar of suffering of Black people is not because of a transgression but because existence itself is considered a transgression. Consequently, the policing of the Black body is a way of confirming, reinstating, and re-inscribing who are the real full citizens of Portugal, who the real human beings are and who are not.

For me, the confirmation that the Black male, in my case, is seen as phobogenic was confirmed in many terrifying instances including my experiences of the state apparatus of antiblack violence. I could talk about when they invaded my home or tried to knock us down with their vehicles after they crossed the road. The latter happened on January 16, 2009 when I was a fly posting in the neighborhood for demonstration against the police killing of my fourteen-year-old Black brother, named Elson Sanches 'Kuku' in 2009. I knew the brother because he was one of the kids that I was responsible for when I was working at Scholl in Amadora. Before I tell the story, I will tell the story of what happened to the 4 brothers on February 5th 2015 to illustrate how Black people are seen in this antiblack country. On that particular day the Militarized Police of Amadora Division conducted an 'operation'[7] in our neighborhood and shot three Black women when they started to shoot into crowd who were protesting because those pigs had beaten up a young Black male. One woman was hit in her chest while she was hanging clothes on the clothes on her balcony. When the residents started to gather in great numbers, they picked up a brother who was soaked in blood and took him to the police station, located a few kilometers outside of our neighborhood. On arrival immediately I saw Jailza Sousa crying with bullet marks on her chest. I saw that she had also collected the shotgun cartridges that had been emptied by police. She told me that she had collected them because she had seen a policeman picking up discarded cartridges and she thought—'if he is collecting them, it is important, so I will do the same'. So, I agreed to go with her to the police department in Lisbon to lodge a complaint, even though we knew such a thing would not result in anything.

At the same time, I was told by a senior colleague of the Association to go to the police station to find out about Bruno Lopes, who had been taken by the police bloodied and beaten. It was not the first time that we had to do this because we know the histories of torturing and the death of brothers across the entire peripheral area of Lisbon. So, I went with my friend and colleague Celso Lopes 'Kromo di Ghetto' and we were followed by other brothers. When we arrived at the police station, they immediately greeted us with a couple of shots that hit Celso Lopes. They then kidnapped and falsely imprisoned us and tortured us physically and psychologically and we were subjected to a constant stream of words, along the lines as—'if we had power, we would exterminate all you *niggers* ... you should be castrated ... this is our country'.

Additionally, they were constantly lauding and celebrating the summary execution of young Black males, in particular Elson Sanches who had been shot in cold blood at a point-blank range by an officer named Diogo Gachineiro of the PSP. I followed the court case and court hearings from 2009 until January 20, 2015. From inside the beast, we heard a police officer calling a right-wing TV Channel Correio da Manhã to send a journalist to come to the police station, claiming that they had stopped an invasion by 'invaders' attempting to rescue a Black man who had been detained. Those media vultures came very quickly and started to broadcast the police narrative which legitimized their actions to the entire country. As the people of our communities received this news, they went *en-masse* to the police station. This is the reason why they stopped torturing us.

We were eventually charged with committing an act of terrorism which our lawyers were latter able to get discharged. Years later the state prosecution charged the entire police station of kidnapping, torturing, falsifying evidence

---

7. They called it operation, but we called it terrorism and hunting of Black lives.

and other crimes. It was the first case of this nature in forty years old Portugal of *Herrenvolk* democracy. On November 25, 2020 we received a confirmation from the Court of Appeal about the conviction of the eight of them. I just want to say that if there is any merit to this victory it belongs to the strength and solidarity of our communities and antiracist movements that mobilized on our behalf.

Another thing that caught my attention was that news and media commentaries were always clearly indicating that for them, the Black body is seen as 'phobogenic'; the Black man, in particular, as a 'sexual predator'. They referred to us as thugs, drug dealers, rapist, parasites and other anti-Black vocabularies. I want to add that at the court hearings, even though we were not the accused, we were treated as such; I felt a deep sense of rage because I was conscious that I was in front of 'white liberty and white justice' (Fanon, 2008: 195) and before a body of judges who displayed only 'paternalistic curiosity' making us 'responsible at the same time for my [our] body, for my [our] race, for my [our] ancestors' (Fanon, 2008: 192).

Even my music, as well as the songs of Kromo di Guetho, were a topic in the court proceedings when the lawyers acting on behalf of police, described me as an anti-system warmonger due to my songs lyrics and my rapper's name 'LBC Soldjah'. Tell me if there is a more disgusting thing to hear than that paternalistic voice of judgment asking: 'do you know the meaning of this words' even after reading that I have a qualification in translation and creative writing. In short, we were not fighting only against those racist pigs but against the entire structure of western White supremacy, White civil society. It was this, which was responsible for what happened to us. Because this country understands itself as White and Christian that is normalized and naturalized by 'a host of information and a series of propositions slowly and stealthily work their way into an individual through books, newspapers, school texts, advertisements, movies, and radio and shape his community's vision of the world' (Fanon, 2008: 131).

With regard to the above court transcription, I want to discuss the question of language since it is through language, in a broader sense, that we reveal our world. According to Fanon 'to speak is to exist absolutely for the other.... To speak means being able to use a certain syntax and possessing the morphology of such and such a language, but it means above all assuming a culture and bearing the weight of a civilization'(Fanon, 2008: 1-2).

The analysis of language proposed by Fanon could yet be extrapolated to policies of language in Africa. In this aspect, regarding to African continent, language has been used since colonial times as tool for colonial domination and alienation. And still operates even after decades of achievement of formal independence by African countries, what is totally 'absurd when you take into account that the majority of the African people speak African languages and that only a very tiny minority... speak French or English or Portuguese' (Thiong'o, 1992: 26). The fact is that the former European colonial powers redesigned their neocolonial map, according to language, in order to protect their symbolic, culture, and economic neocolonial interests and their African allies. The British reorganized its formers colonies in neocolonies of Commonwealth and incorporated yet other countries in it; France did the same through its neocolonial project known as 'France-Afrique'; and the Portugal created Lusophony.

Regarding this aspect, Fanon teaches that the colonial violence from the 'mother country' stems straight from a cynical coalition between knowledge and power. Europeans' languages are at the core of ongoing western epistemic neocolonialism that dominated universities of world, inclusive in African continent—that informed the human rights, international politics, in order to legitimizing western imperialism, neocolonialism, proxy wars, currency policies, multinational corporation extractivism of African raw materials, international institutions like world bank and IMF (International Monetary Fund), psychological warfare on African peoples. So, language has a significant role to play in order to materialize the total divorce from (neo) colonialism.

So, the constant use of the word 'you' in plural to refer to an individual Black male or female demonstrated once again that Portuguese civil society has a fixed concept of 'Black'. There is nothing more exasperating than to be asked: 'How long have you been in [Portugal]? You speak [Portuguese] very well'. This ' imago of the Black' is constantly appearing in movies, novels, books and idiomatic expressions. This fixed concept of 'the Black' is because the bestiality narratives of Black African peoples still breathe and is perpetuated by those who control the means of production and the ideological apparatus of capitalist society.

This disguised anti-Blackness manifests itself systematically in language namely in the school's system. I have been working for more than ten years with young students (primary and secondary level) and I forget how many times that I have to fight teachers who prohibited children with Cape Verdean backgrounds to speak the Cape Verdean language with the argument that they do not understand it and, additionally, that using such 'dialect' diminishes the children's capacity to learn Portuguese. Some parents have internalized this, ultimately banning their children to speak 'creole' at home. This is a paradigmatic example of calling for assimilation that is euphemistically disguised in official narratives as 'integration'—which means literally amputation. One of the most flagrant cases is that of social workers, Whites and Blacks, who have 'forbidden to speak creole' at community centers where the majority of the population (93%) speak 'creole'. But the good thing is that some parents and youth have rebelled against this and forced them to stop with this nonsense. In the school system, one quickly observes that the 'language problem' is a disguised antiblack racism because one sees, as Fanon puts it:

> When I meet a German or a Russian speaking bad French, I try to indicate through gestures the information he is asking for, but in doing so I am careful not to forget that he has a language of his own, a country, and that perhaps he is a lawyer or an engineer back home. Whatever the case, he is a foreigner with different standards. There is nothing comparable when it comes to the black man. He has no culture, no civilization, and no 'long historical past'. (2008: 17)

In short, language is not a problem in the case of some European languages but a 'certain form of existing'. The children that come from Cape Verde, Guinea-Bissau, Angola and even Brazil, suffer because of their accent and their mother languages. Some of them have been torturing their tongues in order to sound and speak like Portuguese. Clearly even after decades of 'independence' the decolonization process is yet a task to be fulfilled. I am saying this because Cape Verde stills 'finds itself face to face with the language of the civilizing nation; that is, with the culture of the mother country [western countries, especially Portugal]' (see Fanon, 2008: 2) and it can be illustrated by the way in which Cape Verdeans treat fellow compatriots from the African continent, especially from West Africa. As stated by Fanon (1963: 162):

> it is by no means astonishing to hear in a country that calls itself African remarks which are neither more nor less than [anti-Black] racist, and to observe the existence of paternalist behavior which gives you the bitter impression that you are in Paris, Brussels, or London.

The only thing that differs in this case is that most of Cape Verdean intellectuals do not consider Cape Verde as an African country because they are trapped in Lusotropicalist and miscegenation theory, subjected to what Fanon calls 'lactification'. This illustrated that Cape Verdeans on the island and abroad have internalized anti-Blackness and internalized fear that leads to the amputation of us.

Another aspect is that Portugal for centuries developed a psychology of starvation in the Cape Verdean mindset and inculcated in us the idea of 'Lisbon as place of escaping' from Blackness. Trapped in this desire to be considered fully Portuguese 'The black who has been to the metropole is a demigod'. For these reasons I want to dig a little bit more into the Cape Verdean 'self-division'. According to Fanon, some of his fellow Martinicans who have lived in France 'returns home radically transformed. Genetically speaking, his phenotype undergoes an absolute, definitive mutation' (2008: 3). To be honest, we observed the same behavior among some of Cape Verdean migrants after returning from Europe and the United States, France and Portugal. In Cape Verde, they make a point to demonstrate to the natives of the island that they have 'assimilated the cultural values of the metropolis ... [and] escaped the bush' (2008: 2). They complain about the island's temperature and most of the men and women return bleached. In a conversation with natives, they were constantly using

> European forms of social intercourse; adorning the native language with European expressions; using bombastic phrases in speaking or writing a European language; all these contribute to a feeling of equality with the European and his achievements. (Westermann quoted in Fanon 2008, 9)

It for this reason that some of Cape Verdeans students in Lisbon like to say that they think that they 'were deceived because we found out that most of them were working as 'mules' in civil construction and other work that White people despise, and lived in in impoverished neighborhoods, occupied and terrorized by racist police department, listening daily the racist 'nigger go back to your country'.[8] The fact is that they hide the reality since they used to talk and walk and send pictures back to islands as if they were living like millionaires.

What caught my attention working with Black communities in Portugal is that some Africans masks their accent when speaking with White Portuguese. Others after few months in Europe claimed that they do not know how to speak their mother tongues. Of course, as explained by Fanon this self-division is a direct result of anti-Blackness, cultural *imago* of the Black as well in the capitalist political economy. The structurally imposed 'self-division', according to Fanon, also appears as affective desire of Black men and women to desire *White love*, which means that there is a cultural imposition of Whiteness as standard of beauty, moral value, intelligence, humanity, reason, and creativity.

Blackness is the opposite of all this. In this manner, complexes of inferiority and superiority are produced. People bleaching their skin and using chemicals (to straighten their hair and cases of 'self-division' 'are the product of a psychological-economic system' (Fanon, 2008: 18).

Another thing that Fanon calls to my attention is the animalization of Black man who is constantly reduced to the 'biological', and to the genitalia. Even before reading Fanon I had heard this in Cape Verde through anecdotes from fellow Africans from Guinea Bissau, Senegal and Nigeria, etc. The Cape Verdean finds out that in Europe they are Africans and despised as such. They discover that the jokes, anecdotes that they used to make in the islands about Blacks were actually about themselves which illustrated the internalization of anti-Blackness. In Portugal, it got to be too much, especially when I was working in the construction industry or confronting White street cats in university settings, as well as dealing with police officers. I dare say that my experience and observations led to the conclusion that the White man has a jealousy of the fantasy of the hypersexual Black men that exist in their imagination as a desire to castrate the Black man.

When we were kidnaped and tortured by the police, one police officer called Hugo Gaspar cried out—'if I had power, I would make a decree to sterilize all you niggers'. The reduction to genitalia appears frequently in anecdotes, jokes and comments such as: 'you *Blacks*, you think that you are more of a man than us'. In fact, a few years ago on a television channel called SIC, which has a comedy program called '*Levanta-te e Ri*', a white comedian, called Fernando Rocha was always doing racist anecdotes about Black men's sexual organs which would make the White audience explode with laughter. We were very attentive to this because every time that such disgusting jokes were made the camera would focus on the Black person in the audience. If the Black person laughed, we cursed them because they were emulating, reinscribing and confirming the degradation of

---

8. In June of 2020 a former colonial combatant killed a father, husband and actor Bruno Candé, cold bloody after screaming 'nigger, go back to your country... I killed a lot niggers like you in Africa'.

Black people. And there is nothing that is more disgusting than to hear: 'you, black people you are so potent sexually', as a kind of complement.

When dealing with police officers, one is astonished by their desire to strike our genitalia. This desire to castrate Black men is global. One hears it from brothers who have spent time in the United Kingdom, France, and Italy. We were told by former combatants of Africa liberation struggles that the Portuguese colonial military used to cut African soldiers' balls after they were killed. One of the most honored of the Portuguese is a former colonial soldier and traitor from Guinea Bissau, called Marcelino da Mata. He is very proud of 'cutting balls' off of the liberation soldiers from Guinea Bissau and Cape Verde.

Moreover, state institutions, such as education, health services, and social services, systematically pathologize Black families. Recently, the European Court of Human Rights declared that Portuguese courts committed human rights violations when it took the decision to remove seven children from Liliana Melo, a Black woman, and give them up to adoption (*Jornal Público*, 16.02.2016). There are more and more examples, which proves that this society does not recognize Black-kinship and family.

I want to finish by saying that Frantz Fanon was fundamental for me because he validated my [our] experiences and gave us a very deep understating of the White supremacist capitalistic, patriarchal, neocolonial and imperialistic monopoly we are facing: 'An answer must be found on the objective as well as the subjective level' (Fanon, 2008: xv). Some people said that Fanon was mad. His is a legitimate rage because he was unlike those intellectuals whose 'research always focuses on others and never on themselves' (Fanon, 2008: 145). I loved the fact that Fanon was shaking us up and not condemning us to fatalism. He rejected the idea that 'Black man [and woman] cannot take advantage of this descent into a veritable hell'. (2008: xii) and that, 'the Black man is supposed to be a good nigger' (2018: 18). This makes us proud of some of our acts since we never stopped to be '*actional*' (2018: 197) because as he wrote 'I must free myself from my strangler because I cannot breathe' (2018: 12).

What I find unambiguous in Fanon's work is that it does not give you a space to have any illusions, he kills them all eloquently and with such a realistic understanding. I say that because I have seen a lot of people running from one place to another to escape racism and I confessed that the idea has crossed my mind. But after reading Fanon you understand that no matter where you go, the same predatory system will be there, even if it manifests itself in another of its multiples faces.

Others try to engulf the pain and rage by becoming intoxicated by representations of Africa's glorious past, especially about Kemet (Egypt). We must remember. Yes, it is important to know about African civilizations that were destroyed by colonialism, but we must bear in mind that not of all of us are descendants of Pharaohs or the multi-billionaire King Mansa Musa of the Mali Empire.

For the great mass of Black peoples discovering an African past does not change their living condition. The people in the African continent who are struggling for better lives, improved access to healthcare, education, and housing are not doing so because they found out that Imhotep was the first genius or that

Timbuktu was the center of intellectual life. In our case, we are fighting because 'we cannot breathe' and this is so across the globe. In short, Fanon taught us that the struggle of Black people is the struggle to realize our full humanity, and when that happens, we will realize the humanity of all human beings on this planet.

What is extraordinary in Fanon's work is that he shows the reader the unheard and underground poisoned waters of our contemporary predatory system and its different nexus of positionality, while also telling you about solidarity among oppressed peoples. More importantly, the struggle must be conducted not on moral terms because power must be confronted with power. As he puts 'We shall see that another solution is possible. It implies a restructuring of the world' (2008: 63). Fanon the doctor, prescribed that 'the true disalienation of the Black man [and Black woman] implies a brutal awareness of the social and economic realities' (2008: xiv) in order to change the whole social structure from the bottom up and without being 'so naive as to believe that the appeals for reason or respect for human dignity can change reality' (2008: 199).

For all of the above, I think that Fanon's works have become fundamental reading for the 21st century. Not just for Africans but for all those who dare to struggle by showing revolutionary love for les *Damnés* for the creation of a 'new humanity'. Undoubtedly, Fanon has become fashionable to speak about, write and even to Whiten Fanon. Instead of speaking about these anemic intellectuals, I stress the necessity of spreading his works among masses. I suggest that a Fanon reading group should be created in every corner of the world and above of all in urban shanties, favelas, hoods, ghettos, *palanques, musseques* and barrios who live in this compartmentalized world will be identified by his words quickly. Fanon wrote about them even without knowing them.

To close, I say that 'no attempt must be made to encase man, for it is his destiny to be set free' (see Fanon, 2008: 205) and 'The only thing in the world worth starting: the end of the world, for heaven's sake' (Césaire quoted by Fanon, 2008: 76).

## Bibliography

Fanon, F. 1968 [1961]. *Les Damnés de La Terre*. Translated by Constance Farrington. New York: Grove Press.

_____. 1980. *Em Defesa da Revolução Africana*. Lisboa: Livraria Sá da Costa Edição.

_____. 2008. *Black Skin, White Mask*. Translated by Richard Philcox. New York: Grove Press.

Jussawalla, F. F., and Dasenbrock, R. W., 1992. *Interviews with Writers of the Postcolonial World*. University Press of Mississippi.

Kromo di Ghetto, 2009. O noz o ez, https://www.youtube.com/watch?v=cv47ivPlXbI.

Mendes, A. 2005. 'Arrastão' pôs em pânico praia de Carcavelos, Jornal o Público,' https://www.publico.pt/2005/06/11/jornal/arrastaopos-em-panico–praia-de-carcavelos-25047.

*Plataforma Gueto.* 2015. 'Vídeo do Genocídio da Policia Portuguesa contra Jovens Negros,' https://plataformagueto.wordpress.com/2015/02/27/video-do-geno-cidio-da-policia-portuguesa-contra-jovens-negros/.

*Portuguese Times.* 1990. '*Na Cova da Moura vivem três mil Cabo-Verdianos, ou seja, sobrevivem na sua condição de condenados da terra*,' Arquivo da Biblioteca António Ramos Rosa.

Rocha, F. 2012. 'Tibúrcio Não Vai Ao Futebol,' https://fr.napster.com/artist/fer-nando-rocha/album/the-best-of-12-years/track/tiburcio-nao-vai-ao-futebol.

Sanches, A. 2016. 'Tribunal Europeu condena Portugal no caso da mãe a quem foram retirados sete filhos,' *Jornal o Público*, https://www.publico.pt/2016/02/16/sociedade/noticia/portugal-condenado-por-tribunal-europeu-no-caso-da-mae-a-quem-foram-retirados-sete-filhos-1723450.

Thiong'o, N. 1992. *Decolonising the Mind: The Politics of Language in African Litera-ture*. Nairobi: East Africa Publishers.

Zenun Almada, F. 2020. 'Os Discursos Sobre a Cova da Moura: uma Análise Crítica e Exploratória a partir de Aguns Conceitos de Frantz Fanon.' Master's thesis in International Studies – Middle-east and North of Africa – ISCTE, https://repositorio.iscte-iul.pt/handle/10071/21783.

# BLACK MIND IN MOTION

Gene Reid

---

*In my own country I am in a far-off land*
*I am strong but have no force or power*
*I win all yet remain a loser*
*At break of day I say goodnight*
*When I lie down I have a great fear*
        *Of falling.*
—Francois Villon

If *Black Skin White Masks* is the groundwork of transcendence of the minds of humanity, then *The Wretched of the Earth* is the military wing that the transcendence will fly on to reach completion. Violence is not the act of rebellion alone as a physical act but also the violence counter to the violence implemented upon the minds and body of the oppressed and the butchery of the state to suppress the idea of freedom. The idea of liberation is embodied in the oppressed who are forced into a self-destructive and walled-in cell of despair: the bottom rung of society with minimum vision of a way out. Fanon's wretched of the earth: where Black on Black crime, drugs, gang warfare upon which the state builds invisible walls of confinement that cannot be crossed without police violence meeting the violator. Unable to shed our Black skin in a society where being Black in itself is a crime, a society built on White supremacy i.e. American capital. To reach a Black consciousness as Fanon projected is a step in the negation of White racist society. It is the idea of self, as whole human being that will uproot the very structure of a society, which feeds the mind that White equals success under the dominance of capital. But the impossibility of that economic transcendence to be 'White' among the Black masses creates an alienation that eats away at the spirit of our Black being; a caustic existence that can and will eat away at the very inhuman foundation at the very root of capitalist society.

Fanon was fighting colonialism, which is a word that we don't hear so much about today. It existed during Fanon's lifetime as an outside force, in his case France, that planted its forces upon a Third World country. The key word is found in the forced relationship of cultural submission. Language, religion, and values of the self are stolen alongside the land and this is embodied in culture and identity. This form of colonized embodiment of the Black mind exists today. In other words, Fanon is as relevant today as ever. If anything, the oppression has become more sophisticated, expressed in the tactics of attack. Malcolm X characterized it as the difference between 'the wolf and the fox'. Today the 'wolf' is the Donald Trump (the Wallace of today) who is confrontational in your face, while the 'fox' is a 'Joe Biden' (the Kennedy type) who can sneak around to undercut the movement. Which is more dangerous? Malcolm thought the 'fox' was harder to confront due to their misleading tactics which will compromise 'the moment' in history to get you on their 'ground' or remove the movement from that fertile 'Black soil' (the news of the grassroots movement from below) onto the 'slippery slope' of reform or compromise. While Trump must go, the electoral politics that allows the vote against Trump will not allow us to shift the ground of the capitalist state to transcend Black/White/Brown existence into new human relationships, beyond the foundation of American slavery. Thus the question remains, how do we change human relationships under the impact of this movement?

## Creation of New Human Relationships

From my experience, the civil rights movement of the 1950s and 1960s created the ground which brought about a 'collision' as new relations developed between Black and White youth through integration. It was an expression of how the 'battle for the minds of man' is the greatest battle of all. It confronted the need to separate the races and control the thought of how one race views another. All the lies our parents and adults told their children came undone when children sat side by side in a classroom and determined that we, Black and White, were not as far apart beyond the color of our skin which was only a shell of an image created to suppress our dreams of a free social existence beyond the labels of 'White' and 'Colored'. The nonviolent movement for civil rights became concrete as an idea of freedom through the 'violent' act of revolution; an idea which took root through a human force, a spirit, which displaced the concrete reality of White supremacy. Fanon speaks to 'national culture' in *The Wretched of the Earth* where the revolution transcends the culture of being Black and is expressed in a 'new language' which is spoken with a clarity of thought among the masses. National consciousness expressed in culture developed through practice as the movement to theory is expressed as a new language! 'But' Fanon adds, "the native intellectual who wishes to create an authentic work of art must realize that the truths of a nation are in the first place its realities. He must go on until he has found the seething pot out of which the learning of the future will emerge' (Fanon, 1968: 225).

The 'Black mind' is under attack, where wartime forms of oppression exist in the inner city of America producing forms of 'PTSD' to where Blacks cannot hold a job—a job requires a certain amount of discipline, to be on time, punch a clock, being a felon, etc.—to the point of an unemployed Black army internally exploding on itself though the self-destructive practice of violence, drug abuse, alcohol, to murder i.e. self-hate reflected in a ghetto form of isolation unable to cross the color line of gangs and race of 'inferiority' which 'has been felt economically'. 'In opposition to rationalism', which is to live a human life, the invisible Black, Fanon argued, 'summoned up the negative side, but... forgot that this negative draws its worth from an almost substantive absoluteness. A consciousness committed to experience is ignorant, has to be ignorant, of the essences and the determination of its being' (Fanon, 1967: 134). Identity needs to be realized and can only be realized when movements take place. The 'taking a knee' during the playing of the American national anthem that Colin Kaepernick made famous and which got him 'fired' from the National Football League is now common-place at 'all' sporting events under the impact of the George Floyd movement. This act of defiance has been realized in consciousness as a new Black reality. There is a southern saying from Black folks that 'nothing comes from the top down but grave-digging!' The state will not uproot the very ground upon which it is built. Only a self-determined consciousness, conscious of its human force, can reach a new concept of human thought and answer Fanon's question 'who am I?' anew. It can change the reality of what is at the root of the 'small prison cell of self' under capital in which we live. To be human demands to know the universal dimension, which can transcend the world as we know it. Fanon looked at the mental illness of the oppressed which we can see in his chapter in *The Wretched of the Earth* on 'Colonial War and Mental Disorders': 'Once again, the objective of the native who fights against himself is to bring about the end of domina-tion. But he ought equally to pay attention to the liquidation of all untruths implanted in his being by oppression' (1968: 309). Fanon wrote extensively of this 'self-destructive' image of the Black world. Black self-movement is beyond eco-nomic liberation, where the Black can't adapt to 'hold a job' or 'migrate' into mainstream White society.

In *Black Skin White Masks*, Fanon brings to light the lived experience of the Black professional who is seen as only a Negro: 'look Mama a nigger' among the French, where you must speak French with the pronunciation of the French-man to be accepted: language reflects education or class status, as he puts it, 'the myth of the nigger-that-eats his-R's' (1967: 21), liking it to being 'locked away, entombed' most of your life in poverty in life and thought. Now you must 'fit in' as the 'invisible force' for change, making your presence known and seen as a 'danger to society' as 'we know it'. The only fear is of the 'change', which will upset that comfort zone of White society. Their last line of defense, beside eco-nomic domination, is the police force which is there to extract all that appears defiant and threatening, with the image alone, 'my being'... is a crime! A lot of us don't know how the other half of society lives, the two worlds, one Black, one White, separate and unequal, which is to the detriment of society as a whole.

The Black world lives in fear of being sacrificed for the 'betterment of society'. FEAR is the first chapter in Richard Wright's book *Native Son*, which still char-acterizes a lot of what we see in these police shootings of Blacks today. Living in fear is a big part of being Black in America. Fear can be an aggressive ten-dency that can lead to a Black individual's reaction to a Black existence that can lead to death by police bullets or by one of our own. To cover up his fear Bigger Thomas in Wright's *Native Son* would bully his homeboys, abuse others, inflict pain to cover up his own inadequacy, including killing his girlfriend, his White employers' daughter who patronizingly attempted to explore and feel Big-ger's Black pain of being entombed in a Black world. But that forced relation-ship of 'kindness' alienated Bigger more and drove him to accidentally suffocate the drunken young woman in a dark bedroom, not wanting to be discovered by the young woman's blind mother, who probably would scream rape. The fear of being seen as a Black 'rapist' by a White world spelled death to Bigger Thomas.

In a lot of Black murders by police, you can smell the fear from Blacks being 'hunted' or confronted for being an object of fear, we fit the profile of being out of place in a White world where normally we are made invisible. Two worlds collide against a 'wall': a movement to suppress social consciousness among Blacks, while we demand recognition, but under racial profiling we must remain invisible. Recognition is a power, a threat to the powers-that-be, because we need to determine our own destiny as Humankind. If 'Black Lives Matter', it is because 'her' life impacts the world. If the movement hits a 'dead end', it would be very disheartening at this time because we have already been through Black electoral politics.

How does Black Lives Matter as a group of activists who has impacted the youth of all colors, from the antifascist struggle to the anarchists, to the sports world, and as an 'organization of thought' give voice to the narrative of the *zeitgeist,* a German word to define spirit or mind, the spirit of the times, as freedom made explicit in history, as the force shown by how ideas of freedom move masses and how beliefs of the time concretize that vision? Of course we need to grapple with actuality as activists but we also need not be stagnant in thought but develop an idealism which can transform reality. In other words, not just fight about our present existence, but also create a new reality. For example, even the concept of 'reform the police' coming out of the movement today could mean many things, and the movement needs to set the narrative rather than let others define it.

The police make their living through carrying out violent acts within the community. 'Black on Black crime' feeds the cops with more overtime and helps to keep the police employed and in control within the community. You might think that police are here to suppress the 'crime wave' but in reality, they feed a wave of violence to keep us divided. I witnessed that during the Gang Truce in Watts as part of the 1992 L.A. rebellion. The cops fed the narrative of the gang truce as an attempt to create organized crime on a greater scale. In other words the truce scared them. The truce reflected too much power in the hands of the people in the community.

In 'The Pitfalls of National Consciousness', Fanon speaks to Black as identity which is just the beginning of a movement to reach independence and which is not the end of the struggle for Black consciousness. In this section Fanon is very critical of the Black 'educated class' and the petty bourgeois elements who become the new ruling class and stop the movement at Black identity without changing social and economic relationships from 'top to bottom'. That reality has held true within this country. In a sense, ever since the murders of Malcolm X and Dr. King. This state's sanctioned form of murder is an attempt to kill the movement by killing the 'peacemakers' as a search for a harsh truth to unite the movement across the color barrier, as a new reality that can destabilize the state structure that White supremacy empowers. The system attempts to kill a movement at its peak by cutting off its head. These murders from within the movement or by the state help to kill the social movement before it can reach the next step of transforming capitalist society from a Black identity to a class identity of Black Mind and thus become closer to freedom. As a critique Black Power became reduced to Black capital which left open the door to class society or old forms of oppression with a Black face under a White mask. I think Fanon holds the keys to that next step with his philosophy of Black Consciousness as self-movement toward to a new humanism.

## Where I Met Fanon: A Black Worker's Reason for Revolution

I 'met Fanon' in spirit, in 1975, while attending the CETA (Comprehensive Employment and Training Act) program at the Watts Skill Center (a self-help program for youth, which paid a minimum wage to learn a trade), in South Central Los Angeles, where I learned to weld. A Caribbean student in the school had a copy of *Black Skin White Masks*, which caught my attention. The cover spoke to me, knowing the cover picture was a critique of Black assimilation into White society where Black skin is not enough to realize Black identity. So I bought a copy and began to 'find myself' within the pages of his writings, which led to a 'shock of recognition' that being Black, poor and a worker wasn't within itself an individual problem but was a social condition under capital that hailed within the 'subject' as Black and labor, its solution in the 'uprising'. Fanon spoke to me '... you are not alone, but there are millions just like you, alienated and self-destructive. Turn that negative energy into a force of reason for change within today's Black world'.

I was born in Alabama into a segregated system of the 1950s and went through integration in 1967. Most Black elected officials voted into office during this period came from within the Black community. In order not to split the Black vote, between more than one Black candidate, the 'block vote' (a pre-vote among Black candidates to determine who would run for office in order not to split the Black vote) was used. My grandfather was chosen to run for the city council and won as the first Black city councilmen in that area of Alabama. A great accomplishment, but 'we', my Grandfather and I, couldn't find common ground with our differences in age and attitude toward the system of White supremacy and to 'racist cops' in our small town. I had issues with my grandfather's conversion to compromise the revolutionary act of a Black being voted into political office in the newly integrated South. Even though I was a troubled Black youth, I felt my grandfather, whom I loved, was complacent in his newly found position of 'power'. This illuminated for me the need for real drastic change of the system. Such change cannot come on capitalist ground; we must set our own ground. The capitalist system will swallow you whole if you attempt change from the top. As Fanon puts it, 'In order to assimilate and to experience the oppressor's culture, the native has had to leave certain of his intellectual possession in pawn. These pledges include his adoption of the forms of thought of the ... bourgeoisie' (1968: 49). I took it very personally. 'Individual experience, because it is national and because it is a link in the chain of national existence, ceases to be individual, limited, and shrunken and is enabled to open out into the truth of the nation and the world' (1968: 200). In so many words, the conditions for the poor and Black people did not change with the Black vote alone; the class question came front and center. The Civil Rights Movement was short-stopped by a new Black leadership that stopped its continued movement. This isn't necessarily about betrayal but about the 'ground' that had shifted. Only 'in the name of the spirit' of the movement should the leader exist. The success of the individual leader must reflect freedom of the whole of society under the impact of the Black consciousness movement for identity.

Now, how do we answer the class question that is not always discrete but, in some ways, made explicit throughout Fanon's writings, even though race is forefront; how do we achieve 'a new Humanism' without attacking relationships at the point of production? Fanon stated 'that the tool must never possess the man' (1967: 231). Alienated relationships at the point of production impact the development of self-identity to self-movement to becoming a conscious human being whose work is at the root of capitalist society. How does that 'tool' extend to Mind? I keep thinking of 'two worlds', and pulling back the curtain, to expose the rock bottom poverty of the working poor and starving jobless families. An exposure that takes us back decades in this country. The 'right to a union' comprises two bosses with 'no rights to the worker'. The answer is the not so simple question of 'TIME', of when does the working day begin and when does it end; forced labor and starvation wages is death to the worker, who creates all we see as wealth in this world. I think that is where the hammer starts to forge its metal about a subject who hungers to reach reason in their lifetime. If 'American' White labor can't confront its racism then the forward movement of all 'labor of color', Black in particular, is derailed in America. While Black labor is struck with the double-edged sword of race and class in which there appears to be a death sentence, 'the dialectic of the Subject' is in reality a liberation of being, 'in the process of becoming' (Dunayevskaya, 1973: 7), from the bottom upward. All those above are moved progressively forward, but labor will need a strong wake-up call for our future to be realized.

Today, the Black masses make up the bulk of the mass of unemployed, imprisoned, and the outlaw brand of the outcast element within society. How do we transcend that Black reality into a new living human existence? What can we concretely do to change that relationship at the point of production to create employment in which computers don't set the pace for a quicker production process and where the human doesn't become the tool enslaved by the machine? If 'machines' controlled by capital's drive for profit create production speedup, then the workers can produce their 'worth' in less time. In other words, the machine should be a tool, not the human being a tool for the machine. So why not shorten the working day? Six hours of work for eight hours of pay can put more workers to work. The capitalist's profit would be impacted! But employing a new fourth shift of workers would require benefits, retirement, sick leave, etc. and cut capitalist profit. Would the politicians, Democratic or Republican, be willing to compromise their profit short of a revolution? If you sit in the capitalist boat, you don't rock the boat for fear of going overboard.

COVID-19 has put the capitalist economic disparity under a microscope. It has exposed a massive gap in class society. 'What's good for Wall Street is not always what's good for Main Street'. Within the first six months of the pandemic 29 million people were collecting unemployment, while the net worth of the 600 billionaires in the U.S. grew by 20%. Jeff Bezos' net worth grew to 43.8 billion dollars.

A racial divide exists. 'Eviction COVID-19 = Murder', said one protest sign held by a Black protester, and it reflects that economic divide as a life and death question:

> No, there is no question of a return to Nature. It is simply a very concrete question of not dragging men toward mutilation, of not imposing upon the brain rhythms which very quickly obliterate it and wreck it. The pretext of catching up must not be used to push man around, to tear him away from himself or from his privacy (to think), to break and kill him [his spirit]. (Fanon, 1968: 314)

Needless to say I had no background in Hegel in 1975 when I discovered Fanon. But I found Hegel was a big part of Fanon's concepts in chapter seven of *Black Skin White Masks* titled 'The Black and Recognition'. In the section titled 'The Black and Hegel', 'Being', 'Consciousness of Self' and 'Other' are spelled out as a movement toward Black Identity as liberation. I needed the Hegelian dialectic to understand Fanon even though Fanon takes issue with Hegel, that recognition needed to be expounded through the additive of color. Fanon deepened that new Black reality into a Black consciousness. Even when the Black slave is 'free' from the master-slave relationship she or he will never be free from the 'jail cell' of their Blackness in a system dominated by White supremacy. So a deepening of the Hegelian dialectic is needed to reach that reciprocity and to recognize the consciousness of self. In other words, the 'Master' is as much a slave to himself as a master to others because he cannot reach his Human side.

> The only means of breaking this vicious circle that throws me back on myself is to restore to the other, through mediation and recognition, their human reality, which is different from natural reality. The other has to perform the same operation. Action from one side only would be useless, because what is to happen can only be brought about by means of both ... they recognize themselves as mutually recognizing each other. (1967: 217)

To help bridge that gap I found Raya Dunayevskaya's philosophy of Marxist-Humanism in 1979. It helped to put Marx, Fanon, and Hegel's philosophy into perspective for me. Being a worker, Marx's philosophical materialism spoke to my labor and Fanon spoke to my Blackness, while Dunayevskaya brought out the subjective union of both, as force and reason of revolution. A link to a new world opened up with Dunayevskaya being the 'red thread' that showed an ideological union of historical significance. The idea of Black and labor as subject and as reason, was made explicit as they became narrators of their own thoughts transcending the 'master / slave' reality while attempting to bridge the gap between practice, theory and revolution. It spoke to the need to create a new Humanism which is what Fanon and Marx were calling for, 'to set afoot a new man' as Fanon puts it. To visualize the whole Human being, not just a 'set of hands'. The butchered lives of Blacks and of labor, alienated, had to be intellectualized in theory and transformed in practice into new social individuals and FREE beings, what Dunayevskaya called 'The self-determination of the fact, reason, and reality, self-developing toward the ideal: 'It is the nature of the fact, the notion which causes the movement and development, yet this same movement is equally the action of cognition" (Hegel quoted in Dunayevskaya, 1973: 42).[1]

No ideal or utopian concepts are an end in themselves, the idea alone will not uproot capitalism or dethrone ruthless rulers who attack and attempt to control the narrative of our identity, whether it is being Black, being women, being a worker, or being all three. The attack upon the idea of freedom, or the mind of the subject, is like the attacks by the state forces—from the police to the armed forces, to the citizen militia—to suppress history, or any movement forward. A conservative way of thinking is to be 'marking time' to maintain 'what is', as oppressive as it might be for the majority of people. The conservatives consider themselves as preservers of civilization. Society moves forward only with the 'whips and kicks' of a consciousness and a forward social movement. Dialectical motion is something that is internal to Human life, which requires thought's growth as masses in motion. For example, the Women's Liberation Movement as subject: When women move forward—beyond men's fear of a whole woman, 'body and mind'—that subjective movement of women moves the whole of society forward. I was watching CBS Sunday Morning on the hundredth anniversary of Women's right to vote on August 18th 2020 and when women got the right to vote, there was a fear that Black women or that all Blacks would get the right to vote against segregation. Segregationists, including some White women, stood against the women's right to vote. And corporations feared that if women got the right to vote, that would end child labor.

How can a subject of revolution be made explicit as a subject, and reflect its multidimensionality as a beacon of light illuminating the way to transcend America's reality under President Trump or Biden? The Idea of freedom in its subjective form needs to be articulated in theory to break chains to our minds and help the freedom fighter, even when that individual cannot see the connection, or the universal repercussions that exist from the revolt, from America to Africa to the Caribbean in the Black World.

## 'America the Beautiful' ... A Nightmare

America has put its stamp upon the world. What is America known for, if not for world domination through production and military might, a glowing example of capitalism? Trump makes America's world relationship more explicit with his

---

1. For a more explicit Marxist-Humanist view on Fanon see John Alan and Lou Turner, *Frantz Fanon, Soweto and American Black Thought*.

'America First' nationalist agenda. Whatever happened to the 'roots of freedom', if they really ever existed in American culture? Freedom can only be imagined within the embodiment of the people. Freedom is not the state that propagates freedom draped in an American flag. The American flag was characterized by Black Americans as 'stars and bars' instead of 'stars and stripes'. The 'stars' that we see are from being assaulted by the police and the 'bars' we see are after being locked down behind prison walls. The system suppresses the rights of immigrant labor of color, the weak and the poor whose voices go unheard. Only when the human spirit takes on life can freedom exist.

As a working-class Black man within the walls of Trump's America, being only a step away from imprisonment or death, I grew up in the Deep South under segregation and saw movements for integration. For me, Black identity or Black Consciousness is not an abstraction. To identify with Fanon's reality in Black thought is a power within itself, to turn a negative identity into a positive concept for change.

> Comrades, let us flee from this motionless movement where gradually dialectic is changing into the logic of equilibrium. Let us reconsider the question of cerebral reality and of the cerebral mass of all humanity, whose connection must be increased, whose channels must be diversified and whose message must be re-humanized'. (Fanon, 1968: 314)

## Bibliography

Alan, J., and Turner, L. 1986. *Frantz Fanon, Soweto & American Black Thought*. New expanded edition. Chicago: News & Letters.

Dunayevskaya, R. 1973. *Philosophy and Revolution: From Hegel to Sartre and from Marx to Mao*. New York: Delacorte Press.

Fanon, F. 1967. *Black Skin White Masks*. New York: Grove Press.

_____. 1968. *The Wretched of the Earth*. New York: Grove Press.

# SETTING AFOOT A NEW PEOPLE: PRISON INTELLECTUALS, NEW AFRIKAN COMMUNISM AND THE MAKING OF MEDITATIONS ON FRANTZ FANON'S *WRETCHED OF THE EARTH*

Toussaint Losier

In the summer of 2011, Sanyinka Shakur, then one of California's most well-known prisoners, circulated two essays that hint at the enduring influence of Frantz Fanon's *Wretched of the Earth*. Born in Los Angeles, he had gained notoriety as the bestselling author of *Monster: The Autobiography of an L.A. Gang Member*. Its gripping narrative detailed Shakur's ruthless street and prison exploits as part of Los Angeles' Eight Tray Gangster Crips, as well as his personal transformation into an avowed revolutionary. While behind bars, Shakur had pledged his allegiance to the New Afrikan Independence Movement (NAIM), a national liberation struggle committed to forging an independent Black nation-state out of the five Southeastern states of the U.S. Emerging after Black activists had struggled for and won the passage of landmark civil and voting rights legislation in 1968, the launch of this movement, as one scholar notes, effectively 'indicted the United States as unredeemable and uninhabitable for the descendants of the country's enslaved' (Onaci, 2020: 2). For these political commitments, prison officials would confine him to the Secure Housing Unit (SHU) of Pelican Bay State Prison, California's infamous super maximum-security correctional facility and the subject of his more recent political writings (Scott, 1993: 352).

Held for 22½ hours a day in long term solitary confinement, Shakur sought to rally other prisoners around the idea of an open-ended hunger strike. Months earlier, a small group of prisoners held in the SHU's 'short corridor' had called for the strike. In the short corridor, corrections officials reserved the most extreme isolation for those deemed to pose the greatest threat to security. Conversely, officials had placed Shakur in the somewhat less restrictive 'long corridor' and it was from here that he wrote his first essay, 'Who Are You', as a pledge of support for the strike call. For him and others he had helped to recruit to the NAIM, their participation was not only an endorsement of the strike's five core demands for changes to California's use of solitary confinement. It was also a recognition that this protest built upon an unbroken line of struggle that had originated in the first armed resistance by African people to the encroaching European slave trade and continued through subsequent moments of militant revolt and struggles for self-determination. For Shakur, the strike would be more than simply an act of resistance to the conditions of their confinement; it would be an affirmation of their New Afrikan national identity (Shakur, 2013: 135-145, 178-184).

While the first essay had been a public declaration of support, the second would be a more private document criticizing those unwilling to join the fight. Written just three days before the strike was set to begin, 'The Reverse Nuremberg Defense' castigated prisoners who professed to be 'about the struggle' but now refused to participate in this collective action, even though they were to be its main beneficiaries. Analyzing both the dynamics of their own oppression as well as the contradictions the strike proposal was exposing amongst prisoners themselves, Shakur used this essay to criticize those held in the SHU, specifically prisoners regularly threatened with transfer to the further isolation of the 'short corridor', urging them to reconnect to a decades-long tradition of collective resistance. Circulated amongst those on the 'long corridor', this second essay hit a nerve. The strike began on July 1st, 2011. By the end of the first day, nearly every prisoner in the SHU was on strike. Within a week, roughly six thousand prisoners across the state of California were refusing food. On the twentieth day, the historic strike ended with an official acknowledgement of prisoners' demands and the first steps towards ending indefinite solitary confinement at Pelican Bay (Shakur, 2013: 178-184).

Beyond the scope of the 2011 hunger strike, these two essays reflect Shakur's own contributions to a New Afrikan Communist school of thought, a body of revolutionary theory deeply informed by Fanon's classic text. More than a decade and half earlier, Shakur had first encountered this book at the outset of his political development and found it quite difficult. 'Admittedly the book was over my head', he writes in his autobiography. 'I couldn't overstand what Fanon was saying' (Shakur, 2010). With the support of his comrades, Shakur continued to struggle with the text, gaining a greater appreciation for its insights as the years passed. In the first essay he circulated that summer, Shakur identified the Algerian revolutionary as a theorist whose work is studied by those within the NAIM alongside the likes of Che and Cabral. He also mentioned Owusu Yaki Yakubu, who although decidedly less prominent, but no less important. In fact, Yaki remained one of the most significant influences on Shakur's own ideological development.

Held for decades in Illinois' most secure prisons, Yaki had cut his teeth as an organizer, jailhouse lawyer, and movement strategist during the 1970s and 80s. Later, he would soon begin circulating letters and then later pamphlets to Shakur and others that offered an interpretation of Fanon altogether different from most academic and popular accounts.

More a study guide than a literary explication, Yaki's *Meditations on Frantz Fanon's Wretched of the Earth: For NAC's and other Activists who struggle against Racism and Neo-Colonialism (Capitalism) and for the 'Setting Afoot' of New People (Socialist/ Communist Humanism)* proposed a thoroughly original approach to reading *Wretched*'s core themes of violence and colonialism, nationalism and independence across individual chapters.[1] Circulated first as letters, Yaki's writings would leave their impression on Shakur and other imprisoned New Afrikans: 'when We started receiving these Meditations, I was so grateful that the Comrad had taken the time to break down Wretched from a New Afrikan Communist perspective' (Shakur, 2010). Published first as a set of essays and then posthumously as a book, *Meditations* would be Yaki's last major intellectual project. Offering what has been described as 'one of the most profound studies of *The Wretched of the Earth*', Yaki's *Meditations* puts forward a novel reconsideration of the place of race, class, and national consciousness within the colonial context (Hudis, no date). It does so by re-examining this and other themes within the broader scope of decolonization in the United States. In doing so, Yaki's work opens up both new interpretations of Fanon's ideas and contributed to the resurgence of New Afrikan thought behind bars in the years leading up to the 2011 Pelican Bay hunger strike and in the years since.

## Baptisms in Blood

Although Yaki had encountered Fanon's classic 'handbook of the Black Revolution', at a young age, it would not be until years later that he felt that he was able to grasp some of its most salient point, particularly on the question of violence. Born James Sayles in 1948, he was the child of working-class parents who had joined more than 5 million other New Afrikans in leaving the South in the aftermath of the Great Depression. In particular his mother's family had come from Mississippi, part of the 'Black Belt' that stretched across the Deep South in which the majority of New Afrikans lived. It was this region that the NAIM would consider its national territory. This had been the crucible for the creation of a new people out of the various West and Central African nationalities during the early 19th century. It was from here that Yaki's parents would be forced to flee, ultimately settling in Chicago. 'Only after political activity', he would later write, 'was i able to reflect on my early years and the story of my family's flight to the North, and make connections to the story of New Afrikan people in the U.S., and the struggle to regain independence' (Yakubu, 2001). Absent an awareness of how his individual experience connected to the broader experience of African peoples in the United State, Yaki was left to navigate the pitfalls of an adolescence on the city's South side.

After dropping out of high school, Yaki would find himself repeatedly arrested by police and then jailed for the first time at the age of thirteen. Henceforward, most of his intellectual and political development would take place behind bars, as confinement marked the remaining balance of his life. In and out of Illinois' juvenile reformatories through his teenage years, it was here that Yaki began to read seriously, primarily Black literature and poetry as well as *The Autobiography of Malcolm X*. While being held in jail on an armed robbery and attempted

---

1. In the subtitle, NAC is an acronym for New Afrikan communist.

murder charge in 1967, it would be conversations with other inmates that would lead him to a deeper engagement with Black Nationalist and Pan-African ideas, including the work of Fanon. 'Yaki was one of those rebels for whom Fanon wrote his *Wretched of the Earth* in the first place', his editors recounted. 'One of those stateless youth who followed Fanon and other liberating voices into taking up the political violence that the white colonist had tried to reserve for himself' (Sayles, 2010: 4). Found guilty, he would spend just over a year in Illinois' Pontiac prison, connecting with other prisoners with whom he continued to read about and debate these ideas. Together, they formed a study group, printed a newsletter, and plotted on how to connect the movement on the streets to their struggles behind bars. But without a clear political line and organizational program holding them together, those in the group tended to drift away upon release. This problem compounded itself when Yaki, following his release in late 1968, attempted to establish an organizational foundation for their activity once the remainder were released. 'For two years I'd been committed to the early vision of the group—but my feet were by then firmly planted on the side of aboveground activity, and now i was hearing calls for 'action'', he later explained. In addition, 'i'd always had these Mau Mau images, and Fanon's depictions of dashes into the forbidden zones, and of baptisms in blood' (Yakubu, 2001). Without much of a plan, Yaki and a friend, Henry Dee, attempted to obtain weapons, which he later termed 'our own infantile version of entering the forbidden zone', only to end up beaten and arrested by police on charges of having killed a young white couple living on the city's more affluent Northside (Yakubu, 2001).

The subsequent murder trial took place just as Chicago was in the midst of a panic over this sort of violence. The panic was fueled by the mainstream press and its fears about 'De Mau Mau', purportedly a loose network of thousands of Black Vietnam war veterans. Originally formed on U.S. military bases in West Germany and South Vietnam on the basis of cultural pride and self-defense, the press speculated, 'De Mau Mau' had served as the base of recruitment for those who now sought to carry out random attacks on white suburban residents. Although a few seemingly unrelated killings had occurred, the city's chief prosecutor quickly cast them as part of a 'nationwide conspiracy to kill whites' (Sayles, 2010: 17). Although Yaki's case was not linked to these killings, it went to trial amidst this hysteria. If the death penalty had not been declared unconstitutional several years earlier, he and his co-defendant would have likely been sent to the electric chair. Instead, a judge sentenced them to 100 to 200 years in prison. Transferred to Stateville, once considered the 'toughest prison in the world', Yaki spent his first several years appealing his case. Although unsuccessful, the practical expertise he gained would help him to make contact with imprisoned members of the Republic of New Afrika (RNA), the most prominent organization within the NAIM. At roughly the same time, another set of connections would bring him in contact with members of the Black Liberation Army (BLA), the armed underground formation that had grown in prominence as the repression facing the Black Panther Party and other revolutionary organizations escalated during the early 1970s.

These new political relationships would inform Yaki's efforts to form a new study group in Stateville prison, composed primarily of imprisoned Black Panthers and other political militants. Organized first as the Stateville Prisoner Organization (SPO) and then as the New Afrikan Prisoner Organization (NAPO), this group would draw close to the RNA's Provisional Government and the Coordinating Committee of the BLA. At first, this new group carried out much of the same work as the old one—political education, circulating a newsletter, and organizing alongside outside organizations—with the added focus of rallying support for prisoners indicted for the killing of prison guards. Through the course of the 1970s, its cadres played a key role in mobilizing public support for these prisoners and laying out the strategy for defense campaigns. This would include the 'Pontiac Brothers', the case of 17 Black prisoners, nearly all of them high-ranking street gang members, indicted for the killing of three guards at Pontiac during the course of twin rebellions there and at Stateville in July 1978. Occurring just after Illinois had reinstated the death penalty, this would be the largest civilian death penalty case in U.S. history.

From behind bars, Yaki would play a pivotal role in the Pontiac Brothers defense campaign. During the first days after the rebellion, he helped to craft the class action lawsuit that challenged the lockdown corrections officials had imposed on both prisons. During the months that followed, he helped to lay out a multi-pronged strategy that sought to mobilize support for the defendants in their own community, while also challenging the state's narrative within Chicago more broadly. Yaki's involvement helped to draw in Chokwe Lumumba, then the Midwestern Vice President for the RNA. A skilled lawyer, Lumumba agreed to represent Larry Hoover, a leader of the Black Gangster Disciple Nation and the case's most notorious defendant. Moreover, Yaki argued that the campaign also needed to attend to the political consciousness of prisoners themselves. Although Hoover would not be among the first group of defendants to go on trial, he was one of the six Pontiac Brothers who called on Lumumba to file a motion that casts them as colonial subjects and linked their prosecution to, as a defense campaign newsletter put it, the 'State's attempt to suppress the New Afrikan Liberation Struggle in total' (Pontiac Prisoner Support Coalition, 1980: 7). This motion would not be successful, but it spoke to the ways in ways in Yaki and others used the trial to raise not only the public's awareness about the inhumane condition prisoners faced behind bars, but also the political consciousness of those on trial for their lives. In the spring of 1981, a Cook County jury acquitted the first group of Pontiac Brothers of the charges against them and prosecutors announced that the charges against the remaining defendants would be dropped. It was a signal victory and one that proved Yaki's defense campaign strategy correct. At the same time, it came at the beginning of a slow ebb in the movement both inside and outside of the prison walls. Over the next several decades, Yaki would find himself be surrounded by younger prisoners increasingly disconnected from the radical ferment of the sixties.

In some sense, Shakur was an example of the potential of this new generation of prisoners. Born Kody Scott and raised in South Central California, he had been thoroughly drawn to the martial camaraderie of gang life by the end of

sixth grade. Over the next several years, he would gain notoriety as a street combatant so brutally violent that his friends dubbed him 'Monster'. Like Yaki, he
would have his first exposure to nationalist politics while behind bars, though in
Los Angeles county jail while awaiting trial for shooting and severely wounding
a rival. Here, Shakur would be recruited into the Consolidated Crip Organization, an attempt by imprisoned gang leaders to infuse revolutionary nationalist politics into a unified gang structure. Now, a member of a quasi-political
Crip faction, he would be given the name 'Sanyinka', meaning 'Custodian of the
Nation'. Once convicted of mayhem and sentenced to seven years in state prison,
he would be shipped to California's Soledad prison in 1984. During only his first
year there, Shakur would experience his own 'baptism in blood' with the stab-
bing of a notoriously racist prison guard. Implicated in the attack, Shakur would
be hit with a twenty-eight-month solitary confinement sentence in the infamous
San Quentin prison (Bing, 1991: 239-240; Scott, 1993: 340-41). 'At that stage', he
later explained, 'i just thought revolution was physical violence. i thought We'd
only need to gather enough people together in order to get free. i had an ill
notion about what We were trying to get free from, and, further, to get free to?'
(Shakur, 2013: 7) Faced with these questions, it would be in near isolation that
Shakur would slowly experience his own political awakening.

Just as this newer generation of prisoners continued to inundate the system,
Yaki would see many of his closest comrades either pass away or scatter upon
their release. At the same time, prison authorities further restricted the number
of papers and books that he could keep in his cell, successively whittling down
what had once been a substantial personal library. 'All this led him to decide
to center himself on one major project which only required two books', his editors later wrote, 'a reappraisal and explanation of Frantz Fanon's greatest revolutionary writing, *Wretched of the Earth*' (Sayles, 2010: 36). This project's primary
audience would be younger militants, who, like Shakur, had, 'picked up *Wretched*
only to put it down before completing it, because they'd found it 'too hard to
read'' (Sayles, 2010: 145). Doing this might in some ways make up for his own initial errors, when, as a youth, he had grasped only Fanon's sharp excoriation of
colonial racism and endorsement of revolutionary violence. Returning back to it,
Yaki hoped that a younger generation would grasp Fanon's deeper commitment
to a liberatory communist thought, while sharpening their own abilities to read
and think critically for themselves.

## A School of New Afrikan Communist Thought

Yaki opened his guide to *Wretched* by offering his own approach to making sense
of the book and its relevance to militants in the United States. From the outset, he suggested that many of those who professed to be experts on or even
just familiar with Fanon's work tended to overlook some of its most profound
insights. Admittedly, the author himself had only gained greater clarity about
some of Fanon's more nuanced arguments after having returned to the text  more
than a decade after having read it for the first time: 'it was at this point that

i could begin to distinguish sections within each chapter, and i then began to number the paragraphs of each chapter—and to read and meditate upon one paragraph at a time, then one section at a time' (Sayles, 2010: 146). Through a practice of reading and reflecting paragraph by paragraph, he began to unravel the complexities often overlooked by a more straightforward appraisal. Take the fact, for instance, that Fanon speaks in several voices throughout the text. He uses the voice of the 'native' under colonialism, the voice of the 'ex-native' or 'ex-negro' who has decided to fight the colonist, and the voice of the person who has overthrown colonialism only to discover the limits of national independence. By speaking through these different voices at different points in just a single chapter, Yaki explains, 'Fanon is carrying us through a process of 'decolonization'—through the stages of struggle for national independence *and* social revolution'. However, he doesn't take us through a 'linear progression' as (western) convention may have it' (Sayles, 2010: 149). Instead, the use of these different voices helped Fanon to register the changing subjective conditions and political circumstances faced as one progressed through a national liberation struggle.

This use of different voices was also an example of the dynamism with which Fanon engaged crucial themes like racism and violence, national consciousness and cultural production. Far from being relegated to just one chapter, these themes reappeared throughout, usually as different manifestations of this broader process of decolonization. 'Don't, for example, read only the first chapter and then think that you know Fanon's position on 'violence', he writes. 'Don't read the eleventh paragraph of the first chapter, without reading the last four paragraphs of the second chapter (or the relevant lines in the third chapter) and think that you understand Fanon's position on 'race' or 'racism'. An incomplete reading means superficial understanding and a distortion of your own development' (Sayles, 2010: 151). To gain a more complete understanding of Fanon's ideas, he suggests that at the very least, particular chapters be read together as parts of a larger whole.

First, one should read the preface by French philosopher Jean-Paul Sartre. Then, one should read Chapters 1, excluding section 1A, 'Violence in the International Context', as well as chapters 2 and 5. These, he contends were one part that went beyond the question of colonial violence and the emergence of revolutionary counter-violence by calling on the forces of decolonization to also attend to all aspects of the personality touched by this violence. Then, one should read Chapters 3 and 4, inclusive of the section on 'Reciprocal bases of National Culture and the Fight for Freedom' as another part focused on the intertwined relationship between race and colonialism, with an eye towards the need to both advance class struggle and a deconstruction of blackness through the creation of a national identity. Lastly, Yaki contended that one should read section 1A, then conclusion, as the final part of the text (Sayles, 2010: 150-1). With its four-parts, this outline would also serve as the rough framework for Yaki's four-part guide to *Wretched*. Most of his *Meditations* would be written during his last decade of imprisonment and first years of freedom beginning in 2004, only to leave the last part unfinished prior to his death four years later.

This unique approach to reading *Wretched* was not simply a matter of what insights could be gained by engaging with Fanon's ideas. It was also about further developing what Yaki termed a 'New Afrikan Communist 'school of thought' (Sayles, 2010: 153). It was New Afrikan, as opposed to black or African American, he argued, because that was our nationality. Terming it communist, as opposed to Maoist or Marxist-Leninist fully accounted for the breadth of scientific socialist ideas on which he and others within this school had drawn. And following Fanon, it was grounded in a revolutionary, socialist humanism. This politics had been central to Yaki's own work on publications like *Notes of New Afrikan P.O.W. Journal* (Books 1-7), *Vita Wa Watu: A New Afrikan Theoretical Journal* (Books 8-12), and *Crossroad: A Captured Combatant Newsletter*. It had also been a cores aspect of other publications circulated behind bars, like *Grassroots* and the *New Afrikan Community Bulletin*. For years, these prison intellectuals and their outside supporters had remained committed to similar project of national liberation and socialist transformation. Although limited in their reach, Yaki and others had remained influential, particularly for younger militants, who, like Kody Scott, had come of age in the wake of the movement's heyday and drawn on these ideas through the course of their own political development. While in solitary confinement, Scott would be introduced to Yaki through imprisoned BLA cadres, who then provided him with some of his first copies of these very same journals and newsletters (Shakur, 2013: 9).[2] 'I received the New Afrikan ideological formulation material and it redeemed me', emphasizes Shakur. 'It gave me answers to all the questions I had about myself in relation to society. I learned about how our situation in this country was that of an oppressed nation, colonized by capitalist-imperialist. The science was strong and precise' (Scott, 1993: 351).[3] So much so that in 1986, Scott began to step away from the Crips and became a conscious citizen of the Republic of New Afrika. Soon thereafter, he adopted the name Shakur, joining Yaki as part of the older prisoner's Spear and Shield collective (Scott, 1993: 352).

Yet despite the strengths of these earlier writings, untangling the complexities of *Wretched* would provide an opportunity to further elaborate on some of this school's core concepts. Approaching this ideological work more systematically would require attending to several key objectives. Taking Sartre's preface as an opportunity to elaborate on them, Yaki began by noting that in the past, he had skipped over this part of the text, assuming that a European writing to a Euro-

---

2. 'This led me to the Black Liberation Army Coordinating Committee (BLA-CC). i got in touch with Sundiata Acoli, who in turn sent me to Owusu Yaki Yakubu, who was using the pseudonym Atiba Shanna at that time, and he began to send me the New Afrikan ideological material and things just cleaned up. What the comrades in the BLA-CC had done was go back and reformulate, rebuild and reboot all the theories of the failed BLM and tie them together in a current ideo-theoretical line that corresponded perfectly to what was happening and what happened and what We should do for the future'. Shakur, *Stand Up, Struggle Forward*, 9.

3. These words echoed George Jackson's description of his own politicization: 'I met Marx, Lenin, Trotsky, Engels, and Mao when I entered prison and they redeemed me. For the first four years I studied nothing but economic and military ideas. I met black guerillas, George 'Big Lake' Lewis, and James Carr, W. L. Nolen, Bill Christmas, Tory Gibson, and many, many others. We attempted to transform the black criminal mentality into a black revolutionary mentality'. George Jackson, *Soledad Brother: The Prison Letters of George Jackson* (Chicago: Lawrence Hill Books, 1994: 16).

pean audience about Fanon's ideas was of little importance to him as a New Afrikan. Now, he realized that this assumption was wrong and that aside from several minor points of disagreement, it was important to include this section in any study of the book as a whole. In a similar manner, Yaki encouraged his readers to reconsider other assumptions about the trajectory of their own struggle. From Sartre's opening description of how colonialism manufactured native elites to play an intermediary role, Yaki pointed to the need for New Afrikan communists to think more concretely about class struggle as a crucial aspect of any process of decolonization. This might require not only a reconceptualization of class within their own colonized context, but also a further commitment to an ideological and theoretical program within a mass-based class struggle. And following prisoner revolutionary George Jackson as well as Fanon, Yaki emphasized that it should not be a 'what to think', but instead a 'how to think' program (Sayles, 2010: 173). Doing so would help to, for example, highlight how just as those in North Africa, European settlers in what would become the United States had manufactured successive generations of elites amongst the colonized. For New Afrikans, this process had begun as early as the 17th century and continued up through the present. More importantly, this process had been an essential part of thwarting the revolutionary socialist and nationalist upsurge of the late 1960s. Calling this moment the 'high tide' of our decolonization struggle', Yaki asserted that it had been met with a counterrevolutionary response that included 'an alliance between colonialism and pseudo-bourgeois and petty bourgeois forces among the oppressed people' (Sayles, 2010: 173). Where those in the NAIM had sought to free the land, this alliance had helped to cement a 'post-neocolonial situation'. By the end of the 20th century, the fruits of this alliance had ripened into the stark inequality marking the distance between the 'new black middle class' and New Afrika's poor and working-class majority (Sayles, 2010: 174).

In addition to rethinking questions of class, the preface to *Wretched* also offered an opportunity to rethink some of the strategic limitations of this last round of struggle. Here, Yaki was concerned with the movement's conception of the revolutionary class. 'Sartre's reference to the peasantry reminded me that Fanon's popularity among bloods in the U.S. in the 1960s rested, in part, upon his characterization of the peasantry and the lumpen as 'revolutionary' and/or as the 'vanguard', he offers. 'While our practice has proven the unsoundness of prior beliefs, We've failed to put the premise to a thorough theoretical analysis, and put it to rest, which will allow this or similar incorrect views to surface again and to disrupt the momentum of the next revolutionary thrust' (Sayles, 2010: 176). This crude approach had failed to appreciate Fanon's nuanced assessment of these sectors of the colonial population, one which noted their capacity for spontaneous resistance. Yet, simply having the capacity for resistance, is not what constituted a revolutionary class. To fit the bill, Yaki asserts, this class needed to identify itself as a class and identify its class enemies. It needed to understand that its members shared common interests and to engage in purposeful action in pursuit of these interests. And it needed to provide leadership for the whole people, reflecting the sort of revolutionary class consciousness that even Fanon's acknowledged still needed to be cultivated in heat of the struggle.

Yaki closed out his assessment of the preface by advancing a critique of Sartre that allowed him to raise a cautionary point about national identity. In particular, he takes issue with the contention that Fanon message to the colonized had little direct relevance to the character of the settler population or the role of citizens of imperialist states in the anti-colonial struggle. Suggesting that Sartre might have been overzealous in his summation of Fanon's ideas, Yaki recalls *Wretched*'s depiction of the Manichean ideology of the colonial system. At the outset, anti-colonial revolt reflects this stark dualism. As the struggle progresses, it must reject and overcome these divisions. In place of a sort of narrow nationalism, people take up a greater political and social consciousness, recognizing that a certain stratum of the colonized population is unwilling to give up their privilege for the sake of an independent nation, while certain segments of the settler population are willing to give their lives in the struggle for national liberation. The barriers that had once seemed fixed in blood and race fall away. 'When Fanon says, early on, that 'What parcels out the world is to begin with the fact of belonging to or not belonging to a given race, a given species'—he's not putting this forth as unalterable reality, but as something that needs to be changed', Yaki writes. 'He's merely describing the Manichean world, the capitalist/colonist world, the imperialist world; he's reflecting the state of consciousness of colonized peoples as they **begin** the struggle to become NEW PEOPLE' (Sayles, 2010: 180).[4] Just as the construction of world capitalism gave rise to the social construction of race, a certain 'species' identified by skin color and the like, so to must these 'species' be deconstructed alongside the deconstruction of capitalism. For Yaki, this meant recommitting to the NAIM's longstanding practice of refusing to identify New Afrikans in racial terms. But it also meant more. Echoing Fanon, the goal was that no one should be identified in these terms, for in the end, the struggle for independence and socialism will progress to the point where one's standing would be assessed not in relation to a fixed notion of race or skin color. In the final analysis, New Afrikan nationals and their allies should be understood in relationship to their social and political consciousness, their commitment or opposition to these broader goals.

## Rebuilding the NAIM

Working his way through the four different parts of *Wretched*, Yaki encourages his readers to approach this text in a dialogical manner. In place of a plain reading of the text, the reader needs to engage with it: asking questions that would not only draw out some of the implications of Fanon's words, but also prompt further reflection on the current state of the NAIM. Beginning with the second part, Chapters 1, 2 and 5, he directly addressed Fanon's near infamous formula-

---

4. Emphasis in original.

tion that 'decolonization is always violent phenomenon' (Fanon, 1963: 35). Quite forthrightly, Yaki noted that since its initial publication, he and others had read this and other aspects of Fanon's writing as simply a call to 'pick up the gun'. 'The people of Africa have suffered for this', Yaki wrote. 'We've suffered for it, and our children and grandchildren suffer for it today' (Sayles, 2010: 183). From its first publication, Fanon's depiction of the means required to defeat colonialism had been taken simply as an endorsement of armed struggle. Offering a different approach, Yaki argued that Fanon's words needed to be read within the context of a colonial relationship, steeped not only in military occupation, but also foreign domination that manifested in various socio cultural, political, and economic forms. Just as colonial violence played out across these different aspects of society, Fanon argued that in order to triumph, the struggle against colonialism also needed to fight with 'all means to turn the scales' across these very same aspects of society (Fanon, 1963: 37). This admittedly would be a violent process, not because it required blood to be spilled. In reality, decolonization was violent because it dramatically attacked the relations between the colonizers and the colonized, bringing an end to the particular species of humanity the colonial world had brought into being.

More importantly, this process of decolonization, however violent provided an opportunity to get to the heart of the matter: the transformation of people's consciousness. 'To paraphrase Fanon', he writes, 'the people can't become self-governing citizens in a truly independent nation without developing their consciousness, no matter how much or how well they 'fight' or how skillful they are in the use of weapons. Failure to grasp this fact accounts for much of the backsliding among would-be activists, and for many of the failures of past attempts at revolutionary transformation on these and other shores. 'National liberation' or 'revolution' is about the transformation of people and their consciousness' (Sayles, 2010: 190).[5] Here, Yaki emphasizes an important point that he would return to again and again: decolonization did not come through the control of territory or military defeat of a foreign power as much as came through—and after—a change in people's consciousness. 'This is the heart of the book, the "key" to it all', he exclaimed, noting Fanon's choice of words in the first chapter alone. 'Decolonization—the revolutionary process is about 'influencing' and 'modifying' people. The revolutionary process transforms 'spectators' into 'actors'' (Sayles, 2010: 210). It demonstrates a new humanity, as the changes that have already begun to touch peoples' consciousness are reflected in their efforts to transform the world. Thus, Yaki writes, even more important than guns and grenades was the need to push people to question everything, to probe meanings and implications, to think critically about the world for we transform ourselves through this process of reflection.

Far from an academic point, it was one he felt had a direct bearing on New Afrikan peoples. Mired in what he describes as a 'post-neocolonial' period, fully

---

5. Emphasis in original.

comprehending this point might help to ensure that any renewed struggle for decolonization would be built on a more stable foundation (Sayles, 2010: 210). 'We have to start this process by finally admitting to ourselves that the old movement is dead', Yaki writes. 'Today the people ARE 'Americans'—even most of the so-called 'radicals' and 'nationalists' ARE 'Americans' at heart. They are consumers and proponents of consumption. They are taken by the 'commodity fetish' (Sayles, 2010: 194). It was imperative that today's revolutionary nationalists commit to rebuilding the NAIM. Fundamentally, this meant coming to grips with a mindset that was being reproduced on a daily basis at work, at home, at church and so on, a way of being to which people were being pressured to conform. Rather than assuming that it would take a fiery speech to get people to take action, it had to be admitted that this mindset had to be confronted. And confronting it and the values that undergirded this mindset would mean more than simply taking a few hours of volunteer work. It would require the attention of full-time cadre, real political workers committed to working amongst the masses of people to carry forward the program of a revolutionary party.

Indeed, Yaki had made this very same point in his prior correspondences with Shakur. In November 1988, California officials had granted Shakur parole four years and nine months into his sentence. By then, he had already deepened his understanding of New Afrikan politics, publishing his first piece of writing, 'Where Does Correct Terminology Come From?' in Crossroad (Scott, 1993: 356). Returning home to South Central, Shakur found his neighborhood and gang life transformed by the influx of crack cocaine. 'One of the first things i got was a kalishnikov ak-47, 7.62×39', he later wrote. 'Needless to say, without the requisite consciousness, the gun & i soon parted company'. By June of 1989, police had arrested him for illegal possession of the weapon, sending him back to prison on a parole violation. From his cell, he wrote to Yaki, only to get a curt response. According to Shakur, 'He said, "i'd rather have one cadre free than 100 ak-47's", It took me years to overstand & appreciate that one sentence' (Sayles, 2010: back cover). Much of the time he would have to meditate on Yaki's words would be in solitary confinement, first in Soledad, and then in newly built Pelican Bay. Soon after his release, police again arrested him, now on charges related to beating up a police informant who refused to stop selling crack cocaine near his home. Pleading guilty, he received a seven-year sentence. Fully aware of his revolutionary politics, prison officials deemed him a threat to institutional security and immediately placed him in the strictest solitary confinement from where he would write and publish his autobiography (Scott, 1993: 379-380; Horowitz, 1993).

In many ways, Yaki's reflections on Fanon's treatment of violence identified some of the pitfalls into which Shakur himself had fallen. 'We know that our people are armed today, as never before (and in many respects, armed by the oppressive state), but their having arms doesn't signal a turn toward the left', he contends. 'Even when We consider efforts by the enemy to disarm the people, it's not the guns in their hands, as such, that's the source of the settler's fear, but the potential threat posed by an armed and politically conscious people' (Sayles, 2010: 212). Shakur's re-arrest and long-term solitary confinement had demonstrated this point. Closing out his meditations on this second part of the book, he notes that with the absence of this consciousness, challenges to the colonial order occur spontaneously, with all of its attendant objective strength and ideological weakness. These challenges would be either ignored or disparaged as simply 'violence' by reformists intellectuals and elites. Instead, it was up to revolutionary cadre to go amongst the people to help educate and organize them so as to intensify the struggle, and most importantly, to transform the way in which they think about themselves and the world. 'More and more I come to believe that We periodically find ourselves having to start from scratch not because our job is hard', Yaki writes, 'but because We don't know what our job is!' (Sayles, 2010: 238) Echoing Fanon's dictum that 'raising the standard' of people's consciousness was the essence of a revolutionary struggle, this, he concludes, had to be understood as the central mission of New Afrikan communists regardless of where they found themselves.

This point would be further reiterated in Yaki's examination of the third part of *Wretched*, Chapters 3 and 4. Initially, he had planned to use this part of his *Meditations* to reflect on Fanon's treatment of class and narrow nationalism. However, he ultimately decided to focus it on the 'race' and its deconstruction. 'This has to be done because of the probability that no effective revolutionary movement (no meaningful transformation of the world) will be generated without incorporating the deconstruction of 'race' process into our theory and practice', he writes. 'The probability exists because 'race' and racism have been the shadows that have historically diverted people's energies and diffused their revolutionary thrusts. This applies particularly to the motion of peoples within what are now U.S. borders, but it is clearly a worldwide phenomenon' (Sayles, 2010: 243). While racism needed to be eliminated, so did all forms of racialism, or referring to people in terms of 'race', as well as narrow nationalism. Instead, a revolutionary nationalism would need to be adopted as part of the struggle against the allies of capitalism, however progressive or radical their rhetoric, that blocked the ways towards socialism and self-determination.

Decades after the upsurge of the 1960s and 70s, this task was an even more urgent one, as the politics of race and skin color continued to shape popular opinion. 'It's no accident that the mass consciousness today is heavily 'racialized', and not revolutionary, just as 'black nationalism' became 'ethnic pluralism' and 'cultural equality' in the form of the rightest tendency of Afrocentricity', Yaki laments. 'The real revolutionary were disrupted and fell by the wayside; the bourgeois forces filled the vacuum, and today the people think that 'racial feeling' is the same as revolutionary thought and practice' (Sayles, 2010: 247). Militants who take 'white racism' or 'white people' as the enemy, too often ignored the problem of economic exploitation and the need for a liberation that ends all forms of social alienation. Despite the sense of empowerment notions of Blackness might confer, they ultimately granted legitimacy to the cultural and biological hierarchies colonialism had marked out as 'race'. 'At bottom', he writes 'so-called 'race relations' are economic relations between groups of people(s), better distinguished as classes and/or as nationalities' (Sayles, 2010: 256). What was needed was a politics that pierced through the mysticism of race and called attention to the material foundations upon which these class and national relations rest. Following Fanon, this meant thoroughly deconstructing and abandoning all racialized thought and instead, seeking a new sense of collective identity grounded in a revolutionary national consciousness, firmly oriented towards the proletariat and the fight for socialism. More particularly, 'New Afrikan' had to mean more than simply a stand in for skin color; it needed to be an identity that referenced one's thought and practice. One that sought to 'set a foot' a new people and in doing so, foster a new humanity.

This conception of New Afrikan identity was relatively heterodox and in the wake of Yaki's death, it is one that Shakur would work to extend. After a series of police arrests and parole violations, Shakur had pled guilty to carjacking and robbery charges in May 2008, receiving a six-year sentence that sent him back to Pelican Bay. There, he would help to establish the August Third Collective, also a communist faction of the NAIM, and promote the New Afrikan Peoples Liberation Army. Even more significantly, he would continue to write, publishing his first book of fiction in 2009, *T.H.U.G.L.I.F.E.*, then a series of political writings. These included a review of Yaki's *Meditations*, lauding it as 'work that will last a hundred years because it is the truth. And it is rich with substance & dialectical-materialist reasoning' (Shakur, 2010).[6] Inspired, he would consciously draw on Yaki's insights not just in his work written in advance of the 2011 Hunger Strike, but also in the months that followed. Written in the SHU, these essays touched on questions of revolutionary politics and patriarchal oppression, class analysis and national identity. Collected alongside a series of interview given during and after his imprisonment, Shakur's writing would be published as *Stand Up, Struggle Forward*, about a year after his June 2012 release from Pelican Bay.

Many of these writings quoted Yaki at length, for, as Shakur notes in one article, 'it was some of his contributions, along with other Comrads in the PG-RNA and NAPO, that were largely responsible for kickstarting the resurgence of the NAIM today' (Shakur, 2013: 54). And reflecting Yaki's own decades-long captivity, this resurgence has been most evident behind bars. In the wake of the last hunger strike, this resurgence would touch the drafting of the August 2012 Alliance to End Hostilities. Prepared by four prisoners in Pelican Bay's Short Corridor and supported by 12 other SHU prisoner representatives, this document called for an end to all violence and hostility between racialized prisoners throughout California. Although broadly representative of those held in the facility, the Short Corridor Collective would draw on the insights of Sitawa Nantambu Jamaa, a New Afrikan prison intellectual and one of the collective's core leaders. When prison authorities refused to meet its demands, the collective called for a resumption of the hunger strike. In July 2013, more than 29,000 men and women throughout California again refused to eat food, with the last 100 ending their fast only after state lawmakers agreed to hold public hearings on the conditions in solitary confinement cells. Through the course of the two-

---

6. Emphasis in original.

month long strike, this resurgence would be reflected even more directly in the ideological leadership of the New Afrikan Revolutionary Nationalism Collective Think Tank (NCTT), itself chaired by Sitawa. Circulated in print and on the internet, the NCTT's writings helped to publicize the hunger strike and through its references to *Meditations*, ground the hunger strike's broader politics in Yaki's reflections on Fanon.[7]

## Conclusion

In 2008, Yaki succumbed to terminal lung cancer, leaving unfinished the fourth part of his *Meditations*. Attending to Chapter 1A and the Conclusion, it consists of a first draft, that ultimately trails into notes on how it should be completed. However fragmentary, Yaki's commitment to both shedding light on Fanon's key insights as well as addressing their enduring relevance to the current state of the NAIM remains central. Much of the failure of the 1960s upsurge, he notes, had to do with the lack of a clear sense of what the objective was as it progressed through 'civil rights', 'black power', and then "'black' skin liberation' (Sayles, 2010: 352). Lacking ideological clarity, each of these movements had gestured in the general direction of where to go but floundered on the question of how and why. Now, before the next upsurge of popular struggle, it was essential to get clear on revolutionary direction. 'We fight today for the same things that we fought for as when Fanon wrote *The Wretched of the Earth*', Yaki explains. 'The contradiction between imperialism (capitalism in a world-dominating system) and REVOLUTIONARY nationalism (i.e. national revolutions that aim to de-link from the world-dominating capitalist system, and to build socialist societies), is still fundamental to the world' (Sayles, 2010: 354). For the remainder of this last part of his *Meditations*, Yaki focused on demonstrating how, for Fanon, the nation went beyond skin color to the forging of a new unity, a new collective consciousness, and sharing a common cause of winning 'self-determined, socialist development' (Sayles, 2010: 381). In nearly complete paragraphs and scattered notes, he demonstrated how Fanon points to the process that might make this new consciousness possible and how, if pursued might transform those considered the 'wretched' into an enlightened, responsible, and self-governing people.

---

7. For example, see NCTT Corcoran SHU, 'Trayvon, Christian, Jason, Gerardo, Kendrec and nine children in Afghanistan: a discussion of race, violence and the authoritarian psychology', *San Francisco Bay View*, June 29, 2012, https://sfbayview.com/2012/06/trayvon-christian-jason-gerardo-kendrec-and-nine-children-in-afghanistan-a-discussion-of-race-violence-and-the-authoritarian-psychology/; N.C.T.T.-Cor-SHU, 'On Racism, Resistance and State Violence—A Discussion on the Politics of Greed and Hate', *San Francisco Bay View*, October 25, 2014, http://sfbayview.com/2014/10/on-racism-resistance-and-state-violence-a-discussion-on-the-politics-of-greed-and-hate/; Michael Zaharibu Dorrough, J. Heshima Denham and Kambui Robinson, NCTT Corcoran SHU, 'Prisoners' Agreement to End Hostilities as the basis for the abolition of 'legal' slavery', *San Francisco Bay View*, December 24, 2014, http://sfbayview.com/2014/12/prisoners-agreement-to-end-hostilities-as-the-basis-for-the-abolition-of-legal-slavery/; NCTT: Zaharibu Dorrough, Heshima Denham, Jabari Scott and Kambui Robinson, 'On Self-Defense against Racist Murder', *San Francisco Bay View*, April 28, 2016, http://sfbayview.com/2016/04/on-self-defense-against-racist-murder/.

According to Yaki's editors, there had been discussions of adding a part 5 and 6 to further extend Fanon's vision into the future. And while no one has yet looked to pick up where Yaki left off, prisoners as a whole have built on some of his insights. On September 9, 2016, the Free Alabama Movement (FAM) marked the 45th anniversary of the Attica rebellion by calling a nationwide prisoners strike. The strike would quickly spread to more than 29 prisons across 12 states. In the years prior, FAM organizers had cut their teeth by leading a series of strikes, hostage takings, other protests that shaken the Alabama prisons system and prompted calls for prison reform. Rather than a cohesive list of demands, grievances driving the national prison strike varied from state to state, and strike activities continued for up to three weeks (Losier, 2018a). At its core, though, the national prisoners strike lifted up the idea that rather than ending slavery, the U.S. Constitution's 13th amendment had simply relegated it to a form of punishment meted out to those deemed criminal—an idea Yaki had helped to promote as a young prison organizer (Scott, 2020: 16-17).

Two years later, Jailhouse Lawyers Speak, a network of incarcerated human rights organizers called for another national strike and issued a list of grievances. Presented to the public, rather than a particular official or bureaucrat, these grievances demanded changes that recognized the humanity of imprisoned men and women. Beginning on August 21st to mark the anniversary of the 1971 assassination of George Jackson, the summer's strike ranged from labor and hunger strikes to sit-ins and commissary boycotts. Ending on the anniversary of Attica, September 9th, the strike effectively overcame some of the barriers that had previously frustrated prisoner organizing efforts and reached at least 16 state and federal prisons. And in contrast to the previous strike, it garnered unprecedented mainstream media coverage as well as the endorsement of more than 200 community organizations, with supporters conducting call-in campaigns, noise demonstrations, teach-ins, and various nonviolent protests (Losier, 2018b).

With the onset of the Covid-19 pandemic, scattered prison strikes rose into a torrent of protest. Beginning on March 17th, 2020, with one of the first reported coronavirus hunger strikes, there has been a consistent demand for basic protections to their health and safety. As officials at prisons, jails, and migrant detention centers have been slow to provide access to personal protective equipment (PPE) and cleaning supplies or require that CDC guidelines around the wearing of masks by guards or physical distancing by inmates, those held behind bars have repeatedly taken action. Over the subsequent 90 days of the pandemic, some 119 instances of protests, hunger strikes, work stoppages, hostage takings, and other attacks on staff had occurred. Much of the same seems likely to continue through the duration of the pandemic (Perilous Chronicle, 2020). And while this emerging prison movement has not demonstrated an avowed commitment to revolutionary nationalism, the basic tenets of Yaki's New Afrikan communism shape its practice. It has eschewed any crude identification with 'skin color', bringing prisoners together across lines of division. And without invoking race, it has grounded itself firmly in the legacy of New Afrikan prisoner struggles, with regular references to George Jackson and the Attica rebellion. It spurred the formation of new groups and collectives committed to politically educating their members. And perhaps, most importantly, this movement has consistently sought to provide prisoners with a platform from which to validate their own humanity, and in doing so, transform themselves and the wider world.

# Bibliography

Bing, L. 1991. *Do or Die*. 1st ed. New York: Harper Perennial.

Fanon, F. 1963. *The Wretched of the Earth: The Handbook for the Black Revolution That Is Changing the Shape of the World*. 1st ed. New York: Grove Press.

Horowitz, M. 1993. 'In Search of Monster,' *The Atlantic*. Accessed January 15, 2021, https://www.theatlantic.com/magazine/archive/1993/12/in-search-of-monster/305739/.

Hudis, P. n.d. *Racism and the Logic of Capital: A Fanonian Reconsideration*. Accessed January 15, 2021, https://www.historicalmaterialism.org/articles/racism-and-logic-capitalism.

Losier, T. 2018a. 'The Movement Against "Modern Day Slavery".' Accessed January 15, 2021, https://www.jacobinmag.com/2018/09/prison-strike-slavery-labor-jls-abolition.

Losier, T. 2018b. 'Make the Nation Look at our Demands': The 2018 National Prison Strike and the Crises of Mass Incarceration.' Accessed January 15, 2021, https://www.europenowjournal.org/2018/11/07/make-the-nation-look-at-our-demands-the-2018-national-prison-strike-and-the-crises-of-mass-incarceration/.

Onaci, E. 2020. *Free the Land: The Republic of New Afrika and the Pursuit of a Black Nation-State*. 1st ed. Chapel Hill: University of North Carolina Press.

*Perilous Chronicle*, 2020. 'First 90 Days of Prisoner Resistance to COVID-19: Report on Events, Data, and Trends.' Accessed January 15, 2021, https://perilouschronicle.com/2020/11/12/covid-prisoner-resistance-first-90-days-full-report/.

*Pontiac Prisoners Support Coalition Newsletter*, 1980. 'Brothers Challenge Court's Jurisdiction.'

Sayles, J. Y. 2010. *Meditations on Frantz Fanon's Wretched of the Earth: New Afrikan Revolutionary Writings*. 1st ed. Montreal: Kersplebedeb Publishing.

Scott, D. M. 2020. 'The Social and Intellectual Origins of 13thism,' *Fire!!!* 5 (2): 2–39.

Scott, K. 1993. *Monster: The Autobiography of an L.A. gang member*. 1st ed. New York: Grove Press.

Shakur, S. 2010. *Sanyinka Shakur on Meditations: A Weapon for Struggle*. Accessed January 15, 2021, https://kersplebedeb.com/posts/sanyika-shakur-on-meditations-a-weapon-for-struggle/.

Shakur, S. 2013. *Stand Up, Struggle Forward*. 1st ed. Montreal: Kersplebedeb Publishing.

Yakubu, O. Y. 2001. *Biographical Outline – O.Y.Y.* Accessed January 15, 2021, http://brothermalcolm.net/TRANSFORMED/PDF/BIO.pdf.

# LOOKING FOR JUSTICE IN A COMPARTMENTALIZED WORLD: MOTHERS AND POLICE KILLINGS IN KENYA

Wangui Kimari

Building on Fanon's discussions of a Manichean colonial world in his seminal book *The Wretched of the Earth*, this chapter details the activist work of mothers whose children have been killed by the police within Nairobi's compartmentalized colonial geographies. It discusses their experiences within these spaces of hunger and violence, and, above all, their work to end alienation and indifference to the oppression they face on a daily basis. Theirs are efforts to make evident colonial violence in a postcolonial world, even as colonialism is regarded as past, and simultaneously demand justice for the killings of their children. As part of their ungovernable activism, their 'rational revolts', they demand recognition, equality and justice, while seeking to undo the violent dichotomies of their colonial worlds. Certainly, by 'penetrat[ing] inside this compartmentalization', they 'bring to light some of its key aspects' but also 'the backbone on which the decolonized society' can be built (see Fanon, 1968: 37-38).

## Mothers

> *A wonderful lesson that all we have, really have, is us. And again, no one is coming to save us. We the wretched of the earth.*
> —Juliet Wanjira, Social justice activist in Kenya

> *The colonized world is a world divided in two. The dividing line, the border is represented by the barracks and the police stations.*
> —Frantz Fanon, *Wretched of the Earth*

### Mama Alex

Mama Alex's son, Alex, was 19 years old when he was killed by the police on his way home from work at 10.30 pm in late October 2017. He lived in the poor urban settlement of Mathare, barely three kilometers from the city center of Nairobi, but that remains one of the 'most difficult urban environments in East Africa' (Muungano Support Trust, 2012: 4). When accosted by the police a few meters from his house, witnesses who overheard this encounter said that after he told the police he was coming from work, they said: 'this is no time for work', and shot him more than 10 times.

When his mother, Sara, went to the shop to buy milk not too long after he was killed, she saw her son lying on the street dead. Reacting to this, she reached for her son, but the police corked their guns at her and she ran back home. She was too scared to go back to this scene until 5 am, and when she did, she met the trail of blood that marked her son's demise, but no body.

When I visited her early in 2018, she had not been able to open Alex's room since he had died. And too afraid for her other 12-year-old son to remain with her in this settlement, she sent him away to live with his paternal grandmother.

When I went to look for her at her house again in early August 2020, she had had to move, and had built her tin shack above another sister's home after they were forced to move by a predatory 'slum' landlord, who had now built a mixture of rough cement tenements and corrugated iron shack dwellings that faced away from their small houses. She told me that they used the police to kill Alex so that they could take their land— roughly a 50 x 5 meter parcel in this poor space, almost a third of what they had tried to cling to for three generations.

I had found her documenting human rights cases in her room, violations that had taken place and continue to take place in this settlement: tragic tales of more police killings, house fires, child defilement and more. Her little notebook, used by children in primary school, was gradually being filled by a litany of violence against and within the community where she grew up.

Mama Alex took up this task informally, hesitatingly, not knowing her power, although others were familiar with it. How she stood up for the homeless man who was shot by the police during the COVID-19 lockdown; one of the lone women in a crowd of young men protesting and burning tires in the street. We know her power from the defiance and solidarity she shares with other mothers like her, even if she has to walk past the spot where her son was shot dead a few years ago to meet them. Mama Alex, in this compartmentalized world, is struggling for justice.

## Mama Gideon Njuguna

Mama Gideon came to the Mathare Social Justice Centre in 2015, a few months after her son, a *boda boda* motorcycle taxi driver, had been killed by the police after he had dropped a client off at 10 pm. His family learned of his death when he did not show up to the police station to bail his brother out on August 5th of that same year. His mother had spoken with him a day before at 10 pm to tell him that this brother was being held at Kariobangi police station, one of the many police posts in his area.

When they called him at 6 am on August 5th, he did not pick up his phone. A few hours later it was turned off. His family went to Kariobangi police station at 9 am, the same day, to see if he had gone there, but they were told that he still had not arrived. His brother, however, who was still detained at this very police station, was later released after his family's efforts. They continued to wait and query, but still Gideon did not make it home. His family then decided to check at all other police stations where poor people like him, from his location, could be arbitrarily detained: they looked for him at Kasarani, Muthaiga and Pangani police stations.

They did not find him for two days. And on the morning of August 7th, his *boda boda* compatriots decided that since they could not find him anywhere, they would go and look for him in the local city mortuary—the destination of last resort for many poor families, but often the first place they know they should look. And this is where he lay dead. When they found him, they could see that he had been shot four times. He did not have any eyes; his sockets were empty. He had also been shot in his mouth—it had a huge gaping hole and was disintegrating—and in his chest.

On September 14th, a month later, his family pieced together some funds for a lawyer, and collaboratively drafted a letter to take to Kariobangi police station to force an investigation into what had happened to Gideon. On the same day they found his *boda boda*; it was in a nearby police station and they were told that some people had brought it on August 5th— they had found it in Kariobangi, some distance from where he worked.

His mother, a vegetable seller in Korogocho market, a woman, like many of her generation, likely displaced by colonialist and then postcolonialist greed from her rural *shamba*, who could not read or write, took it upon herself to find justice for her son. She found and spoke to lawyers and then went to talk to people who lived in the area where they believed Gideon had been shot by the police. From her barefoot and tireless investigations, she heard that her son and two people he was carrying on his *boda boda* were shot dead on the doorstep of some houses in Korogocho on the night of August 4th. Gideon's family knows where those houses are, the faces and stories of those who heard these executions unfold, but the residents do not want to be witnesses—they are too scared; police killings have been normalized and so they too can be killed.

With wavering hope, but unable to turn away, we sought to walk with Mama Gideon; we demanded assistance at the different organizations mandated to report, investigate, and prosecute officers charged with killings and abuse. We did not know what to do as they made her narrate and re-narrate the tragedy of seeing her son in the morgue, a young man who was working to take care of his small family—a wife and new baby, with holes in his face and chest. We took letters from one institution to another, translated for Mama Gideon, followed up, and demanded action. Still, five years later, despite the many extraordinary efforts of a mother—formally illiterate and poor—his family continues to wait for *something*: a recognition, an investigation, a phone call from the authorities charged with investigating his death. Something.

## Mama Nura Malicha

Nura Malicha, the son of Halima Malicha, was killed on February 21, 2015. Like many teenagers in the poor urban ward of Kiamaiko, he worked in the goat market of this location, one of the largest goat abattoirs' in the city. On the day he was killed, he had been working in the morning, as he usually did, unpacking the goats from the trucks that delivered them to his area: vehicles that carried these animals from far off places like Moyale, Marsabit and Garissa.

The trucks, akin to the abattoir where he worked, are part of an industry predominantly ran by Muslim men from North Eastern Kenya, communities that border Somalia and Ethiopia. Because of a localized 'war on terror', as well as histories of state oppression and neglect, they and their ethnic kin are habitually terrorized for embodying what was seen as the phenotype profile of 'terrorist'. We imagine that these are some of the logics that contributed to Nura's execution—still a child at 17 years old. Not only was he a poor urban body in a stigmatized location, but he could also be framed as a threatening foreign body encompassing an ethnic profile often denied documents that would confirm citizenship in Kenya, and, more often than we wanted to recognize, even denied the right to life.

Witnesses say that Nura ran to the road because he heard what he thought was the goat truck arriving. On his arrival, he discerned that it was actually a police truck, and on apprehending it and being apprehended by it, a tragic encounter ensued. The police from Huruma Police Station, a few hundred meters away, chained him and began to beat him. And even though he surrendered to them, on his knees with his hands raised, he was shot dead.

As he lay on the floor of the market bleeding, his mother was called and told that her son had been shot. She rushed to the market and found him as he lay dying. She picked up his head and he tried to speak to her with his last breaths, but only blood and teeth came out of his mouth. Mama Nura recounts this, always, in tears.

In some ways, she is lucky. Two years after his execution, Nura's case was recommended to the courts by the Office of the Director of Public Prosecutions (ODPP). Out of the many thousands of cases of police killings a year, somehow Nura's case had shone through the files and was investigated. When the investigation was complete, police officers at Huruma police station were arraigned in court to be tried for his execution. A significant victory. But, still, an incomplete one.

For a poor woman from a marginalized community in a poor and stigmatized urban area, the steps towards justice are always arduous. How does one get a lawyer in this case—a lawyer that will work for free, for all the years this case may remain in court? What measures will prevent witness tampering and intimidation? Who will keep her and her family safe from the arraigned police officer and his colleagues? And now, how to pick up an almost concluded case from the ruins of the COVID-19 pandemic? These obstacles are proving challenging: three years later, against a pandemic, lack of cooperation from the police force, and 'missing' court documents, Nura's family is still waiting for the case to be concluded and a judgement to be pronounced.

In the meantime, Mama Nura has planted a tree for a son in Mathare. Though shaped by an environmental apartheid, characteristic of a colonial 'world divided in two' (Fanon, 1968), residents plant trees wherever they can to memorialize those killed, and to harvest food, knowledge and medicine. These are ultimately multifaceted struggles oriented around a search for justice in a compartmental-ized world.

The stories that these mothers—of Alex, of Gideon and of Nura—carry, are of premature deaths, of generations intentionally lost, of poor urban dreams vio-lently extinguished. Their foremost crime is to live in the former *cité indigine*, the "native' quarters, the shanty town, the medina, the reservation' [...] a disreputable place inhabited by disreputable people'. Here, as we have glimpsed in the three stories above, 'you are born anywhere, anyhow. You die anywhere from anything. It is a world with no space, people are piled one on top of the other, the shacks squeezed tightly together. The colonized sector is a famished sector, hungry for bread, meat, shoes, coal and light'. It is also hungry for justice (Fanon, 1968: 4).

## A Compartmentalized World

*The colonist's sector is a sector built to last, all stone and steel. It's a sector of lights and paved roads, where the trash cans constantly overflow with strange and wonderful garbage, undreamed of leftovers.*
—Frantz Fanon, *The Wretched of the Earth*

Though Nairobi grew and grew since independence was declared in Kenya in 1963, and Africans could now claim a solid foothold in this urban space not cre-ated for them, the dynamics of the city have remained the same since the colo-nial period. Nairobi was certainly, as one scholar put is, a 'perfect apartheid city without trying' (Londsdale, 2001: 220). This is even though the first actual Master Plan for the city, written in 1948 by South African planners, asserted that:

The Master Plan however, is able to be completely neutral on the subject of racial segregation by being confined to the principles of planning which take their measure on the human and technical needs. It is con-cerned with the satisfaction of wants which all men require such as privacy, open space, education, protection from through-traffic, water supplies, etc. The more attention that can be devoted to what is common to man the more likely are we to concentrate on what can to-day be planned in the light of reason while leaving to political and educational action and to the individual to sort out the rest. If the plan has a bias it is this humanistic one. (White, Silberman and Anderson, 1948: 49)

Nairobi's overall governance certainly did not have a 'humanistic' bias—it was systematically racist. This was the city where, W. McGregor Ross, the director of Public Works from 1900 to 1922, stated that his department did more for oxen than had been done for native housing (quoted in White, 1990: 47). This was also the city where, in 1954, as part of a larger siege against Mau Mau and the independence struggle, the largest urban cordon and search action ever mounted took place and saw Nairobi effectively become a 'closed district': for one month, buses were cancelled, barbed wire enclosures were erected and, on the initial morning of the operation, it was declared that 'no African would leave Bahati,

Pumwani or Kariokor [...] except in the back of a caged lorry' (Anderson, 2005: 200-201).

The *cité indigene* continues to be caged, shaped by class, built on an imperial and racial bias that took over the zoning of the city. In this way, the former native city remains a place of hunger for bread, meat, shoes and coal as Fanon puts it. It continues to be the site where people are physically forced and psychologically compelled 'to stay in their place'. This engenders a nervous condition that is exacerbated by the police borders that remain. In places like Mathare, where both Mama Alex and Mama Nura Malicha come from, their community, which is only three square kilometer in size and of roughly 300,000 people, is surrounded by five police stations and an army barracks. This surveillance prompts us to recall Fanon's reflection in *The Wretched of the Earth* that:

> The colonized world is a world divided in two. The dividing line, the border is represented by the barracks and the police stations. In the colonies it is the policeman and the soldier who are the official, instituted go-betweens, the spokesmen of the settler and his rule of oppression. It is obvious here that the agents of government speak the language of pure force. The intermediary does not lighten the oppression, nor seek to hide the domination; he shows them up and puts them into practice with the clear conscience of an upholder of the peace; yet he is the bringer of violence into the home and into the mind of the native. (Fanon, 1968: 4)

The purveyors of violence into the homes and minds of the 'native' still remain the principal agents of a government of oppression; this is the police. Just as 'in 1952, the 200,000 victims of the repression in Kenya could meet with relative indifference' (Fanon, 1968: 78), so do the contemporary deaths of young people that have been sinisterly occasioned by police gun-speak because of their socio-spatial residence in the wrong section of the compartmentalized city.

Community organizations, long tired of this apathy, have documented disappearances, killings, and abuse. They detail how in three years, between 2013 and 2016, over 850 Kenyans were killed. Many more are missing, and these tallies have not included those documented in previous years. The activists who did this work know that these numbers are only the tip of the iceberg; many other children's names are not brought forward, their families too scared or their bodies never found. They too were met with relative indifference, but their communities and mothers could not and will not be silent.

## Rational Revolts

> *The colonized subject thus discovers that his life, his breathing and his heartbeats are the same as the colonialist.*
> —Frantz Fanon, *The Wretched of the Earth*

> We cannot go resolutely forward until we realize our alienation.
> —Frantz Fanon, *The Wretched of the Earth*

June 2020. They sit in a small room in Mathare. Close to 50 of these mothers have been brought together by the shared grief of having lost a child or husband to police bullets. They come from the poor settlements that house the majority of Nairobi dwellers: Kiambu, Kibera, Mathare, Dandora, Mukuru, Kariobangi and elsewhere. But there are many more like them, who have not had the strength to meet, who are still mourning, or who can't leave their children or work here and in other poor urban neighborhoods to attend these monthly meetings. They all come from what Fanon (1968) refers to as the 'colonized sector'; theirs are the former native quarters, the 'shanty town', which continue to be exposed to hunger, violence, environmental pollution, unemployment, police violence, and disease. The oppression within these geographies is kept in by barracks or police stations, principally because, as the residents have been told continuously throughout the history of this town, they are a different 'species'.

And these meetings of the Mothers of Victims and Survivors Network challenge, above all, the narratives that have made them alienated from themselves and each other. While they individually and collectively try and chip away at economic immiseration and all the dire conditions this brings with it, they meet more formally to humanize each other and their children who, though have been killed, are blamed for their own deaths by the police and an indifferent nation. Because they come from a disreputable place, their children could only be disreputable people—disposable and not to be missed by the larger colonial society.

These mothers began to meet in 2017, walking the same path as mothers in Argentina, Brazil, and elsewhere. They did not know each other previously, but still reached for one another through the shared grief prompted by the sinister violence of a compartmentalized world. In reclaiming their humanity, they 'penetrate inside this compartmentalization' to 'bring to light some of its key aspects'. It is through these actions that also discern and demand that their 'breathing' and 'heartbeats are the same as the colonists', that they reveal 'the backbone on which the decolonized society' can be built, that they know their revolts are rational and that they develop their 'postcolonial imagination [s]' (Fanon, 1968: 10; Gibson, 2017).

When they officially launched their network a few months before this meeting in June, they talked about how their children were being killed like *kukus* [chicken], the grief of burying children who were meant to bury them, and the informal government 'shoot to kill' policy that is only implemented in areas like theirs. But they are determined to be activists, not just for their children, but for their communities as a whole. As they wore red shirts to represent the 'blood that had been shed' and that portrayed boldly the letters 'justice for victims', they danced through the settlement, on the way to plant trees for their departed sons or husbands, singing *moto imewaka* [the fire is lit] and chanting ' killings get back, we are moving forward'.

# Ungovernable protests

*What is also obvious is that the spontaneity of popular actions is not simply spontaneous but the result of ongoing thinking and organising.*
—Nigel Gibson, *Fanon: The Postcolonial Imagination*

On June 8th, 2020, after the killings of three residents of Mathare—including a 13-year-old boy killed on his balcony and a homeless man shot dead on the street for supposedly not adhering to the covid-19 lockdown curfew protocols, over 200 residents took to the streets. With the Mother of Victims and Survivors Network leading the march, the protestors moved through this settlement, stopping to memorialize the places where their children, brothers and husbands had been shot. Defiant in the face of the ban on public gatherings because of the pandemic, they claimed their streets and erected invisible monuments to their children—disreputable persons—where they had been shot.

They led us in song and grief and boldness as we protested, bringing back to life persons long since forgotten by the police officer that killed them. Many expressed that what they feared the most during the pandemic was not the virus, but the police, who like the colonial officer described by Fanon (1968) turns on them even though they are kin. After moving through the whole settlement, reclaiming their community, getting others to join them—mourning, dancing, demanding justice—they were to end their protest at a local police station where, in their own way, they would confront the 'bringer of violence into their home'. And as they approached this notorious space that policed the compartmentalized borders, they lived within; many phones rang with warning: 'they are waiting for you with teargas'; 'batons'; 'don't go there'; ' be warned'.

The police expected that these weapons would be enough to scare women whose lives they have terrorized both in real time and in shadows, their colonial power appearing larger than life. But these mothers had already accepted, and continued to accept together, that their breathing was the same as the police and the colonialists, their heartbeats the same. They would not forget their children, brothers and husbands, and they knew and would name the violence that had extinguished them. And so while the Network made a tactical retreat and decided not to end the march at the police station, they had other objectives: though ending the protest early appeared spontaneous, their revolts were rational, the result of 'ongoing thinking and organizing'. Indeed, they had bigger plans for bigger places.

# Parliament and the President

A few days later, unanticipated by many, the members of this network operationalized a long held plan to protest in the heart of the city, the other side of their colonial world. They knew that for their struggle to be taken more seriously they had to make claims, not just in their areas—the colonized sector— but before the institutions where the fake gestures of post coloniality and democracy were performed for the state. Thus, they made their way, barely a week after their Mathare protest, to the 'colonist's sector... built to last, all stone and steel' and with light and paved roads.

On this day, targeting Parliament, they would converge from different directions; some mothers carrying models of babies in their arms, while others stuffing their stomachs to look pregnant. A few younger women, most of them widows for the same reason, carried two coffins: one for an adult and the other for a child. Embroidered on the masks that they now all had to wear by law were names of children and husbands killed: Christopher Maina, Cosmas Mutethia, Yassin Moyo, Nura Malicha and others. There were also masks for the many nameless and faceless victims. One of the young women helping to carry a coffin had lost two husbands killed months apart. Another had had her husband dragged from a building site and killed in broad daylight and on a public road when she was eight and a half months pregnant.

The impromptu mobilization startled the guards manning the August House. Initially, the Network had made an orderly covid-19 rules adhering assembly outside Parliament. But when they were all together, and with some of their children, they took over the road, demanded justice and collectively mourned for their kin. This House, built during the colonial period, served as the symbol for the maintenance of structural violence in their lives. It convened citizen representatives that had the power to reshape their lives, help rupture the compartmentalization that they lived. Instead, parliamentarians benefited from the exploitation—they, the governing classes, 'travel a great deal...[are] gold mines for airline companies' and who 'may in the same month follow a course on socialist planning in Moscow and one on the advantages of the liberal economy in London or at Columbia University' (Fanon, 1968: 81).

So if they were going to continue like this, fortifying the borders of the compartmentalized world, then they should see the youth that were being killed, see their coffins, hear the mother's grief and demands for justice. Hear their names and stories, neither of which would be hidden any longer in the colonized sector, just as their mothers and wives would not keep their place. Because they are 'natives' that could not be easily 'painted as evil', neither by the police nor the residents of this sector, the public had to watch for as long as the women decided to be there, shaming the colonists, claiming their lives, humanizing their children. Breathing the same air, heartbeats the same, the wretched of the earth unmoved in the colonist's sector then left their coffins for the police to clear.

Less than a month later, the mothers were back with their other children—students, poor urban city dwellers, street hawkers, community activists, feminists, queer allies—to take over the streets. But this anticipated march to commemorate 30 years of a watershed pro-democracy movement in 1990, principally a 'march for our lives', was disrupted by the kind of colonial force naturalized in the Operation Anvil of 1954 mentioned earlier: activist spaces were barricaded from eight in the morning, teargas thrown at those who had gathered early to have tea and who dared to sing freedom songs. Many people were arrested a few hundred meters from their homes on the way to converge at the President's office. Before midday, over 60 young activists had been arrested.

Their singing, marching, convening, carrying pictures of children who were killed, and even their clothing was taken as a threat to the state, and, under the guise of 'not adhering to covid-19 [regulations]', they were arrested and subsequently dumped in a few crowded cells. Still, in these conditions, they sang—they had still managed to invade the colonist's sector.

## Looking for Justice

Our mothers, the mothers and wives of the Network, are not looking for intellectuals to save them, or bourgeois organizations to frame them or teach them 'non-violent' tactics. These women may have never heard of Fanon, although they and their activist children point out loudly, the persistence of empire, a compartmentalized world that limits all aspects of their life. Sooner or later, and more and more, 'they turn away from this nation in which they have been given no place and begin to lose interest in it ' (Fanon, 1968: 169). This turning away occurs simultaneously with the collective education they share and use to foment their own postcolonial imaginations, the 'backbone' on which a decolonized society will be built. Together their material and ideological work—from attending court cases, to helping each other document violations, to sharing food, to memorializing each other's children —is a praxis that is co-created to undermine their present colonial situations. Undoubtedly, by just daring to aspire to other possibilities, and united, they incrementally map out visions of what decolonization could look like.

They come together to look for justice in ways that make sense for them; grieving, offering solidarity to each other at police stations, attending court cases, documenting new victims, building alliances. But they are also protesting in the streets, invading the colonist's sector, no longer afraid of the colonizer and his other face: the police. They make incremental strides, a few steps forward and some back. They see some minor movements by the state to investigate the assassination of their children, but, above all, what grows is the clamour of demands that arise from these mothers whose network grows every day. By coming together, they humanize each other through tragedy. They also intentionally point out the shaky foundations of the barracks, the police stations, the Parliament, and face them, unafraid. In these movements for justice, for community, for dignity, they 'shake off the heavy darkness in which they were plunged and leave it behind. The new day which is already at hand...' the justice they have been looking for, will, no doubt, soon find them 'prudent and resolute' (Fanon, 1968: 311).

## Bibliography

Anderson, D. 2005. *Histories of the Hanged: The Dirty War in Kenya and the End of Empire*. New York: WW Norton & Company.

Fanon, F. 1968. *The Wretched of the Earth*. Translated by Constance Farrington. New York: Grove Press.

Gibson, N. C. 2017. *Fanon: The Postcolonial Imagination*. Cambridge: Polity Press.

_____. 2020. 'Fanon and the "rationality of revolt".' *New Frame*, 14 August. Accessed August 15, 2020, https://www.newframe.com/fanon-and-the-rationality-of-revolt/.

Lonsdale, J. 2001. 'Town Life in Colonial Kenya.' *Azania: Archaeological Research in Africa* 36–37 (1): 206–222.

Muungano Support Trust. 2012. *Mathare Zonal Plan. Nairobi/Kenya: Collaborative Plan for Informal Settlement Upgrading*, University of Nairobi and University of California, Nairobi/Berkeley.

White, L. 1990. *The Comforts of Home: Prostitution in Colonial Nairobi*. Chicago: University of Chicago Press.

White, L., Silberman, L., and Anderson, P. 1948. *Nairobi, Master Plan for a Colonial Capital: A Report Prepared for the Municipal Council of Nairobi*. Nairobi: HM Stationery Office.

# FROM 'CALIBAN' TO 'COCKROACHES': THE CONSTRUCTION OF PROFANE SPACE, WRETCHED OTHERS AND POLITICAL AGENCY IN A POSTCOLONIAL 'GHETTO'

Johannah-Rae Reyes and Levi Gahman

*The sacred space, the tiny sacred island, is thus delimited with the utmost clarity from the infinite profane space. We might say that outside the 'chosen people' everything tended to be reduced to deconsecrated nature, within whose orbit also came the populations condemned by Jehovah to be wiped off the face of the earth.*
—Dominique Losurdo, *Liberalism: A Counter-History*

## Introduction, Overview and Theoretical Framework

This chapter aims to cast light upon structural violence and take seriously both the political agency and critical thought of people who reside in the 'hot spot' (i.e. high crime) community of Morvant (pronounced 'mo-VAH' locally), Trinidad and Tobago. Morvant, which is often referred to as 'Morvant-Laventille' by residents, has been labelled dangerous and high risk by the government due to its poverty and crime rates. Consequently, given it is under-served and resource-poor, across both political and civil society, it is frequently criminalized as a 'hot spot' and stigmatized as a 'ghetto', which are contested terms (in particular, by participants) that we push back against and use advisedly without quotation marks for ease of reading hereafter. Whilst residents have arguably been abandoned by the government, the community is heavily militarized and experiences periodic episodes of state-sponsored violence and disproportionate degrees of police brutality. Incidentally, Morvant is predominantly comprised of Afro-Caribbean/Black and low-income households. Notably, it is where numerous people make their lives, share stories, fall in love, start families, build community, politically organize, and call home.

In late June 2020, three unarmed Afro-Caribbean men who had not committed any crime were gunned down by the Trinidad and Tobago police force in Morvant. The murders spurred mass protests nation-wide, during which another Afro-Caribbean woman from a hot spot community who was speaking out against police brutality was shot and killed by officers. We detail the names and realities of those who were targeted in the sections to come. The killings laid bare both the persistent coloniality of the Government of Trinidad and Tobago (GoTT) and the ways in which race, class, and space in Trinidad are inextricably linked to state violence and alienation.

This piece, by drawing upon the concept of profane space and anti-colonial explicatory insights offered by Frantz Fanon in *Les Damnés de la Terre* (1963), provides an overview of state-sanctioned violence in Trinidad, as well as shares with readers the critical analyses and quotidian realities of community members from Morvant. Here, we return to and reiterate Ato Sekyi-Otu's (1996: 10) call from 25 years ago that 'the time has indeed come to remember Fanon'. The chapter is thus a Fanonian analysis of institutionalized oppression in Trinidad and account of the enduring coloniality of the Westminster-modelled GoTT. It represents six months of engaged participatory action research with residents from differing hot spots who shared their insights and experiences of what life—be it joy or pain—is like in 'd ghetto'. Our ultimate aim is to amplify the voices of community members on their terms, as well as highlight the political agency that is habitually denied to people marked as 'poor', 'criminal', and 'Other' in places deemed 'dangerous' and spaces condemned 'profane'.

## Methods and Fieldwork

Discussions with participants were illuminating as Morvant-Laventille residents clearly articulated their realities and gave deep insight into the community's history, political landscape, cultural norms, and socioeconomic circumstances. The rich descriptions were captured via interviews, focus groups, and transect walks, as well as was part of broader community outreach that Johannah-Rae was conducting as part of Womantra (a local feminist organization) and Black Lives Matter (Trinidad and Tobago). In total, 55 people were included in the project, all of whom were engaged to varying degrees ranging from in-depth semi-structured interviews and oral histories to WhatsApp chats and phone call conversations, to community assemblies and physically-distanced discussions at protests. Interviewees were residents who mobilized for the protests and/or attended community forums and were later asked if they would be interested in speaking at length about the issues at hand. Participant selection was thereby guided by convenience and chain sampling as some interviewees were present at the same demonstrations Johannah-Rae attended or were mutual friends and/or friends of friends. All interviewees were asked for and granted consent, offered the right to withdrawal, and have been given aliases.

The project was designed via feminist research ethics, which meant we were intentional about ensuring that the project was convivial, attentive to power relations and boundaries, guided by the terms and preferences of participants, and inclusive, i.e. gender, disability, age, religion, class, race, etc. were not prohibitive. The majority of interviewees were Afro-Trinidadian, with Dougla participants also contributing. Predictably, conducting fieldwork during flashpoint occurrences of state-sponsored violence in conflict-affected communities whilst following public health recommendations regarding physical-distancing during a pandemic with varying lockdown measures proved challenging. Nevertheless, Johannah-Rae was able to build rapport with and gain valuable insight from residents amidst the protests, during semi-structured interviews, and as a part of the community focus groups, she co-convened as an organizer with BLM. In addition to *in situ* participant observation and resident voices, several other secondary sources (e.g. regional song lyrics, national newspaper articles, local media reports) inform this chapter.[1]

Interviews with residents demonstrated that the static and reductive descriptors often imposed upon ghettos and hot spots were neither fixed, nor discrete. That is, the ghetto is not a monolith and liminality and dynamism characterized the realities of participants' lives more than anything else. This was made patently evident in numerous instances given resident's perceptions of their home communities were mutable, layered, and complex. Accordingly, participant quotes have been written in the way they were colloquially spoken. This is to ensure that the essence and flair of the participant's contributions, situated knowledge, and local dialect is neither diluted nor domesticated by Standard ('proper') English or liberal-Western respectability politics.

We feel this is vital because if researchers wish to meaningfully contribute to community development work, they must become proficient in grounded vocabularies that carry the potential to raise political consciousness and effect radical change via the terms, conditions, and languages of communities themselves. That is, we believe that actually-existing social transformation (i.e. revolution) is born out of local people (and their accomplices) mobilizing knowledges 'from below' and collectively organizing, which must respect and make room for multiple languages, worldviews, and ways of being (Gibson, 2017; Pithouse, 2013; Reyes et al, 2020). In short, sharing resident quotes in their local dialect is meant to signal to readers who are unfamiliar with the emplaced parlance used by participants that every extra minute they spend pouring over and researching the vernacular of Trini Creole is an investment in changing unequal power dynamics, subverting bourgeois decorum, and respecting the voices, languages, and realities of others.

## A Geography of Hot Spots and Ghettos

> *The cruelties of property and privilege are always more ferocious than the revenges of poverty and oppression.*
> —CLR James, *The Black Jacobins*

Trinidad and Tobago is an oil-rich twin-island state in the Caribbean widely recognized for Carnival, calypso, and soca, as well as its racial, religious, and ethnic diversity. The country is a pluralistic, complex, and at times paradoxical society that comes with a sobering history of imperial penetration, dispossession,

---

1. In addition, we draw from our initial essay 'Hot Spots and Kill Shots in the (Post)colonial State' in *ROAR*: https://roar-mag.org/essays/trinidad-tobago-protest/. We also agree that lead authorship here is shared.

enslavement, indentureship, and erasure. Notably, Trinidad and Tobago also carries a proud tradition of creativity, resistance, and collective action (Nurse, 1999). Reports of political corruption, partisan conflict, and violent crime often make the newspapers, as do celebrations of culture, imagination, and diasporic-to-nearby kin (Greenidge and Gahman, 2019). All this said, Trinidad's social relations, cultural landscape, and (petrol) economy remain profoundly shaped by the racism of colonial worldviews and class stratifications of patriarchal-extractive capitalism.

Here, as Caribbean economists George Beckford (1990) and Norman Girvan (2015) would argue, the role of the plantation and its durable legacy and mentalities across regional institutions cannot be overstated. Similarly, as Marxist-Feminist Cecilia Green (2001) and socialist revolutionary Andaiye illustrate (Andaiye and Trotz, 2020), the devastating consequences wrought by neoliberal logics and the privatization of social reproduction upon postcolonial societies must be factored into any examination of state violence. This is not only because of the repercussions austerity carries for people who are laboring in informal economies—but also because of the harm it causes to women and care-workers, not to mention the poverty, deprivation, hot spots, and ghettos it creates.

Hot spots in Trinidad are neighborhoods or wards (e.g. Morvant, Laventille, Beetham Gardens, Sea Lots) with high concentrations of low-income families, informal housing, illicit economic activity, and gang violence (Watson, 2016). In turn, they are problematically stereotyped and regularly homogenized as being 'pest-ridden', 'parasite-infested' ghettos overrun by 'marauding thugs'. Households in hot spots are disproportionately Afro-Caribbean/Black, cash-poor, and neglected by the government, meaning they frequently lack access to basic services like running water and serviceable roads. It is not uncommon for people from ghettos to be disparaged and discriminated against. As a result, hot spots and ghettos are branded as 'disreputable' and 'threatening' spaces by both political and civil society, and consequently, are militarized and heavily surveilled by the state. The condemnatory discourse surrounding hot spots elides the fact that ghettos are home to a diverse array of unique Caribbean thinkers, creators, and cultural producers. Even so, the negative connotations and scorn remain.

In diagnosing social relations in Trinidad, not to mention across the Caribbean as a whole, West Indian journalist Sunity Maharaj (2020) and novelist George Lamming (Fragopoulos, 2011) suggest that while European imperialists no longer hold the reins of power—historical amnesia and the old colonial order endures. Caribbean political economist Lloyd Best (1968) and author V.S. Naipaul (2010) go so far as to describe Trinidad's post-independent class dynamics and racial tensions as competing classes of 'Afro- and Indo-Saxon' elites pitted against not only each other, but also against poor 'yutes' (youth) and ghettos. Both Trinidadian poet Colin Robinson and activist Stephanie Leitch assert the Westminster-modelled state remains doggedly heteropatriarchal (Fraser, 2020). Many argue that whilst countries across the Anglo-Caribbean won their political independence, the racial hierarchies (Henry, 2000), economic disparity (Green, 2001), oppressive gender regimes (Barriteau, 2001), disavowals of Indigenous sovereignty (Jackson, 2014), and socio-spatial segregation that characterized the colonial enterprise and plantation carry on to this day. Indeed, to understand Trinidad, as well as the inherent violence of the state, it is important to take geography into account.

Morvant-Laventille is case-in-point. The community is a complex place where complex people live, much like most communities. The diversity of lived experiences and histories in Morvant cannot be captured in one uniform narrative, though, it is often attempted. That is, Morvant-Laventille should not be wholly reduced to being perceived as a site of violence, criminality, pity, and death, as it is regularly portrayed in the media. Such framings influence residents and non-residents alike. For example, the subject position of 'criminal element', 'police officer', 'politician', and 'thief' are often blurred and can be held simultaneously. Likewise, sometimes the 'gangster' from the ghetto one sees robbing people was a homeless child, abandoned by the state, who had nowhere to sleep but a rug on the step in 'the plannings' (low-income, subsidized urban housing). Meaning, if postcolonial states such as the GoTT earnestly acted on policies to serve the child and secure the material and spiritual well-being of its people, then there would be far fewer sensationalized headlines about 'gangsters', 'ghettos', and 'gun man'.

## The Persistent Coloniality of Police Brutality

> *Ah living right dey.*
> —Joel Jacobs' last words, with hands up, before being killed by the police

On June 27th of 2020 in Morvant, Trinidad and Tobago, three Afro-Caribbean/Black men—Joel Jacobs, Israel Clinton, and Noel Diamond—were gunned down by the Trinidad and Tobago Police Service (TTPS). Jacobs, Clinton, and Diamond were apparently guilty of no offense at the time and had their hands up (Bahaw, 2020). This led to accusations that their deaths were extrajudicial, which ignited mass civil unrest and prompted an investigation into the police. A series of demonstrations against state-sponsored violence and police brutality exploded across the country, which led to the arrest and detainment of over 70 people. Abdul, a resident of Morvant, describes the police killings:

> Dey (the TTPS) decided death to dese men. It look like ah kinda gang related move by the police officers, this is how it come across. Like ah man from one gang, which is de police gang have been killed in dis community and the rest of the police gang came and killed three men in retaliation. Teach dem men a lesson boy! Dey cyah come round we! How different has that been from the rage and ignorance that has prevailed in wit the different gang.

In addition to demanding justice for the three extrajudicial killings, protesters from the community issued a collective response to long-standing issues of state negligence, police brutality, and social denigration that people in so-called hot spots experience (Kerrigan, 2015). The deaths of Joel, Israel, and Noel are a direct result of the same institutionalized racism and classism that sparked the international movement for Black lives after numerous high-profile police killings of Black men and women in the United States. Amidst the 2020 protests in Trinidad, local residents proclaimed: 'This is our George Floyd' (Kissoon, 2020).

Then, on June 30, two days into the mass civil unrest, Ornella Greaves, a 30-year-old pregnant mother of five, was shot and killed during a demonstration along Trinidad's Beetham Highway. Greaves—who already lost her 23-year-old brother Christopher to police violence in 2013—joined the protests to speak out against frequent police abuse in the community (LoopTT, 2020). With respect to Christopher's death, community members in the area at that time recalled armed officers saying they opened fire after 'mistaking' a soda bottle Christopher had in his hand for a pistol. Christopher, before being killed by the TTPS, was reportedly walking home from a shop after purchasing snacks for his children. Just a few years later, without justice being served for her brother and upon having seen the protests against the 2020 killings in Morvant, Ornella felt compelled to speak out and take a stand against the recurrent police brutality. Protesters created makeshift roadblocks, shutting down the traffic on two major highways. Upon arriving at the blockades, police opened fire on the crowd critically injuring Greaves who later passed away in the hospital.

> It was you who shoot me.
> —Ornella Greaves' final words, spoken to an armed police officer

The same racial logics and liberal-capitalist values that fueled colonialism in the past lie at the roots of state violence in Trinidad today. Recognizing the indissoluble link classism has to Trinidad's state-sanctioned racial and gendered violence is particularly salient when it comes to understanding and explaining the types of authoritarian relations and hierarchical social orders that have emerged in the country since independence (Girvan, 2015). That is, whilst Trinidad and Tobago is purportedly in a post-independence era, a closer look at the country's racial, classed, and gender-based violence reveals that the state remains *actively* colonial. Nevertheless, movements, activists, and youth from the West Indies have a rich track record of rising up and asserting their political agency against colonial power and state repression.

Serena and Abdul, both residents of Morvant with whom Johannah-Rae spoke, described the community response to the state-sanctioned murders. Their quotes below are testimonies of political agency 'from below', which government officials refused to acknowledge. That is, state administrators disseminated word across the nation that the uprising was part of a larger conspiratorial plot to 'destabilize the country', that ghetto residents were paid to cause upheaval, and that protestors even shot at police officers. According to both residents and media reports (Neaves, 2020), protesters were neither paid nor did they open fire on the police. Abdul explains:

> Before we knew it we heard dat all over people were protesting. The next
> day it escalated, because people get strength now because they see sup-

port. I cannot verify if men shoot at the police... dais what de police say, given what the police have been saying, it safer to trust in what the people saying.

Abdul, along with several other residents, noted community members were inspired by the initial call for justice that erupted in Morvant when the killings occurred. Word of the collective action against police brutality quickly spread and caught on. Notably, two major gangs ('Rasta City' and 'Muslims') operating in the Port-of-Spain area (the capital city of Trinidad), and which have their own de facto boundaries/territories, negotiated a peace treaty that allowed for unimpeded participation in the protests. Meaning, community members could cross borderlines without either harm or harassment from rival gangs. Serena, a resident from Morvant, offers an overview of the complexities and solidarity:

> I ain't tink it was ah plot yuh know but what I think it was, it was... dey started protesting Morvant. Den it was ah Rasta (versus) Muslim ting so yuh know is ah different kinda... so dey say let us come tuhgeda (together). Rasta and Muslim come tuhgeda (together). A kinda solidarity ting. Let us... I tink so it happen and all de other communities come out. It end up all in South, it end up very far because dis Rasta (versus) Muslim is ah very serious ting... It had some people couldna even come in tong (town or Port-of-Spain) and dat was so bad dey can't even leave their community. Dey hadda wear all dey clothes home. Now within dis protest yuh seeing all dem fellas from Sealots, Duncan, Nelson couldna walk in tong, now yuh seeing all ah dem comin in tong.

At the time of this writing, the Police Complaints Authority (PCA) completed an investigation into the shootings and passed their report on to the Director of Prosecutions (DPP) for further action. Immediately after the shootings, several TTPS officers were placed on leave but no details of the PCA's report were provided to the public (Guardian Media Newsroom, 2020). And whilst the demonstrations have dissipated, the dissidence continues with online forums still being scheduled and supporters mobilizing to pay fines and bail protesters out of jail. The prevalence of the *#blackghettoyutelivesmatter* hashtag in Trinidad in the weeks that followed, as opposed to the more common *#BlackLivesMatter*, explicitly drove home the point that, besides race and gender, both geography and a lack of class privilege are determining factors when it comes to being a recipient of police brutality in the country.

## Slaying Like A State: 'One Shot, One Kill'

> *Sometimes this Manichaeanism reaches its logical conclusion and dehumanizes the colonized subject. In plain talk, he is reduced to the state of an animal. And consequently, when the colonist speaks of the colonized, he uses zoological terms.*
> —Frantz Fanon, *The Wretched of the Earth*

In the wake of the 2020 killings and subsequent protests, Trinidad and Tobago's Commissioner of Police, Gary Griffith, a former military captain who 'serves God' and notoriously implemented and adamantly defended a 'one shot, one kill' use-of-force policy, stated that demonstrators deserved the full force of law enforcement. Moreover, amidst the demonstrations, Griffith, who routinely uses terms like 'cockroaches' and 'savages' when describing hot spot communities and crime, was the state's leading voice arguing that the demonstrations were a 'conspiracy' organized by gangs to destabilize the nation. As noted earlier, Griffith's conspiracy claim was quickly refuted and debunked as contrived speculation, yet he still held firm that using the full brunt of the law against protestors was warranted (Neaves, 2020).

Per Griffith's approach, the police fired live rounds, used chemical irritants, beat demonstrators, and arrested 72 community members who participated in the collective action (La Vende, 2020). The protesters were charged under the Public Health Ordinance Act, which was updated in light of the coronavirus pandemic and provided officers an excuse to detain marchers who did not adhere to social distancing regulations. According to anti-violence organizers, the arrested demonstrators were confined to overcrowded cells—in clear violation of the Public Health Ordinance Act—where they suffered physical abuse at the hands of the police. Local activists, in response, contended that the state was weaponizing COVID-19 against the public.

The current militarization of the police force follows a long history of state violence. The Trinidadian police carries a jarring and exceptionally brutal legacy of caging, maiming, and executing Indigenous, African, and Indian peoples, amongst others (Ottley, 1964). For over 400 years, the mandate of the police force has been to suppress the uprisings of the disenfranchised, displaced, and subjugated in the name of 'law and order', putting the interest of capital over the well-being of the public (Pino, 2009). Here, one need not look any further than the exploitation of local workers and ecosystems facilitated by free trade deals, fossil fuel dependency, and IMF loans to understand the social and ecological damage caused by the increasing neoliberalization of economies and societies across the Caribbean (Barriteau, 1996).

Frustration with politicians, and by extension the ever-neoliberalizing and authoritarian state, emerged multiple times in interviews. Residents felt a sense of betrayal, frustration, and even marveled at the irony sometimes. One participant pointed out the community has been a stronghold for the ruling government for the past 46 years, even in the 'PNM's (People's National Movement, a conservative Afro-majority party) darkest moments'. That is, Morvant has never voted against the PNM. However, when it comes to resource distribution and social welfare, the community lacks basic amenities like a reliable supply of running water and serviceable roads. This is a point source of feelings of betrayal for residents. They feel their loyalty to the conservative, Afro-Caribbean majority party is never reciprocated. This is an example of the oppressive and ongoing colonial realities wrought by fractious partisan (state) politics, state institutions that rebuke class consciousness, and a capitalist-minded ruling class. As Fanon (1963: 12-13) avowed decades ago, nepotistic politicians, 'petty individualists', and a 'sly and shrewd" national bourgeoisie win—the masses do not. Jacob, a resident of Morvant-Laventille, elaborates:

> I believe dat for Laventille what has been a stronghold for the PNM dey should be well taken care of. Dey should be a community dat is well developed not because, dis family should feel sorry fuh dem because dis community is diehard to me, because dis is ah country rich in resources, rich in finances, and the wealth of de rich history of Trinidad and Tobago when it comes to de natural resources, is pitch, rich in oils, rich in developin' our own chemicals...I jus pass through Laventille dis morning and in Caledonia and a young guy is tellin' me dey don't have water for three weeks.

The GoTT, along with its institutions, remain structured along the lines of the British Empire-imposed Westminster model. It has a fraught history and regrettable track record of corruption and failure to protect and assist the people it purportedly serves. That is, abandonment and explicit violence persist, whether it be against women, children, migrants, refugees, the LGBTQI community, Indigenous people, or university students (Reyes and Gahman, 2020). These iterations of state negligence and institutionalized oppression look chillingly familiar, mirroring the practices of colonial governance and plantation culture. The insights from Akil and Charlene below shed light on the manifestations of structural violence community members in ghettos experience via neglect by design. Residents are subjected to chronic waiting for basic goods and services, which is constant and provokes collective action/protest.

> So dey does talk all dey nice talk on television but in de real life I telling yuh if I want to get someting from de Minister of Parliament (MP), most times I hadda be loud and tell de MP who bad man I know and dey will respect yuh and give yuh someting fass fass tuh hush yuh up. When contributing to de community I think dey could do much more in terms of understandin de people better. Iz not about handouts. (Akil)

> I doh work because ah di wheelchair. Yeah I get disability (welfare) and I had meh food card since I make my last child (through the social worker). To tell you the honest truth it (government assistance) is not enough, but I get by. Since I went through what I was through. If is not the teachers, is the principal (offering assistance). Even dis counselor does call me and give me little hampers and ting. The counselor from de Children's Authority. Dat time till now I apply for ah HDC house... dais like 25 years till now. I went through de whole process and all I have tuh do is get ah location and den I'll get my keys... and nothing, I ain't hear nothin... is 25 years. (Charlene)

Fanon (1963) surmised that if social relations, cultural norms, governance, and the distribution of wealth were all not equally rethought after emancipation and divorced from Western worldviews and liberal-capitalist logics—the deprivation and violence that defined imperialism would continue. Fanon (2008) went on to warn of the trappings of nationalism and the Westphalian state, arguing that even if the complexion might change the repression would remain the same. Fanon explains (1963: 93):

> The people who in the early days of the struggle had adopted the primitive Manichaeanism of the colonizer—Black versus White...—realize en route that some Blacks can be 'whiter than the Whites', and that the prospect of a national flag or independence does not automatically result in certain segments of the population giving up their privileges and their interests.

For communities across Trinidad and Tobago at the present moment, as well as throughout the Caribbean and beyond, Fanon's prognostications on lateral hostility, unsafe post-independent institutions (Scholars At Risk, 2018), and members of the postcolonial national bourgeoisie selling out are as seemingly prophetic as they are harrowing.

## Profane Space and Misanthropic Skepticism

As a result of Trinidad's situated race-class-space dynamics, certain groups, as Fanon (1963) theorized, are *imagined to be*, *condemned as*, and *made into* wretched 'Others' who dwell in 'profane spaces' (Losurdo, 2014), e.g. hot spots, ghettos. Decolonial theorist Nelson Maldonado-Torres (2007) refers to this as 'misanthropic skepticism', which is the institutionalized act of doubting—in conjunction with maintaining a fanatical contempt and palpable disgust for—the humanity of others on the basis of difference. It is a means to negatively racialize, and, as Aimé Césaire (2001) explained decades ago, constitutes the 'thingification' of people. The concept of misanthropic skepticism is particularly illuminating given it casts necessary light upon the racial logics, colonial worldviews, and chauvinistic rationalities that have historically been used to legitimize the damning, dispossession, dehumanization, and elimination of Others.

Maldonado-Torres' (2007) insights on misanthropic skepticism, which are heavily informed by Fanon (1963), are particularly germane when analyzing the GoTT's policing regime and discourse surrounding criminality (Kerrigan, 2018). State rhetoric is influential in shaping social norms, respectability politics, and the perception of certain places, as well as who should be included in—or excluded from—full participation in society. The language government officials employ has sway and loaded terms about who is 'good', 'upstanding', or 'law-abiding' produce certain truths (Foucault, 1991). That is, language is power-laden and the rhetoric deployed by the state sets the boundary around who is accepted as a model citizen and who is condemned as a criminal. Community activist Joseph offers this hypothesis about the role language plays in the construction of Trinidad's profane spaces (i.e. ghettos and hot spots) and which justifies state brutalities that are committed against the residents of Morvant:

Iz almost like if dey (the state) have tuh say those words to make other people believe dat what dey doing is OK—dat de way dey treat our community is OK. [The government says:] 'Dey is monsters, dey bad, dey dis and dey dat!' So other people will tink well dey (people from ghettos) are all ah problem and de police handlin de problem.

Relatedly, several participants spoke of being stigmatized because they lived in Morvant, 'd ghetto'. Stigmatized by the state, ruling class, and what Fanon (1963: 9-13) referred to as local 'vulgar opportunists' and 'colonized intellectuals'.[2] Chivonne, echoing the sentiments of numerous residents, explains the debilitating effects being ostracized carries:

> Most of the stresses that I have about growing up here are with public perception of Morvant. It's very hard to get a job. I haven't had a job in so long and it's not for lack of trying. I noticed that every time I get to the stage where they ask where are you from and I say Morvant, then communication stops.

The same discursive dynamics delimit what is seen as a 'safe' community versus what is perceived as a 'threatening' one. In short, discourses can be deployed to define, discipline, and castigate people *and* places. Accordingly, the Trinidadian state's misanthropic skepticism is revealed in its use of labels like 'cockroaches', 'savages', 'thugs', and 'criminal elements', which it recurrently associates with hot spots and ghettos. Totalizing descriptions like these omit the fact that hot spots contain a distinct assortment of differing people, families, relationships, and Caribbean culture. In fact, ghettos throughout the region have produced some of the world's most creative artists, musicians, singers, innovators, poets, political activists, calypsonians, and philosophers (Boyce Davies, 2007; Carmichael, 1966).

Fanon (1963: 4) outlines how dehumanizing discourses can be mapped onto differing *places* as a way to pillory, ridicule, subjugate, and forsake communities:

> the 'native' quarters, the shanty town, the Medina, the reservation, is a disreputable place inhabited by disreputable people. You are born anywhere, anyhow. *You die anywhere, from anything.*
>
> It's a world with no space, people are piled one on top of the other, the shacks squeezed tightly together. The colonized's sector is a famished sector, hungry for bread, meat, shoes, coal, and light. The colonized's sector is a sector that crouches and cowers, a sector on its knees, a sector that is prostrate [emphasis added].

---

2. Whilst Fanon's blistering critique of 'colonized intellectuals' was linked to the dynamics at play in newly liberated colonies during the 1950-60s (i.e. local scholars with class privilege 'betraying' the cause of freedom by prioritizing their own self-interests and individual 'rank')—to think the term is not applicable to 'First World' and White academics (or class-privileged Majority World scholars) in the present-day would be both fraught and a mistake.

Subsequently, the state has a convenient pretext to either neglect or inflict what they claim is legitimate violence upon communities and spaces it deems abject or disreputable. Put differently, space becomes at once racialized and classed, and race and class, in return, become spatialized both discursively—via misanthropic skepticism (Maldonado-Torress, 2007) and damning (Fanon, 1963—and materially, through the actual physical (re)arrangement of space. Institutionalized processes of this nature harken back to the Caribbean's brutal and haunting colonial past, not to mention echo the rhetoric and spatial (dis)orderings of imperialists who besieged the region. Here, Fanon's (1963) insights on space are especially illuminating as he suggests that the dehumanizing and racist ways in which colonizers perceived, constructed, and condemned allegedly 'barbarous Others' afforded them license—from their imperial standpoint—to dispossess, abandon, or kill said 'savages'.

Fanon's (1963: 12) insights on colonial-capitalism's affinity for abandoning Others and austerity, regrettably, continue to carry resonance in contemporary postcolonial societies. For example, when analyzing the Trinidadian police force's present-day 'war on crime', gangs, and the drug trade, Caribbean scholarship (Seepersad, 2013) explains that the surges in organized gang activities stemmed from Structural Adjustment Programs that were being implemented in the 1980s. That is, upon the state slashing social spending and its public sector budget in order to service sovereign debt, liberalize its economy, and cope with plummeting oil prices—countless people across the region were forsaken and left on their own (Pino, 2009). The sentiments expressed in the lyrics below by Morvant-Caledonia resident and popular Trinibad artist, Reiga, represent a large cross section of young men in the community.

> If ah bird, fireworks, we nah rehearse
> kill or be killed thats how di ting work
> Pop di desert Eagle, put the AK first
> Mash pun ends them, Heads start churn
> Heartless world, full setta dirt
> —*Ride fi dem*, Reiga

The realities alluded to in Reiga's prose offers insight into the reasons why men become involved in gang activity. When Reiga says 'kill or be killed that's how di ting work', he is elucidating the reliance there is upon violence in an area that has been deserted by the state. One can replace 'kill' with either the word 'exploit" or 'oppress' to understand the proverbial 'sword of Damocles' Fanon (1963: 16) referenced apropos surviving a purportedly post-independence national context—and world—that arguably remains configured by colonial worldviews.

Reiga's line 'heartless world, full setta dirt' can be interpreted as a statement made from the standpoint of a community in a profane space—i.e. the soil for well-being and making a good living in a ghetto is infertile. This is a reality birthed by historical, structural, and state forces in conjunction with enduring colonial and classist mentalities, which are often elided by government officials, police chiefs, and members of the national bourgeoisie (and even civil society) when speaking of the 'problems' that continue to plague ghettos. Abdul, a local activist explains further the socio-economic response to the state sanctioned violence:

> You'd find that communities like Morvant-Laventille historically we have been at the bottom of the economic ladder and in order to offer some redress because when dis happens ah lot of our people do not have opportunities to develop economy and industry of their own, dat leaves us de criminal industry of course there are ah lot of people that are no part of dat criminal industry but it is an attractive alternative to being broken and poor and hungry so we are where we are today and dis is it.

Essentially, many people from ghettos have been forced to opt for livelihood strategies in informal, illicit, and illegal economies. Moreover, other regional researchers have found that market shocks intrinsic to global capitalism resulted in stagnating domestic Caribbean economies, which opened the door to the drug trade (Harriott and Katz, 2015). Hence, there is an argument to be made that if the Trinidadian police force was honestly concerned with eliminating gang violence and narco-trafficking, they should be taking aim at neoliberal policies, the capitalist state, and its own colonial legacy.

## State Racism and Who Gets to *Be* (Human)

Michel Foucault (1997: 256), while offering insights into the intrinsic racism of the Western liberal state, noted that 'racism is the precondition that makes killing acceptable' and that *state* racism marks the 'break between what must live and what must die'. Whilst important to realize that Foucault was not writing explicitly about either the Caribbean or postcolonial contexts, his analysis of race and the state very much aligns with Audre Lorde's (2018) allegorical 'Master's House' foundation, the edifice upon which Trinidad's Westminster system and social order rests. Members of hot spot communities in Trinidad, surrounded by officers in tactical gear, were and continue to be aware of this precise reality. Akil, a resident of Morvant, shares he and his peers' experiences as young Black men with the police in the community:

> [Police demand]: 'Where yuh living? Go home! Allyuh go inside!'

> Dey might rough yuh up. I know ah lot of yute (youth) men geh rough up physically. I muhself. Yuh know I sitting outside and police pull up. Many times we run eh. We running because yuh want to avoid...

> [Police command]: 'Eh, where you from? Where you from? Stand up there!'

> [Police then typically frisk/pat-down 'ghetto yutes' via what is referred to locally as a 'search down']

> None of us is eighteen none of us is seventeen. Dey (officers) will take pictures ah yuh. Den dey will send yuh home. Police is something yuh try tuh avoid as much as possible, especially at night. If is ah group of young men, if dey have their hair open out... At night dey (police) more aggressive, dey will jump out of their vehicle, pull dey gun, dey know everybody stan up there and is inspection. Ah kinda antagonising, uncomfortable way. Is something that yuh does try to avoid. You will find when men liming dey will more lime somewhere dark where dey could see, so if ah vehicle coming. You position yuhself in ah way you could see whatever coming yuh way.

Reflecting on the limitations posed by Western notions of what it means to *be* human, Jamaican decolonial thinker Sylvia Wynter (2003) avows that the lived experiences of negatively racialized people are profoundly affected, if not scarred, by their recurrent and pervasive encounters with Eurocentric conceptions of 'Man'. Meaning, in the eyes of imperialists and under the ideology of liberalism, what humanity *should* be is predominantly coded as white, male, Christian, bourgeois, and rational. In short, under liberal modernity, the lives of the negatively racialized and 'poor' neither matter nor have worth and are deemed by the powers-that-be, as Fanon (1963), Maldonado-Torres (2007), and Lorde (2018) note, to be rapeable, killable, disposable, and forgettable. Ironically and cruelly, this is a page taken straight out of the white supremacist's playbook.

Consequently, given that people who are negatively racialized under colonial worldviews are thought not to measure up to Western standards of 'Man'—they live with the constant threat of experiencing abuse, humiliation, or even death. Akil continues by speaking of the criminalization and derogatory stigma community members from ghettos face, despite the evidence they offer to both political/civil society and the media of their own political agency and efforts towards justice:

> Most of the time what does be highlighted is: 'man from Morvant dont go there there will rob yuh, they will take yuh money'. Alright! I aint saying no, (but) how about the other good stuff for example the protest? All the media was saying was that them fellas is criminals. Dais all the media do. I aint see the media try tuh justify and say yuh know what... the police was wrong, whether they was criminals or not... that was wrong. I dont think people standing up for that. That's it, we don't have a voice, when it is yuh dont have a voice and people put yuh down and because of the culture of the community the easiest thing to do is get on crazy... They don't help in terms of image then the people that represent us they dont put forward as much, good that is needed for the other parts of Trinidad to see.

Well-known deprecatory and homogenizing narratives like Akil references continue to over-determine ghetto life: e.g. men involved in narcotics dealing and the arms trade; women being involved in gangs, sex work, and rendered financially dependent on men; and poor children 'hustlin' fruits picked from trees in the community, soft drinks, and recycling beer bottles. Whilst these hegemonic narratives contain glimpses of reality, they omit the innovative spirit, creative resistance, and senses of 'homeplace' (hooks, 1990) that also define Morvant.

For example, there is a budding food strip in the community where residents go to get local street food and converse. Chivonne talked about the home-made ice cream at 'the strip' and Abdul talked about enjoying the wings. Statements like this, which are profoundly human and rupture the notion that the ghetto is a profane space, were made regularly during interviews and even on the streets during protests. That is, places condemned as profane, 'wretched', and 'criminal', in many instances, are often as human as they are sacred—depending upon who one listens to. There also remains the fact that localized informal economies see many residents investing in each other given that finding meaningful and dignified work in Trinidad's formal economy is exceedingly and disparately difficult for people from a ghetto.

As argued by numerous Caribbean anti-colonial thinkers (Henry, 2000), a liberal-Western version of humanity continues to debilitate, endanger, and damage Black, Brown, and Indigenous people—including 'Black ghetto yutes'—not to mention is deeply embedded within the punitive capitalist state. As one resident of Morvant asserted:' 'They protestin' in America and killin' we here in Trinidad... ...allyuh [the police force] killin' us here fuh nutin'. Indeed, the GoTT and police brutality and neoliberal logics it endorses—along with its complicit sycophants who feel entitled to calling *certain* poor, Black humans 'cockroaches'—are performing the most belligerent type of 'sickening mimicry'. Fanon (1963: 235) warned us of such obscenities sixty years ago and rightfully called it betrayal:

> Let us not lose time in useless laments or sickening mimicry. Let us leave this Europe which never stops talking of man yet massacres him at every one of its street corners, at every corner of the world.

As Fanon explained about societies that were founded upon the ideals of liberal-capitalist modernity—both racial animosity and class-based animus can *and will* continue to be shrewdly grafted onto the bodies of disobedient and different Others. Just as each will be levied against 'disreputable places'. In detailing the inseparability of class and race in (post)colonial geographies, as well as their role in the social construction of profane spaces, Fanon (1963: 5) writes:

> This compartmentalized world, this world divided in two, is inhabited by different species. The singularity of the colonial context lies in the fact that economic reality, inequality, and enormous disparities in lifestyles never manage to mask the human reality. Looking at the immediacies of the colonial context, it is clear that what divides this world is first and foremost what species, what race one belongs to.

These ongoing colonial (classist and racist) dynamics, for post-independent ruling classes, serve as a rationalization for demeaning, segregating, punishing, and exiling those perceived as Others. It also affords the post-independent national bourgeoisie a convenient means to cast Others into what Fanon (2008) refers to as the 'zone of non-being' (Gordon, 2015). This can be conceptualized as an abyss reserved for the *damned* who must suffer *justifiable* and *deserved*—in the eyes of the state—abandonment, alienation, and anguish. In short, Fanon's (1963: 111) contention that 'the State imposes itself in a spectacular manner, flaunts its authority, harasses, making it clear to its citizens they are in constant danger' is as true today as it was when he penned *Les Damnés de la Terre* some 60 years ago.

Indeed, colonial worldviews and danger in Trinidad still remain and the realities they come with are both materially lived and tangibly sit in places, i.e. geography matters. The Government's deliberate use of connotation-laden designations like hot spot, coupled with the intent underpinning its broadcastings of dehumanizing pejoratives like 'cockroaches'' illustrate how space can be constructed as profane. In short, Prospero, the European patriarch and enslaver, condemns Caliban, the grotesque native and islander, redux. Notably, these dehumanizing machinations and condemnations of particular places have historically been resisted and continue to be confronted, contested, and challenged in Trinidad and across the Caribbean.

## Political Agency, Mutual Aid, Community Care

Residents of Morvant have not been resting idly or going about their days in lackadaisical manners. They are, on a daily basis, endeavoring to make their community a better place. They have invested time, energy, and talent towards the betterment of their community and cultural norms. Abdul offers his assessment of the situation and personal orientation and rationale to engage in social change work:

> Gang violence, teenage pregnancy, unemployment has been some of de problems dat plague the community on an ongoing basis. There are some of us dat are up to the challenge and will not be daunted. We are a community in one of de depressed areas of de country, there are difficult times, there are difficult situations but we grapple with it. Ah good example is dat we had three national league matches in the community, it was well attended and went off incident free... From very young I have approached my life in de community with a sense of responsibility because I knew in terms of the 'feelin' that we were up against.

Based on conversations with residents, there has been a significant number of organizations composed of residents who are trying to develop the community through strategic advocacy and lobbying, creating and maintaining sports teams, and the arrangement of after-school programs. All of this is completed through sponsorships, crowdfunding, and mutuality, i.e. solidaristic out-of-pocket donations from local individuals. The attention paid to youth is a hopeful investment in the future men, women, and others, however they identify, who will constitute the community. Individuals are also doing simple things to set an example and avert the trappings of capitalist consumerism, materialism, and even alpha-male posturing, like Akil, who explains:

> Dais one ah de reasons I does try my best not to wear gold. I does want to wear it. I grow up in it. It does feel nice to put ah big chain around yuh neck but I feel like it does send de wrong message tuh de younger boys. Dey doh have de balance.

Similarly, Charlene, a resident who uses a wheelchair and who joined demonstrations against police brutality when the murders in Morvant took place, explains her motivation for attending the protests:

> Kathy (a friend) say if we not going out and protest? So I say what we protestin' about, den my daughter-in-law was showing me de video. I say 'oh my god dat is murder dem police an dem murder dem men!' I say well I dont mind taking part in the protest for justice because dat was hard for me and all to really... I couldnt make to go his wake. I choose not to go because it was rel hurtful... I got dropped from one in de neighbour de first day. I had got a drop the second day. My daughter carry me down by pushing me in de wheelchair. I had get drop down the road. During the protest I get to find out he had a case going on with the police and dey was owing him over 400 thousand dollars and I say well ok, dat is why dey kill him. He win his case for police brutality. It was just for them to pay the money now but dey fine (find) dey shouldn't have to pay dat to ah little black boy.

Charlene went on to detail the ways that Joel (aka 'Lion'), Noel, and Israel (i.e. the men murdered by the police) acted as a support system for her and her son. All the men, at some point in time, acted as 'father figures', offered financial support in hard times, took her to the bank to collect welfare cheques, and accompanied her on trips to get groceries. Charlene describes the intense pain and heartbreak she seems to be unable to escape: 'Everybody who I get close to, like dey takin dem away from me'. Charlene went on to recount the difficulty she experienced when trying to explain the murders to her son:

> All of them used to say dat was dem son inno. When one not there de next one lookin out fuh him and so dey going. He (Luke, her son) took it hard too. Yes he told me: 'why the police had to kill Israel, Diamond, and Lion?' I say 'I dont know, I cannot answer dat question but dats why we going out there everyday to protest for justice'. Then he say 'dem police wicked' because he watch de video. He say 'oh my gosh! mummy! dem police willfully kill dem'. He say' 'Why boy?' I say, 'sometimes yuh here and sometimes yuh not here'. He just went in his own lil zone. He cry. He say mummy 'everybody who lookin out fuh me dey goin?' I say how you mean 'dey goin'. He say somebody always 'taking dem up'.

Here, the role of gender, social reproduction, and carework must be emphasized (Andaiye and Trotz, 2020). As a result of engaging with women and over the course of the fieldwork, it became clear that women in the community carried the burden of loss, did most the emotional labor, and provided counsel/comfort to their children about the violence and deaths.

Women also simultaneously felt a sense of duty to stand up for and defend their community. Charlene, in her contribution above, exhibited this sense of duty as she performed all these roles as a wheelchair user. Numerous other women from ghettos shared stories of myriad hardships that stemmed from both internal and external sources. Many, too, offered testimony of resilience and agency, in particular through their willingness to engage in collective action, boldly confront state violence, and comfort afflicted community members—all whilst being afflicted and aggressed-upon themselves. In this same vein, Akil shares his observations about the carework and socially reproductive labor that women disproportionately perform when he states:

> I know what a woman goes through to raise children and how that feels. She (his mother) struggle to take care of us and other ladies around (as well). While it [the livelihood strategies for women] might be crazy for people on the outside, it's quite normal for people on the inside [in Morvant].

Akil's mention of 'she struggle' alludes to the difficult realities and systemic marginalization women in the community, not to mention country writ large, are subjected to. Several of the women who contributed to this research shared similar sentiments. That is, the care- and community-building work of women, which secures wellbeing, kinship, and sustains communal bonds in ghettos, is often as thankless as it is life-giving.

As Fanon (1963: 142), not to mention countless women across the Caribbean have contended for generations (Collins and Gahman, 2019), liberation necessitates that women 'be given equal importance to men, not [only] in the articles of the constitution, but in daily life, at the factory, in the schools, and in assemblies'. It is arguable, then, that any revolutionary version of humanity or process of social transformation that is not defined by gender justice, both institutionally and in everyday life—and which does not (re)value socially reproductive labor—is not revolutionary at all.

With respect to emancipatory politics, throughout the duration of this research participants frequently made note of the catch-22 residents from ghetto communities face when exercising political agency and attempting to effect justice, e.g. do social change work, try to improve their communities, have a say on topics in the national discourse. Abdul captures the overarching sentiment when he asserts:

> It gives us the feeling in de streets in de hood and in de community dat de only way to get tings is to protest. Dais what dis kinda (government) lethargy does lead to. Yuh know what? Lewwe light dem up! While burn-

ing tires and blocking roads is nonsensical it (the state) does leave us wit no other choice.

In short, when the ghetto mobilizes to engage with the state, it is breaching the *profane space* to which it has been relegated and seen as a threat. Yet, when the state puts people from the ghetto in its crosshairs and pulls the trigger, it is seen as keeping the peace. This is neither a hyperbole nor a one-time incident—this is the state (Mbah and Igariwey, 2001). Fanon (1963: 76) was correct to equate such vulgar displays of power with the actions of past imperialists and declare:

> The national bourgeoisie, appropriating the old traditions of colonialism, flexes its military and police muscle.

And whilst the violence of (post)colonial institutions persists, as the participants who informed this chapter demonstrated, so too does the political agency and collective care of communities in struggle.

## Conclusion

> Justice does bring ah certain balance to any action or any activity. Even if you deal unjust with your stomach when you eat too much, your stomach will perform an action to bring justice to the system yuh does get a bad feeling, a nausea. Dat in itself is justice. So if within de police service, within de media dat feeling of nausea does not take place den ppl like (TT)BLM would not continue dat nausea, dat feeling of nausea must be felt among us that's the responsibility we must take as activists. So in dat sense I sayin we cyah go to sleep. We have to remain vigilant. We must be so in the mind of de people who want to commit an unjust act, 'ah wonder what BLM will say boy...' Dey hadda think twice! So you become a check tuh balance de ting. (Abdul)

In sum, as Abdul alludes to in the closing quote above, across the Caribbean, the hot spot killings by the TTPS were and continue to be viscerally felt in body, mind, and soul—corporally, psychologically, and spiritually. Indeed, the state violence perpetrated by the GoTT is a haunting reminder of the systemic and naked disregard for human life that was operationalized by colonizers via racial contempt, classist derision, and heteropatriarchal norms for generations on end. The slayings in Morvant also eerily emulate the institutionalized repression and structural white supremacy that define so many other societies and geographies across the world, which continue to disproportionately injure—and end—the lives of both the negatively racialized (e.g. Black, Indigenous) and working-poor. More than half a century ago, Frantz Fanon (1963: 235) trenchantly called upon us to confront and abolish the 'sickening mimicry' of enduring coloniality—along with its attendant hierarchical social relations, liberal-capitalist institutions, and 'colonized intellectuals'. That is, to 'turn over a new leaf' as a means of breathing life into inclusive cultural relations, an economy of tenderness and radical care, and ultimately, a 'new humanity'.

For us, as well as other emancipatory social movements across the circum-Caribbean, not to mention the participants who informed this chapter, Fanon's call for a revolutionary version of humanity—one in which people are neither condemned as' 'wretched' nor killed by the state— remains as exigent as ever. And as the people from the ghetto in Trinidad have shown us throughout this piece, Fanon's hope for a world transformed is something worth fighting for, whatever the geography. To end and to put it bluntly, for anyone who earnestly takes the prospect of actually-existing emancipation seriously, the state will get the critiques, calls for abolition—and riots—it deserves. As for the spirits of Ornella Greaves, Joel Jacobs, Israel Clinton, Noel Diamond and the people of the ghettos who continue to assert their worth under the shadow of a repressive Westminster-modelled state and defiantly refuse to go quietly as 'cockroaches' into the darkness of non-being—their rage is precious. *A luta continua...*

# Bibliography

Andaiye and Trotz, A., eds. 2020. *The Point is to Change the World: Selected Writings of Andaiy*. London: Pluto Press.

Bahaw, D. 2020. 'New Video Emerges in Morvant Police Killing,' *Trinidad and Tobago Newsday*, http://newsday.co.tt/2020/07/09/new-video-emerges-in-morvant-police-killing/?fbclid=IwAR1zIp3QzwH_TwvOvBBj8X-qoCOilmEir3U2i35obUycqNV1UOnxYxjmDuM#.XwpaQPmAtrU.facebook.

Barriteau, V. E. 1996. 'Structural Adjustment Policies in the Caribbean: A Feminist Perspective.' *NWSA Journal* 8 (61): 142–156.

Barriteau, V. E. 2001. *The Political Economy of Gender in the Twentieth-Century Caribbean*. Baskingstoke: Palgrave Macmillan.

Beckford, G. L. 1999. *Persistent Poverty: Underdevelopment in Plantation Economies of the Third World*. Jamaica: University of West Indies Press.

Best, L. A. 1968. 'Outlines of a Model of Pure Plantation Economy.' *Social and Economic Studies* 17 (3): 283–326.

Boyce Davies, C. 2007. *Left of Karl Marx: The Political Life of Black Communist Claudia Jones*. Durham: Duke University Press.

Carmichael, S. 1966. 'Toward black liberation.' *The Massachusetts Review* 7 (4): 639–651.

Césaire, A. 2001. *Discourse on Colonialism*. New York: NYU Press.

Collins, T., and Gahman, L. 2019. 'Recognizing and Undisciplining Feminist Geography in the Caribbean.' *Gender, Place & Culture* 26 (7–9): 988–1000.

Fanon, F. 1963. *The Wretched of the Earth*. Translated by Richard Philcox. New York: Grove Press.

_____. 2008. *Black Skin, White Masks*. Translated by Richard Philcox. New York: Grove Press.

Foucault, M. 1991. *Discipline and Punish: The Birth of a Prison*. London, Penguin.

_____.1997. *Society Must Be Defended: Lectures at the Collège de France, 1975–1976*. New York: St. Martin's Press.

Fragopoulos, G. 2011. 'Reviewed Work: Sovereignty of the Imagination by George Lamming.' *Callaloo* 34 (4): 1113–1115, http://www.jstor.org/stable/41412485.

Fraser, N. 2020. 'NGOs, UWI Guild: PM Should Rethink Recovery Team.' *Trinidad and Tobago Newsday*, https://newsday.co.tt/2020/04/18/ngos-uwi-guild-pm-should-rethink-recovery-team/.

Gibson, N. C. 2017. 'The Specter of Fanon: The Student Movements and the Rationality of Revolt in South Africa.' *Social Identities* 23 (5): 579–599.

Girvan, N. 2015. 'Assessing Westminster in the Caribbean: Then and Now.' *Commonwealth and Comparative Politics* 53 (1): 95–107.

Gordon, L. R. 2015. *What Fanon Said: A Philosophical Introduction to His Life and Thought*. New York: Fordham University Press.

Green, C. 2001. 'Caribbean Dependency Theory of the 1970s: A Historical-Materialist-Feminist Revision.' In *New Caribbean Thought: A Reader*, edited by Meeks, B., and Lindahl, F., 40–72. Jamaica: University of the West Indies Press.

Greenidge, A., and Gahman, L. 2019. 'Roots, Rhizomes and Resistance: Remembering the Sir George Williams Student Uprising.' *Race & Class* 61 (2): 27–42.

Guardian Media Newsroom. 2020. 'Morvant Police-Involved Killing Sent to DPP.' *CNC3*, https://www.cnc3.co.tt/morvant-police-involved-killing-sent-to-dpp/.

Harriott, A., and Katz, C. M., eds. 2015. *Gangs in the Caribbean: Responses of State and Society*. Mona: University of the West Indies Press.

Henry, P. 2000. *Caliban's Reason: Introducing Afro-Caribbean Philosophy*. London: Routledge.

Hooks, B. ed. 1990. 'Homeplace (As a Site of Resistance).' *Yearning: Race, Gender, and Cultural Politics*, 41–49. Boston: South End Press.

Jackson, S. N. 2014. 'To Be Anti-Black Is to Be Anti-Indigenous: Reflections on Emancipation.' *Stabroek News*, https://www.stabroeknews.com/2014/07/28/features/anti-black-anti-indigenous-reflections-emancipation/.

James, C. L. R. 2001. *The Black Jacobins: Toussaint L'Ouverture and the San Domingo Revolution*. London: Penguin UK.

Kerrigan, D. 2015. 'Transnational Anti-Black Racism and State Violence in Trinidad.' *Cultural Anthropology Online, Fieldsights – Hot Spots*, http://culanth.org/fieldsights/692-transnational-anti-black-racismand-state-violence-in-trinidad.

Kerrigan, D. 2018. 'Language-In-Use Living Under Militarisation and Insecurity: How Securitisation Discourse Wounds Trinidad.' *The Journal of Latin American and Caribbean Anthropology* 23 (3): 416–436.

Kissoon, C. 2020. 'This Is Our George Floyd' – Protesters Demand Murder Charges.' *Trinidad Express*, https://trinidadexpress.com/newsextra/this-is-our-george-floyd—protesters-demand-murder-charges/article_4211e8fe-ba32-11ea-83c1-9b2eebcb7358.html.

La Vende, J. 2020. 'Tear Gas in Town.' *Trinidad and Tobago Newsday*, https://newsday.co.tt/2020/07/02/tear-gas-in-town/.

Loop, T. T. 2020. 'Ornella Was Second Family Member to Be Killed in Police Confrontation,' https://www.looptt.com/content/ornella-was-second-family-member-be-killed-police-confrontation.

Lorde, A. 2018. *The Master's Tools Will Never Dismantle the Master's House*. London: Penguin UK.

Losurdo, D. 2014. *Liberalism: A Counter-History*. London: Verso Trade.

Maharaj, S. 2020. 'Our Unfinished Revolution.' *Trinidad Express*, https://trinidad-express.com/opinion/columnists/our-unfinished-revolution/article_f678ba16-be5b-11ea-952f-0f2dff892eef.html.

Maldonado-Torres, N. 2007. 'On the Coloniality of Being: Contributions to the Development of a Concept.' *Cultural Studies* 21 (2–3): 240–270.

Mbah, S., and Igariwey, I. E. 2001. *African Anarchism: The History of a Movement*. Tucson: Sharp Press.

Naipaul, V. S. 2010. *The Mimic Men*. New York: Knopf Doubleday Publishing Group.

Neaves, J. 2020. 'MP: Morvant Protests Organised by Residents, Not Gangs.' *Trinidad and Tobago Newsday*, https://newsday.co.tt/2020/07/11/mp-morvant-protests-organised-by-residents-not-gangs/.

Nurse, K. 1999. Globalization and Trinidad Carnival: Diaspora, Hybridity and Identity in Global Culture.' *Cultural Studies* 13 (4): 661–669.

Ottley, C. R. 1964. *A Historical Account of the Trinidad and Tobago Police Force From the Earliest Times*. Trinidad: Ottley.

Pino, N. 2009. 'Developing Democratic Policing the Caribbean: The Case of Trinidad and Tobago.' *Caribbean Journal of Criminology and Public Safety* 14 (1–2): 214-258.

Pithouse, R. 2013. 'The Open Door of Every Consciousness.' *South Atlantic Quarterly* 112 (1): 91–98.

Reyes, J. R., and Gahman, L. 2020. 'Hot Spots and Kill Shots in the (Post)Colonial State.' *ROAR (Reflections on a Revolution)*, https://roarmag.org/essays/trinidad-tobago-protest/.

Reyes, J. R., Miller, T., Gibbings, R., Cohen, A., Greenidge, A., Chattopadhyay, S., and Gahman, L. 2020. 'Activist Geographies.' In *International Encyclopedia of Human Geography* edited by Kobayashi, A. 2nd ed. Oxford: Elsevier.

Scholars At Risk. 2018. 'University of the West Indies: Use of Violent Force and Arrests of Students During a Nonviolent Campus Protest.' *Scholars At Risk Network*, https://www.scholarsatrisk.org/report/2018-10-17-university-of-the-west-indies/.

Seepersad, R. ed. 2013. *Gangs in the Caribbean*. Cambridge: Cambridge Scholars Publishing.

Sekyi-Otu, A. 1996. *Fanon's Dialectic of Experience*. Cambridge: Harvard University Press.

Watson, D. 2016. '"Hotspot policing": A Comparative Analysis of Sanctioned Acts of Policing Versus Media Representations of Policing in a Stigmatized Community in Trinidad.' *Police Practice and Research* 17 (6): 520–530.

Wynter, S. 2003. 'Unsettling the Coloniality of Being/Power/Truth/Freedom: Towards the Human, After Man, Its Overrepresentation – An Argument.' *The New Centennial Review* 3 (3): 257–337.

# THE POWER OF ABAHLALI AND OUR LIVING POLITIC HAS BEEN BUILT WITH OUR BLOOD

S'bu Zikode

*Talk delivered by S'bu Zikode as part of the virtual speaker series 'Thinking Freedom from the Global South', American University, 17 February 2021.*
[Editor's note: S'bu Zikode has always used the term 'politic', not politics as it reflects a way of speaking in a form of English and feels closer to the Zulu term. Hence the title of this chapter.]

I am deeply honoured to be invited into this space and I do say that I carry the hearts and lives of shack dweller members, Abahlali baseMjondolo with me and I want to take this moment and salute those who have suffered injustices not only in South Africa but across the globe. I do want to salute those who have passed away in their efforts to humanize the world. We have lost 18 activists here in Abahlali and I carry those hearts and I carry that courage with me as I speak to you this morning.

May I first of all take this opportunity to thank the American University's Anti-Racist Research & Policy Center, Department of Critical Race, Gender and Culture Studies and Women's Initiative for giving Abahlali this important opportunity to speak here today. The most powerful forces of oppression operate at a global level, and for this reason the movements that organize resistance need to connect with each other. Our movement is open to the world, and we work to build solidarity with progressive forces everywhere. Which is why I speak with you here. I also want to acknowledge the audience who have taken time to listen and to participate in these conversations. Students have often played an important role in the struggle, and when university trained intellectuals are able to humble themselves and work with oppressed people in a spirit of equality and mutual respect, they can play an important role in struggle too.

Thanks to Professor Irene Calis for your leadership and guidance, and for making this discussion possible.

I also appreciate this opportunity and am honored because I am sharing it with Abahlali scholar and comrade, Professor Nigel Gibson who has introduced me today. For those of you who may not know Professor Gibson, he is not just a Fanon scholar, but was also graduated from the University of Abahlali baseMjondolo with his book *Fanonian Practices in South Africa, from Steve Biko to Abahlali baseMjondolo*. We have much to learn from his work and from the fact that you are very humble and you are grounded and open to work with activists on the ground. That makes you one of us.

Many academics start their work by assuming that impoverished black people cannot think for ourselves and that it is their job to think for us, speak for us and decide for us. Nigel always met us as equals. He understands that we can learn from him and that he can learn from us. This is why he is a comrade professor. And there are very few comrade professors.

I also wish to thank Abahlali, the organization that has entrusted me with this responsibility as well. In our movement all requests to speak at events like this are referred back to a democratic process before being accepted. No member of the movement represents themselves. We speak with the responsibility of carrying a mandate from the movement.

This virtual speaker series 'Thinking Freedom from the Global South' is indeed pushing anti-colonial thought and practice. There are oppressed people everywhere, including the United States. There are also oppressors everywhere, including in countries like South Africa. It is our own elites that murder us when we organize with the simple demand of being recognized as human beings. It is the same in India, Brazil, Zimbabwe and many other countries.

But as we all know since the time of colonialism the countries of the global South have been dominated by the North. There can be no future for humanity unless this is changed and a world of equality between countries and between people is built.

Abahlali baseMjondolo is a radical, mass democratic movement of shack dwellers and other poor people in South Africa. The movement is led by shack dwellers themselves who have often been looked down upon. I remember when we first started, many people did not believe that the poor could think for themselves. They often referred to our movement as *umlilo wamaphepha*—a fire of papers that will not last. Many of these people even from government were also critical and ashamed of the name of our movement Abahlali baseMjondolo (residents of the shacks). They told us that it was ugly and they even persuaded us to change it into some fancy English name that suggests all African people in South Africa are liberated and enjoy their freedom, while in reality millions of us are landless, homeless, living in deep poverty and excluded from official forms of decision making.

It was colonialism that made us landless, that commodified land and built segregated cities. It was colonialism that came with the idea that some people cannot think, that they do not count as human beings and that they can be repressed and subject to violence with impunity when they try to take their places as human beings. More than 25 years after the end of apartheid we remain landless, land remains commodified and cities continue to be segregated, but now on the basis of class. Our humanity continues to be denied, elites continue to think that we cannot think for ourselves and that they should think and speak for us, and when we insist on our humanity, we continue to be subject to violence, even to murder. Hence my topic is the power of Abahlali and the living politic is being paid with our own blood.

For all these reasons our struggle is an anti-colonial struggle. The idea that our languages and cultures are primitive and should be replaced with what are seen as 'modern' languages and practice be rejected at all cost.

Our movement is open to the world. We learn from comrades everywhere. We learn from Brazil, from the Landless People's Movement, we learn from comrades from India, from comrades in South America and elsewhere. We are currently pursuing a program of urban farming on occupied land. The seeds that we used to start this project came from the MST, the landless movement in Brazil. We see this as a beautiful thing. But we also use our own culture and history to build our movement.

I will give one example. In rural villages there is often meetings in which each man is allowed to make his point. That point is not always criticized rather a different view will be raised by someone else. The man who raised the withdrawn point may not be offended by that. This means that no one feels that their dignity has been compromised. Everyone is encouraged to speak and to participate. Through a slow discussion a consensus will emerge about which ideas are best. Often what will emerge will be a mixture of different ideas, or one idea will lead to another one so that in the end the meeting comes to a consensus that has been worked out together. Whoever chairs the meeting facilitates this discussion and is bound to sum up what has been discussed and resolved. The role of the chairperson is not to decide for the people, but to support the process in which people think and decide together.

In the village women may be sitting quietly and not say a word. But women often have the power to influence or send their opinion through their partners or male neighbors outside formal proceedings. This is to say that some men would have received briefing from women prior to getting into the meetings. If he did not raise the particular point he was briefed to raise, he is likely to receive criticism from that woman. So, women do have some power to strategical influence the meetings behind the scenes.

We use the same method in our movement with one major difference. A majority of our members are women and meetings are often run by women. In fact, where they are male leaders, they are chosen by women and they know that they are accountable to women.

This example shows how our movement draws on our culture and history, sometimes advancing it quite radically, to build a movement, a movement that has survived for 15 years despite very serious repression. There are many other examples such as ways to welcome strangers and to resolve serious conflicts peacefully.

One of the colonial ideas that we have to resist from many quarters is the view that poor African people cannot think for themselves. We find this thinking in the ruling party and the state. It is very strong in the universities and in most NGOs.

There are a number of academics who call themselves socialists and are trusted by the left internationally to represent South Africa who are deeply blinded by the idea that the poor African cannot think for themselves. In fact, they have called the idea that we can think for ourselves 'romantic' or even 'Negrophilia'.

Some are so confident that they should be leading the struggle of the oppressed that they have sought to destroy our movement because we have insisted that we will take direction from our members and not from them. They have slandered us, published fraud in their journals, supported state propaganda against us, worked with a front organization for the intelligence services to attack us and, just like the state, used their money to bribe other oppressed people to attack us. They have often thought that they have a right to decide who should represent our movement and struggle internationally. They have contempt for our democratic structures and our own decision making.

Abahlali was formed in Durban in 2005. The movement was formed to fight for, protect, promote and advance the interest and dignity of the shack dwellers and the poor in South Africa, and to create a space for us to build our own democracy and power.

It was formed after promises for development and engagement were made and after promises were broken. It was formed because the lies were put before the truth. In the years before the movement was formed many people, especially young people, had the experience of serious police harassment and violence during their everyday lives. They were often insulted and assaulted. For a number of the people that formed our movement it was this experience that led them to start to be critical of the new democracy. Later there were threats of forced removals to the human dumping grounds for outside of the city.

The final betrayal that led to the formation of the movement was when a piece of land that had long been promised to the residents of the Kennedy Road shack settlement for housing was sold to a local business man. We were told that the African National Congress (ANC) was leading a revolution but profit was put before human needs. The commercial value of land was put before its social value. The living conditions in shack settlements were and still are life-threatening, as noted by the United Nations. There is hardly any water and sanitation, no road access, no refuse collections and no electricity. People are burnt to death in shack fires as they are forced to use candles to light and paraffin stoves to cook. These living conditions put us at all kinds of diseases especially tuberculosis and HIV. Our children continue to die from diarrhea. Today we face a high risk from the COVID-19 pandemic.

Politicians thought they were owning us. Even today when they speak about us, they refer to black impoverished people as 'our people'. They decide for us and go out to speak for us without us. They steal public funds at a huge scale. They have no sense of *ubuntu* (humanism) and do not appreciate the deep responsibility of being trusted to the positions of power.

This is why when we started our movement, we insisted so strongly that we would think and decide for ourselves, and that we would build our own autonomous and democratic power. This is why we created our own philosophy and our politic. Later we discovered that most NGOs also thought that they should own us, decide for us and speak for us.

Both the government and these NGOs, which I refer to as regressive forces, tried to show us to the world as criminals when we insisted on our autonomy. It became clear that for elites in and out of the state it was criminal for us to ask to be recognised as human beings, and to insist on our human dignity.

After 25 years of democracy, shack dwellers still live in the mud like pigs, without access to basic services such as water, electricity and toilets. After 25 years what was supposed to become a rainbow nation witness's regular xeno-phobia and violence against migrants and minority ethnic groups. After 25 years of democracy there are more people living in shacks than before, the poor are poorer than before and police violence is just as bad as it always was.

Our constitutional democracy is being undermined by some of those who claimed to have fought for this democracy. Like in Zimbabwe they wish to make democracy a ticket to reward only for those who claimed to have been in the lib-eration army. The same people who claim to have been in an army of liberation are attacking migrants in the streets. The very same migrants who had hosted them during the olden days. Where is their Ubuntu, where is their humanity?

Our cities have been taken over by political mafias and gangster politicians in suits and ties. They dress so smart that you cannot see them. They are as smart as those who are highly educated and inside they are dirty with indignity. They have been prepared to kill in order to ascend to the positions of power. Some of them have blood on their hands. And that blood has been their ladder to ascend to position to power. They are in power today because they have power to kill people. A number of our leaders have been assassinated. Two ANC councillors are now in jail for killing our leaders.

The price for land, for decent housing and the right to the city, is paid in blood. Brutal and unlawful evictions continue to terrorize our communities. The organized *izinkabi* (hitmen), the Land Invasion Unit of the eThekwini Munici-pality (City government of Durban), the Red Ants of the City of Johannesburg and the Anti-Land Invasion unit of the municipality in Cape Town have sub-verted the law and use violence on landless people. This is what happens when the commercial value of land is placed before its social value. This is what hap-pens when an accountable political leadership is replaced by gangster politicians. This is what happens when a democratic state is replaced by a police state.

So, what we have discovered was that the democracy achieved in 1994 was never for the impoverished people. The elites used the poor and the working class to win power, but they used us as ladders to climb up and replace the old white oppressors. Democracy became an opportunity for the politicians and elites to enrich themselves at the expense of millions of people of South Africa. The question of land, the question of the right to the cities and the question of building a participatory democracy were never resolved.

We were never allowed to participate in decision-making since the onset of our democratic dispensation. We were never allowed to participate in decision-making with regards to our lives and our communities. When we organize to insist on our right to participate in this democracy we were presented as 'the third force' which means agents of foreign powers working with old apartheid forces. We were slandered and violently repressed by the state and the ruling party. Local politicians eventually became dangerous figures in our communities. Today people say sesiyawasaba amakhansela (we are afraid of councillors). How does one become afraid of their own elected representatives? How in our own democracy is one scared of the same people you elect into power? Local council-lors, mostly from the ruling party have been dangerous figures in the streets

The ANC has betrayed the struggle for liberation and become new oppressors. Now new oppressors can be dangerous. They can be very smart because they have learnt from the best. For many years it was very difficult to get progressive people in other countries to understand this. Now, after the Marikana massacre in 2012, and the huge theft when Jacob Zuma was president everyone understands this very well.

However, one thing to appreciate is that Abahlali communities have organized and built our own democracy from below. A democracy that recognises every human being. A democracy that respect every human life. A democracy that encourages participation in decision making. A democracy that celebrates women's power and is committed to self-management.

This is what we call a living politic. It is the politic of truth and it is the politic of principle and courage. It is the politic that is thought from the ground about the reality of our lives. This politic is still not found in big philosophical books of our time. It is found and thought from the humility of ordinary men and women of our time. It is the politic of land. Some refer to it as ''life and death'' as we come from mother earth and shall be buried in the earth when we die.

It is a politic that everyone can understand. It is the politic of decent housing for all, everywhere including in the United States, including in the state of California where I was surprised to meet people sleeping on the streets. There is homelessness everywhere, not only in the global South but in the global North there is poverty. What emerges in the global South has to emerge in the global North so the North and South can meet in humility and humanize the world that needs to be humanized. These politic can be found and thought in the humility of ordinary people. It is the politic of land. And, of course, it is the politic that everyone understands. It is the politic of decent housing for all. It is the politic of good schools, hospitals that heal. It is the politic of libraries. It is the politic of good universities, parks, safe streets and a decent income for all. It is the politic of water. Many of us live without sufficient water in shacks and in rural communities. If we are lucky to have one tap, we share it in our hundreds, yet a middle class or rich person could have up to seven taps in one house in one family. We know water is a natural resource, it is a gift from God. But now the politicians, who want to make themselves as if they were gods, decide who should get it and at what cost. Electricity is also commodified. Mnikelo Ndabankulu, one of the founders of our movement, used to say that we do not need electricity and water but our lives need electricity and water. So those are different things. We do not need just water and electricity, but more than that. It is not us. It is our lives that need water and sanitation, and electricity. There is no compromise in that. That is why whenever we have no water, we connect it ourselves. Where there is no electricity, we make a connection of electricity. Whether you call that theft or crime you are blind because when these fundamental services are denied to people you do not see that you do not see that as theft, you do not see that as crime against humanity.

During these fifteen years of our struggle the self-organization of impoverished communities has been seen as some form of conspiracy. This is done to justify violence on us. Sometimes we are accused of being funded by foreign agencies that aim to destabilize our hard-won democracy. This is also done to justify violence on us. Organizing outside the ruling party and the state and outside of the NGOs has cost us lives. Insisting that land, cities and wealth must be shared has cost us lives. We lost 18 activists between 2009 and 2018. This is why our members started to say that they are in a situation in which they have to accept that their commitment is to land or death. Many of us have scars just for insisting that impoverished people must count in our society.

Although we have deep scars and remain marginalized, today we have a place called home because of our own courage and inkani—which is a kind of strong determination. We have done this through occupying vacant and unused land. That is not crime. Crime is when there are human beings who do not have land, who do not have decent housing. Before you conclude what constitutes criminality, you should start by saying does every human being have decent housing, and have land? Then everything falls into place. We have done this by occupying vacant and unused land. We have connected ourselves to water and electricity. We have built cooperatives and community gardens. We have built crèches for our children and access roads to our settlements. This is called democratic urban planning from below. We are not going to wait for governments, we will do whatever it takes to make sure that our children are safe and have a better future. What choices do you have when your own government has no time for its people? What choices do you have when your local city government or councillor has become a dangerous figure to the same people that have elected him or her into power? What choices do you have when your local councillor spends their time chasing tenders and business deals?

Today we remain a people's movement and the largest to have emerged in post-apartheid South Africa. It is the democracy that we have built ourselves that has given hope to many people in South Africa and abroad. The power of Abahlali and our living politic has carried the values and the treasure of our democracy and we work hard to build the future we want, while we defend our gains. It is important to repeat that the power of Abahlali and living politic has been paid in blood. Fifteen years of our revolutionary struggle has not been easy. We have scars on our bodies. We have scars in our own spirits. We are emotional. We have been through hell for insisting that we are human beings among other human beings. And we love our country as we love humanity. We love our world as we move every human life. So, we've been guilty for showing this, not just for saying this.

Ubuhlali is our philosophy. It is the philosophy of our movement. It is our joy and our pride that can be used to advance democracy, to defend the constitutional democracy that was won in 1994 against a criminal elite in the ruling party and the state, to deepen and expand that democracy. After fifteen years of our struggle we remain committed to building radical democracy from below. We remain committed to the principle that the wealth, the cities and land must be shared. We remain committed to our right to participate in discussions and to make decisions in a way that is shared.

This is the mission that confronts our generation.

Let us work together in our communities, and across the world, to humanize the world.

I want to conclude using this quote which is close to my heart by Frantz Fanon, 'Each generation must discover its mission, fulfil it or betray it'. When these words were said I can imagine at what stage Fanon was, that he was challenging the world and humanity that unless they rise, unless they speak truth to power in the face of severe repression such as the one faced by Abahlali. In the face of all kinds of threat, humanity has to rise. No matter what the consequences are, Abahlali has emerged. Abahlali has discovered its mission, we are in a process to fulfil it or betray it. And each time I read this quote, I was also reminded when I was arrested and charged with several fabricated charges, when I had to reside a whole night in the police cell, when the police attached me in the police cell, when I was hurt and refused medical attention, when I was tortured, I had to decide whether or not to continue leading this strategy of Abahlali. When I appeared in court and saw the red Abahlali T shirts all over the court and corridors of the courts, when I saw massive Abahlali support standing with me immediately the answer came that it was worth continuing. So, the scars that I carry today together with many comrades in Abahlali are the scars, the sacrifices, the offering of humanity, not only to Abahlali members, but to the struggle to human kind all over the world whose mouths are shut who cannot say or express what they want to say. So, at the moment Abahlali are discovering and also fulfilling their mission. So, there are times in our lives when we have to take decisions. And these decisions are not easy. Our families have gone through difficult moments sometimes my kids have been without their father. Sometimes there is a moment when I had to think about what is it that I have not achieved in life because death was unavoidable. Because this hasn't come, we have not fulfilled the mission that we have discovered. We have risen to live but continue to struggle. I am inspired by the very same people that are claimed by many as uneducated, as unthinking. As you know, I get this power from the old women who cannot speak English and that doesn't make them stupid, it doesn't make them people who cannot make their own future.

# FANON AND PALESTINE: THE STRUGGLE FOR JUSTICE AS THE CORE OF MENTAL HEALTH

Samah Jabr and Elizabeth Berger

## Introduction

While it appears that the psychiatrist Frantz Fanon wrote nothing addressing the specific situation faced by the people of Palestine under occupation (A. Cherki, personal communication, July 7, 2019), his prophetic insights remain a source of inspiration to Palestinians even at this time, 60 years after his death (Fanon, 1952/2008, 1959/1965, 1961/2004, 2018).

Fanon's genius arose from his creative integration of two vast human concerns. One is the quest for justice in the face of oppressive control of one population by another—the need for revolutionary change to restore equity to the global population subjugated by colonialist oppression. The other is the understanding that this subjugation is not only political, economic, and military but also profoundly, inherently, and perversely psychological. Fanon saw, in the broad tradition of Marx and Engels but enhanced by the twentieth-century tools of the Freudian tradition, that the physical enslavement of human beings was simultaneously accompanied by the enslavement of their spirits through the loss of their history, dignity, and agency. The brilliance of Fanon was to hold fast to the overriding ethical commitment to the struggle for social and economic justice but to extend his analysis to parse the myriad ways that psychological warfare is an invariable element of this struggle. The covert operations of day-to-day ideology, persuasion, public opinion, bureaucracy, and propaganda as well as the deep persistence of ethnic, racial, gender, national, and class-identification and their various shames and entitlements—all of these slippery intangibles became legible in new ways when viewed through Fanon's discerning lens. With Fanon, it became possible to read between the lines of the oppressor's playbook and to develop a genuinely robust psychology of liberation.

Just as Fanon deconstructed the ideology of the oppressor as a top-down imposition of power and control, he was able to work upward from the psychological reactions of the dispossessed, contextualizing their lived experience as meaningful responses to their powerlessness and defining the outlines of revolutionary solidarity through thinking, feeling, and action. We believe that the situation of Palestine could serve as a protype for such an ongoing struggle viewed in these human terms, extending from the Nakba (Catastrophe) of 1947 until the present day and involving the local population of five million and the global Palestinian diaspora of an additional six million persons.

Both the history of the Zionist enterprise and the history of Palestinian resistance to it are enormous domains; we report here on a much smaller topic, describing developments in Palestine within the field of mental health. We pose the questions, 'What is the contextualized thinking of mental health workers in Palestine? How have Palestinians implemented Fanon's themes in their own practices in the field of mental health? What have Palestinians in mental health been doing to challenge the status quo politically and professionally?' We examine, therefore, some examples from clinical work, research initiatives, solidarity campaigns, and political action that reflect aspects of Fanon's rich legacy.

## Clinical Work

The following vignettes and commentaries describe actual patients or situations familiar to the authors as therapists or consultants; some details have been altered to protect confidentiality.

> *Vignette One:* A woman of 30 was evaluated by a European mental health professional who worked for an international aid organization in Palestine, after the patient had developed dramatic conversion symptoms of weakness and paralysis. This woman lived in a rural village while her husband—who originally had been a farmer on his own land—was currently employed as a laborer in Israel. Because the husband was obliged to travel long distances to find work, he was able to return to his village only one day out of every week. Due to this arrangement, the wife had taken residence in the home of her husband's family. Her husband's brother then found an opportunity to sexually assault her in this residence, precipitating a variety of physical symptoms. A local sheik was called to consult—that is, a man giving the appearance of a religious scholar who in traditional Palestinian culture offers advice and healing. This sheik also abused the woman sexually.

*Commentary:* This case was initially conceptualized by the clinician working for the European non-governmental organization (NGO) in terms of the patient's hysterical response to traumatic assault, a reaction which might be considered quite typical of uneducated persons, with additional note made of the powerlessness of women and the unscientific approach taken by traditional religious healers found in Palestine. The NGO worker's Palestinian supervisor acknowledged aspects of this formulation, but in addition highlighted the role of the colonialist context, in which the absence of the husband was a key feature permitting and setting in motion the patient's victimization. The absence of the husband, in turn, was driven by a cascade of circumstances caused by the occupation: the destruction of local agriculture through land seizure and population resettlement, restrictions on movement, demolition of homes, loss of roadways through which agricultural products are brought to market, and the pervasive disintegration of village economy, community integrity, family cohesion, and way of life.

Against the backdrop of widespread forced cultural and economic impoverishment in Palestine, the *absent husband and father* is commonplace—either intermittently missing as a low-paid laborer in Israel and in its illegal settlements or missing outright as a political detainee. The victimization of the patient and her reactive symptoms, while reflecting an isolated instance of individual trauma, were also part of a larger narrative of a progressively deteriorating familial and social fabric made up of many interlocking threads. Implicit in this vignette is the hidden agent of the occupation in all of its undermining effects.

To underscore the role of the occupation in this genesis of the patient's pathology is neither to absolve the father's brother or the imposter sheik of their respective culpabilities, nor to idealize a mythological Palestinian village of the past as the model of future social reform, nor to deny the persistence of a patriarchal system in Palestinian society (as elsewhere) as a serious problem in itself. To underscore the role of the occupation here is simply to find the occupation present—if not accounted for—as the framework within which psychological experience in Palestine takes place and often the engine driving psychological distress.

> *Vignette Two:* An urban professional woman of 28 presented in psychotherapy for help resolving her ambivalence around relocating to North America—a case of 'brain drain'. She felt guilty about leaving Palestine, especially leaving behind her mother who did not want her to go. On the other hand, the patient had abandoned hope of finding satisfying professional work in Palestine, having been disgusted by the corruption she witnessed in her current employment by a partnership between a Ministry of the Palestinian Authority and an international NGO. In one therapy session, this woman described playing over in her mind a fantasy of apologizing to the native peoples of North America for her own future role, as she saw it, as an occupier of their lands. She perceived the irony of her situation as a member of an occupied population in one country seeking the middle-class privileges enjoyed by the occupier in another country.

*Commentary:* This patient herself had insight into the colonialist dynamics that Fanon illuminated, reflecting an awareness of these pervasive themes in her own psychological life. In the larger perspective, her story reflects a frustration often experienced in the face of existing Palestinian institutions—which typically function under the thumb of Israeli agendas. The resulting cronyism and nepotism within the Palestinian Ministries and elsewhere are psychologically deadening and dismaying for employees; it is often reported that those with the 'right' beliefs and connections are favored as employees because they are more easily controlled than those with innovative ideas, who are less readily manipulated. The woman in Vignette Two is a member of the educated urban elite, in vivid contrast to the woman in Vignette One; from another perspective both patients present differing versions of the same story—they both struggled within a society that has been profoundly damaged through colonialism. The lack of legitimate authority in Palestine, a casualty of the occupation, is a well-spring of psychological insecurity and harm leaving no social group untouched.

*Vignette Three*: A psychologist providing a mental health training program to the staff of a private school close to East Jerusalem was approached by its principal for help with a crisis surrounding the mysterious disappearance of an 8-year-old boy in the community. There had been immediate public speculation that this child had been murdered by the Israelis, with the formation of spontaneous search parties and street demonstrations. The community was filled with conflicting rumors and reports.

These events in real time were dramatically apparent to the public and to school children in an intensely painful and frightening manner.

This crisis vividly brought back memories of the circumstances which had taken place five years before, surrounding the 14-year-old Palestinian teenager Mohammed Abu Khdeir, who had been kidnapped and burned alive by a group of Israeli settlers. The murder of Khdeir and the subsequent events had had an enormous psychological impact on the people Palestine at that time and had been the focus of international news, a television series, and a vast amount of media attention.

The murder of Khdeir in turn was not an isolated instance, but an event that stands out among a backdrop of innumerable assaults on Palestinian children and youth. Khdeir, by providing a specific face and identity as a child victim, represented many. Children in Palestine have been especially targeted by the occupation for generations; night-time home incursions by Israeli forces leading to detention and interrogation under torture of children and adolescents is well-documented as a routine practice. The sequestration of the corpses of Palestinian children and unwillingness to return them to families for burial as another aspect of the behavior of the Israeli forces. These violations of international law and ordinary human decency are familiar to the population of Palestine as ongoing realities (Otman, 2020; Shalhoub-Kevorkian, 2019, 2020).

The psychologist was well aware that the disappearance of the 8-year-old boy had rekindled the collective memory of Mohammed Abu Khdeir and all that he symbolized. In addition, the psychologist was personally involved in the current crisis: the 8-year-old had been at the time of his disappearance a student in a school where the psychologist had provided a similar training program a few years previously. During the period of crisis surrounding this child's disappearance, she was distressed and unable to sleep; she tearfully warned her youngest child to carry her cell phone as she went to school. These personal reactions were fairly normative states of mind in her community.

These were the circumstances surrounding the day in question. In the early morning hours a few days after the disappearance, the body of the missing child was found at the bottom of a canal—the waterway in which the body was recovered was adjacent to the psychologist's home. The child's father maintained in public that a postmortem examination suggested that his son was already dead when his body had been dumped into the water; this emotional but unverified claim reinforced rumors that the child had been murdered.

These events took place just prior to the morning hour when school classes ordinarily began. The principal at the school where the training program was held asked the psychologist whether the school should refrain from mentioning to the students—who were already in a state of uncertainty and agitation—the fact that the body of the child had been recovered. The psychologist felt however that the information should be given to the students and met with a team of school staff to discuss how best to go about it.

The entire school staff and the students were thus informed regarding the recovery of the body. There was an opportunity to share in group discussions in which articulation of feeling by the students was encouraged and contained. These measures settled the school community, provided a structured environment for the expression of strong affects, enhanced constructive resistance to the occupation, and diminished the risk of regressive acting-out by students. The school day then proceeded with reasonable calm and attention to ordinary educational processes.

*Commentary*: Here the psychologist's work reflects efforts to broaden the school's mental health approach from an exclusive focus on individual troubled students to a response to the comprehensive psychological needs of the school as a community. The psychologist had been embedded within the school for over a year as the leader of an in-school training program combining two goals: helping specific children presenting behavioral, learning, or emotional problems and meeting the needs of the school community as a whole. The goal of the training program was to develop skills in communication, emotional awareness, and respectful conflict resolution among all school staff, parents, and the students themselves—to effect a cultural change in the school's entire psychological environment.

Within this program, the clinician/trainer led a small weekly team meeting among the school staff to respond to both individual children and to school-wide mental health issues—issues which often related to the occupation. The school was thus positioned to deal with harsh realities under occupation in ways that are developmentally appropriate to children, constructive for individual and group well-being, and the reinforcing of solidarity. The program had already developed a nuanced crisis-response approach to address periodic surges in violence related to the occupation that had been experienced in previous years through coordinated work with students, school staff, and parents (Abdeen, Jabr, Morse, et al., 2017).

In the current instance, the school staff team meeting provided an opportunity for its members to debrief their emotions with one another and to support one another in their roles within the school. This meeting fortified the school staff as the proper authorities for students and confirmed the staff's commitment to mutual support. It readied the staff to deal with the school as a community in need of facts—to the degree that facts could be known, verified, and acknowledged—as well as a community in need of solace. The feelings of grief, anger, bewilderment, sorrow, fear, and helplessness were acknowledged and named.

The principles of crisis management from a mental health perspective are well recognized. What the legacy of Fanon adds to this body of knowledge are additional elements that identify the parts of the crisis that are generated by oppressive circumstances and strengthen the oppressed to come together in creative solidarity to resist these circumstances. In the case of the death of the 8-year-old boy, the causes and circumstances of the death had not yet been determined. The role of crisis management in such an instance is complex: to identify that the history of the murder of Palestinian children is a legitimate source of powerful community anxieties whenever there is the death of a child, and to identify the current anxieties in relation to that history. In particular, the psychologist helped the school staff and students to recognize how quickly rumors and misinformation can spread within a population that has already been injured by repeated trauma. By naming these anxieties and validating their origins in historical Israeli violence, she was able to help the school community resist becoming further disorganized by unfounded rumors, misinformation, and panic.

The aim of trainer and of the school mental health team was not to draw specific conclusions about the circumstances surrounding the death of this boy, nor to assert whether or not Israelis were responsible for this death. The aim of this mental health work was to support the school community in the shared recognition of their fundamental conditions of life as a backdrop to their current experience. These conditions include damaged community capacities for self-governance, clear communication, flow of responsibility, and human dignity enforced through the rule of law. The mental health trainer assisted the school to reclaim its legitimate authority in these injured domains. In this way, the school was able to acknowledge the ongoing suffering and demoralization engineered by the Israeli government through the downstream effects of its policies, and to mount a resistance to these effects.

## Research

The following discussion of research initiatives in Palestine does not claim to be comprehensive but merely suggestive, painting with a broad brush some of the outlines of this rich history in East Jerusalem, the West Bank, and Gaza. From the beginning, research in Palestine has examined mental health in relation to the context of dispossession, and indeed many thought leaders in mental health have embraced key roles as ambassadors to the world in defining the scope of distress imposed by the political and military occupation.

Notable within this history is the career of the late Eyad El-Sarraj, a psychiatrist who founded the Gaza Community Mental Health Programme (GCMHP) in 1990 and fostered decades of mental health research and training based at that center. Dr. El-Sarraj and his colleagues explored the impact of the occupation on the people of Palestine, especially children, illuminating how reactive symptoms of depression, anxiety, and trauma were pervasive under conditions of periodic war and chronic terror. This research documented the importance of active engagement in political resistance against the occupation as a protective factor for youth mental health, confirming in new and quantitative ways Fanon's emphasis on the redemptive role of group solidarity and personal agency within revolutionary struggles (Punamaki, Quota, and El-Sarraj, 1997, 2001).

Research findings were harnessed by Dr. El-Sarraj in his lifelong efforts to enlighten global opinion regarding Palestine in his capacity as a noted public intellectual. Active research as well as international public advocacy based at the GCMHP continues under its present director, Yassir Abu Jamei (Gaza Community Mental Health Programme, n.d.). Within this broad tradition, until his recent death, the psychiatrist Abdelaziz Thabet and his group in Gaza had published over 100 research articles documenting the scope and nature of symptomatic suffering related to the occupation, exploring how individual mental health intersects the forces of social oppression, in the hope of constructively engaging a global conversation (Thabet, El-Buhaisi, and Vostanis, 2014).

Much of the research in Palestine historically has employed the standard tools and methodologies of Western academic medicine, using internationally-accepted criteria for the diagnosis of specific mental health diagnoses and adopting—at least in part—the framework of the individual case and case prevalence as a platform for bringing the suffering of the people of Palestine to the attention of scholars, policy makers, and communities around the world.

More recently, these tools of Western medicine have themselves been the focus of study and debate in Palestine as elsewhere. Here too the prescience of Fanon is relevant, as Fanon was the first to explore in detail the limitations of the Western clinical approach to the mental health of global populations experiencing colonial oppression. It is important to recognize that Fanon did not succumb to a naïve intellectual model that interpreted all mental disorders as 'nothing but' the consequence of imperialism and colonialism; far from such reductionism, Fanon saw the need to integrate the understanding of individual psychology and pathology with an analysis of the social forces that act upon, with, and through the individual psyche. His meticulous curiosity about and respect for the actual experience of the persons involved in revolutionary struggle demanded new ways of describing and understanding these phenomena. This bottom-up approach required Fanon to reconfigure some of the basic constructs of Western psychiatry.

In this spirit, the Institute of Community and Public Health (ICPH) at Birzeit University in the West Bank, under the leadership of its founder and current director Rita Giacaman, has been a pioneer in both practical and theoretical work to advance such a public health model of well-being (ICPH, n.d.). Dr. Giacaman and her colleagues have studied the impact of the occupation on well-being and sought to develop a conceptual approach that captures the phenomenology of lived experience under chronic violent and war-like conditions, as well as to construct models of healthcare systems appropriate to meet these challenges.

The foundational work of this group has highlighted the imposition of humiliation as a core element of such conditions and the resulting experience of 'feeling broken' as a common and pervasive outcome (Barber, McNeely, El-Sarraj, et al., 2016). The public health framework in Palestine thus connects the dots between the political intentions of Israeli policy and psychological experience on the ground in ways far more pointed and finely-grained than the usual humanitarian protest that war is simply very bad for victimized civilians.

Psychological warfare is acknowledged as a crucial element in the development of political narrative; for example, Rana Nashashibi, the head of the Palestine Counseling Center, has observed in a panel discussion that the 'broken' nature of Palestinians—after being induced by Israeli policy—is then used by Israel as a justification for its oppression (Watch Palestine-Global Panel at Cornell University, 2020). The debt to Fanon is explicitly acknowledged by one of us (SJ), interviewed in the documentary film *Fanon: Yesterday and Today*, suggesting that activism inspired by the theories of Fanon can assist Palestinians in developing new concepts to work through the sense of inferiority inflicted by this oppression (Mazine, 2018).

Inherent in this approach is the conceptualization of active *resistance* to the occupation as a significant social dynamic, a paradigm-shift from the classic focus on personal *resilience*. The Birzeit scholar Lena Meari, for example, has examined the experiences of Palestinians in detention tortured by the Israelis, described by these survivors as a battle of wits and an inevitable hardship to be borne as part of the collective struggle (Meari, 2015). Such researchers are trailblazers concerned with the repair, restitution, and refutation of the colonialist narrative as it plays out in individual humiliation and collective disintegration. By redefining the status of the revolutionary hero-as-actor rather than ill-fated passive victim and by identifying the psychological weapons of the oppressor, the activities of research, training, and clinical work in mental health are reclaiming the narrative and liberating psychological life under oppression.

## International Networks of Mental Healthcare Workers Supporting Palestine

For decades, individual mental health professionals in Palestine have been powerful activists within the Palestinian struggle against the occupation, speaking out both locally and internationally. In 2019, there emerged a single organization, the Palestine-Global Mental Health Network (PGMHN), unifying across disciplines the voice of Palestinian mental health workers within Palestine itself, the state of Israel, and the Palestinian diaspora scattered globally. Its Steering Committee includes a number of individuals who play important leadership roles within governmental and non-governmental agencies concerned with mental health as well as within professional and labor organizations of mental health workers. The Palestine-Global Network's reach among Palestinian mental health workers is augmented by online readers and followers internationally. The mission statement on its website (Who Are We?, 2020) states:

The Network aims to promote the ideals of mental wellbeing, liberation, dignity, and social justice for peoples and societies throughout the planet and for Palestinians in particular. By articulating a professional discourse of personal freedom and respect for human rights, it also aims to increase public awareness of psycho-social issues which affect and hinder colonized people's aspirations for a dignified living. The Network hopes to employ theoretical and pragmatic approaches to promote the understanding of fundamental human needs for liberation, and thus contribute to Palestinian resilience in the face of and resistance to the violence inherent in colonialism.

Here, the founders of PGMHN echo implicitly the contributions of Frantz Fanon in their global reach and their aim to utilize liberation theory and practice to cultivate resistance to colonialism. An endearing and telling detail pays explicit homage to Fanon—the very first book listed in the website's extensive list of print resources, scholarly articles, and documentary films is *Wretched of the Earth* (Books, n.d.).

In solidarity with PGMHN, there have emerged a number of mental health Networks established in other countries aiming to raising awareness and combat misinformation about the Palestinian struggle. The first was the UK-Palestine Mental Health Network (UK-Palestine Mental Health Network, n.d.) followed by the USA-Palestine Mental Health Network (USA-Palestine Mental Health Network, n.d.). Members of both of these English-language Networks are closely allied with Palestinian clinicians living in Palestine/Israel and elsewhere, and all projects launched by these solidarity Networks are jointly undertaken in coordination with colleagues in Palestine. At the time of this writing, a new mental health Network in support of Palestine has arisen in Belgium (Palestine Mental Health Network in Belgium, n.d.) and additional mental health Networks are under discussion and construction in South Africa, France, Ireland, Austria, and Italy.

The origin and group process of each of these international Network is different and dependent upon the varied specifics of the local professional community, but typically each Network has been organized through the efforts of a more-or-less spontaneously-formed central working group of local clinicians who develop a mission statement, establish an internet presence, and embark on a series of projects. Some Networks seek donated funds to support maintaining a website, printing business cards, renting speaking venues, and other modest project-associated costs. Other Networks have opted to avoid fundraising altogether and depend entirely on member volunteerism.

The core concept uniting the various Networks is the belief that our professionalism as mental health workers is intimately related to broad ethical ideals of justice. Concern with racism, colonialism, patriarchy, and economic inequity are therefore inescapably embedded in our daily work as clinicians, as program and policy planners, and as academic theorists—as well as part of our ordinary lives as citizens. All human beings experience moral responsibilities to others, a need to redress wrongs and to protect the innocent. But as mental health workers, we have more specific obligations to understand, to analyze, to speak out, and to agitate on behalf of the dispossessed and the powerless in light of their vastly disproportionate suffering. We possess the professional tools to address these obligations, armed with the interwoven perspectives of psychology, public health, and human rights. Our expertise moreover can be richly fruitful in analyzing propaganda and illuminating the manipulations of psychological warfare which are so central to maintaining systems of injustice. And as mental health workers, we must acknowledge the need for solidarity as a necessary element contributing to our own well-being as psychologically vital creatures; the principles of labor union organizing, based on a shared work ethic and shared needs, is relevant here.

Fanon's contribution to each of these themes has been central and indispensable, insofar as he linked insight into unconscious and symbolic modalities, identifications, and motivations to the devotion to collective revolutionary struggle.

## Network Activism

Specific projects and campaigns undertaken by the various Networks illustrate these themes in action. In carrying out these projects, each individual country has tended to develop its own agenda, although the Palestine-Global Mental Health Network provides guidance through formal and informal ties with the international Networks. The formation of Advisory Councils within some Networks, composed of noteworthy international experts, has added a further dimension of global teamwork and coordinated inter-communication.

Like the PGMHN, several international Networks have devoted web-space to extensive lists of resources such as books, scholarly articles, organizations, and films related to mental health in Palestine; in addition, periodic bulletins sent to the list of Network email subscribers alert them to notable news items, petitions, recent publications, and upcoming events such as film festivals, speakers, and street demonstrations in support of Palestine.

Mental health Networks have in addition organized free-standing public conferences featuring visiting clinicians from Palestine. There have been in addition two separate specialized conferences based on the 'protest teach-in' model—each presenting a panel of speakers on mental health in Palestine—that were held on (or close to) the site of a larger mental health conference being targeted for its collusion with Israeli policy. Finally, there have been screenings throughout the world of the award-winning documentary film *Beyond the Frontlines* directed by Alexandra Dols and featuring one of us (SJ) as its subject (Beyond the Frontlines, n.d.). The screening of the film in many cities internationally has been followed by an audience question-and-answer discussion with both the director and the subject featured in the film present in person.

In an exciting innovation, the Palestine-Global Mental Health Network has partnered with the organization Students for Justice in Palestine at Cornell University in Ithaca, New York to present a video-stream online panel composed of talks by three senior clinicians in Palestine; the panel was moderated by a member of the Palestine-Global Network based in New York. The presentation was viewed online in real time by a live group assembled at Cornell University, as well as a real-time virtual audience linked online. Audience question-and-answer discussion from the floor at Cornell followed the panel presentations. The taped event may be viewed online (*Watch Palestine-Global Panel at Cornell University*, 2020).

Recently, the UK-Palestine Mental Health Network has initiated Café Palestine, an ongoing video-stream series of live online presentations and panels featuring Palestinian mental health experts and organizations. Over a dozen notable presentations have taken place, widely advertised by several Networks, and recorded for later online viewing (Café Palestine Index, n.d.).

In addition to developing a website presence and live in-person and virtual presentations, members of several Networks have published extensively on the subject of mental health in Palestine in both the popular press and in scholarly domains. The authors of this chapter, for example, have co-written a number of papers in academic psychoanalytic/psychiatric journals and book chapters in the field of sociology; often referencing Fanon, we have explored how the Israeli narrative infiltrates the domain of mental health organizational politics, conferences, supervision, and clinical work across the Israeli/Palestinian divide and have advocated clinical and political techniques to combat it (Berger & Jabr, 2020; Jabr & Berger, 2016a, 2016b, 2017, 2021, forthcoming). In addition to these academic works, one of us (SJ) has written hundreds of articles on the well-being of the people of Palestine published in news venues such as the *Middle East Eye*, the *Middle East Monitor*, and the *Washington Report on Middle East Affairs*; a group of these articles have been collected in book form under the title *Derriere les Fronts*, which has appeared in French and also Italian translation (Jabr, 2018).

In a recent journal article, 'The settler's town is a strongly built town: Fanon in Palestine', members of the USA Network's Advisory Council Stephen and Lara Sheehi reported on their experience presenting the work of Fanon to a group of Palestinian clinicians within the state of Israel (2020). The authors describe the stunned silence that arose when a passage from *Wretched of the Earth* was read aloud to this group, and the deep resonance that Fanon's words clearly evoked among them. Their paper explores, through the idiom of Fanon's perspective, the interplay between colonialism and the experiences of mental health practitioners in Palestine.

A number of professionals and clinicians in leadership and advisory roles within the PGMHN and international Networks have published on issues in mental health among Palestinians—the late Abdelaziz Thabet, Rita Giacaman, Yassir Abu Jamai, Alice Rothchild, Hammam Farah, Mustafa Qassoqsi (2010), Martin Kemp, Lama Khouri, Rana Nashashibi, Manal Abu Haq, Yoad Ghanadry-Hakim, Fathi Flefel, Ferdoos Al-Issa, Nadera Shalhoub-Kevorkian, Said Shehadeh, and Maria Helbich are among these Network-affiliated scholars and activists. Several of these writers cite the works of Frantz Fanon as foundational to the analysis of the Palestinian context (e.g. Kemp, 2020; Khouri, 2018, 2019; Sheehi, 2018) and many of their publications engage with principles of liberation psychology that ultimately derive from Fanon.

Other Network programs bring mental health workers to Palestine for direct interaction with colleagues there, guided 'Study Delegations' sponsored by the UK and USA Networks which have taken place over the past several years. Typically, the participants chosen for these delegations are seasoned activists well-familiar with liberation psychology through their own previous participation in anti-colonial and anti-racism movements. The delegation participants travel from their home countries to visit in small groups with noted mental health experts, human rights spokespersons, and heads of organizations—and to experience first-hand the conditions in beleaguered refugee camps, at checkpoints, and in people's homes. The participants also visit activists supporting Palestine who live within Israel. Reading lists including the work of Fanon, discussions following each day's activities, and intensive communications among the group both before and after the Study Delegation help structure the meaning of the experience. The goal of these Study Delegations is to immerse each participant in the realities of life in Palestine and to acquaint them with the extensive factual resources available to them. Once the participants return from the Study Delegation, they are well-prepared to act as community leaders speaking to groups, giving talks and presentations, and writing about these experiences.

Some of the alumni of the Study Delegations go on to join a cohort of mental health workers distributed internationally as Outreach Representatives who are able to connect with their local communities for sharing information, event participation, and event planning. The Networks provide centralized suggestions, support, and encouragement to these community organizers; prototypes of slide-talks about mental health and well-being in Palestine are made available to these volunteers to form a platform for public or professional presentations. Outreach Representatives help connect local communities to national organizations that are, in turn, in touch with Palestinian colleagues. In this way, mental health workers in support of Palestine are able to support one another with a solid grounding in news, information, priorities, and the important intangible of solidarity.

Through other initiatives, several Networks have engaged in extensive 'Don't Go' campaigns related to international mental health meetings and conferences planned to be located in Israel. These campaigns are based in the ethics and philosophy of the Boycott, Divestment, Sanctions (BDS) movement which was launched in 2005 within civil society in Palestine, seeking to raise global awareness of Israeli human rights violations by drawing attention to international corporations, business ventures, academic/professional meetings, and cultural productions that implicitly support the state of Israel through their investment in and participation with Israeli institutions (BDS Movement, n.d.). The Networks' 'Don't Go' campaigns are not formally affiliated with the BDS movement, although these campaigns act in parallel to BDS activities and aim to achieve the same goals through non-violent protest.

Networks have typically begun a 'Don't Go' campaign by noting the general announcement that an international mental health organization intends to hold a meeting in Israel at some future date. The Network then sends a formal emailed letter to the organization's Board of Directors, stating the argument for re-locating this meeting and requesting that the organization reconsider this decision.

The first such 'Don't Go' campaign was initiated by the UK-Palestine Mental Health Network in 2014, requesting that a mental health organization, the European Association of Behavioural and Cognitive Therapists (EABCT), reconsider holding its planned 2015 conference in Israel. The campaign then published a letter of protest that was signed by a number of senior psychologists; the UK chapter of the EABCT passed a resolution condemning the decision (UK Clinical Psychologists Urge Boycott of Jerusalem Conference, 2014). A petition protesting the location was signed by hundreds of clinicians worldwide, with the additional support of the Palestinian Union of Social Workers and Psychologists (Open letter about EABCT conference in Jerusalem, 2015). Ultimately, however, the meeting was held in Israel despite these many coordinated international protest efforts.

The next 'Don't Go' campaign involved members of the UK-Palestine Mental Health Network and the USA-Palestine Mental Health Network, protesting a conference planned in Israel by the Society for Psychotherapy Research (SPR). The authors exchanged letters with the officers of the SPR—at which point the SPR declined to reconsider its choice of location (Jabr and Berger correspondence with SPR, 2016). Following this exchange, there was a published petition signed by 300 mental health professionals protesting the conference in Israel—another example of the principle that even refusals to reconsider can be utilized as opportunities, since these set-backs can be fashioned into newsworthy events to gather support and increase public awareness (Samuels et alia, 2016).

There followed a number of 'Don't Go' efforts. Some of these initiatives were modest in scope, consisting of a single emailed letter asking for reconsideration of location for a planned conference. One such attempt was a letter sent by a member of the Steering Committee of the USA Network to the Innovations in Conflict Resolution and Mediation conference planned for November 2018 in Israel. There was no response to the Network's letter itself, although the invitation to the conference was reportedly the focus of energetic online debate among the hosting organization's website (Synopsis of WMS campaign, n.d.). Similar to this effort was a USA Network letter sent to the International Society for Psychological and Social Approaches to Psychosis, which had planned to meet in Israel in December 2018. There was no response to this letter either (International Society for Psychological and Social Approaches to Psychosis, 2018). A third example was a letter sent to the New Lacanian School of Psychoanalysis, which planned to meet in Israel in June 2019. This letter too received no response (NLS, n.d.).

A somewhat different 'Don't Go' protest model was applied at the University of Rennes in France in December 2018 on the occasion of a conference at the university organized by COPELFI, the Association pour les Conferences de Psychiatrie de l'Enfant et de l'Adolescent en Langue Francaise en Israel—a conference held by a joint association of French and Israeli Child and Adolescent psychiatrists. Objections to this conference were raised by an organization in France, the Groupe de Prefiguration de 2018/Un temps de la Palestine a Rennes, which had been specifically formed for that purpose. The protesters wrote a letter which was then signed by several French political organizations as well as one mental health organization, the USA Network. One of the explicit demands of the protesters' petition was the call for support of another 'Don't Go' campaign currently underway, reflecting international solidarity within 'Don't Go' initiatives (Synopsis of COPELFI campaign, n.d.). As the conference took place at Rennes, members of the Groupe de Prefiguration de 2018 peacefully demonstrated in person among the members of the audience.

In December 2017, the USA Network sent an email to the Members of the Board of a large mental health organization, the International Association for Relational Psychoanalysis and Psychotherapy (IARPP), requesting that the Board reconsider their plan to hold its June 2019 meeting in Israel. The Board responded with an emailed refusal (A reply to IARPP, 2018). The USA Network then engaged the UK-Palestine Mental Health Network and the organization Jewish Voice for Peace to re-issue the original letter calling for reconsideration in the form of an online petition, which eventually was signed by over 1400 mental health workers and professionals globally (Jabr, Berger, Fadil, & Schmidt, 2017). The campaign protesting the IARPP decision accrued additional supportive petitions, including one from the Palestinian Union of Psychologists and Social Workers (PUSWP) representing over 20,000 clinicians in Palestine (Statement from the PUSWP, 2017) , one from a group of clinicians within Israel (Israeli professionals oppose IARPP meeting, 2018), and one from a group of Palestinian clinicians who are citizens of Israel (Palestinian clinicians, citizens of Israel, opposed IARPP meeting, 2018), as well as numerous media reports and articles and letters of support from other mental health professionals and organizations internationally (About don't go, n.d.).

It happened that the IARPP organization had announced plans for its June 2019 international meeting in Israel six months prior to holding its June 2018 international meeting in New York City. The IARPP meeting in New York City provided the USA Network with an opportunity to hold a counter-conference, 'Voices on Palestine', by renting a conference space in the same hotel during a time slot that interfered with no scheduled IARPP speaker. The panel of professionals addressing mental health in Palestine was attended by over 150 mental health clinicians, including members of the IARPP organization—all of whom had been invited to attend ('Voices on Palestine' forum, 2018).

Another protest counter-event was held in Israel by Israeli activists during the IARPP 2019 conference, a meeting focused on the theme of 'why we are not going to the IARPP conference' and exploring the ethical underpinnings of the activists' position. Once again, participants in the IARPP conference were invited to attend.

The authors have reported in a psychoanalytic journal the history of the IARPP protest and the various objections, obfuscations, manipulations, and distortions launched by the IARPP leadership in reaction to this protest; in addition to the IARPP history, this paper discussed a number of attempts to silence the activism of their own members launched by various other mental health organizations when the issue concerns Palestine (Berger & Jabr, 2020).

The various official responses made by organizations to the Network's 'Don't Go' campaigns are themselves of interest to us as mental health professionals and can form the basis of an analysis of settler-colonialist propaganda. In this way, we are able to use our clinical skills to turn the tables by taking Zionism itself as the object of psychological study and exposing the various arguments put forward by mental health organizations supporting the state of Israel. The arguments put forward by organizations that refused to reconsider the relocation of their conferences cluster around various common themes: that Israel is a vibrant democracy and should be vigorously supported; alternatively, that Israel is perhaps indeed morally blameworthy but that mental health professionals should remain 'neutral;' that the mental health organization planning to meet in Israel itself welcomes genuine debate and offers a forum for fair-minded and 'expert' exploration of issues related to political violence or trauma; that the 'Don't Go' movement stifles conversation and individual freedom; that the 'Don't Go' protests are the handiwork of a single individual; alternatively, that the 'Don't Go' protests are the handiwork of a huge, well-funded political organization; that the 'Don't Go' protests are guilty of intimidating mental health workers into giving lip-service to a 'Don't Go' initiative which they do not sincerely support—i.e. that the enormous outpouring of international support for the 'Don't Go' initiatives among mental health workers is thus somehow invalidated.

Most of these arguments in support of mental health organizations meeting in Israel are familiar as variations on stock objections to the BDS movement and objections to anti-colonialist practices generally. These stock arguments support the status quo by denying the reality of the oppression or by admitting the reality while undermining efforts to discuss it. They support the status quo by claiming to represent the voice of Palestinians and by appropriating the Palestinian narrative. They support the status quo by denigrating the authenticity and integrity of the various Networks and the thousands of 'Don't Go' supporters as the conspiratorial handiwork of sinister outsiders or a small unrepresentative coterie of political operatives who magically hold captive the thousands of professional colleagues who have added their signatures to protest petitions. These elements of psychological warfare can be identified and refuted, so that their capacity to deflate and marginalize activism is neutralized and their goal of sapping activist agency and energy is foiled.

Additional 'Don't Go' campaigns offered variations on these themes. In the summer of 2019, the Palestine-Global Mental Health Network initiated a campaign related to a small organization, the European Network for Mental Health Service Evaluation (ENMESH). ENMESH had originally planned to hold a conference for 2021 in Israel, but according to news reports, the chair of its Executive Committee decided to withdraw that plan two weeks after it had been announced (Times of Israel staff, 2019).

The reasons for canceling this conference in Israel were posted on the ENMESH website (ENMESH, 2019). Although this material is no longer found online anywhere, it was briefly visible in very small type on that site during the summer of 2019. The now-inaccessible ENMESH statement read at that time:

At the Board meeting in June 2019 in Lisbon, the Board decided to hold the ENMESH 2021 conference in Israel. After further consultation, and in view of the inadequate resources to handle the type of campaign to which some conferences held in Israel are subject, it was reluctantly concluded that it was not at present possible to host the ENMESH conference in Israel. The decision was a practical decision, not a political or permanent decision, and it is hoped that it will be possible to hold a future ENMESH conference in Israel.

At that point, the Palestine-Global Mental Health Network sent a letter to the Board of ENMESH supporting its decision not to hold its conference in Israel; the letter was also signed by the UK-Palestine Mental Health Network and the USA-Palestine Mental Health Network (Letter to the ENMESH, 2019). The letter to ENMESH stated:

> ...we would argue that your decision is wise not only on practical grounds but more importantly on ethical ones. Your decision underscores the significance of the mental health professions ethic of 'do no harm'. Holding a conference in Israel indirectly supports a government whose abuse and oppression of the Palestinian people has been going on for over 70 years.

The ENMESH Board did not respond to this letter. And unfortunately, shortly after the Networks' letter, there were news reports that ENMESH was considering reversing its position yet once more, in response to a 'huge effort' and 'organized campaign' by pro-Zionist supporters (following pressure, mental health academics may reverse decision to cancel conference in Israel, 2019). By August, 2019, news media indicated that the chair of the Executive Committee had stepped down; the new chair of the Executive Committee had been one of the leaders of the pro-Zionist reaction to the initial cancellation of the Israel conference and indeed had briefly 'resigned in fury'—both of these individuals posted online a joint statement regretting the 'hurt' that may have been experienced as a result of the Board's processes of decision making (Jewish News reporter, 2019).

In the Spring of 2020, a new announcement appeared on the ENMESH website indicating that the 2021 conference would be held in Israel, while avoiding any material that would reveal the history of controversy regarding this plan (ENMESH, 2020).

The ENMESH drama highlights certain phenomena observed in previous 'Don't Go' interactions between Networks and mental health organizations. Most overtly evident, perhaps, are the secrecy with which organizational decisions are made and the erasure of the evidence of internal discussion about these decisions when the topic relates to Palestine/Israel—despite the fact that the media reported that great outrage had been mobilized in defense of reinstating Israel as the site of the cancelled conference. The fiction of organization harmony is preserved although evidence indicates that the facts demonstrate quite the opposite situation.

On an optimistic note, it is reasonable to infer that those within ENMESH who made the initial 'practical' decision to cancel the conference in Israel were mindful not only of the possibility of BDS activism generally but alert to the recent 'Don't Go' campaigns targeting mental health organizations specifically. The ENMESH episode provides evidence that the growing visibility of the 'Don't Go' movement in mental health presents a stimulus for debate that is increasingly difficult to silence.

Beyond the 'Don't Go' initiatives, the Palestine-Global Mental Health Network has recently spearheaded other campaigns that impact Palestinian well-being. One such campaign involves protesting the initiation of a course in 'Cultural Sensitivity' offered by Ariel University, as the Network website describes (Mental health training in the service of Israeli violence towards Palestinians, 2020):

> The Palestine-Global Mental Health Network (PGMHN) strongly condemns the recent decision of the Israeli Ministry of Health to award to 'Ariel University' the bid for organizing and implementing a Continuing Professional Development program in mental health—a program which will be required for Palestinian psychologists who live in Israel, among others. 'Ariel University' is located within the Israeli settlement of Ariel, a settlement built on Palestinian land within the town of Salfit in the West Bank that has been occupied since 1967. PGMHN finds it particularly egregious and cynical that one of the courses claims to address the issue of 'cultural sensitivity' in the context of psychotherapy and mental health services. We view this as yet another attempt to entrench the racist and dehumanizing settler-colonial discourse.

The USA-Palestine Mental Health Network published online a letter in support of this campaign (USA-Palestine Mental Health Network supports Palestine-Global Mental Health Network on Ariel University, 2020). Another supportive letter was signed by over one hundred Israeli mental health professionals as well as three activist organizations—Joining Resistance, Psychoactive, and Academia for Equality—representing many hundreds of additional Israeli professionals and academics (Letter to the Ministry of Health regarding training in culture-sensitive psychology, 2020). This letter was sent to the Israeli Ministry of Health. Several days later, a notice appeared on the website of Ariel University indicating that its training program in 'cultural sensitivity' had been cancelled (E. Rapoport, personal communication, May 19, 2020).

## Challenges Ahead

There would seem to be no end to the challenges to justice and well-being posed by exploitation and oppression worldwide, and specifically the challenges posed by the occupation to the people of Palestine. Indeed, at this time worsening conditions for humankind such as global warming, pandemic illnesses, and the economic consequences of these conditions bode well for the rise of despotic leaders and paranoid public reactions driven by fear. So far, it seems that these conditions bode poorly for the development of thoughtful international coordination to support human rights and human welfare. These broad global issues can afflict the most stalwart of activists everywhere with dismay.

These challenges may be especially pointed with regard to Palestine. Here, challenges may rise up under the very disguise of humanitarianism, such as the field hospital under construction in Gaza sponsored jointly by the Israeli government and an American evangelical Christian organization. In this instance, what would appear to be a generous action to promote health among the people of Gaza is actually an Israeli 'security' measure under the leadership of an Israeli army official who has been charged with crimes against humanity (Jabr, 2020).

Surely the difficulty discerning friend from foe and identifying the motivations behind the welter of everyday developments in Palestine can induce fatigue and discouragement.

To counter hopelessness and exhaustion, we believe that activists must be especially mindful of the strain and trauma that accompany our work. The psychological burn-out of mental health workers is a well-recognized entity related to many factors: over-work, the obligation to contain painful affects, and vicarious as well as direct PTSD. We note as well the feelings of frustration and pain often experienced by activist mental health workers who are barraged by retaliatory hate-speech, intimidation, and personal attacks by the oppressor and the oppressor's sympathizers; Network activists have received anonymous death threats and suffered relentless blacklisting by pro-Israeli entities such as Canary Mission (Berger, 2021).

Less well-known perhaps is a particular suffering that takes place when personal attacks are experienced within the solidarity group—when activists turn their condemnation against one another. With some notable exceptions (Atshan, 2020), analyses of political activism rarely describe or document the phenomenon of discord and ill-will among activists. Historically, of course, there has often been great pressure on liberation movements to present the outward appearance of harmony and unity to the outside world. The incentive to avoid revealing evidence of cracks and strains within solidarity movements is therefore understandable but denying the reality of conflict among activists carries its own risks.

A recent informal poll of Network mental health activists revealed that a significant number of these volunteers spontaneously reported that in-fighting with other activists was the most painful aspect of their political work and the most lingering source of personal burn-out. We believe that attention to the phenomenon of in-fighting falls under our professional role as clinicians to deal honestly with our own counter-transference; giving heed to our in-fighting and dealing with it wisely is also imperative for us as participants in a process of group renewal.

We must not forget that solidarity activists for Palestine are not immune to the foibles of human nature. We all fall prey at times to folly, error, self-importance, envy, impatience, the lure of group-think, and similar states of psychological regression. In addition, it is likely that the Left, as opposed to the Right, is especially vulnerable to in-fighting—which reflects no doubt the fundamental socio-political insecurity of marginalized groups and the consequent tendency towards mutual accusation and mistrust within such groups. There are many dynamics at play within this phenomenon, within which 'identification with the aggressor' is certainly prominent. The Right everywhere is smaller but more powerful, united by shared class-interest and mutually-reinforcing goals; the Left depends upon a coalition of a large number of splintered sub-groups who are often inevitably in a position of jealous jockeying for prestige and leadership voice, often without a strong basis for mutual empathy. Leaders especially can be targeted for attacks within the Left, not only for delivering the wrong message but for delivering the right message with eloquence and talent. Envy of the charismatic leader arises from both conscious and unconscious rivalry, and can be a powerful dynamic in group psychology—especially when the group itself is under perpetual threat. One must remember that whenever power is achieved, someone will try to take it by force.

As activists we believe it is important to acknowledge that we are supremely dependent upon other activists for encouragement and support, insofar as we are already isolated from the mainstream by the marginalized goals of our activism itself. Our alienation from the dominant social context renders us especially vulnerable to the penetrating ostracism and fiery denunciations of our friends. Moreover, as activists, we are especially vulnerable to these dynamics because of our very idealism. We are often unaware of our deep need for heroes and for ideological purity. These drives may lead us to unrealistic thinking and condemnatory attitudes which are profoundly unconstructive.

We suggest that mental health activists take pains to be especially alert to the psychological milieu in which their activism takes place, particularly in its unconscious aspects. The exaggerated and perhaps necessary dependence that the activist experiences in relation to an inner circle of comrades, a core of solidarity, can readily become a tool for power-hungry rivals. And too, the vulnerability to peer encouragement and affection can become a destabilizing factor among group members, with the emergence of a primitive 'bad object' who was only recently a valued colleague. Internal conflicts within an individual or within the group can involve projection of a guilty conscience or an overly-fastidious demand for consistency—leading to outright character assassination. The need for everyone to be equally saintly and self-sacrificing (or self-sacrificing on the same fronts at the same time) may lead to disappointment among comrades, denunciations of a 'super-star', a critic, or an outlier.

Fanon tells us that we are fortified if we bring psychological understanding to our assessment of the players in revolutionary activity, including ourselves. We need to strive for patience and maturity in our dealings with one another and to maintain generosity, empathy, and dignity in our work together. We believe that self-awareness by activists, including awareness of our own potential for injustice, can go far to prevent the inevitable conflicts and cross-purposes that arise within all human groups from devolving into unproductive *ad hominem* attacks, regressive group dynamics, and the search for a scapegoat. But to do this, we must commit ourselves to the development a transparent group culture that acknowledges diversity within solidarity and admits the validity of differing points of view within an overarching commitment. Only through working constructively together can we gain a sense of organic rootedness and ownership over the historical past—however scattered that history may be—as well as the courage to create a new human future.

Fanon's exquisite alertness to the role of *aggression* within the pre-revolutionary and revolutionary context is thus, to our minds, one of his most valuable contributions to this ongoing work. His analysis of the envious spell cast by the narrative of the colonizer and its enforcement through the dynamics of power reveal the many ways that the colonized subject unwittingly participates in his own victimization—manifest, in Fanon's terminology, through the subject's characteristic bodily agitation and emotional alienation. A key role of liberation psychology is to make conscious the many manifestations of this spell, so that self-subjugation can be transformed into an engine of action, rather than unconscious acting-out.

It is here that Fanon is often misread as glorifying violence as the portal to social renewal. We assess this reading of Fanon as a distortion intended to discredit him. Certainly, Fanon supported the right of the oppressed to defend themselves from the violence of their oppression, just as international law supports the right of occupied people to defend themselves from the violence of military occupation.

But in our view, Fanon did not call for violence as a simplistic remedy; rather, he called for clarity in understanding and naming the immense overt and the covert violence embedded in the colonialist situation and in the human reaction to it. Fanon warned us against fratricidal infighting and wild acts of impulsive destruction; he was prescient in his alertness to the dangers of reductive nationalisms and post-revolutionary dynamics that only mirror the recently-dethroned power-elite. He was wary of all psychological defenses that tended to displace the violence of colonialism onto the wrong targets, thereby tragically continuing its damage.

Fanon did not proscribe a rigidly specific model of revolutionary change, but identified the core feature that genuine liberation must involve: the need to acknowledge, to value, and to engage the energetic, open-ended agency within each individual, extended over the fabric of meaningful human connections. We see this agency as the core of psychological life, embedded in each person and in the human collective.

We believe that the spirit of Fanon resides as a guiding illumination for the mental health workers of Palestine and their international supporters—both as a specific struggle and as a prototype for similar anti-colonial and anti-racism movements everywhere. The debt owed to Fanon is direct and acknowledged by many of the leading mental health scholar/activists within Palestine and international colleagues working with them. But beyond this direct line of descent—so to speak—it is possible to see the spirit of Fanon emerging in the everyday practice of mental health work in Palestine. This phenomenon is a testimony to the fact that Fanon articulated universal principles of justice and human dignity which are being defended in Palestine at the level of popular resistance, while aligned with similar struggles the world over. Fanon may have said nothing explicit about Palestine but we are free to imagine what words he might have said, and to draw strength from them.

## Bibliography

A Reply to IARPP. 2018. January 14. Accessed January 28, 2021. https://ukpalmhn.com/2018/01/14/a-reply-to-iarpp/.

Abdeen, S., Jabr, S., Morse, M., Lyman, K., and Berger, E. 2017. 'A Comprehensive Student Support Program in Mental Health.' *Bethlehem University Journal* 34: 43–155. Accessed January 21, 2021, https://www.jstor.org/stable/10.13169/bethunivj.34.2017.0143?seq=1#metadata_info_tab_contents.

About Don't Go. n.d. Accessed January 28, 2021, https://usapalmhn.org/about-dont-go/.

Atshan, S. 2020. *Queer Palestine and the Empire of Critique*. Redwood City: Stanford University Press.

Barber, B., McNeely, C., El-Sarraj, E., Daher, M., Giacaman, R., Arafat, C., et al. 2016. 'Mental Suffering in Protracted Political Conflict: Feeling Broken or Destroyed.' *PLoS One* 11 (5). Accessed May 14, 2020, https://www.ncbi.nlm.nih.gov/pmc/articles/PMC4883798/.

Berger, E. 2021. 'Canary Mission Is Dangerous to Your Professional Health.' *Mondoweiss*. Accessed January 28, 2021, https://mondoweiss.net/2021/01/canary-mission-is-dangerous-to-your-professional-health/.

BDS Movement. n.d. Accessed January 28, 2021, https://bdsmovement.net/.

Beyond the Frontlines. n.d. *Home Page*. Accessed January 28, 2021, https://beyondthefrontlines.com/.

Books. n.d. Accessed January 28, 2021, https://www.pgmhn.org/books.

Cafe Palestine Index. n.d. Accessed January 28, 2021, https://ukpalmhn.com/cafe-palestine/cafe-palestine-index/.

ENMESH. n.d. *Home Page*. Accessed July 11, 2019, http://enmesh.eu/index.html.

———. n.d. *Home Page*. Accessed January 28, 2021, http://www.enmesh.eu/.

Fanon, F. 1965 [1959]. *A Dying Colonialism*. Translated by H. Chevalier. New York: Grove.

———. 2004 [1961]. *The Wretched of the Earth*. Translated by R. Philcox. New York: Grove.

———. 2008 [1952]. *Black Skin, White Masks*. Translated by R. Philcox. New York: Grove.

———. 2018. *Alienation and Freedom*, edited by Khalfa, J., and Young, R. Translated by S. Corcoran. London: Bloomsbury Academic.

Following Pressure, Mental Health Academics May Reverse Decision to Cancel Conference in Israel. 2019. *The Middle East Monitor*. Accessed January 28, 2021, https://www.middleeastmonitor.com/20190809-following-pressure-mental-health-academics-may-reverse-decision-to-cancel-conference-in-israel/.

Gaza Community Mental Health Programme. n.d. *Home Page*. Accessed January 28, 2021, https://gcmhp.ps/.

International Society for Psychological and Social Approaches to Psychosis. 2018. Accessed January 28, 2021, https://usapalmhn.org/intl-society-for-psychological-and-social-approaches-to-psychosis/.

Institute of Community and Public Health. n.d. *Home page.* Accessed January 28, 2021, http://icph.birzeit.edu/.

Israeli Professionals Oppose IARPP Meeting. 2018. Accessed January 28, 2021, https://usapalmhn.org/israeli-professionals-oppose-iarpp-meeting/.

Jabr and Berger Correspondence with SPR. 2016. Accessed January 28, 2021, https://ukpalmhn.com/2016/03/03/jabr-and-berger-correspondence-with-spr/.

Jabr, S. 2018. *Derriere Les Fronts: Chroniques d'une psychiatre psychotherapeute palestinienne sous occupation.* Paris: Premiers Matins de Novembre.

_____. 2020. 'Gaza's New Mental Health Unit: A Project of Psychological Control.' *Middle East Monitor.* Accessed January 28, 2021, https://www.middleeastmonitor.com/20200214-gazas-new-mental-health-unit-a-project-of-psychological-control/.

Jabr, S., and Berger, E. 2016a. 'An Occupied State of Mind: Clinical Transference and Countertransference Across the Israeli/Palestinian Divide.' *Psychoanalysis, Culture, and Society* 21 (1): 21–40. doi:10.11057/pcs.2015-46. Accessed January 28, 2021, https://link.springer.com/article/10.1057%2Fpcs.2015.46.

_____. 2016b. 'The Survival and Well-Being of the Palestinian People Under Occupation.' In *The State of Social Progress in Islamic Societies: Social, Political, and Ideological Challenge.* Book Series in Quality of Life Research, edited by Tiliouine, H., and Estes, R., 529–543. Cham: Springer. Accessed January 28, 2021, https://www.springer.com/us/book/9783319247724.

_____. 2017. 'The Trauma of Humiliation in the Occupied Palestinian Territory.' *Arab Journal of Psychiatry* 28 (2): 154–159. Accessed January 28, 2021, http://arabjournalpsychiatry.com/wp-content/uploads/2017/11/The-Arab-Journal-of-Psychiatry-2017-Vol.-28.pdf.

_____. 2020. 'Silencing Palestine: Limitations on Free Speech in Mental Health Organizations.' *International Journal of Applied Psychoanalytic Studies* 17: 193–207. Accessed January 28, 2021, https://onlinelibrary.wiley.com/doi/abs/10.1002/aps.1630?af=R.

_____. 2021. 'Mental Health Under Occupation: The Dilemmas of "Normalcy" in Palestine.' In *Global Mental Health Ethics*, edited by Dyer, A., Kohrt, B., and Candilis, P., 289–303. Cham: Springer.

_____. Forthcoming. 'The Children of Palestine: Struggle and Survival Under Occupation.' *Handbook of Children's Security, Vulnerability, and Quality of Life: Global Perspectives.* Book Series in Quality of Life Research, edited by Rees, G., Benatuil, D., Lau, M., and Tiliouine, H., Dordrecht: Springer.

Jabr, S., Berger, E., Fadil, R., and Schmidt, C. 2017. 'To the Board of the International Association of Relational Psychoanalysis and Psychotherapy.' Accessed January 28, 2021, https://secure.everyaction.com/hIIcCM7s106Wu9RFASoD_A2.

Jewish News Reporter. 2019. 'Mental Health Experts Sorry for "Hurt" Over Claims of Israel Boycott. *Jewish News.* Accessed January 28, 2021, https://jewishnews.timesofisrael.com/mental-health-experts-sorry-for-hurt-over-claims-of-israel-boycott/.

Kemp, M. 2020. 'The Psychoanalytic Encounter with Settler Colonialism in Palestine/Israel.' *International Journal of Applied Psychoanalytic Studies* 17: 93–125. Accessed January 28, 2021, https://onlinelibrary.wiley.com/doi/10.1002/aps.1651.

Khouri, L. 2018. 'Through Trump's Looking Glass into Alice's Wonderland: On Meeting the House Palestinian.' *Psychoanalytic Perspectives,* 15 (3): 275–299. Accessed January 28, 2021, https://www.tandfonline.com/doi/full/10.1080/1551806X.2018.1491725.

_____. 2019. 'The Normative Unconscious of Nations: A Critical Geopolitical and Psychoanalytic Perspectives on the United Nations Security Council's Counterterrorism Strategy.' *International Journal of Applied Psychoanalytic Studies* 16: 244–257. Accessed January 28, 2021, https://onlinelibrary.wiley.com/doi/abs/10.1002/aps.1635.

Letter to the ENMESH. 2019. Accessed January 28, 2021, https://www.pgmhn.org/news/letter-to-the-european-network-for-mental-health-service-evaluation-enmesh.

Letter to the Ministry of Health Regarding Training in Culture-sensitive Psychology. 2020. English translation by Google. Accessed January 28, 2021, https://www.hebpsy.net/blog_Post.asp?id=4501.

Mazine, H. 2018. *Fanon: Hier, Aujourdi'hui* (Fanon: Yesterday, Today). Accessed February 9, 2021, https://vimeo.com/ondemand/fanonhieraujourdhui.

Meari, L. 2015. 'Reconsidering Trauma: Towards a Palestinian Community Psychology.' *Journal of Community Psychology* 43 (1): 76–86. Accessed January 28, 2021, https://onlinelibrary.wiley.com/doi/10.1002/jcop.21712.

Mental Health Training in the Service of Israeli Violence Towards Palestinians. 2020. Accessed January 28, 2021, https://www.pgmhn.org/news/mental-health-training-in-the-service-of-israeli-violence-towards-palestinians.

NLS. n.d. Accessed January 28, 2021, https://usapalmhn.org/nls/.

Open Letter About EABCT Conference in Jerusalem. 2015. Accessed January 28, 2021, https://ukpalmhn.com/2015/06/13/open-letter-about-eabct-conference-in-jerusalem/.

Otman, A. 2020. 'Handcuffed Protectors? Palestinian Fatherhood-Protection Unlocking Its Chains.' *International Journal of Applied Psychoanalytic Studies* 17: 146–164. Accessed January 28, 2021, https://onlinelibrary.wiley.com/doi/10.1002/aps.1643.

Palestine Mental Health Network in Belgium. n.d. *Facebook Home Page.* Accessed January 28, 2021, https://www.facebook.com/Palestine-Mental-Health-Network-in-Belgium-2281898002075218/.

Palestine-Global Mental Health Network. n.d. *Home Page.* Accessed January 28, 2021, https://www.pgmhn.org/.

Palestinian Clinicians, Citizens of Israel, Oppose IARPP Meeting. 2018. Accessed January 28, 2021, https://usapalmhn.org/assoc-of-arab-clinicians-in-israel/.

Punamaki, R., Quota, S., and El-Sarraj, E. 1997. 'Models of Traumatic Experiences and Children's Psychological Adjustment: The Roles of Perceived Parenting and Children's Own Resources and Activity.' *Child Development* 64 (4): 718–728.

_____. 2001. 'Resiliency Factors Predicting Psychological Adjustment After Political Violence Among Palestinian Children.' *International Journal of Behavioral Development* 25 (3): 256–267.

Qassoqsi, M. 2010. 'The Narrative of the Nakba and the Politics of Trauma.' *Jadal*, 1–4.

Samuels, A., Giacaman, R., Jabr, S., Abu Jamei, Y., Kemp, M., Marton, R., et al. 2016. 'Move This Conference Away from Jerusalem.' *The Independent*. Accessed January 28, 2021, https://www.independent.co.uk/voices/letters/letters-it-s-not-friends-eu-who-peddle-fear-a6905821.html.

Shalhoub-Kevorkian, N. 2019. *Incarcerated Childhood and the Politics of Unchilding*. Cambridge University Press.

_____. 2020. 'Gun to Body: Mental Health Against Unchilding.' *International Journal of Applied Psychoanalytic Studies* 17: 126–145. Accessed January 28, 2021, https://onlinelibrary.wiley.com/doi/abs/10.1002/aps.1652.

Sheehi, S. 2018. 'Psychoanalysis Under Occupation: Nonviolence and Dialogue Initiatives as a Psychic Extension of the Closure System.' *Psychoanalysis and History* 20 (3): 353–369.

Sheehi, S., and Sheehi, L. 2020. 'The Settler's Town Is a Strongly Built Town: Fanon in Palestine.' *International Journal of Applied Psychoanalytic Studies* 17: 183–192. Accessed January 28, 2021, https://onlinelibrary.wiley.com/doi/10.1002/aps.1647.

Statement from the Palestinian Union of Social Workers and Psychologists. 2018. Accessed January 28, 2021, https://www.facebook.com/PUSWP.Palestine/posts/902274599967730.

Synopsis of COPELFI Campaign. n.d. Accessed January 28, 2021, https://usapalmhn.org/synopsis-of-copelfi-campaign/.

Synopsis of WMS Campaign. n.d. Accessed May 15, 2020, https://usapalmhn.org/synopsis-of-wms-campaign/.

Thabet, A., El-Buhaisi, O., and Vostanis, P. 2014. 'Trauma, PTSD, Anxiety, and Coping Strategies Among Palestinian Adolescents Exposed to War on Gaza.' *The Arab Journal of Psychiatry* 25 (1): 71–82.

Times of Israel Staff. 2019. 'European Association Said to Nix Jerusalem Conference, Fearing BDS Pressure.' *Times of Israel*. Accessed January 28, 2021, https://www.timesofisrael.com/european-association-said-to-nix-jerusalem-conference-fearing-bds-pressure/.

UK Clinical Psychologists Urge Boycott of Jerusalem Conference. 2014. Accessed January 28, 2021, https://ukpalmhn.com/2014/12/01/uk-clinical-psychologists-urge-boycott-of-jerusalem-conference/.

UK-Palestine Mental Health Network. n.d. *Home Page*. Accessed January 28, 2021, https://ukpalmhn.com/.

USA-Palestine Mental Health Network. n.d. *Home Page*. Accessed January 28, 2021, https://usapalmhn.org/.

USA-Palestine Mental Health Network Supports Palestine-Global Mental Health Network on Ariel University. 2020. Accessed January 28, 2021, https://www.pgmhn.org/news/usa-palestine-mental-health-network-sup-ports-palestine-global-mental-health-network-on-ariel-university.

Voices on Palestine. 2018. Accessed January 28, 2021, https://usapalmhn.org/voices-on-palestine-forum/.

Watch Palestine-Global Panel at Cornell University. 2020. Accessed January 28, 2021, https://www.pgmhn.org/news/zaaqfrxfaxwg19rkoimklgqoovc8k5.

Who Are We? 2020. Accessed January 28, 2021, https://www.pgmhn.org/about-us.

# READING THE TERM *WHITE SYRIAN* THROUGH FANON: AN ANTI-COLORIST FEMINIST CRITIQUE

Razan Ghazzawi

> *The politicians who make the speeches, who write in the nationalist press, raise the people's hope. They avoid subness of their listeners or readers. Often the national or ethnic imagination is allowed to roam outside the colonial order. Often the national of ethnic language is used. Here again, expectations are raised and the times even these politicians declare: 'We blacks, we Arabs', and take on a sacred connotation. These nationalist politicians are playing with fire. As an African leader recently told a group of young intellectuals: 'Think before speaking to the masses, they are easily excitable.' There is a therefore a cunning of history which plays havoc with the colonies.*
> —Frantz Fanon, *The Wretched of the Earth*

## Introduction: Fanon and the Gendered Politics of *White Syrian* in the Syrian Uprising

With this introductory quote from Fanon on the essential role of words and feelings in times of popular protests, I write this chapter while keeping in mind this legacy and lessons learned from previous popular protests in the Southwest Asia and North Africa region (SWANA). More specifically, I write this chapter with the intention to transfer similar lessons learned from the past decade's protests to future generations in the region and worldwide based on my experience as a previously-incarcerated blogger, feminist community organizer, and a queer nonbinary teacher in times of popular protests, counter-revolutions, war and exile. In this chapter, I talk about the importance of words, terms, and feelings in the 2011 popular protests by focusing on the Syrian uprising and the term 'white Syrian' more specifically —an increasingly used term amongst activists and refugees communities in exile. I argue that the term 'white Syrian', which has been initially used in Syrian intellectuals' writings to build bridges with Black people's struggles by renaming and framing the communities who are surviving Syrian state and allies' different forms of oppressions in the 'liberated areas', Black Syrians, whereas Syrians who live and benefit from the state are called 'white Syrians.' While this was and is the intellectuals' writings directions and intentions, the term nevertheless was quickly used as a shaming and a bullying in activist and organic intellectuals communities and everyday language. In this chapter, I offer an ethnographic and autoethnographic account of how intellectuals' uncritical theorization of who are the 'good' and the 'bad' Syrians could easily become bullying and shaming terminologies that are tactically used against nonconforming revolutionary voices in the uprising. I argue that the term 'white Syrian' has been systematically used by public figures, organic intellectuals, and civil society activists against individuals who do not conform to the norm, and especially against those who demand a different form of protest than the mainstream.

I position myself as an 'insider' blogger-activist, a protestor, and a grassroots queer feminist organizer in Syria since 2005. I also position myself as someone who was called as a 'white Syrian' twice by Syrian male public figures and civil society activists. I also I reflect on conversations and interviews with feminists and indigenous activists who have been discredited from the movement for holding nonconforming anti-military views who were called different terms; 'ramadyeen' (grey people), infisalyeen (separatists), and 'aqallaween' (minoritarians), as means to discredit them as individuals in the movement and as a strategy to belittle their demands and perspectives on what self-determination in Syria look like for them. In doing so, I rely on Fanon's work to challenge the term 'white Syrian' for two reasons: First, through my chats with several activists and writers in the activists communities, I was told that Fanon is the muse behind such term, specifically his book, *Black Skin, White Masks*. While I could not verify this information through desk research nor through reviewing the intellectuals' writings I came across while researching for this chapter, I choose to read the term 'white Syrian' through Fanon nonetheless in the hopes that this chapter could offer an alternative reading of Fanon to Syrian readership on 'white Syrian.'

A second reason why I chose Fanon, is his significant ideas about the role of intellectuals, the critical role of words in times of protest, and his awareness of their feelings. In addition to Fanon's work, I also attempt to develop an anti-colorist feminist critique as a theoretical and an activist engagement and contribution to the discussion on 'white Syrian' and other terms that have been used uncritically by intellectuals to describe the struggle of the people in Syria as 'slaves' in the face of authoritarianism. In doing so, I use feminist methodologies to pay attention to the emotions that result of bullying against killjoy feminists and lesbian, gay, bisexual, transgender, nonbinary, and queer (LGBTNBQ) activists who were framed as 'aggressive', 'angry', 'white Syrians', and 'Assadists' for condemning 'rape jokes' and 'rape culture' within the Syrian activist communities in exile.

Drawing on Carlin Borsheim-Black's work on antiracist feminist pedagogy (2015), I define anti-colorist feminist critique as a form of interrupting everyday colorist language and terminologies within the Syrian activist communities that undermine anti-Blackness and/or perpetuates color/race blindness and post-race discourse. This colorist everyday language and terminologies are built on different assumptions. First, it assumes that 'the people in Syria" are a homogenous group thereby perpetuating the abstract imaginations of 'Syrian people' as 'Arab Sunni cismen.' Second, the uncritical comparison between Arab Syrians and Black people assumes that Black Syrians do not exist, therefore the comparison reifies the very racial discrimination it seeks to dismantle. A third assumption this comparison illustrates is the idea that SWANA (Southwest Asia and North Africa) communities have a shared struggle and that they are one 'Arab nation', is not only a legacy of Arabist exclusionary ideology that have swept the region (perhaps strategically so) since national liberation from European colonialism, but more importantly, it erases the indigenous communities' historical struggle in the SWANA from Kurds, Assyrians, Nubian, Amazigh and others. Therefore, while I use SWANA as an alternative framework than the 'Arab World' or the 'Middle East' in this chapter, this framework does not suggest that Southwest Asia and North Africa are a unified entity, nor do I suggest they have a shared struggle despite the similarities and historical connections. This is another contribution I make to the debate on reading Fanon in Syria; the idea that the armed struggle of the Algerian people against French colonialism could be compared to the struggle for liberation in Syria today from authoritarianism. Here, Fanon is often cited as a 'theorist of violence' in Syrian intellectuals writings, which here I offer a different reading of Fanon not only as a theorist and a revolutionary who was constantly critical of armed struggle, but more importantly, I read Fanon as a carefully nuanced intellectual and a theorist of emotions in protests times.

With these lessons above I have personally learned from my pandemic location in Chicago and witnessing and following closely the Black Lives Matter protests and live Instagram coverages, also talks by leaders of the movement, I locate myself in this chapter as a non-Black queer non-binary feminist of color protestor and teacher, and I hope this chapter is useful for future generations of protestors in the region and worldwide on bullying, shaming, feminist and queer protests, and finally, on notions of transnational solidarity.

## Emerging Revolutionary and Counterrevolutionary Terminologies in the Syrian Uprising

Since the eruption of the popular uprisings and revolutions in Tunisia, Egypt, and the rest of the SWANA region in early 2011, new words and terminologies have emerged. These terms depict the new realities imposed by the popular protest movements on the everyday, but also by experiences of violence and repression from the state (Neggaz, 2013; Taheri, 2011). Some of these terms document and identify new forms of violence that emerged as a response to the uprising. Words like 'Shabbeeh' are now commonly used in English written texts instead of 'thugs.' The Shabbeeh are a group of civilian-contracted personnel who are hired by the state to attack protestors in the early months of 2011. This is done within seconds; therefore the protestors invest a new forms of protest called Tayyara—flying protest; which mean a speedy protest that would make a declaration of slogans to disrupt the status quo imposed by fear of Shabeeha. *Tayyara* then is a form of protest in response to the Shabbeha. Almost all protestors experienced or faced or have been hit by a *Shabeeha*. The term *Shabeeha* became mainstream because they were everywhere, in every protest, corner, shop, campus, and neighborhood. The word therefore became an everyday language within the Syrian activist communities and beyond. Similar words *Hajez* (checkpoint), *Harbiye* (military aircraft), *Fasil* (armed group), *Sadiq* (neutralized), and *Kannas* (sniper), *Chimawi* (Chemical weapons).

However, not all the new words and terminologies have emancipatory intentions and purposes; some new terminologies have been surfaced to describe, or rather target, certain communities or persons *within* the uprising movement in Syria. Not only to attack their views, but also to discredit them from the movement. These terms and words include but are not exclusive to; *Infisali* or 'separatists'—specifically used to target Syrian Kurds with nonconforming views on Syria's future. *Aqallawi* or 'minoritarian', is used against people who are framed as 'minorities' and have nonconforming views on the uprising. As for '*Ramadyeen*' it is for those who are considered not revolutionary enough, such as being anti-militarization and anti-Turkey in certain phases of the war and uprising[1]. Therefore, in this chapter, I argue that terms like 'separatists', 'minoritarian', 'majoritarian', *Ramadyeen*, and 'white Syrian'—a term that is said to be inspired by Fanon's work—as forms of *revolutionary-Tashabeeh* that have been mobilized to silence 'othered' protestors who voice nonconforming political views.

Based on an auto-ethnographic and digital ethnographic study of Syrian social media encounters and updates, and interviews with people who were called 'white Syrians', I argue that while the term 'white Syrian' was first used by Syrian and Lebanese intellectuals to describe people who are allied with the Syrian state officials and the regime and those who are benefiting from this relationship—or what Fanon called in his *Wretched of the Earth* 'colonial intellectuals' and 'colonialist bourgeoisie', the term however traveled to be used randomly and against people who are part of the uprising movements and who are organizing and are active participants in the Syrian civil society. Moreover, I argue that the term 'white Syrian' has been used mostly against women, minorities, and feminine-presenting people. It is important to think carefully about terms and terminologies at times of revolutions and armed social movements because, and as Fanon argued in the opening quote to this chapter.

## Anti-Colorist Feminist Pedagogies

> *The only common denominator between the blacks from Chicago and the Nigerians or Tanganyikans was that they all defined themselves in relation to the whites.*
> —Frantz Fanon, *The Wretched of the Earth*

Why do these terms matter to us as teachers, activists, writers, intellectuals, artists, and community organizers? First, there is an epistemological necessity to address the politics and hegemony of these words and phrases, since they are linguistic and rhetorical examples of the everyday sectarianism, anti-Kurdish

---

1. Interview with an anonymous feminist activist on Messenger.com, July, 2019.

racism, and misogyny, in the everyday social media exchanges and political life of revolutionary activists (Fanon, 2004). The act of mourning and grieving *Othered* communities, pain and not others' (Butler, 2004; 2010) has always been a contested area for many Arab-identified Syrian opposition, intellectuals, and public figures, to meaningfully condemn Turkish-backed invasion of Afrin until very recently.[2] Addressing these terminologies, phrases, words, images, effects, and discriminative everyday logic towards Syrian ethnic, religious, and gender minorities, is significant for the revolutionary project, as these reflections and critiques that come from within the movement are opportunities for the revolutionary project to build an anti-sectarian, anti-racist, and anti-colorist feminist revolutionary pedagogy, language, and political culture as an alternative to the state's project. Second, such terms also reflect a colorist language that is reflective of the anti-Blackness in the Arabic language, culture, and intellectual writings (Abulhawa, 2013; Al Chahhal, 2013; ARM, 2011; Sidqi, 2015). Following the Black Lives Matter protests in 2013 and 2020, it is imperative for the Syrian intellectuals, writers, teachers, artists, and community organizers to be reflective of anti-Blackness and co-optation of Black struggles and thoughts in the Arab and SWANA communities and writings. This chapter therefore contributes to producing anti-colorist revolutionary language in the Syrian social movement.

It took me a while to write this piece after contemplating and questioning the epistemological reasoning behind it, and also thinking about the ethical issues that rise for writing it in English, publishing it in a book that may not be accessible to the intended readers, and equally importantly, how to write 'objectively' about a topic that has 'personally' affected me (Tuck and Fine, 2007). This chapter is written from the positionality of anti-humanitarian intervention public figure -and anti-militarization later—who was called a 'white Syrian', three times in separate events, not by strangers but by friends and mutual friends on social media and in real life. In other words, this chapter is 'personal' in the sense that I have not only experienced being called as such by strangers, but by folks from my community and by friends in the Syrian revolution. I therefore locate friendships as an area for critical scholarly reflections, pedagogical teachings, and theorizations of everyday violence, cultures of activists communities, networks, and virtual communities (Mehta, 2017). Furthermore, during my digital ethnographic fieldwork between 2016 and 2019, along with several virtual interviews I conducted at the time with Syrian and Palestinian feminists, I was told that Fanon might have been the 'muse' behind the term 'white Syrian.' Unable to confirm these speculations by my interlocutors, I thought it would be a good opportunity to read the term through Fanon. After all, he argued that being white is a guarantee of class privilege in the colonies. In the *Wretched of the Earth*, Fanon writes that 'you are rich because you are white, you are white because you are rich' (Fanon, 2004). In *Black Skin White Masks*, he writes in chapter 2 of Mayotte

---

2. Public Syrian opinion that is affiliated with the Syrian uprising has always been supportive of Erdogan due to his 'Syrian refugees welcome' policies and military support against Rojava. This position has changed towards Erdogan in recent years specifically after the anti-Syrian refugees policies and deportations in the summer of 2019.

Capecia's desire to become white, 'one is white if one has a certain amount of money' (Fanon, 1970). In these two examples, whiteness is central to the question of access to power and resources. As I will show in the next section how 'white Syrian' and Black Syrian' are used in the everyday language in activist and refugee communities.

## Three Usages of the *White Syrian* in the Syrian Social Movement

> *Najour, with the help of his lawyer and a Syrian voluntary association that mobilized to assist him in his case, mounted a strong defense in support of his whiteness. The presiding judge supported Najour's claim that Syrians were Caucasian and therefore white and admitted him to citizenship. Najour thus became the first applicant for citizenship, among all ethnic groups, to successfully litigate his status as a white person in a U.S. federal court.*
> —Sarah Gualtieri, *Between Arab and White, Race and Ethnicity in the Early Syrian American Diaspora*

Before discussing the prominent usages of 'white Syrian' by Syrian and Lebanese intellectuals, poets, and media experts, I first want to stress that the term itself has different meanings in different contexts and geographies. The quote above by Sarah Gualtieri (2009) tells the story of one of these meanings through tracing the lynching of Syrian American immigrant Nola and Fannie Romey in 1929 in Florida. In her book *Race and Ethnicity in the Early Syrian American Diaspora*, Gualtieri finds that despite legal rulings that concludes Syrians as 'white persons' for naturalization purposes, 'their whiteness', however, Gualtieri maintains, 'remained unstable, or 'probationary', particularly in the color-conscious South' (Gualtieri, 2009: 113). Syrian American community leader, Salloum Mokarzel, said in 1929 that the lynching was 'one of the saddest tragedies in the history of the Syrians in America' (quoted in Gualtieri, 2009: 114). Gualtieri states that the Romey lynching 'was a crisis in whiteness for the Syrians' (Gualtieri, 2009: 134). It was a moment when many realized that, in Gualtieri's words 'they were 'in between' or 'not quite white'' (Gualtieri, 2009: 134). Moreover, Gualtieri argues that Syrian American attempts to distance themselves from Black and Asian people 'in the discourse on race was one way to protect the boundaries of identity' (Gualtieri, 2009: 134). This history of seeking whiteness by white-passing Syrian Americans is perhaps a good reminder how whiteness in the US could not be sustained for Syrians even in legal means. In Syria, however, and specifically during the 2011 social movement, the term 'white Syrian' emerged in different usages. Below I highlight three prominent ways the term has been used that I noticed in recent years whether in intellectual writings, social media dynamics against feminists, or in the everyday life in the refugee and exile civil society and activist communities.

## 1. Intellectuals' Conceptualizations of *White Syrian* as 'Assadists'

In some of the social media posts and intellectuals writings in local media web-sites and press, 'white Syrian' is a reference to privileges, class privilege and connection with the state. In other words, a discussion on race became a metaphor for class and privilege through the use of 'whiteness.' Syrian filmmaker, Maya Abyad, who published a piece about Syrian racism using a similar approach to 'white Syrian' without engaging with race, or any further conceptualization of 'whiteness' in the Syrian context. However, her article was one of the few to acknowledge forms of white-appealing tendency among some white-passing Syrians in the Damascene middle-upper class communities (Abyad, 2018). Syrian and Lebanese journalists, writers, intellectuals, and civil society activists have been using the term in similar contexts and with similar meaning.[3] Here, we see an example of what Fanon warned from in the earlier quote; mentioning a term that is critical of Syrians briefly without careful and critical explanation. The question of Blackness and anti-Blackness are erased altogether and is substituted with class and state/regime power, where whiteness becomes a form of (upper) class backed by state power, and 'white Syrians' becomes the 'First World within' the Syrian state that is monopolized and controlled by the regime. Blackness is transformed into poor, besieged, and bombarded revolutionaries and their communities. By doing so, the erasure of anti-Blackness is thus perpetuated. Fanon sees this erasure as white normalization. He writes:

> The people discover that the iniquitous phenomenon of exploitation can assume a black or Arab face. They cry treason, but in fact the treason is not national but social, and they need to be taught to cry thief. On their arduous path to rationality the people must also learn to up their simplistic perception of the oppressor. The species is splitting up before their very eyes. They realize that colonists do not succumb to the ambient climate of criminal hysteria and remain apart from the rest of their species. (Fanon, 2004: 94)

Furthermore, in his *Black skin, White Masks*, Fanon posits his analysis of racism on the body as a sight of racial otherness (Fanon, 1970). According to the distinguished queer feminist theorist, Teresa de Lauretis, Fanon constitutes the body as the 'material ground of subject formation':

> the value of Fanon's text, perhaps the thing that makes it most radical today, may slip out of sight and out of mind; namely, its equally insistent emphasis on the subjective and physical impact of racism, the introjection

---

3. See for example the press articles published in Arabic and English by these authors; Omran, 2018; Al Haj Saleh, 2016; Al Haj Saleh, 2019

of racist stereotypes in the individual psyche and their consequent hold on the body-ego. For it is there, in the body, that the 'real effects' of racist discourses and acts are realized, thus constituting what Fanon calls experience lived experience. (Lauretis, 2002: 57)

Otherness to Fanon lies in the body, 'in the lived experience of the bodily ego', in de Lauretis' words. The bodily sensations, the effects, the reactions, and the surfaces of feelings (Ahmed, 2004) is what have led Fanon to add 'sociogeny' to the theoretical frameworks of psychoanalysis. On the body-ego point, de Lauretis argues that Fanon's *Black Skin White Masks* teaches us an important lesson about racism that is often missed by focusing on discursive racism. Indeed, Fanon describes the effect and surfaces of the white gaze on his body in the child-mother scene in *Black Skin White Masks*. Fanon's analysis of the white gaze is centered on the body and how it results in a sense of estrangement and alienation created by the white gaze. Based on the arguments above, I argue that the term 'white Syrian' is used in this context in a way that erases Blackness and anti-Blackness to become a question of class and disposability. On this point, the Black American queer feminist poet, Audre Lorde, reminds non-Black queer feminists of color that their struggle is not the same as Black women's struggle (Lorde, 1997).

## 2. *White Syrian* in Praxis: A Technology of Revolutionary Misogyny

While the first usage was a brief abstract conceptualization of what constitutes a 'white Syrian', here we see the praxis of that 'vague' conceptualization, to use Fanon's words. The term has been used in arbitrary different situations, such as; after expressing a politically nonconforming opinion, or against people who do not conform to 'right (read: gendered) way of socializing,' or for doing academic research. Based on digital auto-ethnographic methods, social media updates, and oral history interviews with two women activists who were called a 'white Syrian' and 'Ramadeyeen,' for opposing sanctions against Syria and for opposing calls for further militarization of the uprising in one of the social gatherings. My point of departure in this form of using 'white Syrian' is used against feminine-presenting people who are imagined as rich and powerful women who are not connected to the revolutionary people's struggles on the ground, but rather imagined as 'detached' serving a high ranking position. Ironically, both of the women interviewed are grassroots activists from ethnic and religious minorities, whereas their bullies are cismale intellectuals and public figures. Another example of this usage of 'white Syrian' can be traced to the women Advisory Board[4]

---

4. For more information about the Women's Advisory Board visit https://specialenvoysyria.unmissions.org/women's-advisory-board

appointed by Staffan De Mistura because their statement recommended lifting sanctions of medical supplies.

Here, I argue that misogyny was masked by a talk about 'class' as a way of discrediting politically a Syrian feminine-presenting activists within the movement. This is exactly what Fanon warned from in the quoted passage at the beginning of this chapter. Indeed, Fanon realizes the importance of the intellectuals' role in times of protests and counter-revolutions and the need to be self-aware of 'vague' writing that can be harmful to other marginalized communities even though the term was meant to be against state oppression. Since the 'white Syrian' has been used against women mostly, Syrian intellectuals should be reading Syrian women's writings and feminists work on anti-racist *and* transnational feminist theories when writing about state oppressions.

Another case study occurred in 2016-2017 when a group of Syrian public figures activists posted on social media a photo of a Syrian woman who was carrying the Syrian official red flag, and 'joked about fucking' her as a form of punishment for her 'loyalist politics' with the regime. Feminists demanded a public apology for the harmful post on social media that might instigate hate and violence against the woman who is identified by a photo and whose home address was being shared in the comments section. The response from the activists' friends is to frame the feminists as 'white Syrians' in social media posts. Instead of challenging these posts publicly, some of the leading Syrian intellectuals who theorized 'white Syrian' had 'liked' the posts and so were complicit in the smearing campaign against feminists in the face of digital 'rape joke' hate campaign against 'women loyalists'. I argue that without feminist revolutionary killjoys (Ahmed and Bonis, 2012), feminist movement in Syria would lack any form of condemnation of rape culture within the Syrian revolutionary movement. Feminist NGOs have not issued a statement in condemnation nor in support of the feminists who were smeared by intellectuals and activists alike. This have resulted in isolating them, shaming them, and excluding them not only from the activist communities, but also from the NGOized feminist movement. Finally, lawsuits were another form of intimidation to any feminist or woman who speaks against 'rape culture,' sexual harassment within the opposition and revolutionary movements in Syria[5].

## 3. *White Syrian* as an 'Othered' Syrian within the Social Movement

To give an example: grieving Kurdish communities pain has been considered by Arab Syrians as an 'Assadist' or a 'white' thing to do in most phases of the war up until recently; an observation made by one of the two Syrian feminists I had interviewed between 2016 and 2018 and have been called *'Ramadiyeen,'*

---

5. Interview with anonymous woman who launched a campaign against sexual harassment within the activities communities, through messenger, April, 2020.

'Akalayween,' and 'white Syrian' after voicing their criticisms to the militariza-tion of the uprising[6]. The silence from self-identified 'majoritarian' revolution-aries (read: Sunni Arab) towards Turkey's President Erdogan's hostile, racist, and expansive policies towards the non-Arab indigenous communities in northern Syria, and specifically against Kurdish communities, has exposed counter-revo-lutionary politics within the Syrian movement; such as sectarianism, anti-Kur-dish racism among Syrian journalists, intellectuals, and human rights advocates within the Syrian civil society[7]. In other words, those who are critical of such mainstream politics are commonly called 'white Syrian,' or 'Ramadyeen.'

## Beyond the *White Syrian*: Fanon and Emotions in Protest Times

Scholars on Syria and other violent social movements have often cited Fanon to situate subalterns' violence throughout the process of decolonization from colonizers. In the previous sections, I showed why the term 'white Syrian' is problematic as a concept and praxis, which what Fanon warned the colonized intellectuals and parties from approaching exciting speeches and words with lit-tle explanation and direction. In an attempt to learn from Fanon's legacy as a revolutionary from an anti-militarization lens, I highlight below two areas where I felt connected with Fanon's work and it resonated with me as a protestor who evolved throughout the past decade as pro subaltern violence in Palestine, Lebanon, and in Syria, until 2013, in Kafranbel, when I learned the woes for such reality. This is when praxis won over my ideology and this is how I became an anti-militarization protestor; through processing feeling of rage, alienation, and anti-war methods, all at the same time, as Fanon argues as I will show later in this section.

## Feelings of Alienation and Rage

One of the things that struck me while reading Fanon's *Wretched of the Earth* is the theorization of: 1: feelings of alienation from one's self (Fanon, 2004: 15); 2: the push for 'objectivity'; and 3: feeling of 'rage' (Fanon, 2004: 17) and 'madness' (Fanon, 2004: 34). In this chapter, I read Fanon as a revolutionary teacher and writer who documented the lives of people, their feelings and illnesses on the everyday during their struggle for self-determination from colonialism. Fanon's recognition of the importance of feelings of rage and madness for the colonized to reach a limit of realization that they are free. When the moment of realization comes, imagination and dreams thrive. The feelings of alienation and rage have

---

6. Interview with an anonymous non-Arab and non-Muslim Syrian feminist activist and refugee in Europe. Interview was made online using Messenger, May 2020.
7. Two conversations with Kurdish Syrian activists in Europe and online.

led to the 'muscular dreams' upon moment of realization, of imagination. Fanon writes:

> The first thing the colonial subject learns is to remain in his place and not overstep its limits. Hence the dreams of the colonial subject are muscular dreams, dreams of action, dreams of aggressive vitality. I dream I am jumping, swimming, running, and climbing. I dream I burst out laughing, I am leaping across a river and chased by a pack of cars that never catches up with me. During colonization the colonized subject frees himself night after night between nine in the evening and six in the morning. (Fanon, 2004: 15)

This passage above resonates specifically with the idea of 'muscular dreams' and how they are connected to being deprived from imagination. This passage reminded me instantly of what a dear friend once told me; I met him in Kafranbel where I lived and worked as a teacher for a year, I remember his face when he told me: 'I actually didn't know I had the right to rights. I didn't know they even existed. The revolution made me realize there is something called rights, and that I have the right to them. I didn't know that before.' What I call the military-carceral-paranoid state in Syria (forthcoming, Ghazzawi, 2023), and the constant fear of surveillance and detention in the country for decades—have all caused a culture of self-censorship, which in turn created a sense of alienation from one's self as a non-Black people of color living under military-carceral dictatorship, which is different from the alienation that Fanon speaks of on Blackness. Fanon's conceptualization of alienation, emotions of anger, and his insistence on dreaming—are all lessons activists and organizers in Syria and the SWANA can take away from reading Fanon today post popular social movements that have erupted in Tunisia in 2011 and that still continue in different forms and scale up until today. The feelings of alienation and rage that Fanon described about the colonized have 'accumulated' rage (Ahmed, 2014), which as Fanon argues, has led the colonized Arab and Black people to affirm their 'new humanity" (Munif, 2013).

Similar to my friend's statement who started to imagine his rights, his demands, and what they look like now in praxis in the everyday life of a social movement in Kafranbel, Fanon speaks of feelings of rage and alienation in a way that resonates in this historical moment and memory today in exile. But he's not an armed man and he chose not to be. Abd chose to be the logistics guy; someone who facilitates communication in the village between aid workers and families in need. He is also the bridge between human rights organizations and the previously detainees. Abd's labour is invisible and unseen, yet his impact on the community and on the civil society at large is recognized by his many followers on his social media accounts. Abd is one of the many people who are essential to the revolution but are rendered unnoticed by scholars today on Syria. Fanon writes describing the revolutionary acts of the everyday as follows:

Giving food for the mujahideen, stationing lookouts, helping deprived families and taking over from the slain or imprisoned husband—such are the practical tasks the people are asked to undertake in the liberation struggle (Fanon, 2004: 19).

There are a lot of messages and lessons nonviolent activists can take away from Fanon are these feelings and emotions of rage, alienation, self-recognition, and imagination. Therefore disagree with many scholars in Syria who mostly cite Fanon on militarization or to come up with a bullying and an exclusionary term like 'white Syrian.'

## Lessons from Anti-Militarization Fanon

As a protestor who have gone through different phases and reflections towards militarization, as a teenager who grew up identifying as a Palestinian, armed struggle is part of liberation where I originally came from. This is the ancestral spirit that had taught me to be critical of west-based demonizing discourses of colonized communities when they decide to take up arms to defend their families and lands. This is exactly the connection I made by reading Fanon as both a supporter of people's right to self-determination by violence from violent oppressors, and at the same time, an immense critic of militarization. In fact, Fanon differentiates between two forms of violence: the violence of the subaltern for self-determination, and the violence of militarization . I do not wish to linger on this point as it is beyond the scope of this chapter, but this is just to point out that in the Syrian context today, Fanon is commonly cited as a theorist of violence and some scholars and intellectuals have focused on Fanon's two infamous books *Wretched of the Earth* and *Black Skin, White Masks* but ignored his *Dying Colonialism* (Fanon, 1994), where he states this clearly, I quote him at length to counter the mainstream reading of Fanon as a theorist of violence:

No, it is not true that the Revolution has gone to the lengths to which colonialism has gone. But we do not on this account justify the immediate reactions of our compatriots. We understand them, but we can neither excuse them nor reject them. Because we want a democratic and a renovated Algeria, because we believe one cannot rise and liberate oneself in one area and sink in another, we condemn, with pain in our hearts, those brothers who have flung themselves into revolutionary action with the almost physiological brutality that centuries of oppression give rise to and feed.

The people who condemn us or who blame us for these dark aspects of the Revolution know nothing of the terrible problem faced by the chief who must take disciplinary action against a patriot guilty, for example, of having killed a notorious traitor or, worse, a woman or child-without having received orders to do so. This man who must be judged in the absence of a code, of any law, only by the conscience that each one has of what is allowable and what is forbidden, may not be a new man in the combat group. He may have given, over a period of months, unmistakable proofs of abnegation, of patriotism, of courage. Yet he must be judged. The chief, the local representative of the ruling body, must apply the directives. He must sometimes be the accuser, the other members of the unit having been unwilling to accuse this brother before the revolutionary court. It is not easy to conduct, with a minimum of errors, the struggle of a people, sorely tried by a hundred and thirty years of domination, against an enemy as determined and as ferocious as French colonialism (Fanon, 1994: 25-26).

The on-going occupation of Kurdish homes in Afrin today by Arab-identified fractions is an everyday reminder how militarization in the contemporary Middle East involves different states funding and sponsoring of armed men to execute domestic and regional gains against its opponents. However, Afrin's story is a reminder but it's not the story of all areas of Northern Syria. Fanon famously argued:

> Leaders will come to realize that hatred is not an agenda. It would be perverse to count on the enemy who always manages to commit as many crimes as possible and can be relied upon to widen. (Fanon, 2004: 89)

As an anti-illiteracy Arabic and English teacher in the liberated areas in the North, specifically in Idleb in 2013, I have experienced and lived with militarization everyday as an unveiled cispassing-woman. I received first a lot of questioning from the Free Syrian Army members on why I am 'a Muslim Sunni woman but unveiled.' They wanted to make sure I am 'not Alawi' and a 'supporter of the regime and their spy.' I do not call myself secular because political secularism has a different yet equally oppressive history in Syria, as does political Islam (starting from the Muslim Brotherhood). While my objection for this framing as a 'Sunni Muslim' to forgive me being an unveiled person, it was the easiest way out for my colleagues who were with me during these encounters. 'They do not understand your secularism, Razan', the late Raed Fares used to tell me. 'They will in time, right now, in wartime, you gotta win one battle at a time.' Raed was not just an activist, he was a community leader. He designed the whole town's projects, solved many people's problems, created jobs, Raed Fares was a movement, and his movement still lives on till today. I, however, disagreed with him. But I understand that even he did not have the energy to do this work of convincing the Free Syrian Army every time simply because I felt this was one of my contribution to the revolution. My everyday activism, if you will. To be a non-'Sunni Muslim" unveiled person and to be accepted as such. I was successful throughout the time when the FSA was controlling the area until late 2013 and early 2014 when ISIS and Al-Nusra started to co-opt the uprising and occupy the North, the communities living in the area along with the hundreds of thousands of internally displaced communities.

## Conclusion: Towards an Anti-bullying Revolutionary

## Feminist Ethics

In this chapter, I have tried to reflect on revolutionary terminologies that were initially coined to critique what Fanon would call the 'colonial bourgeoisie' or the 'moderate politician' but have actually been used against the feminist activists in the movement by bullying male revolutionaries on issues related to sanctions, militarization, rape culture, and sexual harassment. I have also argued that the term has become mainstream and has been used in the everyday encounters amongst Syrian refugee communities as a bullying mechanism against 'othered' Syrians. By laying out the different and harmful ways which have been used to exclude some voices and demands from the movement, I invite Syrian intellectuals to take Fanon's advice and avoid hasty comparisons and legitimizing bullying when coining terms to describe people, not *structures* of domination and violence, and work towards writing and organizing against bullying culture within the movement, especially against nonconforming voices and demands.

In the second section of the chapter I lay out three lessons to take away from Fanon's *Wretched of the Earth* for nonviolent protestors and organizers in the Southwest and North African region and beyond, arguing that everyday revolutionary activities that are invisible and unseen labour but are essential part of the movement as Fanon rightly asserts. Here, I invite scholars and academics on Syria to carefully read Fanon.

## Bibliography

Abyad, M. 2018. 'Racism, Sectarianism or Sexism? On Damascus and the Syrian Demographic Barcode | SyriaUntold | انحكت ما حكاية.' Accessed September 8, 2020, https://syriauntold.com/2018/10/03/racism-sectarianism-or-sexism-on-damascus-and-the-syrian-demographic-barcode/.

Ahmed, S. 2014. *Cultural Politics of Emotion*. Edinburgh University Press.

Ahmed, S., and Oristelle, B. 2012. 'Feminist Killjoys (and Other Willful Subjects).' *Cahiers du Genre* 53 (2): 77–98.

Al Haj Saleh, Y. 2016. 'The World in Syria/ Syria in the World.' الجمهورية.نت. Accessed September 8, 2020, https://www.aljumhuriya.net/ar/35336.

———. 2019. 'Fascist in Damascus and Other Fascists.' المتمدن الحوار. Accessed July 22, 2020, http://www.ahewar.org/debat/show.art.asp?aid=634990.

Alkhazen, J. 2013. 'Syria the Victim.' The National Coordination Committee for Change. Accessed July 22, 2020, https://syriancb.com/2013/11/سورية-الضحية/07.

Badrakhan, A. 2019. 'The State's Position on Sex: What Is Lawful to White People Is Not Lawful to Black People.' برس حرية. Horrya Press. Accessed July 22, 2020, https://horrya.net/archives/116246.

Borsheim-Black, C. 2015. '"It's Pretty Much White": Challenges and Opportunities of an Antiracist Approach to Literature Instruction in a Multilayered White Context.' *Research in the Teaching of English* 49 (4): 407–429.

Butler, J. 2004. *Precarious Life: The Powers of Mourning and Violence*. London: Verso.

_____. 2010. *Frames of War: When Is Life Grievable?* London: Verso.

Case, K. A. 2016. *Intersectional Pedagogy: Complicating Identity and Social Justice*. Routledge.

Fanon, F. 2004 [1961]. *The Wretched of the Earth*. Translated by Richard Philcox. New York: Grove Press.

_____. 1970. *Black Skin, White Masks*. Paladin London.

_____. 1994. *A Dying Colonialism*. Grove/Atlantic, Inc.

Freire, P. 2018. *Pedagogy of the Oppressed*. Bloomsbury Publishing USA.

Gualtieri, S. 2009. *Between Arab and White: Race and Ethnicity in the Early Syrian American Diaspora Book*. Berkeley: University of California Press.

Hooks, B. 2014. *Teaching to Transgress*. Routledge.

Lorde, A. 1997. 'The Uses of Anger.' *Women's Studies Quarterly* 25(1/2): 278–285.

Mehta, A. 2017. 'Right-Wing Sisterhood: Everyday Politics of Hindu Nationalist Women in India and Zionist Settler Women in Israel-Palestine.' PhD thesis, SOAS University of London.

Munif, Y. 2013. 'Frantz Fanon and the Arab Uprisings: An Interview with Nigel Gibson.' https://www.jadaliyya.com/Details/26906.

Neggaz, N. 2013. 'Syrias Arab Spring: Language Enrichment in the Midst of Revolution.' *Language Discourse & Society* 2(2): 11–31.

Sidqi, B. 2015. 'The Black Syrian and the Sleeping Racisms.' القدس العربي. Accessed July 31, 2020, https://www.alquds.co.uk/ال-السوريون-السود-واستيقاظ-العنصريات/.

Taheri, A. 2011. 'The "Arab Spring" Has Toppled Some Despots and Enriched the Arab Political Vocabulary. But What Are Its Limits and What Should Western Democracies Do to Help It Achieve Its Objectives?.' *American Foreign Policy Interests* 33 (6): 273–277.

Tuck, E., and Michelle, F. 2007. 'Inner Angles: A Range of Ethical Responses to/with Indigenous/Decolonizing Theories.' In *Ethical Futures in Qualitative Research: Decolonizing the Politics of Knowledge*, edited by Denzin, N. K., and Giardina, M. D., 145–168. Left Coast Press.

# VOICE OF THE REVOLUTION: RADIO AND WOMEN'S EMPOWERMENT

Annette Rimmer

## Introduction

> *Decolonisation never takes place unnoticed, for it influences individuals and modifies them fundamentally. It transforms spectators crushed with their inessentiality into privileged actors, with the grandiose glare of history's floodlights upon them.*
> —Fanon, *The Wretched of the Earth*

The jury is still out with regard to the contested concept of 'decolonization' and whether it is trivialized and overused today in discourses about anything other than bloody struggle (Tuck & Yang, 1993). Indeed, there are those who question its existence and its possibility in a world crushed by racism and inequalities: 'we cannot decolonize while relying on colonial logics of commodification of labour and space' (Adebisi, 2020). At time of writing, Covid 19, the #metoo movement, and #BLM are global issues. 'Black Lives Matter', according to Dei (2017: 40) has become 'part of a revitalized politics of intersectionality... shedding light on the necessity to re-theorize Blackness and how internalized stereotypes of the 'angry Black woman' or 'Black beast' feed into institutions that govern us and police us'. hooks (2015: 277) has challenged academic notions of decolonization for 40 years:

> no need to hear your voice when I can talk about you better than you can speak about yourself. No need to hear your voice. Only tell me about your pain. I want to know your story. And then I will tell it back to you in a new way. Tell it back to you in such a way that it becomes mine, my own. Re-writing you, I write myself anew. I am still author, authority. I am still colonizer, the speaking subject, and you are now at the center of my talk.

Acknowledging the contentious nature of these concepts, the chapter characterizes womanhood as crushed and colonized, made wretched by masculinity. Furthermore, the emotional toll of intersectionality is still overlooked (Nayak, 2015). It is the story of a group of women who train as community radio producers and presenters at *Shout FM*, an urban community station in Northern England. It recounts the barriers to their engagement, not least the notion that they live within a *culture of silence*, (Freire, 1970) a silence enforced by societal 'norms' and violence (Solnit, 2017). Women's radio silence is conceptualized as a metaphor for their muted societal presence, reminiscent of lives under colonial rule where domination is overt, the vernacular used against them is the 'language of pure force' and the colonizer 'is the bringer of violence into the home and into the mind of the native'. (Fanon, 1961: 29)

The chapter holds high the pedagogies of oppression, love and transformation (hooks, 1994; Freire, 2014: Darder, 2017) and the politics and practice of *empowerment*, a notion: 'simultaneously bedecked in the sequins of market glitterspeak or the vibrant patchwork of postmodern socialisms' (Fielding, 2006: 399), and plagued by cynicism. References to empowerment are made with an understanding of that cynicism and that its definition often runs: 'too close to contemporary neo-liberal notions of self-help and self-responsibility, glossing over the structural inequalities that hamper personal and social development''(Mullender, Ward and Fleming, 2013: 69). Additionally, empowerment through radio activism, is 'not simply a process of imposing imported methods' making people operate more happily within the status quo, but of challenging societal orthodoxies, as Gibson (2016: 375) remarks on Fanon's brand of psychiatry. Womanhood's empowerment must challenge patriarchal culture and value systems.

The main purpose of the chapter is to explore the potential of feminist radio pedagogy and activism to break women's silence and enable their transformation into *privileged actors*. It embarks from a position that womanhood has no single identity, but in its various forms, its confidence has been crushed and silenced. In their narratives the women come to voice their own intersectional identities and challenge preconceived notions of womanhood; pornification, racial stereotyping and objectification. The process of feminist radio pedagogy; problematizing, learning together and building relationships raises consciousness and confidence to assert their 'right to self determination' (Fanon, 1961: 62).

## Rationale, Socio-political and Gendered Context

After a period of redundancy and depression, I responded to an ad in *The Big Issue* [a homelessness magazine], offering free radio production training. This led to a kind of radio epiphany, an exodus from one life into another, in radio production. As an educator, radio volunteer and community development worker, I wanted to find out if radio had the same impact on others, after all, women represent the 'key constituency for community work and community action...against gendered violence, trafficking, body surgery, self-mutilation and the overall 'pornifiction of the media' (Popple, 2015: 65).

Between 2014 and 2018, 12 community radio volunteers from *Shout FM*, a radio station based in a crumbling Victorian house in Northern England, offered me their radio stories. Their ages range from 20 to 70+ and they introduce themselves as:

> *Ayisha*: Poet, writer and community activist, lone parent. I'm a British Asian.
> *Jessica*: Welsh background, from the LGBTQ community and have Asperger's.
> *Liz*: Carer with 3 children and 9 grandchildren.
> *Loraine*: Retired, happily married LGBTQ activist and Grandma in my 70s.

*Sasha*: Young adult from a West African background.

*Vee*: Musician and collector of music, Phenobarbital baby.

*Collette*: Radio presenter into doing serious and not so serious shows. Mixed race -Black African white English. I sometimes say Black English.

*Kimi*: I love music. Carer and mother. I'm brown and hate being stereotyped.

*Marie*: Blogger and carer to my Irish Mum until she died. I'm mixed race—interested in all cultures.

*Madonna*: Living life to the full. Football fan. Grandfather from Sierra Leone.

*Kate*: I came out in my 20's, I'm a trade unionist, activist and a singer song-writer.

*Priceless*: I'm a Jamaican woman with daughters and an interest in aircraft.

The narratives were collected in the context of the Conservative government's austerity agenda, increased global, national and local poverty, particularly impacting upon women (Alston, 2018); increased mental distress (Agenda, 2020) and the #metoo 'outpouring of pain' by women abused in the male dominated, individualistic, competitive context of corporately owned media (Brockes, 2017: 50). Tarana Burke, founder of #metoo referred to a culture of silence about abuse, a culture perpetuated due to women being 'drenched in shame' (2017: 5).

## Community Radio: Its History and Potential

The introduction to this book reminds us that Fanon's title comes from the rallying cry: 'Debout! Les damnés de la terre' (Arise, the damned of the earth). *Radio Debout* was at the heart of the French occupy movement in 2016. It covered the uprising and offered support, guidance and was viewed as more trustworthy than mainstream media. It is arguably 'tinkering its way back against the overriding force of computer-mediated technologies...it holds the potential to empower ordinary people at the local community level' (Poulain, 2016; Radio Debout, 2021).

In his chapter: *This Is the Voice of Algeria*, Fanon (1965) conceptualizes radio as a tool of French state oppression, but also of colonial resistance and defiance, opening up endless possibilities in the struggle for information, self-identification, self-determination and ultimately, revolution: 'radio will have been, for many, one of the means of saying "no" to the occupation and of believing in the liberation. The identification of the voice of the revolution with the fundamental truth of the nation has opened limitless horizons'. (Fanon, 1965: 97) Examples of radio activism are abundant in the majority world (Paranjape, 2007; Noronha, 2003; Pavarala, 2015) with some in the U.S. (Dunbar-Hester, 2014), but there are few in Europe. The *Father* of community radio is said to be Zane Ibrahim (2000) who initiated *Bush Radio* in South Africa. In *Tarzan doesn't live here anymore* , he commends grassroots radio as an essential element in 'reconstructing our emotionally blunted population...which would be considerably easier if we didn't have to deal with that horror of horrors—the aid agencies' (Ibrahim, 2000: 203). His rage is palpable with regard to the new colonialism in the form of development agencies with entrenched white liberal, missionary style attitudes: 'So, this is a serious cry for help; Tarzan, if you're out there, please come back and save us" (204) Black controlled radio began in South Africa, illegally as part of the struggle against apartheid. When it was licensed in 1994, it was the first time in history that Black people could be formally trained as broadcasters. Launched on National Women's Day it was:

> a symbol of appreciation for the role women played during the struggle for liberation. Our mission...to ensure that communities take part in producing ethical, creative and responsible radio...reaffirm their dignity and identity and promote social responsibility and critical thinking. (Ibrahim, 2000: 200)

Ooty Radio Station in the Nigiri hills of South India is an important source of news, education and entertainment, due to the mistrust of corporate news outlets and satellite channels associated with the local political parties. Ooty radio is the only place where many women in rural communities can hear their own traditional (Kota) songs. 'Tribal women are fond of listening to (Tamil) film songs whilst they cook...but missionaries condemn such radio stations as "unchristian"'(Jayaprakash & Shoesmith, 2007: 51). Similarly, Fanon describes the dominant Radio-Alger as the voice of the occupier, establishing and perpetuating his own reality, sustaining the occupants' culture: 'the voice of France in Algeria constitutes the sole center of reference...it is a daily invitation not to forget the rightfulness of his culture' (1965: 71). There are many examples of the women at *Shout FM* discussing the denial and misrepresentation of women's voices on radio. Priceless points out her important role as a broadcaster with a Caribbean accent: 'it's good to be relatable—so being on radio—"oh I know that song"— hearing a voice like yours—it's like "wow I can do that too", because sometimes the intimidation is never hearing a voice like yours and thinkin' "that's not for me I can't do that".' (2017). But dominant forces fear marginal voices, as Fanon quips: 'the settlers say that without wine and the radio, we should already have become Arabized' (1965: 72). 'When natives took over the radio waves, *The Voice of Fighting Algeria* brought the nation to life and endowed every citizen with a new status, *telling him so explicitly*' (1965: 96).

*Radio Dabanga* in Darfur reported the rape of over 200 women by Sudanese army personnel and enabled some of the survivors to broadcast their accounts as warnings to others and alert the world to this brutality. (Akasha, 2014) The importance of hearing unheard narratives cannot be over-estimated particularly with reference to refugees: 'Storytelling is part of people's everyday life, a cultural and intersubjective experience to the core in which a person draws on the cultural repertoires at their disposal to make sense of, imagine, and negotiate with others in the world around them'. (Sigona, 2014: 370). In group discussion, the importance of this was raised often: "everyone's got a story to tell and a lot of these stories are hidden and I think on the radio you can open those stories so that anybody that's going through anything, you can give that information out on the radio'. hooks criticizes mainstream education and media for 'subscribing to a form of social amnesia with regard to Black history' (1994b: 31). Solnit (2017) argues that:

> Violence against women is often against our voices and our stories. It is a refusal of our voices, and of what a voice means; the right to self-determination, to participation, to consent or dissent, to live and participate, to interpret and narrate. (2017: 19)

In the U.S., Black radio informed and unified communities, especially during times of crisis. Serving as the voice of African Americans nationwide it became a unifying force immediately after Dr King was assassinated. It 'came of age' the night King died. (Johnson, 2004: 355) In Los Angeles, Stevie Wonder's KJLH FM, became an important alternative political voice when police officers were acquitted after the brutal beating of Rodney King in 1991. Johnson describes its role as activist, mediator and change agent. She describes a community that was burning and Black people desperate for a forum through which to express their rage and anger... 'KJLH FM became that forum' (2004: 263). Since then, KJLH FM has continued to provide a forum for the outpouring of pain and anger by the Black community. The police killing of George Floyd in 2020 prompted it to broadcast reflections: 'on the societal structures that still enforce systematic racism' (KJLH Facebook, 2020). Dunbar-Hester narrates the setting up of a community radio station in the U.S. in order to: 'unbuckle' the bible-belt airwaves: 'by giving real people the tools to find their voice and use it in our democracy...plus it will be a hell of a lot of fun!' (respondent cited in Dunbar-Hester, 2014: 49)

In Britain the political and empowerment potential of community radio has been largely overlooked since its inception in the 1980's. It is generally non-profit, non-governmental (though regulated by government) and tasked with serving communities of geography, identity or interest. Some argue that it aimed to control unregulated 'pirate' stations, mainly produced by minority groups and young people. Kenlock (2013) maintains that the loss of radio controlled by and for the Black community, created a cultural void for Black Britons. The notion of Government (and market) colonization of community radio is reflected by Gaynor and Obrien, (2017) and there are well argued cautions about romanticizing alternative or participatory media (Dagron, 2007). Acknowledging this, for the group at Shout FM, radio becomes a way of: 'giving *lesser* people (I don't know how you are going to phrase this) but people like myself who aren't of the mainstream—giving lesser people a chance' (Collette, 2014).

## Barriers to Engagement—It's Hard to Break the Silence

> *Oppressed people are silenced, alienated and a mere object of the director society . . . having no voice, they inhabit the culture of silence and only when that silence is broken can the oppressed society as a whole cease to be silent toward the director society.*
> —Freire, *Pedagogy of the Oppressed*

Whilst Fanon and Freire are frequently contrasted (Tuck & Yang, 1993), there is a symmetry which speaks to the lived reality of oppressed groups, often diminished and silenced by violence and fear. In the chapter 'Concerning Violence', Fanon asserts that the global war game-playing with rockets brandished, does not frighten nor deflect the colonized peoples as they are used to living in 'an atmosphere of doomsday' (Fanon, 1961: 63) Aside from the hegemony of masculinity surrounding technical issues and women's ongoing caring roles; a major barrier to engaging women in radio training is gendered abuse and its immense impact on women's mental health. During the global pandemic of Covid-19, life worsened significantly for women locked down with violent, abusive men. Men's violence against women was already the leading cause of the premature death for women globally but the pandemic led to a doubling of the number of women killed in Britain (Grierson, 2020; Counting Dead Women, 2020 and The Femicide Census, 2020):

> For many women and girls, the threat looms largest where they should be safest. In their own homes... We know lockdowns and quarantines are essential to suppressing COVID-19. But they can trap women with abusive partners. (United Nations Secretary-General, António Guterres, 2020)

As Priceless recounts, after her brutal marriage: 'I was going on without hope'. Alysha refers to her marriage as imprisonment: 'I was told "No—women don't go out—women don't go out!"' (2017). Kate brings in the notion of women being silenced by internet trolling and others carry cruel memories of a school education which left them unprepared to deal with sexism, racism and poverty. Collette, expelled from school at 13, refers to herself as a 'lesser person' (2014). Priceless remembers: 'On the day of the radio training appointment I didn't go—I was terrified, but understanding this, the radio trainer persisted: "Priceless, where are you, did you get lost, you need to come." The rest is history' (2017).

Solnit (2017) argues that abuse enforces women's silence, forbidding them to narrate their own stories and identities. Sasha raises the notion that women's silence is also perpetuated by shame, not just of the abuse, but shame about breaking their silence, particularly in minority communities, which may already feel besieged by racism:

> ... from a Nigerian point of view women are very much shamed into silence. It's a shame if you make it known that your husbands beating you and not only is it a shame, it's like just get on with it. It happens, it's been happenin'—it happened for your grandmother, it happened for your mother... (raises voice) JUST GET ON WITH IT. That's life, that's men for you—and that's the kind of attitude –they kind of make you feel shamed and they kind of normalise the whole situation. (2014)

The dailyness of emotional abuse is pointed out by Liz, a lone parent:

I'd lost all that—all that confidence, when you're caring 24/7—it's not lifting, washing and dressing its more the emotional part of it—because its drugs, alcohol and mental health and it was the emotional part of it draining me and it was becoming groundhog day and I was tired and I was depressed and I was going on a real low. (Liz, 2017: Lines 39 to 43)

Loraine recounts why she and other LGBTQ women stayed silent about their identity for fear of having their children removed: '...that was a real worry which is why a lot of women stayed hidden' (2014, lines: 157–162). She comments that such suppression contributed to her depression.

Healicon (2016) points out that the majority of women who have experienced sexual violence tell no one and the cultural myths surrounding rape, leading to feelings of self-blame and 'an overwhelming sense of shame'. (55) Spivak's 1988 argument in 'Can the Subaltern Speak?' has become a mantra for those working to facilitate the empowerment of women. As she notes, the key ingredient of empowerment is not being *given* a voice but *demanding* a voice. Gill's (1993) research showed up inequalities in the boy's club of mainstream radio which still resonate. In *Justifying Injustice; broadcaster's accounts of inequality in radio*, she uses discourse analysis to explain the absence of women's voices and concludes that it looks:

> less like the result of a lack of applications from women, and more like a deliberate policy not to employ women—because of audiences' alleged preference for men rather than a woman's voice. (Gill, 1993: 76)

Not only are women shrouded in low confidence about producing and presenting radio, but their fear of technical learning is palpable: 'when you walk into the radio studio and you see all that equipment, you think...oh my god—am I going to be able to do that?' (Liz, 2017: Lines 110-116).

Whilst many British community stations lack diversity, and do not see their role as *working against subalternity*, some are stepping up to the mark, and arguably making more progress than public and commercial media. Manchester, England has 13 community stations, some specifically serving minority ethnic or LGBTQ communities (*Legacy 90.1FM*; *Gaydio 88.4FM*). Nevertheless, there is still little focus on equalising the contribution of women.

In addition to the more obvious low confidence and technical barriers, the women report complex, nuanced, intersectional issues, found in the dailyness of life (Lorde, 1984), which impact on their identities and challenge the presumed homogeneity of womanhood. Goikoetxea (2019: 206) examines the subjective aspects of intersectionality which are impossible to disaggregate. Fanon's (1961) arguments about the mental health effects of violence and colonialism remain pertinent and synthesize with well documented histories of women's mental health since the medieval witch trials. (Szasz, 1973; Showalter, 1987; Usher, 1991) these works foreground the notion of psychiatrization as a method of pacifying and controlling women who refuse conformity to submissive gender roles.

Similarly, Fanon highlights that the methodical denial of identity and perpetual violence, are a breeding ground for mental disorder. Whilst the colonial 'native cure' sought to: 'pacify and make him thoroughly a part of a social background of the colonial type' (1961: 200). What emerges from the radio women, is their need to find and establish their own identity, as if it has somehow been denied, reshaped or stolen. As Fanon (1961: 200) notes, in its: 'systematic negation...and furious determination to deny the other person all attributes of humanity, colonialism forces the people it dominates to ask themselves: 'In reality, who am I?'' Kimi was an aspiring actor, but left the career disillusioned and angry, after being offered only 'stereotyped roles', parts where she had to wear a hijab or sari or burqa: 'just because I'm brown', Kimi (2017) relates dealing with her anger, not with violent revolution or militant feminism, but by seeking counselling. Self blame and individual pathology is common amongst colonized people, it is an intended consequence of oppression. Biko (1978: 29) asserts the importance of conscious identity; of Knowing one's place in the world. After years of apartheid, he maintained that: 'the first step is to make the Black man come to himself; to pump back life into his empty shell; to infuse him with pride and dignity...this is the definition of Black consciousness'. Collette recounts: 'If I gave certain Black people a lift in my car I would hide my [music] CD'S by white artists as they would have a dig at me for being a Coconut'. (2017) The goal of intersectionality is not to find the different ingredients that make up identity, but to understand; stay with and 'inhabit the inevitable tensions' within it (Nayak & Robbins, 2019: 206).

Fanon proclaimed the 'new horizons' offered by radio, but in order to engage women, the trainers and the curriculum must understand and address the complex and corrosive interactions between racism, poverty, misogyny, refugeeism, disability and more. Ledwith (1997: 47) cautions that 'attempting to explain the vast diversity of experience of oppressions according to universal theories has resulted in a fragmented understanding of this complexity'. Fanon refers to colonialism demanding 'the expulsion of self' (1965: 65). In the women's stories and analysis there is much talk of hiding one's true identity, silently planning until such a time as it is safe to escape. Priceless observes:

> ... you see these women, their clothes look good and happy, but you never know the storms that's brewing on the inside—because I've lived in silence for years during my abuse with my ex and everyone thought I had the perfect marriage and my children—(puts on another voice) 'Oh your beautiful children, your beautiful marriage' and no-one has ever known, until I break the silence ... and move away, because no-one knew—everyone thought everything was OK until I step away from that marriage. (Priceless, 2017: lines: 85–94)

Fanon (1965: 66) maintains that women's silent existence borders on 'quasi absence' but she is building up her defense mechanisms, 'deepening her consciousness of struggle and preparing for combat'.

## Unveiling Women's Voices

Aside from the important relational aspects of women's empowerment fulfilled by community radio, the medium offers the unique opportunity of *disembodiment*. There are well documented accounts of damage done to women by media misrepresentation, objectification, pornification and by its power to define and homogenize womanhood (Levo-Henriksson 2007; Usher, 1997). Only when women have the opportunity to create their own media will they stop being: 'passive recipients of media misrepresentation' (Levo-Henriksson, 2007: 58). Maria concurs:

> I find it really nice to just be a voice. There's a power in that 'cos it's just you and what you want to say, sometimes maybe people hold back with their judgments if they can't see you. I think that could be something that could apply not just to a racial thing—you know how people see you and make assumptions. I do think that whoever you are and whatever you look like, radio can be a way of people just hearing your voice and maybe liking what you say. (Marie, 2017. Lines: 71-85).

Other positive features of being heard and not seen, are raised by the women, such as the use of body language, so frequently misinterpreted and judged in what Treat et al (2016: 985) call 'maladaptive cue-utilization patterns...particularly among men'. As noted by Croft (2010) in *The Secret Body Language of Girls*, women discuss body language as small gestures of resistance: '... it's not like in meetings cos nobody can see my hands on hips, or my fist clenched! ... and Nobody can see you going like this either'. (Rude gesture with fingers & laughter) (Group session, 2017, Lines:140-145).

In *Algeria Unveiled* (1965: 46), Fanon analyzes women's veiled bodies as shrouded in mystique and eroticism by the colonialist, who dreams of raping her, but the rape is: 'always preceded by a rending of the veil. We here witness a double-deflowering...never of consent or acceptance, but of abject humility'. With his focus on unveiling; on mystique and exoticism; the 'frightened attitude of the Algerian woman', Fanon is highlighting intersectional concerns well-rehearsed by Black feminist scholars (Crenshaw, 1991; Nayak, 2015). However, his assumptions that European white women are afforded respect (as if they are not also brutalized by men) and that they see Algerian women as shameless and amoral, requires further analysis. Radio offers women a veil which shields them from the *male gaze*, objectification and judgement, whilst enabling their wisdom to be heard, just as: 'the niqab protected me, I liked hiding from men. I could see them, but they couldn't see me' (De Fao, 2018).

Renault (2011) understands Fanon as seeing, in the radio movement, the *discourse of rupture*, an alternative voice which challenges the mainstream:

> the emergence of the *words* of the colonised...that each man feels rising within him...the defence strategy of the colonised subject who, still powerless to emit his own words, refused to listen to the master's voice...The

power to then name oneself by one's own name, bringing men towards freedom...bringing them to speak themselves (Renault, 2011: 114).

In aiding the discovery and amplification of women's voices, radio becomes, what Stuart Hall alluded to as a: 'critical site of social action, where power relations are both established and potentially unsettled... where socialism might be constituted' (Hall, 1981: 72).

That *lightbulb moment*; the notion of realisation; of positioning one's self in the world, a raised consciousness through dialogue with, learning from and listening to other women, is alluded to in critical theory as 'transformative' (hooks, 1994). 'Interaction which is respectful restores dignity and self-esteem, reverses the process of alienation by accepting individuals in their wholeness...' (Ledwith, 1997:72) After overcoming the barriers to radio engagement the women discuss their lightbulb moment:

> For many years I was silenced and its difficult –to break out of it when you're going through it. But the minute you realize you are being oppressed or silenced—that's the first wake up call for the individual—then its onwards and upwards and getting yourself out of it. Nobody can get you out of it, you can only get yourself out of it. (Ayisha, 2017: Lines: 318-323)

> It's been happenin' for years but there's a point in your life when you just can't take any more. (Priceless, 2017: Lines 93-94)

> ... and it's like a spark, a light switch goes on and you think 'I can't do this anymore, I'm gonna walk'. (Liz, group discussion, 2017: Lines: 115-116)

Fanon sees this 'mental liberation' as the radical change in consciousness required to revolt and break out of oppression, beginning with: 'the revolution in our minds, questioning everything that has been hitherto taken for granted... what had been normal for so long is fundamentally shaken' (Gibson, 2011: 3). None of the women here would say that their 'lightbulb' moment came to them without the support of others.

> We cared—if someone wasn't here we'd say where's so-and-so this week and we'd ring them. The radio training makes you make friends and share problems. (Loraine, 2017)

## Feeling Ten Feet Tall

> *You're gonna do live shows! I didn't dream of me doing that, being there lettin' my voice project out into the atmosphere.* —Priceless

At *Shout FM*, women are trained collectively using dialogic learning, providing a safe space to problematize and 'to dream'.Seller (2003: 26) The process of anti-colonial and anti-sexist training becomes an antidote to their hated traditional schooling which Macedo calls 'Literacy for Stupidification' (1993: 183), and McLaren claims is predatory: 'schools are vigorous mechanisms for the reproduction of dominant race, class, and gender relations and the imperial values of the dominant socio-political order' (1995: 229). Instead, radio training focuses on learning through friendship and shared experience. As Pallas posits:

> When individuals who have been oppressed by colonialism over a sustained period of time feel solidarity with those in similar situations to themselves, they begin to find a common purpose linked to the personal feeling of catharsis that comes with reclaiming their state (*Critical Legal Thinking online blog*, 2016).

hooks (2008: 293) sees this process as feminist pedagogy, challenging the masculinist focus of 'hardness and toughness which prevents acknowledgement of the enormous grief and pain in Black life'. She also censures educationalists for shutting down the magic and fun in active learning. In radio, where technical skill is equated with masculinity, the antidote is relationship building and a leveling of power between learner and tutor. The technical 'work objects' in radio—i.e. operating the mixing desk or editing, become almost a side issue when conveyed through a relationship involving care, fun and laughter...and inevitably mistakes by tutor and learner. This 'pedagogy of love' (Freire, 1997; hooks, 1994, Darder, 2017) is referred to by Dunbar-Hester (2014: 55) as: 'the work of pedagogy in technological activism'.

Anecdotal evidence from examining radio schedules, is that radio programmes broadcast by women in community radio are more likely to be group affairs and include discussion, interviews and awareness-raising: 'You bring education into your show—to show that Muslims aren't all terrorists etc. On my last show I had someone doing American native drumming'. (Loraine, 2017: lines: 92–97). Kate and co-presenter host a show serving the LBGTQ community, others include regular features on issues like abuse and female genital mutilation; a variety of unrepresented languages, such as Pidgin English and music, such as Lollywood film tracks. Vee, a disabled presenter, hosts a disability rights show and Liz, a carer's show.

'The *radio revolution* sounds preposterous, yet the Arab Spring has become known as the Facebook Revolution'(Netherly, 2011 online blog). Overall, community radio emerges at the very least, as a template for the engagement and empowerment of women through radio. It is a site of anti-colonial feminist pedagogy and social action in which diverse cultural identities are realized, through friendship, dialogue, laughter and solidarity.

> What Community Radio is about is giving 'lesser' people...people like myself who aren't of the mainstream—giving lesser people a chance. I got a really nice text the other week from someone who'd listened to my show and they thought it was really good. That makes you feel *10 feet tall!* (Collette, 2014: Lines 366-376)

# Conclusion

> *The fruitful use that can be made of the radio can well be imagined.*
> —Fanon, '*This the Voice of Algeria*'

Emergent from the women's stories, is the notion that there is no one *womanhood*, but a rich array of identities within the group and within each woman. The concept of empowerment is consistently framed as collective and relative—it is only effective when it can be used to help others. Radio is seen as: 'the power of bringing the community together so we can think: 'there's more to life than just your own individual misery'. (Madonna, 2017: lines 214-216). Inviting radio guests who represent charities or campaigns is an essential use of radio: 'it's about empowering me to empower other disabled people' (Vee, 2014). Individually, some define empowerment as *creativity*—it is for some, their first experience of having creative space, support and friendships. Jessica describes her radio show as: 'my own little creation', after years of loneliness which she describes as akin to 'a physical pain'. In particular, the advantage of radio is in its disembodiment, being heard and not seen. Women of color feel specifically strengthened to be themselves, unbound by racial or gendered stereotypes. The thrill of restored confidence and the privilege of having a voice on radio is palpable.

In the sixty years since *Wretched of the Earth* and fifty years since *Pedagogy of the Oppressed*, there has been much critique, updating and adaptation, particularly by feminist scholars (Lorde, 1991; hooks,1994; Burman, 2019). Fanon's ideas about women resonate with critical and feminist pedagogy and fit neatly into the ontology of a chapter about silence, voice and empowerment; despite his perception of women being occasionally romanticized and her role in struggle idealized. *Black Skin, White Masks*, is arguably more perceptive and described by Baucom (2001: 15) as 'diverse acts of listening', it 'is often less Fanon's text than a compilation of those voices to which he has inclined his ear and a record of his responses to what he has been hearing'. This locates Fanon's relevance in anti-colonial, grassroots work today. Community radio is one example of how a group of ordinary women can be heard in the process of analyzing their lives and identities, modernizing his ideas in a way which takes care to address the nuanced, daily pains and joys of diverse womanhood.

At time of writing, women's groups are still being trained at *Shout FM* during the COVID-19 pandemic. Though the training takes place mostly online, the camaraderie and feelings of solidarity, are still present, and much needed to combat isolation. The backdrop of Black Lives Matter demonstrations brings TV images of slave-owner statues being brought down and the *Topple the Racist* website (2020) is crowdsourcing a list of more targets. Whilst most feminist scholars do not wish to untopple the male canons of social theory; there is an argument for an epistemology of womanhood to take its rightful place on the plinth. The narratives of these ordinary women reflect their struggle and serve to redefine their identities; challenging much more than the male orthodoxy of radio. It is heart-rending to note their incredulity upon rediscovering their voice and finding new skills:

I never ever in a million years thought I could do my own radio show—no more than I could have been a beauty queen. (Collette, 2014: Lines 277-283)

It's the first time I've really done something that I can honestly say that without any contradiction that I'm good at it. I just love it. I just love my show and the great thing is it's all been off my own bat, no body's told me what to do or what to put in it, it's all come from my ideas it's been great to be able to channel my ideas into something that's actually tangible, it's audible. (Vee, 2014: Lines: 506-516)

Sixty years after Fanon women still have multiple reasons to revolt and alternative radio offers them a means of refusal to *imitate the mainstream*, which has, arguably, *done what it set out to do*, in keeping them down. It is time for Black and white women's histories to be told; to "affirm the lives of Black queer and trans folks, disabled folks, undocumented folks, folks with records, women and all Black lives along the gender spectrum' (Black Lives Matter, 2020).

Women's voices have been universally silenced and power and audibility go hand in hand. (Solnit, 2017) Community radio may not lead to decolonizing, or unsilencing womanhood; nor to a vociferous woman's revolution, nor is it the panacea for gender or race oppression; the complex, historical, deep-rooted, structural issues involved in women's silencing. However, the chapter characterizes radio as a significant metaphor for women's empowerment and suggests that community radio projects are potential sites of activism for change. In Fanon's terms, such projects find women at the beginning of their 'the battle for liberation' (1965: 65). His resonance for today lies in his uncovering the real identities of colonized people; his amplification of unheard stories which challenge the: 'interlocking, interdependent nature of systems of domination' (hooks, 2008: 290).

Like the toppling of statues, the narratives are political acts and we must turn over a new leaf: 'we need a political act now that speaks for the people that didn't have the power. That is a new type of sculpture' (Van Hensbergen, 2020).

## Bibliography

Adebisi, F. I. 2020. 'Foluke's African Skies Blog'. Accessed November 6, 2020, https://folukeafrica.com.

Agenda. 2020. 'Often Overlooked: Young Women, Poverty and Self-harm.' Accessed June 7, 2020, https://weareagenda.org/wp-content/uploads/2017/03/Often-Overlooked-Young-women-poverty-and-self-harm-2.pdf.

Akasha, Y. 2014. 'Darfur Radio Station Exposes the Use of Rape as Weapon of War.' *Guardian Newspaper*. Accessed June 12, 2015, https://www.theguardian.com/world/2014/dec/11/-sp-darfur-rape-radio-dabanga.

Alston, P. 2018. 'Statement on Visit to the United Kingdom.' *United Nations Special Rapporteur on Extreme Poverty and Human Rights*. Accessed November 19, 2018, https://www.ohchr.org/Documents/Issues/Poverty/EOM_GB_16Nov2018.pdf.

Baucom, I. 2001. 'Frantz Fanon's Radio: Solidarity, Diaspora, and the Tactics of Listening.' *Contemporary Literature* 42 (1, spring): 15–49.

Black Lives Matter. 2020. Accessed June 6, 2020, https://blacklivesmatter.com/about/.

Brockes, E. 2018. 'I Wanted to Flood the Red Carpet with Badasses.' *The Guardian Newspaper*.

Burke, T. 2018. Interview by Brockes, E. (2018): 'I Wanted to Flood the Red Carpet with Badasses.' *The Guardian Newspaper*, January 15, 2018.

Burman, E. 2019. *Fanon, Education, Action. Child as Method*. London: Routledge.

Crenshaw, K. 1991. 'Mapping the Margins: Intersectionality, Identity Politics, and Violence Against Women of Color.' *Stanford Law Review* 43(6): 1241–1299.

Croft, M. 2010. *The Secret Body Language of Girls: Decoding the Far-Too-Subtle Body Language of Women*. London: Pavilion.

Curry Jansen, S., Pooley, J., and Taub-Pervizpour, L., eds. 2011. *Media and Social Justice*. Basingstoke: Palgrave Macmillan.

Dagron, A. G. 2007. 'Call Me Impure: Myths and Paradigms of Participatory Communication.' In *The Power of Global Community Media*, edited by Fuller, L., 197–207. Basingstoke: Palgrave Macmillan.

Darder, A. 2017. *Reinventing Paulo Freire: A Pedagogy of Love*. London: Routledge.

De Fao, A. 2018. 'After the Niqab, What Life is like for French Women Who Remove the Veil.' *The Independent*, February 27, 2018. Accessed June 29, 2018, https://theconversation.com/after-the-niqab-what-life-is-like-for-french-women-who-remove-the-veil-91192.

Dei, G. J. S. 2017. *Reframing Blackness and Black Solidarities through Anti-Colonial and Decolonial Prisms*. New York: Springer International.

Dunbar–Hester, C. 2014. *Low Power to the People: Pirates, Protest, and Politics in FM Radio Activism*. Cambridge: MIT Press.

Fanon, F. 1961. *The Wretched of the Earth*. London: Penguin.

_____. 1965. *A Dying Colonialism*. New York: Grove Press.

_____.1967. *Black Skin, White Masks*. New York: Grove Press.

Fielding, M. 2006. 'Empowerment: Emancipation or Enervation?' *Journal of Education Policy* 11 (3): 399–417.

Freire, P. 1970, 1972 and 1977. *Pedagogy of the Oppressed*. London: Penguin.

_____. 1997. *Pedagogy of the Heart*. New York: Continuum.

Gaydio Radio Manchester. 2021. Accessed January 8, 2021, https://www.gaydio.co.uk/.

Gaynor, N., and O'Brien, A. 2017. 'Community Radio, Democratic Participation and the Public Sphere.' *Irish Journal of Sociology* 25 (1): 29–47.

Gibson, N. C. ed. 2011. *Living Fanon: Global Perspectives*. New York: Palgrave.

_____. 2016. 'Tunis Connections: Concatenations and Missed Opportunities, Bond, Fanon, Foucault.' *Journal of Asian and African Studies* 51 (3): 370–386.

Gill, R. 1993. 'Justifying Injustice; Broadcaster's Accounts of Inequality in Radio.' In *Discourse Analytic Research: Repertoires and Readings of Texts in Action*, edited by Burman, E., and Parker, I. London: Routledge. Accessed August 31, 2015, http://www.heron.dmu.ac.uk/2006-02-28/0415097207(75-93)51895.pdf.

Hall, S. 1981. 'Notes on Deconstructing 'the Popular.' In *Cultural Theory, An Anthology*, edited by Szeman, I., and Kaposy, T. [2011]. Oxford: Blackwells.

Healicon, A. 2016. *The Politics of Sexual Violence: Rape, Identity and Feminism*. Basingstoke: Palgrave Macmillan.

Hooks, B. 1994. *Outlaw Culture: Resisting Representations*. New York: Routledge.

_____. 2015. *Yearning: Race, Gender and Cultural Politics*. London: Routledge.

Ibrahim, Z. 2000. 'Tarzan Doesn't Live Here Anymore.' *International Journal of Cultural Studies* 3 (2): 199–205.

Jayaprakash, Y. T., and Shoesmith, B. 2007. 'Community Radio and Development: Tribal Audiences in South Asia.' In *The Power of Global Community Media*, edited by Fuller, L. K. Basingstoke: Palgrave Macmillan.

Johnson, P. 2004. 'Black Radio Politically Defined: Communicating Community and Political Empowerment Through Stevie Wonder's KJLH-FM, 1992–2002.' *Political Communication Journal* 21 (3, July–September): 353–336.

Katrak, K. H. 2006. *Politics of the Female body, Post-Colonial Women Writers of the Third World*. Rutgers University Press.

Kenlock, N. 2013. 'After the Demise of Choice FM, Is It Back to Pirate Radio for Black Britons?' *GuardianOnline*. Accessed May 18, 2014, http://www.theguardian.com/commentisfree/2013/nov/14/demise-choice-fm-pirate-radio-black-britons-capital-xtra.

KJLH-FM. 2020. Accessed July 6, 2020, https://www.facebook.com/radiofreekjlh/.

Ledwith, M. 1997. *Participation in Transformation. Towards a Working Model of Community Empowerment*. Birmingham: Venture.

Legacy 90.1 Radio Station Manchester. 2021. Accessed January 8, 2021, https://legacy901.com/.

Levo-Henriksson, R. 2007. 'Media as Constructor of Ethnic Minority Identity: A Native American Case Study.' In *The Power of Global Community Media*, edited by Fuller, L. Basingstoke: Palgrave Macmillan.

Lorde, A. 1984. *Sister Outsider: Essays and Speeches*. Place: Crossing Press.

Luke, C., and Gore, J., eds. 1992. *Feminisms and Critical Pedagogy*. New York: Routledge.

McLaren, P. 1995. *Critical Pedagogy and Predatory Culture: Oppositional Politics in a Postmodern era*. London: Routledge.

Macedo, D. 1993. 'Literacy for Stupidification.' *Harvard Educational Review* 63 (2): 183–206.

Mullender, A., Ward, D., and Fleming, J. 2013. *Empowerment in Action; Self-Directed Groupwork*. Basingstoke: Palgrave Macmillan.

Nayak, S. 2015. *Race, Gender and the Activism of Black Feminist Theory Working with Audre Lorde*. Hove: Routledge.

Nayak, S., and Robbins, R. 2019. *Intersectionality in Social Work: Activism and Practice in Context*. London: Routledge.

Netherly, D. 2011. 'International Broadcasting Revolution.' Blog. Accessed April 3, 2017, http://insidestory.org.au/broadcasting-revolution/.

Noronha, F. 2003. 'Community Radio: Singing New Tunes in South Asia.' *Economic and Political Weekly*, May 31: 2168–2172.

Pallas, J. 2016. 'Critical Legal Thinking Blog.' Accessed January 8, 2021, https://criticallegalthinking.com/2016/01/20/fanon-on-violence-and-the-person/.

Paranjape, N. 2007. 'Community Media: Local is Focal.' *Community Development Journal* 42 (4, October): 459–469.

Pavarala, V. 2015. 'Community Radio "Under Progress".' *Economic & Political Weekly* 1 (51, December 19): 14–17.

Popple, K. 2015. *Analysing Community Work: Theory and Practice*. Maidenhead: OUP.

Renault, M. 2011. 'Rupture and New Beginning in Fanon: Elements for a Genealogy of Postcolonial Critique.' In *Living Fanon: Global Perspectives*, edited by Gibson, N. C. Basingstoke: Palgrave Macmillan.

Poulain, S. 2016. 'Revolt in the Air—Radio Activism, Protest and Politics.' Accessed June 8, 2020, http://explosivepolitics.com/blog/revolt-on-the-air-radio-activism-protest-and-french-politics/.

Radio Debout. 2021. Accessed April 2, 2021, https://www.radiocampusparis.org/radio-debout/.

Seller, A. 2003. In *Action for Social Justice in Education*, edited by Griffiths, M. [1998]. Maidenhead: OUP.

Showalter, E. 1987. *The Female Malady*. London: Virago.

Sigona, N. 2014. 'The Politics of Refugee Voices: Representations, Narratives, and Memories.' In *The Oxford Handbook of Refugee and Forced Migration Studies*, edited by Fiddian-Qasmiveh, E., Loescher, G., Long, K., and Sigona, N. Oxford: Oxford University Press.

Solnit, R. 2017. *The Mother of All Questions*. Chicago: Haymarket.

Spivak, G. C. 1988. 'Can the Subaltern Speak?' In *Marxism and the Interpretation of Culture*, edited by Nelson, C., and Grossberg, L., 271–313 and 271–313. Basingstoke: Macmillan and Chicago: University of Illinois.

Szasz, T. S. 1973. *The Manufacture of Madness*. London: Palladin.

Tuck, E., and Yang, K. W. 2012. 'Decolonization Is Not a Metaphor.' *Decolonization: Indigeneity, Education & Society* 1 (1): 1–40. Accessed October 10, 2017, *http://www.decolonization.org/index.php/des/article/view/18630/15554*.

Usher, J. 1991. *Women's Madness: Misogyny or Mental Illness?* London: Harvester Wheatsheaf.

———. 1997. *Fantasies of Femininity, Reframing the Boundaries of Sex*. London: Penguin.

Van Hensbergen, C. 2020. 'When We Tear Down Racist Statues, What Should Replace Them?' Accessed January 7, 2020, https://www.wired.co.uk/article/topple-racist-statues-uk.

Webb, L. M., Allen, M. W., and Walker, K. L. 2002. 'Feminist Pedagogy: Identifying Basic Principles.' *Academic Exchange Quarterly* 6 (March): 67–72.

# PART II:
## STILL FANON

when faced with
criminality. We ▮▮ see

a permanent state

We have seen
the

world, bulldozing the masses,

The guard
knows
he is configured by the
colonizer,
considers it
a sword of
authority.
He is
the
muscles of the

persecutor.
the police

do not signify: "Stay where you are." But
rather "Get ready

'Blacked-out-poem' by Leah Kindler based on Fanon's *The Wretched of the Earth.*

# PAKISTAN: THE IMMEDIACY OF FRANTZ FANON

Ayyaz Mallick

*The time had come to (re-)read [the classics] .... Not in the piety of an eternal return to the founding texts, but rather as a necessary detour towards our own present, via byways on which one might meet forgotten companions, discover hidden elective affinities and disconcerting astral attractions.*
—Daniel Bensaïd , *An Impatient Life: A Memoir*

Pakistan is not the first place which comes to mind when we think of Frantz Fanon, nor is Fanon the first revolutionary you would think of when it comes to Pakistan. But the classics are classics, among other reasons, precisely because of the immediacy with which we feel their appeal in times and climes far removed from their formulation. Indeed, it is this immediacy and, in fact, this viscerality of Fanon's description of a colonial world 'divided into compartments', the quest to 'turn over a new leaf', along with—let's say—those famous descriptions of the 'working day' (Marx) and 'reification' (Lukács) which continue to affirm their status as classics today—their capacity to puncture the self-satisfaction of the present and awaken us to its inescapable nightmares, the slaughter house of history which seems to have become our fate today like a bad infinity.

It is this theme of 'immediacy' around which I would like to organize this (semi-autobiographical) reflection on Fanon and Pakistan. 'Immediacy' of course—along with its dialectical counterpoint: mediation—is a fulcrum around which much, if not all, of Fanon's oeuvre may be understood. Indeed, Fanon's 'subversive fidelity to Hegel' (Gidwani and Kumar, 2019: 155), his rebellious flights of argument with—among others—Sartre and Senghor, his elective affinities with Gramsci, can all be organised around the theme of immediacy-mediation. And among these custodians of humanity's critical and revolutionary impulse, it is Fanon whose fidelity to the particular, whose insistence on 'the labour of the negative' (Hegel quoted in Hudis, 2017: 870), distinguishes his oeuvre and makes him so amenable to travel and translation across our tortured present. 'Immediacy' is thus a theme without whose understanding it is difficult, if not impossible, to grasp the fullness of Fanon's dialectical humanism and, dare I say, his *universal* vision of emancipation.

I will also lean on the authority of Fanon and his insistence on the moment of immediacy to justify the semi-autobiographical tenor of this essay, not as an exercise in narcissism, but instead as an act of opening out and into the world: 'consciousness of the self', Fanon reminds us, '[as] not the closing of a door to communication... [but as] its guarantee' (Fanon, 1968: 199).[1] The 'self'—not unrelated to 'immediacy'—is of course another key leitmotif in Fanon—his plunge into the depths of the (colonized) person, an excavation of her 'thingification' and its 'sociogenesis' an ineluctable moment in his wider oeuvre (Gordon, 2015). However, while I will rely on my encounters with Fanon (or, better still, with Fanons) to talk about Pakistan, I will not do so in the critical psychiatric register that he deploys. I narrate my own experience of Fanon to demonstrate the many ways he remains *actual* in Pakistan in his existential, sociological, and political dimensions. On this short journey, we will also (briefly) encounter the different Fanons who have made their way to Pakistan and the conditions of possibility of his travels and translation as such. We will thus shed light on two distinct, but related, senses of Fanon's immediacy: one, and most importantly, the warnings, the familiarity, and indeed the viscerality of Fanon to our classically post-colonial nightmare in Pakistan; and two, in a more submerged manner,[2] the more epistemological (and political) reflections on the importance of the moment of immediacy in Fanon's 'dialectic of experience' and the many dangers and diversions awaiting us on this tortured road to enlightenment. It is these multi-sided actualities, the many immediacies of Fanon, that will eventually bring us back to the question of mediation, and some of the (dare I say) troubling insights I see emerging from Fanon for Pakistan today.

The semi-autobiographical tenor of the essay and its reading of the Martinican therefore is not intended as self-congratulatory satisfaction in my recovery of a 'pure' Fanon; but, and just as with Bensaïd's poignant vignette above on reading and re-reading the classics today, it is a necessary detour on the byways and side-streets of revolution, the moment of pause in the heat of struggle, where we take account of our forces (both material and intellectual), and search for forgotten companions who too have affirmed the 'open dimension of every consciousness' and, therefore, 'the universalism inherent in the human condition' (Fanon, 1952: xvi, 206 ).[3] In short, it is an act of return as a necessary point of departure, a looking back to look forward.

## Baleful Footnotes, Baneful Inconsequence: The Class Which is Not (Even) a Class

I remember the exact moment I encountered Frantz Fanon for the first time. It was sometime in 2011, I was reading Biochemistry at Oxford, but had taken up a habit of meandering half-aimlessly through the many social science and humanities libraries of the city. It is in one of these wanderings through the library of

---

1. In-text citations of *The Wretched of the Earth* henceforth abbreviated to (WE: page number).
2. Mainly because others have done this before much more ably and thoroughly. See, for example, Sekyi-Otu (1996) and Gibson (2003).
3. In-text citations of *Black Skin, White Masks* henceforth abbreviated to (BS: page number).

the Politics & IR Department, half-eyed musing over the stacks, that one curious title caught my eye: *The Wretched of the Earth*.

On the cover (the Penguin Classics edition): a (black) man sitting on some kind of wooden or cement plank attached to a wall, clothes hung loosely on a lithe (wasting?) body, one exposed leg dangling over the platform, another drawn up towards his chest, elbow resting on the drawn up knee, and hand resting on a capped head in a way that hid one eye, signalling either despair or tiredness (maybe a bit of both), while the other eye half-askance seemed to be asking: will you simply pass this by or actually read it?

Not one to simply ignore strangers with curiously-titled books, I turned over to the back cover. Here, words and phrases from an assessment from *The Independent* jumped out: 'the cool heat of rage', 'classic text', 'inspiration for anti-colonial movements'. Curiouser still. No choice but to check it out.

Later that evening as I turned my attentions to Sartre's preface and then Fanon's first chapter, what would strike me was not the (so-called) justification of violence, but the heat, the sheer brightness of the words—many of which seared themselves in my mind's eye: 'our victims know us by our scars', 'shame, as Marx once put it, is a revolutionary sentiment', 'France was once the name of a country, we should take care it does not become the name of a nervous disease', 'decolonisation is a program of complete disorder', 'total, complete, and absolute substitution' (WE: 12, 25, 27).

As I kept reading however, and this might sound surprising considering Fanon's reception in popular culture and indeed prevalent trends in the academe, it was not the ruminations on violence or racial Manicheism which would stay with me. Much of this of course was because of my own social upbringing. A middle-class *Muhajir*/Urdu-speaking boy who had grown up in Karachi at the height of the urban militancy of the 1990s—a combination of ethnicized turf wars, gun-toting youth, wanton killings and torture, and military and paramilitary operations—violence, its advocacy, or an excavation of its sociological and psychological roots, hardly shocked me. Nor did the descriptions of compartmentalized cities, dividing lines policed and haunted by various self-proclaimed guarantors of order, elicit much surprise. I had grown up, after all, in a *mohalla* [neighbourhood] where the evening round of street cricket would be followed by a night-long curfew, active gun battles between the police/paramilitary and the *mohalla* militias, and a taken-for-granted—indeed naturalized—demarcation of territories between the Urdu-speakers and the various 'others' who laid claim to Karachi —from the Pashto-speaking migrants to more indigenous Sindhi-speakers.

No, what struck me in that first, uninitiated reading—and indeed has stayed with me ever since—were those deliciously disparaging descriptions of that most useless of all useless social groups: the national bourgeoisie of the (post-)colony. It was as if Fanon—this man reeling from the failures of his many attempts to become *a man*, writing with the accumulated rage of centuries of humiliation, distilling the red-hot experiences of an arduous armed struggle, and (though I did not know this at the time) in the premature twilight of his life—it was almost as if he delighted and reveled in inventing new descriptors for this motley crew of 'baneful inconsequence' (Sekyi-Otu, 1996: 154).

To understand *this* immediacy of Fanon, a bit of a background: I had been part of a generation of young Pakistanis—especially those from its 'core' areas—whose politicization had happened through the recently concluded, pro-democracy Lawyers' Movement. In the late 1990s and early 2000s, we had grown up under the martial rule of Pakistan's latest military dictator (the fourth since the late 1950s) and a country where every political problem seemed to dissolve itself into the contradiction of (military) dictatorship versus (civilian) democracy. Indeed, I and many like me in their late teens and twenties had come out on the streets in 2007 to redeem that one irrefutable promise we believed guaranteed to us by God, Independence, and the Constitution: government of the people, by the people, and for the people. Many of us had taken beatings at the hands of the police, doused (in classic colonial fashion) by powerful jets of water cannon, forced to be underground on nights of heightened danger, or—more prosaically—written blogs and protested outside Pakistan embassies abroad in a quest to get rid of General Musharraf —America's 'most allied ally', latest avatar of Truman's cynical pronouncement: 'he may be a bastard, but he is our (i.e. the US's) bastard'. The 2000s themselves had passed by amidst increasing religious millenarianism (despite the so-called 'War on Terror'), the wholesale mortgage of Pakistan's economic sovereignty to IMF dictates, a neoliberal bonanza of an economy predicated on import-based consumption, a proliferating range of military operations in 'peripheral' areas, a khaki aristocracy and its assorted minions with tentacles in all crevices of the country's politics and economy, and a pantomime of freedom enacted every day on the booming private media, a daily titillation of exposes, scandals, and transgressions of one elite actor after the other, serving the purpose not of the accountability of said callous elite, but of a circus of dissimulation.

And thus, when in 2007 a Supreme Court judge—who had previously taken a stand against privatization of state enterprises and against the soldiers of the night who had taken to 'disappearing' people in broad daylight—refused to resign on the dictates of the Generalissimo, the dammed reservoir of rage and discontent had burst. Led by the young (especially those in 'core' cities such as Lahore and Karachi), the movement erupted on streets, key universities and colleges, and public squares to first demand the restoration of the forcibly removed judge and, eventually, to demand an end to military rule itself and the restoration of democracy. Poems and poets who had written and sung against previous military strongmen had become fashionable again, a long poem—by jailed lawyer and politician Aitzaz Ahsan—becoming the anthem of the movement: *ryasat ho gi maa ke jaisi*, 'the state shall be like a mother'. It is in this moment of insurgency that Benazir Bhutto—living symbol of struggle against the dictatorship of the 1980s—had returned to Pakistan, her previous sins forgotten amidst much popular acclaim and hope, and then proceeded to become a martyr—joining her father Zulfiqar Ali Bhutto, hanged by the previous military dictator, to become yet another symbol of Pakistani masses' long and tortured struggle for democracy.

General Musharraf was finally forced out of the presidency in 2008, general elections were held, and democracy restored. For many—including myself—this was a moment of much hope, the great redressal and restoration of the universe's balance: the military was back in the barracks, a civilian (Bhutto's widower) took over as President, the upright judges reinstated, and rule of the people, for the people seemed restored on the back of a popular movement. Predictably, we were being set up for even greater disappointments. Pakistan entered another debilitating IMF program on the back of a deep balance of payments crisis (exacerbated by the effects of the global financial crash), US drone attacks in northwestern regions increased, the millenarian violence of the religious right penetrated the mosques and bazaars of core Pakistani cities, military operations in peripheral areas took on a new intensity, and disappearances of activists and intellectuals became an open state policy. Government instead of being returned to the people became a means of their immobilization and silencing, a melancholia all-the-more menacing for following on the footsteps of those moments of exhilaration where we had confronted the might of a dictatorship and, at least seemingly, defeated it. The long night of praetorian rule had given way to various disguised and open forms of coercion and austerity. And instead of living and making the fullness of time, here we were stuck in the bad infinity of circular time. The more things changed the more they seemed to remain the same.

It is amid this disorientation that 'The Pitfalls of National Consciousness' came to me as that douse of cold water, whereby 'man [sic] is at last compelled to face with sober senses his real conditions of life' (Marx and Engels, 1848: 16). Here was no consolation in the slow cajolings of liberal democracy or its incremental promise of progress. Nor was there the pessimism which would consign our condition to some culturally-ordained disposition to authoritarianism among the black and brown peoples of the world. No, Fanon compelled us to look at the post-Independence ruling bloc in its face, and not in its self-proclaimed satisfactions as upholders of 'civilian rule' or 'democratic values'. Fanon asked us to take account of its rhythms of accumulation, its inability to forge a productive base sufficient for an expansive hegemonic project, its grovelling obsequiousness to imperialism as a function of material inadequacy, and finally its cynical deployment of the cudgels of authoritarianism, patriotism, and religion as born out of a social deficit.

Here then was Fanon, fifty years later, throwing down the gauntlet with uncanny prescience: what was the Pakistani ruling bloc's hegemonic project? What spatial and social bases of (sustainable) accumulation is it based on? What vision has it offered toiling masses beyond the crumbs and obfuscations of patrimonialism, praetorianism, and religion? What coherent understanding of national culture has it produced that would truly and democratically value all of Pakistan's myriad oppressed classes, nations, and languages?

For Pakistan's ruling classes have neither had the capacity nor the willingness to form any viable and coherent hegemonic project of their own since Independence in 1947. Initial forays into a project of Import Substitution Industrialization (ISI) in the 1950s and 60s were itself funded majorly by the US as part of its Cold War project to build-up Pakistan (and its military) as a regional bulwark against communism. Any project of sustainable industrialization sub-sequently floundered on the fluctuations of international aid and—even more debilitatingly —on the neocolonial exploitation of East Pakistan (now separated as Bangladesh)—East Pakistan provided 60% of foreign exchange and 40% of the market for West Pakistani industrialists in this period (Nations, 1971: 21-22). And once this neocolonial relationship was broken after a brutal civil war in 1971, even this anemic vision of ISI was left in the doldrums. With the worldwide eco-nomic downturn of the 1970s following close upon the heels of the '71 crisis and then the ravages of neoliberalism, any integral project of sustainable accumula-tion—based at least minimally on land reforms, industrialization, nationaliza-tion of key sectors, and internally-focussed development—had been foreclosed.

For coherence and saving grace then, the Pakistani ruling bloc had been drawn even more closely into the poisoned embrace of the US imperium and its vari-ous regional partners. Aid for facilitating the various regional machinations of global imperialism (first, anti-Soviet 'jihad' in Afghanistan in the 1980s and then the so-called War on Terror) and an export of its labouring classes to various Western and Gulf countries becoming the most important sources of economic stabilization and core media of Pakistan's dependency on the world-system. The confluence of praetorianism, patrimonialism, and imperial coddling turned the military into its own mighty corporate empire worth over $20 billion, with deep penetration into each pore of the state apparatus (Jalal, 1990; Blom, 2011: 31)—this in turn led, as Fanon forewarned, to 'a crystallisation of the caste spirit' and 'drawing-room generals, [who] by dint of haunting the corridors of powers come to dream of manifestos' (WE: 163). It is in this context of a narrow, almost non-existent hegemonic project, an anemic productive base, an expanding mil-itary-industrial complex, and a reliance on imperial patronage for any kind of economic and social coherence, that a military-dominated authoritarianism had become a defining feature of the Pakistani polity. No consolation to be received here in the seductive promises of liberal democracy, nor in the simple binary of dictatorship versus democracy. For the civil-military faultlines of the Pakistani polity were not simply a zero-sum game to be reduced to an eternal oscillation between democracy versus dictatorship, but this faultline itself was integrally conditioned and perpetuated by these wider conditions of possibility. 'Every-thing must be started from scratch', Fanon was saying to us (WE: 142).

It is thus Fanon's descriptions of the deprivations and depravations of the post-Independence ruling bloc that unveiled these considerations for me. For nowhere in The Wretched is Fanon at his most impatient, his most impassioned, and his most eviscerating than in his exhortations to skip this 'completely useless phase in the history of under-developed countries' (WE: 142). The plethora of terms deployed to describe its 'precocious senility' tell a story in themselves about this social group whom—tellingly—Fanon does not even deign to dignify with the designation of a class. At various points therefore, he calls them 'a trade union of individual interests', 'members of a gang', 'a caricature', 'a bourgeoisie in spirit only', 'a caste', 'little greedy caste', and to add a final insult to injury: a motley crew 'which has not yet [even] the homogeneity of caste' (WE: 134, 136, 139, 142, 144).

In fact, these tendencies towards incoherence, caricature, and senility had become even more pronounced in the post-1980s conjuncture of structural adjustment, and especially since the onset-in-earnest of neoliberal restructuring in 2000s. As production became increasingly subject to the rhythms of the world market, taxes on the privileged decreased or remained stagnant, productive bases were eroded by privatization and shifts to a more services-based economy,[4] the social bases of the ruling bloc threatened to narrow even further. Here was Fanon telling us about a ruling bloc 'unable to bring about coherent social relations', and thus in a bid for mass pacification and indeed to manage contradictions within the ruling bloc itself, resorting to a state that 'does not... reassure the ordinary citizen, but rather one that rouses his anxiety' (WE: 132).

A ruling bloc internally disoriented, suffering from recurring crises of accumulation, is thus lent coherence by a combination of imperialist dependency, military-dominated authoritarianism, and a shallow ideological cocktail of religion, praetorian nationalism, and imitation. So, on the one hand, with their constant balance of payments of crisis and need for imperial patronage, and in a new conjuncture with the global imperium's power coordinates shifting, Pakistan's ruling bloc has been playing a balancing game between competing imperial and sub-imperial powers: the US, China, Saudi Arabia, Turkey, and others. Twist and shift, they turn here one moment only to turn to another next moment, all in a quest to sell their laboring classes, their land, and—most often—their military services to the highest bidder. Thus, where the military was happy to mortgage its services to various Gulf dictatorships in a bid to quell the Arab spring, it has also competed with other dominant fractions over a bid to offer services and become junior partners for the increasing Chinese investment in Pakistan (Mashal, 2011; Ghumman, 2016). On the other hand, there is also a bid to maintain US-linkages especially as the so-called 'Great Game' in neighboring Afghanistan winds down and the prospect of future US aid and military equipment diminishes. Here then is the Pakistani ruling bloc's veritable dance over the hot coals of imperialism, jumping from one dependent 'alliance' to another, unable to balance or maintain any on a sustainable basis, and with ruinous consequences for all involved.

Weak hegemony would thus need the bluster of pomp and show to prop it up. And so we encounter those clownish behaviors, that utter stupidity, which compelled Fanon to call the national bourgeoisie of the (post-)colony 'a bourgeoisie in spirit only' (WE: 144). A recent headline and news story would suffice here to make my point (Hussain, 2021):

---

4. The service sector now accounts for close to half of the country's GDP, up from a quarter of GDP in the 1950s. Since the 1980s, as a percentage of GDP, investment in manufacturing has been in a secular decline, while the services sector has seen the most investment head its way. In the absence of substantive land-reforms and declining agriculture too, this is a recipe for a low-productivity economy with weak absorption of labor mainly through atomized, personalized, and insecure arrangements. In short, a most unstable basis for a coherent hegemonic project if there ever was one. See Jan (2016); Munir and Naqvi (2017); Kardar (2018); Waheed and Ghumman (2019).

---

### PAKISTANI BUILDER MAKING 'EXACT' COPY OF PARIS IN GUJRANWALA

*Scheme to have world's second biggest Eiffel Tower*

A developer is launching a 'complete' replica of Europe's popular city of Paris outside Gujranwala.... Le Paris will have its own 200m Eiffel Tower, which will make it the biggest replica in the world. The original Eiffel Tower is 324 metres tall. If built, Le Paris's Eiffel Tower will outdo Bahria Town Lahore's replica, which stands at 80 metres. The housing scheme will also have replica Arc de Triomphe and a road it is calling Shanzelize street (after Avenue des Champs–Élysées).

France's AREP Group and Renzo Piano Building Workshop will be undertaking the town planning, design and architecture.

'Pakistanis will not have to go to Europe,' said Bilal Sandhu, the marketing manager. 'The city will give affordable houses but will be replete with facilities just like the real Paris.'

---

Consider too that in recent years, Pakistanis have been the third biggest foreign investors in Dubai's real estate market (second only to Indians and the British) (AFP, 2016)—this in a country with a housing shortage of between 11 to 12 million currently and growing by 700,000 each year.

See how Fanon speaks to us here: '... in order to hide this stagnation and to mask this regression, to reassure itself and to give itself something to boast about, the bourgeoisie can find nothing better to do than to erect grandiose buildings... and to lay out money on what are called prestige expenses' (WE: 133). In the absence of any integral hegemonic project, with no coherent long-term vision to offer, what we have therefore is a 'permanent wish for identification' with the mother country (WE: 143), a reliance on glitz and glamour, shallow compensation via the built environment, symbolic paeans to Pakistan's arrival on the 'world stage'. This was a social group that, having skipped the industrious and creative phase of the Western bourgeoisie, 'identifies itself with the decadence of the bourgeoisie of the West': 'it is in fact beginning at the end' (WE: 123). Here is that pathology of imitation, 'this absence of all ambition' (WE: 122), the total lack of gumption and creativity, which led Fanon to desist from conferring upon this compendium of clowns the dignity of even calling them 'a class'.

PAKISTAN AND FANON | 181

What we had (or indeed, have) therefore is a ruling bloc which cannot live up to its own promises. Its constant betrayals of its own paeans to Constitutionalism, the sanctity of democracy and the vote, floundering not simply due to a subjective will to compromise with the praetorian guard, but rooted in an anemic productive base. Its subjective idealism thus rooted in the inadequacy of its own material coordinates, its congenital cowardice, its total abdication of responsibility, its utter lack of creativity, stemming from a constitutive inability to transcend its own conceit i.e. its inability to either forge any sustainable productive base and, relatedly, to give enough (material and ideological) concessions to the masses for any coherent hegemonic project. Here then was a social group permanently afraid of the shadow of the people, and even of its own myriad contradictions, its ontological cowardice born out of a social incapacity to rule in its own name and for its own project—and ever-ready therefore to take refuge behind that heady cocktail of patriotic bluster, theological dissimulation, and—when things come to a head—happy to taunt the people from behind the boots of one strong-man General or the other. To speak with Marx of *The Eighteenth Brumaire*, Pakistan's ruling classes were 'bound to fear the stupidity of the masses so long as they remain conservative, and the insight of the masses as soon as they become revolutionary' (Marx, 1852: 63). And thus was (formal) democracy in Pakistan, and the elites who had come to become its bearers, condemned to alternate between a sense of tragedy and a sense of farce.

Here too Fanon had warnings for us: 'the state… seeks to impose itself in spectacular fashion', the people shall be 'hemmed in and immobilised' (WE: 137). Eventually, then what we get is 'a dictatorship of the national-socialist type', a 'fascism at high interest', where people are asked 'to fall back into the past', and 'to become drunk on remembrance' (WE: 135: 138). No wonder then that Ahmed Faraz, leading custodian of Urdu poetry's dissident tradition, was compelled to put it thus (and suffer exile for it to boot):

> *Naara-e-hubb-e-watan maal-e-tijarat ki tarah*
> *Jins-e-arzaan ki tarah deen-e-khuda ki baatein*

> (Love for the country trades like an object for sale
> And God's religion like a cheap commodity)

It is of course that other explicator *par excellence* of the postcolonial condition Ngugi wa Thiong'o who once designated African literature of the immediate post-Independence period as 'a series of imaginative footnotes to Frantz Fanon' and especially to the chapter on 'The Pitfalls of National Consciousness' (Thiong'o, 1993: 66). To this then I am compelled to add, with appropriate apologies to Ngugi, that the Pakistani ruling bloc may be characterized above all else as a series of baleful footnotes to Frantz Fanon's nightmare.

Here then was the first immediacy of Fanon in Pakistan: a caste of baneful inconsequence, a post-colonial condition as a series of baleful footnotes to *The Wretched of the Earth*.

## Viscerality: The Density of Immediacy

I had grown up, as mentioned earlier, in a Karachi riven by intense ethnic conflict. For people of my generation and background in Karachi, being *Muhajir* (Urdu-speaking migrants from India) was *the* source of social and political identity—itself sitting in varied and uneasy articulations with the valences of class and the official Islamic nationalism of Pakistan. However, while the Muhajir ethnicity had emerged, and indeed been *forged*, in the 1980s as 'beleaguered' and in need of protection/assertion (Verkaaik, 2016: 853), this was not a dominant feeling through the 1990s and 2000s. Muhajir militancy since the 1980s had asserted and concretely territorialised its claims through space, culture, and society—after all, and despite counter-claims by several competing groups, we had Karachi, a 'Muhajir city', 'our city'. Thus, while we felt resentment towards the state and many people around me had been involved in the urban militancy, our everyday life in those decades was not structured by an immediate and direct feeling of injustice.

However, as I was to learn through an increasing awareness of Pakistan's officially-denied peoples' history, this was a substantially different situation compared to Pakistan's other minority ethnicities/nations—the Baloch, Sindhis, and Pashtuns among others. For it is these peoples, and before them the Bengalis of former East Pakistan, who had been victims of the ruling bloc's geo-strategic adventures, repeated military operations, and profligate rapaciousness. An opposition to the militarized oppression of 'peripheral areas' or 'smaller provinces' of Pakistan had already been an integral part of the pro-democracy movement of 2007-8—the latter being preceded in important ways by a renewed nationalist movement in Balochistan province from the mid-2000s onwards over issues of provincial autonomy, self-determination, and resource extraction. In that heady moment of insurgency and beyond, as conversations opened and links formed between activists and intellectuals from different (and often siloed) social and geographical milieus, what struck me was the sheer erasure of history, memory, and experience that had been inflicted upon peripheral Pakistan and its long struggle for recognition, autonomy, and dignity. Here were peoples whose glorious anti-colonial history found no space in the official narrative of the 'Pakistan Movement', their political leaders and reformers vilified as 'anti-nationals' and 'foreign agents', their mother tongues relegated to the status of 'regional' languages, their resources robbed (often at gunpoint) by state and imperialism, and their lands instrumentalized for myriad regional (mis)adventures and imperial wars.

Of course, like all people of the Left, I too knew about the stratifications of, for example, tribalism among the Baloch and those of class and caste among the Pashtuns. Here, however the structuring principle of class, exploitation in relations of production and reproduction, is given density by—and often produced *through*—the patina of ethno-linguistic difference. At an everyday level, the alienations of land, labor, language, and legibility (to the state and mainstream society at large) were thus the registers through which the uneven rhythms of class were produced in Pakistan. Themselves conditioned by older, colonial patterns of economic geography and uneven development, these were the joints and fractures through which the iniquities of class played out in our post-colonial present. As such, while a joint (class) struggle cutting across the injuries of nationality remained a cherished aim of the Pakistani Left—and one with not insignificant precedents in the past (cf Toor, 2011; Akhtar, 2018)—it remained one which would require a delicate labor of working through those characteristic 'traditions of long-dead generations', the many alienations of land, labor, and language, which continue to 'weigh like a nightmare on the brains of the living' (Marx, 1852: 5).

On the Left, especially those from 'mainstream' areas of the country, we read and learnt about these histories through the generation of stalwarts who had lived through Pakistan's own 'long 1968' and the coercive-suppressive machinations of the ruling caste since then. We knew the figures on investment and extraction, the statistics on relative poverty, the numbers of hospitals, clinics, schools, and universities, the availability of clean water and the prevalence of disease(s), the ethnically-skewed recruitment into the civil and military services, the distribution of military cantonments and paramilitary check posts, the spatial spread-concentration of the nihilistic violence of the religious right—in short, we were well-aware, at least in the calculative-quantitative sense, of the many markers of social welfare, (under)development, and oppression proven in study after study to be distributed along starkly unequal linguistic and regional lines in Pakistan (cf Khan, 2019). However, it was only through experience of political work and teaching, travels and encounters with students, intellectuals, laborers, and political workers from all over the country, and indeed through the medium of the Internet and social media, that I (and I suspect many like myself) gained an appreciation of the sheer existential and experiential weight of these histories of visible, linguistic, and often epidermal iniquity.

For example, while core Pakistani cities have themselves undergone a steady process of militarization (in Karachi from the 1980s onwards, in other places post-9/11) (Shirazi, 2012), the situation takes on a qualitatively different hue in peripheral areas. In the Balochistan province, a nationalist insurgency has been on-going—with various lulls and breaks—since at least the 1970s, if not even earlier with the province's annexation in 1948 and repeated betrayals of the Baloch by the Pakistani state and ruling bloc (Ahmad, 2014a). Fueled by desperate underdevelopment and a rapacious robbery of the province's natural resources (gas, copper, and more recently, its deep-sea coastline), large numbers of Baloch have taken to the mountains in an armed bid to secure self-determination or, at the very least, the provincial autonomy guaranteed by the Pakistani constitution.

It is however in the everyday spatial markers of iniquity that the hot rage of the Baloch towards the Pakistani state can be most palpably felt and understood. Baloch cities are wanton playgrounds for the erection of the Pakistani state's phallic symbols (missiles, statues etc.), walls and compounds are canvasses for paintings of giant Pakistani flags and 'national' (i.e. state-sanctioned) heroes, land is up for sale for various extractive endeavors (most involving the military's own network of mining, construction, and transport companies), roads and neighborhoods dotted by paramilitary check posts, insurances not of 'security' but of a daily renewal of denigration and colonization, colleges and universities breeding grounds of sexual harassment by officials due to the confluence of patriarchal impunity and military surveillance, and—even more sinisterly—a black hole from where young Baloch are abducted and 'disappeared' regularly by a deliberately confusing cocktail of intelligence agencies and state-sponsored proxy groups. To give just one example, the federal government has recently been planning to 'fence' the Baloch coastal city of Gwadar to secure the deep-sea port being developed with considerable Chinese investment (Kakar, 2020a). 'Development', as is often the case, confirming the worst fears of the local population and the destruction of traditional economies linked to maritime rhythms (Jamali, 2014).

This then is that 'web of three-dimensional violence'— 'violence in everyday behaviour, violence against the past that is emptied of all substance, and violence against the future' (Fanon, 1960: 654)—a concatenation of economic deprivation, linguistic-cultural erasure, and everyday humiliation which gives existential—and indeed, a visceral—impetus to the Baloch resistance. This is 'a world divided into compartments, a motionless, Manicheistic world' where the native is 'hemmed in' and 'learns to stay in his place' (WE: 40). 'A primary Manicheism' rules social and spatial relations—here the truth stands naked, no compensation received via appeals to God and nation, the 'dividing line, the frontiers are shown by barracks and police stations' (WE: 29). In this 'world of statues', soldiers of the night frisk away the young and even the women, to disappear regularly into the voracious pits of the Pakistani state. 'Ontology is made impossible in a colonised society', Fanon tells us, no reciprocity of mutual recognition or 'being-for-the-Other' is here possible, a 'feeling of non-existence' implying a tonicity and tension of the muscles, a constant smarting from the daily deprivations of alienation and dehumanization (BS: 89, 118). Here, an articulation of politics along the lines of ethnicity is not therefore any 'false consciousness', nor the dive into the particular a sinister diversion from the 'real' and 'universal' struggle of class (as some among the Left would have us believe). It is the starkness of the injustice itself, the viscerality of a colonial situation which plays out through all-too obvious perceptual and indeed embodied iniquities, in short it is the density of immediacy itself, which compels 'consciousness [and practice] ... to get lost in the night of the absolute, the only condition for attaining self-consciousness' (BS: 112). Where a recognition of equality and dignified reciprocity is withheld, where claims to nation, development, civilization, and universality are wielded as cudgels for alienating labor, land, and language, a dissident consciousness and practice must find its way through a 'negativity [that] draws its value from a virtually substantial absoluity' (BS: 113).

No wonder then that the Fanon we encounter here, and that has often been taken up by the Baloch resistance, is the Fanon who speaks to the 'delirious Manicheism' of the colonial situation (BS: 160), who explains—if not prescribes—as response to the existential weight of 'violence in its natural state', an 'absolute line of action' whereby the 'colonised man finds his freedom in and through violence... [which] enlightens the agent because it indicates to him the means and the ends' (WE: 48, 65).[5] 'To the lie of colonial situation,' Fanon reminds us, 'the colonised reply with an equal and forceful lie of their own' (WE: 39). And thus, it remains—overdetermined by the weight of state repression and the inadequacies of the Pakistani Left in general—that the Fanon encountered in these spaces is one not of mediation and hegemony, but of the immediacy of violence and counter-violence, a 'spontaneous impetuosity which... is condemned, in so far as it is a doctrine of instantaneity, to self-repudiation' (WE: 107). As one political worker once put it to me succinctly: '[his] strategic and internationalist messages have been ignored and Fanon has been reduced to *shar'i jawaaz* [theological justification] for getting involved in militant [i.e. armed] acts'. A partial uptake of Fanon, as prophet and purveyor of violence, devoid of his emphasis on an invigorating and dialectical arc of experience, is here mediated by the dense conjuncture of deprivation, isolation, and oppression at the hands of the Pakistani ruling bloc on the one hand, and—critically—the long eclipse of a strong, anti-colonial Left in 'mainstream' Pakistan since the 1970s/80s.[6] The missing intellectual, generational, and organizational mediations of the wider Left thus feeding into a debilitating social and geographical isolation of the Baloch movement, and the latter thus condemned to a ruinous cycle of visceral deprivation, violence, counter-violence, and—indeed—of internecine, lateral violence.

A different articulation of immediacy, conditioned integrally by its own specific history and spatiality, may be seen in the case of the Pashtuns of Pakistan. Here, while the Pashtuns have suffered immensely from the Pakistani ruling bloc and imperialism's instrumentalization of their lands for various *jihadi* and (post-9/11) anti-*jihadi* wars, this is also an ethno-linguistic group with greater—though uneven—absorption into the structures of the Pakistani state and its allied rhythms of accumulation and regional differentiation (Ahmed, 1998). In the post-9/11 moment, with Pashtun areas bearing the brunt of US drone attacks, Pakistani military operations, and religious neo-fundamentalism, a whole generation of war-displaced young Pashtuns grew up in 'core' Pakistani cities (Kakar, 2020b). Here, they joined already existing networks of a large Pashtun working class, faced prevalent stereotyping as 'religious fanatics' and 'independent tribes' [*azaad qabaail*], while also bearing the brunt of 'counter-terrorism' surveillance, harassment, and extra-judicial killings by police. Access to the virtual (i.e. social media and Internet) and the spaces of the urban in 'core' Pakistan proved a mediatory moment for the linking up of young Pashtuns from disparate tribal and geographical backgrounds, and for discovery of their common experiences of war, displacement, and instrumentalization at the hands of unaccountable state policies. Where traditional Pashtun parties failed to live up to this nascent anti-war consciousness, a new and powerful movement, the

---

5. I make this necessarily generalized claim based on conversations with young Baloch nationalists and intellectuals, and their experiences of encountering Fanon as part of internal debates. Of course, much nuance and qualification can be added here, but this must await a more detailed enumeration of Baloch nationalism, its historical and contemporary valences, and its intellectual and political lineages. For example, see Ahmad (2014b).

6. I have discussed these missing mediations of the Left in Pakistan in greater detail elsewhere. See Chapter 5 in Mallick (2020a).

Pashtun Tahaffuz Movement (Pashtun Protection Movement, PTM), emerged in 2018 with an intensity that caught everyone off guard.[7] Since its meteoric rise, and despite much state repression and propaganda, the PTM has gained mass support among Pashtuns through courageous and public campaigns against enforced disappearances, unaccountable military operations, the instrumentalization of Pashtun lands in various imperial and regional (mis)adventures, and—indeed—has sought a renewed social contract between the Pakistani state and oppressed nations therein (Nasar, 2018).

In a Fanonist register, it is interesting to note both the spatial registers of the PTM's oeuvre and the potentials and lessons this offers. Stefan Kipfer, in his conjunctive reading of Fanon and Henri Lefebvre, has pointed to how Fanon's politics of emancipation eschews the one-sided-ness of urban- or rural-bias, while aiming to embed itself in—and thus, transform—multiple levels of the social totality: from the colonial city and its everyday embodied injuries, to transformation of the (sub-)national geographies of uneven development, and finally to a complex transformation of the inter-national and internationalism itself (Kipfer, 2011). It is here that the PTM's mediation of the rural-urban and core-periphery dialectic in contemporary Pakistan is instructive. For, as mentioned earlier, the PTM itself is the product of a conjuncture overdetermined by the so-called War on Terror and the associated patterns of displacement, migration, and spatially-extended networks of labour, loss, and memory that now link 'traditional' Pashtun spaces (i.e. western and north-western Pakistan) with core urban spaces in Pakistan. Here, the catalyzing effects on consciousness and practice of the urban areas are crucial, serving as a medium for the discovery of common experiences among a new generation of displaced and war-weary Pashtuns, while also signalling a reformulated and indeed re-spatialized national question in Pakistan. Pashtuns often form the most obvious underclass among Pakistan's urban laboring classes, and thus bear the brunt of the ruling bloc's narrow accumulation machine predicated as it is on real estate speculation and attendant coercive demarcations and displacements of space. For example, it is no surprise that the extrajudicial killing of the young Pashtun man, Naqeebullah Mehsud, in Karachi which served as catalyst for formation of the PTM was carried out by Rao Anwar, a police officer notorious for acting as strongman for the sleazy alliance of bureaucrats (both civil and military), politicians, and land 'developers' and speculators making their blood-soaked millions at the peri-urban periphery.[8]

Where PTM organizers and mobilizers have continuously had to 'fall back to the countryside' in order both to escape state repression and 'to learn their lessons in the hard school of the people', this has also been accompanied by a

---

7. I have discussed the social and spatial bases of PTM, its emergence, and politics previously (Mallick, 2020b). Therefore, I will only briefly flag some of the Fanonist resonances of the PTM's oeuvre here.
8. Between 2011 and 2018, Senior Superintendent Police of Malir District (Karachi) Rao Anwar killed 444 people in 'encounters'. As per the police's own records, 'not a single policeman was even injured, let alone killed, during the 745 encounters' (Zaman and Ali, 2019). Also see Anwar (2019).

politics in the urban core (WE: 100-1).[9] While this 'return' to the urban might not signal (as in Fanon) the 'crowning point of the dialectic' (WE: 102), it is a key mediatory moment in bringing visibility and organizational depth to the movement, and indeed in forging unity among Pashtuns from disparate backgrounds themselves. Indeed, where the urban became a key orientation and terrain for articulation of the Pashtun 'partisan universal' (cf Sekyi-Otu, 1996: 118), this also has the potential for the PTM forging alliances with other oppressed groups and classes in the core. As such, the urban (as space and orientation) has been a key mediator in providing density, proximity, and articulation to the immediacy of Pashtuns' post-9/11 deprivations. However, in its integral linkages to other social groups, such articulations of Pakistan's reformulated national and urban question also have the potential to become a mediatory moment towards 'a second harmony' (ibid: 121) i.e. 'a concrete universal' which emerges from within the historical, spatial, and indeed experiential specificities of differentially-marginalized social groups, the dialectical sublation of immediacy into a concrete and insurgent universality.

This then is another Fanon we encounter in Pakistan: often one-sided and partial, but always bringing to our attention the density of immediacy itself. Telling us to 'beware of crossing our arms in the sterile attitude of the spectator', but conversely to join the people 'in that fluctuating movement which they are just giving shape to' (BS: 164; WE: 183). Here is the Fanon imploring us to understand, in all its constitutive historical, spatial, and experiential joints, the viscerality of immediacy, not as a moment of self-enclosed particularity, but for building on 'the open dimension of every consciousness', the 'progressive infrastructure... [of] the path to disalienation' (BS: 206, 161); that is, with an eye ultimately on the question of mediation and, therefore, of hegemony itself.

## Mediation or Barbarism: Fanon's Final Warning

As should be clear from the above, Pakistan today is characterized by two, intractable and mutually reinforcing realities. On the one hand, there is a ruling bloc increasingly facing a crisis of legitimacy and coherence, one generated not simply by their subjective prejudice, their breath-taking lack of courage and creativity, but integrally conditioned by a social deficit, their rootedness in an anemic productive base, and—by dint of that debilitating feedback loop between tied interests and path dependency—their material incapacity to transcend their own conceit. We have discussed briefly how this lack of coherence, baked into the very constitution of the Pakistani state and ruling bloc since Independence, has led to one ruinous dependency on (sub-)imperial powers after another. That the US imperium's military interventions in the Afghanistan-Pakistan region arrived at opportune moments for the Pakistani ruling bloc (first with the 1980s

---

9. For the interesting and instructive social and spatial trajectory of a district-level organizer of the PTM, see Sattar (2020).

Afghan 'jihad' and then the 2000s 'War on Terror') now lays the basis of an uncertainty that is all the greater as inter-imperialist competition at the global level heats up. Thus, it is that—in the absence of an integral hegemonic project and, relatedly, a coherent accumulation strategy, one of course that would require this caste of baneful inconsequence to transcend its own congenital deficits—the Pakistani ruling bloc and especially its militarized core are forced into a grotesque dance over the hot coals of imperialism: turning one moment to the US, then to China, then to Saudi Arabia, and most often to the IMF, to fulfill their insatiable appetite for aid, guns, and patronage.

On the other hand, we have large parts of the citizenry, for long forcibly denied the very status of citizenship and the most basic of democratic rights, but now in an increasingly insurgent mood to not just claim citizenship and representation, but indeed to restructure the very covenant between state and society itself. After a long hiatus, with more and more women staking their claim in public and virtual space, on campuses, and in urban life, and thus facing brutal patriarchal backlash in response, we have an increasingly vocal feminist movement challenging the many gendered injuries and exclusions perpetuated in the name of property, propriety, and nationalism (Newsline, 2019; Rasheed, 2019). On the other hand, a renewed student movement—gaining strength from the courage of the women at its forefront—has emerged. A confluence of unrelenting campus militarization, a fear-induced patriarchal backlash against the increasing visibility of women on campuses, and denial of even the semblance of democratic rights (student unions being effectively banned in Pakistan since 1984 —another gift of the US-backed Zia dictatorship) fueling what is fast becoming a youth insurgency. That the latter is conditioned integrally by the ruling bloc's fraying hegemony and its lack of absorptive capacity goes without saying.

In addition to the above, we have already discussed the case of the Baloch and Pashtun movements. The Baloch movement itself seems to have entered a new phase—one led by the young and the women, building decentralized committees of mobilization all over the province, and increasingly in no mood of dealing/compromising with the tribal and nascent bourgeoisie leadership who have continually sold the nationalist cause for a few crumbs from tables on-high (BMR, 2020). Pashtun mobilization, given a new lease of life by the PTM, is now sustained by a steady supply of volunteers, organizers, and the young permanently scarred by unrelenting war on their lands, and the many injuries of displacement and rootlessness born out of the confluence of underdevelopment and militarized violence. Predictably, to the Baloch, to the Pashtuns, and to the increasingly assertive youth even in 'core' Pakistan, the ruling bloc has responded in the only way it knows: a blitz of propaganda and coercion, uniformed robots and soldiers of the night, trained in the tradition of the old colonial armies, wholly incapable of understanding the strength of popular sentiment and collective will. All movement, all dissent for them a conspiracy. Their focus not the situation, but merely the interpreters of the situation—their structural and, therefore, historical blindness making them singularly incapable of comprehending that it is *they* who are the crisis, *they* who are the situation.

What we thus seem to be approaching—and in fact, may even have arrived at—is the culmination of a *longue durée* crisis of the ruling bloc. The old ruling classes cannot keep ruling in the same way. The new shows glimpses of its emergence but remains hampered by a terrain of unevenness—an unevenness which, as we have seen, lends a particular salience, a visceral immediacy to the myriad insurgencies and assertions which have arisen among various social groups in Pakistan over the last few years. Thus, it is that an alternative hegemony—centered on exploited classes, oppressed nations, and invisibilized genders—has to work through a terrain where older patterns of uneven development persist but have been reworked and indeed respatialized in specific ways. As such, where the integral organizations of the Left and working classes have undergone a long eclipse, and where a social terrain is structured through fractures and joints—often along ethnic-national lines—it is no surprise that the most intense challenges to the prevailing carousel of wealth, pelf, and corruption continue to emerge along those lines. However, where the shifting social and spatial bases of accumulation, and associated networks of labor, production and reproduction, are linking the urban-rural and core-periphery in new ways, no politics of the (sub-)nation can remain and succeed in its magnificent, but aloof, self-ensconsement. Here we are faced with a delicate dialectic: one which cannot ignore the terrain of the particular and its moment of immediacy, and indeed must deepen it substantively; but one which—even where it takes its departure point from the terrain of (separate) partisan universals—is condemned to isolation, involution, and ultimately failure, if it fails to undergo a 'mutual transformation in convergent points of struggle or processes of organizational condensation' (Kipfer and Hart, 2013: 338), a relational socio-spatial imbrication of partisan universal(s), the sublation of immediacies into a concrete universality; in short, if it fails to achieve that most cherished crowning point of the (Fanonian) dialectic i.e. the function of mediation and, therefore, of hegemony.

This is exactly the point at which Fanon has warnings for us. For on the one hand, he dismisses prophets of a pre-given or abstract unity, 'certain pharisees... wishing to skip the national stage' (WE: 198), philistines whose untethered universalism is abstract to the extent it fails to come to grips with the depths and densities of immediacy itself. Fanon thus advocates for a 'national consciousness, which is *not* nationalism', one which is 'national, revolutionary, and social' in the very same moment, and 'is the only thing which will give us an international dimension' (WE: 117, 119, emphasis added). The national, the immediate, and the particular, must thus deepen itself, connect to the rhythms of iniquity and exclusions within, work its way through that '*substantial* absoluity', a 'rapid step to be taken from national to social and political consciousness.... [and] a doctrine concerning the division of wealth and social relations' (BS: 113, emphasis added; WE: 163-4). On the other hand, hear his salutary warning too: 'what can be dangerous is when they [the people] reach the stage of social consciousness before the stage of nationalism. If this happens, we find in under-developed countries fierce demands for social justice which paradoxically are allied with often primitive tribalism' (WE: 164).

Here is Fanon throwing down the gauntlet, one which needs to be translated with much care to our context and conjuncture in Pakistan. For here we have a post-colonial state home (and, many would claim, a prison) to *multiple* nations with the accumulated weight of their own histories, spatialities, and languages. The accidents of geography and the machinations of history having brought us together in a situation where the very structuring of the social terrain determines an uneven—even if often mutually reinforcing—development of consciousness and practice. Indeed, it is this very unevenness which provides grist to the many insurgencies of class and nation(s) we witness simmering in Pakistan today. The danger too however lies in the possibility of these insurgencies out-of-sync, times and spaces out-of-joint, thus missing out on the moment where partisan universals achieve that second harmony, the function of mutual imbrication and mediation, i.e. that of a truly *pluri*-national unity *from below*, without which each insurgency, each rebellion stemming from its visceral immediacy, each stirring of that inimitable human quest for freedom, will wither on the poisoned vine of isolation and involution.

Here then is the great danger and opportunity of the present moment of crisis in Pakistan, both an opening to forge something truly new from below, one which casts off the accumulated muck of past generations, but which in its oppressive weight continues to determine the many discordances of time, space, consciousness, and insurgency. Any inadequacy in living up to this momentous historical task however, a failure to relegate that useless caste of baneful inconsequence to its rightful place in the dustbin of posterity, threatens to deliver us to the same bad infinity of theological dissimulation, patriotic fraud, and militarist barbarism, but this time with a usurious interest added to it.

For when a people insurgent but only unevenly, and no longer willing to being ruled in the same old manner, faces a ruling bloc incapable of ruling, unable to reinvent itself, and unwilling to enact its long overdue exit from the stage of history, then it might well be that we become fatefully condemned to live out Fanon's final warning, that Virgilian call of wrath and despair: 'if I cannot deflect the will of Heaven, then I shall move Hell'.

## Bibliography

AFP. 2016. 'Pakistanis Third Biggest Foreign Investors in Dubai Property.' *Express Tribune*, May 4.

Ahmad, M. 2014a. 'Balochistan Betrayed.' In *Dispatches from Pakistan*, edited by Madiha, R. T., Qalandar, B. M., and Vijay Prashad, 150–167. Minneapolis: University of Minnesota Press.

_____. 2014b. 'Home Front: The Changing Face of Balochistan's Separatist Insurgency.' *Caravan* (July Issue).

Ahmed, F. 1998. 'The Integration of Pashtuns.' In *Ethnicity and Politics in Pakistan*, edited by Feroz, A., 212–228. Karachi: Oxford University Press.

Akhtar, A. S. 2018. *The Politics of Common Sense: State, Society and Culture in Pakistan*. Cambridge: Cambridge University Press.

Anwar, N. H. 2018. 'Receding Rurality, Booming Periphery: Value Struggles in Karachi's Agrarian-Urban Frontier.' *Economic and Political Weekly* 53 (12): 46–54.

Bensaïd, D. 2013. *An Impatient Life: A Memoir*. London: Verso.

Blom, A. 2011. *Pakistan: Coercion and Capital in an 'Insecurity State'*. Paris: IRSEM.

BMR Team. 2020. 'Birth of a Movement: Transformation of Bramsh Solidarity Committees.' *Balochistan Marxist Review* .

Fanon, F. 2008 [1952]. *Black Skin, White Masks*. Translated by Richard Philcox. New York: Grove Press.

_____.2018 [1960]. 'Why We Use Violence: Address to the Accra Positive Action Conference, April 1960.' In *Alienation and Freedom*, edited by Jean Khalfa and Robert J. C. Young. Translated by Steven Corcoran. London: Bloomsbury Academic.

_____.2001 [1968]. *The Wretched of the Earth*. Translated by Constance Farrington. London: Penguin Books.

Ghumman, K. 2016. 'PML-N Unwilling to Share CPEC Control?' *DAWN*, July 18.

Gibson, N. 2003. *Fanon: The Postcolonial Imagination*. Cambridge: Polity Press.

Gidwani, V., and Kumar, S. 2019. 'Time, Space, and the Subaltern: The Matter of Labor in Delhi's Grey Economy.' In *Subaltern Geographies*, edited by Jazeel, T., and Legg, S., 142–166. Athens: University of Georgia Press.

Gordon, L. R. 2015. *What Fanon Said: A Philosophical Introduction to His Life and Thought*, New York: Fordham University Press.

Hudis, P. 2017. 'Frantz Fanon's Contribution to Hegelian Marxism.' *Critical Sociology*, 43 (6): 865–873.

Hussain, B. 2021. 'Pakistani Builder Making "Exact" Copy of Paris in Gujranwala.' *SAMAA*, January 25.

Jalal, A. 1990. *The State of Martial Rule: The Origins of Pakistan's Political Economy of Defence*. Cambridge: Cambridge University Press.

Jamali, H. 2014. 'A Tempest in my Harbor: Gwadar, Balochistan.' In *Dispatches from Pakistan*, edited by Tahir, R. M., Memon Q. B., and Prashad, V., 168–184. Minneapolis: University of Minnesota Press.

Jan, M. A. 2016. 'Deindustrialisation and Beyond.' *The News on Sunday*, December 11.

Kakar, R. 2020a. 'Fencing of Gwadar.' *DAWN*, December 26.

_____. 2020b. 'Demystifying the PTM.' *DAWN*, February 23.

Khan, D. 2019. 'The Political Economy of Uneven State-Spatiality in Pakistan: The Interplay of Space, Class and Institutions.' In *New Perspectives on Pakistan's Political Economy: State, Class and Social Change*, edited by McCartney, M., and Akbar Zaidi, S., 130–152. Cambridge: Cambridge University Press.

Kipfer, S. 2011. 'The Times and Spaces of (De-)Colonization: Fanon's Countercolonialism, Then and Now.' In *Living Fanon: Global Perspectives*, edited by Gibson, N., 93–104. New York: Palgrave Macmillan.

Kipfer, S., and Hart, G. 2013. 'Translating Gramsci in the Current Conjuncture.' In *Gramsci: Space, Nature, Politics*, edited by Ekers, M., Hart, G., Kipfer, S., and Loftus, A. West Sussex: Wiley-Blackwell.

Mallick, A. 2020a. 'The (Un)Making of the Working Class in Karachi, 1980s–2010s.' PhD diss., York University.

_____. 2020b. 'From Partisan Universal to Concrete Universal? The Pashtun Tahaffuz Movement in Pakistan.' *Antipode* 52 (6): 1774–1793.

Marx, K. 1852. *The Eighteenth Brumaire of Louis Bonaparte*, www.marxists.org.

Mashal, M. 2011. 'Pakistani Troops Aid Bahrain's Crackdown.' *Al Jazeera*, July 30.

Max, K., and Engels, F. 1848. *Manifesto of the Communist Party*, www.marxists.org.

Munir, K., and Naqvi, N. 2017. 'Privatization in the Land of Believers: The Political Economy of Privatization in Pakistan.' *Modern Asian Studies* 51 (6): 1695–1726.

Nasar, S. U. 2018. 'War, Masculinity, and the Pashtun Long March.' *Daily Times*, March 8.

Nations, R. 1971. 'The Economic Structure of Pakistan: Class and Colony.' *New Left Review I* 68: 3–26.

Newsline Admin. 2019. 'How Can the Younger and Senior Generation of Activists Bridge the Divide within the Women's Movement and Effect Real Change?.' *Newsline*, March Issue.

Rasheed, U. 2019. 'What Made Aurat March Possible?.' *The News on Sunday*, March 17.

Sattar, A. 2020. 'Baghawat ke Muqadmaat: PTM Worker Se Ghar Walay Kia Sulook Kartay Hain? [Cases of Sedition: How are PTM Workers Treated by Their Family?].' *Independent Urdu*, February 25.

Sekyi-Otu, A. 1996. *Fanon's Dialectic of Experience*. Cambridge: Harvard University Press.

Shahid, K. 2018. 'Growing Economic Disparities.' *DAWN*, October 7.

Shirazi, S. 2012. 'City, Space, Power: Lahore's Architecture of In/Security.' *The Funambulist*, October 22.

wa Thiong'o, N. 1993. *Moving the Centre: The Struggle for Cultural Freedoms*. London: James Currey.

Toor, S. 2011. *The State of Islam: Culture and Cold War Politics in Pakistan*. London: Pluto Press.

Verkaaik, O. 2016. 'Violence and Ethnic Identity Politics in Karachi and Hyderabad.' *South Asia: Journal of South Asian Studies* 39 (4): 841–854.

Waheed, M. W., and Ghumman, A. A. 2019. *Pakistan at 100: Growth and Investment*. Washington: World Bank Group.

Zaman, F., and Ali, N. S. 2019. 'Dawn Investigations: Rao Anwar and the Killing Fields of Karachi.' *DAWN.com*, March 12.

# ALL QUIET IN THIS NON-SETTLER-POSTCOLONY

Ato Sekyi-Otu

*Truth is a bacchanalian revel wherein no member is sober.*
—Hegel

At the end of the 'Fanon Fifty Years After' Colloquium held at Rhodes University in July 2011, some of the South African participants burst into song: 'That's Why I am a Socialist'. It is difficult to imagine such seditious exuberance—to say nothing of the commitment the song avows—enacted in the placid halls of a Ghanaian university or indeed at any public forum in this country. Why is that so? The following musings are an oblique attempt to answer that question.

## Rethinking the Discursive Conditions of Revolt with Fanon

In a memorable passage in 'Concerning Violence'. Fanon evokes a time in the anti-colonial struggle when an 'extraordinary vocabulary' of political subjectivity and solidarity, one of 'brother, sister, friend' comes into being. Presaging the demise of 'a whole material and moral universe', this new language comes to discredit and supplant yesterday's survivalist solipsism, the depraved individualism of 'everyone-shits-for-himself'. (Fanon, 1968: 46-48). But that ascendant vocabulary of the unitary racial-national community will in its turn be contested by the disclosure of rifts and divisions in the social body, and, as a consequence, the emergence of a new understanding of antagonism and solidarity. In *Fanon's Dialectic of Experience*, but also in my more recent work, I followed Fanon—or so I imagined—in reading this story of pivotal shifts in the nascent postcolonial subject's self-understanding as signaling an unambiguous gain in 'the successive enlightenment of consciousness' (Sekyi-Otu, 1996: 111-123; Sekyi-Otu, 2019: 9, Fanon, 1968: 143). From that perspective, Marikana 2012 was an emblematic event in the process whereby the people are compelled, as the *Communist Manifesto* puts it, 'to face with sober senses the *real* conditions of life'. Perhaps I overstressed the unified, coherent, full moon nature of that enlightenment, to say nothing of its putative blessings. In so doing, I risked forgetting Fanon's allusion to the 'penumbra' (Fanon, 1968: 144-145) that, paradoxically, beclouds this enlightenment even as it unveils hidden realities, and even as it purports to replace its forebears without debts and traces, the penumbra that is an insuperable and by no means deleterious feature of the formation of social knowledge. In what follows, I indirectly revisit Fanon's understanding of the nature of these pivotal discursive shifts by characterizing them as *moments*. With Hegel—his semantic intent 'slightly stretched' in defiance of literalist originalism—I construe 'moment' as signifying not a discrete stage or point in a successive order of time, but rather a latent and structural feature of a form of thought and practice in a moving body of countervailing properties. Such a structural feature typically assumes a dominant and defining status at a determinate epoch or place of human experience. Alternatively, it undergoes relative effacement or disavowal in a particular context. It is a dogmatic progressivism, to say nothing of ignorance of the auspicious complications of created things, that sees either the salience of such a feature or its relative effacement as a 'done deal' or an unmixed blessing.

## The Visible and the Inaudible

In the past few years throughout the world, from Chile to Lebanon (even before the deadly explosion of 4 August, 2020), insurgent bodies have been assembling on the streets screaming bloody hell, denouncing inequities and injustices in the social order and demanding redress. South Africa has witnessed continuing protests from below, the proliferating 'rebellions of the poor', and the multi-pronged demands of the #MustFall movement. Everywhere, it seems, except in the African non-settler-postcolony such as Ghana. In the by now regular enumeration of events and scenes of protest, this non-settler-postcolony is conspicuous by its absence. Occupy has had no local equivalents. Not even George Floyd's untimely dispatch to the land of the ancestors awakened this nation from its accustomed stupor or sparked the kind of widespread protests that occurred elsewhere in the world. It is significant that the only group to raise its voice and stage a protest after the lynching of George Floyd was one whose name, Economic Fighters League, echoes South Africa's Economic Freedom Fighters. Even more uncharacteristically for this country, the protestors' signs and placards connected the killing of Floyd and other African Americans with injustices and instances of police violence in Ghana. However, that protest and the discursive connections it voiced was an isolated occurrence. Yet if this society is hopelessly destitute of insurgent discontent and mobilized protests, it is not because of lack of material evidence, evidence of things seen—from structural features of the social order to conjunctural events—which should instigate such protests. Consider some of these structural phenomena and conjunctural events that would elsewhere regularly provoke the people's discontent and send them screaming into the streets.

## Hidden in Plain Sight: Geographies of Inequality

Contrary to those who pretended not to see, it did not take coronavirus to make the virus of radical inequality in the social body manifest. The virus merely confirmed the visible social organization of opulence and destitution, one as stark as Fanon's description of the settler-colonial world as 'a world divided into compartments'. Unmistakable is the spatial geography of cities where 'sprawling poor neighbourhoods lacking basic utilities coexist with well-furnished gated communities' (Graham, 2016); children's schools with insufficient desks, materials and decent sanitation, and elite ones bearing the telltale moniker 'International' in their names. But if the topography of inequality is as stark and unmistakable here as it is in the settler-colony where 'race became spatialized and space racialized' (New Frame, 2020a), that lived chiasmus, as a defining feature of social reality, does not obtain in the non-settler-colony and its postcolonial successor. Consequently, the *analogy* as a discursive convention is not registered either in popular social consciousness or even in academic studies of inequality. Of course, Ghanaian scholars have cogently detailed this geography of inequality and its consequences in studies replete with pictorial juxtapositions of vast differentials in residential neighbourhoods and the amenities made available to them (see Owusu, Oteng-Ababio, Owusu, and Wrigley-Asante, 2016) Yet when I pointed out to some of the authors of these studies at a 2018 conference the startling similarity between spatialized (albeit non-racialized) inequality in Accra—powerfully portrayed in their own work—and Fanon's description of the racialized 'geographical ordering' of the colonial world, the invitation to consider that analogy was greeted with silence. But neither is it the case that the analogy—and the perceptual vocabulary that might trigger it—is registered in popular social consciousness, functioning as a defining trope of grievance and discontent. Unlike post(?)apartheid South Africa, there is here no living collective, 'popular memory' of racialized space as a central, indeed constitutive, feature of injustice, (New Frame, 2020b). There is no such mnemonic template that may serve as a powerful weapon of criticism directed at postcolonial geographies of inequality; an analogizing discourse that instigates and is instigated by a *humanist* criticism of oppressive and constrictive spatial conditions of existence. Could it be that a critical humanist apprehension of such spatial arrangement is more readily available, precisely, in a place where it is (re)lived as an offending continuation of racialized space in the settler colony. Living memory of racialized space as metonym for the structure of social power and organized inequality is precisely what might provoke that humanist criticism, that denunciation, to borrow Saidiya Hartman's Fanonian phrase, of 'human nature caged in a narrow space' (2018: 465) with all its material effects and psycho-existential consequences. Imagine what force such a *combined discursive mode*—the articulation of grievance against current spatialized inequalities with living and livid remembrance of the racialized divisions of the recent past—would be generated especially in this season of the pandemic.

For already in the postcolony as everywhere in the world, but especially in the postcolony, the pandemic has made inequalities and the geography of class injustice a demonstrable, incontrovertible fact. Everywhere, the plague has been a revelation or rather a re-unveiling of social truths, truths regarding organized crimes of inequity in the social body and its vital organs, truths challenging the claim that 'we are all in this together'. Confuting the homily of one suffering humanity unmodified, the virus has made cruelly manifest the special agony of the poor, those without the privilege of a viable residence to be quarantined in, those with pre-existing conditions of ill-health made even more virulent by the pathogens of neoliberal privatization and the abolition of public goods in the recent past; those for whom social distancing is not an option and home is no haven. Covid's class epidemiology and differential consequences have not gone unnoticed by the subaltern. Consider the outburst of some fishermen in Cape Coast to the effect that the virus is a problem for the rich who travel overseas and bring it back with them to their secluded residences: class consciousness gone visceral and vengefully reductionist. Or the truculent refusal of an anonymous Ghanaian writer on social media who will not obey lockdown instructions crafted, he figures, to make the world safer for the one-percent snuggled in decadent isolation in their luxurious living rooms teeming with postmodern gadgets. Or a letter from a Ghanaian immigrant in London unwilling to heed the siren song inviting lost souls like him to return home, answering that invitation with this disloyal trope of social difference, 'Your 'Ghana' is Different from Mine', and detailing a seven-ladder scheme of social hierarchy in Ghanaian society as disincentive against the romance of return (Opuku-Agyemang, 2019). The pandemic, then, is the privileged moment when the open secret of class—and other organizing axes of social division—irrupted, unmistakably, upon life and consciousness. Everywhere, from the heartlands of advanced capitalism to the impoverished regions of the Global South we are witnessing attestations of the compelling material need for a radical transformation of society sparked by the wrenching re-unveiling of social truths. Unfortunately and characteristically, in *this* postcolony, this time of disclosure is likely to be squandered, the incipient albeit inchoate expressions of class discontent and particular wrongs doomed to fall short of insurrectionary mobilization. That may be because those pre-existing conditions of inequity, stark as they are, have escaped insurgent articulation and discontent for so long.

So it is with the emblematic instance of gender injustice. Especially notable yet unremarked in popular public discourse, even before the pandemic, are the more deleterious gendered effects of socioeconomic inequities, the specific gravity of injustice in the material conditions of life for women. One scandalous example is the crisis of affordable accommodation for single young women living and working in urban areas. Usurious rental arrangements, often with stipulations of multi-year advance payments, force struggling young women to seek the succor of 'sugar daddies' in exchange for sex. Yet when one such woman outed herself in a 2018 CNN interview with Christiane Amanpour, she, not the male predator or the usurious landlord, still less the constraining relations of gender injustice, became the object of opprobrium and moralizing hectoring in the media. Here is a hypothetical question: Would a case such as this one incite a more significant *political* outrage—not the misdirected moralism it produced here—in a postcolony with a lingering history of socioeconomic divisions and inequities which, in addition to being gendered, are racialized? What difference would it make if the woman in question were a *black* woman? A woman bearing the historical weight—the specific historicity—of that status and designation? Would gender injustice and the degradation visited on women sting more deeply, if they were apprehended as products of the 'racial formation of inequalities?' (Andrews, 2016)

We are faced with a more generalizing question. What does it take for visible structures of inequity and iniquity to engender organized antagonism? What would it take for palpable injustice to speak in tongues of outrage, political outrage, articulation of the 'the common pain and the general wrong', as Ama Ata Aidoo's *Anowa* calls it? What does it take to rouse palpably suffering bodies from this insufferable docility? Perhaps the visible, here inequity living in plain sight, made manifest in social space—as transparent and unmistakable as the 'geographical arrangement' of the colonial-racial order Fanon unforgettably evoked—perhaps the visible devoid of identitarian signifiers, unremarked in perceptual language, is well-nigh obscured, its offending effect rendered inaudible.

## Concerning Violence

If the pandemic has revealed or rather re-unveiled the open secret of vast social inequalities, the enforcement of injunctions for its containment has unleashed a spate of police brutality, disclosing anew the intrinsic violence of state power, now as always directed principally at the subaltern.

It is a fine morning in August 2020. At a street corner in Cape Coast in the central region of Ghana, a team of policemen beat to the pulp, mercilessly bloody a hapless young man supposedly guilty of violating some Covid-19 restrictions, although he appeared to be in full compliance, mask and all. The violence is administered with an earnestness that makes the comportment of Derek Chauvin, George Floyd's killer—one hand cavalierly in his pocket as he knelt on Floyd's neck—a model of enlightened punishment. The bystanders just look on. There is no video recording of the ghastly affair by any onlooker. No audible outrage. No report of the incident in the local, to say nothing of the national, media the day after. No demonstrations and denunciations of police brutality. No questioning of the Public Order Act, the enabling instrument of police violence. What does it take for such savage deployment of power to call forth the people's resistance? Consider the following disconcerting facts on the ground, facts bristling with outrageous irony: The scene of this police brutality is adjacent to the Cape Coast Metropolitan Building where women and men were on that morning exercising their quintessential civic democratic duty, registering to vote in the forthcoming national elections, reaffirming in so doing their rights as citizens and their status as inviolable persons. It is also within walking distance from 'Cape Coast Castle', the obscene name for the demonic place where Africans, captured and sold with the complicity of our villainous chiefs and merchants, were once incarcerated before being exported to the Americas. Primal site of racial and colonial violence, the 'castle' is so close in physical space to the site of police brutality visited upon an enfranchised citizen that fine August morning, yet so far away in lived time, it seems, to function as a mnemonic trigger, spark that work of 'traumatic memory' (Fyfe and Stenberg, 2019) which might incite fury with current inhuman exercises of power sanctioned by our very own democratically appointed agents of the state. Forgotten connectedness, inaudible signs of disapproval; tragic ironies of chronotopic import that fail to provoke the political outrage they richly deserve. When poet Kwadwo Opoku-Agyemang says of the relationship of the populace to the 'castle' that 'We kneel because it stands' (Opuku-Agyemang, 1996: 9) he is speaking of the trained kowtowing of the spirit induced by collective amnesia that permits the legacy of the edifice to persist, unrecognized, and makes the citizenry acquiesce to contemporary violations by the state and its security agencies without a murmur.

Thus cognitively distanced from the history of the enslavers' dungeon, this atrocious brutality and others that regularly occur around the country do not provoke the outrage that might be triggered by a sense of their obscene continuity with racial and colonial violence. Unconnected with being black and the violence that gave birth to blackness, the brutalization of our fellow citizens by the police does not instigate insurgent chants of Black Lives Matter. That is why, strictly speaking, charging the action of the government of Ghana (after the killing of George Floyd) with hypocrisy for 'claiming solidarity with Black people globally against injustice and state violence when it is guilty of doing the same against *Black* people at home'[1] (Kwarteng, 2020), contains a certain category mistake. For while violence committed by Ghana's police is indeed atrocious, it is not directed against *black* lives. Missing here is the lived experience and perceptual vocabulary that would make that charge stick and sting by virtue of connecting violent acts against African Americans and those inflicted on people at home as being in some fundamental sense wrongs inflicted on *black* people.

And here the left universalist would be tempted to welcome that missing linkage and suppose that, thus racially-unindexed, 'subtracted' from the 'identitar-

---

1. Emphasis added. It is true that next door in the much less docile nation of Nigeria, some of the participants in the recent 2020 widespread protest against police brutality perpetrated especially by the Special Anti-Robbery Squad (SARS) articulated an identification with BLM by marching under the conjoined slogan #SARSMUSTEND #BLACK LIVESMATTEREVERYWHERE. Is it pointless quibbling to ask whether this is identification by analogy or affiliation or assimilation? If it is the third, wouldn't that be rather out of place? Even if we take 'blackness' to connote not ethnos, still less epidermis, but rather a world-historical socio-structural position and, consequently, a political commitment answering to that shareable position, does identification by assimilation work in this instance? Does it work given that Nigeria is a black majority nation, with a black political class and a black majority government, and black officers as culpable agents of state violence—and for that very reason are not normally and internally designated black? Isn't the more apposite slogan be what the predominant voices of the #ENDSARS protest in fact declared—'Nigerian [Human] Lives Matter'. That would make an identification, on the part of those who connect the protest with Black Lives Matter, one of analogy or even affiliation, rather than one of assimilation, thereby rendering the adopted slogan's connotation, ultimately, a-racial. But each such mode of identification, whether it is implicit or explicit, has its risks and strengths. For example, the risk involved in the a-racialism inherent in identification by (mere) analogy, is that of tendentious appropriation by the usual suspects, right-wing ideologues. See how they turn Martin Luther King's injunctive dream and prophetic demand —'not by the color of their skin …'—into a history-amnesiac dogma of radical solipsism. On the other hand, the strength of identification (of local forms of violation and resistance) with BLM by analogy or affiliation only, is that it brings the stuff squarely home, makes internal power relations, local public institutions and authorities, indigenous collective and individual agents, recognizably and irrevocably accountable for oppressions and injustices. And it does so in the name of the determinate civic codifications of human rights, namely, the human rights of Nigerians. All the same, my musing regarding the potential force of combined discursive modes makes me wonder how much more powerful the rhetoric of resistance, the language of the Nigerian protests, would be if (as in South Africa) the history of the present and popular memory of that history had at its core the reality of racialized violence definitive of settler colonialism; for in that case apprehension of continuities by analogy with today's state-sponsored violence would be all the more galvanizing, all the more outrage-inducing. As for Ghana, the prospect of such a galvanizing recollective and reconnective practice is even more remote. The iconic instance of colonial state violence ritually invoked at Independence Day celebrations is that of the killing of three army veterans by the colonial police while they were on their way to presenting a petition to the Governor of the Gold Coast on 28 February 1948. That is Ghana's Sharpeville Massacre and its Soweto Uprising conjoined. That is this nation's epic roll call of martyrs.

ian object' as Badiou might say (Swyngedouw, 2014: 132), the language of protest will be compelled to skip the 'moment' of particularity and inescapably speak in the name of universality, in the name of violated humanity. The trouble is that, yes, in *this* non-settler-postcolony, local injustice and state violence do not spark outrage voiced in the name of the shared particularity of *racial* wrongs, wrongs inflicted on *black* people; but neither do they of necessity incite an insurgent invocation of humanity, a rhetoric of resistance containing that interrogative maxim I have referenced in *Left Universalism* as a native idiom of ethical universalism: 'Is s/he not also a human being?' Or incite that maxim uttered not as a tame moral disapproval but as a potent political act? Can it be that only where the particular agony of lives lived *as* black lives is the defining fact of social existence, will that exclamation of universality also be heard in protest? Can it be that one is the other's condition of possibility, that what lets the trumpet of the universal sound as a seditious act is a lived experience of the harrowing particular? Is living memory of brutalization *as* racial wrong precisely what is needed to instigate livid criticism of the general wrong, or at the very least what gives such criticism a certain intensity? Consider the fact that whereas police brutality unleashed in the enforcement of Covid-19 restrictions sparked opposition and demonstrations in South Africa with its living tradition of traumatic memory—consider the angry protests after the police shooting of the disabled sixteen-year old Nathaniel Julies on 26 August, 2020—recurring incidents of police violence in Ghana have been greeted with criminal silence. With memory of the violence which forged this polity as part and parcel of the world system of the racial polity repressed, with the 'lived experience of blackness' effaced as defining mark of social being, the people of this non-settler-postcolony are as destitute of black consciousness as they are of that insurgent transracial 'social and political consciousness' which Fanon envisaged as the goad towards the goal of a 'new humanism'.

## Scandals of Political Economy and Consequences of Indeterminate Criticism

As I said at the beginning of these musings, you are unlikely to hear 'That's Why I am a Socialist' at a public forum anywhere in these parts. There is hardly a Left to speak of in this postcolony, one whose members will dare sing such a song or to whom doing so comes naturally; a Left armed with an organizing rhetoric of resistance. That may be because the non-settler-postcolony is bereft of a perceptual vocabulary and denotative convention with which to name the system of socioeconomic arrangements and attendant policies that vividly spell the subordination of the national interest and well-being to particular interests—name and mount opposition to them.

Consider some recent cases of privatization of state-owned enterprises and transactions involving multinational manufacturing companies and financial institutions—and the tepid responses they received. The year 2018 saw the privatization of the Electrical Company of Ghana. This in defiance of opposition from workers and trade unions, dire predictions of job losses, and exponential increase in user fees. Elsewhere, privatization measures that are seen to bring more hardship to the people, especially the poor, or are viewed as being injurious to the national interest have been met with spirited mobilized opposition. Successful protests against attempted denationalization and privatization measures by Carlos Mesa in Bolivia in 2003 come to mind. In Ghana, also in 2018, a new auto policy featuring such forfeiture of the popular-national interest came into being. In exchange for restricting the importation of second-hand cars, the policy grants multinational car manufacturers a ten-year tax holiday. Thus VW cars will be assembled by a local branch plant and principal dealership. The policy demonstrably delivers a body blow to the life of local used-car dealerships, sabotages the prospects of a domestic automobile manufacturing industry, and, most importantly, aggravates the problem of affordability for ordinary people in the vital area of transport. Yet, if there was any organized opposition to this capitulation to foreign monopoly capital and deference to the tastes and 'no worries' pockets of the national elite, news of that opposition has escaped public dissemination. An even more recent and egregious instance of the surrender of the national interest to foreign control and colluding domestic interests is the case of the Agyapa Royalties Transaction completed in 2020, a case concerning revenues from the mining industry. According to a critical statement by two knowledgeable analysts, it is a ' transaction by which 75.6% of royalties payable to Government over the life of a number of mining operations are being assigned to a Jersey incorporated company and its Ghanaian affiliate' (Ansah and Tsikata, 2020). A shameless example of state capture and conflict of interests, principals of that affiliate are closely associated with the President and party in power; so is the private legal firm that superintended the negotiation of the deal and billed the government for its services. Commenting on the transaction and the less than earth-shaking response it has so far generated, one observer writes as follows: 'Elsewhere, an entire people would march to Parliament and demonstrate daily until this naked rape is abrogated. Not in tribal and partisan Ghana' (Ghanaweb, 2020). Indeed. But perhaps elsewhere, there would be a pre-existing discursive formation, shaped by living history, at the disposal of the people and activists alike with which to call things by their name and mount opposition to such transactions, such products of 'toxic collusion'.

That last phrase, significantly, has to do with South Africa. It is a critic's characterization of the system of political-economic relations, class alliances and alignment of interests, forged after the formal ending of apartheid, the system from which the Marikana massacre of August 2012 sprung (Higginbottom, 2017). More specifically, Andy Higginbottom describes this system's principal feature as the 'co-option and alliance of a black elite that cooperates with multinational capital and has aligned its own advance with multinational capital' via the domains of government, state and the corporate sector (Higginbottom, 2017: 15). Following a discursive tradition that goes back to the Freedom Charter, Julius Malema and the Economic Freedom Fighters have distilled this description into a graphic nomenclature, identifying the system's central generative motor as *white monopoly capital* (Ford, 2019), a concept first articulated by the

South African Communist Party in 1962. That denotation places criticism of the system under the discursive rubric of 'racial capitalism'. And it is that discursive rubric which is absent as a usable weapon of criticism of neo-colonial political-economic transactions and arrangements in the non-settler-postcolony such as Ghana. Perhaps unavoidably absent. Still, here is the question or rather family of questions: What would be the effect of a critique of neo-colonial political-economic policies (such as those I named above) founded on collusive transactions and demonstrably injurious to national-popular interests, if that critique could call on such a discursive tradition and denotative vocabulary? Would scrutiny or exposure of the operations of multinational manufacturing and finance capital and the enabling role of local interests and elites via state capture pack a more powerful rhetorical heft, were the signifier, white monopoly capital, available? What work would perception of the people's wretched conditions of existence as the consequence of exploitation caused by the self-serving collaboration of the elite with white monopoly capital do? Is thinking exploitation in relation to the 'political economy of blackness' (Burden-Stelly, 2020) forged by racial capitalism the true 'weapon of theory' (Cabral) for the insurgent activist? In that case, the answer to Michael Walzer's dismissive view of the concept of racial capitalism and his assertion that 'the key issue is exploitation, not racism' (Walzer, 2020) would be the following: Exploitation is indeed 'the key issue'. Fanon would not disagree. Does he not evoke, approvingly, that moment of disenchantment when the romance of a racial-national community as an undivided whole is shattered by the upsurge of particular interests? In goading accents Fanon recounts the subaltern postcolonial subject's 'discovery' that what is at stake in the emerging new reality is 'the iniquitous fact exploitation;' that the matter of that fact, so to say, is transracial; and that the 'treason' of the elites as they go about the sordid business of accumulation without restraint is not racial-national but rather social, the consequence of a social relation (Fanon, 1968: 145). However, that 'discovery' does not entail, first, reducing structural locations in relations of socioeconomic power to Walzer's strawman of 'racism'. Still less does it warrant the binary opposition from which Walzer seems to want us to take our discursive bearings—critique of racial subordination or critique of (a-racial) social exploitation. In the paradigmatic context of South Africa, the 'effectual truth of the matter', as Machiavelli would put it, is that the critique of exploitation *is* the critique of the socioeconomic conditions of existence in which the *black* majority in particular are mired: a conception of the racial constitution of exploitation. Paradoxically, the a-racial or transracial phenomenon of exploitation and exploitative class interests is, in this context, concretely registered, precisely, in the impoverishment of members of a specific racialized group. The transracial cause here produces racialized consequences. In the event, the indictment of exploitation owes its particular sting to a perceptual vocabulary that identifies it with the systemic damage to black lives and livelihoods caused by the alliance, however asymmetric and fraught with tensions, between the black elite and white monopoly capital. What is at work here is a racialized instance of a social universal, a black-eyed experience, so to speak, of the injuries of class. And this is what makes that Fanonian moment of 'discovery'—the disclosure that antagonistic divisions and interests within the social whole is a transracial fact native to 'the history of societies'—potentially and especially galvanizing instead of being paralyzing.

Consider how this articulation of discursive modes informs criticism of Cyril Ramaphosa's programme and its consequences in South Africa, as reflected in the following statement by Irving Jim of the National Union of Metalworkers of South Africa:

> Ramaphosa may manage to create a semblance of unity between the black capitalists who are created and survive by stealing from the government through tenders, those who are beneficiaries of 'shares' from imperialism and White Monopoly Capital like himself and White Monopoly Capital itself. The trouble, however, is that poverty, unemployment and inequalities suffered by the majority black and African working class will deepen. (Jim, 2018)

Moreover, Irving Jim connects the collusive alliance of 'black capitalists' and 'white monopoly capital' with the state violence employed to 'regulate ... the behavior of striking workers and their communities' as operative parts of one exploitative and oppressive system. The potential consequences of this discursive articulation for critical judgment and action are significant. Ramaphosa's programme before and after Marikana, for all its contingent circumstances, is not entirely fortuitous; it is an intelligible programme and thus an intelligible object of insurgent politics, rather than the target of sanctimonious homilies delivered on Sunday mornings or of moralizing criticisms of 'corruption' as is the norm in a place like Ghana. It provokes a critical practice whose rationality consists, precisely, in the conjunction of the multiple structures and operations of power as interrelated parts of a functioning whole—racialized capitalism. As a complex matter of sociohistorical causality, structural reproduction and lived reality, then, *racial* capitalism is the thing from which critical practice in the settler-postcolony takes its bearings (see Táíwò and Bright, 2020). Perhaps only where capital's continuing dominion in the postcolony is so registered, only where *racial* capitalism is lived not only as capitalism's *fons et origo* but as its very quintessence, will the universality of its iniquity, its specific gravity upon African lives and livelihoods, and the rationality of revolt against it, be made compelling.

## Concluding Questions of Theoretical Practice

Anyone longing for insurgent politics in a place like Ghana may be forgiven for harbouring a truly perverse sentiment: apartheid envy. Why perverse? You would think that in the absence of a history of racial rule in its direct form and lingering consequences, there is nothing but class to confront as the organizing principle of social power and the material cause of social misery; consequently, patently, that there is nothing to lose but the chains of class. Of course, the settler colony was a class society and the non-settler colony was part and parcel of what Charles has designated as the global system of the 'racial polity'. So who save the bizarre sadomasochist would tout the harsh school of apartheid as a necessary crucible of insurgent, emancipatory politics in the postcolony? The very thought is ghastly. However, the dubious fortune of the postcolony that did not undergo settler colonialism as a pre-existing condition, that knew the racialization of the social order only in the shape of indirect rule, the postcolony that was, as a result, denied the lived experience of race as the dominant contradiction in social reality and social consciousness, is that it is today mired in the most grievous injustices but bereft of a perceptual language and visceral tradition of antagonism, protest and revolt. So it is that over the all-too visible geographies of inequality, conspicuous privilege and destitution, toxic collusions between capital, state and class to the detriment of the people, recurring practices of state violence, over transparent evidences of these structural and conjunctural faultlines, a deafening silence reigns. Our ears strain in vain to hear the scream of refusal and resistance, desperately desire to hear, with a witness of another native land at another time, 'the only cry you want to hear/for it is all the city can say' (Césaire, *Cahier*). It may well be that this stubborn culture of docility in the face of scandalous structures of subjugation and recurring incidents of brutalization is a perverse manifestation of Ghanaian exceptionalism, the ethos and habitus peculiar to this nation of jolly sufferers, rather than a generic pathology of the non-settler-postcolony. As I write (October 2020), Nigeria is the scene of unstoppable demonstrations that began as protests against rampant police brutality but are now naming material suffering and social inequality as reasons for insurgent discontent. Perhaps the magnitude of the fault-lines, matching the colossal size of that nation, is too great and pervasive to go forever unopposed; too onerous for the people to keep on enduring the paradox of inequity and iniquity hidden in plain sight. But if the degree of imperturbable quiescence here in Ghana is special, arguably something of a national peculiarity, Ghana may well typify, on the other hand, the growth of compensatory practices that, as they unfailingly do elsewhere, take the place of insurgent political mobilization. For the void created by this inaudible and unarticulated commonality of social misery and the atrophy of an emancipatory politics that would attend to it, that void *will* be filled. As they say, nature abhors a vacuum. So does our human social condition. In a place where the global Occupy Movement is unheard of and Tahrir Square some extraterrestrial location, that void will be occupied by other discursive and material practices: defeatist satire, the witticism of resignation, sardonic references to official state promises that will never be delivered; a culture of survivalist solipsism. As reported by the late Ernest Wamba-dia-Wamba in a dialogue with Michael Neocosmos, in the Democratic Republic of Congo the pragmatics of existence has distilled that culture of self-reliance into an inimitable artform, an informal 'people's constitution', the essence of whose articles is the injunction 'do what you can do on your own'. Walk, don't bother waiting for public transport (Wamba dia Wamba unpublished paper). Such vernacular exercises in everyday-life-as-irony are, recognizably, the common currency in Ghana. They are an oblique indictment of the failed state and its non-delivery of public goods; indictment, however, that does not issue in organized protest; atomized coping practices in place of insurgent collectivity. Above all, that void is filled by the votive community of enraptured believers. Ghana, quintessential scene of this political quiescence in the teeth of multiple structures of subjection, is today ranked among the most religious nations of the world, a land teeming with tithe-eating pastors and noise-polluting places of worship offering a haven for what Peter Tosh called 'vexation of the soul'. And rivalling the balm of the votive community is the lure of ethnic identity and allegiance. A particularly egregious instance of the latter is the reactivation of Asante ethnic chauvinism, with all its royalist and supremacist vocabulary, refashioning a mode of solidarity that is introverted, essentially anti-national and inimical to class consciousness and mobilization, indeed pre-empting all popular-national articulations of discontent, social subjectivity and solidarity.[2] We have here the separating attachments of ethnicity and modes of identity which stand little chance of being harnessed even as shared national registrations of grievance. All the more unlikely that you will encounter in this context social criticism and political action oriented to or generative of 'insurgent universality' (Tomba, 2019)

I have thus been provoked by the dispiriting stupor of my homeland into wondering if an effectual radical politics does not require as a discursive 'moment' a certain nominalist identitarianism, one, that is to say, not tethered to any metaphysics of difference. In so doing, I am debating not only with myself but also with the kind of universalism espoused by Badiou. Confronted with the speechless void of this society—a void that remains stubbornly untroubled even after the world-convulsing spectacle of the lynching of George Floyd, even after coronavirus has illumined cruel social truths in this and every society—has left me seriously rethinking the discursive conditions of insurgent politics. It has strengthened the suspicion I voiced in *Left Universalism* to the effect that Badiou's normative 'new militant subject', one dispossessed of all referents of particularity, is a-human and apolitical. But if the 'identitarian object' is, *pace* Badiou, irreplaceable, it need not function in the service of an absolutist separatism or in opposition to the universal as generalizable particular, if not a presupposition.[3] It may well be that postcolonial discontent is more powerfully audible,

---

2. As noted above, a critic of the Agyapa Royalties Transaction blames its enactment and the absence of protest against it on 'tribal and partisan Ghana'. Even more reductively, a frequent criticism blames it all on the 'Akyem Mafia', that is, the collective egotism of the ethnic group (the Akyems of Eastern Ghana) to which the President, leading members of his administration and indeed principal architects of the deal belong. Predictably, former President John Mahama's echo of that barb sparked anger on the part of some Akyem chiefs and leaders. Totally missing here is a critique of the deal as a *class* transaction, a collusive deal between a fraction of the national bourgeoisie wielding state power and foreign capital to the detriment of national economic self-determination. Similarly, the collapse and closing of seven banks for insolvency and questionable practices in 2018—resulting in customers' loss of their deposits—was lambasted in some quarters as an assault on *Asante* businessmen, since a prominent banker who is an Asante was owner of one of the banks in question. Criticism of the class genealogy of state capture and economic malfeasance are here deflected into the dead-ends of ethnic-reductionist, personalized, and moralistic denunciations of corruption, greed and inter-ethnic envy. You will listen in vain for a language of scrutiny, contestation and protest that, like reactions to the 2008 subprime crisis, indexed the banks' principal victims as a social collectivity—racialized class victims of finance capital.
3. Working in dialogue with my idea of the 'partisan universal', Ayyaz Mallick has proposed, as a critical corrective to disembodied, context-unindexed universalism—eminently vulnerable to tendentious appropriation by right-wing ideologues—the 'concrete universal' as the 'point of arrival' of thought and practice that is oriented to the generalizable particular. See Mallick, 'From Partisan Universal to Concrete Universal? The Pashtun Tahaffuz Movement in Pakistan', *Antipode* 56: 6 (2020).

generative of revolt, ultimately of emancipatory politics, where that discontent is articulated, as in the settler-postcolony, in a vivid perceptual vocabulary born of the obdurate racialized organization of social power and conditions of human existence. Critique without a visceral perceptual vocabulary bespeaking the exclusions and violations, the concrete material conditions of life lived by a determinate human community is vacuous, ineffectual, dead on arrival. However, that visceral perceptual vocabulary and the rhetoric of resistance it spawns are not without risks. Shorn of thought—universalizing thought with respect to its objects and ends—such a vocabulary risks reification of the products of history, mystification of the agents, relations and ends of which it speaks. As a famous utterance has it: 'Thoughts without content are empty, intuitions without conceptions are blind'. Faithful to Fanon's commitment to the principle and practice of democratic enlightenment, we must hold onto the idea that a nascent emancipatory politics *gives proof of its rationality to itself* —not to some external overseer of the concept—in virtue of that labour of connectedness which, 'beginning with a [particular] case (*à partir d'un cas*)' (Fanon, 1968: 146, 2011: 538) achieves a 'self-generated' universality (Neocosmos, 2017) as a result of the auspicious complication of its objects. The challenge for radical politics, then, is how to attend to the cries of one determinate community of suffering humanity and, in so doing, hear the agonized panting of all those other sentient beings who can't breathe.

# Bibliography

Andrews, K. 2016. 'Black Is A Country: Building Solidarity Across Borders.' *World Policy Journal* 33 (1, spring): 15–19.

Ansah, K., and Fui, T. S. 2020. 'Statement on the Agyapa Royalties Transaction.' *Ghanaweb*, August 19.

Burden-Stelly, C. 2020. 'Modern U.S. Racial Capitalism: Some Theoretical Insights.' *Black Agenda Report*, August 19.

Fanon, F. 1968. *The Wretched of the Earth*. Translated by Constance Farrington. New York: Grove Press.

_____. 2011. *Œuvres*. Paris: Découverte.

Ford, G. 2018. '*NYT* Joins Campaign to Purge the Term, "White Monopoly Capital" in South Africa.' *Black Agenda Report*, February, 8.

Fyfe, J., and Maximillian, S., 2019. 'Unsettled Landscapes: Traumatic Memory in a Croatian Hinterland.' *Space and Polity* 23 (3): 299–318.

Graham, Y. 2016. 'Ghana's Socio-Economic Transformation and the Imperative for Equitable and Inclusive Development.' *Social Watch*.

Hartman, S. 2018. 'The Anarchy of Colored Girls Assembled in a Riotous Manner.' *South Atlantic Quarterly* 117 (3, July): 465–490.

Higginbottom, A. 2017. 'The Marikana Massacre in South Africa: The Results of Toxic Collusion.' Paper delivered at *XVIII Congresso Columbiano de Historica, Medellin, Columbia*, October 12.

Jim, I. 2018. 'New Era in War on Workers: The Ramaphosa Presidency in South Africa.' *The Bullet*, February 18.

Kwarteng, K. 2020. 'Pan-Africanism Begins at Home.' *Africa Is A Country*, September 21.

Neocosmos, M. 2017. 'The Creolization of Political Theory and the Dialectic of Emancipatory Thought.' *Journal of French and Francophone Philosophy* 25 (2): 6–25.

New Frame. 2020a. 'Brutal Evictions Worsen South Africa's Urban Crisis.' *New Frame*, editorial, July 10.

_____. 2020b. Editorial, August 5.

Opuku-Agyemang, K. 1996. *Cape Coast Castle*. Accra: Afram Publications.

Opoku-Agyemang, S. 2019. 'Your "Ghana" Is Different from Mine.' *Ghanaweb*, January 21.

Owusu, G., Martin, O., Adobea, O. Y., and Charlotte, W., 2016. 'Can Poor Neigbourhoods Be Correlated with Crime? Evidence from Urban Ghana.' *Ghana Journal of Geography* 8 (1): 11–31.

Sekyi-Otu, A. 1996. *Fanon's Dialectic of Experience*. Cambridge: Harvard University Press.

_____. 2019. *Left Universalism, Africacentric Essays*. New York: Routledge.

Swyngedouw, E. 2014. 'Where Is the Political? Insurgent Mobilisation and the Incipient "Return of the Political".' *Space and Polity* 18 (2): 122–136.

Táíwò, O. O., and Liam, K. B. 2020. 'Reply to Walzer "Racial Capitalism" is the Kind We've Got.' *Black Agenda Report*, August 19.

Tomba, M. 2019. *Insurgent Universality: An Alternative Legacy of Modernity*. Oxford: Oxford University Press.

Walzer, M. 2020. 'A Note on Racial Capitalism.' *Dissent*, July 29.

Wamba-dia-Wamba, E., unpublished paper. In dialogue with Michael Neocosmos, 'The Struggle for Africa: History, Culture, Philosophy, Politics.'

# THE STILL WRETCHED OF THE EARTH: A CRITIQUE OF IMAGINARY DECOLONIZATION

David Pavón-Cuéllar

This chapter is about the *still-wretched of the Earth*. It is about those who have not been liberated by what is described here as an *imaginary decolonization*. It is about the victims of neocolonialism—the peoples of the Third World, a world that continues to exist as it was conceived in the past, although now it is named differently.

This chapter is about something as charged as the Third World, for which we have fought so hard, and not about something as new and neutral like the Global South, which can make us forget our struggles in a past that is still our present. There will be no subtle distinctions on the following pages between underdeveloped, developing and emerging countries. These distinctions, like those that erase the class struggles within each society, can be very useful, but they distract us when we try to think about the fundamental division between the oppressed and the oppressors, the looters and the looted, the First World and the Third World, and the neocolonial powers and their victims in underdeveloped countries that continue to be seen as underdeveloped (i.e. eternal infants), although now they are termed more respectfully.

Underdevelopment and the Third World have not been overcome with politically correct words. Imaginary decolonization has not actually liberated anyone from colonialism. The looting, exploitation and oppression of the colonized peoples do not cease (see Bond, 2006; Ceceña, 2009). These peoples continue to develop rich countries (see Kar & Schjelderup, 2016; Hickel, 2017). The rich continue to enrich themselves at the expense of the poor by impoverishing them and by keeping them in poverty (see Laplante & Hillali, 2018).

The wretched of the Earth are still here. Their situation is not very different from that of their parents, grandparents and great-grandparents, whom Frantz Fanon wrote about. Many of Fanon's ideas still allow us to think about the peoples of the Third World, who can still learn a lot about their situation through the book, *The Wretched of the Earth*, which Fanon has left to them.

## Change Everything so that Everything Stays the Same

David Macey (2012) has pointed out how, in *The Wretched of the Earth*, 'impressions of what Fanon had seen of the newly independent states of Africa merge into a nightmarish picture of colonial Algeria' (2012: 451). These two visions reflect the historical context in which Fanon found himself, both when dictating his book in 1961 and when writing—between 1956 and 1959—some texts that he included in it. The writing of *The Wretched of the Earth* coincided with the Algerian War of Independence and with the decolonization of most of the African countries, including: Sudan, Tunisia and Morocco in 1956; Ghana in 1957; Guinea in 1958; and Cameroon, Senegal, Madagascar, Somalia, Niger, Burkina Faso, Gabon, Chad, Mali, Nigeria, Mauritania, Ivory Coast, Democratic Republic of the Congo and other states in 1960.

While carefully observing the first few years of independent life in various African countries, Fanon is still fighting for the liberation of Algeria, which will be consummated in July 1962, a few months after the publication of *The Wretched of the Earth*. This work is located in the revealing transition between colonial and postcolonial or neocolonial times. The former times had not ended when the latter had already begun. Both times coexisted and could be compared to each other and analyzed in the same historical space.

In addition to being astonishingly insightful, Fanon's analysis is best placed to discover what is and is not changing with the independence of the former colonies. The discovery is bleak. Not only did continuity prevail over discontinuity, but discontinuity itself appeared as a means of continuity.

Fanon shows how the colonial system, threatened by the liberation movements, is paradoxically reconstituted thanks to the independence of African countries. It is as if decolonization was necessary to perpetuate colonialism. History seemed to follow Tancredi's famous formula in Lampedusa's *The Leopard* (1960): 'If we want things to stay as they are, things will have to change' (1960: 40).

Colonialism had to change in order to remain the same. In order for the oppression and exploitation of Africa to continue, the great transformations that took place between 1956 and 1960 were needed. We understand that these transformations have not satisfied Fanon—that they have disappointed, afflicted and saddened him. They were confirmations of the weight of repetition and its 'dehistorizing root', although they were also, at the same time, a 'radical' point of support for the hopeful liberation of the 'subject in historicity' (De Oto, 2003: 147-152).

Without the hope that Fanon placed in the future, his vision of the present would have been totally discouraging. This vision makes clear that the victory of the liberation movements did not mean the conquest of what they were fighting for. The freedom of the African peoples remained on the horizon—always far away, moving further and further away as they advanced towards it. By its own temporality, by the eternalization of its present, this reality remains the same today as always, and Fanon knew it well since he was an 'accomplished realist', as Nigel Gibson (2003: 204) has well noted.

## Fanon and Neocolonialism

Fanon refers to the militant who realizes that 'while destroying colonial oppression, he contributes to building another apparatus of exploitation' (Fanon, 1961:

138-139).[1]. At first glance, the new oppressors and exploiters are no longer White, but native. First, during the war of liberation, the native exploiters are those who do business related to the war. Later, in the newly independent nations, they occupy the empty spaces left by the colonists to continue, like the colonists, the oppression of the African people.

The new Indigenous oppressors and exploiters of Africa are identified by Fanon using the generic label of *national bourgeoisie*. Fanon offers a ruthless portrait of this rising class: It is a 'useless and harmful' class that does not even correspond to a 'true bourgeoisie', since it is, rather, a 'small caste with long teeth, greedy and voracious', lacking 'inventiveness and great ideas', a 'caricature' and not a 'replica' of Europe's bourgeoisie (Fanon, 1961: 168-169). Unlike the European bourgeois, the African parvenus do not build or innovate anything. Nor do they transform society. They do not take risks or fulfil any historical mission. Ultimately, for Fanon, the African bourgeois 'is literally useless', merely taking and preserving the colonial 'heritage' of economy, thought and institutions (1961: 169).

The colonial inheritance is reproduced by the Third World national bourgeoisie. This reproduction, as Fanon shows, is not only formal. The bourgeois of Africa did not only think, act and dominate as the colonists did; the reproduction of colonialism is real since the African national bourgeoisie perpetuated colonial structures by fulfilling an indispensable function that made it possible for those structures to continue to operate. As Fanon (1961) explains, the bourgeoisie in Africa become mere 'intermediaries' and 'business agents of the Western bourgeoisie' (1961: 148-149). This First World bourgeoisie remains the true bourgeoisie of the Third World. The African bourgeois are only 'representatives' of the European bourgeoisie (1961: 171).

Europe continues to colonially dominate the African peoples through the Indigenous bourgeois. These bourgeois not only act as colonists, but represent, serve and work for the new colonists. The African bourgeoisie, according to Fanon's terms (1961), sells itself to foreign companies, 'combines its interests' with those of those companies, is internally 'connected' with Europe, and exports to European banks 'the benefits of exploitation' of the African peoples (1961: 160-166). Thus, after independence, everything continues to be approximately as it was under colonialism.

Colonial structures do not stop working after the victory of imaginary decolonization. After their independence, the African countries maintained a relationship of dependency on the European countries. The former metropolis still ruled its former colonies, now indirectly, through the bourgeoisie 'whom it feeds' and the national armies 'framed' by European experts (Fanon, 1961: 167). Commercial transactions remain under the control of Europe. Africa's industry is only allowed to develop in 'assembly factories' (1961: 169). Africans are still the 'small farmers of Europe, specialists in raw products' (1961: 148). The economy

---

1. The translations in this chapter to *Les damnés de la terre* are mine.

of the Third World remains 'directed' by the First World through 'loans and gifts, demands, concessions and guarantees' (1961: 161). Everything of importance remained the same: threats, manipulation, coercion, domination, plunder and so on. Dependency continues after independence.

The imaginary decolonization does not allow the Third World to liberate itself from colonialism, but only to renew it. This was how neocolonialism arose, as conceived by Fanon (1961), who had already spoken of a 'neocolonial structure' (1961: 161). Neocolonialism, for Fanon, is the sad outcome of the struggles for liberation. Latin-American and African peoples free themselves from the degraded colonial structure only to surrender, unarmed, to a brand new neocolonial structure.

Neocolonialism is not only a renewal of what preceded it, but it also seems to be the rehabilitation, revival, revivification and reinvigoration of a colonialism that was unbearable and unsustainable in its older forms. Forms should be changed to preserve content. In order not to destroy itself, the colonial system tried to 'fix itself' or 'reform itself', as Sartre says in 1956, when he introduces the concept of 'neocolonialism' (Sartre, 1964: 25-48).

The neocolonial is like an evolution of the colonial that seeks to avoid a true anticolonial revolution. This was well understood by Fanon, who surely read Sartre's 1956 text and stated a year later that 'the characteristic of neocolonialism is to prevent revolutionary situations by introducing evolutionary methods into its system' (Fanon, 1957: 463). What Fanon did not yet understand at the time, and what he would discover later, is that neocolonial evolutionary methods could include formal independence and imaginary decolonization, which allowed the perpetuation of real colonialism.

The point is that the perpetuation of colonialism was and continued to be inevitable, perhaps not so much for itself as for what underlies it. Fanon (1961) recognizes what is really fundamental when he refers to capitalism as 'forced to camouflage' and today as 'adorned with the neocolonial mask' (1961: 148-149). Neocolonialism, like colonialism, is a manifestation of the same capitalist system that needs its colonial device first, followed by its Third-World twist.

## Latin American Lesson

The Third World is what capitalism uses to supersede the colonial order as a kind of replacement solution (i.e. a continuation of colonialism by other means). What is tragic is that this continuation could go on indefinitely. This risk of an eternalization of colonialism through neocolonialism is substantiated in some of the references to Latin America in *The Wretched of the Earth*.

The Latin American case is sometimes used by Fanon as an example of a danger that threatens independent African countries. The danger is that of an imaginary decolonization that leads to colonialism as an inescapable logic, in a time without time and in a kind of eternity that closes the horizon and makes any attempt at liberation fail. The latter is verified in the smallest details of the history of Latin America. For example, in Brazil, the capital was well understood to be a colonial concept that must be 'desacralized'; that is why Rio, which was 'an insult to the Brazilian people', was abandoned as the capital, but very soon Brasilia became the same, 'a capital as monstrous as the first' (Fanon, 1961: 178).

The example chosen by Fanon has a precise function in his argument about the capitals of the Third World but can also serve to illustrate a global problem in the history of Latin America. Brasilia is one of those typical Latin American roads that only serve to lead people astray—to wear themselves out, waste time and return to the starting point. The whole is like a colonial maze from which it is not possible to escape. In the end, Latin Americans are always at the beginning, fighting for their independence, even though many Latin American countries have been independent since the 19th century.

The Latin American history of the last 150 years seems to have been useless. Latin Americans are still at the beginning of everything. The reason for this is very simple, and Fanon expresses it clearly. The peoples of Latin America have left their history in the hands of their local bourgeoisies, who 'are useless', and therefore, once these privileged castes disappear, 'we will realize that nothing has happened since independence, that everything must be retaken, that one must start from scratch' (Fanon, 1961: 169).

The Latin American lesson for Africa is that people must not let the bourgeoisie decide their destiny. When this bourgeoisie decides for the people, it simply drags them into its inertia, its degradation and its reaction and regression, and it makes them stumble and fall. This fall can take many different forms. Fanon (1961) refers to at least two of them that are characteristic of Latin America: (a) the 'neglected Latin American fascism' that saves itself 'the parliamentary phase' (1961: 165), and (b) the 'depravity of the national bourgeoisie' that 'practically turns its country into the First World brothel', with 'the casinos in Havana and Mexico City, the beaches of Rio, Copacabana, and Acapulco, the young Brazilian and Mexican girls, the thirteen-year-old mestizas' (1961: 149-150). Thus, oppressed and prostituted by their local bourgeoisies, the Latin American peoples have been reduced to a neocolonial subjugation against which Fanon wants to warn the African peoples.

Fanon offers a sad image of Latin America. Unfortunately, the image is faithful and currently remains. There is an indisputable persistence of fascist tyrannies, sex tourism and other situations referenced by Fanon. Perhaps the modes and places have changed, but the reality is approximately the same. There is very little, perhaps nothing, that has advanced in half a century.

After *The Wretched of the Earth*, almost all Latin American countries, including the three mentioned by Fanon (i.e. Brazil, Mexico and Cuba), had the propensity to return again and again to the starting point. In Brazil, just as João Goulart's promising reforms were interrupted and reversed by the 1964 coup d'état, so also the fascist regime of Jair Bolsonaro neutralized the achievements of the progressive governments of Lula and Dilma. Mexico, although still benefiting from the conquests of the Revolution of 1910, has been struggling in vain for several decades against the reactionary tangle that prevents the revolutionary advance from being carried out. The gesture of the Cuban Revolution of 1959 was certainly most hopeful, but finally the island was paralyzed, as if suspended, so as not to fall again.

## Third World, Underdevelopment, Dependency and Neocolonialism

Latin American countries are still trapped in neocolonialism, which has also clearly unfolded on the African continent and in Southeast Asia. All such cases exhibit neocolonial forms of historical functioning such as paralysis, stumbling, relapse, regression, repetition, self-inflicted harm, useless self-immolation, strenuous conflicts and vicious circles. The only beneficiaries of all this are the national and First World bourgeoisies, which now, as in 1961, continue to be allies who divide up the loot and enrich themselves at the expense of the supposedly emerging countries.

Most of the emerging countries are not truly emerging. If they are defined by their emergence, it is because they constantly emerge, because they do not finish emerging, because they do not really emerge. As much as they develop, they still remain underdeveloped. The same is true of other underdeveloped or developing countries. The problem is that development is never absolute, but it is relative to a situation and a position in the global structure of capitalism. This was explained very well in the theories of dependency, which are still as valid now as they were half a century ago.

As dependency theorists taught us, underdeveloped countries are tied to their dependent status (Marini, 1974). It is in dependency that the former colonies develop under the new imperialism (Dos Santos, 1975). This is why they only manage to develop their underdevelopment (Frank, 1974). Underdeveloped countries are increasingly underdeveloped, changing without changing, because they are condemned to a 'uniform, static, immobile' situation that is a reality and not just an 'image' attributable to the theories of dependency, as Robert J. C. Young (2001: 54) optimistically claims.

It goes without saying that immobility does not imply an ahistorical vision. There is a history of underdevelopment. First, former colonies were deliberately underdeveloped by the colonial powers (Rodney, 1973). The underdeveloped countries then had to maintain their underdevelopment to adequately fulfil their role in the global capitalist system (Salama, 1972). Under capitalism, underdeveloped countries can only develop in a dependent, subordinate, neocolonial way (Nkrumah, 1967). They can only move under the conditions of neocolonialism (Zea, 1971; Macías Chávez, 2015). They can only advance along the paths of the neocolonial maze, increasingly lost but without advancing at all, always returning to the starting point (see Haag, 2011; Langan, 2018).

Finally, colonialism is always here, perhaps transforming itself, but persisting. Its past is the present and future for the countries that were once colonized. It is as if their colonial history decided their fate. What is certain is that practically all former colonies are still suffering aspects of this neocolonialism that was evoked by Fanon in 1961 and officially defined that year in Cairo, by the Conference of

African Peoples, as 'the survival of the colonial system in spite of formal recognition of political independence in emerging countries, which become the victims of an indirect and subtle form of domination by political, economic, social, military or technical means' (All-African Peoples' Conference, 1961: para. 2).

## Expressions and Explanations of Neocolonialism

The neocolonial situation has the most diverse expressions (e.g. those identified by Fanon). It would be impossible here to mention them all, but a few are worth remembering. At the base, there is the persistent lack of sovereignty of the former colonies, the enrichment of the First World at the expense of the Third World, the unstoppable exploitation of Africa, Latin America and South and Southeast Asia, the international division of classes and labor, unfair trade, the haemorrhage of wealth from the south to the north, the systematic looting of the natural resources of poor countries, the exploitation of their cheap labor, their dependence and their economic fragility and the external debt. In the superstructure we have extreme inequality and abysmal social gaps, systemic racism, destroyed cultures, wars caused and sustained by the First World and by local oligarchies, massive forced migrations, the death, drowned in the Mediterranean or thirsty in the deserts of the southern United States.

Neocolonialism, with its well-known superstructural expressions, can be explained in part by the economic base or infrastructure on which it rests. This typically Marxist explanation is found, for example, in dependency theories. However, although necessary and fundamental, the economic explanation is insufficient. It is particularly so in this case since neocolonial logic continues to operate like colonial logic, which, as Fanon (1961) well warned, inverts the relationship between base and superstructure, making 'the cause a consequence', as the 'economic infrastructure is also a superstructure' (1961: 43).

To paraphrase Fanon, poor and exploited African people are poor and exploited because they are African, which does not exclude that they are African because they are still poor and exploited. They have not become like those rich exploiters who can Whitewash and Europeanize themselves. On a global level, neocolonialism is based on the looting of wealth, but this exploitation of the Third World is also based on political, cultural-ideological and psychosocial factors that are determinants of neocolonial logic. Some of these factors were identified by Fanon and remain current in the African, Latin American and Asian contexts.

On the political level, there are various means by which the First World still exercises its power over the Third World, including the strategy of division and rule, of 'opposing peoples against each other', thus fueling regional, tribal and religious conflicts (Fanon, 1961: 156). On the cultural-ideological level, favoring these conflicts, are the emptiness, weakness and fragility of the 'national consciousness' of the former colonies (1961: 145-146). Finally, on the psychosocial level, the one that interests us most here, Fanon mentions two factors that underlie these deficiencies in national consciousness: (a) the 'spirit' of the Third

World bourgeoisie, and (b) the 'mutilation of the colonized man' (1961: 146). Let us examine separately these two psychosocial factors, which are at the very foundation of the superstructural factors that explain neocolonialism in Fanon's explanatory model.

## Spirit of the Bourgeoisie in the Former Colonies

We have previously commented that the Third World national bourgeoisie, as conceived by Fanon, is characterized by its uselessness, lack of historical mission, harmfulness, internal connection with Europe and responsibility in the perpetuation of colonial power. Fanon (1961) explains these characteristic features by what he calls 'the spirit' of the former colonies' bourgeoisie (1961: 146, 149). The term 'spirit' is understood here as something psychosocial, determined by society and explicitly situated on the 'psychological plane' (1961: 149). Although Fanon is suspicious of psychology and has been warned against the danger of psychologizing racism and colonialism, he is particularly sensitive to the psychological plane, perhaps due to his training and experience as a psychiatrist. This expertise allows him to probe the deepest psychosocial factors that have turned the Third World bourgeoisie into an accomplice and agent of neocolonialism.

Fanon considers that the role of the former colonies' bourgeoisie has been determined not only by its submissive, humble attitude towards foreign companies, but also by its 'narrow vision and lack of ambition', as well as by its 'joyous spirit' by which it 'hides its construction phase to launch itself into enjoyment' (Fanon, 1961: 149, 161). The bourgeois of the former colonies want to reap the fruits without deserving them (i.e. without having sown, without having made any effort). They intend to avoid the bourgeois struggles and reach the end for the party of the victorious class.

The joyous spirit results, according to Fanon, from the identification of the Third World bourgeoisie with the European bourgeoisie in a late stage—a 'negative and decadent' phase—without having gone through the 'first stages of exploration and invention' (1961: 149). Identifying itself with the old and tired European bourgeois, the underdeveloped young bourgeoisie suffers from 'early senility' and is 'already senile without having known either the petulance or the fearlessness or the voluntarism of youth and adolescence' (1961: 149, 161). This allows an understanding of many of the problems of the bourgeois of the former colonies, such as their lack of 'ideas, dynamism and invention', their panic at 'initiatives that involve a minimum of risk' and their wastefulness in 'ostentatious expenses' such as mansions and luxury cars (1961: 149-151). It is about appearing to be what they are not, having what they do not deserve and being prematurely what they are not ready to be.

The underdeveloped bourgeois don't want to bother themselves with anything other than enjoying their lives. They are not willing to work to create anything but prefer to limit themselves to imitation. Their 'laziness' and 'mimicry' makes them recklessly embrace everything European, even 'the most rotten roots of colonialist thought', including, paradoxically, racism (Fanon, 1961: 157). Although they belong to peoples who are victims of racism, the bourgeois of the former colonies have no problem being racists themselves. They also don't mind being exploiters. This makes Fanon say that 'exploitation can present a Black or Arab appearance' and that 'it happens that Blacks are whiter than Whites' (1961: 138-139).

If Fanon thinks that non-Whites can be whiter than Whites, it is because he is clearly distinguishing two kinds of whiteness: (a) a biological or corporal one, consisting of the colour and pigmentation of the skin, and (b) another symbolic, psychological or psychosocial whiteness, which is rooted in the spirit, attitude and relationship with the other. Qualifying Fanon's phrase, then, it happens that Blacks are more symbolically White than biologically White. These two ways of being White can be distinguished through two different terms, as Bolívar Echeverría (2010) has done with the concepts of 'whiteness' (*blancura*) and 'whiteyness' (*blanquitud*), the first designating the colour of the skin and the second a subjectivity that is historically associated with that skin colour and underlies capitalist European modernity (2010: 58-64).

As Echeverría shows, capital is not a colourless entity, but has a spiritual, ideological or symbolic coloration. Capital is White. It is pale, blond and light-eyed like colonialism, whatever the color of the bourgeois who embodies it.

## The Mutilated Human Being in the Former Colonies

Along with the White spirit of the Third World bourgeoisie, the second psychosocial factor that Fanon places at the foundation of neocolonialism is the mutilation of the colonial subject. This mutilation is the effect of the colonial violence exposed in the famous first chapter of *The Wretched of the Earth*. As Fanon shows, colonialism is an extremely violent system that hurts its victims and amputates important parts of their being. These victims fail to recover, even centuries after their nations have achieved formal political independence, as in Latin American societies, which are still deeply injured and maimed by the Spanish, Portuguese and French colonialism of the 16th to 20th centuries.

The colonial damage inflicted in the past puts the former colonies in a position that is vulnerable to neocolonialism. Neocolonial devices attach to existing colonial wounds but, in turn, prevent them from healing and keep them open, thus ensuring the perpetuation of vulnerability and neocolonialism. This perpetuation is also the reproduction of the colonial violence exposed by Fanon.

Colonial violence is reproduced through neocolonial violence. Both are the same violence that is not only real (e.g. the military interventions of the United States and its allies in Korea, Guatemala, Vietnam, Nicaragua, Iraq or Afghanistan), but also symbolic or ideological (e.g. the racist and xenophobic speeches that have been recently accentuated in the extreme right). For Fanon (1961), it is the violence that 'dehumanizes and animalizes', that sees the African, the Asian or the Latin American as the 'absolute evil', as the 'enemy of values', as a 'corrosive element, destroying everything that comes close to it', or as a 'deforming element, disfiguring everything related to aesthetics or morals' (1961: 44-45). As Fanon (1952) shows in *Black Skin, White Masks*, all this violent colonial and now neocolonial denigration allows an 'inferiorization' of the non-European that is the correlate of the 'superiorization' of the European (1952: 75).

Both objectively and subjectively, and both economically and culturally-ideologically, colonial powers have risen, enlarged, and been enriched at the expense of their colonies by diminishing, lowering and impoverishing them. The problem is that the inferiorized assume their inferiority; they take it for granted and they identify with it intimately. As Fanon (1952) says, there is an 'internalization or, better, epidermization of this inferiority' (1952: 8). The African, the Asian or the Latin American end up convincing themselves of their inferiority and act accordingly by denigrating themselves, stumbling over themselves, seeking failure, sabotaging themselves and bowing down to the European or the American, which obviously favours the persistence of the neocolonial logic.

In addition to inserting itself into the colonial wounds of the colonized subject, neocolonialism relies on the internalization of inferiority and the assimilation of colonial violence by its victims. This assimilation gives rise to 'fratricidal struggles', 'suicidal behaviour' and various forms of 'collective self-destruction' (Fanon, 1961: 55, 59). The violence that should be directed against the colonial and neocolonial powers turns instead against the colonized subjects themselves. This occurs for various reasons; among them, one, emphasized by Fanon, that is too simple and evident: 'the Indigenous people are among them' and appear to each other 'as a screen', since 'each one hides the national enemy from the other' (1961: 295).

Since it cannot be easily exercised against the First World or against the capitalist system, violence is unleashed on the fellows of the Third World, who are the concrete beings at hand. The result is the high levels of criminal and political violence in African and Latin American countries. It is no coincidence that these countries are the most violent in the world. Here, violence is a colonial heritage and a neocolonial phenomenon.

## Condemned by Men

Neocolonialism is as violent as colonialism. Its violence is fundamentally structural (Galtung, 1969). It is true that it comes from the capitalist structure, but it is as colonial as this structure. It is, as Fanon (1961: 297) says, a 'direct product of the colonial situation'. It is violence specific to former colonies, and it is specifically suffered by colonized subjects—by subjects mutilated by colonialism and now by neocolonialism (Pavón-Cuéllar, 2019).

There are countless examples of human beings suffering neocolonial violence today. All of them continue to be victims of others, 'condemned by men', as Fanon (1961: 283) rightly says. The still-condemned of the Earth show that decolonization has been a purely imaginary process in the former colonies. This is as true now as it was in 1961. Neocolonialism continues to colonially oppress Third World subjects such as marginalized Indigenous people, rejected migrants, and exploited labourers—three cases discussed next.

Of course, Indigenous people, migrants and laborers do not suffer the same oppression in different places. Neocolonialism does not treat the various Indigenous peoples the same. The neocolonial exploitation of labor is not the same in India or Bangladesh as it is in Brazil or Mexico or in Lesotho or Nigeria. Asian migrants in Australia have different experiences than Africans in Europe or Mexicans and Central Americans in the United States. Although there are so many differences between these cases, there are also intimate connections, profound coincidences and insistent repetitions that allow a glimpse into the global character of neocolonialism.

## Marginalized Indigenous People

Indigenous people continue to be marginalized in their own territories. Decolonization did not return these territories to them. The best lands—the humid and fertile valleys—have generally been monopolized by the national bourgeoisies, large White or Mestizo owners, or by foreign fruit or grain companies.

The Indigenous people must work for the new owners or remain confined in the mountains or on sterile soils. It is common for them to live in the greatest misery, suffer from hunger and die of curable diseases. They often do not have easy access to healthcare and education. Their living conditions tend to be worse than in urban centers. When they go down to the cities for a better life, Indigenous people are victims of all kinds of racism, both discriminatory and segregative. It is as if they remind the others of their colonized and neocolonized condition. Perhaps it is partly because of this that they are systematically excluded, inferiorized and despised by beings Whiter or more Whitened than they are, more westernized or modernized, or wealthier and more empowered.

Non-Indigenous people of the Third World tend to interpret the role of colonists in their relationship with Indigenous people. The First Nations often suffer the same marginalization as in colonial times. It is infrequent that imaginary decolonization has improved their place in society; rather, it made the marginalization worse.

## Exploited Laborers

The luckiest marginalized Indigenous people are those who manage to rise to the level of exploited laborers in mines, plantations or urban factories. They often work for foreign companies and leave their lives there. It is not uncommon for them to have workdays of more than 12 hours, to be reduced to a condition of semi-slavery and to lack the most elementary labor rights. They receive miserable wages, earning per day, week or month less than what is earned per hour in the First World. They are exploited, producing very high rates of surplus value and profit. Most of the wealth they produce ends up being concentrated and consumed in the neocolonial metropolises of Europe and North America.

Exploited laborers enrich the First World and the bourgeoisies of the Third World. In exchange they receive a few crusts, just enough to stay alive. Their lives are usually spent in unsanitary conditions. In spite of everything, they surpass their previous marginalization to a certain degree, have a better alimentation and sometimes access certain health and education services.

The laborers may even be able to Whiten and abandon the Indigenous conditions that made them victims of racism, but the price they pay is very high. They suffer alienation, depersonalization, loss of identity, self-dispossession, cultural misery, proletarianization, disassociation, loneliness and vulnerability. The big cities of poor and emerging countries are hellish for the working class. Crime rates are extremely high. Depression is as common as homicide, addiction, prostitution, rape and sex trafficking.

## The Rejected Migrants

Just as the luckiest Indigenous people are those who rise to the level of exploited laborers, so the luckiest exploited laborers are those who rise to the top of rejected migrants. These migrants are like the elite of the wretched of the Earth in the current neocolonial stage. Only they manage to savor at least a little of the peace and prosperity of the neocolonial powers. It is the greatest success imaginable, but it is almost impossible to achieve.

Accessing the First World is increasingly difficult. There are more and more immigration barriers. Europe, the United States and the other rich countries have become an impregnable great fortress with ever-higher walls. The purpose of these walls is very simple: to not share wealth, to keep poverty out, to protect loot stolen from poor countries and to protect it obviously from the same poor countries and their miserable and hungry inhabitants.

Migrants must expose themselves to the greatest dangers on their journeys to neocolonial powers. They must first cross other poor countries where they are murdered, kidnapped, raped, prostituted, sold and enslaved, as is the case with Central Americans crossing Mexico or with those from sub-Saharan countries crossing North Africa. Then migrants must traverse the Mediterranean or the deserts of the southern United States. When they do not drown or die of thirst, hunger or heat, they risk being detained. Finally, once they arrive in the First World 'paradise', they will become migrants who are systematically rejected by society and by the government, as well as persecuted by the immigration services and by the new extreme right, neo-Nazi groups or white supremacists. They will often live in constant fear of being deported. This will make them accept all kinds of abuse. Sometimes, they will be physically assaulted and will suffer the same racism—the same discrimination and segregation—that they had already suffered, at first, as Indigenous people in their own countries. Other times they will not have the same rights as citizens of the countries in which they are located. Their socioeconomic (i.e. income and living) levels will invariably be lower than that of the rest of the population. They will not stop being below—always below—where colonialism and now neocolonialism put them.

# In Conclusion

Rejected migrants, exploited laborers and marginalized Indigenous people make up millions of Third World peoples. They are some of the current victims of neo-colonialism—of the neocolonial powers and of their representatives in the Asian, African and Latin American national bourgeoisies. Those Indigenous laborers and migrants are, thus, part of the still-wretched of the Earth. They are children, grandchildren and great-grandchildren of the mutilated people Fanon referred to in 1961. They are no less mutilated. They are no less wretched.

The still-wretched of the Earth continue to suffer hunger and misery. They die more easily and sooner than the rest of humanity. They suffer more from the consequences of economic crises and climate change. They continue to pay First World bills. They continue to give infinitely more than they receive. They are still despised by others and by themselves. And they are more numerous than they were before.

The still-wretched of the Earth need from their allied intellectuals the continued reading of Fanon in a militant, politically committed way, and not just for academic research or reflection. Thanks to the same acuteness that excites scholars, Fanon can be extremely helpful in struggles against capitalism, against new forms of imperialism, for decolonization and for the emancipation of the Third World. We have to keep fighting, together with Fanon, for these causes, thinking about them and talking about them. We must continue to call them by their names. There is no reason to change the names of things when things remain the same. In a way, there is still nothing left behind.

We may stop talking about capitalism to talk about neoliberalism. Neoliberalism, however, unleashes capital and liberates it, allowing it to be increasingly savage, brazen and cynical, to the point of becoming neo-fascist. The current globalization of this neoliberal capitalism is the consummation of colonialism. Similarly, imperialism triumphs and disguises itself in the new global consensus.

The so-called 'Global South' should not serve to make us think that our struggles are other than those of the Third World. Both struggles are the same, and we need to be aware of the struggles of the past because of their teachings. Past defeats can also make us stronger. As Walter Benjamin (1940: 260) put it, 'the sinews of our greatest strength' is 'the image of enslaved ancestors rather than that of liberated grandchildren'.

We cannot get to the future without going through the past—a concept that was very well understood by Fanon, perhaps thanks in part to what he learned from both Marxist and Freudian traditions. It is possible that these traditions helped teach Fanon to conceive practice not as an external application of theory, but as an indispensable internal moment of theory that allows for deepening and knowing reality in all its material complexity (Pavón-Cuéllar, 2017). Thus, overcoming the division of mental and manual labor with its capitalist and colonial expressions, Fanon was an insightful intellectual thanks to—not in addition to or despite of—being a tireless and dedicated fighter.

It was through his struggle, for example, that Fanon learned to grasp reality in all its complexity and to not simplify it or think about colonialism without also thinking about racism, imperialism and capitalism. This distinguishes him from postcolonial or decolonial scholars who give in to academic fashions and neglect capitalism when considering coloniality. Perhaps it is possible to forget capital in the amphitheatre or in the library, but not in the world, not on the street, and not in the social and revolutionary movements.

Contrary to popular belief, we need practice in order to have a faithful representation of the world in all its complexity. This complexity involves various systems of oppression studied by Fanon (e.g. capitalism, imperialism, colonialism and racism). Of course, there are also systems that Fanon overlooked or even reproduced that we must think about today. To think about these systems properly, however, we must think about them at the same time as the other systems. This is something that is also better understood in practice, when we have to confront neoliberal neofascism with its knotting of classism, racism and colonialism, as well as ableism, ageism, sexism and heterosexism. No matter how complex it may be, this knotting is perceived with the greatest clarity by those who go through experiences such as those of marginalized indigenous people, exploited labourers and rejected migrants.

## Bibliography

All-African Peoples' Conference. 1961. 'Statement on Neocolonialism.' Accessed September 27, 2011, https://www.pambazuka.org/global-south/africa-all-african-peoples-conference-statement-neocolonialism.

Benjamin, W. 1968 [1940]. 'Theses on the Philosophy of History.' *Illuminations*, 253–264. New York: Schocken.

Bond, P. 2006. *Looting Africa: The Economics of Exploitation*. London: Zed Books.

Ceceña, A. E. 2009. 'Caminos y agentes del saqueo en América Latina.' *Observatorio Latinoamericano de Geopolítica*, http://geopolitica.iiec.unam.mx/index.php/node/147.

De Oto, A. 2003. *Fanon: política y poética del sujeto poscolonial*. Mexico City: El Colegio de México.

Echeverría, B. 2010. '*Modernidad y blanquitud.*' Mexico City: Era.

Fanon, F. 1952. '*Peau noire, masques blancs.*' Paris: Seuil.

———. 1957 [2015]. 'L'indépendance nationale, seule issue posible, El Moudjahid 10, septembre 1957.' In *Frantz Fanon, Écrits sur l'aliénation et la liberté*, edited by Khalfa, E. J., and Young, R., 461–466. Paris: La Découverte.

———. 1961 [2002]. '*Les damnés de la terre.*' Paris: La Découverte.

Frank, A. G. 1974. 'El desarrollo del subdesarrollo.' *Pensamiento Crítico* 7: 159–172.

Galtung, J. 1969. 'Violence, Peace, and Peace Research.' *Journal of Peace Research* 6 (3): 167–191.

Gibson, N. 2003. *Fanon: The Postcolonial Imagination*. Cambridge: Polity Press.

Haag, D. 2011. *Mechanisms of Neocolonialism: Current French and British in Cameroon and Ghana*. Barcelona: Institut Català Internacional Per la Pau.

Hickel, J. 2017. 'Aid in Reverse: How Poor Countries Develop Rich Countries.' *The Guardian*, January 14, 2017, https://www.theguardian.com/global-develop-

ment-professionals-network/2017/jan/14/aid-in-reverse-how-poor-countries-
develop-rich-countries.

Kar, D., and Schjelderup, G. 2016. 'New Report on Unrecorded Capital Flight
Finds Developing Countries Are Net-Creditors to the Rest of the World.'
*Global Financial Integrity*, https://gfintegrity.org/press-release/new-report-on-
unrecorded-capital-flight-finds-developing-countries-are-net-creditors-to-
the-rest-of-the-world/.

Lampedusa, G. 1960. *The Leopard*. New York: Pantheon.

Langan, M., ed. 2018. *Neo-Colonialism and the Poverty of 'Development' in Africa*.
London: Palgrave Macmillan.

Laplante, M., and Hillali, M. 2018. *Le pillage du monde par l'Occident: la face cachée
du capitalisme*. Paris: L'Harmattan.

Macey, D. 2012. *Frantz Fanon: A Biography*. London: Verso.

Macías Chávez, K. C. 2015. 'El neocolonialismo en nuestros días: la perspectiva de
Leopoldo Zea.' *Universitas Philosophica* 32 (65): 81–106.

Marini, R. M. 1974. *Dialéctica de la Dependencia*. Mexico City: Era.

Nkrumah, K. 1966. *Neo-colonialism: The last stage of imperialism*, New York: International Publishers.

Pavón-Cuéllar, D. 2017. *Marxism and Psychoanalysis: In or Against Psychology*. London: Routledge.

Pavón-Cuéllar, D. 2019. 'Violencia colonial y daño subjetivo en el presente Latinoamericano.' In *Sujetos y contextos de las violencias en América Latina. Aportes
teóricos y evidencias empíricas*, edited by García Lara, G. A., Cruz Pérez, O., and
Ocaña Zúñiga, J., 17–34. Mexico City: Porrúa.

Rodney, W. 1973. *How Europe Underdeveloped Africa*. London: Bogle-L'Ouverture.

Salama, P. 1972. *El proceso de subdesarrollo*. Mexico City: Era.

Sartre, J.-P. 1964. *Situations V. Colonialisme et Néo-colonialisme*. Paris: Gallimard.

Young, R. J. C. 2001. 'Neocolonialism.' In *Postcolonialism: An Historical Introduction*, 44–56. Malden: Blackwell.

Zea, L. 1971. *Latinoamérica: emancipación y neocolonialismo: Ensayos*. Caracas:
Tiempo Nuevo.

# OF SIGNS, SYMPTOMS, AND STEREOTYPES: FANON, INSTITUTIONAL RACISM AND INSTITUTIONAL SUBJECTIVITY

Miraj U. Desai

There has been much rightful focus on institutional racism of late in everything from law and politics to health and education. However, often absent in discussions on institutional racism that focus on individual actors, groups, or policies is the following: If institutions can systematically exclude, bias, imprison, or worse—if they can *act*—then there is something else, something more elusive also occurring. Institutions can, in effect, behave in ways that we normally only attribute to individuals. That is, they can become a subject *unto themselves*, an *institutional subject*, endowed with institutional subjectivity or consciousness, that haunts the institution itself. Such an embedded, institutionally racist subjectivity demands more of our critical attention, even in fields not given to investigating in these ways and fields that Fanon himself would have been familiar with: health care, medicine, psychiatry, and psychology. This chapter is my attempt, as a psychologist, to sociodiagnose (Fanon, 1952/1967: 11) these issues, which I hope may shed light on similar problems outside of these fields and bring greater focus to such institutional syndromes.

## Institutional and Disciplinary Diagnoses

Frantz Fanon was a psychiatrist. This is true. Fanon's psychiatric eye was never too far from his political mind, or his vision of the work ahead (e.g., Fanon, 1961/ 2004; 2018; Gibson & Beneduce, 2017; Gordon, 2019b; Marriott, 2018; McCulloch, 1983). Yet, his life and work have been far less engaged within psychology and psychiatry (e.g., Adams, 1970; Bulhan, 1985; 1998; Burman, 2016; Desai, 2014; Giordano, 2011; Hook, 2005; 2012; Lebeau, 1998; Metzl, 2009; Robertson & Walter, 2009; Sikuade, 2012; Utsey et al, 2001) than in other disciplines like philosophy or cultural studies. Fanon himself had an ambivalent and complicated relationship to the *psy*-fields. Indeed, one of the integral aspects of his oeuvre is that, when he begins with or utilizes psychology, he arrives at a place beyond it. In doing so, psychology—or psychology as conceived of in a certain individualistic, reified, or socially naïve way—is left behind and what emerges is a transformed, delimited use of the psychological that is now considered in relation to everything else—the social, the political, and even the geographical (Desai, 2014; Hook, 2005). How else could one interrogate such a complex and deeply embedded phenomenon like racism, which scoffs at attempts to understand and excise it using only one frame of entry? A beast whose tentacles move in endless directions requires the same dexterity to confront its reach.

Through these multi-perspectival maneuvers, racism becomes further exposed. It is not just an individual matter, an individual subjectivity matter, or even an interpersonal matter. It seeps down into the groundwater and up into the buildings. Racism is the invisible and visible. It whispers with a yell, such that those who are forced to hear it are simultaneously told that what they heard does not exist, and, yet, it remains, quite literally, everywhere. Race, racism, and racial hierarchy have—to borrow that painfully descriptive of phenomenological terms—become *sedimented* (Husserl, 1954/1970: 361). Racialized norms are sedimented within structures, cultures, institutions, habits, narratives, discourses, symbols, and subjectivities; and, as Fanon's gift for needling the thickets of the lifeworld revealed, they reach even down to the storybooks (Ahmed, 2007; Al-Saji, 2013; Buck, 2004; Desai, 2018; Fanon, 1952/1967; Gordon, 2017; 2019b; Henry, 2005; Hook, 2012; House, 2005). Racist encounters themselves are found to entail more than the particular instance, and are constituted instead, in part, by generations of hatred, ignorance, and exploitation, such that when a little child becomes frightened at the sight of Fanon, a Black man, the child's fright is already overdetermined by what came before him, and before them (Fanon, 1952/1967). History is a culprit and an accomplice.

Psychology is a discipline that theoretically might help investigate such phenomena as racism, for instance, by addressing how racism is taken up, perceived, mediated, negotiated, and acted upon in everyday life—but as Fanon found, psychology's typical methods and theories were limited in dealing with these matters, ignored them, or could have been used in the service of perpetuating them (Bulhan, 1985; Gibson & Beneduce, 2017; Maldonado-Torres, 2017). In its efforts to compile objective facts, psychology had missed the fact that society had created, collectively, race and racism *as objective facts*, which permeate everything to the extent that they appear as 'just the way things are'. Such a psychology, given that it often operates on the basis of a presumed static world—or as Husserl says, presupposes the ground of the world (Husserl, 1954/1970: 257-8; see also Davidson & Cosgrove, 2002; Davidson & Cosgrove, 1991)—then not only continues to operate on the tacit acceptance and imbrication of a racist world, but falls behind in its task of revealing such a world and its accomplices, including the *collective* and *institutional* subjectivities, that help make it possible.

Drawing on Fanon, phenomenology, and contemporary social science research, this chapter attempts a corrective by offering a sketch of institutional bias, racism, and *subjectivity* in particular. Institutions, it will be argued, possess their own form of subjectivity that relates to but goes beyond their members: an institutional subjectivity. An institution becomes its own gaze, its own subject, that is more powerful and less accountable (or even visible) than an individual person. It becomes a train without the need of a specific conductor or riders.

To develop this sketch of institutional subjectivity, I will first return to an important Fanonian description of collective racist processes. Then, I will attempt to describe the ways in which these processes relate to a collective subject, or what Edmund Husserl (1950/1999) calls a 'personalit[y] of a higher order' (1950/1999: 132), which achieves, sustains, and spreads racist reality, including through 'thingify[ing]' people (Fanon, 1964/1967: 14). I then briefly describe what it is like to be on the other side of thingification before traveling to one particular personality of a higher order—the clinic—to elucidate the presence of *institutional* subjectivity therein.[1] This institutional perspective, I contend, is often an elusive aspect of contemporary forms of bias and oppression, taken to extreme lengths in law enforcement, immigration, and other domains.

Part of Fanon's enduring message was to take no one and nothing for granted. One form of taking nothing for granted involves interrogating the ways in which harmful social structures invade all of life, including psychological life. This is illustrated directly by Fanon through delineation of how bias, racism, and racist tropes become sedimented within varying levels of human organization, such as collectives, communities, and yes, clinics. The chapter suggests that such a focus on institutions and the subjectivities that go along with them—their minds and designs, their specters and shadows—may aid in the interrogation of biased, oppressive, and authoritarian trends in society.

## 'In Every Society, in Every Collectivity Exists…'

I begin with one of Fanon's passages appearing in his chapter on *The Black Man and Psychopathology*, which points towards the collective dimensions of racism and racist aggression (Fanon, 1952/1967; 1952/2008). I have previously used it to elucidate the structure of Fanonian psychopolitical investigations (Desai, 2014),[2] but here I will employ it for a different purpose: to present how Fanonian psychopolitical investigations lead one back to collective subjectivities. Per Fanon (1952/1967):

> In every society, in every collectivity, exists—must exist—a channel, an outlet through which the [energy] accumulated in the form of aggression can be released … each type of society, of course, requiring its own specific kind of catharsis. The Tarzan stories, the sagas of twelve-year-old explorers, the adventures of Mickey Mouse, and all those 'comic books' [aim at releasing] collective aggression. The magazines are put together by

---

1. A note on method: This evolving project first began with an original empirical phenomenological study of cultural incongruence within mental health clinics and centers, in which we observed a hidden architecture within the clinic that contained preferential norms and biases related to Euro-American and efficiency cultures (Desai, Paranamana, Restrepo-Toro et al, 2021). Subsequent phenomenological analysis led to a sense that at play is not just individual provider subjectivity or even group subjectivity, but something more spectral, a subjectivity that is attached to an institution and in some cases, though not necessarily, a building. In the present paper, I then turn to Fanonian and Husserlian resources, as well as literature on race and racism, to help flesh out this picture. In the end, though, my overall approach is not to be considered theoretical in the traditional use of that term in social science. It is ultimately focused on the things themselves, which always remain primary, and to which one's limited thoughts remain secondary. Further, informing my reflections are my peers and my experience of being subjected to racist hate and racial profiling in the post-9/11 world, by individuals, collectives, *and* institutions.
2. Here, the word 'psychopolitics' to characterize Fanon's approach was initially drawn from the work of Lebeau (1998) and Hook (2005).

white men for little white men. This is the heart of the problem. In the Antilles—[and there's no reason to believe the situation is any different in the other colonies]—these same magazines are devoured by the local children. In the magazines the Wolf, the Devil, the Evil Spirit, the Bad Man, the Savage are always symbolized by [Blacks] or Indians; since there is always identification with the victor [or good guys], the little [Black child,] quite as easily as the [little white child], becomes an explorer, an adventurer, a missionary 'who faces the danger of being eaten by the wicked Negroes. (pp. 145–6, translation modified in brackets mostly via Fanon, 1952/2008: 124-5)

In this passage, Fanon makes a central point about racist processes: a collective will seek, create, and *sanction* collective objects of aggression. The good people of the world must vanquish the evil. Fanon notes how Black children, being children, naturally identify with the good in this good-versus-evil saga. Seeds of aggression are therefore tragically planted within and towards themselves, which reach full toxicity when they later realize they were the 'evil enemy' all along. I have earlier detailed this latter process as it unfolds in the life of the person of color (Desai, 2014), but my interest here is to return back to the other side—the initial preconditions for mass racist processes.

Embedded within Fanon's passage above is an emphasis on a *collectivity*: 'In every society, in every *collectivity*, exists—must exist...' an outlet for '*collective aggression*' (p. 145, emphases added).[3] Being a collectivity, it is not just about one or two people or one or two perspectives fomenting racism, but a collective, not a singular. It is a mass movement of consciousness towards the creation of a racist world of things. This type of collective, far outstripping any single person, places mines in the field of experience—mines of alleged objectivity about the moral imperative of whiteness and the moral decrepitude of color which are ready to ignite, or be wielded, in the haunting words of Elijah Anderson (2015). There is a great benefit to be had by those who are on the right side of the equation—a side that is relatively free of mines—and who thus do not require the energy needed to confront, dodge, heal from, or survive the mines (Ahmed, 2007; Al-Saji, 2013; Buck, 2004). From Fanon's description, then, it is clear that even well-intentioned white persons can benefit from this world structuring. Equality is not entirely possible between things and people. Thus, even if this or that person may hold humanistic beliefs, there is still something amidst the mist that creates things of people of color, because it can. It can 'thingify' (*chosifier*)[4] them, in the words of Fanon (Fanon, 1964/1967: 14; Fanon, 1952: 256, modified), and that

---

3. Nearby this passage, Fanon (1952/1967) invokes similarly collective language of 'collective catharsis' and a psychopoliticized rendering of the Jungian 'collective unconscious' (pp. 144-5), which, for Fanon, is little more than the acquired and culturally imposed 'prejudices, myths, [and] collective attitudes of a given group' (p. 188, 191). See also Bernasconi (2019).
4. In the original, Fanon is indicting a you or *tu*—you thingify or 'tu chosifies'—but later I will present a re-reading of this you/*tu* as an institutional other, and not just a straightforward reading of you as an individual or even sets of individuals.

produces real economic, political, and affective inequalities (Ahmed, 2007; Buck, 2004; Gordon, 2008; Hook, 2012), as well as a distortion of the sense of past and of the range of possibilities in life (Al-Saji, 2013; Gordon, 2017).

Collectives can produce reality. That is, when there reaches a critical mass that thingifies people as some-thing, it becomes reality, and is considered to be as objective as anything else around, like this blade of grass or that branch of a tree. If enough people perceive, think, label, and describe immigrants as evil diseased leeches or Black persons as criminals, then that becomes a sedimented reality unfurled onto lived spaces from TV shows to news footage to political discourse to what parents teach their children, and how children mock other children, and how the mocked children start viewing themselves—such that when both sets of children become adults, they may carry vestiges of this deep within the recesses of their mind, subtly and, determinatively, influencing their perception, well-being, and decision-making (including within health care, Hall et al, 2015).

These socially condoned versions of reality and sanctioned forms of aggression proliferate and sediment, including within varying levels of human organization, such as families, peer groups, shared living spaces, institutions, neighborhoods, cities, cultures, nations, and empires. Each of these perceive, judge, and mete out realities. They have capacities for perspective, perception, judgment, and action. Human they are, unfortunately; but human they are not, entirely. And they fuel the overdetermination that individuals within these spaces must endure and overcome—the wall they hit, get pushed into, or thrown up against.

## Collective Layers, and the Collective that Layers

Evidence regarding such collectively racialized processes of intentionality and constitution, is, quite literally, all around. In recent times, in our own agonizing corner of the world, we have seen Black persons (re)inscribed as criminals and thugs, East Asian persons carved as backwards, disease-carrying viruses, Latinx persons labeled as invading thieves and miscreants, Middle Eastern and South Asian persons marked as enemies and threats, and all of the above as just, well, inferior. The list goes on. This has resulted in renewed acts of violence towards these communities, and/or paranoia, fear, and suspicion towards them, and/or degrees of privilege for those free of experiencing each form of racist depravity. Each of these collective objectifications can, in turn, be linked to previous instances, here and globally, including when these were the basis of official colonial policy.

The *sedimentation* of racism is an appropriate analogy not just because it invokes images of the layered nature of soil, but also because of how such layers crush those underneath them, eventually turning them into fossils or fuel, without breath or oxygen, as Fanon (1952/1967: 226) searingly observed. The sheer weight of the gravitational forces 'suffocate human experience' (Desai, 2014: 70).[5] These meanings, percepts, and objectifications are sedimented in so much of the world, entrapping people within them, covering over the person with something else or something that has been placed there not by someone, but by someones. To borrow a phrase from law enforcement: you are being surrounded. *Collective subjectivities surround.* Thus, not too far from sedimentation—a racist story where the savage is like such and such; a skin color that does not just mean but *is* this or that (foreign, exotic, dangerous, dirty, diseased, lecherous, lazy); the norms of normality, productivity, and beauty that are brought down from on colonial high (Desai, 2018: 8)—are collective subjectivities that constitute and apprehend them. This seems to be an obvious point—that collective norms and values relate to collective processes of constitution (McIntyre, 2012)—but its obviousness can become obscured within a quite Western psychologized frame of viewing conscious life or subjectivity as only an individual psychological issue (embodied or otherwise). We remain in need of a wider and more robust praxis that also allows for addressing collective subjectivities. Racism, too, requires such dexterity, as Fanon has shown us.

## We-Subjectivit(ies) and Personalities of a Higher Order

I turn now to various resources within phenomenology that may offer some useful resources for interrogating this process of the collective, intersubjective constitution of the world (Carr, 2019; Husserl, 1950/1999; 1952/1989; 1954/1970; McIntyre, 2012). One important implication from this work is that individuals are certainly not the only beings that can be called a subject. A community can be a subject, a 'we-subjectivity', as Husserl coined: 'Constantly functioning in wakeful life, we also function together, in the manifold ways of considering, together, objects pre-given to us in common, thinking together, valuing, planning, acting together. Here we find ... we-subjectivity...'. (Husserl, 1954/1970: 109).[6]

Carr (2019) importantly noted how the wisdom of our ordinary language often understands this phenomenological insight about the capacity for a community or a collective to be a subject, and not just in a metaphorical sense. One regularly hears utterances like, ' 'Parliament decided', 'Germany invades Poland', the electorate can't make up its mind'. (2019: 251). These examples are not only illuminating but take on added significance in the present discussion on colonial and oppressive personalities of a higher order.

---

5. In a presentation for Fanon's 95th birthday, Lewis Gordon (2020) pointedly described the ways in which breath, and the lack thereof, is a central aspect of Fanon's work and also the multiple pandemics of 2020, not just COVID-19 but colonialism, racism (including anti-Black police brutality), and crass economic extraction. Gibson and Beneduce (2017) also described such Fanonian themes of breath and constriction within the American context of police brutality and the Black experience (2017: 18).

6. I am applying McIntyre's (2012) skillful editing of Husserl's buried yet important passage on we-subjectivity in the *Crisis*.

A community is a subject, a we-subject, and as such it is endowed with the power to constitute a world (McIntyre, 2012)[7]—that is, 'to disclose it as such-and-such—to give it 'sense', to make sense of it' (Drummond, 2008: 55, bolding removed). As McIntyre's helpful commentary observed: 'A community is char-acterized as a *we-subject* and thus by *how and what it constitutes*. In this regard, a community achieves its character ... not by how it is experience*d* but by how it experience*s*' (2012: 90). It may follow, then, that a community is not just some-thing out there to be experienced; it experiences *back*. Communities also have a 'common experience and understanding of how things are or ought to be', including what is good, bad, or otherwise (2012: 61, 86). It may follow, then, that a person does not just co-constitute a community; the community can constitute them back, attribute sense or value, and act accordingly.

I suggest that when a community's experiencing is loving, caring, and welcom-ing, this communal subject can instill a mutually supportive space, or a beloved community, in the words of Dr. King (King, 1958). When a community's experi-ence is destructive and hateful, this we-subject can be antithetical to life, a be-hated community. Or, it could be an objectifying, be-thinged community, or a begone community—as in, 'You, be gone!' Such a community comprises its mem-bers, but any community, according to Husserl, cannot be reduced to the mere sum of its individuals (Drummond, 2008). It becomes its own thing, its own 'personality of a higher order' (Husserl, 1950/1999: 132). With regard to racism, individuals can collectively make a racist community, but an equally disturbing implication of the above is that the racist community then becomes a beast of its own—an emergent phenomenon that is not the mere sum of its parts. It becomes a train, with scores of riders—but a train, nonetheless.

The anguish and humiliation that Husserl, of Jewish heritage, had to endure from Nazi authorities in his own late life (e.g., Ahmed, 2007; Drummond, 2008) speaks to this dark side of communities and personalities of a higher order. In this same time period, one of Husserl's historical counterparts, psychoanalyst and eventual Jewish exile Sigmund Freud (1930/1961), was preoccupied with the question of whether these communal forces of aggression and destruction could or would be overcome through the loving embrace of community—that is, the 'other of the two 'Heavenly Powers', eternal Eros' (1930/196: 112). He added a haunting concluding line to this passage in 1931, once the rise of Nazism was more apparent: 'But who can foresee with what success and with what result?' (1930/196: 111-2).

Consciousness, subjectivity, perspective, point of view—whatever we want to call it—is not restricted to individual psychological varieties. Collectivities are endowed with perspectives, 'a shared understanding of the world' (Drum-mond, 2008: 53), that have very real impact and consequence. A community is not just an aggregate of individuals, nor is it always a readily identifiable or

---

7. McIntyre's (2019) concise rendering of constitution in the Husserlian sense is relevant to the current discussion: 'To 'constitute' an object...roughly means to experience it 'as' a particular object of a certain sort' (2019: 62).

exact formation. It can be elusively operating in the background: at one moment blurring out minority voices, lives, bodies, and perspectives, while in another, more overtly authoritarian moment, forcefully reasserting its will and dominance over them. Mass racial or religious backlash against minority communities, for instance, frequently occurs after sociohistorical events such as 9/11. These are not just one instance of subjectivity but multiplicities converging, and agreeing, on the nature of their perception of others who fit a particular description or profile.

Fanon leveled the global nature of anti-Blackness and other forms of racism with penetrating psychopolitical insight, including how they become rooted within collective structures, institutions, and systems of meanings. Paget Henry's (2005) excellent piece on Africana phenomenology situates the Fanonian contributions well for the current discussion on communal constitution and we-subjectivity. Fanon's account of the state of being a Black person in the world, for instance, as the state of being projected as all things base by European intersubjective consciousness, is described by Henry as thus:

> It is a state of enforced negrification in which colonized Africana peoples lost their earlier cultural identities and became identified by the color of their skin. The outer form of this state is the substituting of an epidermal identity in the place of a cultural one. The inner content of this outer transformation is the socio-historical reality of being forced to live as the unconscious, liminal shadow, the repressed and undesirable side of the imperial European subject that had racialized its identity as white. (2005: 12)

The imperial-European-subject-that-projects is not only a singular perspective but, translated in terms of the present case being built, is indicative of a personality of a higher order (c.f., Hook, 2012: 86). The Black person thus faces two very different we-subjectivities: 'One with his fellows, the other with the white man' (Fanon, 1952/1967: 17), the latter of which seeps into and radically distorts the former (Henry, 2005), including by demarcating a 'sterile', 'arid', and hellish 'zone of nonbeing' (1952/1967: 8).[8] Part of Fanon's project entails investigating the psychopolitical ramifications of colonial and racist structures and the psychopolitical possibilities for transformation.

## The Sedimented (of the) Earth

These reality-producing and 'nausea'-inducing (Fanon, 1952/1967: 112) racial ideologies, embedded in such an expansive way, can lead to existentially excruciat-

---

8. Pertinent for our purposes here, Henry too makes explicit reference to a 'We' in his discussion of Fanon via connection to Du Bois' related account of double consciousness and twoness: The Black person is stuck between two We's. Weate's (2001) discussion also shows how Fanonian and related accounts of racism and difference challenge the notion of shared community as a given, and instead positions shared community as an ideal or deferred universal.

ing conditions for those on the other side of them. 'I am overdetermined from without', proclaims Fanon. 'I am the slave not of the 'idea' that others have of me but of my own appearance' (1952/1967: 116).

To be 'overdetermined' is to be already there before you appear. It is arriving 'too late' (Fanon, 1952/1967: 121) to a world already structured in advance by sociohistorical processes and hierarchies (Al-Saji, 2013). As Ahmed (2007) noted via Fanon: '...histories of colonialism [make] the world 'white', a world that is inherited, or which is already given before the point of an individual's arrival. This is the familiar world, the world of whiteness, as a world we know implicitly ... a world 'ready' for certain kinds of bodies ... a world that puts certain objects within their reach' (Ahmed 2007: 153-4; also Al-Saji, 2013: 7-9). This is a world containing sordid racist narratives and tropes and the thousands of 'details, anecdotes, [and] stories' that are 'woven' about (Fanon, 1952/1967: 111). The clinician Fanon's own 'objective [self-]examination' would thus reveal his true 'ethnic characteristics': from 'cannibalism' and 'intellectual deficiency' to 'racial defects' and 'slave-ships' (1952/1967: 112). These threads and needles had been sedimented over years of conflict and exploitation—or especially now, during an election year—or just any old day.

The individual other's gaze can instantiate the collective racist perspective, which treats you, and those who appear like you, *as if* you were that object. This is objectification or 'thingif[ication]' that introduces to the situation an object that is dead (Fanon, 1964/1967: 14). This object is real but not alive. It is alive in terms of its impact on a situation (and its capacity to move and multiply), but it is not humanly alive. You are seen as such and such, and you become stone; or rather, I become stone. I become what you see me as, and then, to you, I disappear. Everything that may be near or dear about yourself—your capacity for love and kindness, your gifts and personality, your history and memories, the way you are known to your friends or siblings, that time when you sacrificed for your neighbor, that time when you contributed to your neighborhood, your innocent desire, as Fanon mourned, to build a world together (Fanon, 1952/1967: 113)—all these disappear because of your appearance. You are 'one of those', or worse, a criminal, a dirty foreigner, a backwards savage, an extremist, a global leech, an alien, an illegal, an enemy. A nothing.

I lived in New York City in the early part of this millennium—before, during, and after the 2008 global economic crash, and around the same time the now infamous 'if you see something, say something' message about spotting suspicious or dangerous public activity was prevalent. Of course, one could see plenty, just on the news, of sanctioned economic exploitation within the financial industry (leading to untold distress)—but what the collective was being told to spot instead were Black and brown bodies, to stop, frisk, search, and suspect in the name of security (leading to untold distress). As Ahmed (2007) described, stop and search has both political-economic and affective consequences: 'Stopping is both a political economy, which is distributed unevenly between others, and an affective economy, which leaves its impressions, affecting those bodies that are subject to its address' (Ahmed, 2007: 161). Some don't get stopped, and others do, such as those 'DWB (driving while black) or looking Arab in a U.S. airport' (Mahendran, 2007: 192).

The idea that none of this affects mental health is absurd. But until very recently, one would rarely see these types of discussions featured in the main halls of national mental health boards or associations, except among groups on the periphery. Environmental destruction, exorbitant greed, modern-day segregation, and mass incarceration are virtually nowhere to be found in diagnostic manuals. Prisons, to be sure, are to be found not within manuals but as using manuals, because prisons are among the largest—if not the largest—providers of mental health services in the U.S. They are becoming, in many ways, the proxy 'community mental health' system—that is, the place where people with mental health challenges are kept and returned to (Davidson et al, 2004; Gibson & Beneduce, 2017: 219; Steinberg et al, 2015). It is to the institution of the health or mental health clinic that we now turn.

## The Sediment Under, Around, and In the Building

Thus far, I have attempted to describe how subjectivities of an order higher than the individual live on and bear considerable weight on the world and on people (Carr, 2019; Husserl, 1950/1999; 1954/1970; McIntyre, 2012). These spectral forms of subjectivity may appear peculiar at first glance, a peculiarity which has left them without a standard disciplinary home. Of course, this lack of a home is not new terrain for an anti-racist activist or investigator, as mentioned at the outset. Very little of what Fanon himself interrogated fits comfortably within one analytic frame, and indeed the capacity for multi-perspectival movement, or a shifting of 'registers', improvisation, or transcending disciplinary dogmatism, was an integral part of his approach and contribution (Al-Saji, 2013; Bhabha, 2004; Desai, 2014; 2018; Gordon, 2006; 2019a; b; Henry, 2005; Hook, 2005, p. 476).

Personalities of a higher order can often be difficult to access or describe. One cannot simply go talk to them. Our recent research on one particular higher-order personality—the institution—suggests that one can begin to perceive these spectral phenomena through their workings in the world (Desai, Paranamana, Restrepo-Tor et al, 2021). For instance, there has been increasing attention to the role of institutional racism and bias in perpetuating everything from health to legal disparities, including mortality rates, access to health care, and justice system involvement[9]—starkly witnessed in 2020 through massive disparities in COVID-19 sickness and death among Black and brown communities (SAMHSA Office of Behavioral Health Equity, 2020; Webb Hooper, Nápoles and Pérez-Stable, 2020) and the ghastly public displays of police brutality towards Black persons.

---

9. The notion of institutional racism dates back to the pioneering work of Ture and Hamilton (1967), which continues to influence contemporary accounts (e.g., Feagin & Bennefield, 2014; Henry, 2010; Metzl & Hansen, 2014).

There are often institutions at the center of these types of issues. I suggest that with institutional bias and racism comes an institutional subject. This institutional subject, being a personality of a higher order, is made up of individuals, but also becomes its own thing, as we saw above in our discussion of communities. It becomes a train—with interchangeable riders, but a train nonetheless—that moves along without the need for any specific member or conductor. The train has compartments, as well, in what Hook—following Levi-Strauss—might describe as a 'momentum of structure' (Hook, 2012: 123), barreling down the tracks.

Ahmed (2007) described some of the internal socialization processes within the institution, and the ways in which the initiate can soon become a part of it, including its sense of We:

> Becoming a 'part' of an institution, which we can consider the demand to share in it, or even have a share of it, hence requires not only that one inhabits its buildings, but also that we follow its line: we might start by saying 'we'; by mourning its failures and rejoicing in its successes; by reading the documents that circulate within it, creating vertical and horizontal lines of communication; by the chance encounters we have with those who share its grounds. To be recruited is not only to join, but to sign up to a specific institution: to inhabit it *by turning around as a return of its address*. (Ahmed, 2007: 158)

The 'it' in Ahmed's (2007) passage is what concerns us here, because, as noted above, such supra-individual entities can attribute meaning and act accordingly. Regarding the institution as 'it', what also comes to mind is Freud's (1923/1960) initial German text *Das Ich und das Es*. Although translated as *The Ego and the Id* in English, more helpful for our purposes would be the basic German sense of the terms that Freud himself poetically meant in the original (Mills, 2004): The I and the It. The subject and what lies beneath the surface. Perhaps, then, my aim here is to describe, as a form of sociodiagnosis (Fanon, 1952/1967: 11), both the institution as 'I' and the institution as 'It': first by establishing that an institution has or is an I, with We's within, and then delineating aspects of the institution's It—that is, the institutional subject and what lies beneath the surface.[10] We may find that these issues could even suggest the need for an *institutional* phenomenological reduction that explicitly illuminates the subject matter at hand.

All told, institutions, as subjects, can attribute meaning and act in their own preferred ways but without responsibility for the acts. This is because the actions often refer to no one, that is, no single person, even if you were to go looking. Conversely, the individual members can, and often do, then act through what is

---

10. Here we do not necessarily ascribe to the Freudian metapsychological interpretation of these terms, but nonetheless find the more everyday senses to be helpful, and suggestive of horizons for further phenomenological clarification.

merely 'on the books' (Robeson, 1958: 86), and thus they too act without the burden of responsibility for the action (Gordon, 1995).[11]

## Institutional and Psychopolitical Syndromes

Dr. Fanon of course spent considerable time and energy working in health and mental health institutions, which occasioned ample opportunities for him to reflect on what happens within them—but also to observe that what happens within them may be reflective of structural processes both within *and* outside them, such as in more overtly sociopolitical institutions (Fanon, 2018; Gibson & Beneduce, 2017; McCulloch, 1983). I hope to do the same here.

To support the development of our ongoing account of institutional subjectivity and bias, I turn now to Fanon's powerful essay on the North African Syndrome (Fanon, 1964/1967), in which he details forms of bias within the medical space of the clinic. Constantly confronted with what they perceived as vague symptoms without a clear organic basis among their Arab patients of North African origin, doctors in France relied on harmful stereotypes—for instance about their alleged constitutional laziness and avoidance of work—to fill in the explanatory blanks regarding patients' symptom presentations. In one such example, the 'North African's pain, for which we can find no lesional basis, is judged to have no consistency, no reality. Now the North African *is* a-man-who-doesn't-like work. So that whatever he does will be interpreted *a priori* on the basis of this' (Fanon, 1964/1967: 6).

In my rereading, I see this process as reflective of the individual providers in question;

and yet, it goes beyond them. Replace one or two providers, or even the entire regime, and the next one that comes in will most likely be liable to the same biased conclusions, which themselves are related to collective racist views and disciplinary tendencies beyond the clinic. I read these biases and prejudices as having become inscribed within the institution and maybe even the building—they have been institutionalized, as it were. Thus, I contend that Fanon is speaking not just of a racist gaze but of an institutionally racist gaze and an institutionally biased gaze. This biased gaze, or subjectivity, creates a thing out of its patients. It is what the 'North African *is*' (Fanon, 1964/1967: 6).

Thus, the North African patient was there long before any actual North African person arrived on the scene. Further, the North African thing was there long before any actual North African person arrived on the scene. Fanon's (1964/

---

11. Gordon (2019b) frames a parallel ethical problem of the lack of accountability within institutions that consider persons of color as less-than or non-beings: 'If they regard blacks and other groups of color as neither selves nor others, and the institutions of power are used to preserve that separation, the result would be people in a 'zone of non-being' or a non-place in which ethical and moral relations do not apply. Under such conditions, there isn't accountability for harm done to people in such netherworlds, for 'harm' properly happens against those to whom one is accountable' (p. 8 of online publication). Harm is sanctioned or even 'banal' to borrow the classic Arendtian (1963) word.

1967) second thesis from his essay described this predetermined clinical situation and perspective as follows:

SECOND THESIS.—*That the attitude of medical personnel is very often an a priori attitude. The North African does not come with a substratum common to his race, but on a foundation built by the European. In other words, the North African, spontaneously, by the very fact of appearing on the scene, enters into a pre-existing framework.* (1964/1967: 7)

This pre-existing framework not only seeks and bestows thinghood, but, as Fanon (1964/1967) would go on to describe, ignores the person's social context, and the systemic oppression therein, which would have provided a fuller context of their suffering. Fanon does paint a broader picture of the North African's life as a migrant for the reader. He fills in the blanks left out by the clinic's perspective by describing how much of a North African's life in France is marked by intolerable blankness that may lead them, or any human, to writhe in unspeakable pain—and not a pain that is easily captured by a search for an organic lesion, with the truth being that the lesion was everywhere and larger than what could fit under a microscope. 'Without a family, without love, without human relations, without communion with the group ... he will feel himself emptied, without life, in a bodily struggle with death, a death on this side of death, a death in life' (Fanon, 1964/1967: 13).

Fanon's (1964/1967: 10) use of 'situational diagnosis'—a clinical practice he psychopoliticizes in the essay—originally required ascertaining what the story of the person's life was. Fanon's response: 'It would be better to say the history of his death. A daily death' (1964/1967: 13). Thus, the North African thing, being a thing, was already dead, before any North African person arrived on the scene. In this France, the prognosis of death was already inscribed prior to the patient's symptom presentation.

In contemporary landscapes and literatures, we know that institutional bias remains a key avenue through which racism impacts health, mental health, and wellbeing (e.g., Bailey et al., 2017; Fernando, 2017; Metzl, 2009; Metzl & Hansen, 2014; Vera & Speight, 2003; Williams, Lawrence and Davis, 2019). Though expressing commitments to diversity, health institutions, and the we-subjectivities therein, remain structurally prone to relying on stereotypes. In a recent news article on racial bias in the era of COVID-19, health disparities expert Margarita Alegría noted the connection of bias to efforts to 'maximize profits', succinctly noting: 'There's not enough time *not* to stereotype patients...You attribute people's characteristics and behavior based on their group'. This tendency, she says, fails to realize how any lack of engagement may be related, for instance, to financial, transportation, and other serious barriers (O'Donnell & Alltucker, 2020: para 11-16). The North African Syndrome redux.

One focus of my colleagues' and my current empirical research is to examine the ways in which bias lives on or reconfigures in the current landscape—specifically within the *hidden* norms of institutions and their policies, procedures, rules, requirements, and codes of conduct, and in who is afforded the status of an ideal or preferred member (Desai, Paranamana, Restrepo-Toro, O'Connell et al, 2021). In one empirical phenomenological project, we investigated potential sources of mental health disparities for communities of color in the U.S. (Desai, Paranamana, Restrepo-Toro, O'Connell et al, 2021). We focused on one specific source: cultural conflict or incongruence between mental health providers and their clients of Asian or Latinx background. Our interview guide was intentionally simple and, being phenomenological, focused on everyday situations in the clinic, including providers' specific accounts of their work with these clients and any disjunctures encountered. Though beginning with this point of provider-client contact and individual conflicts therein, our attention soon became redirected towards the structures in which this contact took place.

A clue emerged that began to alert us to the presence of biases within the clinical we-subjectivity when we started noticing that individual providers noted similar reasons for when their process reached disjunctures or broke down—when the client was not verbal, did not admit to an illness or problem, did not accept services, or had a presenting problem that did not fit within the individualist ethos of the clinic. That is, these seemingly isolated conflicts were indicative of a pattern—and beyond a pattern, a mental health clinic culture, and beyond a culture, a structure with a hidden architecture that preceded, surrounded, and influenced the reality in the clinic. This 'pre-existing framework', in Fanon's (1964/1967: 7) words, that the client walked into was marked by largely Euro-American norms and biases regarding mental health (e.g., illness model, individualism, results orientation) and expectations about correct conduct (e.g., verbal, proactive, compliant).[12] This hidden architecture was not just a simple matter of mere preference. It was a force that received its potency, in part, by being inscribed within policies, procedures, and bureaucratic requirements for efficiency. There was indeed no system without them.

In other words, the institution and the institutional subject possessed a pre-existing framework, preferred adherence to its ideal norms, and demanded efficiency. These were therefore what you, as a client, had to do or be for the system to work optimally for you rather than, in some cases, against you. Local variation, creativity, and resistance were still possible in this context, especially by open and flexible clinicians; but there was a larger machine with which to contend, which itself was related to much larger economic machines outside and inside the clinic. As Fanon's own former colleague Alice Cherki (2017) recently observed, the modern era is 'governed ... by the principle of efficiency' (Cherki 2017: x; see also Gibson & Beneduce, 2017: 14).

The continued horizon of this work is to further examine and address—not just in health care but in other societal domains—the ways in which institutional rules, policies, procedures—and subjectivity—inculcate bias *inculpably*. Why

---

12. Fanon himself had become quite aware of the problem of presupposing culturally incongruent frameworks in psychiatric practice. See Fanon (2018), Gibson and Beneduce (2018), and Bulhan (1998) for accounts, including Fanon's development of a critical ethnopsychiatry. Similarly, Sikuade (2012) shows how Fanon's work anticipated and presaged many recent transformations within contemporary psychiatry itself.

inculpably? Because at their origin is a personality of a higher order, a ghost *of a machine*, a subject who does not have a discernible face. If one tries to locate the mastermind, one may find nobody at all.

## Acknowledgments

I thank Nigel Gibson for his leadership in bringing together this edited collection, as well as for his overall inspiration, kindness, and editorial care. I also thank Hanétha Vété-Congolo and the Caribbean Philosophical Association for inviting me to present these ideas at the celebration-cum-intervention to honor Fanon's 95th birthday. Several helpful comments and questions were offered by participants that helped clarify my thinking. I also thank Usha Rungoo, Larry Davidson, Michael Seifried, Jeremy Forster, and Tom Meager for discussions, feedback, and helpful reviews.

## Bibliography

Adams, P. L. 1970. 'The Social Psychiatry of Frantz Fanon.' *American Journal of Psychiatry* 127 (6): 809–814.

Ahmed, S. 2007. 'A Phenomenology of Whiteness.' *Feminist Theory* 8 (2): 149–168.

Al-Saji, A. 2013. 'Too Late: Racialized Time and the Closure of the Past.' *Insights* 6 (5): 2–13.

Anderson, E. 2015. 'The White Space.' *Sociology of Race and Ethnicity* 1 (1): 10–21.

Arendt, H. 1963. *Eichmann in Jerusalem: A Report on the Banality of Evil*. New York: Penguin.

Bailey, Z. D., Krieger, N., Agénor, M., Graves, J., Linos, N., and Bassett, M. T. 2017. 'Structural Racism and Health Inequities in the USA: Evidence and Interventions.' *The Lancet* 389 (10077): 1453–1463.

Bernasconi, R. 2019. 'Frantz Fanon and Psychopathology: The Progressive Infrastructure of *Black Skin, White Masks*.' In *Race, Rage, and Resistance: Philosophy, Psychology, and the Perils of Individualism*, edited by Goodman, D. M., Severson, E. R., and Macdonald, H., 34–45. London: Routledge.

Bhabha, H. K. 2004. 'Foreword: Framing Fanon.' In *The Wretched of the Earth*, edited by Fanon, F., vii–xlii. New York: Grove Press.

Buck, C. 2004. 'Sartre, Fanon, and the Case for Slavery Reparations.' *Sartre Studies International* 10 (2): 123–138.

Bulhan, H. 1985. *Frantz Fanon and the Psychology of Oppression*. New York: Plenum Press.

‗‗‗‗‗‗. 1998. 'Revolutionary Psychiatry of Fanon.' In *Rethinking Fanon: The Continuing Dialog*, edited by Gibson, N., 141–175. New York: Humanity Books.

Burman, E. 2016. 'Fanon, Foucault, Feminisms: Psychoeducation, Theoretical Psychology, and Political Change.' *Theory & Psychology* 26 (6): 706–730.

Carr, D. 2019. 'Intersubjectivity and Embodiment.' In *Husserl's Phenomenology of Intersubjectivity: Historical Interpretations and Contemporary Applications*, edited by Kjosavik, F., Beyer, C., and Fricke, C., 249–262. New York: Routledge.

Cherki, A. 2017. 'Foreword.' In *Frantz Fanon, Psychiatry, and Politics*, edited by Gibson, N., and Beneduce, R., ix–xiii. London: Rowman & Littlefield.

Davidson, L., and Cosgrove, L. 1991. 'Psychologism and Phenomenological Psychology Revisited, Part I: The Liberation from Naturalism.' *Journal of Phenomenological Psychology* 22 (2): 87–108.

———. 2002. 'Psychologism and Phenomenological Psychology Revisited Part II: The Return to Positivity.' *Journal of Phenomenological Psychology* 33 (2): 141–177.

Davidson, L., Staeheli, M., Stayner, D., and Sells, D. 2004. 'Language, Suffering, and the Question of Immanence: Toward a Respectful Phenomenological Psychopathology.' *Journal of Phenomenological Psychology* 35 (2): 197–232.

Desai, M. U. 2014. 'Psychology, the Psychological, and Critical Praxis: A Phenomenologist Reads Frantz Fanon.' *Theory & Psychology* 24 (1): 58–75.

———. 2018. *Travel and Movement in Clinical Psychology: The World Outside the Clinic*, London: Palgrave Macmillan.

Desai, M. U., Paranamana, N., Restrepo-Toro, M., O'Connell, M., Davidson, L., & Stanhope, V. 2021. 'Implicit Organizational Bias: Mental Health Treatment Culture and Norms as Barriers to Engaging with Diversity.' *American Psychologist* 76 (1): 78–90.

Drummond, J. J. 2008. *Historical Dictionary of Husserl's Philosophy*. Lanham: Scarecrow Press.

Fanon, F. 1952. 'Le « syndrome nord-africain ».' *Esprit* 187 (2): 237–248.

———. 1952/1967. *Black Skin, White Masks*. Translated by C. L. Markmann. New York: Grove Press.

———. 1952/2008. *Black Skin, White Masks*. Translated by R. Philcox. New York: Grove Press.

———. 1961/2004. *The Wretched of the Earth*. Translated by R. Philcox. New York: Grove Press.

———. 1964/1967. 'The "North African Syndrome".' In *Toward the African Revolution: Political Essays*, edited by Fanon, F., 3–16. Translated by H. Chevalier. New York: Grove Press.

———. 2018. *Alienation and Freedom*, edited by Khalfa, J., and Young, R. J. C. Translated by S. Corcoran. London: Bloomsbury Academic.

Feagin, J., and Bennefield, Z. 2014. 'Systemic Racism and U.S. Health Care.' *Social Science & Medicine* 103: 7–14.

Fernando, S. 2017. *Institutional Racism in Psychiatry and Clinical Psychology*. Cham: Palgrave/Springer.

Freud, S. 1923/1960. *The Ego and the Id*, edited by Strachey, J. Translated by J. Riviere. New York: W.W.Norton & Co.

Freud, S. 1930/1961. *Civilization and Its Discontents*. Translated and edited by J. Strachey. New York: W.W. Norton & Co.

Gibson, N., and Beneduce, R. 2017. *Frantz Fanon, Psychiatry, and Politics*. London: Rowman & Littlefield.

Giordano, C. 2011. 'Translating Fanon in the Italian Context: Rethinking the Ethics of Treatment in Psychiatry.' *Transcultural Psychiatry* 48 (3): 228–256.

Gordon, L. R. 1995. *Bad Faith and Antiblack Racism*. Atlantic Highlands: Humanities Press.

———. 2006. *Disciplinary Decadence*. Boulder: Paradigm Publishers.

———. 2008. 'A Phenomenology of Biko's Black Consciousness.' In *Biko Lives! : Contesting the Legacies of Steve Biko*, edited by Mngxitama', A., Alexander, A., and Gibson, N., 83–93. New York: Palgrave Macmillan.

———. 2017. 'Phenomenology and Race.' In *The Oxford Handbook of Philosophy and Race*, edited by Zack, N. Oxford University Press [e-book].

———. 2019a. 'Bad Faith.' In *50 Concepts for a Critical Phenomenology*, edited by Weiss, G., Murphy, A. V., and Salamon, G., 17–24. Evanston: Northwestern University Press.

———. 2019b. 'Frantz Fanon.' In *The Oxford Handbook of Phenomenological Psychopathology*, edited by Stanghellini, G., Broome, M., Raballo, A., Fernandez, A. V., Fusar-Poli, P., and Rosfort, R. Oxford University Press. doi:10.1093/oxfordhb/9780198803157.013.22 [e-book].

———. 2020. 'What to Do in Our Struggle to Breathe: Fanon's Relevance in Our Time of Multiple Pandemics.' *Fanon at 95: A Twenty Day Celebration*, Bowdoin College [Online].

Hall, W. J., Chapman, M. V., Lee, K. M., Merino, Y. M., Thomas, T. W., Payne, B. K., Eng, E., Day, H., and Coyne-Beasley, T. 2015. 'Implicit Racial/Ethnic Bias Among Health Care Professionals and Its Influence on Health Care Outcomes: A Systematic Review.' *American Journal of Public Health* 105 (12): e60–e76.

Henry, P. 2005. 'Africana Phenomenology: Its Philosophical Implications.' *The CLR James Journal* 11 (1): 79–112.

Henry, P. J. 2010. 'Institutional Bias.' In *Handbook of Prejudice, Stereotyping, and Discrimination*, edited by Dovidio, J. F., Hewstone, M., Glick, P., and Esses, V. M., 426–440. London: Sage.

Hook, D. 2005. 'A Critical Psychology of the Postcolonial.' *Theory & Psychology* 15 (4): 475–503.

———. 2012. *A Critical Psychology of the Postcolonial: The Mind of Apartheid*. London: Routledge.

House, J. 2005. 'Colonial Racisms in the "Métropole": Reading Peau noire, masques blancs in Context.' In *Frantz Fanon's Black Skin, White Masks*, edited by Silverman, M., 46–73. Manchester: Manchester University Press.

Husserl, E. 1950/1999. *Cartesian Meditations*. Translated by D. Cairns. Dordrecht: Kluwer Academic Publishers.

———. 1952/1989. *Ideas Pertaining to a Pure Phenomenology and to a Phenomenological Philosophy. Second book: Studies in the Phenomenology of Constitution*. Translated by R. Rojcewicz and A. Schuwer. Dordrecht: Kluwer Academic Publishers.

———. 1954/1970. *The Crisis of European Sciences and Transcendental Phenomenology*. Translated by D. Carr. Evanston: Northwestern University Press.

King, M. L. 1958. *Stride Toward Freedom*. New York: Harper & Brothers.

Lebeau, V. 1998. 'Psychopolitics: Frantz Fanon's Black Skin, White Masks.' In *Psycho-politics and Cultural Desires*, edited by Campbell, J., and Harbord, L., 113–123. London: UCL Press.

Mahendran, D. 2007. 'The Facticity of Blackness: A Non-conceptual Approach to the Study of Race and Racism in Fanon's and Merleau-Ponty's Phenomenology.' *Human Architecture* 5 (3): 191–203.

Maldonado-Torres, N. 2017. 'Frantz Fanon and the Decolonial Turn in Psychology: From Modern/Colonial Methods to the Decolonial Attitude.' *South African Journal of Psychology* 47 (4): 432–441.

Marriott, D. S. 2018. *Whither Fanon? : Studies in the Blackness of Being*. Stanford: Stanford University Press.

McCulloch, J. 1983. *Black Soul, White Artifact: Fanon's Clinical Psychology and Social Theory*. Cambridge: Cambridge University Press.

McIntyre, R. 2012. 'We-subjectivity': Husserl on Community and Communal Constitution.' In *Intersubjectivity and Objectivity in Adam Smith and Edmund Husserl*, edited by Fricke, C., and Føllesdal, D., 61–92. Frankfurt: Ontos Verlag.

Metzl, J. M. 2009. *Protest Psychosis: How Schizophrenia Became a Black Disease*. Boston: Beacon Press.

Metzl, J. M., and Hansen, H. 2014. 'Structural Competency: Theorizing a New Medical Engagement with Stigma and Inequality.' *Social Science & Medicine* 103: 126–133.

Mills, J. 2004. 'The I and the It.' In *Rereading Freud: Psychoanalysis Through Philosophy*, edited by Mills, J., 127–164. Albany: State University of New York Press.

O'Donnell, J., and Alltucker, K. 2020. *Medical Bias: From Pain Pills to COVID-19, Racial Discrimination in Health care Festers*, June 15, 2020. Accessed July 14, 2020, https://www.usatoday.com/story/news/health/2020/06/14/festering-racial-bias-health-care-factor-covid-19-disparities/5320187002/.

Robertson, M., and Walter, G. 2009. 'Frantz Fanon and the Confluence of Psychiatry, Politics, Ethics and Culture.' *Acta Neuropsychiatrica* 21 (6): 308–309.

Robeson, P. 1958. *Here I Stand* (2nd Imp.). London: Dennis Dobson.

SAMHSA Office of Behavioral Health Equity. 2020. *Double Jeopardy: COVID-19 and Behavioral Health Disparities for Black and Latino Communities in the U.S*, 2020. Accessed July 15, 2020, https://www.samhsa.gov/sites/default/files/covid19-behavioral-health-disparities-black-latino-communities.pdf.

Sikuade, A. 2012. 'Fifty Years After Frantz Fanon: Beyond Diversity.' *Advances in Psychiatric Treatment* 18 (1): 25–31.

Steinberg, D., Mills, D., and Romano, M. 2015. *When Did Prisons Become Acceptable Mental Healthcare Facilities?* Stanford Law School Three Strikes Project. Accessed July 15, 2020, https://law.stanford.edu/publications/when-did-prisons-become-acceptable-mental-healthcare-facilities/.

Ture, K., and Hamilton, C. 1967. *Black Power: Politics of Liberation in America*. New York: Random House.

Utsey, S. O., Bolden, M. A., and Brown, A. L. 2001. 'Visions of Revolution from the Spirit of Frantz Fanon: A Psychology of Liberation for Counseling African Americans Confronting Societal Racism and Oppression.' In *Handbook of Mul-*

*ticultural Counseling*, edited by Ponterotto, J. G., Casas, J. M., Suzuki, L. A., and Alexander, C. M., 311–336. Thousand Oaks: Sage.

Vera, E. M., and Speight, S. L. 2003. 'Multicultural Competence, Social Justice, and Counseling Psychology: Expanding Our Roles.' *The Counseling Psychologist* 31 (3): 253–272.

Weate, J. 2001. 'Fanon, Merleau-Ponty and the Difference of Phenomenology.' In *Race*, edited by Bernasconi, R., 169–183. Malden: Blackwell.

Webb Hooper, M., Nápoles, A. M., and Pérez-Stable, E. J. 2020. 'COVID-19 and Racial/Ethnic Disparities.' *JAMA* 323 (24): 2466–2467.

Williams, D. R., Lawrence, J. A., and Davis, B. A. 2019. 'Racism and Health: Evidence and Needed Research.' *Annual Review of Public Health* 40 (1): 105–125.

# FANON, MOVEMENT AND SELF-MOVEMENT

Nigel C. Gibson

## Now is the Time

*Each generation must out of relative obscurity discover its mission, fulfill it, or betray it.*
—Fanon, *Les damnés de la terre*[1]

*Don't expect to see any explosion today. It's too early ... or too late.*
—Fanon, *Black Skin, White Masks*

Sixty years after Fanon's death, movements across the world stand up to the systemic racism and structural violence at the heart of 'Western civilization', no longer believing in its shibboleths. My focus here is Fanon as a thinker of movement and self-movement in a practical and necessary sense, and these are essential categories to understand Fanon as a person, as a clinical practitioner and as a political revolutionary. Working through the idea of self-movement, I will also discuss the questions of spontaneity and organization, the centrality of the rationality of revolt, and Fanon's conception of ideology as ways of thinking about Fanonian practices.

Fanon lived at a great turning point in history: the birth of the 'Third World' and the global struggles against colonialism. Now, sixty years since his death, there is almost nobody, apart from his son, Olivier, who knew him personally. One could say former FLN leaders who are still alive, like former President of Algeria Bouteflika, did meet Fanon, but that does not say very much. Indeed, once in power, the FLN did not promote the study of *Les damnés de la terre*. In contrast, Fanon was kept alive in the first decades after his death by activists and revolutionaries from the Americas and Africa who found his writings speaking to them. And one could say the same about a new generation today who are asking new questions as they discuss Fanon. In *Les damnés de la terre* Fanon writes similarly of revolutionary memories across the generations that are held among the oppressed: of the mothers who 'still hum to their children the songs which accompanied the warriors as they set off to fight the colonizer', and of the chil-

---

1. Since I prefer the first English title The Damned to the Grove Press translation The Wretched (and would prefer the Internationale use the better translation of Les damnés de la terre as The Damned of the Earth), I refer to Fanon's work as Les damnés de la terre throughout.

dren who 'know by heart the names of the elders who took part in the last revolt' (2004: 69). The memory of revolt, kept alive across the generations, also becomes part of the history of grassroots organizations. In Abahlali baseMjondolo (the shack dweller movement in South Africa), for example, many members are too young to have been politically active against apartheid, but many can trace a link back to those movements and even further back. Some have become aware of a lineage dating back to the 1906 Bambatha rebellion against the British.

In contrast, there is the freshness of historic discontinuity expressed in the opening lines of the chapter on National Culture in *Les damnés de la terre*: 'Each generation must out of relative obscurity discover its mission, fulfill it, or betray it'. Or, as Lenin puts it in his *Philosophic Notebooks*, the world does not satisfy a new generation who decide to change it by their activity (see Lenin, 1961: 213). There is also something very liberating about this that is grounded by Fanon's insistence in the introduction to *Black Skin, White Masks* that 'every human problem cries out to be considered on the basis of its own time' (2008: xvi). And Fanon insists, 'I am resolutely a man of my time'. Rather than repeating the old, a new generation of revolutionaries might not have to be forced into *a priori* conclusions about how a struggle *should* be fought and thought (1968: 206-207). And they can think from that ground about their situation afresh and they can see what Fanon and other liberatory thinkers can offer.

Fanon is resolutely a man of his time and a man of his place, but he is also often out of time and out of place (see Macey, 2011: 39). A work like *Black Skin, White Masks*, published in 1952, is one example. There he argues that 'only a psychoanalytic interpretation of the Black problem can reveal the affective disorders responsible for this network of complexes' (Fanon, 2008: xiv); but then, he adds, the alienation of the Black is not alone an individual issue. Alongside Freud's phylogeny and ontogeny, he says, there is sociogeny, which includes how the social structure and meanings, including racialization, are 'formed and internalized resulting in self-negation' (Nissim-Sabat, 2010: 42). He calls for a socio-diagnostics since it is society that brings the person into being. Thus the internalization of objectification and reification had to be understood socially (and materially), and the quest for disalienation and healing would have to be multidimensional. Of a new generation today raising voices of freedom—engaging Fanon's lived experience of the Black body, of the Black body in space, of the Black body objectified and reified, and also the Black body liberated and free—his thought remains remarkably alive to questions unthought by him in the time.

Fanon's war experiences (during World War II), the racist structure of the French military, and the everyday racism of the French people were essential to his break with French society. His idea of an 'emptied life' (1967: 13) experienced by the colonized and discussed in 'The "North African Syndrome",' remained an important theme that returns in the discussion of Algerian criminality in the chapter titled 'Colonial Wars and Mental Disorders' in *Les damnés de la terre*. There he refers back to a scene that he witnessed when he was 18 years old:

I remember one horrible scene. It was in Oran in 1944. From the camp where we were waiting to embark, soldiers were throwing bits of bread to little Algerian children who fought for them among themselves with anger and hate. Veterinary doctors can throw light on such problems by reminding us of the well-known 'peck order' which has been observed in farmyards. The corn which is thrown to the hens is in fact the object of relentless competition. Certain birds, the strongest, gobble up all the grains while others who are less aggressive grow visibly thinner. Every colony tends to turn into a huge farmyard, where the only law is that of the knife (1968: 308).

Fanon returned to France as a student in 1947 but he did not hold France in the same high esteem as those Antilleans he discussed in *Black Skin, White Masks*. As he put it in a letter to his family dated April 12, 1945: 'Why had I left Fort-de-France? ... To defend an obsolete ideal'. He then goes on to explain, 'if you are informed of my death at the hands of the enemy, console yourselves but never say, "he died for a just cause" ... Because we must no longer look to this *false ideology*, behind which secularists and idiotic politicians hide, as our beacon. I was wrong' (quoted in J. Fanon, 2014: 34, my emphasis).

*Black Skin, White Masks*, then, 'represents seven years of experiments and observations' dating from 1944 to 1951, from which he concludes that the Antillean (slave to their inferiority) and the White (slave to their superiority) 'behave along neurotic lines' (2008: 41-42).[2] The Antilleans discussed in *Black Skin, White Masks* are those who have internalized White values: they are civilized, unlike the 'savage' African. Arriving in the metropole, the French-educated Antillean find out that they are deluded. Using a sociodiagnostic psychoanalytic approach, Fanon sets out to uncover the anomalies of affect. So while Fanon does not deny that the experience of alienation is experienced individually, he insists that one needs to understand it socially. And to understand it, one has to consider the production of mystifications which fastens the Black to images of Blackness, 'snaring, ... imprisoning them as the eternal victims of an essence, of a visible appearance for which they are not responsible' (2008: 18). Clinically, the Black who has internalized the inferiority complex and wants to be White needs to be gradually liberated from this unconscious desire—*and* also be made aware that it is the society that promotes the inferiority complex. 'As a psychoanalyst', he says, 'I must help my patient to bring to consciousness their unconscious, to no longer be tempted by a hallucinatory lactification, but also to act along the lines of a change in social structure' (2008: 80, translation altered). This world, the bourgeois world, which speaks of universal man and human rights, is racist to the core and must be thoroughly opposed.

---

2. Richard Philcox (who translated the 2008 edition) consistently translates *l'homme noir* as the Black man but it is not clear that Fanon is using the term to mean male but rather 'man' as in human. I have preferred to change Philcox's translation to the Black, Blacks or Black people.

# I: Bourgeois Society is Sick

*Life acquires a sense, a transcendence, an object: to end exploitation, to govern themselves by and for themselves, to construct a way of life.*
—Fanon, *L'an V de la révolution algérienne*

Marie-Jeanne Manuellan, who was a Communist and broke with the party after the Suez Crisis, became Fanon's assistant, typing *L'an V de la révolution algérienne* (*A Dying Colonialism*) in the spring of 1959.[3] The book, written in the fifth year of the Algerian revolution, took its title from the idea of a new dating system born from the French revolution. The Algerian revolution was similarly a new beginning. It was making history as Fanon mapped the radical changes in people's consciousness engendered by their involvement in the struggle. Fanon understood that theory begins from reality and needs to transcend the given society. Thus he was concerned not only with destroying the old society but with creating the new, which he expressed in the preface in stark terms: 'Because we want a democratic and a renovated Algeria, because we believe one cannot rise and liberate oneself in one area and sink in another, we condemn, with pain in our hearts, those brothers who have flung themselves into revolutionary action with the almost physiological brutality that centuries of oppression give rise to and feed' (1965: 25).

In the conclusion to *Black Skin, White Masks*, Fanon damns bourgeois society. Echoing the conclusion to the later *Les damnés* about its motionlessness and deadness, he explains that bourgeois society is synonymous with 'any society that becomes ossified in a predetermined mold, *stilling any development*, progress, or discovery. For me bourgeois society is a closed society where it's not good to be alive, where the air is rotten and ideas and people are putrefying. And I believe that a man who takes a stand against this just death is in a way a revolutionary' (2008: 199, my emphasis). In his essay 'The "North African Syndrome",' published just before *Black Skin, White Masks*, Fanon writes that the Arab immigrant's pain and suffering is total and lived in the flesh as a pain without a lesion. 'It is a pain that is everywhere. The French doctor cannot find a cause. Threatened in their affectivity, social activity, and membership of the city' (1967: 13). The North African lives a living death, a daily death lived in 'profound inauthenticity' (Macey, 2011: 35). Anyone who takes a stand against this living death is a revolutionary.

*L'An V de la révolution algérienne* opens with the revolution as the new reality that is 'changing humanity'. In this struggle, he adds, 'the immense, oppressed masses of the colonies and semi-colonies feel that they are a *part of life for the first time*. Life acquires a sense, a transcendence, an object: to end exploitation,

---

3. *L'an V de la révolution algérienne*, year 5 of the Algerian revolution, is Fanon's purposeful and literal title. Written in the 5th year of the revolution, it refers to the revolutionary calendar that his French readers would know. I prefer the title to *A Dying Colonialism* and will refer to the book in its original French title here.

to govern themselves by and for themselves, to construct a way of life' (1965: 1, my emphasis). 'Life acquires a sense, a transcendence': this is Fanon's philosophy of liberation,[4] 'a project to combat all forms of alienation' as Lilia Ben Salem (who took extensive notes from Fanon's course on Society and Psychiatry at the University of Tunis in 1959-60) puts it (Fanon, 2018: 515). Fanon's idea of human liberation was a total outlook—social, political, and psychological—where becoming alive breaks up old routines and 'opens the door to the future'. For Fanon, the revolution represented a leap in consciousness and in existence because both are made by 'the masses with their own hands' and it is they who would then turn 'their energy and their experience to the tasks of building, governing, and deciding their own lives for themselves' (1965: 2). That was Fanon's project.

Writing *L'an V de la révolution algérienne* from inside the revolution, Fanon was understated when he spoke of the brutality of the French. Perhaps the intended French readership was one reason, but perhaps it was more the focus on the radical changes taking place which French brutality could not stop. In 'Colonial Wars and Mental Disorders', in *Les damnés de la terre*, he returns to *L'an V de la révolution algérienne* reminding us, 'we have already pointed out that a whole generation of Algerians, steeped in wanton, gratuitous homicide with all the psychosomatic consequences that this entails, will be the *human legacy of France in Algeria*' (1968: 251, my emphasis, translation altered). Visiting the overcrowded refugee camps on the Moroccan and Tunisian borders, as a doctor and psychiatrist in 1959 (see Gibson and Beneduce, 2017: 215-219), Fanon worked under awful conditions made worse by French planes strafing the border. The notion of a 'cure' for the suffering seemed impossible. Fanon's basic treatment for those in the camps, as well as exhausted militants in the field, was sleep therapy, rest, and time—adding, the latter 'may appear unscientific' (1968: 264).

It was during one of these visits to the border that Fanon's car was blown up. I mention this to underscore the reality of the situation and also Fanon's vigilance. Everyone thought it was a terrorist attack, though no terrorist organization claimed responsibility and there remains uncertainty about whether it was a bomb or a car crash. Fanon was thrown out of the vehicle and fractured his spinal vertebrae. He was taken to a local hospital and then arrangements were made to take him to Rome. The GPRA (the Provisional Government of the Algerian Republic) representative in Rome, Taïeb Boulharouf, was to meet Fanon at the airport but that morning Boulharouf's car was detonated when it was hit by a football from children playing nearby. Newspapers also mentioned a Libyan in a Rome hospital. From inside the hospital Fanon noticed an article mentioning him and giving his room number. He insisted on being moved. He wasn't wrong;

---

4. I am reminded of Fanon's statement in *Black Skin, White Masks* that 'philosophy never saved anybody' (2008: 12), that is philosophy which grasps only at theoretical problems. Fanon's philosophy of liberation is a philosophy of praxis.

that night, gunmen gained admission to the hospital and entered his original room (see Geismar, 1969: 144, Macey, 2012: 392).[5]

From Fanon's writing in *Les damnés de la terre* it is clear that for him the revolution does not end with the removal of the colonialists. In fact it is then that the revolution enters a most important phase and the question becomes instead how to bypass neocolonialism. In contrast to the emphasis on movement and self-movement in *L'an V de la révolution algérienne*, *Les damnés de la terre* also highlights how the threats to still the revolution continue externally and also emerge internally. In this practical sense Fanon was a student of revolution. According to the Marxist psychiatrist Jean Ayme, with whom Fanon stayed in Paris in 1956, Fanon went through Ayme's library including the unpublished transcripts of the first four Congresses of the Communist International, which, Alice Cherki (2006: 94) states, 'had a special fascination for Fanon' . Reading Lenin's writings on the early years of the revolution were enlightening. Here Lenin was constantly reminding the party that it could not 'introduce socialism'. Rather, he insisted, the revolution was 'not the product of a decision of our Party, but ... created by the masses of the people themselves under their own slogans, by their own endeavors' (1936, 321). Lenin's ideas that 'socialism cannot be introduced by a minority, a party' (1936: 320) and that the 'new democracy' had to be based on enlisting everybody 'to the government of the state while working to eliminate exploitation and the apparatus of repression' (1936: 320) have resonances with *Les damnés de la terre*. Indeed, the echo of this libertarian Lenin is also found in C.L.R. James' 'Every Cook Can Govern' (in James, 1977: 160-174), published in the same year Fanon visited Paris.

## II: Spontaneity and Organization: Fanon, C.L.R. James, and Lenin

*That famous dictatorship, whose supporters believe that it is called for by the historical process and consider it an indispensable prelude to the dawn of independence, in fact symbolizes the decision of the bourgeois caste to govern the underdeveloped country first with the help of the people, but soon against them. The progressive transformation of the party into an information service is the indication that the government holds itself more and more on the defensive. The incoherent mass of the people is seen as a blind force that must be continually held in check either by mystification or by the fear inspired by the police force. The party acts as a barometer and as an information service. The militant is turned into an informer.*
—Fanon, *Les damnés de la terre*.

---

5. Fanon's biographers Cherki, Geismar, and Macey have different analyses of the attacks. Macey wonders whether Fanon warranted the attention of *La Main Rouge*. Reluctantly he concedes that Fanon was involved in high level FLN meetings in 1959 as a 'specialist' drawing up a political program and proposals for the FLN's statutes to be approved by the CNRA. 'According to the specialists', writes Macey (2012: 392), 'the goal of the war was "the liberation of the national territory"' and 'the social and economic revolution form a whole... and do not constitute two distinct stages'.

In *Whither Fanon* David Marriott links Fanon to Lenin by way of C.L.R. James' *Notes on Dialectics*, connecting James' writings on the question of spontaneity and organization with Fanon (Marriott, 2018: 263). Marriot contends that for Fanon and for C.L.R. James, 'organization is what *both* secures and thereby ruins mass spontaneity as innovation' and that 'for both men spontaneity and usurpation are one and the same movement' (2018: 270). Fanon might agree with James that, as Marriott quotes, the 'party has to be negated because in its current form (the one-party state) it represents 'the incorporation into bourgeois, capitalist society of the nearly two-hundred-year-old efforts by the labour movement to create a party to take over the state. Instead the state takes over the party' (2018: 270). In the colonies, the European form of vanguard party organization was virtually unquestioned. Fanon calls this a fetish form (1968: 108) uncritically imported into the colonies, becoming the perfect organization for the aspiring anticolonial national bourgeoisie whose desire, Fanon argues, is to take the place of the colonizer. For James the new ruling class, formed by the Stalinist counter-revolution, is intimately linked to nationalized property, which becomes a fetish form (James, 1980: 33); likewise for Fanon, the call by the elites for nationalization does not offer 'a new program of social relations' but 'the transfer into indigenous hands of privileges inherited from the colonial period'. And for Fanon the one-party state becomes the perfect form: 'The single party is the modern form of the dictatorship of the bourgeoisie, unmasked, unpainted, unscrupulous, and cynical' (1968: 165).

On these points Fanon and James agree. But where James counter-poses spontaneity to the vanguard party form of organization as absolute opposites, Fanon does not reduce organization to the vanguard party. In the context of the colonial police state his criticism of the weaknesses of spontaneity necessitates organization, even perhaps a centralized one, even if later in *Les damnés de la terre* Fanon advises that the party must be 'decentralized in the extreme'. For Fanon, the question of organizational form is contextual rather than absolute. In other words, for Fanon, the contradiction between spontaneity and organizational form by no means exhausts the question of organization or the question of realizing liberation. At the same time Fanon equates making a fixed particular of spontaneity with making a fixed particular of the party form or leader's personality.[6] And when he famously says that 'each generation must discover its mission, fulfill it or betray it', one should also consider this in terms of new forms of organization that emerge in the revolutionary movements as important expressions of social change.

---

6. On the 1979 revolution and 1983 counter-revolution (within the revolution) in Grenada see Brian Meeks (2001) which discusses the revolution's dominant ideology in terms of 'Jamesianism' and 'Leninism' (153-156) and the growing disconnection between the party leadership and the mass of the people as the context for the counter-revolution—namely the murder of Maurice Bishop and those who had liberated him from house arrest. In an analysis written a few months later, James' emphasis—surprisingly in light of how he has been associated with spontaneity—turns back to a vanguardism in the shape of a leader or the army: 'A mass movement needs leadership and if a political leader does not give it people turn to another organization, often the army' (James, 1984: 304).

This discussion connects to 'the theoretical question' that Fanon raises in *Les damnés de la terre*, which, he adds, 'has been posed for the last fifty years' about whether the bourgeois phase could be skipped' (1968: 119). Indeed the question is connected with the contradiction Fanon marks within spontaneity, titling the second chapter of *Les damnés de la terre* 'Spontaneity, Its Strengths and Weaknesses'.

Around the same time C.L.R. James was studying Lenin's philosophic notebooks on Hegel, which are the basis for his 1948 *Notes on Dialectics* (James, 1980), he was developing his thesis on the 'Negro Question' based in part on thinking through Lenin's political writings,[7] especially after the October revolution, and the revolutionary specificity of the Black dimension in the USA. James' 1948 essay 'The Revolutionary Answer to the Negro Problem in the United States' (James, 1996: 138-147) was based upon three principles: 1. That 'the Negro struggle, the independent Negro struggle has a vitality and validity of its own'; 2. That it 'is able to intervene with terrific force upon the social and political life of the nation'; and 3. That it 'is able to exercise a powerful influence upon the revolutionary proletariat'. At the same time James wrote an introduction to a translation of three of Marx's 'humanist' essays written in 1844, which were being discussed within the Johnston-Forest Tendency.[8]He again connects this back to Lenin. James argues that Lenin's *Can the Bolsheviks Retain Power* (an ironic essay title since the Bolsheviks did retain power but in the opposite way to what Lenin was arguing), written immediately *before* the revolution, 'said openly what Marx was writing' in the humanist essays. Indeed, what Lenin writes there on the eve of revolution has a remarkable resonance with how Fanon ends 'Misadventures of National Consciousness'[9] in *Les damnés de la terre*. James quotes Lenin: 'The most important thing is to inspire the oppressed and the toilers with the confidence of their own strength' and 'an honest, courageous move to hand over the administration to the proletarians and semi-proletarians' where 'they begin to work for themselves, and not under the whip of the capitalist, the master, the official'. 'Only then', James continues quoting Lenin, 'a million new fighters will arise, who until then had been politically dormant, languishing in poverty and

---

7. The period reflects the Johnson-Forest Tendency deep study of Lenin connecting the 'National question' and the 'Black question'. In addition, in his 1947 essay 'Lenin on Agriculture and the Negro Question', James notes Lenin's 'interest and knowledge' of the 'Negro question' going back to his work *Capitalism in Agriculture*, published in 1900, which was 'no more "theoretical" discussion' but the 'driving force of the Russian revolution' where it [the revolution] 'said openly what Marx was writing' in the humanist essays. Indeed, what Lenin writes there on the eve 'penetration of capital into the Russian countryside' was disrupting 'traditional relations' and creating social differentiation and proletarianization (1996: 130-131). While the abolition of slavery in the US, continues James (who is summarizing Lenin), 'did not entirely abolish all traces of the old chattel slavery', he saw similarities between it and the remains of feudalism in Russia.
8. J.R Johnson was C.L.R. James and Freddie Forrest was Raya Dunayevskaya.
9. I prefer to translate the title of Fanon's third chapter, 'Les mésaventures de la conscience nationale', literally as the misadventures of national consciousness. One reason is because the idea of misadventures gestures to Merleau-Ponty's important 1955 work *Adventures of the Dialectic* that includes, he says, 'errors through which it [the revolution] must pass' (1973: 204). On 'errors' also see the latter section on 'failure' in Fanon and note Hegel's idea that 'only out of this error does the truth arise' and that error, when it is 'absorbed, ... is a necessary dynamic element of truth' which is important to C.L.R. James and quoted in *Notes on Dialectics* (1980: 92).

despair, having lost faith in themselves as human beings' (quoted by James, 1984a: 66-67).[10]

In the essay Lenin argues, 'Is there any other way to teach the people to manage their own affairs and to avoid mistakes than by actual *practice*, than by immediately proceeding to genuine popular self- government?' (Lenin, 1943: 274, my emphasis). He then goes on to criticize what he calls the administrative mentality of the party intellectuals: 'The most important thing at present is to abandon the bourgeois-intellectual's prejudice that only special officials, who by their whole social position are entirely dependent on capital, can perform the work of administration of the state'. (1943: 287) Again, we can see connections with Fanon's argument about the specific problem of the relationship between the intellectuals and the masses, their elitism and bourgeois sensitivities. Thus the need for the intellectuals and militants committed to the revolution to develop relationships 'inside the people' learning through 'actual practice' expressed in the idea that the struggle is a school.

Whether Fanon read James is beside the point.[11] Rather there are important parallels, which might be considered 'in the air' especially when considering Fanon's idea of stretching Marxism.[12]

## Slightly Stretching Marxism?

> *In the colonies the economic substructure is also a superstructure. The cause is the consequence; you are rich because you are white, you are white because you are rich. This is why Marxist analysis should always be slightly stretched every time we have to deal with the colonial problem.*
> —Fanon, *Les damnés de la terre*

Fanon's slight stretching of Marxism is connected to the idea of rethinking who the revolutionary forces are in a specific context. Lenin had asked a similar question after the collapse of orthodox Marxism in Europe in 1914 when the socialist parties supported the imperialist 'World War'. He argued anti-imperialist struggles for national self-determination could become what he called the 'bacillus' for revolution. Lenin had in mind not only anticolonial struggles like the Irish rebellion of 1916 but also the Black dimension in the United States. Critical of the chauvinist 'aristocracy of labor' produced in the imperial metropoles which had become the 'bulwark' of a conservative and chauvinist social democ-

---

10. Quoted by James (1984: 66-67). These quotes appear in James, Dunayevskaya and Stone *Invading Socialist Society* (1947) (https://www.marxists.org/archive/james-clr/works/1947/invading/). The direct quote comes, *Can the Bolsheviks Retain Power*, in Lenin *Selected Works*, volume VI https://archive.org/stream/in.ernet.dli.2015.189959/ 2015.189959.Vilenin-Selected-Works--Vi_djvu.txt See also*https://www.marxists.org/archive/lenin/works/1917/oct/ 01.htm*

11. There are two copies of C.L.R. James' *Black Jacobins* in Fanon's Algiers library. Both copies are uncut and thus unread (P. I. R. James, is mistakenly listed by Gallimard as the author of its 1949 edition of *Les Jacobins noirs* (Paris: Gallimard, 1949). Peter Hudis notes that Fanon 'crossed paths' with Raya Dunayevskaya in Lyon in the summer of 1947 (see Hudis, 2015: 22).

12. On Fanon and Marx see Gibson (2020).

racy, Lenin was also critical of his radical comrades (including Luxemburg) who considered national liberation struggles 'bourgeois'. Lenin's idea of uncovering revolutionary forces meant going 'lower and deeper' into the mass of the impoverished peasantry and working class, whether they were formally employed or not. Fanon's idea of stretching Marxism can be considered in a similar vein based on concrete situation which for Fanon, took on a spatial dimension.

In *Les damnés de la terre* Fanon argues that colonial society is a racist society, which he describes as 'a motionless, Manicheistic world, a world of statues' (1968: 50)[13] where the urban colonized petit bourgeois and numerically small colonized urban working class were at best only interested in coming to terms with it, with the goal of becoming part of it.[14] Instead, Fanon argues, it was those outside the urban areas, the landless peasants and those who had moved to the urban peripheries, living in the bidonvilles (tin shack towns) and shanty towns, where one could find populations who have continually resisted and where an elemental opposition to colonialism has flourished.

Fanon's 'slight stretching of Marxism' can be considered a recreation of Marxism, i.e., a designation of the social composition of revolutionary forces in a specific context. Nowhere is this more concrete than with Fanon's revision of what Marxists called the lumpenproletariat. Since the term lumpenproletariat has been associated with an unthinking reactive mass (lump) of impoverished people, the term, often shortened to lumpen, is considered derogative. In fact it translates simply as 'raggedy proletariat'. Fanon takes up the concept of the lumpenproletariat anew in 1950s Algeria where a growing number of rural people had been forced off the land and traveled to the urban areas in search of work.[15] This process has continued to speed up over the past sixty years so that the majority of the world's population now resides in urban areas, with the number of people surviving through informal employment and living in 'informal' housing growing exponentially, making the 'lumpenproletariat' a significant part of the global working class. Rather than dismissing the urban poor and their daily struggle to survive,[16] Fanon rethinks their revolutionary potential and limitations in 1950s Algeria.

For Fanon spontaneous action is incredibly powerful but also, as the tactics of the enemy change, it can ruin itself; and as it becomes exhausted it can turn in on itself. There is a need, in short, for self-reflection and clarification as well

---

13. Fanon's use of the term Manichean in *Black Skin, White Masks* may be indebted to Simone de Beauvoir's *The Second Sex* (2011: 476) published in 1949: 'The essence of Manichaeism is not only to recognize two principles, one good and one evil: it is also to posit that good is attained by the abolition of evil and not by a positive movement'.

14. He includes 'tram conductors, taxi drivers, miners, dockers, interpreters, [and] nurses' among this faction who are for the 'colonial machine … to run smoothly'. He calls them a privileged 'bourgeois' fraction of the colonized people (1968: 109).

15. In his last psychiatric article, 'Day Hospitalization in Psychiatry', Fanon characterizes the economic situation of female and male patients in the day hospital program in Tunis (2018: 483-488). Many are unemployed or day laborers with the 'wives of unemployed men represent[ing] the highest proportion of hospitalized women' (2018: 488). As well as a high number of Algerian refugees in the program there are a large number of people who live in the shanty-towns.

16. A point made, for example, by Mike Davis in *Planet of Slums* who sees very little chance of solidarity among the 'slum' dwellers in a daily war of survival.

as strategic organization. This is not simply a call for a vanguard party to lead. Rather, like Lenin's argument in the conclusion of *What Is To Be Done* it is the spontaneity of the masses who 'demanded political consciousness on the part of the leaders' (1960: 518).[17]Likewise for Fanon, the problem is not at all spontaneous action *but the political leaders' inability to understand it* and to connect with it. One turning point in *Les damnés de la terre* is his consideration of the militant in the political organization who appreciates the rationality of revolt and the gulf between it and the nationalist political leadership. This militant is a crucial figure because it is they who also want clarity from the political leaders to give action its direction and articulate at least a 'minimum humanist program'. It is they who leave the political groupings in the colonial urban areas and embrace the rising of 'the damned of the earth'. Fanon sides with these militants because they are in touch with the rationality of revolt.[18]

## III: The Rationality of Revolt

> For us, that Martinican, whose journey through French culture made him an Algerian revolutionary, will remain the very living example of a universalism in action and the highest approach to be human as yet realized in this inhuman world.
> —Francis Jeanson, *La révolution algérienne*
>     Wherever there is movement, wherever there is life, wherever anything is carried into effect in the actual world, there Dialectic is at work.
> —Hegel, *Logic*

'The battle of reason is the struggle to break up the rigidity to which the understanding has reduced everything', the Fanon scholar, Sekyi-Otu, quotes Hegel (1996: 151) in *Fanon's Dialectic of Experience*. For Fanon this battle of reason becomes the rationality of revolt that moves us past the rigidity and stillness of colonial Manicheanism. This is not the doomed-to-fail battle over 'reason' that Fanon details in chapter five of *Black Skin, White Masks* where 'reason' plays cat and mouse with him and walks out when he walks into the room (see Fanon,

---

17. In another essay, 'Guerilla Warfare' (written in the context of the 1905 revolution) Lenin argues that the problem of the lumpenproletarian spontaneous armed action is actually a problem of the elitist social democrats who 'proudly and smugly [declare] "we are not anarchists, thieves, robbers, we are superior to all this, we reject guerrilla warfare".' Instead the actions need to be understood as a new form of revolt with which the revolutionary organization needs to engage. Lenin warns, 'Every new form of struggle, accompanied as it is by new dangers and new sacrifices, inevitably "disorganises" organizations which are unprepared for this *new form of struggle*' (Lenin, 1972: 220 ).

18. Again, this has resonances with Lenin's critique of the Bolshevik leadership prior to the October 1917 revolution. In his *April Thesis* presented to the All-Russia Conference of Soviets of Workers' and Soldiers' Deputies after he returned from exile, among Lenin's theses' demands were the end to the war, the nationalization of all land, and all power to the soviets in a 'commune state'. If the party rejected them he threatened to leave it and 'go to the sailors' who were far more revolutionary than his Bolshevik Marxist colleagues.

2008: 99, 1967: 119).[19] Here he is walled in by this White instrumental reason[20] and one can see a critical connection with Fanon's critique of struggles that have been fought in terms of the master's values (including the master's tools), or what we could also call 'bourgeois values' (2008: 194-195).

## Listening as Praxis

By praxis, I mean Fanon's thoughtful engagements—social, political, clinical (the three terms, of course, intimately connected)—with the world around him, namely the racist and (neo)colonial world. In that short decade between 1952 and 1961, from his first published article to his last publication, Fanon wrote three books, published numerous articles and edited a revolutionary newspaper. This work was connected to practice, experience, and continued self-reflection as he thought through and ana- lyzed new situations and refused *a priori* conclusions. Fanon was an original thinker whose analyses are grounded in the concrete.[21] What he did in *Black Skin, White Masks* and continued to do was radically differ- ent from what had come before as he challenged grounding notions of the fields of psychoanalysis, psychiatry, and philosophy.[22]

The rationality of revolt, Fanon argues in *Les damnés de la terre*, is 'not a ratio- nal confrontation of points of view ... It is not a treatise on the universal, but the untidy affirmation of an original idea propounded as an absolute' (1968: 41).[23] Thus rather than battling normative (White) reason and its liberal assumptions, the rationality of revolt is the affirmation of the uprisings of the damned of the earth, those who don't count or are seen as good-for-nothings and beyond the pale of reason. For Fanon, it is the struggle of these masses of objectified and dehumanized people who count. The rationality of revolt is where the 'thing' who has been colonized 'becomes human during the same process by which it frees itself' (1968: 36). This double movement, the destruction of the colo-

---

19. See Lewis R. Gordon's (2015: 47-52) excellent discussion of Fanon's critique of 'reason' in the *L'Expérience vécue du Noir* chapter in *Black Skin, White Masks*.

20. Here it is important to remember lines from Césaire's *Notebooks of a Return to My Native Land* which Fanon knew by heart: 'Reason, I crown you wind of the evening. Mouth of order your name? To me it is the whip's corolla. Beauty I call you petition of stone. But ah! the raucous smuggling of my laughter. Ah! my treasure of saltpetre! Because we hate you, you and your reason, we invoke dementia praecox flamboyant madness tenacious cannibalism. Treasure, let us count: the madness that remembers the madness that screams the madness that sees the madness that is unleashed' (Césaire, 1995: 93).

21. Long before Benedict Anderson, argues Anne McClintock (1999: 289), 'Fanon recognizes the inventedness of national community'. Indeed Fanon heralds the new nation, made real through the struggle to 'invent souls'. 'This is one example of political education, which is both non-linear and dialectical. The nation is fabricated and invented through the struggle. The fragments, and 'scattered acts', lose 'their anarchic character', as he puts it in 'This is the Voice of Algeria', are organized into a national and Algerian political idea (1965: 84). It is through the struggle that the people become new subjects, inventing the nation in motion

22. Fanon's first published articles, 'The Black's Complaint: The Lived Experience of the Black' (La plainte de Noir: L'Expérience vécue du Noir') published in Esprit in May 1951 (and republished as the fifth chapter of *Black Skin, White Masks* as The Lived Experience of the Black) and 'The "North African Syndrome",' are phenomenological cri- tiques of racist normalizations. Understood narrowly, neither is political not psychiatric but both express Fanon's unwill- ingness to remain within disciplinary confines. Both articles demand action. For a discussion of the interrela- tions of politics and psychiatry in Fanon's works see Gibson and Beneduce (2017).

23. On the question of universalism based on Fanon's critique see Ato Sekyi-Otu: *Left Universalism, Africacentric Essays*.

nial society and the creation of a new society, is of course the problematic of *Les damnés de la terre* and one that remains for us to work out. At first, there is a seamless character to the double process, as Fanon argues in the opening pages of *Les damnés*: movement and self-movement encourage movement and self-movement. And self-movement becomes synonymous with making history and becoming historical. Thus what Fanon calls a new humanism is a politics of becoming, the transformation of the paralyzed and thingified beings into human beings through their own actions: 'Decolonization never takes place unnoticed, for it influences individuals and modifies them fundamentally'. This modification is a product of history-in-the-making, transforming 'spectators crushed with their inessentiality into privileged actors'. Fanon describes the new humanism being introduced by a new people out of the struggle itself, and 'with it a new language and a new humanity' bringing 'a natural rhythm into existence'. In short, 'decolonization is the veritable creation of a new humanity' which 'owes nothing of its legitimacy to any supernatural power; the "thing" which has been colonized becomes human during the same process by which it frees itself' (1968: 36). But Fanon is not saying that the process is automatic. Rather we find out that the process is a tortuous one, one beset by misadventures and one that will need commitment, reflection and time; a new and anticapitalist conception of time as the space for human development. At the same time, as David Marriott puts it (2018: 244), Fanon's 'attempts to forge a new humanism remained incomplete'. In a certain sense this has to be; a movement of becoming is always incomplete. For me, this is an essential element of Fanon's anti-formalist dialectic.[24]

The challenge to hear the rationality of revolt, to hear the new language, is not automatic because it involves a commitment to the new kind of listening that has to cut through prejudices and assumptions.[25] As a 'practicing psychiatrist Fanon spent much of his time as a professional listener' (Baucom, 2001: 15) as can be seen, for example, in the case notes in the final chapter of *Les damnés de la terre*. And much of Fanon's writing is a compilation of voices as well as responses to what he had been hearing. Fanon's thinking, the notion of working out new concepts, in other words, is grounded in his engagement with the world. One can see this in his writing, developing new concepts from his earliest published writing onward.

In the chapter 'Medicine and Colonialism' in *L'an V de la révolution algérienne*, Fanon connects hearing symptoms speak to hearing quotidian resistances in daily life: 'It is necessary to analyse, patiently and lucidly, each one of *the reactions* of the colonised', he argues, warning that '*every time we do not understand*, we must tell ourselves that we are at the heart of the drama, that of the impossibility of finding a meeting ground in any colonial situation' (1965: 125, my emphasis).

---

24. Indeed, not Fanon's dialectic alone, but to the dialectic of negativity itself. As Raya Dunayevskaya argues, 'The dialectic would not be the dialectic and Hegel would not be Hegel if the moment of encounter with the Absolute Idea was a moment of quiescence ... Far from the unity of the Theoretical and Practical idea being an ultimate, or pinnacle, of a hierarchy, the Absolute Idea is a new beginning ... rooted in practice as well as in philosophy' (1980: 163-4). This is also how I understand Fanon's idea to 'humanize the world'.

25. See Fanon's 'The "North African Syndrome"' as one early example.

Fanon describes the colonized distrust of colonial hospitals in Algeria. The colonized say, 'I don't trust them and would refuse to be taken to the hospital until it was too late'. The European doctor's response is that these people's beliefs are irrational. The reality that 'the patient would usually die ... would strengthen the group in its original belief in the occupier's fundamentally evil character' (1965: 124). In 'Medicine and Colonialism' Fanon describes a father who has scratched his son's forehead in the 'traditional' way because his son was complaining of a headache. This action is 'from a strictly rational point of view', adds Fanon. But when he goes to the European doctor he is insulted and the father admits that 'this insulter is right ... I was wrong to make those scratches. For, as a matter of fact, my son has meningitis and it really has to be treated as a meningitis ought to be treated' (1965: 126). But the father must also refuse. He must refuse 'to admit that he owes his son's life to the colonizer's operation' (1965: 128). His notion of understanding continues to resonate.[26]

Just as in France where the North Africans' visit to the doctor's office is an alienating one, the patient is facing the technician as colonizer. Their body is tense and muscles contracted. They speak in monosyllables, giving nothing away (1965: 126-127). Even in a case where a father knows his son has meningitis he must cover his son's dose of antibiotics with a visit to the traditional healer, since that expresses that he is 'acting, from a strictly rational point of view, in a positive way' (1965: 126).

For Fanon, the colonized's resistances to French medicine is a reaction essential for psychological and cultural survival. In *Les damnés de la terre*, as in *L'an V de la révolution algérienne*, the colonized are not simply a dominated people, they 'constantly' cling to 'a way of life which was in practice anti-colonial' (1968: 136). This 'permanent struggle against omnipresent death' (1965: 128) is a struggle against the negation of their being. Thus the act of refusal or the rejection of medical treatment is not a refusal of life, but a 'greater passivity before that close and contagious death'. Of course Fanon warns that 'consciousness remains rudimentary' (1968: 136) and a 'complete reinterpretation of events' is called into being by the 'hard lesson of facts' (1968: 134).

But we also must remember, Fanon intones in *Les damnés de la terre*, that 'a colonized people is not just a dominated people'. Unlike the French under German occupation who remained human beings, in a colonial situation there is not simply domination dehumanization. In Algeria, 'the Algerians, the veiled women, the palm trees and the camels make up the landscape, the natural background to the human presence of the French' (1968: 250). Nobody could have put it better, argued Joby Fanon: 'in French Algeria, the only humans were the French' (J. Fanon, 2014: 120). The racist and dehumanizing structure that explains Fanon's

---

26. For example in our period of the COVID pandemic, where the distrust of hospitals and vaccines, for example, among Black and Brown people in the United States, are spoken of in Manichean terms. On distrust of the COVID-19 vaccine in Britain among young Blacks, see 'Survey says 64% of young black people in England are "vaccine hesitant"', *The Guardian*, March 16, 2021, https://www.theguardian.com/society/2021/mar/16/survey-says-64-of-young-black-people-in-england-are-vaccine-hesitant.

description resonates with the daily struggle for Black life in the metropolitan North and the postcolonial South where the struggle to breathe is a daily one and where it is only through struggle and self-consciousness that 'the racial and racist dimension is transcended' (2008: 95).

In short, any attempt to understand what is going on must shift the ground of reason because, as Fanon puts it in the colonial situation, 'the truth objectively expressed is constantly vitiated by the lie of the colonial situation' (1965: 128). For Fanon, truth requires not just a recognition of failure but also an understanding that the failure to understand means being prepared to listen carefully and critically, aware of meaning and context and eschewing the will to fit the responses of the colonized into a ready-made scenario.

Fanon begins with an absolute based on the reality of the Manichean colonial situation: 'the impossibility of finding a meeting ground'. This is just a beginning and it could also become an abstraction that effectively limits any further development if the radical intellectual, on this new ground, does not also bring their own self-critical reflection to bear. This constant engagement is what the radical / militant must also learn. In *Les damnés de la terre*, the militant fleeing bourgeois nationalist politics 'discovers in real action a new form of political activity which in no way resembles the old' (1968: 145). This new politics expresses the new space on which the new society must be built and in the conclusion of the chapter on spontaneity he says that it is the insurrection that '*proves to itself* its rationality' (1968: 145, my emphasis) as it uncovers new knowledge and 'unknown facts, which brings out new meanings and pinpoints the contradictions' (1968: 146). It is a movement from practice as a form of theory when 'spontaneity discovers the power of thought along with its physical might' (Dunayevskaya, 1980: 172). This becomes both the challenge to intellectuals and the measure of the misadventures of national consciousness.

On the first page of the chapter 'Misadventures of National Consciousness', Fanon immediately pinpoints a central contradiction, namely, the incapacity of the national bourgeoisie, the unpreparedness of the nationalist elites, their lack of ties to the mass movement, and indeed their cowardice. These are all elements of why they are incapable of 'rationalizing popular praxis' (1968: 149).

The rationality of revolt is therefore neither given beforehand nor immediately comprehensible. Rather, it is living. Fanon introduces the idea within the anticolonial struggle arguing that retrogression is the inevitable result of the incapacity to 'rationalize popular praxis': the 'retrograde steps with all the weaknesses and serious dangers that they entail are the historical result of the incapacity of the national bourgeoisie to rationalize popular praxis, that is to say their incapacity to attribute it any reason' (1968: 149, translation altered). In the midst of the revolution Lenin's idea that the revolutionary struggle doesn't erase differences, but enlivens them,[27] becomes important for Fanon as he focuses on

---

27. See Lenin, 'Speech On The Report On The Activities Of The Central Committee May 4, 1907' (*Collected Works*, 12: 446): 'Our old disputes, our theoretical, and especially our tactical, differences are constantly being converted, in the

the retrogression within the political movements themselves. A few years earlier, in 1958, all had agreed on Pan-Africanism. Now, in 1960, Fanon argues that the greatest challenge to African liberation is not colonialism but the lack of a liberatory ideology that measures up to the new politics and new subjectivity that is being expressed by the anticolonial movements. The leaders' incapacity to rationalize popular praxis was a problem of recognizing the newness of this praxis and work out new concepts on that basis. Remember earlier, Fanon talked about the development of a new person and a new language. In *Les damnés de la terre* he expresses this, sharply connecting it to new forms of organization: 'The very forms of organization of the struggle will suggest to him a different vocabulary. Brother, sister, friend—these are words outlawed by the colonialist bourgeoisie, because for them my brother is my purse, my friend is part of my scheme for getting on' (1968: 45).

## On the Question of Failure: The Political Education of the Militant

> *The essence of the revolution, the true revolution which changes humankind and renews a society is… the oxygen which brings about and sustains a new kind of human being.*
> —Fanon, *L'an V de la révolution algérienne*

In *What Fanon Said* Lewis Gordon contends that with Fanon, 'the message of the failures … is systemic' and because of the systemic failure, the system has to be totally uprooted. With this struggle, Gordon adds, 'Fanon calls for a pedagogy to build (*édifier*, "to edify, "to build"), through the tremors of beckoning bodies, a questioning humanity' (2015: 69-70). What I want to discuss here are the failures *within* the anticolonial struggles which are highlighted in *Les damnés de la terre* and that mark the book as quite different from *L'an V de la révolution algérienne*, written just two years earlier. Here concrete reflections of that immediate moment of political failure are in need of edification with Fanon warning that the idea that liberation could be achieved 'in one fell swoop' is a great weakness (1968: 138). Whereas the colonized are the corrosive element of 'Western civilization', the colonized rationality of revolt is the 'poetry of the future' (as Fanon quotes Marx in the conclusion to *Black Skin, White Masks*). The need to totally uproot the system and build through the 'questioning humanity' of everyone continues to be an important lesson for all revolutionary movements and especially those that want to divorce the struggle from the working out of how to create a new society. The new society, Fanon insists, has to be made by conscious human beings from situations riven by crises. Learning from mistakes becomes essential to open up, rather than to silence, thinking: 'We all have

---

course of the revolution, into the most downright practical differences … Practical experience does not erase differences of opinion; it sharpens and vitalises them'.

dirty hands', Fanon says, recognizing that humanizing human beings will be done through practice, political education, and also through mistakes. In other words, involving everyone in the work of political administration is part of the work of putting the idea of involving all in the practice of popular administration (see 1968: 314). Going forward is difficult and requires careful and concrete studies. If a government 'really wants to free the people politically and socially ... there must be an economic program; there must also be a doctrine concerning the division of wealth and social relations'. Fanon warns that such a program is opposed to any 'demagogic formula' or 'collusion with the former occupying power'. In fact the content of this program will not be set up by the leadership or by a group of intellectuals behind closed doors. Instead it must be realized through discussion and practice, based on an idea of humanity as people become 'more and more clear minded' demanding this program (1968: 203-204).

The militant, and the militant's education, is a constant feature throughout *Les damnés de la terre*. The militant learns through practice, realizing that 'while they are breaking down colonial oppression, they are building up automatically yet another system of exploitation' (1968: 145, translation altered). This realization has to be reflected on as the militant demands that the leadership draw up a program and set of objectives (1968: 170). But it is Fanon's critique of the militant who wants to sink differences to get things done that is an important educational moment. Fanon explains, 'It sometimes happens at meetings that militants use sweeping, dogmatic formulas. The preference for this shortcut, in which *spontaneity and over-simple sinking of differences* dangerously combine to defeat intellectual elaboration, frequently triumphs' (1968: 199, my emphasis). So we have an example of a situation that many have experienced inside movements, the tactical sinking of differences and the suppression of intellectual elaboration. Fanon calls it a 'shirking of responsibility'. Part of the difficult work of intellectual elaboration, Fanon argues, is to clarify a situation and then explicate goals and vision, thereby explaining differences. Moreover, Fanon explains that the militant learns and also shares their learning through failure: 'When we meet this shirking of responsibility in a militant it is not enough to tell them they are wrong. We must make them ready for responsibility, encourage them to follow up their chain of reasoning, and make them realize the true nature, often shocking, inhuman, and in the long run, sterile, of such oversimplification' (1968: 199, translation altered) In other words, Fanon sees an important pedagogy in the militant's 'failure'. It is not at all about shaming the militant but about learning from the error (absorbing and uplifting it as a dynamic of truth as Hegel puts it), and sharing and developing the intellectual elaboration in the social setting by making it a 'collective affair'.

Thus, failure and learning from failure are essential elements of political education and one can't help but think back to Marx's discussion in *The 18th Brumaire*, of revolution constantly criticizing itself and returning to what seems to be accomplished, deriding 'with cruel thoroughness the half-measures, weaknesses, and paltriness of their first attempts' (Marx 1963: 19). Thus, Fanon warns: 'We African politicians must have very clear ideas on the situation of our people', adding that 'this clarity of ideas must be profoundly dialectical' because 'the awakening of the whole people' and 'the people's work in the building of the nation will not immediately take on [their] full dimensions' (1968: 193).

The new society will not be achieved magically overnight but will take time and work. This is partly 'because the spirit of discouragement which has been deeply rooted in people's minds by colonial domination is still very near the surface. People's enlightenment will take time and come through new experiences. In addition, the concept of time also shifts—time not measured by production or the seasons, but by building a society based on human relations'. As Marx puts it, where time can be measured 'as the space for human development' (Marx 1989: 493). Fanon adds, 'The yardstick of time must no longer be that of the moment or up till the next harvest, but must become that of the rest of the world' (1968: 193-194). He goes on to explain this practically from the bottom up. 'Development' is not about having a plan that experts decide is the most efficient but about involving everybody in discussion and treating the worker as a human being, 'even if it takes them twice or three times as long'. This time is not lost, Fanon explains: 'The fact is that the time taken up by explaining, the time "lost" in treating the worker as a human being, will be caught up in the execution of the plan. People must know where they are going, and why'. Rather than the worker being measured by the 'output of energy, or the functioning of certain muscles', the idea of treating the workers as a human being means involving them in decision making, 'using their brains and their hearts [rather] than with only their muscles and their sweat' (1968: 193, 191-2). Humanity is a yes, Fanon proclaims in *Black Skin White Masks*, yes to freedom, and no to *any* exploitation.

## IV: Motion and Motionlessness

> *Was my freedom not given me in order to build the world of the You?*
> *At the end of this book we would like the reader to feel with us the open dimension of every consciousness.*
> *My final prayer:*
> *O my body, always make me a man who questions!*
> —Fanon, *Black Skin, White Masks*

As I have argued, movement and self-movement are essential categories to understand Fanon as person, as activist, and as intellectual. Fanon moved throughout his adult life. As a young adult he left Martinique to join the Free French in early 1943 but didn't get further than Domenica. He made it out the following year, traveling to North Africa and then to France. By the time Fanon returned to France and began study in Lyons in 1947 he had already experienced different cultures of racism and colonialism in the French Empire from the metropole to the Antilles and North Africa (see House, 2005: 45).

Movement and self-movement are essential elements to Fanon's praxis, and to the goal of disalienation, and to the freedom of the human being. In his medical thesis, written after a draft *Black Skin, White Masks* was rejected for political reasons, Fanon quotes Jacques Lacan that 'Not only can the human's being [l'être de l'homme] not be understood without madness, but it wouldn't be the human's being if it didn't carry within it madness as the limit of its freedom' (quoted in Gibson and Beneduce, 2017, 13). Fanon then argues, as he does in *Black Skin, White Masks*, 'the human is human insofar as they are entirely turned toward the future'. He continues, 'we [will] approach the problem of history from a psychoanalytic and ontological angle. We will then show that history is nothing but the systematic valorization of collective complexes' (quoted in Gibson and Beneduce, 2017, 42). In Fanon's resignation letter from Blida-Joinville Psychiatric Hospital in 1956, he returned to this idea, and the need to change the world, arguing that taking care of madness is about returning freedom to the mad: 'Madness is one of the means by which the human being can lose their freedom'. In other words, freedom is the goal and it needs to be consciously and intentionally created. Fanon had tried to encourage this at Blida-Joinville Psychiatric Hospital by promoting patient autonomy, trying to 'attenuate the viciousness of the system' (Fanon, 1967: 52), and breaking up institutional alienation and hierarchies through critical sociotherapy programs. But the reality that colonial Algeria was pathological meant that humanizing the hospital in a dehumanizing society became an 'illogical' goal. Thus, in the resignation letter, he adds that since the social structure in Algeria is actively attempting to 'decerebralize' the people, it must be replaced (Fanon, 1967: 53).

Travel, Miraj Desai argues, provided Fanon opportunities 'to see the social structure as such ... [and] also led to increasing "self" awareness ... show[ing] the extent to which the self was bound up within a surrounding world that did not support their well-being' (Desai, 2018: 40). In chapter five of *Black Skin, White Masks*, 'The Lived Experience of the Black' (L'Expérience vécue du noir), Fanon says that he has to become a sensor, 'investigating my surroundings; I am interpreting everything on the basis of my findings' (2008: 99). These experiences and his analyses and self-analyses in North Africa, in France, and also in Martinique, are reflected in the book and continue into his work in Algeria inside the clinic and then inside the Algerian revolution.

Fanon's was a critical mind in motion intimately connected with bodily experience. Though classical psychoanalysis of the time tended to ignore the body, it is worth remembering that Freud always maintained that the Ego was a body ego. This idea of the Ego as a body ego was of course true for Fanon who considered the body schema and body ego, in contrast to Freud, sociogenically and phenomenologically. Sociogeny includes the social structure and meanings, including the internalization of objectification. Fanon opens 'The Lived Experience of the Black' by recounting his experience of reification on a train (itself a symbol of movement, modernity, and colonization), 'Look, un Nègre'.[28] He is fixed by the child's look which disrupts his self-image with the other's vision. Having come 'into this world anxious to uncover the meaning of things', he is immediately objectified and 'locked in this suffocating reification' (2008: 89) by the words

---

28. I prefer using the French word Nègre / nègre because of its multiple derogatory and less derogatory meanings in *Black Skin, White Masks*. Clearly Fanon is using it purposefully here.

and the racial gaze of a young child, 'Sale [dirty] nègre'. (The opening words mirror Roumain's famous poem with its reference to Les damnés de la terre, 'Sale
nègres'.) 'Or simply', Fanon continues, 'Look, un Nègre. The child points at him,
calling to their mother,"I'm scared"' (2008: 91). Fanon is the phobic object. This
objectification immediately denies Fanon freedom of motion. He is paralyzed
by the White gaze and put together by another. Fanon argues that the image
of the Black, in popular culture, plays an essential role in how the child deals
with what can be considered the good and bad parts of the self: 'The White person can project *psychic dirt* interpersonally, across the colour divide... the Black
person's use of skin colour for that purpose is doomed to failure' (Davids, 2011:
134, my emphasis). Because this option is not open, 'the Black person ... has to
resort to intrapsychic projections' (Davids, 2011: 134). The opening of 'The Lived
Experience of the Black' is all about objectification and the denial of free movement: 'the difficulties of elaborating his body schema', where 'all around the body
reigns an atmosphere of certain uncertainty' produced by the epidermal racial
schema (2008: 90, 92). 'I slip into corners', Fanon continues, 'I was walled in ...
I was hated' (2008: 95-97) in a society where Blackness is a source of evil, and
Whiteness is the measure of 'civilization'. In this situation it is not surprising that
Whiteness and Whitening become the ego ideal: 'Don't pay attention to him,
Monsieur', the White mother says to Fanon, 'He doesn't realize that you're just
as civilized as we are' (2008: 93).But what the child expresses is a social truth,
what Fanon calls the 'myth of the Negro' (2008: 96), a set of socio-cultural racist
stereotypes that are 'pre-rational' (see Hook, 2020: 313). Thus, Fanon is always
already a Black man. Wherever he goes, he is marked. Fanon responded with reason and when the White man agreed that 'the Negro' was a human being, he
added, 'under no condition did he want any intimacy between the races' (2008:
99). The 'Lived Experience of the Black' is not only a critical account of racial
objectification it is also the 'integrating of the denigrated' (Davids, 1996: 230).
Fanon becomes a constantly questioning body with long antennae (2008: 96),
wary of the objectification and reification that are internalized from a young
age and often expressed in the destructuring of the body (2008: 139), where self-
loathing and self-deception is constantly present.[29] Fanon argues that a 'genuine
new departure can emerge from ... this descent into a veritable hell' though most
Blacks will not be able to do so (2008: xii). Fanon thus had to be path breaking, taking himself as the subject of the questioning body, as Fanon puts it in
the conclusion to *Black Skin, White Masks*. He has made progress, 'O my body,
always make me a man who questions', underscoring how the work of questioning comes from reflection on body experience. The certain uncertainty means
questioning everything, even one's own conclusions. It is this spirit of question-

---

29. This objectification, internalized from a young age, can be psychologically traumatic, Fanon argues, and is often
expressed in terms of self-withdrawal (quoting Anna Freud,2008: 33. Taken alongside his engagement with the phenomenology and lived experience of the objectified body with its real material effects of oppression, the questioning
body has becomes a source for new critical engagement about sexuality and gender and a potential space of affirmation engaging Fanon's question, 'Who am I?'

ing norms, even norms which were unquestioned by Fanon, that gives his work an aliveness as new generations engage him with new questions about reification and identity.

Rather than looking for any accommodations, *Black Skin, White Masks* represents Fanon's break with bourgeois society. Similar to the conclusion in *Les damnés de la terre* where he writes that Europe is 'motionless', he concludes *Black Skin, White Masks* by arguing that the air of French bourgeois society is rotten and its 'people are putrefying' (2008: 199). One finds in the first pages of Aimé Césaire's *Notebooks of a Return to My Native Land* similar descriptions of zombie-like life in Fort-de-France, the capital of Martinique. It is an inert town, writes Césaire, a crowded town without sociality, 'this strange crowd that does not cram up together, does not mingle' (Césaire, 1995: 75). The motionlessness is repeated in the Algerian context in 'Letter to a Frenchman' written while Fanon was still at Blida-Joinville Psychiatric Hospital. As in Césaire's poem, the 'motionless fellah' whose life has stopped is connected to material reality: 'Empty basket, empty hope, this whole death of the fellah. Two hundred fifty francs a day. Fellah without land'. And he importantly adds, 'Fellah without reason' (1967: 50).

The lack of movement and self-movement, the lack of hope and land, the inertia and pauperization, is also viewed spatially in *Les damnés de la terre*. The same oppressive lack of movement, of space, of air, and of light, governs life for the majority of the population. The colonizer's town is described as full of movement, space, food and clothes, contrasted to the pauperized and hemmed-in bare life of those in the colonized zones: crushed, suffocated, and encased by violence and force, Fanon recapitulates the image from Oran that he witnessed years earlier: 'Every colony tends to turn into a huge farmyard, where the only law is that of the knife'. Governed by this daily violence, they are moved along but they are denied self-movement. This order to remain in place and not move exists alongside forced removals and evictions. The movement toward the urban areas, and the existence of the shantytowns and 'informal' settlements are expressions of what Fanon calls a biological necessity, or a struggle to survive. What Lewis Gordon calls the Black's 'illicit appearance' in (White) 'civil society' is another expression of the continuous racial ordering. The neocolony, the ghettos, the shantytowns, and the redlined zones remain the places of 'ill-repute' and those who live there are considered a continued threat. While the neocolonial bourgeoisie hide behind securitization and retreat to their gated communities, forced removals, including gentrification, refashion the urban areas but they do not disrupt the ontology of the zones, which are constantly brought to mind by the police murders of Black people.

## Fanon and Africa in Motion

> *To put Africa in motion, to cooperate in its organization, in its regrouping, behind revolutionary principles. To participate in the ordered work of a continent—that*

*was really the work I had chosen.*
—Fanon, 'This Africa to Come'

*Fanon can say that in the world in which he travels 'I am endlessly creating myself'*
—Marriott, *Whither Fanon*

In the short period between when Ghana became the first independent 'Sub-Saharan' nation on March 6, 1957 and by the end of 1960, nineteen other African nations had become independent. Nkrumah was first appointed Prime Minister of the Gold Coast in 1952 under British 'supervision'.[30] And Britain also managed Kenya's independence by the end of December 1963, making sure that 'Mau Mau'[31] would take no part in it and that land would remain commodified. Like Britain, France would maintain a supervisory role in all except Guinea, which voted against De Gaulle's Constitutional referendum to remain in the 'French Community' in 1958. Congo gained independence on June 30, 1960 but the Belgians continued to play an important role in the emergent 'Congo crisis'. In less than six months President Lumumba was arrested and then was assassinated on January 17, 1961.

In the summer of 1960 Fanon took part in a reconnaissance mission to set up a base in the south of the Sahara. The notebooks from the trip reveal Fanon feeling, experiencing and listening to the African revolutions as 'the untidy affirmation of an original idea propounded as an absolute' (1968: 41).

Reading these travels, one can get the sense of Fanon's acute attunement with the continent. On the move there is a new rhythm and a new sensibility: 'In every corner arms make signs to us, voices answer us, hands grasp ours ... Things are on the move' and 'if one listens with one ear glued to the red earth one very distinctly hears the sounds of rusty chains' (1967: 179). He writes of his traveling companion, Chawki: 'one can say anything to them but they need to feel and touch the Revolution in the words uttered'.[32]

Fanon reads histories, reliving 'the old Empires' and understanding how the region has been 'worked over by so many influences'. He warns that the Revolution 'will require a great deal of rigor and cool thinking',[33] and that mentioning 'Islam and race ... require extra caution'. He ends the first section of the notes with a most profound critique that would be developed in *Les damnés de la terre*.

First, he argues,

---

30. Nkrumah would become Prime Minister of Ghana in 1957, President in 1960 and the Convention Peoples' Party became the one-party state in 1964. The military coup against him took place on 24 February 1966.
31. The Kenya Land and Freedom Army
32. He had expressed himself in similar terms in an answer to Francis Jeanson about a sentence in *Black Skin, White Masks*, 'I cannot explain this sentence. When I write things like that, I am trying to touch my reader affectively, or in other words irrationally, almost sensually. For me, words have a charge'. Fanon's writings were always performative. He dictated and discussed *Black Skin, White Masks* with his wife Josie. She was the first active audience. And his newly translated plays, which we should remember he wanted destroyed, indicate the importance of performance.
33. Cool thinking reminds us of his introduction to *Black Skin, White Masks* where he speaks about writing the book while wary of zealousness and needed to cool to address the situation (see Gordon, 2015: 20-21). This is in stark contrast to the oft-repeated notion from the 1960s and 1970s, especially in the US, that Fanon was a man of rage.

Colonialism and its derivatives do not, as a matter of fact, constitute the present enemies of Africa. In a short time this continent will be liberated. For my part, the deeper I enter into the cultures and the political circles the surer I am that the great danger that threatens Africa is the absence of ideology. (1967: 185)

These sentences should be read carefully. Colonialism is not the present enemy, he says. A year earlier he had argued in *L'an V de la révolution algérienne* that French colonialism in Algeria was finished and that a new Algeria was 'no longer in future heaven' (1965: 30) but already in existence where the Algerian masses were 'storming heaven'.[34] Here he adds an important qualification, that the danger to the realization of a new society is not simply colonialism, its maneuvering and dirty tricks, but the absence of a unifying liberatory ideology. He set out to answer this problem in *Les damnés de la terre*.

Thinking about the lack of ideology, he continues: 'For nearly three years I have been trying to bring the misty idea of African Unity out of the subjectivist bogs of the majority of its supporters'. The United States of Africa, he adds, is supposed to be achieved 'without passing through the middle-class chauvinistic national phase with its procession of wars and death-tolls'. The problem is how to develop a liberatory ideology inside the popular struggle as well as how to analyze the counter-revolution within the revolution. In the front of his mind was the systematic execution of the radical leaders of the African revolutions, Lumumba (in the Congo) and Abane (in Algeria), the latter murdered by the Algerian revolutionary organization, the FLN.

In his last conversation with Sartre and De Beauvoir in July 1961, he said, 'I have two deaths on my conscience which I can never forgive myself: Abane's and Lumumba's'. De Beauvoir reports that 'if he had forced them to follow his advice they would have escaped with their lives' (de Beauvoir, 1992: 317). In 1960 Fanon had planned to meet Félix-Roland Moumié, the young leader of the UPC (Union du Peuple Camerounais), who was born a year after Fanon in 1926. The 1960 notebooks begin with Moumié's murder: 'On September 30th we met on the Accra airfield. He was going to Geneva for some very important meetings. In three months, he told us, we would witness a mass ebbing of colonialism in Cameroon'. Fanon continues in short staccato sentences:

> In Rome, two weeks later, we were to have met again. He was absent. His father standing at the arrival in Accra saw me coming, alone, and a great sadness settled on his face. Two days later a message told us that Felix was hospitalized. Then that poisoning was suspected ... A few days later the news reached us: Felix Moumié was dead. We hardly felt this death. A murder, but a bloodless one. There were neither volleys nor machine guns nor bombs. Thallium poisoning. It made no sense. Thallium! How was

---

34. A phrase from Marx about the Paris Commune in his *Civil War in France*, a work which resonates in Fanon's *L'an V de la révolution algérienne*.

one to grasp such a cause? An abstract death striking the most concrete, the most alive, the most impetuous man. Felix's tone was constantly high. Aggressive, violent, full of anger, in love with his country, hating cowards and maneuverers. Austere, hard, incorruptible. A bundle of revolutionary spirit packed into 60 kilos of muscle and bone. (1967: 179-180)

Just weeks later Lumumba was murdered. In his article 'Lumumba's Death: Could We Do Otherwise?' published in *Afrique Action* in February 1961, Fanon predicted that with Lumumba's death 'Africa is about to experience its first great crisis over the Congo'. By the end of the year Fanon would be dead at thirty-six. Moumié and Lumumba were thirty-five.

The three murders—Abane, Moumié, Lumumba—continued to be on Fanon's mind when he was writing *Les damnés de la terre*. As Lou Turner and Kurtis Kelley argue in Chapter 15 of this volume, 'Africa's first political crisis in the Congo, differences over violence versus non-violence were quite beside the point'.[35]

In the months after Lumumba's murder, Fanon was writing the first chapter of *Les damnés de la terre*, 'On Violence', a draft of which was published in *Les Temps modernes* in May 1961. In early April Fanon wrote to his publisher, François Maspero, saying that his health had slightly improved and that he had 'decided to write at least something' (2018: 689). What that something would be is much less than he wanted but it would become a world-famous book. Slightly improved but still terribly sick Fanon completed *Les damnés de la terre* in a ten-week period between April and July 1961. As well as a work deeply embedded in its moment, it was completed in a race against time. Fanon had wanted to do something much more. Indeed, his original plan was to title it *Algiers-Cape Town*, 'based on the armed revolution in the Maghreb, the development of consciousness and national struggle in the rest of Africa' (2018: 685).

While David Macey makes a point that much of the material in *Les damnés de la terre* was produced before 1961 is a text based on 'emotion' and rarely justified with 'hard facts',[36] I view the work as Fanon's powerful critical and analytical synthesis from inside the revolution with one nodal point being his working out of the notes from the reconnaissance mission the year before. In the notes he argues that to consider the problem of the lack of ideology, 'We must once again come back to the Marxist formula. The triumphant middle classes are the most impetuous, the most enterprising, the most annexationist in the world'. And he forewarns two major concerns connected with the problem of the lack

---

35. Lumumba had supported Nkrumah's 'non-violent', positive action strategy and Ramdane Abane, as the leader of the FLN, supported armed struggle.
36. Macey notes the speech given by Fanon presented at the Second Congress of Black Writers and Artists, in Rome, during Easter 1959 organized by *Présénce Africaine*. The case notes made at Blida-Joinville Hospital and from his psychiatric work in Tunis and for the FLN and other material included in his chapter on 'Colonial War and Mental Disorders'. His now-lost lectures, believed to be on Sartre's *Critique of Dialectical Reason* (Macey, 2012: 449) or a draft of the third chapter of *Les damnés de la terre* delivered to officers of the Algerian Liberation Army at Ghardimaou on the Algeria–Tunisia border (see Zeilig, 2016: 6)]. Opines Macey, 'Between April and the beginning of July, Fanon worked fast against the clock... Little or no research was done. His impressions of what he had seen of the newly independent states of Africa merge into a nightmarish picture of colonial Algeria. Fanon's hopes and fears for the future are expressed with powerful emotion, but he rarely justifies them with hard facts'. (Macey, 2012: 451)

of ideology developed in *Les damnés de la terre*: First, the critique of the hollowness of the idea of African unity highlighted by narrow nationalism expressed in the 'Ghana-Senegal tension, the Somali-Ethiopia, the Morocco-Mauritania, the Congo-Congo tensions' (1967: 187) is summed up in *Les damnés de la terre* as the retrogressive movement from the promise of nationalism and African unity 'to ultranationalism, to chauvinism, and finally to racism' (1968: 155). And second, in *Les damnés de la terre* Fanon refers back to Marxist formula in 'the theoretical question, which has been posed for the last fifty years'. Fanon is referring to a discussion of the debates about the 1905 Russia revolution that were grounded in Marx's analysis of the failure of the 1848 revolutions (namely, that the working class was used and then pushed aside by the bourgeoisie in their struggle with Feudal power) and the possibility of 'skipping the bourgeois phase' and calling for 'revolution in permanence'.[37] Fanon begins this discussion with the composition of the national bourgeoisie in the colonial countries and is damning. It is 'incapable of great ideas or of inventiveness'. It is a 'little greedy caste, avid and voracious, with the mind of a huckster, only too glad to accept the dividends that the former colonial power hands out to it' (1968: 175). It should be remembered that when Fanon is saying that the national bourgeoisie is useless, and a mimic of the European bourgeoisie, he is not saying that the European bourgeoisie is useful. Indeed, when he says the national bourgeoisie is cynical, it is a reflection of the agedness and sterility of bourgeois Europe. The European bourgeoisie is senile; the national bourgeois, its caricature, is senile before its time. Like the European bourgeoisie its interest is finance capital and get-rich-quick schemes. Fanon, in other words, is not hoping for the emergence of an authentic bourgeois, rather that the bourgeois 'stage' should be avoided at all costs.

## Enlivening Differences, Reading *Les damnés de la terre*

Lenin's idea that the revolutionary struggle doesn't erase differences, but it enlivens them is especially clear in Fanon's critique of anticolonial politics in *Les damnés de la terre*. The problem of the lack of ideology is expressed at the nodal point of the book, namely the last few pages in 'Spontaneity: Its Strengths and Weaknesses' and in the next few pages of 'Misadventures of National Consciousness'.

To be spontaneous is an expression of human freedom denied by oppression. Here one can see a connection between Fanon's clinical practice and his political practice (see Gibson and Beneduce, 2017). But then spontaneity has to be deepened since it can become reified, mesmerized by the power and excitement of its opening act. The revolt, in other words, has to become political. 'In their [the masses] weary road toward rational knowledge', Fanon argues in the conclusion

---

37. Marx's conception of the revolution in permanence was not limited to a critique of alliances with bourgeoisie. Clearly it related to revolution itself as ongoing, as he argues in the 1844 manuscripts: 'Communism is not the goal of human development' but rather the form in which '*positive* Humanism, beginning from itself' can emerge.

to the spontaneity chapter, 'the people must also give up their too-simple conception of their overlords', warning that the masses who shout treason at the new Black or Arab exploiters need to understand that the treason 'is not national' but 'social' (1968: 145). Here we have an important explanation of what Fanon means by the lack of ideology. That treason is social and not national is then connected to a new problem: nationalism itself, which needs to be 'enriched and deepened by a very rapid transformation into a consciousness of social and political needs, in other words into humanism' (1968: 204). Concluding the chapter on spontaneity, he argues that the relationship between the radical intellectuals, militants, and masses can become the basis for a 'new politics' (1968: 147) if the new reality of the nation is lived and experienced and exists only through movement. As I have argued, this action is not devoid of thought: in fact, it is the action and the movement itself, diagnosed and reflected on itself, that produces new thought and uncovers new contradictions. This action is not simply spontaneous, as though the actions have no history; rather it is conscious. Fanon develops the argument from *Black Skin, White Masks*: 'To induce humans to be actional [with] ... respect of the fundamental values that make the world human, that is the task of utmost urgency for those who, after careful reflection, prepare to act' (2008: 200, 197, translation altered). It is action that flows from preceding and repeated collective thought and action. It is the action of 'muscles and brains', of theory and practice, that enlivens political differences. As he concludes the spontaneity chapter, 'the essence of the fight which explodes the old colonial truths and reveals unexpected facets ... brings out new meanings and *pinpoints the contradictions* camouflaged by this reality' (1968: 147, my emphasis).

It is the revolutionary movement—the self-movement of masses of people—that creates, reflects back and develops the rationality of revolt. And Fanon was convinced that this was the challenge to intellectuals: to 'return' to where the people actually are.[38] In contrast to the stasis of the colonial Manichean zone, it is a zone of motion and instability where things are in flux and constantly moving. It is history in the making and in doing so it enlivens political and ideological differences. The idea is essential to Fanon and essential to Fanonian practices.

## VI: A New Humanism and the Question of Time

> *Total liberation is that which concerns all sectors of the personality.*
> —Fanon, *Les damnés de la terre*

The European liberal thinker's reaction to Fanon's *Les damnés de la terre*, and to Fanon's conception of anticolonial violence, emulates the same syndrome, namely their incomprehension of the colonized's life of 'daily death' (1967: 13) in

---

38. This idea is echoed in Cabral's injunction to 'return to the source' and Walter Rodney's idea of 'grounding' (*The Groundings with my Brothers*), which, as he put it begins with 'sitting down together to reason to 'ground', as the Brothers say' (1969: 64), 'and getting in touch, working with the people' (1969: 63).

a system built on and sustained by violence. Fanon agreed with Aimé Césaire's argument about why Europe's humanistic bourgeoisie could not forgive Hitler. It wasn't the crime in itself but 'the crime against the white man, the humiliation of the white man, and the fact that he applied to Europe colonialist procedures which until then had been reserved exclusively for the Arabs of Algeria, the "coolies" of India, and the "niggers" of America' (Césaire 2000: 36). Thus, Hitler was not dead but could be found in the years following the end of World War II in the torture, beatings, murders, exterminations, and concentrations camps of Madagascar, Vietnam, Kenya, and Algeria.

Fanon saw how action against colonial violence not only destabilized the colonial regime but also destabilized colonial hegemony and destructured it as all-powerful and commanding. For Fanon, French colonialism in Algeria is totalitarian (1968: 41). It settles into the center of the Algerian, expelling the self to 'rationally produce mutilation'. As Patricia Lorcin argues (2006: xxii), 'France's relationship with Algeria is one of violence, a violence central to the Franco-Algerian colonial experience from its inception in 1830 to its close in 1962 ... forcibly reshap[ing] collective and individual identities' through conquest, settlement, and expropriation. Thus, to think that colonialism is reformable is illogical,[39] as Fanon points out in his resignation in November 1956 letter from Blida-Joinville Hospital to the resident general of Algeria, 'Socialist' Robert Lacoste. That same year, 1956, in his presentation to the Negritude conference in Paris, he argued that colonialism's aim 'is rather a continued agony than a total disappearance of the pre-existing culture' (Fanon, 1967: 34). Under these conditions, he later adds in 'Algeria Unveiled', the individual's breathing is an observed, occupied breathing. 'It is a combat breathing' (1965: 65). And it is this struggle for survival, for breath, that undergirds *Les damnés de la terre.* Only through this revolt and resistance can a new culture (which includes a breathing of life into cultural forms that have been crushed and disfigured after years of colonial rule)—what he calls a combat culture—emerge (1968: 168).

Fanon's new humanism is a politics of becoming, based on the fundamental transformation of paralyzed Black and colonized subjects into new human beings through the liberation struggle. To Pramod Nayar's (2013: 93) argument that Fanon's 'new humanism is more inclusive, and collective, and rejects the individualist humanism of the Europeans', I would add that Fanon has a conception of a non-alienated individual as the individual not only socialized through the struggle but born within the struggle. Thus it is also this 'liberated individual who undertakes to build the new society' (1967: 114). But he also recognizes that for the racialized and colonized mental health is always a double struggle: individual and social (2008: xv).

But how does Fanon humanize these seeming abstractions? (Bamyeh, 2010). For Fanon this was a pressing issue. It is only through practice, through move-

---

39. Here we might think of the contemporary discussions about reforming the police in the United States as similarly illogical.

ment, that humanity can be affirmed. His psychiatric and political work overlap in a working principle, to humanize all the senses in an all-sided way, to humanize all human relations. In *Black Skin, White Masks*, Fanon writes of the eye becoming a human eye: 'The eye is not only a mirror, but a correcting mirror', Fanon argues, that 'must enable us to *correct cultural mistakes*' (2008: 178, my emphasis). The human eye not only reflects but creates 'a sunset that turned the robe of heaven a bright violet' (1967: 197), and 'lets itself be carried away by Césaire's vermiculate howl' (2008: 178).

What does the eye see, what does it look at, what does it correct? It sees fear in the 'eyes of the oppressor' and moreover it sees 'Africa on the move' (1967: 179): the colonist's look 'no longer shrivels me up nor freezes me, and his voice no longer turns me into stone' (1968: 45). The connection between movement and the confrontation with the oppressor is as important as making cultural corrections. It is this movement that creates discursive changes but Fanon also warns that the colonist knows that 'no phraseology can be a substitute for reality' (1968: 45) which speaks directly to us when the discursive becomes a substitute for real change. It is important to follow Fanon's focus returning to cultural corrections and to material reality, as he immediately reminds us in *Black Skin, White Masks*: 'The Black problem is not just about Blacks living among Whites, but about the Black exploited, enslaved, and despised by a colonialist and capitalist society that happens to be White' (2008: 179).[40] Fanon is not disavowing the primacy he gives to racialization; rather, he is returning to the structure he points out in the introduction: 'true disalienation of the Black implies a brutal awareness of the social and economic realities. The inferiority complex can be ascribed to a double process: First, economic. Then, internalization or rather epidermalization of this inferiority' (2008: 15). Without addressing social and economic realities you could end up with some de-racializing reforms, creating a capitalist Black society as Biko prophesized for South Africa: 'This is one country where it would be possible to create a capitalist black society, if whites were intelligent, if the nationalists were intelligent. And that capitalist black society, black middle class, would be very effective . . . South Africa could succeed in putting across to the world a pretty convincing, integrated picture, with still 70 percent of the population being underdogs' (Mngxitama, Alexander, and Gibson: 2008: 41-42). Fanon simply and starkly expresses the shortcomings of a decolonized capitalism: 'The people find out that the iniquitous fact of exploitation can wear a Black face, or an Arab one' (1968: 145).

Thus Fanon admonishes in *Les damnés de la terre* that to politically educate the masses is to build their confidence in their own decision-making, reinvigorating democratic practices of self-government. Again there is a continuity with *Black Skin, White Masks* with Fanon concluding that the work is 'to induce [men and

---

40. In his 1956 presentation to the first Congress of Black Writers and Artists in Paris, he argues that racism 'is only one element of a vaster whole: that of systematized oppression', adding that it would be thus incorrect to consider racism as a 'mental quirk, as a psychological flaw' (1967: 38). There has to be, instead, a total uprooting of this morbid system.

women] to be actional, by maintaining in their circularity the respect of the fundamental values that make the world human' (2008: 197). In *Les damnés de la terre* the move from the reified, dehumanized things produced by colonialist and capitalist society to actional human beings is practical work that becomes the measure of authentic decolonization: 'to try, relentlessly and passionately, to teach the masses that everything depends on them ... that there is no famous man who will take the responsibility for everything, but that the demiurge is the people themselves and the magic hands are finally only the hands of the people' (1968: 197). How is this work done? The question is not simply a technical one. It is about creating space for confidence and consciousness to develop among people who have been silenced, ignored and denied a name. As I have argued, by the end of *Les damnés de la terre* Fanon is aware and also concerned that this is going to take time and he calls it a major theoretical problem. Remember that he used similar language while referring to the question of 'skipping the bourgeois' phase: but where that had to be proved through action here he returns to the question of movement and motion. For him, the revolution innovates, 'but it is consciousness that needs help':

> The important theoretical problem is that it is necessary at all times and in all places to make explicit, to de-mystify, and to harry the insult to mankind that exists in oneself. There must be no waiting until the nation has produced new men [and women]; there must be no waiting until men [and women]are imperceptibly transformed by revolutionary processes in perpetual renewal. It is quite true that these two processes are essential, but consciousness must be helped. (1968: 305)

We are once again back to issues of political education and consciousness-raising based not on doctrinaire repetition but on careful listening and engaged thinking aimed at giving the people the confidence to speak for themselves.

Fanon argues that those with technical knowledge sometimes gleaned from the elite institutions should put that knowledge into the service of the people. When Walter Rodney spoke about 'groundings with my brothers' he did not pretend that he did not have a PhD or did not have 'professional' knowledge; the work of Fanon's militant intellectual is not to eschew what they have learnt and simply rely on knowledge of the people as though they do not live in the material and discursive reality of colonialism, racism, and exploitation. He calls this opportunism. Rather, the militant should be self-assured so that they can also listen and learn together as well as contribute and teach, knowing that the goal is the building of self-confident social action as well as the practical and mental liberation needed for people to take active roles in running the newly liberated nation. And, when the militant doesn't understand, they need to take a step back, reconsidering that they are at the heart of the problem: 'There must be an idea of [the hu]man and of the future of humanity; that is to say that no demagogic formula and no collusion with the former occupying power can take the place of a program' (1968: 202-203). Sixty years after Fanon's death, the rationality of revolt is expressed by the maturity of the uprisings challenging militant intellectuals to engage with them on their terms in solidarity and thought. The very maturity of the revolt itself offers an idea of the future of humanity. The decommodification of land and water, of the rivers and the minerals, requires a rethinking as Fanon puts it. And here, movements of people thousands of miles apart often offer similar views. The movements come up against the violence of the state and corporations to silence them and to silence humanity's future. In this long struggle, there are defeats and there are victories, as Fanon put it in *Black Skin, White Masks* (2008: 196). Each has to be carefully analyzed and criticized as we continue to think with Fanon.

# Appendix: A Note on Fanon's Library

In 2011 Olivier Fanon donated part of his parents' library to the Centre National de Recherche Préhistorique Anthropologiques et Historique (CNRPAH) in Algiers. The center created a catalogue, which is now reproduced with annotations in Khalfa and Young's edited volume *Frantz Fanon, Freedom and Alienation* (Fanon, 2018). I had the opportunity to look at the collection, which was still in boxes, with Matthieu Renault, when I was in Algiers for the conference 'Africa Today and Fanon' organized by CNRPAH in 2013.[41] Apparently the books were left behind when Fanon and his family left the country in January 1957. So we can deduce that books with a publication date later than 1956 are not Fanon's but were added later by Josie. For example, the library donated to CNPRAH includes six books by Freud: five of them are published on or before 1948 and one could assume they were purchased when Fanon was a medical student. There is nothing by Ferenczi or Klein, in whom Fanon became interested and purchased everything he could by them while at Tunis, where Alice Cherki tells us, Fanon liked to frequent the bookstore owned by a Monsieur Levy. All this is to say that one should be wary of taking this library to be anything other than containing a sample of Fanon's books and in addition we should be aware that this is not Frantz Fanon's library but Frantz and Josie's library. Of the 1400 books in the collection, there are roughly 440 that were published in or before 1956. There can be no certainty which of the 440 were Frantz's and which were Josie's (assuming that they didn't share books). In addition, it is clear that while there were many books from Fanon's days in France (and referenced in *Black Skin, White Masks*), there were many important works from that period that aren't in the collection. In other words, essential books that Fanon would have definitely owned, like Césaire's *Notebooks of the Return to My Native Land*, Senghor's *Anthologie de la nouvelle poésie Nègre et malgache de langue française*, Sartre's *Anti-Semite and the Jew* and *Being and Nothingness*.

In the reproduction of the catalogue listed by Khalfa and Young (Fanon, 2018) there is an added complication. In the main section of the catalogue there are some Marxist works, but there is also, without explanation, a separate section, titled 'Marxism and Political Brochures'. This subdivision is created by the editors and was not in the original CNRPAH catalogue created by F. Boulkroune and S Khouider.

Marx's work in this library includes his major political writings, *Class Struggles in France*, *The Eighteenth Brumaire*, *The Civil War in France*, *The Communist Manifesto*, as well as *The Contribution to the Critique of Political Economy*, and *Wages Prices and Profit*. Engels' listing includes *Anti-Duhring* (critiqued by Fanon in *Les Damnés*) and *Origin of the Family*. Also listed is Engels resumé of Marx's *Capital*

41. My report on visiting the library can be found at http://readingfanon.blogspot.com/2013/06/unpacking-fanons-books-and-putting-them.html.

*On Capital* which includes 5 pages from Luxemburg *Études sur 'le Capital', Suivies de deux études de Franz Mehring et de Rosa Luxemburg* (1949). This is the only writing from Luxemburg in the collection. Lenin's listing includes *State and Revolution, Left Wing Communism: An Infantile Disorder, Imperialism: the Highest Stage of Capitalism, Notes on the National Question, Two Tactics of Social Democracy in the Democratic Revolution, The Collapse of the Second International* and *Alliance of the Working Class and Peasantry* (a collection of Lenin's political writings on the peasantry) all of which have a resonance with Fanon's arguments in *Les damnés*. Fanon extensively marked up the sections on national and social chauvinism in Lenin's *The Failure of the Second International*, which would be developed by Fanon in his critique of national consciousness. This is not to say that Fanon was a Leninist or simply a synthesizer; rather he was a revolutionary theoretician, actively thinking from inside the revolutionary movement.

## Bibliography

Bamyeh, M. A. 2010. 'On Humanizing Abstractions the Path Beyond Fanon.' *Theory, Culture & Society* 27 (7–8): 52–65.

Baucom, I. 2001. 'Frantz Fanon's Radio: Solidarity, Diaspora and the Tactics of Listening.' *Contemporary Literature* XLII (I): 15–49.

Césaire, A. 1995. *Notebooks of a Return to My Native Land*. Translated by Mireille Rosello. Newcastle: Bloodaxe Books.

_____. 2000. *Discourse on Colonialism*. New York: Monthly Review.

Cherki, A. 2006. *Frantz Fanon: A Portrait*. Ithaca: Cornell UP.

Davids, M. F. 1996. 'Frantz Fanon: The Struggle for Inner Freedom.' *Free Associations* 6 (2): 205–234.

Davids, M. F. 2011. *Internal Racism: A Psychoanalytic Approach to Race and Difference*. London: Red Globe Press.

Davis, M. 2005. *Planet of Slums*. New York: Verso.

de Beauvoir, S. 1992. *Hard Times: Force of Circumstance, II*. New York: Paragon.

_____. 2011. *The Second Sex*. New York: Vintage.

Desai, M. 2018. *Travel and Movement in Clinical Psychology: The World Outside the Clinic*. New York: Palgrave.

Dunayevskaya, R. 1980. 'Hegel's Absolute as New Beginning.' In *Art and Logic in Hegel's Philosophy*, edited by Warren E. Steinkraus and Kenneth L. Schmitz, 163–178. Atlantic Highlands: Humanities Press.

Fanon, F. 1963. *The Damned*. Translated by Constance Farrington. Paris: Présence Africaine.

_____.1965. *A Dying Colonialism (L'an V de la révolution algérienne)*. New York: Monthly Review.

_____. 1967. *Toward the African Revolution*. New York: Grove Press.

_____. 1968. *The Wretched of the Earth*. Translated by Constance Farrington. New York: Grove Press.

_____. 2008. *Black Skin, White Masks*. Translated by Richard Philcox. New York: Grove Press.

_____. 2018. *Alienation and Freedom*, edited by Jean Khalfa and Robert J. C. Young. London: Bloomsbury.

Fanon, J. 2014. *Frantz Fanon, My Brother: Doctor, Playwright, Revolutionary.* Lanham: Lex- ington Books.

Geismar, P. 1969. *Frantz Fanon.* New York: Grove Press.

Gibson, N. C. 1999. *Rethinking Fanon: The Continuing Dialogue.* Amherst: Humanity Books.

_____. 2020. 'Fanon and Marx Revisited.' *Journal of the British Society for Phenomenology* 51 (4): 320–336.

Gibson, N. C., and Beneduce, R. 2017. *Frantz Fanon, Psychiatry and Politics.* Johannesburg: University of Witwatersrand Press and Lanham: Rowman and Littlefield International.

Gordon, L. R. 2015. *What Fanon Said.* New York: Fordham UP.

Hook, D. 2020. 'Fanon via Lacan, or: Decolonization by Psychoanalytic Means...?.' *The Journal of the British Society For Phenomenology* 51 (4), 305–319.

Horton, R. 2018. 'Frantz Fanon and the Origins of Global Health,' https://www.thelancet.com/jour-                    nals/lancet/article/ PIIS0140-6736(18)32041-5/fulltext.

House, J. 2005. 'Colonial Racisms in the 'Métropole': Reading Peau noire, masques blancs in Context.' In *Frantz Fanon's Black Skin, White Masks: New Interdisciplinary Essays*, edited by Max Silverman, 46–73. Manchester: University of Manchester Press.

Hudis, P. 2015. *Frantz Fanon: Philosopher of the Barricades.* London: Pluto Press.

James, C. L. R. 1977. *The Future in the Present.* London: Allison and Busby.

_____. 1980. *Notes on Dialectics: Hegel, Marx, Lenin.* London: Allison and Busby.

_____. 1984a. *At the Rendezvous of Victory.* London: Allison and Busby.

_____. 1984b. 'The Grenadian Revolution: From Self-defence to Self-destruction.' *Communist Affairs* 4 (2): 301–304.

_____. 1996. *C. L. R. James on the 'Negro Question,'* edited by Scott McLemee. Jackson: University of Mississippi Press.

Lenin, V. I. 1936. 'Report on Revising the Programme and Name of the Party' (March, 1918). In *Selected Works*, Vol. viii. New York: International Publishers.

_____. 1943. 'Can the Bolsheviks Retain State Power' (October 1917). In *Selected Works*, Vol. vi. New York: International Publishers.

_____. 1960. 'What Is To Be Done' (1902). In *Collected Works*, Vol. 5, 347–530. Moscow: Foreign Languages Publishing House.

_____. 1961. 'Conspectus of Hegel's Book, The Science of Logic' (1914–1915). In *Collected Works*, Vol. 38. New York: International Publishers.

_____. 1965. 'Guerilla Warfare' (September 1906). In *Collected Works*, Vol. 11, 213–223. Moscow: Progress Publishers.

_____. 1977. 'Speech on the Report on the Activities of the Central Committee May 4, 1907.' *Collected Works*, Vol. 12, 442–447. Moscow: Progress Publishers.

Lorcin, P. M. E. 2006. *Algeria & France 1800–2000: Identity Memory, Nostalgia.* Syracuse: Syracuse University Press.

Macey, D. 2011. 'I Am My Own Foundation Frantz Fanon as a Source of Continued Political Embarrassment.' *Theory, Culture & Society* 27 (7–8): 33–51.

‗‗‗‗‗‗‗‗. 2012. *Frantz Fanon*. London: Verso.

Marriott, D. 2018. *Whither Fanon: Studies in the Blackness of Being*. Stanford: Stanford UP.

Marx, K. 1871. *The Civil War in France*, https://www.marxists.org/archive/marx/works/1871/civil-war-france/.

‗‗‗‗‗‗‗‗. 1963. *The Eighteenth Brumaire of Louis Bonaparte*. New York: International Publishers.

‗‗‗‗‗‗‗‗. 1989. 'Economic Manuscripts of 1861–63.' *Marx-Engels Collected Works*, Vol. 32. New York: International Publishers.

McClintock, A. 1999. 'Fanon and Gender Agency.' In *Rethinking Fanon: The Continuing Dialogue*, edited by Nigel C. Gibson, 283–293. Amherst: Humanity Books.

Meeks, B. 2001. *Caribbean Revolutions and Revolutionary Theory: An Assessment of Cuba, Nicaragua and Grenada*. Kingston: University of West Indies Press.

Merleau-Ponty, 1973. *Adventures of the Dialectic*. Evanston: Northwestern UP.

Mngxitama, A., Alexander, A., and Gibson, N. C., eds. 2008. *Biko Lives! Contesting the Legacies of Steve Biko*. New York: Palgrave.

Nayar, P. 2013. *Frantz Fanon (Routledge Critical Thinkers)*. New York: Routledge.

Neocosmos, M. 2017. 'The Creolization of Political Theory and the Dialectic of Emancipatory Thought: A Plea for Synthesis.' *Journal of French and Francophone Philosophy* XXV: 6–25.

Nissim-Sabat, M. 2010. 'Fanonian Musings: Decolonizing/Philosophy/Psychiatry.' In *Fanon and the Decolonization of Philosophy*, edited by Elizabeth A. Hoppe and Tracey Nicholls, 39–54. Lanham: Lexington.

Phillips, A. 1984. 'A Missing Page in American Labor History.' In *The Coal Miners' Strike of 1949–50 and the Birth of Marxist-Humanism in the US*. Chicago: News & Letters.

Rodney, W. 1969. *The Groundings with my Brothers*. London: Bogle-L'Ouverture.

Sekyi-Otu, A. 1996. *Fanon's Dialectic of Experience*. Cambridge: Harvard UP.

‗‗‗‗‗‗‗‗. 2019. *Left Universalism, Africacentric Essays*. New York: Routledge.

Senghor, L. S. 1948. *Anthologie de la nouvelle poésie nègre et malgache de langue française*. Paris: PUF.

Ulloa, M. 2007. *Francis Jeanson; A Dissident Intellectual from the French Resistance to the Algerian War*. Stanford: Stanford UP.

Young, R. 2005. 'Fanon and the Turn to Armed Struggle in Africa.' *Wasafiri* 20 (44): 33–41.

Zeilig, L. 2016. *Voices of Liberation: Frantz Fanon*. Chicago: Haymarket Books.

# SECTION III
# FANONIAN PRACTICES

# SECTION A:
## FANONIAN HOMES

there is not one

day

the

compartmentalized world,

of

economic       inequality, and

enormous disparities       manage to mask the

human reality.

what divides this world is

what race one belongs to.

You are rich because you are white, you are white because you

are rich.

the       issue   is

the       capitalist society,

difference in status.

the       cannons and machines.

the facto-

ries, the estates,   the bank

the "ruling class."                       and

The violence

'Blacked-out-poem' by Leah Kindler based on Fanon's *The Wretched of the Earth*.

# WHEN BLACK LIBERATION MATTERED: FRANTZ FANON IN THE THEORY AND PRACTICE OF PAN-AFRICANISM IN THE BLACK POWER ERA, 1965-1975

Lou Turner and Kurtis Kelley

In this chapter, we subject the revolutionary implications of Fanon's thought to his own dialectical method as a new generation of Black radical theorists and activists who discovered those implications in the late 1960s and '70s, at a historic moment not unlike the scope of our contemporary one. In doing so, we demonstrate why Black radical America became the first 'home' of Frantz Fanon, not only as a revolutionary icon, but also as a philosophy of revolution. It was a time when Black Liberation mattered. As Amiri Baraka observed in 1966, at the beginning of the Black Power era, 'we must act now, in what I see as an extreme 'nationalism', i.e., in the best interests of our country, the name of which the rest of America has pounded into our heads for four hundred years, *Black*' (Baraka, 2009: 106). The question underlying our historical recreation of Fanonian dialectics of liberation is: Can Black Liberation matter again?

The historiographic method deployed in this chapter makes it incumbent to acknowledge the multiple intermergings developed in our research and theoretical work. Our work intersects multiple crises of police anti-black violence and anti-racist uprisings, in 2020, against the backdrop of a once-in-a-hundred-years pandemic, COVID-19. At the time of this writing, the 2020 uprising is still defining a new epoch of black liberation. Delimited by the Black modernist moment of post-World War II, anti-colonialist, anti-imperialist struggles, 2020 marks the sixtieth anniversary of the death of one of the key figures of Black modernism, the African American anti-racist writer Richard Wright, in France, rumored to be the target of US intelligence 'black-ops'. By the beginning of the following year (1961), the US Central Intelligence Agency (CIA) colluded with Congolese neocolonial puppets of European and US imperialism to assassinate Patrice Lumumba, the first premier of the independent Democratic Republic of the Congo. By the end of that year, Frantz Fanon lost his battle with leukemia, while hospitalized at the Clinical Center of the National Institutes of Health, in Bethesda, Maryland, under CIA watch (Fanon, 2018: 783).

However, 2021 not only marks the sixtieth anniversary of the death of Frantz Fanon but of the publication of his revolutionary last testament on the vicissitudes of the decolonization process in which he participated and whence he developed his unique insider's view of the dialectics of liberation. That these three men—Wright, Lumumba, and Fanon—knew each other may be surprising or unusual from our 21st century vantage point. However, the circles and networks of Black radical thinkers and political leaders in the Third World epoch were close-knit as they organized themselves in the aftermath of the anti-fascist World War II, which swiftly turned into anti-colonial and anti-racist liberation struggles across three continents, Africa, Europe and North America. When carefully excavated, this period reveals a veritable trans-Atlantic jet stream of revolutionary ideas blown to life in Black mass struggles for liberation, disclosing dialectical linkages in the development of shared theoretical perspectives. That is the burden of this chapter.

## Black Working Class Origins of a New Pan-Africanism

Black Marxist-Humanist autoworker Charles Denby reported on Black proletarian solidarity in the early days of the African revolution in the midst of its first great crisis. In a column titled 'Race and Class', he wrote for the June-July 1962 issue of the Marxist-Humanist newspaper *News & Letter*, for which he was editor, connecting his own African American genealogy to African liberation more than a decade ahead of Alex Haley's *Roots*.

> In the early years of my life [in rural Lowndes County, Alabama], it was a common thing among Negroes to discuss their relation to those in Africa. Many of the older ones would remember to which tribe in Africa they belonged while the younger ones would not understand their dialect. But it was practically impossible for any Negro not to have a feeling of close kinship as he sat and listened to the stories of slave ships that the old ones told. I can remember my grandmother telling me about how people were put on the block for sale. She told me how she was sold in Virginia while her mother stood screaming. She never saw her mother again. (Denby, 1962)

Through his Black proletarian perspective, Denby understood the relationship between Africans and Africans in America as a two-way road to liberation. The reason for his recollection becomes more apparent further on in his column when we read that its actual focus was the 1960-61 crisis in the newly independent Democratic Republic of the Congo that culminated in the tragic assassination of its first Prime Minister Patrice Lumumba, and the different class attitudes toward it among Black workers and the Black middle-class:

> Where the middle-class Negro was quiet as a tomb, the working-class Negro first began to speak his mind during the assassination of Lumumba, lining up solidly behind Lumumba and his nationalist movement. The workers in my shop eagerly followed all developments both in the Congo and in the UN, warmly supporting the demonstrations before that body, holding it responsible for the murder. (Denby, 1962)

In *For the People: Black Socialists in the United States, Africa and the Caribbean*, Daryl Russell Grigsby singles out this passage in order to make the point that 'Black auto workers, Denby noted, were not so consumed in their own problems to miss the connection between racism at home and imperialism overseas' (Grigsby, 1987: 49). In this chapter, we appraise several such connections of post-World War II Black radicalism and nationalism to the thought of Frantz Fanon:

- Richard Wright (1950s)
- Armed Black Self-Defense of Robert Williams (late 1950s)
- Black Panther Party (late 1960s through the early 1970s).

Such an appraisal requires that we periodize these transnational linkages,[1] recognizing that the materialist basis of Black working class existence and consciousness underwent historic transformations during the capitalist restructuring that began in the mid-1970s as the US economy deindustrialized and purged Black labor from traditional manufacturing and industrial production relations.[2]

## Radical Notes of a Native Son

In the seldom-cited 1951 work on the Black freedom struggle in the United States, French anarcho-syndicalist writer and historian Daniel Guerin shared critical remarks he got from Richard Wright on the page-proofs of the French edition of Guerin's *Negroes on the March* (Guerin, 1956: 68, note):

> The rhythm of American industrial development can be used as a gauge for measuring the exact pace of the rhythm of Negro progress. For example, after the Civil War, and while America was still mainly an agrarian country, the Negro kept better pace with American progress than he does today. Between 1865 and 1900, American industrial progress advanced rapidly; and it was precisely during this period when the American Negro was thrust backward under the terror of the Ku Klux Klan... This should be emphasized more than you have done. Negroes in America lose sight of this important point of comparison, and it is from this that their over-optimism comes.[3]

It is not clear whether this note was only inserted in the English edition of Guerin's book, that it documents Wright's critique of the 1951 text means that it

1. We should not proceed without acknowledging this notion of trans-national exchange of revolutionary ideas as the original meaning of 'diaspora'. See George Shepperson, *Independent African: John Chilembwe and the Origins, Setting and Significance of the Nyasaland Native Rising 1915* (with Thomas Price). London: University Press, 1958 (5th edition 1987); and 'African Diaspora: Concept and Context' in *Global Dimensions of the African Diaspora*, Joseph E. Harris (ed.) Wash., D.C., 1993. Also, see Elliot Skinner, 'The Dialectic between Diasporas and Homelands', in Ibid.
2. The qualifier 'traditional' signals the regional particularities of capital's disposal (purge) of Black labor in the North and Midwest at the same time its super-exploitation of Black, mostly women's, labor (sweated labor) proceeded hothouse style under new capitalist production relations in the South. See Turner, 2010.
3. Essentially, Wright's comments are a biopsy of the material/ideological infrastructure of what Sundiata Cha-Jua calls the black nadir. Cf. Cha-Jua, 2010.

likely predates Wright's contact with Frantz Fanon by two years. In 1953, Fanon wrote to Wright that having 'circumscribe[d] in the most complete way [the] human breadth' of Wright's message that he (Fanon) was 'working on a study bearing on the human breadth of your works' (Ray and Farnsworth, 1973: 150).[4] As the organizer of the 1956 Paris Congress of Negro Writers and Artists, Wright invited Fanon to speak at the first Congress[5] sponsored by *Présence Africaine* of which Wright was also a founding member of the editorial board. In his paper, 'Racism and Culture', Fanon credits Wright, in his first novels, with providing 'a very detailed description' of the 'phantom-like' existence of the Black experience. Fanon then pivots decisively to ground his psycho-existential spectral analysis of racial phantoms in a historical materialist framework of capitalist development akin to Wright's critical commentary above:

> Progressively, however, the evolution of the techniques of production, the industrialization, limited though it is, of the subjugated countries, the increasingly necessary existence of collaborators, impose a new attitude upon the occupant. The complexity of the means of production, the evolution of economic relations inevitably involving the evolution of ideologies, unbalance the system. Vulgar racism in its biological form corresponds to the period of crude exploitation of man's arms and legs. The perfecting of the means of production inevitably brings about the camouflage of the techniques by which man is exploited, hence of the forms of racism.
>
> It is therefore not as a result of the evolution of people's minds that racism loses its virulence. No inner revolution can explain this necessity for racism to seek more subtle forms, to evolve....
>
> In the very heart of the 'civilized nations', the workers finally discover that the exploitation of man, at the root of a system, assumes different faces. At this stage, racism no longer dares appear without disguise....
>
> Racism, to come back to America, haunts and vitiates American culture. And this dialectical gangrene is exacerbated by the coming to awareness and the determination of millions of Negroes and Jews to fight this racism by which they are victimized. (Fanon, 1969: 35-36)

That Fanon's first ideological 'home' as Black America actually begins with Fanon adopting the Black radical intellectual tradition of figures like Du Bois and Richard Wright as his ideological 'home away from home'. Although never cited in his works, W.E.B. Du Bois, especially his concept of double conscious-

---

4. By 1953, most of Wright's work was available in French, a fact attested by Wright's works that Fanon lists in his note to Wright. For a bibliography of Richard Wright's work in French, see Davis and Fabre 1982. Fanon's Wright study is not extant, although Wright's novel *Native Son* plays a crucial dialectical role in Fanon's 1952 *Black Skin, White Masks*.

5. Fanon also gave a paper at the 1959 Second Congress of Black Writers and Artists, in Rome. He incorporated that paper into the second part of chapter four of *Wretched of the Earth*, 'On National Culture', entitled 'Reciprocal Bases of National Culture and the Fight for Freedom'. Cf. Fanon, 1966: 190.

ness, theorized in *Souls of Black Folk*, is alluded to throughout *Black Skin, White Masks* and is *transcended*. The most significant appropriation that Fanon makes of Du Bois' *Souls* is the existentialist literary-philosophic first-person voice Du Bois uses in the first chapter, 'Of Our Spiritual Strivings', which Fanon resorts to in chapter five of *Black Skin*, 'The Fact of Blackness' (Fanon, 1967: 109).

Fanon's intellectual lineage branches out from Hegel and Marx to Du Bois and Karl Jaspers to Alexandre Kojève and Gabriel Marcel to Sartre, Merleau-Ponty and Lacan, to René Ménil and Richard Wright, to Senghor and Césaire. This rich dialectical tradition delineated a sharp differentiation of *Black existentialism* in Fanon's studies of Caribbean and African colonialism, on the one hand, and the Black in France versus the Black in America, on the other. By the late 1960s, this mapped the increasing radical proclivity that formed the reception of Fanon across the geopolitical landscape of Black Power in the US by a new generation of black intellectual-activists, i.e., the receptivity of a cohort of what Antonio Gramsci called 'organic intellectuals' (Gramsci, 1976: 12, 20)[6] outside of academia. With the emergence of the Black Power Movement, it was not long before these organic activist-intellectuals and the university students they inspired were storming the ivy walls and ivory halls of academia with demands for Black Studies.

African American anti-racist resistance honed Fanon's dialectics of liberation to a laser sharp focus, as we will see in the section on Fanon and Black Power in America. However, in the next section, Pan-Africanism opened wide the aperture of the dialectics of continental African liberation in his thought. In other words, where Fanon's and Wright's rendezvous with the radical modernity of the African American experience is instructive in revealing Fanon's dialectical recycling of Wright's African American lived experience in the discursive formation of his existential psychology in *Black Skin*, Pan-Africanism was determinative in the revolutionary dialectic of *Wretched of the Earth*. Despite increasing recognition of the latter (Ahlman, 2010), the African American radicalization of Fanon's thought remains unexplored terrain. Both would exert a profound ideological pull on Black radicals and nationalists, especially those aligned with the Black Panther Party in the propulsion of the historic moment of Black Power. In the next section, we examine the rich organizational ground of revolutionary Pan-Africanism that arose with national independence in Africa and gave Fanon a new transnational stage on which to project his developing theory of anti-colonial revolution.

With the publication and wide dissemination of his work through radical presses in the US, his theory of revolution influenced the consciousness, practice, and organizing of Black radicals and nationalists. In fact, so profound was the effect of his dialectics of liberation on African American and Afro-Caribbean nationalists, it would travel with them back to 'the continent' and the 1974 Sixth

---

6. Gramsci's point is that in order to be 'organically the intellectuals of [the] masses', intellectuals must have 'worked out and made coherent the principles and problems raised by the masses in their practical activity, thus constituting a cultural and social bloc' (Gramsci, 1976: 330).

Pan-African Congress, in Dar es Salaam, Tanzania, where it was organizationally deepened, and propelled a new stage of Pan-African revolution over the next decade. Before turning to Fanon's reception in the Black Power circles of the late 1960s up to the 1974 Six-PAC, we must take an organizational detour to comprehend the ideological context in which Fanon's thought would assume the global prominence it did for Black Nationalists.

## Pan-Africanism: Fanon's Organizational Detour

*I have two deaths on my conscience, which I will not forgive myself for: that of Abane and that of Lumumba.*
Fanon[7]

*Our old disputes, our theoretical and tactical differences, always get transformed in the course of the revolution into direct practical disagreements.... Practice does not erase differences but enlivens them.*
Lenin, The Fifth Congress of the RSDLP[8]

The rising tide of anti-colonial nationalism in Asia and Africa in the decade following the Second World War grew in response to the shifting global capitalist order and the changing forms of Western colonialism intent on maintaining control over its overseas territories.[9] By the late 1950's, anti-colonial Pan-African nationalism throughout the continent was manifested in a number of widely shared principles. These concepts included 'Africa for the Africans', which called for a rejection of white colonial control; 'United States of Africa' that politically linked various regional federations across the continent; rejection of violence as an organizing strategy; rejection of colonial economic systems and the promotion of some form of African communal economics or socialism (Legum, 1965).

Pan-African conferences organized in the first half of the 20th century in Western metropoles revealed a cross-section of ideological and strategic views on national liberation from colonialism and opposition to racial domination of African-descended peoples in Western societies. Black scholar-activist W.E.B.

---

7. Quoted in de Beauvoir (1992). Abane Ramdane was the Kabyle revolutionary and architect of the 'Battle of Algiers', who was the leader of the left wing of the Algerian National Liberation Front (FLN) and who was murdered in internecine ideological strife within the FLN in 1958. Patrice Lumumba was the first premier of newly independent Congo, assassinated by US CIA-supported Congolese puppets of European political and corporate mining interests, January 1961 (Turner, 1999).

8. Vladimir Lenin's closing statement at the May 14, 1907 session of the Fifth Congress of the Russian Social-Democratic Labor Party (RSDRP), held in London, to discuss the ongoing 1905 Russian revolution. (Quoted in Dunayevskaya, 1991: 8)

9. David Ranney examines the new global economic institutions formed at the 1944 Bretton Woods Conference, where it was decided that US currency would serve as the international reserve currency, and where the IMF (International Monetary Fund), the World Bank, and the GATT (General Agreement on Tariffs and Trade) were formed to regulate the new capitalist world order. The institutionalism of postwar capitalism structured the debt that African countries incurred stemming from neocolonial relations with their former colonial masters. Neither national independence, nor attempts at establishing economic blocs and ultimately the Organization of African Unity, in 1963, could deliver postcolonial Africa from the fate of neocolonialism and being sucked into the vortex of predatory debt that these international economic institutions enabled (Ranney, 2003).

DuBois gained his Pan-African institutional footing at the First Pan-African Conference in 1900 held in London, corresponding to his participation in the 1900 Paris Exposition.[10] The subsequent four Pan-African Congresses held before World War II reached a turning point with the Fifth Congress, held in Manchester, England, in 1945. By the Fifth Congress, the demand for African self-governance had grown considerably in volume. Trinidadian Marxist, CLR James, who did not attend the 1945 Congress, summed up its significances: 'It was attended by over two hundred delegates from all over the world, the great majority of them engaged in trade union work or other types of work connected with the organization of the masses of workers and farmers in Africa' (James, 1978: 78). For James, the young Kwame Nkrumah represented a new radical nationalism steeped in black proletarian organizing methods of general political strikes that he would deploy to such effect in achieving independence from Britain for the Gold Coast. Inspired by Gandhi's organizing methods in India against British colonialism, in the immediate aftermath of World War II, militant non-violent mass strike organizing emerged at the Fifth Pan-African Congress out of a long Pan-African history of loyal opposition petitioning for colonial rights. In the 1950s and early 1960s, these methods would carry Nkrumah, as well as other African nationalist leaders, to power.

However, the historical conditions and administrative apparatus of different colonial regimes also elicited violent methods from other African nationalist movements in places like Kenya and Algeria. Within the same period of gaining national independence, these dual nationalist organizing ideologies—active non-violent organizing and violent insurrection—cropped up among newly independent African states, which determined the political conditions of support for national liberation movements. Ideological differences also lay behind various multilateral efforts to forge African regional unity, leading to the formation of different and at times opposing regional blocs. Across the historical and ideological continuum of Pan-Africanism, the respective histories of the colonial modalities of racial subjugation conditioned these ideological differences. Upon achieving national independence, these ideological differences morphed into the violent contradictions that fomented the tragedy of Africa's first political crisis—the assassination of Congolese nationalist leader Patrice Lumumba, in the very heart of Africa. Fanon warned a year before the publication of *Wretched of the Earth*:

> What must be avoided is the Ghana-Senegal tension, the Somali-Ethiopia, the Morocco-Mauritania, the Congo-Congo tensions... In reality the colonized states that have reached independence by the political path seem to have no other concern than to find themselves a real battlefield with wounds and destruction. It is clear, however, that this psychological explanation, which appeals to a hypothetical need for release

---

10. See the powerful reproductions of Du Bois' Paris Exposition infographic exhibit in Battle-Baptiste and Rusert 2018.

of pent-up aggressiveness, does not satisfy us. We must once again come back to the Marxist formula. The triumphant middle classes are the most impetuous, the most enterprising, the most annexationist in the world (not for nothing did the French bourgeoisie of 1789 put Europe to fire and sword). (Fanon, 1969: 187)

In the meantime, Nkrumah forged a 'political path' to independence by drawing on the political education and experience he gained in the US, in Britain, and in political organizing among working-class and urban elites in the Gold Coast. According to Christian Høgsbjerg,

> Nkrumah brought to this work what had never been done before. To theoretical study, propaganda and agitation, the building and maintaining of contacts abroad, he added the organization politically of Africans and people of African descent in London. He helped to found a West African National Secretariat in London for the purpose of organizing the struggle in West Africa. The leading members of this were Africans, and thus Africans with roots in Africa began to take over from the West Indians who had hitherto been the leaders. Most important of all, he was the leading spirit in the formation of the Colored Workers' Association of Great Britain. Through this organization, he linked together the students and the workers from Africa and the people of African descent living in England, organized them and carried on political work among them. (Høgsbjerg, 2016)

By the 1950's, the center of anti-colonial Pan-African discourse and *praxis* had returned to the African continent. Prominent among the factors that explain this transition was the beginning of the Algerian revolution for independence from France that began in 1954 with coordinated armed attacks on police and military installations in conjunction with general mass political strikes. In Ghana, Nkrumah and the Convention People's Party (CPP) organized a campaign of nonviolent 'positive action' around general political strikes joined to mass trade union and economic strikes. In a 1951 pamphlet, 'What I Mean by Positive Action', Nkrumah explained positive action:

> The adoption of all legitimate and constitutional means by which we could attack the forces of imperialism in the country. The weapons were legitimate political agitation, newspaper and educational campaigns and, as a last resort, the constitutional application of strikes, boycotts and non-cooperation based on the principle of absolute non-violence, as used by Gandhi in India. (Macey, 2012: 564-65, n34)

Although rarely acknowledged in Black social movement discourse, the early Civil Rights Movement's non-violence methods were not an unmediated appropriation of India's Gandhian model. African American movement leaders found Pan-African models in the continent-wide early African independence movements, from Accra to the anti-pass demonstrations organized by the Pan-African Congress (PAC) in South Africa. The apartheid regime's brutal repression of the non-violent anti-pass law campaign organized by the PAC, led by Robert Sobukwe, was a turning point in Black South African methods of struggle. The African National Congress (ANC) moved to the Algerian model of armed struggle with Nelson Mandela's organization of uMkhonto we Sizwe (Spear of the Nation), the armed-wing of the ANC, after the March 21, 1960 Sharpeville massacre. In fact, the December 16, 1961 MK campaign had all the hallmarks of the FLN's 1954 attack on French colonial military and police installations. When African American civil rights organizers and Black Nationalists debated the merits of violence versus non-violence, over the course of the 1950s and '60s, it was yet another reflection of the two-way road to revolution between Africa and Black America.

In the case of Nkrumah, when violence broke out in Ghana, Nkrumah was imprisoned for sedition. Upon his release from prison in the wake of the CPP winning a large majority in the legislative assembly, Nkrumah agreed to form a government and was made 'leader of government business'. With the CPP's continued insistence on immediate self-rule over the institutions of government, a cleavage opened between the professional urban intelligentsia, led by Nkrumah, and the traditional tribal chiefs backed by the British colonial administration. (Fanon spent some time examining this phenomenon in chapter two of *Wretched*, 'Spontaneity: It's Strengths and Weaknesses'.) Prior to the July 1956 Gold Coast elections, the United Nations conducted a referendum on the disposition of British and French Togo, with residents of the former electing to join the Gold Coast.[11] The transformation of Ghana into a full parliamentary system based on one-man-one-vote led to the CPP gaining majority representation in the new legislative assembly. On August 3, 1956, the majority-CPP assembly passed a motion in favor of immediate independence *within* the British Commonwealth.[12] On March 6, 1957, the former     British Gold Coast became the independent nation of Ghana. Nkrumah and the CPP pursued centralization of political power in the capital to the exclusion of local or regional power, a move that drew the opposition of traditional chiefs.

In the course of Ghana's path to independence, Nkrumah and other African leaders entertained dangerous illusions about the imperialist intentions of Britain, other European powers, and the international institutions controlled by the strategic interests of the Cold War super-powers, the US and the Soviet

---

11. The illusions Nkrumah and other African leaders entertained about the good faith auspices of the UN and Britain would plague their missteps in the Congo crisis in 1960-61, resulting in the assassination of Patrice Lumumba. Tragically, Lumumba, too, shared in illusions about the United Nations and the chances of playing the Cold War superpowers off each other.

12. When Charles de Gaulle came to power in France the following year (1958), he fabricated a similar neocolonial multilateral apparatus called the 'French Community', which newly 'independent' nations, like Senegal, joined. Only Guinea voted 'no!' to being a part of the' 'French Community', in the 1958 plebiscite.

Union.[13] The transnational spaces in which these illusions and realities ideologically clashed were in a series of Pan-African conferences and congresses that ultimately led to founding the Organization of African Unity (OAU), May 25, 1963. The transnational institutions and organizations that involved activist-intellectuals like Frantz Fanon shaped the global spread of Pan-African nationalism. These institutions included the First Congress of Negro Writers and Artists, in 1956 and again in 1959, and the All-African Peoples' Conference (AAPC) in 1958. These conferences afforded Fanon the chance to form vital international and institutional relationships with representatives from numerous African continental and diasporic groups, including from the United States (Legum, 1965: 41-45). So imbued with the Pan-African idea of continental unity of independent African states, in the summer of 1960     while on a reconnaissance mission to open a southern munitions supply route into Algeria's interior, Fanon reflected on a new Pan-African idea, in his logbook:

> To put Africa in motion, cooperate in its organization, in its regrouping, behind revolutionary principles. To participate in the ordered movement of a continent—this was really the work I had chosen....

> For nearly three years, I have been trying to bring the misty idea of African Unity out of the subjectivist bogs of the majority of its supporters. African Unity is a principle on the basis of which it is proposed to achieve the United States of Africa without passing through the middle-class chauvinistic national phase with its procession of wars and death-tolls. (Fanon, 1969: 187)[14]

Whether Fanon was aware or not, the historic moments when Africa, *as a continent*, moved in a single unitary direction over the course of its long human history are so scarce as to be virtually non-existent. Even in such moments as the trans-Atlantic slave trade, or the earlier trans-Sahara slave trade, or 19th century western imperialist colonialism, Africa had its outliers from the larger trends. Nevertheless, there was no region or country, which was not affected or influenced by the anti-colonial struggles of the 1950s and 1960s. The entire continent was in motion, from Cape to Cairo.

---

13. Behind the veneer of UN neutrality, the Soviet Union supported the Nigerian government in its genocidal war against the Igbo people's quest for autonomy during the Biafra civil war, 1968-70. This was in the period of the Soviet Union's invasion and repression of Czechoslovakia's drive for autonomy.
14. Note that Fanon's 1960 mission through Cameroon and Mali was an outgrowth of the proposal for the creation of an All-African People's Revolutionary Army, or African Legion, at the Accra 1958 AAPC. As Young observes, 'The African Legion was conceived as a transnational army corps which would intervene to help in any particular struggle, an idea which Fanon enthusiastically embraced as it constituted an offer of support for Algeria (the April 1960 Positive Action Conference recommended 'the formation of an African volunteer corps to fight side by side with their Algerian brothers')' (Young, 2005). Cuba first put such an idea into practice under the leadership of Che Guevara, in 1965, in the Congo (Turner, 1997). Again, in 1987-88, Cuba committed military solidarity to Angola at the Battle of Cuito Cuanavale, succeeding for the first time in defeating the South African Defense Force (SADF) and forcing the de Klerk government to negotiate with the ANC to call free elections in South Africa.

The ideological role played by Fanon within Pan-African political spaces proved to be pivotal at various points, particularly at the 1958 All-African People's Conference. Held in newly independent Ghana and chaired by its first Prime Minister and President Kwame Nkrumah, this conference was pivotal for the next two decades of Pan-African struggle. Importantly, the first AAPC convened soon after the First Conference of Independent African States, also held in Accra in 1958, which featured Ghana, Liberia, and six other majority Muslim and Arab countries (Egypt, Tunisia, Libya, Sudan, and Morocco). The question of anti-colonial African sovereignty was not part of the official discussion. However, at the All-African Peoples' Conference held in December of that year, revolutionary organizations and parties throughout Africa participated, including the FLN and Fanon. Perceived by many to be the leader of the FLN delegation, Fanon's speech before the conference was a departure from the general diplomatic tenor of the other African representatives in privileging the role of violence in African decolonization. According to Robert Young, the title, 'All-African People's Conference', 'inadvertently linked it to I.B. Tabata's Non-European Unity Movement whose origins lay in the All African Convention of 1936 held in Bloemfontein' (Young, 2005). Fanon attended five Pan-African conferences in 1960 alone.

Differences persist over Fanon's impact at the December 1958 AAPC. Some such as Emmanuel Hansen and Peter Worsley (1969) claim that Fanon's determinative speech on violence occurred two year later, at the April 1960 Accra Positive Action Conference, while Robert Young claims that his speech at the 1958 AAPC marked a new direction in Pan-Africanism:

> Fanon made a powerful statement of the FLN's position of uncompromising militancy, will, and use of violence to achieve its ends. Fanon was later to claim great success for his intervention.... Fanon's language here carries its typical poetic charge, but his claim was not unrealistic, given that his speech was received enthusiastically by his fellow delegates and widely reported in newspapers around the world. Indeed, in many ways Fanon's intervention constituted the decisive event of the whole gathering....

> The tone and tenor of Fanon's famous Accra speech was reported more fully, and no doubt more faithfully, by Stan Grant: 'Another speaker, Dr. Omar of Algeria told the Conference that in the fight for freedom, the African now had to resort to any available devise [sic], including 'force and violence'. He said that they had gathered in Accra in unity 'to prevent the dangers of the future'. 'In our fight against colonialism and imperialism, we must constitute ourselves into a national front, against inhumanity and poverty'. 'The colonial structural resemblance [sic] could be seen at its worst in Algeria. The enemy is powerful and there is the possibility of continuing its maneuvers to cripple our plans for freedom'. ... Dr. Omar was wildly cheered as he concluded by saying: 'And in our fight for freedom, we should embark on plans effective enough to touch the pulse of the imperialists — by force of action and, indeed, violence'.

Fanon's intervention succeeded in changing the tone of the conference, putting the issue of violent military resistance at the forefront of debate and anti-colonial consciousness. Though the official final resolutions continued to affirm non-violence, the tenth Conference Resolution on imperialism and colonialism stated:

'That the All-African People's Conference in Accra declares its full support to all fighters for freedom in Africa, to all those who resort to peaceful means of non-violence and civil disobedience, as well as to all those who are compelled to retaliate against violence to attain national independence and freedom for the people' (Young, 2005).[15]

Less noted in the meagre scholarship on the Pan-African conferences in the first decade of the African revolutions is the discussion of African socialism. This dimension of Pan-Africanism would become decisive for the turn that Black Power nationalists in the US would make with the 1974 Sixth Pan-African Congress. In *Wretched*, Fanon pursued a post-independence discourse on socialist development and warned against authoritarian over-reach, which he described as nothing less than forced labor that did come to plague Third World 'socialist' societies.

At the 1960 Accra Positive Action Conference, Fanon's discussion of the ongoing Algerian revolution and the role that violence plays within the anti-colonial Pan-African struggle again caused a tangible shift in the room and in the future path of Pan-African solidarity and struggle, both on the continent and throughout the diaspora. Emmanuel Hansen reproduced Peter Worsley's in-person account of Fanon's speech at that conference and the excitement it generated:

In 1960, I attended the All-Africa People's [Conference] in Accra, Ghana [sic]. The proceedings consisted mainly of speeches by leaders of African nationalism from all over the continent, few of whom said anything notable. When, therefore, the representative of the Algerian Revolutionary Provisional Government, their Ambassador to Ghana, stood up to speak I prepared myself for an address by a diplomat—not usually an experience to set the pulses racing. I found myself electrified by a contribution that was remarkable not only for its analytical power, but delivered, too, with a passion and brilliance that is all too rare. I discovered that the Ambassador was a man named Frantz Fanon. At one point during his talk he appeared almost to break down. I asked him afterwards what had happened. He replied that he had suddenly felt emotionally overcome at the thought that he had to stand there, before the assembled representatives of African nationalist movements, at a time when

---

15. Raya Dunayevskaya goes further in her characterization of the historic reach of the AAPC and contends, 'The first All-African People's Conference, in 1958 when Ghana was the only independent state, disclosed not just Pan-Africanism but the making of a Negro International' (Dunayevskaya, 1983: 28).

men were dying and being tortured in his country for a cause whose justice ought to command automatic support from rational and progressive human beings. (Worsley, 1969: 30-31; quoted in Hansen, 1977: 51)[16]

Fanon's leadership at the 1958 AAPC meeting caused a significant shift in the embrace of violent tactics within the Pan-African liberation movement. He was named FLN Ambassador to Ghana in 1959. According to George Houser, a leader within the American Committee on Africa (AAOC) who attended all three AAPC conferences, the FLN delegation's 'leader' at the first conference was once quoted as stating that 'nonviolence is out of date' (Houser, 1989: 73).[17] Despite Nkrumah supporting nonviolence during his keynote speech, Fanon undoubtedly impressed upon the entire conference the importance of supporting revolutionaries who utilize violent methods as a vital tactic of the struggle for a united and free Africa (Houser, 1989). At the second AAPC conference, held in Tunis the following year, the issue of non-violence was an afterthought. As the FLN waged their struggle in nearby Algeria, the delegates at the 1959 Tunis conference erupted once again in support of the Algerian revolution. This followed the FLN's Ahmed Boumendjel's invitation to Africans from across the world to come to Algeria to aid in their fight and learn strategies that would help them wage their own struggles for liberation in their home countries (Houser, 1989).[18]

While the connection between Malcolm X, other US-based Black revolutionaries, and the AAPC deserves more scholarly attention, one interesting thread of that relationship is important to note here. George Houser, director of the ACOC, attended all three of the AAPC meetings. Through his US-based work with the ACOC, Houser and fellow member William X. Sheinman, a board member of the National Urban League, worked with Pan-Africanist governments and organizations involved in the ACOC to bring young students from various countries to meet political activists and intellectuals, as well as to tour the US. The ACOC and the Kenyan-based African American Students Foundation (AASF), organized by Kenyan trade unionist and nationalist leader Tom Mboya and the US-based Sheinman to meet with students from East Africa as early as 1960, recruited Malcolm X. They were joined by the likes of Lorraine Hansberry, Jackie Robinson, and Congressman Charles Diggs.[19] Nkrumah himself had chosen Tom Mboya as the Chairman of the first AAPC conference (Houser, 1989: 72). African students from the same governments and organizations, who may have been influenced by the writings and speeches of Fanon

---

16. Both Worsley and Hansen mistakenly attribute Fanon's remarks to the wrong Accra conference and year. The first All-African People's Conference at which Fanon electrified the 200 attendees was held in Accra, December 8-12, 1958, not 1960. Fanon spoke at the conference on December 10, 1958. George Houser, Executive Director of the American Committee on Africa, who attended the conference, wrote an unpublished report on the All-African People's Conference without any mention of Fanon's speech.

17. Although Houser does not name the FLN delegate, other sources corroborate that Fanon was the FLN delegate who addressed the conference concerning violence.

18. Just such a call was what impelled Black Panther leaders and activists, seeking refuge from US authorities, to repatriate to Algiers in the late 1960s and early '70s (Mokhtefi, 2018).

19. This is the program in which Barack Obama's Kenyan father won a scholarship to attend the University of Hawaii.

through the AAPC and other Pan-African institutional settings, formed vital ties with Malcolm X through the organizing efforts of organizations like ACOC and AASF. In her account of her encounter with Fanon in Accra, in August 1960, Elaine Mokhtefi recounts Fanon's interaction with African students at the World Assembly of Youth, which he addressed. One of the student leaders in Fanon's company, when Mokhtefi met him, was 'Maurice Mpolo, the militant Congolese minister of youth...who represented President Patrice Lumumba.... A few months later Mpolo would be executed alongside Lumumba' (Mokhtefi, 2018: 41).

In the final analysis, the debate over non-violence versus violence within the Pan-African movement was a product of the 'lack of ideology' that Fanon observed in the leadership circles of the Pan-African conferences and capitals. The opacity this posed for seeing the imperialist machinations within their midst led to African nationalist leaders becoming unwitting, and, in the Congo, witting tools of European imperialist or Cold War super-power designs in Africa. Fanon came to see that with Africa's first political crisis in the Congo, differences over violence versus non-violence were quite beside the point. Lumumba had been more a partisan of Nkrumah's positive non-violent action than Fanon's use of tactical violence, whereas Fanon's comrade and FLN leader Abane Ramdane, murdered in FLN fratricidal conflicts, in 1958, was the tactician of the famous 'battle of Algiers'. Both, as Fanon confessed to Jean-Paul Sartre and Simone de Beauvoir, in Rome, in 1960, were two deaths that haunt his conscience. Both were victims of African leaders' ideological opacity, or utter lack of theory, regardless of their position on violence and non-violence. After two years of intense immersion in Africa's Pan-African political landscape, Fanon made the decision to write *Wretched*. Just how his articulation of the dialectics of liberation, following his Pan-African detour, played out in a new political environment, viz., at the turning point of emergent Black Power nationalism out of a decade of uninterrupted civil rights struggles in the US, is quite another matter.

## Black Power: The Black Panther Party's Fanon

From the beginning, Fanon cast the 'American Black' as the subject of his philosophy of revolution. In the penultimate chapter of *Black Skin*, 'The Black and Recognition', we read of the failure of the 'French Black' to descend 'into a real hell', i.e., into 'a zone of nonbeing..., an utterly naked declivity where an authentic upheaval can be born' (BS: 10). As in the 'Introduction' to *Black Skin*, Fanon, in the Hegelian moment of his dialectic ('The Black and Hegel'), asserts, 'The former slave needs a challenge to his humanity, he wants a conflict, a riot. But it is too late: The French Black is doomed to bite himself and just to bite' (BS: 221). At which point he pivots decisively:

> I say 'the French Black', for the American Black is cast in a different play. In the United States, the Negro battles and is battled. There are laws that, little by little, are invalidated under the Constitution. There are other

laws that forbid certain forms of discrimination. And we can be sure nothing is going to be given free.

There is war, there are defeats, truces, victories.

'The twelve million black voices' [referring to Richard Wright's work by that name] howled against the curtain of the sky. Torn from end to end, marked with the gashes of teeth biting into the belly of interdiction, the curtain fell like a burst balloon.

On the field of battle, its four corners marked by the scores of Negroes hanged by their testicles, a monument is slowly being built that promises to be majestic.

And, at the top of this monument, I can already see a white man and a black man *hand in hand*. (BS: 221-222)

Nearly a decade later, the 'American Negro...cast in a different play' becomes

Already certain minority groups do not hesitate to preach violent methods for resolving their problems and it is not by chance (so the story runs) that in consequence Negro extremists in the United States organize a militia and arm themselves. (WE: 63)

This reference, in Fanon's 1961 *Wretched of the Earth*, is probably to news reports of a March 25, 1959 press conference called by Robert F. Williams at which the author of *Negroes with Guns* asserted the right of self-defense of Black democratic rights (Singh, 2004: 191).[20] The intersection of Williams and Fanon, two ideological progenitors of the Black Power Movement, the Black Panther Party in particular, requires we take a closer, more dialectical look at how black America became Fanon's first ideological home in the liberation struggles of the 1960s and '70s.[21]

Black Panther Party co-founder Bobby Seale tells a story that by now has become almost apocryphal that he introduced Huey P. Newton to Fanon's work (Seale, 1991: 25). However, Kathleen Cleaver's insider account sets the context of Fanon's reception in the Black Power Movement in more objective light:

His [Fanon's] books became available in English just as waves of civil violence engulfed the ghettos of America, reaching the level of insurrection

---

20. Another source may also have been Chester Himes. In *Conversations with Chester Himes*, the African American expatriate author referenced several times in *Black Skin* recalls, 'everyone knows the CIA was interested in Fanon. They went to Fanon's assistance in the last years of his life to show that they had good will. Took him over to America and put him under medical treatment. By the way, he wrote a long article on my Treatment of Violence which his wife [Josie Fanon] still has, and which I've thought I might get and have published. Because he had the same feeling, of course, that I have.... Julia Wright [Richard Wright's daughter] told me that she had read it and that his wife has it' (Fabre and Skinner, 1995: 78).

21. Neither France nor the francophone African diaspora ever became the ideological home of Fanon; de Gaulle banned *Wretched* at the time of its publication in 1961. The ban remained in effect through the 1960s when Fanon's thought could have found new life in the spring days of the near-revolution in France in 1968. His thought also never became a factor in the francophone Caribbean. *Wretched* had only sold 3,000 copies in France by the time of its U.S. publication in 1965, where it went through five printing alone in its first year of publication.

in the wake of the assassination of Dr. Martin Luther King, Jr. in 1968....
*The Wretched of Earth* became essential reading for Black revolutionaries
in America and profoundly influenced their thinking. Fanon's analysis
seemed to explain and to justify the spontaneous violence ravaging Black
ghettos across the country, and linked the incipient insurrections to the
rise of a revolutionary movement. (Kathleen Cleaver, 1998: 214; also see
Turner and Alan, 1986)

The fast-paced timing of events, both theoretical and practical, explains the context in which Fanon's revolutionary thought found a 'home' in the U.S. The
1959 announcement by Robert Williams that he and other black North Car-
olinians had taken up armed self-defense reaffirmed and deepened for Fanon
the view he had of the radical character of 'Blacks in America', in his 1952 *Black
Skin*. Along with Kathleen Cleaver's assessment of the militant landscape Fanon's
work entered, the 1965 publication of the first U.S. edition of the *Wretched of
the Earth* appeared on the scene precisely at the time when serious ideological
schisms opened in the political leadership of the Civil Rights Movements. The
radicalization of Black students and urban workers perpetuated the schisms. As
Kathleen Cleaver observed, the U.S. publication of *Wretched* in 1965, and *Black
Skin* two years later, was circulating on the waves of Black mass revolt by the time
the winds of change had whipped them into a perfect storm in the wake of the
assassination of Martin Luther King, Jr., in 1968.

Grove Press' initial 1965 edition went through multiple printings, before coming out with a new 1966 Evergreen Press edition, which burned through more
than a dozen printings that year. The most popular 1968, pocketbook, pulp edition soared to at least sixteen printings. Despite the lack of a date in Bobby
Seale's account of when he read *Wretched* six times before introducing it to Huey
Newton, the year is likely 1965 or 1966, corresponding to his and Newton's
founding of the Black Panther Party (BPP) in October 1966, corresponding to
the 1965 publication of *Wretched* by Grove Press.

## Internal Colonialism

Nikhil Pal Singh notes that while the relationship of Fanon to the ideological
formation of the BPP is often referenced in BPP scholarship, 'Works about the
1960s that actually mention Fanon often do so in passing, implying that his influence did not extend beyond supplying aphorisms for would-be revolutionaries'
(Singh, 1998: 67).[22] Thus, the dialectic of Fanon's thought is seldom engaged in

---

22. Although Singh accurately critiques the shortcomings of BPP scholarship for glossing over the significance of the
Fanonian contribution to the formation of Black Panther ideology, his uncritical allusion to Henry Louis Gates' anti-
radical literary Fanonism and other cultural studies interpreters of Fanon is surely misplaced in assessing the radicalization of the BPP. This may be a consequence of Singh's 'long civil rights movement' thesis (Singh 2004: 2). The so-
called 'long civil rights movement' thesis seems more intent on reading Stalinism into Civil Rights and Black Power
movement narratives than in analyzing the new socioeconomic context of the post-war period. A new *transformative*
politics arose in response to the capitalist restructuring that commenced between the end of the second and beginning

BPP scholarship. In light of the title of Singh's discussion of Fanon and the BPP in his essay, i.e., 'Decolonizing America: Fanonism Reconsidered', apparently he attribute the origin of the internal colonialism thesis to Frantz Fanon.

Notwithstanding Kwame Ture's (Stokely Carmichael's) and Charles Hamilton's articulation of an internal colonialism position in their work *Black Power* in the same period (1966-67) as Seale and Newton, the Oakland-Bay Area provenance[23] of a Fanonian internal colonialism thesis still holds. Bay Area radical Robert Allen, in *Black Awakening in Capitalist America* (1970), developed the theory further. Despite Allen's criticism of Ture's and Hamilton's book as 'liberal reformism', following their analysis of the 1964 Mississippi Freedom Democratic Party (MFDP), in Allen's estimation, they nevertheless made a 'radical departure' when they 'concluded that it was necessary to 'build new forms outside the Democratic Party'. According to Allen, this 'radical departure' involved their advocacy of the Lowndes County [Alabama] Freedom Organization (LCFO) and its Black Panther logo as 'the model...of such a new form' (Allen, 1970: 247). Having initially discussed the MFDP and LCFO in a chapter on the social context of Black Power, Allen (1970: 60-65) then poses Fanon's de-colonization dialectic as an internal colonialism thesis in the U.S. in the same context.

Again, the Black proletarian perspective of autoworker Charles Denby is again instructive. Denby provides the backdrop against which developments, such as the Lowndes County 'Black Panther Party', emerged and the political consciousness of the Black rural working class evolved. In the spring of 1965, the Selma-to-Montgomery march passed through Lowndes County. During the model changeover hiatus at Chrysler, when his Detroit auto plant shut down, Denby traveled to Lowndes County and wrote about the situation in the County's segregated schools and about the displacement of Black sharecroppers

---

of the fourth quarter of the 20th century. The latter signaled an end of the Civil Rights-Black Power era and the beginning of what Sundiata Cha-Jua calls a 'new black nadir'. On the 'long civil rights movement' debate, see Cha-Jua and Lang 2007: 265-88. Singh is more insightful in pointing out the 'substantive references to the American context' in *Wretched* that were 'prescient precisely in identifying the political examples out of which the Panthers would fashion themselves (Singh, 1998: 68). Michael Clemons and Charles Jones (2001) provide a less eclectic reading of the Fanon-BPP relationship. Jeffrey Ogbar (2004: 85) conflates Fanon's class analysis of the African peasantry with the Black Panther's position on the black lumpen-proletariat. The Panthers avoided this fallacy because Fanon's proposal of the lumpen as potentially revolutionary is distinct from his analysis of the peasantry as a revolutionary subject. Finally, Singh (2004) seems to have appropriated without attribution the title of Amiri Baraka's "Black' Is a Country' essay from his 1966 collection, *Home: Social Essays* (2009: 101-06).

23. The question of the conceptual provenance of the internal colonialism thesis is complicated by Harold Cruse's 1962 treatment in his essay 'Revolutionary Nationalism and the Afro-American' (Cruse 1968). The essay originally published in *Studies on the Left* 2 (3), 1962, followed Cruse's excursion to Cuba in 1960 in a delegation of Black left intellectuals and artists, sponsored by the Fair Play for Cuba Committee (Singh, 2004: 186). Fanon may have been aware of the April 1960 *New York Times* advertisement that launched the Fair Play for Cuba Committee, representing another of his connection to the Americas. The likelihood stems from the sensation it caused among left intellectuals like Jean-Paul Sartre and Simone de Beauvoir. Robert Williams' support for FPCC is another strand connecting him to Fanon. The meeting between Fidel Castro and Malcolm X at the Hotel Theresa, in Harlem, New York, in late summer 1960, was celebrated enough to also have come to Fanon's attention. Amiri Baraka's essays on his experience during the 1960 FPCC Cuba trip is recounted in 'Cuba Libre', in his 1966 book of essays, *Home*. In it, he features FPCC organizers, Richard Gibson, who had worked for CBC News, and was later outed as an unrepentant informant for the CIA. Gibson was memorialized, as a US intelligence agent in Richard Wright's little known novel *Island of Hallucination*. The genealogy of Cruse's 'domestic colonialism' thesis derives from his critique of the Communist Party's old 'Black Belt' thesis. When Cruse does reference Fanon, it is in his 1968 Introduction to *Rebellion or Revolution?* His aim then was to criticize American Marxists and black moderates like J. Saunders Redding for not having 'envisioned the popularity of Frantz Fanon's ideas among the young black generation of 1968' (Cruse, 1968: 23).

and tenant farmers from white-owned land because they dared to vote and allow civil rights marchers to camp on their land. Denby's Detroit-based Marxist-Humanist newspaper, *News & Letters*, carried the first appeal for support of the of the Lowndes County movement in its June-July 1965 issue. The issue also announced the first meeting of former Lowndes Countians living in Detroit, who organized support for the newly formed Lowndes County Christian Movement for Human Rights following the Selma-to-Montgomery march.

Denby reported on the elections held in Lowndes County, November 1965, in which seven African Americans were elected to public office as a result of the Lowndes County movement that had been organized in March of that year. It was this election, whose Black slate carried for the first time as its symbol the black panther, which was adopted a year later by Huey Newton and Bobby Seale, in Oakland, California, as the emblem of the Black Panther Party. Denby also reported there were similar freedom organizations in other rural Black Belt counties in Alabama.[24]

It is safe to say that Fanon's critique of the national bourgeoisie and its leaders provided the framework for Allen's critique of African American leaders. It is nonetheless problematic that Allen conflates nation with the colonial state in citing Larry Neal's Fanonian discussion of 'Black Power in the International Context.[.footnote]The title of Larry Neal's essay derives from the second part of Fanon's famous first chapter of *Wretched* on violence, 'Violence in the International Context'.[/footnote] Where Neal maintains that Ture's attempts to 'internationalize our struggle are dialectically consistent with the thrust of Afro-American history' and 'connects the Afro-American *nation* to the larger context of the world-wide struggle' (Neal, 1968: 141 emphasis added). Allen (1970: 60) substitutes 'colonial model' for 'nation' in quoting Neal. While a dialectic exists between the colonial and the national theses, they are not synonymous. Theses on the national question date from Marx's and Engels' writings on the Irish and Polish questions in the 1860s,[25] if not earlier in their 1850s writings on revolution in Spain and revolts in India and China in the wake of the 1848 revolutions. These and Marx's earlier writings from the 1840s on the Jewish Question made their way into debates in the Second International between Rosa Luxemburg and Vladimir Lenin, and in the aftermath of the 1917 Russian Revolution in the Comintern (Communist International) of the Third International. The internal colonialism thesis is almost singularly the contribution theorized by Frantz Fanon during the emergence of the Third World revolutions, particularly the African revolutions of the post-World War II period of the 1950s and early 1960s.

Despite representing distinct questions, Black Power ideologues often conflated two other terms of the Fanonian dialectic, viz., the violence of coloniza-

---

24. As head of the Lowndes County Association in Detroit, Denby also led the campaign to purchase 200 acres of land for displaced black sharecroppers living in a 'tent city' because they had been evicted by white landowners.
25. It is a long overlooked fact of the radical black intellectual tradition that the pre-Marxian origins of the black national question actually dates from such figures as Gabriel Prosser, Denmark Vesey and David Walker inspired by the Haitian Revolution (1791-1804), and later by such proto-nationalists as Martin Delany.

tion/decolonization processes with his views on the so-called lumpen-proletariat as a revolutionary force. Black Power theorists posited the internal colonialism thesis sociologically, irrespective of debates over the supposed revolutionary potential of the urban lumpen-proletariat. Although it is often assumed that Black Panther ideologues Seale, Newton, David Hilliard and Eldridge Cleaver espoused a unitary lumpen position, V.P. Franklin (2007: 553-60) contends otherwise. The lived experience of actual political practice and the organizational life of the BPP led Seale and Newton to revise their estimation of the revolutionary potential of the lumpen, even as Eldridge Cleaver persisted in arguing for their revolutionary role. What few proponents of the lumpen position and Black Power historians seem to grasp is what is self-evident in Fanon and later among the BPP leadership, viz., that *praxis*, not the abstract espousal of undigested theories, determines the dialectics of organization that guide work with class fractions of the Black working class.

## Eldridge Cleaver's Fanon: Role of the Lumpen

In pamphlet #6 that he wrote for the BPP, *On the Ideology of the Black Panther Party*, Eldridge Cleaver (June 1970) raises the question of ideology and social motion, which was a hallmark of *Wretched*, viz., the question of dependence on Eurocentric theories. After all, it was Fanon's parting challenge to African nationalists to 'Leave this Europe where they are never done talking of Man, yet murder men everywhere they find them, at the corner of every one of their own streets, in all corners of the globe' (WE: 252). Cleaver makes the argument[26] that the question of ideology and ideological dependency had to be confronted by Black radicals who must 'rely on our own brains in solving ideological problems as they relate to us'.

> For too long Black people have relied upon the analyses and ideological perspectives of others. Our struggle has reached a point now where it would be absolutely suicidal for us to continue this posture of dependency. No other people in the world are in the same position as we are, and no other people in the world can get us out of it except ourselves. There are those who are all too willing to do our thinking for us, even if it gets us killed. However, they are not willing to follow through and do our dying for us. If thoughts bring about our deaths, let them at least be our own thoughts, so that we will have broken, once and for all, with the flunkeyism of dying for every cause and every error—except our own. (Eldridge Cleaver, 1970)

---

26. It was the argument Steve Biko, (1978) made in South Africa the same year, 1970. Throughout Biko's writings, the Fanonian influence is unmistakable.

Although he is known as a dogged proponent of the revolutionary role of the lumpenproletariat, citing Fanon as the voice of authority, it was actually in the area of ideology that Cleaver's theoretical contribution to Black radicalism resides. All of his work, including the counter-cultural *Soul on Ice*, represents a critical exploration of the role of ideological hegemony in cultural and political struggles over power and identity. His critique of orthodox Marxist-Leninist thought and his advocacy of the BPP's declaration of independence from the 'jungle of opinion' of left interpretations of Marxism was along the lines of Fanon's admission that when it comes to the Third World, Marxism 'must here be thought out again' (WE: 33). Cleaver attributes to Newton the articulation of 'the ideology and methodology for organizing the Black Urban Lumpenproletariat'.

> Armed with this ideological perspective and method, Huey transformed the Black lumpenproletariat from the forgotten people at the bottom of society into the vanguard of the proletariat. (Cleaver, 1970)

Cleaver raised the question of ideology more than any other theorist to engage Fanon's thought in this period. As we will see later, when we examine how James Forman engaged the role that Fanon attributes to ideology, the issue is Fanon's alarm over the *absence of ideology* in the political circles of the African liberation movements in which he moved. Cleaver's take on ideology stemmed more from a Maoist position of the correct ideological handling of contradictions among the people. Ideology is more instrumental for Cleaver than problematic. Therefore, his pragmatic assessment of ideology as a 'social glue that holds people together' is understandable but hardly sufficient to fill the philosophic lacunae in the Black liberation movement that was four years away from commencement of the historic capitalist restructuring that would spell the end of its radical Black proletarian base.

Despite Cleaver's inflated abstractions on the role of ideology, there were nonetheless elements that were unique and organic to Cleaver and to others. For example, his prognosis that 'a new strictly American ideological synthesis will arise, spring up from the hearts and souls of the oppressed people inside Babylon' (Ibid.). In his search for a new ideological synthesis, Cleaver turned to Fanon as 'a major Marxist-Leninist theoretician who was primarily concerned about the problems of Black people, wherever they may be found' (Ibid.). The common cause that Cleaver found with Fanon is that he, like the BPP, subjected Euro-American Marxism to criticism for its 'lumping all third world peoples into the category of Lumpenproletariat and then forgetting them there' (Ibid.). What Newton and Seale realized after reading Fanon was that Fanon's analysis of what was, in effect, a new urban class formation of the colonial-imperialist epoch had its global counterpart in capitalist urban centers of the U.S. This was a new globalized radical consciousness that preceded the impending stage of capitalist globalization on horizon.[27]

Cleaver exemplified this new globalization of revolutionary class forces when, upon being hounded out of imperialist America, he set up shop in post-independence Algeria, an independence for which Fanon had fought and given his life. The urgency of Cleaver's ideological advocacy of his position on the lumpenproletariat may be readily lost in the various errors he made in his argument. We, then, risk missing the original and organic theoretical position he sought to work out in addressing the new subjective reality that by now has become the most fundamental crisis of the Black community. The Black community has become an internal colonial repository wherein capitalism disposes of and concentrates the Black working class into so-called 'underclass' ghettos, forgotten zones of manifest degradation, violence, and potential revolt. Cleaver was prescient when he theorized that 'Black people's lumpenproletarian relationship to the means of production and the institutions of the society' (Ibid.) makes them incapable of manifesting rebellion against the capitalist means of production. The question Cleaver raises, but was unable to answer, is —How are the lowest and deepest strata of the Black working class to revolt against capital outside of the point of production?[28]

## James Forman's Fanon: Theorizing the Vanguard Role of the Black Working Class

James Forman is the Black Power theorist who best epitomizes the impact of Fanon on the radical theory and practice of what Harold Cruse called 'the young Black generation of 1968' and, as a consequence, on the question of the revolutionary potential of the Black lumpenproletariat. At the end of *The Political Thought of James Forman*, we read in a December 21, 1969 letter Forman wrote to Donald and Flora Stone:

> As you know, I willingly worked for the Black Panthers because I saw in them an extension of Frantz Fanon's concept of the lumpen proletariat as being the most revolutionary force in the colonized situation, but since most of the Black workers face employment off and on and many are unemployed I think it much better to talk in terms of organizing black

---

27. Marx theorized new objective stages of capitalist development as forerunners of and points of departure for theorizing new subjective stages of class and anti-colonial forces that inevitably arise from and against it. This becomes a truncated dialectic however in periods of revolutionary motion when the formation of new class forces anticipate in their historical material character a new objective stage of capitalist accumulation, or alternatively the resumption of an old stage of accumulation in a new form. The many symptoms in this interregnum, as Gramsci theorized it, range from postmodernism to postcolonialism to postracism.

28. This is the question that Marxist-Humanist worker-intellectual Gene Ford and I sought to find an answer in the aftermath of the 1992 Los Angeles rebellion. Could the value-form that social relations assume in capitalist society be stripped away by class forces who are not for the most part engaged in value production and whose capacity (power) is not, despite their increasing number, *directly* 'disciplined, united, organized by the very mechanism of the process of capitalist production itself' (Marx, 1976: 789).

workers, but keeping the accent on the youth.... We must learn from the Black Workers and they must become the leaders of the revolutionary movement. (Forman, 1970: 188)

Forman's conclusion was a prognosis of the changed labor market demographics that industrial capital would exploit in the midst of the Black urban revolts and economic downturns of the late 1960s. Labor historian Philip Foner described the socioeconomic basis of this new militancy of the young urban poor who entered the auto shops in Detroit at the end of the 1960s this way:

> The UAW itself estimated in 1969 that nearly 30 percent of its members at Chrysler were under 30, at General Motors 33 percent, and at Ford nearly 30 percent; the percentages of workers with less than five years' seniority were 51 at Chrysler, 41 at Ford, and 40 at General Motors. Late in 1967 and in 1968, a new element was added to these young workers—the hard-core unemployed, dropouts from the ghetto schools. The *New York Times* of August 13, 1967, reported that the heads of the big three auto companies and Walter Reuther were working with militant Black nationalists and that the 'purpose of the alliance is cooperation in the prevention of another riot'. One result of the Detroit power structure's sudden interest in the ghetto was the announcement by the auto companies that they would drop all 'educational' qualifications for employment, train ghetto people with government financing, and bring them into the plants. Several thousand young Blacks actually were hired. They moved into the hardest jobs, the foundries, assembly-line work, and press work. None went into the skilled trades. (Foner, 1982: 411)

The 1969-70 downturn in auto sales led to massive lay-offs of these new hires and triggered the last national strike against General Motors, in the 20th century. Organizing Black caucuses within the unions and the sharp class struggles at the point of production, by 1975, set the stage for the commencement of capital's restructuring and industrial purge of Black labor (Turner, 2010: 7-19).

More than any other radical intellectual-activist of his generation, James Forman grappled with the theoretical significance of Fanon's thought and revolutionary *praxis* for the Black working class and Black Power youth movement. Forman traveled to Martinique, in 1969, to interview Fanon's family and friends for a biography on Frantz Fanon that never came to full fruition (Forman, 2009).[29] Forman's position on the Black working class as a revolutionary democratic force that should not be limited to the lumpenproletariat becomes clear in his letter to Donald and Flora Stone from his trip to Martinique.

---

29. The drafts, research notes, correspondence and interviews for Forman's unrealized work on Fanon archived in the James Forman Papers, held in the Library of Congress, compiled in 2009. https://findingaids.loc.gov/db/search/xq/searchMfer02.xq?_id=loc.mss.eadmss.ms010125&_faSection=overview&_faSubsection=did&_dmdid=.

Then, a member of the League of Revolutionary Black Workers, Forman gave a comprehensive survey of Fanon's *Wretched*, on April 13, 1971, in Detroit, at a venue called the Control, Conflict, Change Seminar. At the conclusion of his treatment of chapter two of *Wretched*, on 'Spontaneity: Its Strength and Weakness,' Forman asserts, illustrating with what importance he assigned the analysis of capitalist production to any discussion of class strata and fractions in the Black community:

> The implications of the chapter, Spontaneity: Its Strength and Weakness, are enormous for all colonized people, for too often the masses of people are led by bourgeois reformists similar to the leaders of nationalist parties that Fanon describes. It is necessary for revolutionaries to break with these forces and root themselves in the largest sector of the colonized population. Inside the United States, this sector is working class people, but at the same time, no one who is thinking of revolutionary action can ignore the unemployed. Here I differ with Fanon and Marx for I do not think that unemployed workers should be lumped into the category of lumpen proletariat. At the same time, Fanon's dictum about the need to work with lumpen    proletariat in African countries has its counterpart in the United States for there are many colonized people who have been forced into robbery and vandalism as a way of life due to the lack of employment and *this is going to increase as automation accelerates*. (Forman, 1971: 14-15 emphasis added)[30]

Neither Marx nor Fanon of course 'lumped' the unemployed indiscriminately into the category of the lumpen. However, so adamant is Forman in distinguishing the unemployed from the lumpen, while rationalizing a subordinate, instead of leading, role for the lumpenproletariat in the vanguard of the revolutionary democratic Black working class that he went so far as to flag his departure from Fanon and Marx on the question. This distinguished him from other ideologues in the Black Power Movement, as well. More importantly, Forman understood 1) the relationship of expanding industrial automation to the increasing immiseration of the Black working class, ultimately producing a new class formation for which sociologists would give the name 'underclass' by the end of the 1970s,[31] and 2) he anticipated capitalism's coming industrial purge of Black labor in the decade 1975-85.

---

30. James Forman, 'A Talk on Frantz Fanon's *The Wretched of the Earth*', given at the Control, Conflict, Change Seminar, April 13, 1971, sponsored by the Ad Hoc Action Group, Detroit, Michigan. We are indebted to Abdul Alkalimat for bringing this rare, mimeographed publication to our attention.
31. Black sociologist William Julius Wilson was, in the late 1970s and '80s, mainly associated with the problematic term 'underclass'. However, it was actually Gunnar Myrdal, author of the 1944 Carnegie Foundation-funded study *An American Dilemma: The Negro Problem and Modern Democracy*, who coined the term in an essay in a Sunday, Special Supplement of *St. Louis Post-Dispatch*, 'The Underclass in the Great Society', January 26, 1965.

# George Jackson's Fanon: Dialectics of Socialist Revolution

*George Jackson's discovery of the dialectic of liberation in that hellhole, San Quentin Prison, can by no means be brushed aside as 'accidental", or as a Black Panther reduction of philosophy to such political Maoisms as 'power comes out of the barrel of a gun'. ... For good and sufficient reason the Hegelian dialectic has been called 'the algebra of revolution.*
—Raya Dunayevskaya (2018)

Soledad Brother George Jackson (1990: 10) theorized Fanon's colonial thesis explicitly as the 'Black Colony' in place of the 'Black Community', in *Blood in My Eye*. This most overlooked theorist of the Black Power Movement made several seminal theoretical contributions, among them, his quite dialectical conceptualization of U.S. 'fascism corporativism' (Jackson, 1990: 129). More than James Forman, George Jackson made Fanon's colonialism thesis the basis for analyzing the *strategic location* of the Black working class in the structures of capitalist accumulation and therefore its place in the vanguard of the international struggle for socialism.

> The principal reservoir of revolutionary potential in Amerika lies in wait inside the Black Colony. Its sheer numerical strength, its desperate historical relation to the violence of the productive system, and the fact of its present status in the creation of wealth forces the Black stratum at the base of the whole class structure into the forefront of any revolutionary scheme. Thirty percent of all industrial workers are Black. Close to 40 percent of all industrial support roles are filled by Blacks. Blacks are still doing the work of the greatest slave state in history. The terms of our servitude are all that have been altered.
>
> The Black Colony can and will influence the fate of things to come in the U.S.A. The impact of Black revolutionary rage actually could carry at least the opening stages of a socialist revolution under certain circumstances—not discounting some of the complexities created by the specter of racism. However, if we are ever going to be successful in tying Black energy and rage to the international socialist revolution, we must understand that racial complexities do exist. (Jackson, 1990: 10-11)

Jackson's analysis situates the Black working class struggle for democratic socialism in a more international historical context of capitalist accumulation than other Black Power ideologues, a context that is also more dialectical. So that when he points to the historical development of capitalist accumulation and its corresponding political forms of bourgeois rule, Jackson immediately points to their dialectical opposite:

> Monopoly capital can in no way be interpreted as an extension of old bourgeois democracy. The forces of monopoly capital swept across the Western world in the first half of this century. But they did not exist

alone. Their opposite force was also at work, i.e., 'international socialism'—Lenin's and Fanon's—national wars of liberation guided not by the
national bourgeois[ie] but by the people, the ordinary working-class people. (Jackson, 1990: 136)

Perhaps the most thoroughgoing theoretical engagement George Jackson has
with Fanon is on the question of revolutionary consciousness and *praxis*. It is
an engagement that sets the stage for our next discussion of Fanon's impact on
the psychology of black identity and research in Black mental health. As we will
see, Fanon inspired a new generation of radical Black psychologists, like William
Cross, and the psychological researchers and social scientists who established the
Fanon Research & Development Center at the Charles R. Drew Postgraduate
Medical School, Department of Psychiatry & Human Behavior, housed in Martin
Luther King, Jr. Hospital, in South Central Los Angeles.

While criticizing the historic and strategic failures of left, trade union, and
communist tendencies for their 'general retreat to avoid full commitment [and
for writing] the discomfort out of revolution', Jackson articulated a *dialectic of
organization*. On his view, 'people begin to express their disgust at the demagogic
and reformist maneuvers of the vanguard parties [and] discover in real action
a new form of political activity which in no way resembles the old' (Jackson,
1990: 26-27). Whereupon he renders a long quotation from Fanon on the teleol-
ogy of violence and revolutionary consciousness. The historical work of reason
is, in Fanonian terms, violence that is an 'absolute line of action. For the militant is also a man who works' (WE: 66). Having mastered the Hegelian dialectical
method in *Black Skin*, Fanon pushes the dialectic further in *Wretched*. The existential psychology of *Black Skin* gives way to the dialectics of liberation and to
*liberation psychology*. For Fanon, the individuality that assumes historic shape in
the struggle for national liberation falls in with that reality which was supposed
to be its negation, i.e., the violence of colonial occupation and by opposing and
negating that reality realizes its own purpose.

> The native discovers reality and transforms it into the pattern of his cus-
> toms, into the practice of violence and into his plan for freedom. (WE: 46)

What George Jackson grasped in Fanon was that because the colonized subject
becomes conscious of himself as the absolute reality of the nation, i.e., gains
national consciousness, the 'new facts which the native will now come to know
exist only in action' (WE: 117). More importantly, George Jackson was wary of the
'pitfalls of national consciousness' of which Fanon warned.

> [I]f nationalism is not made explicit, if it is not enriched and deepened
> by a very rapid transformation into a consciousness of social and political
> needs, in other words into humanism, it leads up a blind alley. (WE:
> 162-63)

# By Way of a Conclusion

*Everything can be explained to the people, on the single condition that you really want them to understand.*
—Frantz Fanon

*The philosophy of praxis is consciousness full of contradictions in which the philosopher himself...not merely grasps the contradictions, put posits himself as an element of the contradictions and elevates this element to a principle of knowledge and therefore of action.*
—Antonio Gramsci

In the U.S. in the late 1960s and early '70s, a new generation of Black radicals discovered the revolutionary dialectics of liberation of Frantz Fanon. It was a time when the Black Power Movement was emerging out of the contradictory limitations of the Civil Rights Movement, when the Black Arts Movement was becoming the cultural expression of a new Black consciousness, and when the insurrectionary knowledge of Black Studies began to challenge the intellectual hegemony of academic disciplines and discourse. Frantz Fanon was a conspicuous presence in this great irruption of revolutionary Black consciousness in America and the globalization of its influence.

There is no mystery why the Black Power generation gravitated to Fanon's revolutionary thought. He had comprehended the revolutionary dialectic at the core of the Black experience and in doing so challenged the duplicity of Western Enlightenment humanism with the inhuman reality of the lived experience of Black men and women living in the shadow of the racialized world constructed by the Enlightenment's white supremacist overseer. The narrative of this world, Fanon tells us, is therefore a tale told by idiots, and having proclaimed it, he had the burden of proving it. The racial narrative of this world is found in the hundreds of pages of words that assailed him with idiot expressions like 'understanding among men', 'the brotherhood of man', 'love and understanding', etc. (BS: 9). This tale, Fanon declares, is why he wrote *Black Skin, White Masks*.

The natural law of racism negates the humanity of Black people and casts them into 'a zone of nonbeing...where an authentic upheaval can be born' (BS: 10). The zone of nonbeing confronts all who would dare to be human with a test, with a challenge to their humanity. By overcoming or transcending this challenge to their humanity, they have their humanity realized and reaffirmed. It is in the struggle *to be human* against the 'zone of nonbeing' that Black men and women become human. Fanon claims, 'In most cases, the Black man lacks the advantage of being able to accomplish this descent into a real hell' (BS: 10). The whole of *Black Skin* is devoted to finding a way out of the zone of nonbeing. Even at the end of *Black Skin*, the Black man and woman are still unable to 'accomplish [a] descent into a real hell' where he/she can experience 'an authentic upheaval', a real liberation, except in that former European colony that had decided to catch up with Europe and had become a monster.

From the impossibility of Black people realizing their humanity, Fanon returns to the discussion of what constitutes humanity. Humanity is not only the 'possibility of recapture or of negation' (BS: 10). Human consciousness 'is a process of transcendence', a transcendence that is 'haunted by problems of love and understanding' (BS: 10). Therefore, humanity is not only a negation, a *no*; humanity is also a *yes*. The human condition is a condition of up-rootedness and dispersion (diaspora); and human beings become baffled and confused by the conditions of their own existence. As a consequence of this confusion, humanity is 'doomed to watch the dissolution of the truths that [they] worked out for [themselves] one after another' (BS: 10).

Humanity, Fanon declares, 'has to give up projecting onto the world an antinomy that coexists with [them]' (BS: 10). Antinomies are antithetical statements—contradictions—whose negation or synthesis constitutes the truth not found in either of the opposing propositions alone. Antinomies and their truths, Fanon argued, have dissolved because humanity entertained the false belief that they could coexist as humanity with the antinomy of human being and nonbeing, the antinomy of white and black, and thereby affirmed an authentic humanity for themselves. Humanity cannot live with the antinomy of white and black, of human being and nonbeing, and expect to coexist with such a dehumanizing dichotomy as the truth of human existence and not be doomed to watch as such truths dissolve one after another. This dissolution inevitably leads to the recognition that Black human beings *are* human beings, but only if their liberation also means their liberation from themselves. Here, then, is not only the origin and germination of a Black psychology of liberation but of a philosophy of revolution.

Today, Fanon's image and ideas are representative of a new age of radical humanist revolt against the inhumanity of white supremacy. His image stares from public murals and social media memes. His ideas on not breathing breathe life into a movement for the liberation of black lives from white supremacy. First appearing in social media in response to the police chokehold lynching of Eric Garner in New York, in 2014, Fanon's image and meme, 'When we revolt it's not for a particular culture, [but] simply because, for many reasons, we can no longer breathe', resurfaced with the knee-to-the-neck lynching of George Floyd in Minneapolis, May 25, 2020. Coming as it did in the midst of the COVID-19 respiratory disease pandemic, which does not allow its victims to breathe, the iconography of Frantz Fanon invited representations of another kind of breathing. What Fanon called 'combat breathing' is the second breath that comes with revolt.

Fanonian iconography in revolutionary Black Arts is the expressive vehicle in which Fanon made his appearance on the streets of cities across the global. The 2019 film 'Fanon: Yesterday, Today' by Hassane Mezine is a documentary compilation of Fanonian iconography, memes and radical engagements yesterday, today. It should be viewed with Raoul Peck's 2021 innovative documentary 'Exterminate all the brutes' because it is a project that comes between Peck's film 'The Young Karl Marx' and his Fanon film project. Together, Mezine and Peck imagine in the propulsion of the motion of the present historic moment the revolutionary breadth and breath of the full scope and meaning that Fanon gave to his most controversial articulation of the 'naked truth' of colonization and decolonization, viz., 'absolute violence' (WE: 30, 31). From the start, Fanon talks about the aesthetics of violence

> [A]esthetic expressions of respect for the established order serve to create around the exploited person an atmosphere of submission and of inhibition, which lightens the task of policing considerably... In colonial countries, [t]he policeman and soldier, by their immediate presence and their frequent direct action maintain contact with the native and advise him by means of rifle-butts and napalm not to budge. It is obvious here that the agents of government speak the language of pure force. [They are] the bringer of violence into the home and into the mind of the native...
>
> The violence which has ruled over the ordering of the colonial world, which has ceaselessly drummed the rhythm for the destruction of native social forms and broken up without reserve the systems of reference of the economy, the customs of dress and external life, that same violence will be claimed and taken over by the native at the moment when, deciding to embody history in his own person, he surges into the forbidden quarters...
>
> The natives' challenge to the colonial world is not a rational confrontation of points of view. It is not a treatise on the universal, but the untidy affirmation of an original idea propounded as an absolute. (WE: 31-33)

Specters of Frantz Fanon haunt us as much today, on the 60th anniversary of his death and the publication of his greatest work of revolutionary dialectic, *The Wretched of the Earth,* as they inspired that first generation of Black radicals and nationalists whose revolutionary *praxis,* daring, and thought made imperialist, neocolonialist America Fanon's first *'home'.* In a book of essays by that same name, *Home,* Amiri Baraka expresses this dialectic of yesterday, today in the following poem:

> *We are unfair*
> *And unfair*
> *We are black magicians*
> *Black arts*
> *We make in black labs of the heart.*
>
> *The fair are fair*
> *And deathly white.*
>
> *The day will not save them*
> *And we own the night*
> — Amiri Baraka

# Bibliography

Ahlman, J. 2010. 'The Algerian Question in Nkrumah's Ghana, 1958–1960: Debating "Violence" and "Nonviolence" in African Decolonization.' *Africa Today* 57 (2, winter): 67–84.

Allen, R. L. 1970. *Black Awakening in Capitalist America: An Analytic History*. Garden City: Anchor Books.

Battle-Baptiste, W., and Britt, R., eds. 2018. *W.E.B. Du Bois's Data Portrait: Visualizing Black America, The Color Line at the Turn of the Twentieth Century*. New York: Princeton Architectural Press.

Baraka, A. 2009a. *Home: Social Essays*. New York: Akashi Classics.

————. 2009b. 'Black' Is a Country.' *Home: Social Essays*, 101–106. New York: Akashi.

Biko, S. 1978[1970]. 'Black Souls in White Skins?' In *Steve Biko: I Write What I Like*, edited by Aelred Stubbs, 19–26. New York: Harper & Row.

Cha-Jua, S. 2010. 'The New Nadir: The Contemporary Black Racial Formation.' *The Black Scholar* 40 (1, spring), 38–58.

Cha-Jua, S., and Clarence, L. 2007. 'The "Long Movement" as Vampire: Temporal and Spatial Fallacies in Recent Black Freedom Studies.' *Journal of African American History* 92 (2): 265–288.

Cleaver, E. 1970. *On the Ideology of the Black Panther Party*, http://peacecomrade.org?2010/06/10/on-the-ideology-of-the-black-panther-party-by-eldrid.

Cleaver, K. N. 1998. 'Back to Africa: The Evolution of the International Section of the Black Panther Party (1969–1972).' In *The Black Panther Party [Reconsidered]*, edited by Charles E. Jones. Baltimore: Black Classic Press.

Clemons, M., and Charles, J. 2001. 'Global Solidarity: The Black Panther in the International Arena.' In *Liberation, Imagination, and the Black Panther Party*, edited by Kathleen Cleaver and George Katsiaficas. New York: Routledge.

Cruse, H. 1968. 'Revolutionary Nationalism and the Afro-American.' *Rebellion or Revolution?*, edited by Harold Cruse. New York: William Morrow.

Davis, C. T., and Michel, F. 1982. *Richard Wright: A Primary Bibliography*. Boston: G.K. Hall.

Denby, C. 1962. 'Race and Class.' *News & Letters*, June–July.

Du Bois, W. E. B. 1903. *The Souls of Black Folk: Essays and Sketches*. 2nd ed. Chicago: McClurg.

Dunayevskaya, R. 1963/1983. *American Civilization on Trial: Black Masses as Vanguard*. Fourth expanded edition. Detroit: News & Letters.

————. 1991. *Rosa Luxemburg, Women's Liberation and Marx's Philosophy of Revolution*. Urbana: University of Illinois Press.

————. 2018. *Philosophy and Revolution, from Hegel to Sartre, and from Marx to Mao*. Delhi, India.

Fabre, M., and Robert, E. S. 1995. *Conversations with Chester Himes*. Oxford: University of Mississippi.

Fanon, F. 1966. *Wretched of the Earth*. Translated by Constance Farrington. New York: Grove Press.

_____. 1967. *Black Skin, White Masks*. Translated by Charles Markmann. New York: Grove Press.

_____.1969a. 'Racism and Culture.' *Toward the African Revolution*. Translated by Haakon Chevalier, 35–36. New York: Grove Press.

_____. 1969b. 'This Africa to Come.' *Toward the African Revolution*. Translated by Haakon Chevalier, 177–190. New York: Grove Press.

_____. 2018. *Alienation and Freedom: Frantz Fanon*, edited by Jean Khalfa and Robert Young. Translated by Steven Corcoran. London: Bloomsbury.

Foner, P. 1982. *Organized Labor and the Black Worker, 1619–1981*. New York: International Publishers.

Forman, J. 1970. *The Political Thought of James Forman*. Detroit: Black Star Publishing.

_____. 1971. 'A Talk on Frantz Fanon's *The Wretched of the Earth* Control, Conflict, Change Seminar.' April 13, 1971, sponsored by the Ad Hoc Action Group, Detroit, MI.

Franklin, V. P. 2007. 'Jackanapes: Reflections on the Legacy of the Black Panther Party for the Hip Hop Generation.' *Journal of African American History* 92 (4, fall): 553–560.

Gramsci, A. 1976. *Selections from the Prison Notebooks of Antonio Gramsci*. Edited and Translated by Quintin Hoare and Geoffrey N. Smith. New York: International Publishers.

Grigsby, D. R. 1987. *For the People: Black Socialists in the United States, Africa and the Caribbean*. San Diego: Asante Publications.

Guerin, D. 1956. *Negroes on the March: A Frenchman's Report on the American Negro Struggle*. Translated and edited by Duncan Ferguson. New York: George L. Weissman.

Hansen, E. 1977. *Frantz Fanon: Social and Political Thought*. Columbus: Ohio State University Press.

Høgsbjerg, C. 2016. 'Remembering the Fifth Pan-African Congress.' *Leeds African Studies Bulletin* No. 77 (2015/16), April, https://lucas.leeds.ac.uk/article/remembering-the-fifth-pan-african-congress-christian-hogsbjerg/.

Houser, G. 1958. 'A Report on the All African People's Conference Held in Accra, Ghana December 8–13, 1958.' Michigan State University Special Libraries Collections, PWACOAAAPC58opt.pdf (msu.edu).

_____. 1989. *No One Can Stop the Rain: Glimpses of Africa's Liberation Struggle*. New York: Pilgrim Press.

Jackson, G. 1990. *Blood in My Eye*. Baltimore: Black Classic Press.

James, C. L. R. 1978. *Nkrumah and the Ghana Revolution*. London: Lawrence Hill.

James, F. P. 2009. Library of Congress, https://findingaids.loc.gov/db/search/xq/searchMfer02.xq?_id=loc.mss.eadmss.ms010125&_faSection=overview&_faSubsection=did&_dmdid=.

Legum, C. 1965. *Pan-Africanism: A Short Political Guide*. New York: Praeger.

Lenin, V. I. 1977. *Collected Works*, Vol. 12. Moscow: Progress Publishers.

Macey, D. 2012. *Frantz Fanon: A Biography*. London: Verso.

Malcolm X. 1960. [Photo] 'Meeting with students from East Africa at a welcoming program for students brought to the United States to study by the African

American Students Foundation.' Photo courtesy of Cora Weiss, from the private collection of Cora and Peter Weiss, African Activist Archives, African Studies Center, Michigan State University, East Lansing, MI, African Activist Archive (msu.edu).

Marx, K. 1976. *Capital: A Critique of Political Economy*, Vol. 1. Translated by Ben Fowkes. New York: Penguin.

Mokhtefi, E. 2018. *Algiers, Third World Capital: Freedom Fighters, Revolutionaries, Black Panthers*. London: Verso.

Neal, L. P. 1968. 'Black Power in the International Context.' In *The Black Power Revolt: A Collection of Essays*, edited by Floyd B. Barbour. Boston: Extending Horizons Books.

Ogbar, J. 2004. *Black Power, Radical Politics and African American Identity*. Baltimore: Johns Hopkins University Press.

Ranney, D. 2003. *Global Decisions, Local Collisions: Urban Life in the New World Order*. Philadelphia: Temple University Press.

Ray, D., and Farnsworth, R. M., 1973. *Richard Wright: Impressions and Perspectives*. Ann Arbor: University of Michigan Press.

Seale, B. 1991. *Seize the Time: The Story of the Black Panther Party and Huey P. Newton*. Baltimore: Black Classic Press.

Shepperson, G. 1987. *Independent African: John Chilembwe and the Origins, Setting and Significance of the Nyasaland Native Rising 1915* (with Thomas Price). London: University Press.

_____. 1993. 'African Diaspora: Concept and Context.' In *Global Dimensions of the African Diaspora*, edited by Joseph E. Harris. Washington: Howard University Press.

Singh, N. P. 1998. 'The Black Panthers and the 'Undeveloped Country' of the Left.' In *The Black Panther Party [Reconsidered]*, edited by Charles E. Jones. Baltimore: Black Classic Press.

_____. 2004. *Black Is a Country: Race and the Unfinished Struggle for Democracy*. Cambridge: Harvard University Press.

Turner, L. 1997. 'Lumumba, Fanon, Che and the Congo.' *News & Letters*, Jan.–Feb.

_____. 1999. 'Fanon and the FLN: Dialectics of Organization and the Algerian Revolution.' In *Rethinking Fanon: The Continuing Dialogue*, edited by Nigel Gibson. Amherst: Humanities Books.

_____. 2010. 'Toward a Black Radical Critique of Political Economy.' In *The Black Scholar*, Vol. 40, No. 1, 7–19. Springer.

Turner, L., and John, A. 1986. *Frantz Fanon, Soweto and American Black Thought*. Chicago: News & Letters.

Young, R. J. C. 2005. 'Fanon and the Turn to Armed Struggle in Africa.' *Wasafiri* 20 (44): 33–41.

Worsley, P. 1969. 'Revolutionary Theories.' *Monthly Review* 21 (May): 30–31.

Wright, R. 1941. *12 Million Black Voices: A Folk History of the Negro in the United States*. New York: Viking Press.

# FANON, POSTCOLONIAL CRITICISM AND THEORY: NOTES IN LATIN AMERICAN CONTEXTS

Alejandro de Oto

## Part One

When returns take longer than expected, before considering them as such, it seems necessary to imagine them as processes. The three elements of the title aim at emphasizing that there is something important for our work in the social sciences and humanities. Unlike Borges' well known Encyclopedia series, which Michel Foucault quotes at the beginning of *The Order Of Things, our title is not alphabetical, and it is far from being in ruins.* A couple of decades after Fanon's return to the Latin American arena of critical thought, it is far from producing the stupor of finding ourselves in the limits of our thought.[1] Today we meet a kind of conceptual and theoretical common sense, formed by two important terms: Fanon and postcolonial criticism. The second part of the title is stated in plural since, in the form of hypothesis, it is possible to think that there is another method rather than heterogeneous reading and writing contexts in the articulation of the three elements in the first part of the title.

This introductory section aims to create the space for a brief recount of the possibilities for research and criticism materials in the studies evoked under the generic label of postcolonial studies, considered in relation to the Fanonian spectrum,[2] particularly in Argentina and generally, in Latin America.

---

1. After exposing the classification imagined by Borges in an also imaginary Chinese encyclopedia Michel Foucault writes: 'In the wonderment of this taxonomy, the thing we apprehend in one great leap, the thing that, by means of the fable is demonstrated as the exotic charm of another system of thought, is the limitation of our own, the stark impossibility of thinking *that*'. (Foucault, 1968: xvi).
2. The list of entries that connected Fanon's thought to the postcolonial criticism in its varied forms is relatively extensive. As it can be seen in the second part of this text, most of this connection occurred in English language writings. From mid-nineties up to the present, there have been several compilations about Fanon. These rescued what could be referred to as a heterogeneous map of post-colonialities and theories converging into his writing. In this reflexive context, the particularly outstanding works are those by L.R. Gordon, T. Sharply-Whiting., Renée T. White (1996), Anthony Alessandrini, (ed.) (1999); Nigel C. Gibson (ed.) (1999) and Lewis Gordon, L. (2015). In this book, Gordon traces a precise cartography of those who have, and still do, studied Fanon systematically. Regarding the 'Fanonian spectrum', the issue has been partly theorised in three works in which I have participated. In 2003, I referred to this figure by evoking Derrida's *Spectres of Marx* in a less rigorous way. However, in two recent articles written with Leticia Katzer, this notion was deepened by placing the Fanonian zone of 'non-being' in contact with deconstruction (2013); (2014).

The recent presence of Fanon in the Latin American arena, mainly marked by academia,[3] is the result of particular ups and downs. It is worth noticing that during the late nineties' unfolding of cultural studies and some incipient registers of postcolonial criticism,[4] Fanon intermingled with the texts destined to reflect on the problems of cultural identities, of subaltern subjectivity and the racialization process, a concept that would remain in force during the following decade. Nonetheless, this was not given as the result of a critical revision of the intellectual histories, or of those theories that, in Latin America, had dealt with salient writing issues such as liberation, disalienation, revolution and decolonization, among others. On the contrary, it was a return linked with processes of the academic formation of some postgraduate students, who in those years came in touch with the heterogeneous weave of the postcolonial criticism written in English, finding in it a persistent emergence of references to Fanon.

A decade earlier, in the eighties, with certain disparities, Latin American academia had witnessed the poststructuralist unfoldings[5] in different disciplines. With them, the problem of criticism to those subjects who had founded the modern experience was placed in the center of discussion, thus directly affecting the notion of a relatively homogeneous historical subject—articulated in class, for example, as a nuclear category of social analysis. This consequently brought a revision of the methodologies of analysis, thus giving place to what, at the beginning of the decade, Clifford Geertz had called 'blurring genres' when writing about the ways in which the social thought was prefigured. Such progressive movement provoked a fundamental change in the knowledge of the social, as the methodological certainties and the allocation of sense gradually gave room to reflexive processes on which it imposed a configuration process of the observed

---

3. This issue is worth mentioning since it is particularly proper in order to understand the ways in which Fanon's writing enters the space of theory as an exception. It is necessary to observe that most part of this reflection is centered on dissimilar experiences, several in Argentina. The hypotheses, conversations, and possible connections to different Latin American contexts are posed here as an invitation to further exploration. Some Brazilian and Colombian discussions on the circulation of Fanon's writing are introduced in this text, thus inviting the reader to explore the works that approach them. Some of the central features of the readings in Argentina and Brazil during the sixties are shared. The significant exception in Argentina is the absence of the racial dimension which constituted a relatively constant presence in Brazil, Colombia and Cuba.

4. It is worth mentioning that this was a surreptitious return, almost secret, among those who took seminars connected to Edward Said's writings and then, read other books, like *The location of culture* by Homi Bhabha, appearing in English at the beginning of the decade. Between these two writings, several reasons were woven to provoke, by the late nineties and the turn of the century, Fanon's emergence as a crucial passage of our critical libraries. García Canclini introduces a different stance, as he argues that Fanon's return for certain Latin Americanists and North American cultural studies was amnesic in relation to the readings on Fanon occurring on the continent during the sixties and seventies. This position can be read in Néstor García Canclini (1995). Without strictly opposing this reading, it is important to observe that there is no continuity between the contexts of reading during those previous decades, referred to by Canclini, and the present when we read Fanon together with Said, Bhabha and the like Gramsci's case, part of Canclini's reference, is quite different. On the contrary, Gramsci gradually received more impulse in those works by intellectuals like José Aricó, whose analytical acuity responded to a weave that did not break the link with those pasts in the 1960s, 1970s and 1980s. Nonetheless, Aricó suffered a luck similar to Fanon's, since his works were lost during the eighties and were to be re-ignited (using Edward Said's words) during the last decade in those writings by Raúl Burgos (2005), Martín Cortés (2015) and Guillermo Ricca (2016). The latter leads a deep and sensible discussion on the opening horizon of Aricó's work.

5. It is relevant to observe that this term is frequently used in the United States academia. During the 1980s, with important regional variations in Latin America, references were directly to those authors who were thought of as encompassed rather than characterized en bloc. It is evident that French contemporary philosophical thought is part of this process, though it is clear that differences between its practitioners are highly marked.

social practices around their own objects of study as well as the tasks related to research.

As this happened, with unevenness and shades depending on particular spaces, the research material and texts left apart two decades earlier returned in a distinctive way, which was characterized by a new configuration of the very same material and texts. Hence, the discussion of issues like colonialism and its presence in the processes of subjectivity production became evident in the nineties, and even stronger by the turn of this century. It came to the stage favored by the circulation of the writings generically called poststructuralist, and also by the effects on these writings in varied fields, such as ethnography, literary criticism and cultural studies, among others. It is worth noticing that the fact of being favored is not a main reason for its impact because it is possible to list a relevant series of works that, influenced by the dimensions of the poststructuralist frames, rejected Marxist criticism of the historical process. Illuminated by the records, these works also rejected the stories of political militancy during the sixties and the early seventies, particularly in Argentina. In addition, these works one could list an important series of works that, influenced by the dimensions of the poststructuralist frameworks, rejected as a whole both the Marxist critiques of the historical process, as well as the writings linked to the histories of political militancy in the 1960s and early 1970s, illuminated by the records, in the Argentine case especially, of the philosophy of liberation, the theology of liberation, the idea of the revolution in the third world, the Sartrean readings of the militant intellectual and so on. Here, the issue in question is that if asking about Fanon's return and, more timidly, about other anti-colonial writings, it is possible to describe it as a return rather than as emergence.

When revising the circulations of texts critical of colonialism, it is possible to draw a definite dividing line, considering the specific contexts around the late seventies and early eighties. This line, among other possible things, is a way of describing the discontinuity of determined processes. It has an effect that would be appropriate to describe as water on the sandy beach. In other words, it defines the moment in which the ground of theory and political practices stops acting as positivity that contains writings like the Fanonian ones. It can be observed in this metaphor that the soil, which contained and organized the anti-colonial writings in Latin America, became so permeable that those old statements, loaded with sense, with the capacity to draw a political articulation and to produce a plausible description of the world, are lost in the porosity of an ideological ground and of those social practices that cannot hold them. This is because the weave has been displaced towards negotiations of sense in sensitive democratic contexts, towards new forms of social subjectivization supported on the social processes that do not claim, for example, the univocality of certain categories such as historical subject or conscience. Above all, in the context of knowledge, a disengagement is produced among significant practices connected to political activism, the issues and problems specific to a discipline, and their epistemological deployment.

The bond between the different genres of social thought and their political articulation stops being evidence *per se*. That is to say, the naturalization of all knowledge as political, as if it guaranteed a specific result, halts and enters a more opaque zone where its representational transparency vanishes into deep genealogies. In this sense, writings like the Fanonian ones, previously read in those contexts of strong antagonisms where heterogeneity was not a dimension to highlight since other utopian objectives were privileged, little by little start losing restraint. For example, when observing the ways in which Fanon's writing appears in magazines of political discussion during the sixties, particularly in Argentina, the issues that encourage its circulation are the 'revolution in the Third World' and the 'anticolonial struggle' in terms of national emancipations from colonialism, and 'the social struggle' in terms of socialist transformations.[6]

With relative efficacy, these choices produce the convergence of concrete demands of a political practice with the categories and concepts that are unfolded in the texts. Certainly it is not about a mimetic relation between the general context and the concepts since it would be a naive way of thinking about it. It is about an epistemological dimension that organizes knowledge in functional dependence of certain statements working as a demand of the real in front of the text. The text has a relative weight in itself, and privileges what it refers to, which serves as the location of validation for the readings and writings that depend on the text. This operation works with relative fluency in most political literature of this period, in Latin America and beyond. However, this description, which adjusts to a certain idea of the effect produced by the contexts in the forms of appropriation and circulation of a text, does not adequately describe the developments that are internal to the very fields where such writings take place.

Let us take as an example the planes of incidents that organize themselves around notions such as alienation, culture, conscience, revolution, and colonialism. Along the pressure of the context to turn each of these terms into referents, they are transmitted in the social thought as concepts or descriptions of what happens and what is real. Though concrete, since each term of this series leads to historical dimensions well known in the twentieth century, it is necessary to emphasize that they describe positions within writing, inside the specific field of its emergence. In this sense, the anticolonial writing, or the criticism to colonialism, refers to the dimension of historical experience and is at the same time a surreptitious organization in the way each new statement about colonialism will be produced and understood.

This does not refer to Fanon's writing only, but to the set of interventions that configured the space of criticism of colonialism. However, when considering his writing exclusively, what is at play is the possibility of identifying, or not, scansions, certain orders, planes, discontinuities, where the units of sense seem to even out all roughness, all salient. How would one compare a black body, for instance, with a revolution? How would one give value to the materiality of the bodies under colonialism when it is about the disalienation of minds? These

---

6. See De Oto, A. (2013: 35-60).

questions are intentionally posed since they strongly invoke the plane of the homologations between the subject and the disalienation organized in the anti-colonial writing. They also make possible different ways of reading and integrating specific writings within the network of concepts and categories that form the mesh of contention.

The hypothesis in this work suggests that this mesh is constituted by conceptual units with the size of revolution, alienation, a new man, and a new humanism. During the two decades after Fanon's death, all the micro-cosmos of events of the radicalized body are drained in the sand. It is relevant to highlight that these are not units restricted to the Fanonian text, but they are above all, conceptual units that the practices of reading produce in this mesh. For this reason, it would not be accurate to speak about emergence. All that had been drained in the sand during that time did not return when the force of the big units was still visible. Even more important is the fact that it did not return when the criticism of these units was pronounced while they were stalked by the social processes as well as the specific transformations within the discourses of philosophy, and within the social, political and cultural theories during the last two decades of the Latin American twentieth century. This was a process that almost destroyed Fanon's writing and its numerous effects on the academic arena of the long eighties.

If there was a moment in which Fanon's writing had crossed the threshold of the political compromises of militancy, then with it were his writing abandoned the public consideration and the academia. If it had once inspired reflections on the revolution of the Third World, once it failed, then the other did too. If the program had to think of that complex object called national culture, once the idea of its possibility disappeared, the Fanonian writing accompanied it. One could admit that Fanon's writing somehow contributed to Latin American thinking, particularly to those reflections regarding the foundations of liberation theology, which recognized the subject's alienated character, and identified the stories it evoked towards humanism. It also contributed to those reflections considering the proper philosophy of liberation, which found in this writing a pillar for the discussion of its ontological status (whether it was possible or not to philosophies on a continent that was not emancipated, but subjected). However, in this present, by the end of both decades, few possibilities for the inscription of the mentioned issues remained. It was rather a paradoxical effect produced because Fanon's writing was, and still is part of a minor literature, in the very same sense the figure has for Deleuze and Guattari. In other words, it is the writing of an author who is definitely part of a marginal group and expresses himself in a dominant language. At the same time, his individual problems complete themselves in a discourse of political content and take with him the mark of representation of a type of collective enunciation he depends on. Fanon, like several authors who thought of colonialism, listened to and comprehended the nature of the threats of his present.

This mark somehow went unnoticed once the primarily European philosophical reflection became admitted an extensive criticism of the well-known illusions of modernity, representation and its centered and universal subjects. For a reason that would be eventually understood as specific to the geopolitics of knowledge, in these Latin American vicinities it was assumed that everything connected to the modern narratives and their dreams of instrumental reason, or to their idea of social totalities, had to leave together with the discourses and theories that had given them a frame and contention. In other words, if Marxism had been the extensive object of criticism, there would be no apparent reason for supporting its units of analysis updated to the colonial use of writing like the Fanonian one. There would also be a need to identify the purpose for narrating the mastery of colonialism at a moment when, at a global scale, there was hardly space defined by it. The sense of giving credit to the discussions on the national culture and other similar objects was also questioned when the focus was on the dissolution of the processes that gave an entity to modernity itself. In the nineties, globalization, from the left and the right, put emphasis on the transnational processes, including subalternity as an analytical category. Even more significant would be the question about the sense of sustaining the historicity that inhabited Fanon's texts and other writings when it was evident that the defeat of a generation who had imagined the social change here and there questioned those that had been their instruments of comprehension and ways of action.

At best, Fanon appeared in those writings connected to biographical recounts of intellectuals, and in those was a university professor who remembered the potent echoes, above all, of his text *The Wretched Of The Earth* (1994 [1961]: 7), a manifesto that did not stop reminding the reader of the modern character of genre and questioning it. It is necessary to observe that *The Wretched Of The Earth* does not resist a contrast with processed information in the terms of practiced social sciences. Its tone, its rhythm, is that of a hammer striking over each truth assumed as such, over each certainty of the conditions that befall those it calls colonized. In a universalist gesture, the text reverses the colonial proposition: if there is something new in the world, that is the imagination emancipated from the old colonial societies. Though with a certain peculiarity, this text could absolutely take part of the extended register of manifestos known in Latin America and the Caribbean. It has been largely debated on what could be named as an extended examination of conscience, or the pulse of the pamphlet that tries a performative word[7] and a legacy, a will.

Each of these forms weaves the tension between his writing and the reason why it remained forgotten and seeped into the sand. During the sixties and the seventies, those who disputed that legacy, in a sense suggested by Derrida in *Specters Of Marx*, challenged each element of the series—conscience, pulse and testament—by turning this writing into an unusual tool in use, able to anticipate the social play, without considering its performative character. In doing so, it participates in the genre inaugurated by *Communist Manifesto* a century earlier, while escorting the processes of modernity from a critical side, and certainly defining the movements of an emancipatory history still to happen. This issue is

---

7. To read about the role of *Manifesto* as genre, see C. Maíz (2014).

crucial in order to understand what Fanon states in *The Wretched Of The Earth* is everything that happens without happening. This is not a rhetorical trick, but a description of the effects that the Fanonian writing produces and performs. It is not a utopian or apocalyptic register specific to the written word of the manifestos, which describe old worlds and augur new ones. This is not infeasible because of the impossibility to think his text in this key, since the remains of critical humanism quickly unfold in it, but because the performative effect of his writing directs to the least definite zones, to the least stabilized zones of a concept, of a category, or even of a radical statement. If Fanon's writing provides some novelty, in general terms, it is not for its rhetoric efficacy, not a crossroads that would gain value by the turn of the twenty-first century on this continent, and would connect our own postcolonial memory to his, in the difficulty of giving a name to what had no concept beyond the representational limits of the civilizing or colonial discourses: the colonial experience and the racial experience of the body.

Nevertheless, the moment—the colonial experience and the racial experience of the body—did not arrive. The disputes about the legacy stopped by the end of the sixties. The echoes of discussions which had placed Fanon on the foreground of a long line of Latin American readings and writings vanished. They remained as the remains of a wreck. Though the names of Salazar Bondy, Leopoldo Zea,[8] Enrique Dussel, and Paulo Freire, could be evoked among others, they only pointed to the emptiness of writings in conversation with Fanon's. During the sixties and seventies, the dispute with the legacy had taken place in the field of revolutionary theories and in the comprehension of colonialism, a subsidiary of modernity. It is worth asking if this could have happened in a different mode. The question is right if one is acknowledging the risks that counterfactual thought implies. However, this aspect was crucial to keep the already discussed level of minor writing, and above all, the epic tone of its enunciation. In other words, it seems that by keeping the particularity of his writing, its radical singularity, the impossibility to become something different, was kept. Therefore, his enunciations acted as departure points for a moral rather than problematic issue that aimed at describing the complexity of the present. Fanon was partly responsible for this, since his writing addressed intellectuals and, in that community,

---

8. Augusto Salazar Bondy and Leopoldo Zea were two main figures in the Latin American philosophical arena. They encouraged the discussion about the character of the intellectual activity on this continent. (See his brief work *¿Existe una filosofía de nuestra América?* [Is there a Latin American philosophy?] (1968)). Salazar Bondy claims that the authenticity of an American philosophical thought absolutely rests on how far we can place ourselves from cultural alienation. This shows certain Fanonian circulation within the text. From this work, Leopoldo Zea writes his criticism in perhaps his best well-known text, *La filosofía americana como filosofía sin más* [Latin American philosophy as simply philosophy] (1969). With a remarkable freedom of movement, Zea reads Fanon and Sartre to think that the Latin American philosophy is constructed in dispute with the colonial condition of subalternity. Both readings depict a chapter in Latin American philosophy, and in the role, sometimes surreptitious and others evident, Fanon plays in it. Years later, in *Crisis* magazine, Salazar Bondi publishes 'Diálogos indianos entre Bartolomé de las Casas, Frantz Fanon, el cacique Hatuey y Ginés de Sepúlveda' [Indian dialogues among Bartolomé de las Casas, Franz Fanon, Cacique Hatuey and Ginés de Sepúlveda] (1974). In this text', 'Frans', the black character, expresses a claim against Bartolomé's humanism and a call to the indigenous Hatuey, i.e., to other consciences.

assumed a position in order to prescribe a form of unfolding.[9] At the beginning of the eighties, those aspects, among them the programmatic tone of his texts, made impossible to connect these texts with quotidian life, with the routines in which our existences are unraveled. It was impossible to ordinarily go to work, or even travel, with his texts in the pocket.

The epic and programmatic tones had been auratically incorporated to his writing not only thanks to his own efforts, but also to Sartre's, since in the well-known preface to *The Wretched Of The Earth,* the writer marked it as an enemy's book. This became a fiction that would lengthily affect the readings of the time by taking it away from the possibility of approaching and perceiving it as part of everyday life, which never asks structural or decisive questions, but is solved in a person's micro experiences. What is more, his writing turned strange to the readers as this book became something like a tool to examine the political consciousness of metropolitan intellectuals,[10] assertively bringing it back to the scholarly community (Catelli, 2013).

The destiny of monuments, though insignificant, is almost always quite different from the one imagined by their authors, and by their most conspicuous readers, like in this case. Though it can be deduced, what Fanon expected is unknown. However, it is certainly known what the readers do and what they did with his texts, as these are the material they work with.

It seems a closure of his writing, in philosophical terms, occurred. It was provoked not only by the complexity of the contexts in which it circulated, but mainly by the fact that it remained linked to a predominant perspective of the time, which exhausted the reservoir of questions about its distinctiveness. Therefore, it could not be considered in other conversations, not even in an almost surreptitious register.[11] This is intentionally observed, though being conscious of the register at play. Fanon's irruption in the Latin American emancipatory theories during the sixties and seventies never reached its articulation with the processes of racialization that his own writing suggested to study. On the contrary, his participation was admitted due to the filiations with the emancipatory

---

9. The reflections brought into play in this passage are provoked by Laura Catelli's suggestive text' La ciudad letrada y los estudios coloniales: perspectivas descoloniales desde la 'ciudad real' [The lettered city and the colonial studies: decolonial perspectives from the 'real city'] (2013). Catelli explores the limits that the postcolonial studies field faces, even today, due to the little attention paid to Walter Mignolo's call on semiotics made in the nineties. She works on the basis of the problematization of Angel Rama's notion of lettered city, in conversation with the colonial city and the colonial bodies racialized by Fanon. She points to them as objects of a possible semiosis that can give an account of the repertoires they play while bringing to the forefront those materialities and practices they evoke and refer to. When Fanon writes analytically, he works like the one described by Catelli, as he offers a world of signs, representations and practices that overflow the walls of the lettered city. However, Fanon's register is ambivalent. In *The Wretched of the Earth,* he addresses the intellectuals and urges them to submerge in the materiality of life. At the same time, he tries to restitute an *ethos* which metaphorically seems to send the intellectuals to the lettered city.

10. Judith Butler runs with this idea in one of the texts presented and analyzed in Akal Edition of*Piel negra, máscaras blancas* [Black skin, white masks] (2009: 199).

11. Though the focus has been mostly placed on my work experience in Argentina, it is necessary to remark that the circulation of Fanon's texts varied from country to country. Javier Arévalo Méndez's thesis on Cultural Studies (Universidad Javeriana), provides a map of the work by Colombian black intellectuals reflected on the problem of whitetude in contact with the Fanonian readings. Among them, it is possible to highlight the reference to Sancy de Jesús Mosquera Pérez (1954-2011), a Chocoan intellectual, founder of Franz Fanon Centre, which disappeared after his death. (Arévalo Méndez, 2015: 12).

discourses and the revolution, rather than the narrow analytics of the modes of production of the racial differences in colonial contexts. A problem for some readers in Colombia and Brazil was the issue of maintaining the racial dimension of the Fanonian criticism, though kept as subject categories, mainly anchored in essentialist registers or in strong ontologies of identity. Nevertheless, the resonance of the racial dimensions of the Fanonian analytics on colonial society and the modern subjectivity taken from the group of interventions of the time will remain occluded by a persistent and resistant image of the heuristic potential of his writing cancelled or sealed in the past of its emergence.[12]

Stated in a more radical way, his writings went to the archives of materials with which the history of critical thought of colonialism was eventually to be constructed. However, it is necessary to refer to this as a closed file, indifferent to new configurations.

It is well-known that the problem of reading practices is that they derive towards the scene in which the text and its scaffolds are the object of a specific and contextual performativity anchored in concrete materialities. Though this dimension will not be discussed, it is worth considering it in order to think about the previously mentioned problem of closed archives. The hypothesis of the problem focuses on the production of a sort of double closure of the Fanonian writing. The main closure derived from the bonds between the militant practices, between the contexts of 'use' affiliated to the political struggles, and the factual dimension where these texts were woven in a fabric from small publishers connected with highly-politicized reading groups, to journal and magazines of radical criticism embracing certain key concepts to contemporary thought. Terms or markers like 'Third World', 'alienation', 'revolution', 'liberation', among the most conspicuous ones, were key. They characterized the prominent points of the heterogeneous discursive practices, and at the same time, in relatively rigid interpretative codes, they integrated writings like Fanon's. These dimensions delineated clear limits in Argentina. A comparative work needs to be done in order to know whether in other sociocultural spaces similarities were possible[13] or not. Fanon's writing remained relatively circumscribed to this series of markers. The second closure, which deserves being considered for the purpose of analysis, has to do with the contexts of reading and circulation, where his poetics was unconsidered or sometimes seen irrelevant to the core of the categorical and conceptual discussion that these terms represented. On the contrary, these poetics emerged as an obstacle during the debates about Fanon's writing. Depending on the conditions, some associations were made between the revolutionary leader, with a Che Guevara's style, and the romantic positions that were born in those relations.[14] It is worth noticing here that at the beginning of the eighties, his poetics, which had once worked as a source of inspiration, was the one that

---

12. In order to be precise, I remark that, though my work focuses on readings made in Argentina, after preliminary explorations, it is possible to intuit certain similarities in other contexts. The case of Brazil is referred to in notes 12 and 15.

13. In order to introduce a contrast with the case of Brazil, see Guimarães (2008).

14. This is a classical movement that Albert Memmi expresses in 'The impossible life of Franz Fanon'. (1973)

kept apart readers and exegetes when the revision of the instruments of analysis came into crisis with the criticism of modernity.

Anyway, a trajectory of this type is not fair on the heterogeneity of the articulations that Fanon's writing puts into play. However, it is interesting to observe that in the context of its uses, for example in Brazil and in Argentina, Fanon was introduced by Sartre. From there, it was welcomed warmly by Glauber Rocha's cinematographic production and Paulo Freire's pedagogy in the late sixties (Guimarães, 2008: 100-107)[15] and it found strong echoes in Renate Zahar's work in the seventies.[16]

To sum up, in this research it is estimated that the weak integration of Fanon's writing into the context of knowledge of the social, professionally practiced, affected his writing by turning it into a potent uniqueness and, at the same time, into a minor part in the social sciences and humanities. On this plane, its destiny was, at best, its stabilization in the archives as a source.

These annotations and suggestions contribute to understanding how Fanon's work fell into a kind of oblivion. The worlds and ways his writing referred to did not resonate with the same effect.

## Part Two

By the early eighties, the criticism of modernity, mainly in the academic arena, became stronger in the space opened by postcolonial criticism. This was seen as a kind of novelty whose center remained in the reflection on those conditions created for the emergence of subjectivities in the context of imperial, colonial and modern national histories.

This movement brought with it poststructuralist theory, which placed the issue of difference as its central nucleus. It called into question the figures around whom explanations about the modern historical subject had been organized in most trajectories of philosophy and other fields during the twentieth century. Nonetheless, postcolonial criticism, though in its specificity and its general dimension, introduced what could be considered a 'difference of the difference'. Not only did it endorse the thought of difference, which could be characterized as a reflection on the modes of subjectivity production, but it also introduced the colonial dimension of the global contemporary culture as a second level in these modes. It was global since it detected an affection that was not to be limited to one region or a unique group of stories only. That colonial dimension transformed the criticism of modernity into the criticism of forms and configurations that colonized the modern experience, and also into the criticism of the conceptual limits represented in statistical terms.[17] In other words, a mark was

---

15. For a more extensive reading about the relation between Freire and Fanon, see Fernández Mouján (2017).
16. For a recent research on the reception of Fanon in Brazil, maybe the most important study in Portuguese up to the moment, see Faustino Mendes (2015).
17. This means that concepts and categories act per se in most social theory as the idea of representativity of a statistical sample does though statistics have very important methodological and conceptual qualms. It does not immediately

woven. It was a mark that defined the complete field of reflections on colonialism, namely the low representativeness of concepts and categories of social theory when aiming at expressing or explaining what is subsumed in the modern forms of social experience.

There were several consequences of this movement. Particularly, there were two that are fundamental for the comprehension of the re-introduction of Fanon into global discussions. The first consequence has been already mentioned. It is the evidence of a limit which could be referred to as the ethnocentricity of the social theory (this denomination is assumed when describing a set of complex intellectual practices of specialized knowledge about the social). It put in place a second order of importance to the processes that were not the object or source of reflection, particularly those texts, stories, narrations that did not conform to the library authorized by the theory. In this sense, Fanon's case is paradigmatic. The second dimension has to do with representation, though in a different way. When thinking about the colonial problem as a kind of civilization failure,[18] almost as Césaire had noticed it on the initial pages of *Discourse On Colonialism*, postcolonial criticism as movement did not only point out that the diverse interventions in the global arena of the social theory limited the representations to a relatively narrow cultural sphere, but it also brought into discussion the figure of representation itself, though in a different way this criticism had been processed in the philosophical field.

The difference is, specifically, the 'difference of the difference'. The proceeding did not precisely aim at involving all the interventions in the postcolonial field. Nonetheless, it eventually did, and provoked a distinctive configuration of archives and the organization of the social theory library on a different basis. When postcolonial criticism asked about the representativeness of concepts and categories, and perceived representation as a historically as well as culturally situated process—which could be described as practice affecting the configuration of the archives—it consequently altered the epistemic privileges and destabilized the assertion of the unquestioned character of the universal in each discipline. If difference had become the main theme in poststructuralist trajectories, with postcolonial criticism, it acquired a new meaning since it implied a kind of curl within a curl. Not only did it displace the ontological and teleological dimensions of concepts and categories, either in the order of language or in the order of the systematization of theoretical thinking, but it also analyzed them on the basis of colonialism, a process external to the dominion they conformed. By so doing, the structure of the representation that organized them was unveiled.

---

infer from a sample representing a total group of a population of data. If it did, it would know what they are about, and then, there would not be much to do. Inferences on this plane are always threatened by this paradox. However, in almost all modern disciplines of knowledge that work the social as their object, most of their concepts and categories have acted, and in some disciplines they still do it, as if this paradox did not exist. This is highly marked in humanities. It is as if, for example, qualitative and quantitative differences that put into action all the colonial processes were only secondary and subsidiary phenomena of a central core of temporality and of social experience, so well-known that is naturalized.

18. This refers to the famous third paragraph in Aimé Césaire's *Discourse on Colonialism*. It indicates that the bourgeois regime in Europe has been unable to solve neither the proletarian problem nor the colonial one.

Through these lines of thought, it seems sensible that the writings, which had been closed or sealed with their contexts of emergency or the moral and political urges of a time, became active parts of reflection and abandoned the biographical register in which they had been frequently approached.[19]

Obviously, this allowed not only the incorporation of eccentric writings to the canon, but also the expansion of theoretical and epistemological imagination. It was not simply the return of what had been oppressed in knowledge but of different ways for the configuration of the research arena and its materials.

In a reversible manner, these ways were also possible thanks to the dissemination of the writings similar to those by Fanon. Beyond the operations that placed them as a kind of epochal closure, the writings, or research material, became a prolific field for cultural imagination open to new relations. The most significant one was undoubtedly that of racialization processes, which Fanon had explored with strong phenomenological tones and had been unnoticed by the perspectives centered on the discussions about the Third World revolution.

This last dimension was likely the most influential on the readings about Fanon. During the eighties, these came mainly from North American academia, which Latin American scholars came in contact with.[20]

Thence, Fanon gradually returned to the Latin American arena. He did so together with the postcolonial readings and the epistemological decolonial turn, which converted his work into a unique piece in the decolonizing library. He was invoked in the conversations of postcolonial theory with the registers of the philosophies of liberation, which have always had great intellectual relevance on the continent. It was a return vested with the qualities of an emergence, since the problems that this writing allowed to relieve articulated themselves in a very problematic confluence of postcolonial criticism, decolonial criticism and the registers of a postcolonial phenomenology which unfolded among the thinkers of the Caribbean during the nineties.[21]

In this context, the most outstanding problem in Fanon's writing was undoubtedly race, not as a study issue, but as a form of conceptualizing the processes of racialization inscribed in most social relations in the region, in

---

19. Though this problem is not approached here, it is worth noticing how writings which are considered eccentric in relation to the intellectual and conceptual canons of some disciplines, are many times integrated to these by means of the biographical effect. In other words, the peculiarity of the author's life provides the legitimacy for his/her admission rather than the complexity of the writings. It is frequent to observe this procedure, which is no more than a sample of the geopolitics of knowledge taking place in the contemporary world. Hence, the biography indicates the complexity of a life, and becomes a factor of stabilization when these authors' writings represent an epistemological risk to the discursive order of a discipline, its modes of enunciation and its epistemic privileges. Exaggeratedly, it could be said that the biography works as a Freudian fetish destined to decrease the anxiety that produces the difference. This turn has been thought by Bhabha to observe the way in which the colonial discourse stabilizes, by means of the fetish, the racial difference (sexual in Freud), and therefore reduces the anguish it produces. The bibliography does not present any similar exercise indicating something alike in relation to the biography, but it suggests that the incorporation to an order may occur, in this disciplinary case, because the universal is stabilized in it and admits the difference only as a colourful unfolding of the difference.

20. For detailed successive waves of works about Fanon, see Gordon (2015) and De Oto (2003).

21. Somehow, the Caribbean Philosophical Association and its congresses, which regularly populate the academic scenery of the last fifteen years with Fanonian issues and problems, had the base mark of that colonial phenomenology. However, this is not the only philosophical register at play in it. In order to see the nature of the Association, visit its web page: http://www.caribbeanphilosophicalassociation.org/

anthropological and sociological terms as well as in historical and epistemological ones.

This dimension certainly molded the way of prioritizing the categories of socio-historical analysis with strength. Therefore, it did not revolve around the analysis of a stated—rather than demonstrated—process by which the colonial societies could be explained in a kind of history subsumed in a global revolutionary time. At the same time, it did not alter the configuration of knowledge provided by such notions. Apart from showing itself absent in a large part of the specialized literature, the issue of race in Fanon mainly exposed that this absence articulated a conceptual and categorical hierarchy, and according to this, it arranged the bodies. To the thematic problem, the ontological issue was added, and to it, the epistemological one. Almost immediately, reading Fanon meant dealing with all these absences seen as constitutive of social thought. In that framework, Fanon turned a specific warning that claimed there was a structural flaw in our archives and conceptual reservoirs. In his writing, race and the processes of racialization acquired this status. From then onwards, towards our present, the accurate emergence of race in his writing and in the genealogical nodes of the postcolonial and decolonial registers constituted a claim that suggested shaking the epistemological foundation which had been organized by the closed archives of colonialism and social theory. Hence, the work needed to be done was to open these archives for new heuristic, hermeneutic and configurational operations, and therefore, to reconstruct the archives in a way different from that of colonialism.

## Acknowledgements

A first version of this work was published in the magazine *Intersticios de la política y de la cultura latinoamericana*, [Interstices of Latin American politics and culture: 6: 11). Reproduced here with the permission of the editor.

## Bibliography

Alessandrini, A. C., eds. 1999. *Frantz Fanon. Critical Perspectives*. London, New York: Routledge.

Arévalo Méndez, J. A. 2015. 'Amir Smith Córdoba. Del blanqueamiento a la negritud.' Tesis de Maestría en Estudios Culturales [Amir Smith Córdoba. From whitening to negritud. Thesis of Master Studies in Cultural Studies], Dir. Eduardo Restrepo.Bogotá: Universidad Javeriana, 12.

Burgos, R. 2004. *Los Gramscianos argentinos. Cultura y política en la experiencia de Pasado y Presente* [The Argentine Gramscian. Culture and Politics in the Experience of 'Past and Present' Magazine]. Buenos Aires: Siglo XXI.

Butler, J. 2009. 'Violencia, no violencia. Sartre en torno a Fanon' [Violence, Nonviolence: Sartre on Fanon], *Piel negra, máscaras blancas* [Black Skin, White Masks], 193–216.Translated by I. Álvarez Moreno, P. Monleón Alonso, and A. Useros Martín. Madrid: Akal.

Catelli, L. 2013. 'La ciudad letrada y los estudios coloniales: perspectivas descoloniales desde la 'ciudad real' [The Lettered City and the Colonial Studies: Decolonial Perspectives from the 'Real City']. *Vanderbilt e-Journal of Luso-Hispanic Studies* 9: 56–76.

Cesaire, A. 2000. *Discourse on Colonialism*. Translated by J. Pinkham. New York: Monthly Review Press.

Cortés, M. 2015. *Un nuevo marxismo para América Latina, José Aricó: traductor, editor, intelectual* [A New Marxism for Latin America, José Aricó: translator, editor, intelectual]. Buenos Aires: Siglo XXI.

De Oto, A. 2003. *Frantz Fanon. Política y poética del sujeto poscolonial* [Franz Fanon. Politics and Poetics of the Postcolonial Subject]. México D.F.: El Colegio de México.

_____. 2013. 'Usos de Fanon. Un recorrido por tres lecturas' [Uses of Fanon. An Itinerary in Three Readings]. *Cuyo, Anuario de Filosofía Argentina y Americana* 30 (7): 35–60.

De Oto, A., and Katzer, L. 2014. 'Tras las huellas del acontecimiento, Entre la zona de no ser y la ausencia radical' [After the Traces of the Event, Between the Zone of No-being and its Radical Absence], *Utopía y Praxis Latinoamericana* 19 (65): 53–64.

Fanon, F. 1963. *The Wretched of the Earth*, preface by Jean Paul Sartre. Translated by C. Farrington. New York: Grove Press.

Faustino Mendes, D. 2015. 'Por que Fanon, Por que agora': Frantz Fanon e os fanonismos no Brasil.' Tesis de doctorado en Sociologia [Why Fanon, Why Fanon Now: Franz Fanon and fanonisms in Brazil, Doctoral Thesis in Sociology], Universidade Federal de São Carlos, São Carlos.

Fernández Mouján, I. 2017. *Elogio de Paulo Freire* [Tribute to Paulo Freire]. Buenos Aires: Noveduc.

Foucault, M. 1970 [2005]. *The Order of Things. An Archeology of the Human Sciences* (Tavistock English Translation from French). London: Routledge.

García Canclini, N. 1995. *Consumidores y ciudadanos: conflictos multiculturales de la globalización* [Consumers and Citizens: Multicultural Conflicts of Globalization], 13–28. México: Grijalbo.

Gibson, N. C., eds. 1999. *Rethinking Fanon. The Continuing Dialogue*. Nueva York: Humanities Books.

Gordon, L. 2015. *What Fanon Said: A Philosophical Introduction to His Life and Thought*. Nueva York: Fordham University Press.

Gordon, L., Sharply-Whiting, T., and White, Renée, T. 1996. *Fanon: A Critical Reader*. Oxford: Blackwell Publishers.

Guimarães, A. S. A. 2008. 'Recepção de Fanon no Brasil e a identidade negra' [Reception of Fanon in Brazil and Black Identity]. *Novos estudos* 81: 99–114.

Katzer, L., and De Oto, A. 2013. 'Intervenciones espectrales o variaciones sobre el asedio' [Spectral Interventions (or variations on sieging)], *Tabula Rasa* 18: 127–143.

Maíz, C. 2014. 'El manifiesto: expresión apocalíptica de lo moderno,' De Marx al posboom latinoamericano' [The Manifesto: Apocalyptic Expression of the

Modern, From Marx to the Latin American post-boom]. *Cuadernos del CILHA* 15 (1): 73–91.

Memmi, A. 1973. 'The Impossible Life of Frantz Fanon.' Translated by T. Cassirer and G. Twomey. *The Massachusetts Review* 14 (1): 9–39. Accessed July 15, 2020. www.jstor.org/stable/25088315.

Ricca, G. 2016. *Nada por perdido, Política en José. M. Aricó* [Nothing lost, Politics in José M. Aricó]. Río Cuarto: UniRío.

Salazar Bondy, A. 1968. '*¿Existe una filosofía de nuestra América?*' [Is there a Latin American philosophy?]. México: Siglo XXI.

_____. 1974. 'Diálogos indianos entre Bartolomé de las Casas, Frantz Fanon, el cacique Hatuey y Ginés de Sepúlveda' [Indian dialogues among Bartolomé de las Casas, Franz Fanon, Cacique Hatuey and Ginés de Sepúlveda]. *Crisis* (12): 37–39.

Zea, L. 1969. *La filosofía americana como filosofía sin más* [Latin American Philosophy as Simply Philosophy]. México: Siglo XXI.

# PROMOTING SEDITION: THE IRISH LANGUAGE REVIVAL IN THE NORTH OF IRELAND—POWER, RESISTANCE AND DECOLONIZATION

Feargal Mac Ionnrachtaigh

## Introduction

It is worth stating in introducing this paper that I'm greatly indebted to the resourceful Fanonian intellectual Nigel Gibson, the driving force behind this timely publication, who persevered with insisting on my inclusion in this wonderful collection despite my having missed countless deadlines. I first met Nigel at the Fanon 50th anniversary conference in Paris in 2012 and was subsequently hosted by him in Boston a couple of times thereafter where I spoke to his students about Fanonian practices in Ireland. We had many deep discussions on Fanon where Nigel helped shape and inform my developing understanding of Fanon's radical humanism and his transformative philosophy of liberation.

This paper represents the work of an engaged activist involved in what Gramsci (1971: 405) called the Philosophy of Praxis 'that is full of contradictions, in which the philosopher himself (or herself) understood individually and as an entire social group, not only grasps the contradictions' but also understands his/her role 'as an element of the contradiction and elevates this element to a principle of knowledge and therefore action'. Fanon likewise emphasized the link between knowledge and action since without the 'knowledge of the practice of action' deriving from 'living inside history' nothing remains but a fancy-dress parade (1968: 147). This dual-developmental role, thus, constitutes a defining feature of critical social research where 'it moves beyond the resources of theory into praxis, recognizing the self-as-academic as the self-as-participant' (Scraton, 2007: 240).

I am a product of the anti-colonial struggle and language revival. Born into an activist republican family during the 1981 Hunger Strike, my father had learnt Irish and become politically conscious while interned in the early seventies. Both my parents played prominent roles in the Anti-H-Block movement and subsequent struggles within the West Belfast republican community. In the late 1960's, a cohort of radical activists built their own self-help Irish language speaking neighborhood, before establishing an illegal Irish-language 'hedge school'. My parents chose to send me to this school which to their minds symbolized a community-based manifestation of decolonizing resistance.

My secondary schooling also had particularly formative impact. I attended *Meánscoil Feirste*, the North's first Irish-medium secondary school, which met with outright hostility from the Tory government in London. As pupils, we engaged in a concerted and ultimately successful international campaign for recognition, which arrived as part of the peace process. I had always understood the link between the prison struggle and language revival, as many of my class-mates' parents has been imprisoned during the conflict. Similarly, a few of my most influential teachers had learned Irish in Long Kesh.

On 11 January 1998, loyalist paramilitaries shielded by the British security apparatus, murdered my eldest brother as part of a campaign of terror against the nationalist community. A well-respected community youth worker Terry Óg's murder triggered a wave of emotion, with an estimated ten thousand people attending the funeral (see McKittrick et al, 1999; De Baróid, 2000). Terry Óg's life, the trauma of his murder, as well as the public expression of solidarity, iden-tity and community in its aftermath, indelibly shaped my own personal and political journey. It compelled me to better understand the processes of historic injustices, and structural inequality that affect communities like my own in West Belfast. Ultimately, it inspired my grassroots community activism centered on the Irish language revival.

My research sought to understand what motivated defenceless and brutalized young prisoners, confined all day in a cell covered with their own excrement with only a blanket for clothes, to both learn and utilize the Irish language as a means of struggle? Similarly, what inspired unemployed parents in deprived working-class nationalist areas under British military siege, to send their children to an Irish school? Furthermore, how do we explain the contemporary radical surge in the Irish language movement? Much of this discussion brings us ultimately to the question of ideology.

In its widest definition, 'ideology' describes the process by which people understand and develop perspectives on the world around them (Eccleshall, 1992: 24). In terms of counter hegemonic ideologies, George Rudé (1980) identified an inherent 'sort of 'mother's milk' ideology, based on direct experience, oral tra-dition or folk memory and not learned by listening to sermons or speeches or reading books' (Rudé, 1980: 28). This inherent ideology interacts with 'ideas and beliefs that are 'derived' or 'borrowed' from others'. These can often overlap with the 'inherent' beliefs of one generation becoming ingrained in basic group cul-ture thus inculcating beliefs 'that were originally derived from outside by an ear-lier one' (Rudé, 1980).

The potential for such 'derived' elements to be 'effectively absorbed' depends on how well the ground has been prepared in specific historical contexts (Rudé, 1980: 35). I argue that this theory of ideological development elucidates the growth of the Irish language revival and the plethora of grassroots campaigns and regenerative, decolonizing projects emanating from the bottom up. In prioritiz-ing the previously occluded narratives of activists, 'history-makers' and what rad-ical Brazilian educationalist Paulo Freire calls 'agents for change', this paper aims to contribute to 'an insurrection of subjugated knowledge' (Pilger, 2006: 13) and to Fanon's philosophy of liberation. These activists' accounts, however, could not be meaningfully understood or considered in isolation from a wider historical context that explores the relevant economic, political and socio-cultural structures that shaped Ireland's brutal colonization and its location within a wider understanding of imperialism and *cultural shift in colonial and neo-colonial contexts*.

## Imperialism, Colonialism, Neo-colonialism and Decolonization

Imperial ambitions shaped an expansionist impulse in England and other 'technologically superior' western powers. 'Colonialism', therefore, 'almost always [constituted] a consequence of 'imperialism', forging processes wherein 'one state controls the effective political sovereignty of another political society', through force, political collaboration and/or economic, social, or cultural dependence (Said, 1993: 8). Imperialism thus represents 'the most powerful force in world history over the last four or five centuries, carving up whole continents while oppressing indigenous peoples and obliterating entire civilizations', fostering a 'process whereby the dominant politico-economic interests of one nation expropriate for their own enrichment the land, labor, raw materials, and markets of another people' (Parenti, 1995: 1). This economic process typically found expression in racist and supremacist ideology (Curtis, 1984: 65). Furthermore, Aimé Césaire described how 'millions' were 'skilfully injected with fear, inferiority complexes, trepidation, servility, despair, abasement'. Indeed, Fanon (1961: 171) commented how, 'deep in the minds of the natives':

> As if to show the totalitarian character of colonial exploitation the settler paints the native as a sort of quintessence of evil. Native society is not simply described as a society lacking in values, but also the negation of values ... the enemy of values ... the absolute evil ... corrosive ... destroying ... disfiguring (1961: 32)

This mental subordination is unleashed through a cultural bomb, which delegitimizes identity amongst the colonized. In his seminal work on colonial oppression, Alberto Memmi stressed how cultural colonization involved a wholesale transformation on the part of its victims:

> The crushing of the colonized is included among the colonizer's values. As soon as the colonized adopts these values, he similarly adopts his own condemnation. In order to free himself, at least so he believes, he agrees to destroy himself...just as many people avoid showing off their poor relations, the colonized in the throes of assimilation hides his past, his traditions, in fact all his origins which have become ignominious (1965: 165).

This phenomenon emerged most clearly where 'colonized people' found themselves 'face to face with the language of the civilizing nation; that is, with the culture of the mother tongue' (Fanon, 1970: 14). Writing of Kenya in the 1950s.

Ngugi wa Thiong'o (1997: 9) described how 'the physical violence of the battlefield was followed by the psychological violence of the classroom', wherein language became 'the means of spiritual subjugation.' This manifested itself in imperial education systems, where linguistic domination epitomized colonial power structures. Indeed, Britain outstripped 'the other empires in the reach of its [educational] ambition, the imperial language was represented as carrying its liberal and decent qualities on to the world stage in order to take its rightful place' (Crowley, 1996: 48).

The British had perfected compulsory Anglicization over a hundred years earlier, in their 'first colony', Ireland, drafting 'a blueprint for the consequent models of language and colonialism practiced throughout the world' (Crowley, 1996: 4). After 1831, the Irish national school system instituted a regime of corporal punishment to prevent the speaking of Irish. Irish people's active involvement not only constituted psychological transformation but also facilitated the wider imperial aim of creating culturally English, indigenous, colonial élites (Anderson, 1991: 93). In effect, colonialism convinces its victims that this process is 'natural' or 'legitimate', rather than engineered by the colonizer and unequal power relations. As a result, 'symbolic violence' cultivates complicity and implicit consent, encouraging the native population 'to collaborate in the destruction of their (own) instruments of expression' (Bourdieu, 1991:45). Predictably then, the colonized attribute greater worth to the 'dominant language', leading them, by necessity, to become active participants in jettisoning their traditional cultures (May, 2002: 310).

Neo-colonialism describes the continued economic exploitation of former colonies, which reached acute form under neoliberal globalization. European imperial powers adopted neocolonialism after World War II, by grudgingly replacing blatant colonial rule for 'independence', while maintaining control of profitable resources (Parenti, 1995: 8). 'Decolonization' arguably represents a 'misleading term', implying 'that Britain voluntarily gave up formal control over its colonies, when the reality was that it was forced out of many'. Nevertheless, 'decolonization' ensured that 'independent' countries 'continued to allow British companies to exploit their economic resources' (Curtis, 2003: 236). Furthermore, neocolonialism entailed 'the removal of a conspicuously intrusive colonial rule', thereby obstructing 'nationalist elements within the previously colonized countries' in mobilizing 'anti-imperialist sentiments' (Parenti, 1995: 8). More crucially, neocolonialism also nurtures a native political elite, leaving the imperialist interest 'free to concentrate on accumulating capital—which is all they really want to do' (Parenti, 1995: 8). According to Ghanaian intellectual, Kwame Nkrumah (1964: 101):

> Colonialism is crude, essentially overt, and apt to be overcome by a purposeful concert of national effort. In neo-colonialism, however, the people are divided from their leaders and, instead of providing true leadership and guidance which is informed at every point by the ideal of the general welfare, leaders come to neglect the very people who put them in power

and incautiously become instruments of suppression on behalf of the neo-colonialists.

Fanon (1961) named this grouping the 'nationalist bourgeoisie', who rode to power through the cross-class 'national liberation struggle' before reconciling with the exploitative colonial economic regime after formal 'independence'. Nevertheless, resistance continued amongst 'working people, peasantry and proletariat' against the 'flag-waving native ruling classes' whom they denounced as 'collaborators of imperialism' (Thiong'o, 1997: 2). Modern South Africa represents a case study in neocolonialism, where the 'symbolic trappings' of freedom and democracy exist within the most unequal society on earth (Pilger, 2006; Klein, 2007; Gibson, 2012).

In Ireland, 'neo-colonial international forms of cultural dominance' compounded the historical legacy of English colonialism. The island's partition in 1920 established a northern settler-colonial statelet and a socially conservative, culturally protectionist neo-colonial southern state, where reactionary native élites donned 'the gowns and wigs of the British system... employing the unmodified devices of the old regime upon themselves' (Ó Croidheáin, 2006: 17). Southern Ireland exhibited the customary neocolonial traits of civil war, economic dependency and a 'retreat from revolution' (Kiberd, 1995: 263). As such, the Irish language revival was stripped of its emancipatory content and manipulated in 'the interests of the propertied classes' to strengthen the grip of a reactionary establishment linked to the autocratic Catholic Church (Ó Croidheáin's, 2006: 161).

A neocolonial reading of modern Ireland demands 'that each state's claim to the monopoly of violence within their territories be rigorously thought through in light of their own very arbitrary and violent foundations'. Notably, 'violence' here does not equate to armed insurrection, but the structural legacy of neocolonialism:

> the phenomenon of violence must be understood as constitutive of social relations within the colonial capitalist state, whose practices institutionalise a violence which, though cumulative, daily, and generally unspectacular, is normalised precisely by its long duration and chronic nature. Unlike insurgency, which is usually represented as sporadic and of the nature of a temporary 'crisis', the violence of the state operates through its institutions continuously, producing the material effects of poverty, unemployment, sickness, depopulation, and emigration. That these phenomena are generally not seen as state-mediated effects of capitalist and colonial violence forces us to recognise that the violence of the state belongs in its capacity to control representation, both political and cultural (Lloyd, 2003: 48).

This crucial control of 'representation' allows mainstream academia to obscure Ireland's colonial experience within an uncritical narrative of modernization, which also includes a 'literally state-censored media' that 'celebrate the passage from Ireland's domination by British colonial capital to its domination by the participation in the neocolonial circuits of global capitalism' (Lloyd, 2003: 48).

Furthermore, with respect to continued language shift and indigenous cultural decline, 'Anglo-American mass culture and multinational industry provides the engine' for English to gain 'dominance in global culture' (Lloyd, 2003: 48). Internationally, Anglo-American economic and political dominance elevates English as the language of global Capital. Furthermore, its monopoly of film/media, science, technology and the information/Internet age creates a 'rationalisation process whereby the unequal power relations between English and other languages are explained and legitimated'. 'English Linguistic Imperialism' or 'Linguicism' perpetuates social, economic, political and cultural inequalities between English and other languages and their speakers (Phillipson, 1992: 287—288).

The work of Michael Krauss (1992) predicts that, given the current rate of language shift, ninety percent of the world's languages will be either lost or forced into the final stages of decline during the twenty-first century, mostly through contact with a majority language within the structures of neoliberal and neocolonial domination, including the 'cultural nerve gas' of electronic mass media (Krauss, 1992: 8). Nevertheless, minoritized cultures and languages will 'continue so patently to play a significant (even central) part in many of the political disputes in the world today' (May, 2002: 316) because global capitalism conditions this very linguicide.

Processes of colonialism invariably inspired struggles for decolonization. This reference to 'decolonization', however, refers not to the granting of 'formal independence', but rather to 'authentic decolonisation' or the generation of the strategies of survival and resistance amongst colonized or subordinate groups (Caute, 1970: 52).

The colonial process generated Memmi's 'mythical portraits' of the colonized as 'innately lazy, barbarous, bestial, amoral, bellicose etc.' (Mac Síomóin, 1994: 45). Hence, decolonization typically commenced with an inspiring counter narrative. The appeal to 'national consciousness' entailed a battle for 'legitimacy and cultural primacy' (Said, 1993: 239). Such hegemonic mirroring therefore constituted a survival strategy against the reduction of the colonized to abject material and psychological poverty. In Ireland, academic criticisms of such decolonizing narratives as simplistic, mythological, essentialist and even 'racialist' (Comerford, 2003: 141), consciously avoid the colonial context that conditioned them.

Unsurprisingly, 'culture' becomes a dominant paradigm of decolonization and its aim to 'reclaim, rename, and re-inhabit' a 'decolonized identity' along with the closely associated 'redevelopment of the native language' (Said, 1993: 273). The liberating aspect of such a linguistic revival, according to Memmi (1965: 151) stems from the willingness to make sacrifices in the process: 'he will forgo the use of the colonizer's language, even if all the locks of the country turn with that key; he will change the signs and highway marking, even if he is the first to be inconvenienced.' The revolutionary humanism implicit in such agency and the transformation of the colonized subject into decolonized human being represented a central project of Ireland's revolutionary project.

Under colonial domination, any attempts by the colonized to reclaim 'a voice' immediately involve 'reclaiming, reconnecting and reordering those ways of knowing which were submerged, hidden or driven underground' (Tuhiwai Smith, 1999: 69). Fanon (1961: 193) recommended that native intellectuals rehabilitate and produce a 'national culture' as 'a special battleground' in a three-stage struggle. Firstly, the intellectual acknowledges and rejects their own cultural, colonial assimilation. The intellectual then returns to their roots, by recognizing and recalling their historic past. In the final phase, the intellectual aims to revive and awaken their people and realign themselves with their cause while producing a relevant yet revolutionary national literature (Fanon, 1961: 178-9).

Moreover, Fanon argued that any effort to awaken 'national culture' also 'means in the first place to fight for the liberation of the nation, that material keystone which makes the building of a culture possible. There is no other fight for culture which can develop apart from the popular struggle'. Thus, national culture represents the 'whole body of efforts made by a people in the sphere of thought to describe, justify and praise the action through which that people has created itself and keeps itself in existence' and 'the most complete and obvious cultural manifestation' of the struggle. Fanon's theoretical template clearly elucidated priors and future anti-colonial struggles, with relevance to the last century of revolutionary struggle in Ireland (Fanon, 1961: 187-97).

Similarly, Fanon's controversial and widely misunderstood conceptualization of revolutionary violence speaks to the Irish experience, where the cultural revival culminated in the 1916 Easter Rising. This trend was to extent personified in Pádraig Pearse who wrote that 'bloodshed is a cleansing and sanctifying thing and the nation which regards it as the final horror has lost its manhood. There are many things more horrible than bloodshed; and slavery is one of them' (Rees, 1998: 197). Fanon (1961: 74) used similar language, 'at the level of individuals, violence is a cleansing force. It frees the native from his inferiority complex and from his despair and inaction; it makes him fearless and restores his self-respect.' How is non-violence possible under a situation conditioned by systemic colonial violence?

It's worth distinguishing between 'nationalist independence' phases of anti-colonial struggle and decolonization itself which represents an ongoing process. Independence is not 'a magic ritual but an indispensable condition for men and women to live in true liberation, in other words to master all the resources necessary for a radical transformation of society' (Fanon, 1961: 74). Fanon's was a revolutionary humanism reflected in the revolutionary tendency within the Irish struggle for freedom. Both acknowledged the necessity for national liberation under the colonial regime but sought to expand beyond the narrow confines of nationalism, which if not 'explained, enriched, deepened, if it does not very quickly turn into a social and political consciousness, into humanism, then it leads to a dead end' (Fanon, 1961: 74).

# Retreat, Resistance and Revolution in Ireland

> *Decolonisation never takes place unnoticed, for it influences individuals and modifies them fundamentally. It transforms spectators crushed with their inessentiality into privileged actors, with the grandiose glare of history's floodlights upon them.*
> —Fanon, *The Wretched of the Earth*

English intervention in Ireland from the sixteenth century onwards, established a precedent for a process of political, cultural, and economic subjugation that would reach global proportions in the succeeding centuries. While allowing for variation across space and time, the cultural subordination of the Irish operated within a wider expansionist project based on exploitation and economic profit on an aggressive colonial model that reached its apogee in the vast future empire of the early twentieth century.

The Tudor conquest witnessed 'an outpouring of justifications for colonization and conquest' (Canny, 1973: 581): a moral crusade to civilize the culturally inferior Irish. Moreover, this process provoked a tradition of native resistance, which generated a reciprocal intensification of English brutality, with the colonizer 'now absolved from all restraints in dealing with' the natives (Curtis, 1984: 21). The eventual political subjugation of Gaelic society in the early seventeenth century also represented 'the triumph of the English language, law and politico-administrative institutions throughout Ireland, and the defeat of the whole institutional edifice of the Gaelic political and social order which had been sustained and mediated through the Irish language' (Ó Tuathaigh, 2005: 42).

One of the leading architects of the 1609 Ulster plantation, Sir John Davies, claimed 'that the next generation will in tongue and heart and in every way else become English; so as there will be no difference but the Irish sea betwixt us' (Ó Fiaich, 1969: 105). When Ulster's natives sought to overturn this dispensation in 1641, the resulting Cromwellian campaign ushered in an unprecedented legacy of genocide, destruction, land confiscation and enslavement, based on a religious and racial supremacism 'not far removed from those which Nazis used about Slavs, or white South Africans use about the original inhabitants of their country. In each case, the contempt rationalized the desire to exploit' (Hill, 1970: 113).

The subsequent Williamite wars and early eighteenth-century Penal Laws instituted an English-speaking Protestant hegemony generated a process of language shift to 'English, the language of power and of all the avenues to advancement, soon gathered momentum among those who aspired to improve their condition or to progress and participate fully in the life of the country under the new order' (Ó Tuathaigh, 2005: 42). The Catholic Church essentially facilitated this cultural assimilation in the interests of its own survival and increased status (Crowley, 2000: 84). This assimilationist tendency also found forceful political expression after the 1800 Act of Union amongst leading constitutional nationalist leaders, most notably Daniel O'Connell.

Indeed, the period of the Union witnessed Ireland's use as a laboratory for colonial practices in coercion and education that the British imperial state would employ globally. The National School system's imposition of 'civility' in 1831 marked the formal ostracization of the Irish language under an educational system that Pádraig Pearse would later describe as '*The Murder Machine*'. This is illustrated by the notorious mandatory morning assembly recitation in state classrooms;

> 'I thank the goodness and the grace
> Which on my birth have smiled;
> And made me in these Christian days,
> A happy English child' (Kiberd, 1993: 29)

This Anglicization operated within an environment of violent punishment for children caught speaking Irish both in the classroom and the home, with Irish children internalizing a sense of shame about their indigenous culture and non-literate parents (Nic Craith, 2001: 103).

Nevertheless, more than half the population remained Irish speaking according to the census of 1841 (Hindley, 1990: 15). The Great Hunger 1845-51 effectively 'decimated Irish-speaking Ireland through death and emigration' (Ó Tuathaigh, 2005: 43). This conjunction between economic and cultural domination would operate globally.

Arguably, an ideology of decolonization first appeared in Ireland before the famine with the romantic nationalism of the Young Irelanders and the decolonizing narrative of its leader Thomas Davis, whose manifesto of 'nationhood' employed the concept of hegemonic mirroring by claiming continuity with the past as evidence of a distinct national identity and citing the Irish language as the key to national revival. This would become a source of inspiration for a future generation of cultural and political activists, including Douglas Hyde's whose inspirational decolonizing manifesto led to the formation of the Gaelic League in 1893. The League pro-actively aimed to eradicate inferiority by advocating the revival of the spoken language, a deliberate project of decolonization 'by a group of intellectuals and artists' designed to prevent a 'rupture in cultural continuity' and ultimately undo 'the shame of defeat, dispossession, humiliation and impoverishment—the classic colonial condition' (Ó Tuathaigh, 2005: 47). This followed hard on the heels of Michael Cusack's formation of the Gaelic Athletic Association (GAA) in 1884, which envisaged the emancipation of the Irish poor from the 'dehumanisation, degeneracy and depoliticisation' of colonial sports while providing a 'nationalizing idiom, a symbolic language of identity filling the void created by Anglicisation' (Whelan, 2005: 150).

Within this decolonizing context, the League's radical educational policies emphasized instructional classes as well as more overt political campaigning aimed at increasing the language's status. By 1900 the Irish language had been accepted as a mainstream optional subject within the British National School System, to be taught during school hours. In 1904, the league's bilingual policy for primary schools in Irish speaking areas was accepted (Ó Croidheáin, 2006:

99). Arguably, the largest achievement was when Irish became a compulsory matriculation subject in the National University of Ireland after Gaelic league activists utilized its network of supporters in lobbying the university authorities (Comerford, 2003: 141).

In this period, the Irish language movement naturally converged, as happened in numerous anti-colonial struggles, with the growing forces of nationalism, which led to a dramatic increase in support. Gaelic League branches increased from 120 in 1900 to 985 in 1906, with membership peaking at 75,000. (Hutchinson, 1987: 178-9) In many ways, Pádraig Pearse realized future global paradigms for decolonization in early twentieth-century Ireland. Pearse became the first exponent of Irish-medium education. He established *Scoil Éanna* and *Scoil Íde* to combat the 'mental enslavement' of the national schools, which he argued consolidated British colonialism; 'Education should foster; this education is meant to repress. Education should inspire; this education is meant to tame... The English are too wise a people to educate the Irish in any worthy sense' (Pearse, 1976: 6). Similarly, Pearse gradually synthesized the cultural and political struggles, writing in retrospect that the Irish revolution with the League's formation (Crowley, 2000: 216) Indeed, six of the seven signatories of the 1916 Proclamation were members and all but two of the officers of the League's *Coiste Gnótha* were involved (Ó Huallacháin, 1994: 72).

The cultural revival's centrality to the subsequent independence struggle inspired imprisoned republicans to utilize the language as an educational and political weapon of struggle to challenge 'the colonial ideology of the British empire' (Ó Croidheáin, 2006: 156-157). This set an historical precedent for future generations of struggle. In response, the British Government declared the League 'illegal including its meetings and persons organising them or attending were liable to prosecution by a court under Army jurisdiction'. (Ó Huallacháin, 1994: 75) Paradoxically, this merely strengthened popular resolve and at the first public meeting of Dáil Éireann, held at the Mansion House in Dublin in January 1919, proceedings were conducted primarily in Irish. (Ó Gadhra, 1989: 57)

The eventual triumph of counter-revolutionary forces with the Anglo-Irish Treaty and southern civil war irrevocably divided the language movement with the Gaelic League itself went into sharp decline after 1922 (Lyons, 1973: 636). Despite the revivalist background of many within the pro-Treaty leaderships, the existing pro-British, colonial mentality remained in most state institutions and the revival receded to the background (Ó Snodaigh, 2006: 12). In essence, the Free State 'counter-revolution' retained the same administrative system and ultimately the same personnel as under colonialism. Anglicized Catholicism became the dominant Irish identity as a 'politically conservative government battled against radical ideas in the shape of revolutionary socialism and republicanism' (Ó Croidheáin, 2006: 120). Emptied of its emancipatory potential, right-wing nationalists manipulated the language as an ethnic symbol to re-define 'the interests of the propertied classes' and strengthen the grip of a reactionary political establishment on the one hand and the autocratic Catholic Church on the other (Ó Croidheáin, 2006: 161)

Thus the 'flag waving nationalist bourgeoisie' disregarded hopes for genuine social, political and cultural change with a view to maintaining the status quo. Indeed, despite rhetorical commitment to the language and native-speaking Gaeltacht regions, the Free State failed to provide legal or administrative services to the native speakers (Lee, 1985: 674).

The 'disturbing retreat into a conservative type of cultural protectionism' alienated a whole generation of radical activists and intellectuals who might well have backed a more progressive cultural program (Ó hÉallaithe, 2004: 165). Concomitantly, the decolonizing project which had inspired the Irish revolution 'lost an important ally when the intellectuals turned their backs' (Ó hÉallaithe, 2004: 165) and a fearful and reactionary Free-State administration failed to promote the liberating aspirations of revival as a means of decolonization. As Smyth (1999: 37) summarizes:

> Despite the best efforts of its liberal and left wings, radical decolonisation was commandeered by a nationalist bourgeois elite which tried to arrest the process at the point where it assumed control of the state apparatus left vacant by an offshore power. The drive towards an essential national identity in the years after 1922 actually reinforced social and political hierarchies even as it claimed to be an agent of liberation from such hierarchies.

It is hardly necessary to again distinguish between 'nationalist independence' and decolonization, which constitutes an ongoing process linked to struggle against the protracted injustices and inequalities of neocolonialism. Fanon himself also describes how 'during the colonial phase, the people are called upon to fight against oppression' whilst 'after national liberation, they are called upon to fight against poverty, illiteracy and underdevelopment. The struggle, they say, goes on. The people realize that life is an unending contest' (1961: 74)

One of the most interesting critics of the new Free State, Máirtín Ó Cadhain would inspire a whole generation of activists with his famous rallying call that 'the re-conquest of Irish is the re-conquest of Ireland and the re-conquest of Ireland, the salvation of Irish' (Ó Cathasaigh, 2002). Based on widespread poverty, Ó Cadhain pointed to a revolution betrayed in that formal independence had brought the Irish people no closer to liberation (Mac Síomóin, 2006). In the 1930s, the land-rights movement Muintir na Gaeltachta argued that the language revival couldn't be divorced from wider political and socioeconomic issues. As Ó Cadhain outlined:

> It is the duty of Gaelic revivalists to be socialists. The Gaelic-speaking population in the Gaeltachts make up a class that is the most abandoned and the most oppressed of the Irish people. Their salvation and the salvation of the language are one and the same thing to me. But this is not possible without the reconquest of Ireland—Ireland and its productive resources to be taken back into the control of the people. To me the revolution that is necessary for the reconquest is necessary also for the salva-

tion of Gaelic language. Therefore, any action which raises the spirit and enthusiasm of the Gaelic-speaking public is part and an important part of the reconquest (Mac Síomóin, 2006).

In the early 1960s, Ó Cadhain, then a lecturer at Trinity College Dublin, helped found the radical Irish-language campaigning group, MISNEACH, which used public protest and direct action to pressurize the Free State. This inspired the Gaeltacht Civil Rights Group who successfully campaigned for Raidió na Gaeltachta in 1972. Indeed, Ó Cadhain came to Belfast in 1964 to speak at the West Belfast Cultural hub, Cumann Chluain Ard, again inspiring a new generation of activists to create an urban Gaeltacht that planted the seed for the contemporary revival movement in the North of Ireland.

## The North: Hidden Ulster, Prison Liberation and Community Revival

Brendan O'Leary is arguably correct in his conclusion that 'the creation of Northern Ireland was an outcome of settler colonialism' (2019, 360). The Unionist regime prevented the nationalist third of the population access to political power, employment and housing thereby relegating them to a subordinate status. (Farrell, 1976) Unionism considered the Irish language a threat and the Gaelic League 'an anti-British counter-culture dominated by republican separatists' to promote 'sedition and disloyalty under another name' (Andrews, 1997: 56). The Unionists' 1923 Education Act substantially negated the achievements of the Gaelic league over the previous twenty years, cutting funding and even censoring text books. Despite pressure from extreme loyalism, the Unionist government felt it strategically 'better to keep a control by means of regulations over activities of this character than to drive them underground where they will undoubtedly tend to germinate and exert a baneful influence' (Andrews, 1997).

In short, the Unionist regime viewed any advance for the language as an attack on British cultural hegemony. In 1948, the Public Health and Local Council Act which prohibited the erection of Irish street signs, after nationalist councils erected signs in Omagh and Newry. Future Stormont Prime Minister, Brian Faulkner, couldn't 'tolerate the naming of our streets in a language which is not our language' (Maguire, 1991: 11). Furthermore, the Public Order Legislation (1951) and the Flags and Emblems Act (1954) enabled the Stormont government to physically subdue any cultural or political expressions of Irishness.

Despite official opprobrium, however, voluntary language activists continued to provide Irish classes and other aspects of the cultural revival, thereby creating independent bastions of cultural activity or 'a hidden Ulster of revivalism which enjoyed hardly any relations with statutory authorities and which was entirely alienated from the culture of the state' (De Brún, 2006: 11). After 1928, Ardscoil or the Gaelic League's Belfast headquarters became a mainstay for the language movement, which acted as an ideological umbrella for nationalists, republicans, and socialists, many from working-class backgrounds. In 1936, 'two unemployed young men Seamus Maxwell and Liam Rooney, set up Cumann Chluain Ard in an old, covered gateway in Kane Street beside Clonard Monastery in West Belfast.' When the club became 'Irish only' in 1953, it effectively 'set up an alternative Irish language movement, more outspoken than the mainstream Gaelic League, which many of them looked upon as being too mild and bourgeois' (Mac Seáin, 2006: 4).

Within this milieu, a core of idealistic young activists emerged with the extraordinary idea of creating an urban Gaeltacht in West Belfast, which sought to

> construct a set of values and an institutional framework that could bring a modern independent Irish-speaking society into existence, using what remained intact and worthwhile of pre-colonial Gaelic Ireland. Preservation and development of the Gaeltacht and on the establishment locally of a variety of Irish-speaking institutions in the belief that they may coalesce, creating the nucleus of this new society (Andrews, 1991: 98)

While this initiative took nine years to come to fruition in 1969, the core group 'never wavered in their determination to realize their goal' and succeeded 'without one penny of grant aid or government subvention' (Nig Uidhir, 2006: 138). Indeed, despite the opposition of Belfast Corporation, these Shaw's Road activists deployed their practical skills and philosophy of self-reliance to rebuild Bombay Street off the Falls Road, which had been burnt to the ground by loyalist pogromists, supported by the state police force. To activists like Mac Seáin, 'the struggle for the Shaws Road Gaeltacht wasn't enough on its own and we needed to go amongst the community in its hour of need. We did this as Irish language activists which raised the status of the language in the community' (Mac Ionnrachtaigh, 2013: 90).

In addition, inspired by the politics of Máirtín Ó Cadhain, these activists established the North's first Irish-medium nursery school in 1965 (Mac Seáin, 2006: 4). Indeed, despite threats of legal action, they established Bunscoil Phobal Feirste on the Shaws Road in 1971. This initiative 'would propel the Irish language onto a dynamic and exciting course that would contribute to a language shift in Ireland during the reminder of the millennium' (Nig Uidhir, 2006: 140).

These same activists soon brought their model of self-help best practice to the deprived Upper Springfield area of West Belfast, pioneering a series of community co-operatives to provide employment for local people including Gáráiste an Phobail (The People's Garage), Ballymurphy enterprises and Whiterock industries. The architect, Seán Magaoill designed all these projects, including the Shaw's Road Gaeltacht houses, Bombay Street and the Ballymurphy Tenants Association.

> Ballymurphy was totally marginalised and excluded; it has massive social problems and was completely neglected by the council and the state. At this point, myself and Seamus Mac Seáin were working on Ballymurphy. We were completely focused on it. The only way we could help the community was to bring back some of their self-respect and show them that

they could rebuild the place themselves (Dúchas Oral History Archive interview, 10 Feb 2014).

The violent conflict soon undermined these efforts, however. Loyalists shot Garáiste an Phobail manager, Seamus Mac Seáin five times in November 1974, killing his co-worker, Geraldine Macklin. Mac Seáin would survive and subsequently help found the *Andersonstown News* newspaper, the West Belfast cultural centre, Cultúrlann McAdam Ó Fiaich, and the North's first Irish-medium secondary school Coláiste Feirste.

While a generation of language activists pioneered initiatives reflective of civic republicanism and radical humanist philosophy amongst some of the North's most deprived communities, those same communities bore the brunt of state repression and many young people responded through engagement in armed struggle through the IRA. Throughout the twentieth century political prisoners had engaged with the Irish language while incarcerated. After the introduction of internment without trial in 1971 a new generation of working-class republicans followed in this tradition in the cages of Long Kesh, where 'a group of dedicated language activists came through inspired by the writings of Pearse, Freire and Fanon' (Interview with Jake Mac Siacais in Mac Ionnrachtaigh 2013). Once again, prisoners drew strength from the language to challenge the prison authorities and, by implication, British rule in Ireland.

Centred in Cages 10 and 11 or the Gaeltacht huts, the language became a focal point of prisoner life. In addition, through the course of their political education, prisoners drew political inspiration from African and Latin American anti-colonial struggles. The Irish language operated within a developing decolonization, as prisoners 'recognised the lengths the imperialists went to destroy the language and from this reasoned that it must be important'. Jim McCann not only learnt the language, 'but I learned why I had went to jail and what was keeping me in jail and more importantly we learned how to begin breaking all these things down' (Mac Ionnrachtaigh, 2013). The prisoners had become 'knowing subjects' not 'recipients' of knowledge, thereby achieving 'a deepening awareness both of the sociocultural reality which shapes their lives and the capacity to transform that reality' (Freire, 1972: 51).

After March 1976, the British state decided to transform the prisons into a political battleground and a focal point for their new criminalization policy. The construction of the new high-security Maze H-Blocks coincided with the removal of political status, which meant labeling prisoners as criminals held in singular cells and made to wear uniforms. When Kieran Nugent from Belfast refused to wear the prison uniform, thereby becoming the first 'Blanketman', a prolonged period of protest began that culminated in the death of ten prisoners on hunger strike in 1981 (see Beresford, 1987, McKeown 2001). The language's centrality to the protest owed a great deal to arrival in the H-Blocks of a number of fluent speakers like Jake Mac Siacais, Bobby Sands and Séanna Breathnach. In this respect the education acquired in Long Kesh appeared fundamental to the viability of the prison struggle in the H Blocks (Mac Ionnrachtaigh, 2013). Mac Siacais identified the language as 'totally invaluable in the terrible conditions to lift the spirit of the lads and help build their identity... Irish took off on the basis of security and ended up as the spoken language of the Blocks... ...within a year and a half, there was 300 prisoners with fluent Irish.'

The language, therefore, represented a liberating and transformative power. This widespread use of the Irish language actually increased and yielded a yet more powerful political resonance during the most enduring periods of the protest when there was an intensification of prison warder brutality. As republican ex-prisoner Peadar Whelan (Whelan, in O'Hagan, 1991: 4) articulated:

> Learning and speaking Irish became a crucial part of our struggle against criminality and helped form our identity. We had to fight to learn and speaking it was a form of resistance. Every time we spoke Irish, we were telling our enemy that we were Irish republicans, protesting and struggling. We weren't going to let them silence us...Irish was a weapon we used against the screws leaving them feeling totally frustrated and excluded. Our expression of identity left them feeling totally powerless. Knowledge is power and ignorance diminished their sense of power and control.

The language's galvanic effect on the prisoners' struggle conforms to Buntman's (2003: 236) 'emancipation' wherein resistance is 'not simply about saying no, reacting, refusing, resisting, but also and primarily about social creativity, introducing new values and aims, new forms of co-operation and action'. Crucially these processes emerged organically during the Blanket protest and not as the result of any grandiose political strategy from the republican leadership. In the best Fanonist sense, prisoners transformed themselves through struggle, as Máirtín Ó Maolmhuaidh (Mac Ionnrachtaigh, 2013) pointed out 'the language helped and transformed all those who learned it in prison.'

Long Kesh, therefore, conforms to Buntman's (2003: 8) description of Robben Island or the 'paradox of a site of repression being used to undo the material and symbolic origin of the power of the repressive apparatus' while simultaneously proving that 'events and patterns within prisons can and do shape political dynamics beyond the prison walls'. Therefore, republican prisoners' deployment of the language in their struggle not only confirmed Feldman's (1991: 216-17) view as 'transcendental power' that was 'first and foremost directed at the prison itself' and subsequently transformed 'the cell into a pedagogical space' and an 'act of personalized political appropriation', its importance actually transcended the prison's physical confines reverberating in the language revival movement outside.

> In the H-Blocks with no books, no paper, no pens, no professional teacher, young Irish men living in filthy conditions, frequently beaten, stripped naked...but unbowed, taught each other Irish by shouting the lessons from cell to cell. And as one hunger strike was followed by the other, the people outside heard those lessons too and they determined to carry on the cultural struggle—each one from where he/she was (Pádraig Ó Maolchraoibhe, 1986: 9).

The Long Kesh Prison struggle transformed the Irish language revival in the six counties, particularly through Irish-medium education (Mac Ionnrachtaigh, 2013). Inspired by the prisoners' example Eoghán Ó Néill and others helped form 'Gaels against the H-Blocks and Armagh, we were visible at hundreds of marches in the campaign against Long Kesh, we would have Irish banners and posters and shout Irish slogans aloud' (Mac Ionnrachtaigh, 2013). In short, the prison struggle reignited the emancipatory potential of the language. Others viewed language activism as a 'worthwhile means to play a role in a non-violent way yet progress the same objectives...that was why a lot of people connected with the revival and Irish medium education in general (Mac Ionnrachtaigh, 2013: 158).

In addition, through a plethora of different forms of activism the Irish language took on an added relevance amongst many ordinary working-class people who had not previously been associated with it. In 1982, the republican movement's political wing, Sinn Féin, formed its Cultural Department, *Roinn an Chultúir,* to oversee the organization of scores of additional language classes throughout Belfast and a controversial campaign to create bilingual street signs, which remained illegal under aforementioned legislation, the 1948 Stormont Public Health and Local Council Act (Ó hAdhmaill, 1985). As one of the founders of Roinn an Chultúir, Terry Enright, explained the rationale of

> implementing the Bobby Sands dictum about everyone having their own part to play and so on. This coincided with the reinvigorating impact of scores of released prisoners from Long Kesh who were fluent Irish speakers and motivated around the language and more than willing to commit their time ...we recruited people who could go in to the various working-class areas and take classes where people were comfortable, whether it be in their own living room or the local community centre...the key was to utilise it to break their alienation in a time of immense poverty, oppression and degradation etc.; also to create community solidarity by encouraging people to leave their homes and stop watching popular soaps at the time like Dallas etc. We saw it as a great opportunity to promote a liberating education amongst ordinary people and build confidence and self-worth in people who usually had very little... The first proper campaign was the Irish street names which was of course illegal (Mac Ionnrachtaigh, 2013: 160-1).

The name project developed as working-class communities contributed generously, securing 'one of the first tasks of the culture of resistance... to reclaim, rename, and reinhabit the land.' (Said, 1993: 273). For example, activists erected one hundred and sixty signs and raised fifteen hundred pounds in Twinbrook, an area with seventy per cent unemployment (Naíonra na Fuiseoige, 1988: 15). This appears all the more impressive when we consider that 'many of the organisers were arrested, and many of the signs removed by the RUC and British Army' (Ó hAdhmaill, 1985: 7). These examples correspond to people-centered decolonization that sought to engender 'critical consciousness' amongst structurally oppressed working-class communities with a view to transforming 'the subject from feelings of hopelessness and inferiority to hope and self-awareness thereby developing his capacity to become an "agent for change"' (Freire, 1972b: 75).

Similarly, republican language activists organized education seminars which linked Irish to the wider 'national struggle'. Ó Maolchraoibhe summarized the ideological rationale for their project of 'reconquest', since due to 'the Coca-Cola culture, I don't think we can exist as a separate people without our language. Now every phrase you learn is a bullet in the freedom struggle. Every phrase you use is a brick in a great building, a re-building of the Irish nation'. He continued,

> the process of decolonisation will have stopped half-way if, the day we succeed in driving the English from our shores, what is left behind is an Irish people possessed of the language, culture and values of the English. To be completely free we must not only remove the British presence but also reject the materialism, individualism and opportunism of the capitalist system which has been imposed on us (Ó Maolchraoibhe, 1985: 3-6).

The alienation of nationalist working class from the British state became total, with the Irish language clear example of this opposition (Ó hAdhmaill, 1984). The state effectively labelled this revival subversive by denying official recognition to Irish medium schools. The educational movement came to represent a counter-hegemonic 'education for emancipation', which promoted a counter-hegemonic cultural and linguistic alternative where power lay with the community. Ex-prisoners promoted this education system all over Belfast and throughout the North in Derry, Tyrone, Newry, Armagh, Fermanagh. In this respect their decisive intervention echoed the classic Shaws Road approach of 'Na hAbair é, Déan é' (Don't say it, Do it).

Another ex-prisoner, Pilib Ó Ruanaí, the current CEO of Iontaobhas na Gaelscolaíochta (Irish Medium Trust Fund) and key founder of *An Droichead* Irish Medium School and Cultural Centre in South Belfast, stated 'The vision of Irish medium education had completely inspired me as a vision during that period. It was almost like an awakening of consciousness that made me realize the importance of other ways to take forward the struggle' (Mac Ionnrachtaigh, 2013: 169). Unable to subvert these initiatives, the British state attempted to strategically divide the language movement by providing financial assistance to a cross-community Irish language initiative where British official Brian Mawhinney spoke of 'taking the Irish language out of politics' (Mac Ionnrachtaigh, 2013: 207). This came to fruition in 1989 with the Ultach Trust, recommended by the Cultural Traditions Group (O'Reilly 1998) and represented the first state assistance for Irish language development in the North, which Sinn Féin's Bairbre de Brún criticized as 'a cynical tactic to give money to 'respectable Irish speakers' rather than revivalist organisations'(Mac Ionnrachtaigh, 2013: 181). Many accused the state of falsely portraying the Irish revival movement as sectarian and thereby explaining state discriminatory practices as a consequence of the language's association with republicanism (O'Reilly, 1998: 108-9). The Douglas Hurd principles (1985) already denied state funding to groups that 'have the effect of improving the standing and furthering the aims of a paramilitary organization, whether directly or indirectly' (Ibid: 115). West Belfast Irish-language organization, Glór na nGael, subsequently had its funding removed in August 1990. This decision would not only impact on community development but also removed funding from seven of the eight Irish nursery schools in Belfast. De Brún argued that 'the discriminatory and anti-Gaelic policies of the British government' had made the language into 'contentious issue' or a 'controversial issue'. The government removed grants from Glór na nGael, refused to give financial recognition to Coláiste Feirste and 'trampled on the prisoners' cultural rights'. She continued that the Irish language issue 'involves Gaels, Irish people, and identity in a state that is still a product of the long history of colonialism (Mac Ionnrachtaigh, 2013: 187-88).

British state policy during the final years of the Troubles created a pattern of intransigence met by resistance that fuels radical Irish language activism to this day. One of the younger generation of activists and future Dream Dearg spokesperson, Ciarán Mac Giolla Bhéin, described how the Coláiste Feirste campaign facilitated his own radicalization:

> There was something exceptional about the Meánscoil. We, as pupils, cleaned the school and our parents went out at nights collecting money in the local clubs on the road. Everyone was totally committed to the project and organising sponsored cycles and sponsored mountain walks etc. on our behalf and for the sake of our education. Although we knew that we were involved in a struggle, this help gave us the confidence that we would succeed and that's exactly what happened in the end. Therefore, when I eventually left school, I felt it my duty to put something back into the struggle' (Mac Ionnrachtaigh, 2013: 205-6).

Coláiste Feirste as it is now known received official recognition in 1996, following an international campaign, where it became an issue of 'parity of esteem' during the peace process (O'Reilly, 1999: 132—33). However, the British government arguably only ever acceded to popular pressure and the potential for reputational damage internationally. Crucially, activists in these campaigns in the late 1980s and early 1990's forged a language rights campaigning discourse that would powerfully re-emerge amongst a new generation.

## A 'New Era' for the Language Untangling the New Northern Ireland

> 'On behalf of our party, let me say clearly and slowly...we will never agree to an Irish Language Act at Stormont and we will treat their entire wish list as no more than toilet paper. They better get used to it'
> —Unionist MP Gregory Campbell at the DUP part conference, November 2014

The 1998 Good Friday Agreement promised that the language would be 'encouraged and facilitated in public and private life' (Muller, 2010: 70). In addition, the Education Order (NI) placed a statutory duty upon the Department of Education to facilitate Irish-medium education (Mac Ionnrachtaigh, 2013). However, no sooner was the ink dry on the GFA, when a senior British civil servant, Tony Canavan, wrote in an internal policy document. 'What these worthy sentiments might mean in practice is a matter of interpretation and we could argue that our interpretation is as valid as anyone else's' (Mac Ionnrachtaigh, 2013: 196). In addition, the Irish language's development was impeded by its statutory promotion being linked to that of the Ulster Scots dialect. This permitted Unionism to mimic nationalist arguments of 'parity of esteem', thereby frustrating proportional allocation of resources. In effect, the British government formulated a policy of 'minimalism in the protection, promotion, or development of the Irish language, and disproportional generosity in the promotion of Ulster Scots' (Mac Ionnrachtaigh, 2013: 230).

More recently, the British Government has followed a similar policy regarding the long-standing demand for an Irish Language Act, which would grant similar legal protection as enjoyed by Irish speakers in the South of Ireland, and Welsh and Scottish Gaelic speakers. Having agreed to enact legislation at Westminster, following the internationally binding 2006 St Andrews Agreement, the British Government then delayed public consultation, before announcing a second consultation process that extended until after the restoration of devolution at Stormont in May 2007, thereby facilitating a Unionist veto over any future legislation. Unionist intransigence has its roots in the age-old settler-colonial psyche, as articulated in the Democratic Unionist Party's submission to the consultation process: 'The Irish language serves no communicative purpose in Northern Ireland, but simply the promotion of a political cause. An Irish Language Act is divisive, would alienate the majority population in Northern Ireland and would be a complete waste of money' (DUP Party submission see: http//www.dcalni.gov.uk).

The Irish Language Act campaign has faced continual racist opposition, facilitated by the British Government whose first consultation document in 2007 defined Irish as 'controversial' because unionists held 'genuine fears and concerns' about 'the erosion of their British identity'. Thus, the state excuses discriminatory views as 'genuine fears', thereby denying rights to Irish speakers. Furthermore, the British position epitomizes the monolingual counterargument of 'powerful languages' internationally, who disingenuously portray minority rights as a threat to the majority. Arguably, the demand for rights does not render minoritized languages 'controversial', real controversy should reside in their continued denial (May, 2002: 312).

Nonetheless, state support post-GFA has clearly benefited bottom-up community activism, resulting in the formation of Comhairle na Gaelscolaíochta in 2000 and Iontaobhas na Gaelscolaíochta (Irish-Medium Trust Fund) in 2001 to provide financial support and expand Irish medium provision (Muller 2010: 51). Across more than eighty schools, more than 7000 northern children currently receive their education primarily through Irish (Irish News, 11-3-21). Nevertheless, the establishment, development and long-term sustainability of Irish-Medium schools still largely depend on bottom-up voluntary endeavors. Consequently, many activists criticize statutory organizations like Comhairle na Gaelscolaíochta, stating that a more pro-active developmental approach would bear greater fruit. (Mac Ionnrachtaigh, 2013)

Rapid growth and state recognition also creates the potential for institutionalization, assimilation and elite manipulation which becomes particularly pertinent in processes of conflict resolution, which often yield greater avenues of state recognition and funding (Ó Croidheáin, 2006: 315). Theorists of institutionalization point to 'a loss of radical impetus within a social movement without the achievement of real gains' (Hourigan, 2006: 127). In these processes, 'popular organisations always face the danger of becoming an appendage of state clientelism as mass participation withers' and 'are often incorporated into the state as local mediators with a power to distribute resources' (Harris, 2007: 14).

This usually occurs when 'political elites' use 'social capital to divide and conquer a movement network and marginalize dissent within the public sphere' (Hourigan, 2006: 138). In essence, 'the structures created by the dominant strata to implement their hegemony' consume oppositional ideologies (Gledhill, 2000: 92). Indeed, 'elites may even be able to manipulate such reactive oppositional discourses to their own advantage' (Gledhill, 2000: 92). In a more general analysis of the capacity of the advanced capitalist and neocolonial state to carry out this function, Stuart Hall points to the 'purposeful construction and manipulation of popular consent' that neutralizes opposing forces and incorporates 'some strategic elements of popular opinion into its own hegemonic project' (Scraton, 2007: 226).

Clearly, the financial mainstreaming of the Irish language sector, post-GFA, brings with it the danger of 'rule by quango', or over-reliance on the state playing the role of a 'benign benefactor'. (Williams, 2000: 17) Eoghan Ó Néill also identified the potential for polarization between 'respectable' and 'radical' activists:

> If you look at Wales, two separate movements developed the more the revival grew. Now they have a respectable side and a radical side. In the Irish language community today, there is a lot of the respectable side but I'm not so sure that the radical side is as abundant as it was twenty years ago. The emphasis must be put on the new generation coming through the Irish schools to create additional radical activists (Mac Ionnrachtaigh, 2013: 221).

Despite the differing circumstances of more overt and pro-active state support, the Welsh example provides an interesting comparison in institutionalization, where Williams (Muller, 2010: 59) identifies a 'deep ambiguity... about the dominance of government in language revitalization because of the tendency of institutionalization to create dependency, severing control of language promotion from the community.' Notwithstanding the merit of such comparisons, the existing minimalism and outright hostility toward the Irish language in the North undermines too direct a comparison with Wales.

From the re-established of the Power-Sharing Stormont Assembly in May 2007, Political Unionism signaled its opposition to language rights when taking the Department for Culture, Arts and Leisure (DCAL) ministry and effectively vetoing the fundamental demand for an Irish Language Act. Edwin Poots pointed to the failure of the Irish Language Act and increased funding for Ulster Scots as evidence of the DUP's successful obstructionism. (Muller, 2010: 132) His party colleague, Gregory Campbell, who assumed ministerial responsibility in April 2008, promised to develop a single strategy for Irish and Ulster Scots 'that narrows or eliminates the disparity' between both. Campbell's successor in June 2009, Nelson McCausland reveled in his flagrant intransigence towards the language. (Mac Ionnrachtaigh, 2013)

Frustration with the 'new dispensation' led to activists publicly criticizing the nationalist political parties. In January 2008, Eoghan Ó Néill questioned Sinn Féin and the SDLP's avoidance of the DCAL ministerial brief, asking 'was it... because they have their own agenda... and that the welfare of the Irish language would have to wait'. He concluded that 'the six Nationalist ministers are failing to show leadership and the Irish language community will pay the price' (*My translation*) (*LÁ Nua*, 28 Jan 2008). When Foras na Gaeilge stopped the paper's funding in 2008, with eight jobs lost, the editor labelled *LÁ Nua* as a 'victim of power-sharing', because it 'gave voice to criticism from many in the Irish language community who were disappointed at the way the Irish language was being treated in the 'new dispensation' between Sinn Fein and the DUP' (*AN*, 17 Dec 2008).

Within neocolonialism, leading social actors from the subordinate community gain limited state autonomy in a skillful strategic framework that absolves the powerful of direct responsibility, thereby casting 'local mediators' as 'instruments of suppression on behalf of the neo-colonialists' (Nkrumah, 1964: 101). In the six-counties, this phenomenon has fostered internal divisions, disunity and confusion within republican/nationalist civil society. Ironically, therefore, minoritized language communities often find that they 'had it better when the iron fist was still in fashion', when the 'source of their misfortunes' was more tangible and they were wholly self-sufficient rather than dependent on state support (Fishman, 2005: 9). Muller (2010: 132) argues that this reflects the 'double bind in which many minoritized language communities find themselves. How far can they go in criticizing the parties most likely to act in a positive manner on their behalf?' This very conundrum emerged regarding Irish Medium Education, when Sinn Féin's minister, Caitríona Ruane, held the education portfolio in the reconvened power-sharing executive of 2007.

As a fluent Irish speaker, Ruane took immediate action by approving development proposals for three Irish medium schools, including Gaelscoil Éanna, which British Direct Rule minister, Maria Eagle, had rebuked in late 2006. However, in February 2011, the inherent contradictions in the consensus politics of the 'New Northern Ireland' led Coláiste Feirste to take a Judicial Review against the Department because of its continued refusal to provide transport services. Despite the provision of over 2020 dedicated buses to post-primary schools, with some Grammar schools allocated ten such buses, the Department of Education refused to provide transport to the Falls Road school, thus forcing pupils from Downpatrick to travel upwards of five hours a day on public transport (*Andersonstown News*, 2011). The Board of Governors' chairperson, Seán Mistéil stated that, 'the Department's withholding of bus services is an outrage… an injury inflicted on children on many levels', claiming that 'discriminatory treatment of Coláiste Feirste students will cripple the growth of the IM sector, in direct violation of Article 89 of the Education Order 1998' (*Andersonstown News*, 2011).

However, amidst widespread bemusement, Ruane's department stated that the refusal was 'practical', as its statutory duty to 'encourage and facilitate IME' was non-enforceable under the merely 'aspirational' GFA (*Andersonstown News*, 2011). Nevertheless, in his landmark ruling of October 25 2011, Judge Seamus Treacy announced that 'DE has failed to give proper weight and consideration' to its statutory obligations, which are 'intended to have practical consequences and legislative significance' (*Andersonstown News*, 2011). Treacy's dismissal of the DE argument that the 'proper discharge of this duty' would 'set a precedent in respect of other education sectors to whom this statutory duty is not owed' has opened the door for additional rights-based campaigning for the Irish language movement (Mac Ionnrachtaigh, *AN*, 5 Nov 2011).

These divisions within republican civil society, predicted by Fanon for anti-colonial struggles in his 'Pitfalls of National Consciousness' chapter in *Wretched*, were perhaps unavoidable under a peace process, which often imposes consensus politics over the rights of those on the downside of power relations. In this context, post-Agreement ideological jargon elevates new agendas such as 'good relations' and 'shared future' in a manner that entrenches 'cross-sectarian social-relations' that derive their power 'from an alliance between cross-sectarian polit-ical entrepreneurs, a new cross-sectarian middle-class, civil service, and bureaucratic elite' (McKearney, 2010: 17). Thus, a peace process orthodoxy emerged that embodies a 'new social and institutional ossification of sectarian-ism' where progressive, oppositional activists must choose to 'generally remain silent or to become apolitical' (McKearney, 2010: 17). The assimilationist ortho-doxy of the 'New Northern Ireland' arguably seeks to impose the State's terms of reference at all costs while obscuring unequal power relations.

Indeed, DCAL's launch of the 'Líofa 2015' ('Fluent 2015') initiative, in Septem-ber 2011, demonstrated that the language movement had not escaped this all-per-vasive discourse. The Sinn Féin minister, Caral Ní Chuilín, an ardent supporter of Irish and republican ex-prisoner, announced the commendable aim of encour-aging a '1,000 people from all walks of life across the north to sign up to be fluent in Irish by 2015' (*Irish News*, 6 Sep 2011). Nonetheless, the media essentially com-mandeered the project's launch to promote the assimilationist discourse, a move encapsulated in Ní Chuilín's own stated intention, to introduce 'measures aimed at depoliticizing the Irish language and returning it to a status where it can be practiced and enjoyed by people of all backgrounds and traditions' (*Irish News*, 6 Sep 2011). This remark eerily echoed the relentless NIO discourse of 'depolitici-sation', when Brian Mawhinney sought to 'take the Irish language out of politics'. This 'depoliticization' agenda portrays the Irish language movement as sectarian, thus incongruously blaming discriminatory state policy on links with national-ism and republicanism.

Unsurprisingly, this sparked intense debate within the Irish language com-munity, with many critically engaged activists viewing Líofa as a 'merely a sym-bolic, yet highly political move' and 'the latest example of the New Northern Ireland trying to 'hijack' our language movement by imposing its own terms of reference on how we promote the language' (Mac Ionnrachtaigh, 2011). This critical analysis provoked concerted responses from Sinn Féin activists, one of which described such critics as 'elitist Gaeilgoiristas' (Kearney, 2011). Clearly, as Muller (2010: 230—231) argues, 'former advocates of independence, now seem-ingly supporting institutions which reinforce interlocking relations may experi-ence unease and insecurity', ultimately leading to 'defensive/aggressive action to stifle criticism in the media and in the community; to vilify analytical commen-tators as 'negative'; to sideline particular NGO's; to withdraw funding and so on'.

Indeed, the inherent consolidation of an all-pervasive state hegemony, typical within conflict resolution processes, makes a culture of critique a pre-requisite for any meaningful transformational change. For example, Feilim Ó hAdhmaill promotes a more nuanced understanding of the dialectical relationship between the state and civil society in the protracted struggle for social change. 'If we can-not have challenge, critique, rational debate, and indeed, disagreement, without feeling threatened with abuse and marginalization we simply reinforce a culture of quiet, unquestioning acceptance, within our communities, stunting even fur-ther the potential for change and progress' (Mac Ionnrachtaigh 2013). In argu-ing for the independence of the language movement, Ó hAdhmaill indicates that this 'democratic dialectic' (Harris, 2007: 17) should provide a complimen-tary rather than conflictive dynamic: 'We shouldn't be careless with our allies but then neither should we allow our vision, our needs, our demands, to be con-strained by them. A healthy society allows campaigning and lobbying and cri-tique to flourish; through that we get change' (Mac Ionnrachtaigh, 2013).

The relationship between activists exercising limited forms of state power and those civil society organizations and movements campaigning for structural change is similar the world over. Yet, radical social change through this 'demo-cratic dialectic' requires 'considerable skills in analysis, negotiation and power brokering, and the ability to distinguish that which is illusory' (Muller, 2010: 10). The absence of such issue-based alliance building and an inability to main-tain a counter-hegemonic ideological fervor amongst activists could, I argued in 2013, ultimately lead to the consolidation of hegemonic power structures and the assimilation of the Irish language movement.

In periods of stagnation, institutionalization can cultivate the aforementioned disunity and disillusion, gifting the initiative to the state. During this same period, Foras na Gaeilge, the island-wide arms-length body which manages state funding for the Irish language, underwent an intensive 'rationalization' process stemming from decisions of the North-South Ministerial Council to reconfig-ure state support for Irish language NGO's (Muller, 2010: 135). Precipitated by the spectacular collapse of the Celtic Tiger in 2008, then Minister for Gaeltacht and Rural Affairs, Eamon Ó Cuív, promised to make 'significant savings' by 'collapsing' and 'merging' Irish language organisations as part of savage Government spending cuts (Mac Ionnrachtaigh, 2013). Consequently, the implementation of this divisive state 'rationalization' methodology could ultimately result 'in growing isolation and competition over social resources based solely on each organisation's immediate needs', which made it easier 'for the state to incorporate some and attack others, controlling certain social movements to strengthen its own hold over civil society' (Harris, 2007: 14).

This period of stagnation, regression and division provided the Irish language movement with a salutary reminder that the greatest impediment to the assimilationist designs of both states in Ireland, is the historic capacity of the Irish language community to maintain its independence through radical campaigning and grassroots organisation. The original inspiration came in January 2014 when language activists based in South of Ireland organised a rally after the Language commissioner resigned from his post due to the governments' refusal to live up to its legal obligations regarding state services for the Irish Language. Thousands attended the rally in Dublin on 15 February under the theme 'Dearg le Fearg' (Red with Rage) and a rally named 'An Lá Dearg' (the Red Day) was announced for 12 April in Belfast (*Irish Times*, 16 February 2014).

Several thousand people descended on West Belfast for this political rights rally and the campaign statement spoke of 'anger at the failure of the Power Sharing Executive at Stormont and the Peace process to protect Irish language rights and deliver on the commitments made in international agreements to equality for its speakers' (Ní Chathail, 2014). It continued:

> Sixteen years on from the Good Friday Agreement, we still have young Gaels being treated like second class citizens and being denied transport access to our schools; 8 years on from the commitment in an international agreement at St Andrews to enact an Irish language act, we are still being denied rights protection; and earlier this year our limited resources and infrastructure were put in serious danger by savage government cuts. People are clearly saying 'enough is enough'.

Leading the rally were parents from North Belfast whose children were still denied travel provision from a Sinn Féin led Department of Education three years after the landmark Justice Treacy High Court ruling. These parents were followed by a rural community in South Derry who had two development proposals for a standalone local Post-Primary school rejected by the same minister. In the immediate aftermath of the rally, campaign organisers met with North Belfast parents and engaged the support of the Human Rights NGO, the Participation and Practice of Rights Network with a view to organising a grassroots campaign for travel services.

In June 2014, the Tuistí an Tuaiscirt #busanois (Parents from the north#bus-now) campaign staged a five-mile walk to school along the safest non-contentious city route to highlight the absurdity of the government's three-mile radius bus-pass stipulation. A subsequent parents' survey and research report showed that 'the failure to provide transport was costing parents in north Belfast a combined annual bill of approximately £31,400', and 'acting as a deterrent in terms of parents choosing where to send their children after primary school'. Additionally, '79% of parent's' in north Belfast Irish-medium nursery and primary schools stated 'that existing transport provisions are a significant obstacle to sending their children to Coláiste Feirste' — which was the only Irish medium education secondary school in the north of Ireland at the time (PPR website, September 2014). Speaking to the *Irish News*, a parent from the campaign Nicola McMaster said:

> For parents there are two key issues—safety and cost. Some parents from north Belfast are paying over £20 a week on bus fares to enable their children to attend Irish medium education. The response of the Department is that some of us live within 2.9 miles and should walk to Coláiste Feirste—but that 2.9 miles is actually a walk to Coláiste Feirste through the Shankill and past the Twaddell camp. The only reasonable way to walk is so long it would basically mean our kids could not attend Coláiste Feirste. This is unacceptable. We are not asking for anything we don't have a right to. The government has a duty to promote Irish medium education and that also means providing adequate and appropriate access to the only Irish Medium Secondary school in the north of Ireland. The government have done it before with Integrated Education, and it is time Irish language speakers were afforded the rights which were promised in the Good Friday Agreement. We're asking the Minister to act quickly. Solve this issue before the new school term in September. That is within his power, and it is his responsibility. (*Irish News*, 13 Aug 2014)

The Department of Education bowed to the pressure and agreed to allocate a budget of a maximum £70k per annum for a period of three years to provide the buses for the North Belfast children. The importance of this victory wasn't lost on the emerging activist base who gained great confidence from the participatory methodology. The Director of Participation and the Practice of Rights, Dessie Donnelly, praised the 'creativity and determination of the parents and students throughout this campaign' who managed to 'produce a result that not even a successful court case could produce three years ago' while demonstrating 'the power of people working together to defend and promote rights' (PPR, Sep 2014). This campaign, Donnelly continued, was about 'so much more than a bus, and Irish language rights campaigners should pay attention to, and use, this precedent in their own campaigns elsewhere' (PPR, Sep 2014). This success was followed by the South Derry Irish-medium Post-Primary school proposal for Gaelcholáiste Dhoire finally being approved in December 2014 thus vindicating the importance of public campaigning and protest action.

# 'The Straw that Broke the Camel's Back':
# An Dream Dearg campaign

> We are the risen people who will not stop until we receive the respect, recognition and rights that we are entitled to as citizens. Our message is loud and clear, no government and no settlement and no new political arrangements that facilitates the discrimination and exclusion of Irish speakers.
> —Ciarán Mac Giolla Bhéin speaking at An Dream Dearg Political Rally, 17 May 2017

Despite notable victories, the key question of Irish speakers' rights remained marginal to the mainstream political discourse within a deeply sectarian two-party state where ''shared society' rhetoric and 'good relations' policies obscured the persistence of deepening inequality and cultural discrimination (Mac Ionnrachtaigh, 2013). Unionist politicians continued to denigrate the Irish language, with Gregory Campbell's notorious 'Curry my yogurt a can coco coaler' the most obvious example (BBC NI, November 4, 2014).

Prior to the May 2016 Assembly elections, Arlene Foster signalled that her party would take the education portfolio and 'stop squandering money on Irish-medium schools which cater for as few as 14 pupils…but build an education system that does not play favourites but is fair to every sector' (*Irish News*, April 16, 2016). In response, many in the language movement, through the national language NGO, *Conradh na Gaeilge*, sought to pressure Sinn Féin into taking the education and culture portfolios. Despite getting 43 MLAs (Members of the Legislative Assembly) and over eighty local community organisations to publicly support the call, the DUP secured both portfolios with Sinn Féin taking Finance and Infrastructure. *Conradh na Gaeilge*'s northern advocacy manager, Ciarán Mac Giolla Bhéin, echoed the widespread disillusionment: 'we had faith that the parties would be true to their word, but today's announcement shows that these parties and their representatives have failed to fulfil their promises regarding these demands' (*Conradh na Gaeilge*, 2016). In the following weeks a cross-party executive agreed a five-year programme for government 'which didn't specifically or at all mention an Irish Language Act as a likely outcome of their power-sharing arrangement' (Ó Liatháin, Slugger O'Toole, 10/9/17).

Within days, the DUP blatantly contravened the European Charter on Regional and Minority Languages, when Peter Weir removed all visibility of the Irish language from the Education Department website, logo and administrative functions, while the DUP Minister for Agriculture, Environment and Rural Affairs (DAERA) renamed the fisheries protection boat 'Banríon Uladh' Queen of Ulster and declared DAERA'a new department with a fresh identity and logo' that 'adopts a single language policy'(*Belfast Telegraph*, Sep 29, 2016). Weir rescinded funding for two Irish-medium special needs nurture units—a decision overturned by a Judicial review by one the schools in question (BBCNI, 22 July 2016). These continuous public attacks inspired language activists to call a public meeting for the last week in November, ten years to the day from the signing of the St Andrews Agreement, which promised an Irish Language Act. According to the new campaign's head of communications, Pádraig Ó Tiarnaigh:

> We actively sought out to recruit and to entice into the room those passionately involved with the language, but a wide section of people with a wide range of skill sets; in linguistic skills, in education, in media, in social media, in community organising and in community development. We agreed to come together and agree basic principles and targets on which we all agreed—focusing on the 95% of joint-thought we all shared, and leaving the usual 5% of internal politics and possible differences on other social issues at the door;... a new generation of emerging bottom-up activists resembling a contemporary, socio-linguistic focused update of the Gramscian organic intellectual; fulfilling much of his criteria regarding co-operative organisation and active, practical social application and participation (Ó Tiarnaigh, 2017)

Over the following period 'scores of voluntary activists began weekly meetings—discussing branding, networks, launches—all as part of a larger longer-term strategy' and 'the #dearg or #red theme leading on from the Lá Dearg campaigns in 2014 and the traditional 'fáinne' adopted on a red background to denote the call for language rights from the Irish language community' was encapsulated in the campaign name 'An Dream Dearg' meaning the 'Red Gathering (Ó Tiarnaigh, 2017).

This organising operated within a mounting political crisis generated by the Renewal Heating Initiative (RHI) scandal which saw over £490million of public money squandered with intense scrutiny on the DUP First Minister of Stormont Executive, Arlene Foster who had adopted the scheme while finance minister (BBCNI, 23/10/19). On 23 December 2016, the DUP Minister for Communities, Paul Givan, removed the annual Líofa scholarship grant scheme of £50,000, which helped disadvantaged young people to attend the summer courses in the Donegal Gaeltacht. This flagrant discrimination offered *An Dream Dearg* the perfect opportunity for action, 'as Screen shots of the translated email quickly ricocheted around Twitter and Facebook. Hundreds of tweets directly targeted party leaders (many of whom we have previously met and lobbied), requesting condemnation, all using the #Líofa tag' and forcing the story into the main news headlines' (Ó Tiarnaigh, 2017). Between Christmas and New Year's Day 'social media became a tool not only to hold the DUP to task, but to hold apparent partners in government, and those in opposition, to account also' (Ó Tiarnaigh, 2017).

By the time of An Dream Dearg's publicly launched its campaign on 6 January 2017, Arlene Foster had already refused Sinn Féin's demand to temporarily step down due to the RHI scandal. Ó Tiarnaigh asserts that 'the movement began to grow and transcend the physical room' with 'new spaces ... created, namely on WhatsApp social media group messaging', where 'sub-groups set about launching the Facebook page and the 'red logo', with co-ordinated, timed and staggered sharing 'thunderclaps' ensuring the maximum exploitation of Facebook's net-working algorithms' (Ó Tiarnaigh, 2017) . The skilful use of social media twinned with clear goals propelled the campaign to public prominence: 'We are An Dream Dearg. You are An Dream Dearg. Anyone who believes in rights, respect and recognition for all is An Dream Dearg. Join this open network of Irish Language Activists from all corners and background (Ó Tiarnaigh, 2017). Within days, the nationalist *Irish News* reported that over 12,000 had adopted the red logo on social media accounts, including famous sportspeople and a range of political party leaders as 'the digital political landscape turned red' (Ó Tiarnaigh, 2017).

An Dream Dearg deliberately framed 'the debate in a way that the normal person on the street could see a community was being wronged, that the basic decision was corrupt, to create a sense of natural unease around the discourse' (Ó Tiarnaigh, 2017). Ó Tiarnaigh describes these young activists as 'digital natives' who developed 'transmedia activism and transmedia organising' to bring 'new narrative forms and distribution techniques to human rights' campaign organising (Ó Tiarnaigh, 2017). Drawing on the experiences of the Arab Spring, Peter Beamont (*The Guardian*, Feb 25, 2011) highlights *The Twitter Effect* or the *Facebook Revolution* as central to communities organised themselves digitally and successfully communicated their message to a global audience:

> Precisely how we communicate in these moments of historic crisis and transformation is important. The medium that carries the message shapes and defines as well as the message itself. The instantaneous nature of how social media communicate self-broadcast ideas, unlimited by publication deadlines and broadcast news slots, explains in part the speed at which these revolutions have unravelled, their almost viral spread across a region.

As the Líofa scandal garnered unprecedented media coverage, An Dream Dearg announced a public demonstration, 'bursaries not boilers, for 12 January at Department for Communities head offices in central Belfast. With Stormont's reputation in tatters, the Sinn Féin leadership faced mounting pressure from the republican community and its grassroots.

On 9 January, Deputy First Minister, Martin McGuinness, publicly resigned his position thereby collapsing the Stormont institutions. His resignation letter focused on the DUP's role in the RHI scandal and 'negative attitude to nationalism and to the Irish identity and culture', wherein, 'for those who wish to live their lives through the medium of Irish, elements in the DUP have exhibited the most crude and crass bigotry' (*Irish News*, 10/1/2017). Indeed, Sinn Féin's Minister for Finance then called Givan's decision on Líofa 'straw that broke the camel's back' (*Irish News*, 10/1/2017). In this emerging 'organic crisis', An Dream Dearg had arguably exploited the 'dialectic between reactionary and progressive forces in search of a solution, a new order' (Gill, 2003: 33). Líofa necessitated and accelerated 'the breakdown of those 'truce lines' handed down from the past rounds of movements struggles, and thus also the eruption of those antagonisms and contradicions which they held in check' (Cox & Gunvald Nilsen, 2016: 97). Givan publicly rescinded the Líofa decision via Twitter the morning An Dream Dearg protested at his offices, stating 'My decision on the Líofa Bursary scheme was not a political decision. I have now identified the necessary funding to advance this scheme' (BBCNI, 12 Jan 2017). He then contradicted himself by tweeting that he would not 'allow Sinn Féin to use that £50,000 as a political weapon against us in the upcoming election as a tool to rally their troops, and so I've taken that away from them (BBCNI, 12 Jan, 2017).

Armed with a tangible political victory, An Dream Dearg immediately shifted public focus to the outstanding demand for an Irish Language Act. Ciarán Mac Giolla Bhéin told the hundreds of protesters outside Givan's Bedford Street office that 'The Irish-language community are no longer willing to accept being treated as second class citizens' and 'are Dearg Le Fearg (red with anger) at the repeated failure of authorities to protect and promote our rights' (Irish News, Jan 11, 2017). In a clear message to Sinn Féin, he then declared that 'we want no party to enter into an agreement for government without a guarantee that the rights of Irish speakers will be enshrined in legislation' as 'we don't want to be in the position again where a minister can take a decision like this' (Irish News, Jan 11, 2017).

On 28 January, An Dream Dearg launched a 'short video humanising and personalising the community need for protective legislation' which went viral within days being viewed over 200,000 times with a post interaction of over one million' (Ó Tiarnaigh, 2017). In response to growing public momentum behind an Irish Language Act, Arlene Foster retorted that she would never agree because 'more people speak Polish than they do speak the Irish language in Northern Ireland' (BBCNI, Feb 6, 2017). She then infamously stated that 'if you feed a crocodile it will keep coming back for more' before refusing to 'reward bad behaviour, and to capitulate to manufactured demands' (BBCNI, Feb 6, 2017). Such inflammatory rhetoric only attracted greater international media attention on the grassroots campaign, such as Al Jaezera and the Washington Post (Ó Tiarnaigh, 2017). Nevertheless, Sinn Féin's new northern leader, Michelle O'Neill still refused to draw 'any red line issues for a return to Stormont' (Irish News, 16-2-17). An Dream Dearg commenced co-ordinated public protest at Stormont, Derry's Guildhall and then Newry, where 'over a 100 people thronged on City Hall' on 20 February (Ó Tiarnaigh, in NVTV 2017). Ó Tiarnaigh stated that Irish speakers 'cannot be held hostage to 'political consensus' and we call on all political parties who support us to affirm their commitment that they will not be part of any future arrangement that facilitates the active discrimination of Irish speakers' (Irish News, 20-2-17). Cracks emerged in Sinn Féin's public position, however, prior to the 2 March poll, when local West Belfast MLA and former Hunger Striker, Pat Sheehan told a Youth Assembly organised by Glór na Móna that an Irish Language Act represented a red line: 'we are not going back into the Executive, unless the outstanding agreements are implemented '(Belfast Telegraph, Feb 23, 2017) BBCNI's Nolan Show publicised this statement the next morning, with the Sinn Féin leadership refusing to publicly back Sheehan.

The assembly elections the following week delivered a devastating blow to political unionism as the largest ever nationalist turnout vindicated Sinn Féin's decision to collapse Stormont. After ten years of falling turnout, the traditional base returned to the voting booths, driven, perhaps above all else, by unionist intransigence. The swing back towards Sinn Féin in republican heartlands like West Belfast and East Tyrone suggested that many previously disillusioned supporters sought to give the DUP a bloody nose. The unionist *Newsletter's* political editor, Sam McBride, rightly commented that 'Northern Ireland is today waking up to a fundamentally altered political reality: unionism is no longer a majority in the Stormont chamber for the first time since the creation of the Province a century ago' (*An Phoblacht*, March 4, 2017). Historian Eamonn Phoenix argued in the *Irish News* that 'the RHI scandal; Arlene Foster's strident anti-nationalist rhetoric; Paul Givan's pointed removal of Irish language bursaries and the all-pervasive shadow of Brexit' had mobilised nationalism 'as never before' with the result shocking 'Unionism to its core' with 'political and, especially, the psychological implications ... as the centenary of Partition approaches in 2021' (*Irish News*, March 6, 2017).

Then, on 31 March, Glór na Móna received email notification that our youth funding application to the Education Authority's extended provision youth scheme had been unsuccessful. Speaking to BBCNI Newsline, I stated that 'our community is reeling at this disgraceful decision that we were only informed by the Education Authority of at 4.35pm on Friday afternoon, effectively putting four professionally-qualified youth workers on the dole from Monday onwards with the result being a 'total 65 hours per week of youth work practice' being 'axed, forcing the immediate closure of four Belfast-based clubs'. (BBCNI, April 4, 2017) The Sinn Féin MLA and former Minister of Finance, Máirtín Ó Muilleoir described this as 'worse than the líofa decision' with 'the Irish language was used as a punch bag' with the termination of 'hard-won provision across five youth clubs in Belfast' for a 'burgeoning sector... traditionally under-provided for by the mainstream education authorities'. He also asked for an urgent meeting with the Education Authority CEO and called on 'Taoiseach Enda Kenny to stand up to this assault on the Good Friday Agreement' (Sinn Fein, Feb 4, 2017). Meanwhile, the young people from Glór na Móna and An Dream Dearg activists called an immediate public meeting in Coláiste Feirste. Katy Rose Mead, a sixteen-year-old activist at the time, neatly captured the intersection of class and culture in her moving description of a community mobilised through collective commitment to equality of opportunity:

> When the funding was cut from our youth workers in Glór na Móna, we were active right away, designing banners and writing slogans on them. We organised meetings with the younger children from the club to explain to them what happened and why it had happened. Then we prepared them for the public meeting... I can remember the night of the public meeting in Colaiste Feirste and I recall walking down the Whiterock road by myself and I was dressed in my Dream Dearg shirt and was so nervous... because I knew that I was opening the evening... I was nervous

but also incredibly proud. When I saw 500 people packed into the room, I was still very angry, but my overriding emotion was pride... people from all sorts of backgrounds... teachers, students, pupils, ... people who hadn't spoken a word of Irish in their lives but they were all there for one reason, because our community was being targeted and discriminated against and that's when I realised that everyone in that room was a Gael, even those who hadn't spoken a word of Irish in their lives, they were all there to support the cause.

Amidst an electric atmosphere, only young people and youth workers who lost their posts spoke, following An Dream Dearg policy where politicians aren't given platforms to speak on behalf of the movement. The sight of a mobilised and determined community organising democratically from below constituted 'living inside of history' where the 'making of history by those excluded from History' puts an emphasis on 'a new humanism concerned with real living individuals and real social relations' (Gibson, 2017: 592). An Dream Dearg activist and youth worker, Conchur Ó Muadaigh, epitomised this 'critical engagement with the rationality of popular praxis':

> Our youth club was built from nothing and the decision to cut us was highly political and this was the legacy of the orange state. When a civil servant sits in a room and cuts an Irish language youth club, it isn't an unsuccessful application but a conscious political decision to exclude and was indicative of the discriminatory and hostile attitude of governments in the north. Youth services for young people cannot be separated from the wider campaign for language rights in the north of Ireland. The decision and the callous disregard for our youth workers and our youth clubs clearly indicates the negative approach of some within that system. They think we are not a community; they think we aren't organised. They think we are a bunch of people who sing songs and learn tin whistles. ...We are a community, we are alive, we are young people, we are students, we are youth clubs, we are cycling clubs, we are everything.... we are human beings. We have rights, we have human rights and language rights and we will not take this lying down. Let there be no ifs or no buts about that (Glór na Móna, Facebook 2017).

Just two days later, over 800 protesters 'brought Academy Street in Belfast to a standstill in a vibrant and colourful display of vocal opposition to the Education Authority's removal of funding from Irish medium youth services' (Glór na Móna, 2017). Hundreds of children and young people handed over a 1000 letters and staged a thirty-minute sit-in protest in the EA head offices much to the disbelief of government officials, where they demanded the immediate restoration of this youth provision and an urgent meeting with the Department of Education and the EA. Ó Muadaigh explained that 'disgraceful decisions have consequences and we are bringing our frustration and the widespread anger felt in the community since these services were removed to the doors of those responsible'. (Glór na Móna, 2017). The EA Head, Gavin Boyd, agreed to meet with the young people and immediately restored and increased the funding for the Glór na Móna youth project. As Director of Glór na Móna, I welcomed the additional funding allocation as 'an encouraging step towards securing a more strategic, coherent and long-term approach to Irish-Medium youth provision' which 'gives practical effect to its statutory duty to encourage and facilitate Irish medium education' (Ibid). Off the back of high-profile victories, An Dream Dearg planned for a public march and rally in Belfast on 20 May. Describing the planning process and the wholly horizontal organising methodology, activist Gráinne Ní Ghíllín stated:

> For months, we came together every Wednesday night in the Culturlann (West Belfast Cultural Centre) at 7pm to plan, to clarify our demands, to make sure everyone understood what we were demanding... From the outset, I was very encouraged that all this wasn't being organised centrally by a small clique, that everybody, everywhere in the Irish language community were getting involved in this and declaring to the world that we are An Dream Dearg that every one of us was part of an Dream Dearg... that it doesn't involve one certain place and or a small clique of people, that it involves everyone who wants to be part of it... (NVTV Documentary, 2017)

Ciarán Mac Giolla Bhéin explained:

> ...we never wanted to retain power amongst a small group but rather the vision was to share power amongst everybody... that everyone could achieve the changes they wanted to see in society themselves and because of that empowerment process, everyone felt personal ownership of the campaign and it ensured that people persisted because this involved long hours. People worked over the weekend, kept an eye on social media, did interviews regularly, designed posters, were doing meetings across the 6 counties, coming together for days of action at the weekend. It involved a lot of time but because people felt as much ownership of it as anyone else, they were happy to do it and I think it's a model that other movements and campaigns can learn from (NVTV Documentary, 2017).

Similarly, Ó Tiarnaigh emphasised how 'everyone was an activist, everyone was a spokesperson, everyone was in charge, including all those who sat foot in the room or engaged online and created both physical and virtual spaces with the same inclusive methodology' (Ó Tiarnaigh, 2017). An Dream Dearg thus corresponds with Gibson's (2012: 9) Gramscian contention in the South African context that movements are 'dialectical', often requiring 'a moment or an event when the sufferings, indeed the human resistance, of the oppressed become manifest through a real poor people's movement that becomes historical when their subjectivity changes the objective situation'. In understanding this through a Fanonian lens, Gibson (2012: 9) argues that 'such a moment is not a product of intellectual will or of a charismatic leader' but rather requires organisation, 'not of the vanguardist type, but a practice of self-organisation intimately connected to the organisation of thought in the most open and democratic sense' and that 'opening of space for this thinking is the precondition from which new subjectivities can and do emerge' (Gibson, 2012: 9).

According to Ní Ghíllín, 'very early in the process... we realised that we had to do something big, something public to put us in the centre of things' (NVTV documentary). Describing the ground-breaking and radical decision to bring the rally to Belfast City Hall, Mac Giolla Bhéin explained 'that was very powerful and symbolic. City hall had been the epicentre of anti-Irishness here for a long time. That's where the parliament of the Orange State had sat and where the authorities decided to make this place a cold house for the Irish language from the first day'. He continued that 'we were advancing our political demands relating to rights, legislation, to status and recognition for the Irish language but as well as that and just a importantly, we were celebrating the miracles performed by the Irish language community in this state' (NVTV Documentary, 2017).

On 20 May 2017, somewhere between twelve and fifteen thousand Gaels marched from An Chultúrlann, West Belfast Cultural Centre on the Falls Road to Belfast City Hall (*The Irish News*, May 2017). The rally heard passionate speeches from young children, teenagers, single parents and comrades from *an Ghaeltacht*. Mac Giolla Bhéin rightly declared that 'there is no doubt that the Irish language is now at the very centre of the current political crisis in the north and An Dream Dearg are stating clearly that no political institutions or future political arrangement are tenable in the absence of a rights based Irish Language Act'. Crucially, he added that 'people like us, a chairde, can—and do— change things for the better... We are the risen people who ... will no longer wait to have our rights bestowed on us. We will continue to organise, to protest, to lobby and to fight without cessation until we get our rights (Mac Giolla Bhéin, 2017, in *An tUltach*).

Sinn Féin duly announced that an Irish Language Act now represented a 'redline' for the restoration of Stormont. On 15 June, Gerry Adams couldn't 'compromise on an agreement that has already been made' before rhetorically asking 'if there is no Acht na Gaeilge, how on earth could you put the institutions back in place' (An Dream Dearg FacebookThe Irish language Act then became the key stumbling block in talks to restore devolution. In August, Adams told Conradh na Gaeilge that 'there won't be an assembly without an Acht na Gaeilge. The DUP know that the two governments know that. This right, which has been denied people here, is available everywhere else on these islands' (BBCNI, Aug 30 2017). An Dream Dearg's campaign had propelled the Irish language to the political epicentre and exposed the failings of the sectarian reconstruction of the Orange state that the new Stormont embodied. Writing in the *Irish Times* that September, prominent Irish journalist, Eamonn Mallie described the 'demand for a free-standing Acht na Gaeilge' as 'today's "One man, one vote' of the Civil Rights campaign of over half a century ago' because it had become 'emblematic of a homogeneous, radicalised nationalist community attitude for which nothing short of full-blooded "parity of esteem" will guarantee a restoration of a devolved government' (*Irish Times*, Sep 4, 2017).

By the spring of 2018, Mary Lou McDonald succeeded Gerry Adams as Sinn Féin leader, embarking on an intensive period of negotiations to break the political deadlock at Stormont. After a leaked draft agreement on February 14 included an Irish Language Act, the DUP unilaterally collapsed the talks despite Sinn Féin announcing that they had 'reached an accommodation' (BBCNI, Feb 14, 2018). Under intense pressure, however, Arlene Foster stated that 'We do not have a fair and balanced package...I respect the Irish language and those who speak it but in a shared society this cannot be a one-way street (BBCNI, Feb 14-2018). After eighteen months, in January 2020, and with the Brexit deadline looming, the British Government pushed through an agreement. The New Decade, New Approaches agreement received cross-party support on 11 January 2020 and the Northern Ireland Executive was re-established with immediate effect (BBCNI, 11-1-20).

Crucially, this new agreement included an Irish 'language bill' with 'legislation to create a commissioner to recognise, support, protect and enhance the development of the Irish language in NI and to provide official recognition of the status of the Irish language in NI' (RTE, Jan 11, 2020). While falling considerably short of An Dream Dearg's demand for a stand-alone rights-based Irish Language Act, many legal experts argued that 'the legislation provides a strong and robust institutional model in making provision for a Commissioner and best practice language standards', which 'provides an appropriate structure that could be effective if not actively frustrated' (Holder, 2020). An Dream Dearg tentatively welcomed the initiative as 'an historic development for the Irish language community by potentially providing legal protection to our community for the first time in the history of a state, which has discriminated and excluded us for almost a century. This progress rests solely on our grassroots community led Dream Dearg campaign, which empowered communities to challenge the status quo and speak truth to power'. Key then to this major political concession was the reality 'that ordinary people can make change happen from below. We are proud to have played a positive role in enabling civil society to reclaim its democratic voice in holding those with power and responsibility to account'. The statement continued, however, that 'it is a start and an advancement but is not our final destination. But we no longer sit at the back of the bus. We will not return to the margins but will continue to campaign vociferously for the fulfilment of all our outstanding rights and a democratic and socially just future for our communities'. In a clear reference to previous Unionist intransigence, the statement also made it clear that 'if political vetoes are used, however, to obstruct and hinder rights and resources for our community then the new arrangements and its current reincarnation are set to fail and fall again'. (An Dream Dearg FaceBook, January 2020).

The implementation of the new agreement, like so much of its associated Programme for Government, fell victim to the coronavirus pandemic as Stormont relinquished 'strategic decision making to Westminster' and its herd immunity Tory cabal (Donnelly PPR, July 7, 2020). The executive's shambolic handling of the Covid Crisis has been 'plagued by a division which has marred the devolution project from the beginning and prevented the full implementation of the now 22-year-old peace agreement' (Ibid). Indeed, both the Irish language legislation and the parallel Irish Language strategy have been subject to age-old obfuscation and delay with Conradh na Gaeilge initiating judicial review proceedings against the Stormont Executive on 1 April 2021. Ó Muadaigh criticized the 'constant delay' and pointed out that 'an Irish language strategy' was 'required by law' and that '14 months on from New Decade New Approach' and despite the executive signing off on 'a suite of other strategies' they 'cannot agree to even discuss a timetable for such a strategy, never mind the strategy itself' (BBCNI, April 1, 2021). The following day, a report by the Council of Europe's committee of experts pointed out that the NDNA legislation, 'while welcome' did not 'offer the comprehensive approach a law and strategy would provide' where 'express provision for specific language rights, such as in the fields of education, access to public services, public signage and cultural activities' (BBCNI, April 2, 2021).

At the time of writing, Stormont teeters once more on the point of collapse again with political unionism in disarray as mass loyalist rioting in opposition to the Brexit Protocol mars the political landscape. Amidst growing momentum for a referendum on Irish unity, it is widely recognised that unionism appears 'confused and directionless, lurching dangerously from one populist cause to another without consideration for the longer term ramifications' (Manley, 2021). An Dream Dearg undoubtedly contributed to this crisis, as it 'exposed and laid bare the sectarian nature of the Unionist political establishment and how rooted the ideology is in empire and oppression of the "other".' The campaign proved 'how inherently weak, vulnerable, chronically unstable and sensitive our institutions are to concerted pressure, oversight and mobilisation' that it didn't 'take much for them to be swept aside' (Mac Giolla Bhéin, Lessons for Change, August 2018). Yet beyond its assault on Unionism, an Dream Dearg represented 'a vibrant Irish language movement... which is prepared to debate the issues, create its own agenda, challenge the "common sense" views of the world and indeed make its own history' (Mac Ionnrachtaigh, 2013: 218).

Through the campaign, 'individuals and communities' played a 'transformational... part in the revolutionary process of changing the general relations of power in Irish society', while simultaneously challenging the current global Anglo-American cultural hegemony (Ó Croidheáin, 2006: 18). As an autonomous counter-hegemonic 'social movement from below', An Dream Dearg fits Cox and Gunvald Nilsen's definition regarding 'the organisation of multiple forms of locally generated skilled activity around a rationality expressed and organised by subaltern social groups', which has successfully challenged 'the constraints that a dominant structure of needs and capacities' imposed 'upon the development of new needs and capacities' (2014: 72). An Dream Dearg has created 'a critical theory of knowledge', (Freire, 1972: 68-9) that promotes active participation, empowerment and purposeful action, easily conforming to a Fanonian ideology of decolonisation that 'can continue to imbue the language movement with that radical edge that provides succour from the dangers of complacency and institutionalisation' (Mac Ionnrachtaigh, 2013). This ideology, thus, constitutes 'one of the most effective instruments for keeping the revolution from becoming institutionalised and stratified in a counter-revolutionary bureaucracy; for counter-revolution is carried out by revolutionaries who become reactionary' (Freire, 1972a: 118). The horizontal organising methodology also generated 'a resurgence of young people engaging with politics, in the broadest sense of the word' who now 'feel that they have power and that they can effect change in the here and now' (Mac Giolla Bhéin, Lessons for Change, August 2018). This praxis should condition a new 'civic republicanism' that encourages 'civic values once again' and 'human freedom' (Walsh, 2011: 98). Ó Murchú argues that this republicanism should represent

> ...the liberation of people, liberation from the understanding that they are dependent, that things happen to them, that they have control over their own cultural future. It means empowerment of people to the freedom of having the choice, a choice of language; and of having a right, language rights (Walsh, 2011: 98).

This corresponds with the idealism promoted by the progressive strand of the Irish-Ireland movement of the last century, which promoted concepts of 'civic virtue and political integrity' that 'reflected the enlightenment republicanism of Rousseau', which 'rejected self-interest' in favour of 'self-sacrifice for the common good' (McCluskey, 2011: 157). Conversely, the contemporary northern movement has created an alternative discourse which prioritises a 'dynamic, competent, positive, creative' approach with an 'energetic mentality that breeds a self-respect and self-confidence' through community empowerment (Ó Tuathaigh, 2011: 100). This revival movement can also inspire and herald a new model of 'development' that is 'more holistic and more inclusive of economic, social, cultural, environmental and linguistic aspects of a community's life', leading communities to 'engage more closely with the meaning, process and outcome of development' (Walsh, 2011: 407). The Irish language movement thus becomes a key contributor 'to a more participative process where communities take control of their own development, rather than being guided by an external model inappropriate to their particular circumstances' (Walsh, 2011: 407—8).

The crisis of neo-liberalism, the Covid pandemic, and the associated socio-political upheaval provides progressive activists and movements with a unique opportunity to influence developing debates. In the Irish context, An Dream Dearg indicates that such debates should be rooted in inclusive democratic practice; be non-party political and strictly non-hierarchical. This may well require a new methodology and creative thinking on how best to forge genuine participation, ownership and empowerment. Any civic republicanism must draw its support 'from among the more disadvantaged sections of society' and 'demand a fundamental change to the existing status quo' (McKearney, 2011: 214). The Irish-language community revival must continue to play a transformational and integral role in this endeavour. Crucially, however, a progressive future for the language movement rests on its positioning 'as part of a generalised movement against oppression of all kinds, rather than in splendid isolation' (Ó Cathasaigh,

2011: 29). For social movements exclusively wedded to 'specific social sectors often fail to develop lasting social solidarity and a united political strategy' (Harris, 2007: 14).

If the language movement is to align itself with an emerging counter-hegemonic politics of the left, it must '"join hands" with other groups engaged in oppositional projects' which can 'in turn can lead to alterations in the form and direction of collective action towards more encompassing movement projects seeking to achieve more radical forms of change'.(Cox and Nilsen, 2014: 72) In August 2018, Mac Giolla Bhéin, when sharing a panel in West Belfast with Thapelo Mohapi from Abahlali baseMjondolo South African Shack Dwellers movement, reflected how the 'key lesson of our campaign is that power resides with communities and people—not with political parties and institutions. The question is how do we join the dots between that vibrant, community-led, powerful campaign and other progressive movements'. He continued that 'if we, tomorrow, get the strongest Irish Language Act there is but we have food banks opening up in communities like these then we have not made any progress'. This work will ultimately involve, as Henry Giroux (2002: 54) posits, 'connecting private issues to broader structural and systemic problems both at home and abroad' with a view to bringing 'diverse social movements' together and producing 'long-term organisations that can provide a view of the future' thus developing 'a more comprehensive notion of politics'.

Nevertheless, successful resistance struggles 'may entail strategic acquiescence; the recognition that limited compliance may expand the scope for other strategies of resistance' (Buntman, 2003: 252). These strategies must move beyond defeatist rhetorical grandstanding. Resistance is 'not simply about saying no, reacting, refusing, resisting, but also and primarily about social creativity, introducing new values and aims, new forms of co-operation and action' (Buntman, 2003: 252). Grassroots activism, therefore, requires an adequate understanding of these relationships, to develop strategies appropriate to the existing dialectic (Harris, 2007: 23). This understanding will be crucial in the future conversation on a United Ireland. Our language movement has shown that participatory, democratic forms of activism that oppose socio-economic inequality and cultural assimilation provide a staging post in the wider struggle for a new Ireland. We must recognise, though, that radical 'decolonisation requires fundamental social and economic change' (Gibson, 2012: 138) and heed Fanon's prescient warning that 'national consciousness, national renaissance, etc, become empty slogans, cynically repeated at rallies and anniversaries' unless developed into a 'humanism' that 'addresses the elemental needs of the mass of the people and includes them in the very discussion of the nation' (Gibson, 2012: 138). Interestingly, Fanon's trepidation about the limitations of 'flag-waving' nationalism was preceded by the cogent analysis of Irish revolutionary socialist, James Connolly as far back as 1901 when he pointed out:

> ...If you hoist the green flag over Dublin Castle, unless you set about
> the organization of the Socialist Republic your efforts will be in vain.
> England will still rule you. She would rule you through her capitalists,

through her landlords, through her financiers, through the whole array of commercial and individualist institutions she has planted in this country and watered with the tears of our mothers and the blood of our martyrs (Mac Bhloscaidh, 2021).

Moreover, according to Irish Marxist historian, Fearghal Mac Bhloscaidh, 'this generation faces an historical conjunction that last arose a century ago' and 'our task is to reshape the very nature of Irish society and realise the ideals of that subverted revolution' before stressing that 'without this mass mobilisation, relentless democratic pressure and the clarion call of a just society we will have forsaken an epoch-defining opportunity' (Mac Bhloscaidh, 2021). The continual crisis at Stormont, the outworking of Brexit, the Covid pandemic and the rekindling of the Scottish independence question has created a new context, a unique space and a compelling momentum for political change. The challenge facing us, however, is whether republicans, socialists and progressives of differing opinions, persuasions and affiliations can recognise and exploit the revolutionary potential contained in this unique set of historical circumstances.

Grassroots campaigns, movements and working-class communities can set the agenda for a national debate that could begin the process of forging a mass movement for social change and transformation. By building relationships based on solidarity and trust, we can influence and challenge each other in harnessing a revolutionary moment. A conversation about building this kind of dynamic within republicanism at its broadest degree will require bravery, political maturity and an acknowledgment that there is no simple answer or one-size-fits-all approach to revolutionary change. There is a strength and resilience in admitting collective vulnerability and the need to widen circles and include new ideas, strategies and methodologies of struggle. In this hour of opportunity, any attempt to realise James Connolly's Socialist republic must surely involve republicans, socialists and radicals imagining a future whereby building on what we agree on takes precedence over bickering and squabbling about what divides us.

## Bibliography

Adams, G. 2017. 'Speaking on *BBC The View* on Dream Dearg.' Facebook (7) Watch.

Ainsworth, P., and Morris, A. 2017. 'Scrapping of Irish Language Bursary "Straw That Broke the Camel's Back".' *The Irish News*.

An Dream Dearg Statement. 2020. 'Historic Development for the Irish Language Community but St Andrews Commitment Remains Unfulfilled.' (7) An Dream Dearg – Posts | Facebook.

Anderson, B. 1991. *Imagined Communities: Reflections on the Origin and Spread of Nationalism*. London.

Andersonstown News. 2011. 'Buses, Buses Everywhere But Not Even a Single One for Falls Road Irish Language College .'

Andrews, L. S. 1991. 'The Irish Language in the Education System of Northern Ireland: Some Political and Cultural Perspectives.' In *Motivating the Majority:*

*Modern Languages in Northern Ireland*, edited by R. M. O. Pritchard, 89–106. London.

_____. 1997. 'The Very Dogs in Belfast Will Bark in Irish: The Unionist Government and the Irish Language, 1921–43.' In *The Irish Language in Northern Ireland*, edited by A. Mac Póilin, 49–94. Belfast.

Bayview Media Documentary. 2017. 'Dream Dearg – An Lá Dearg.' Dream Dearg – Lá Dearg on Vimeo.

BBCwebsite. 2014. 'Curry My Yoghurt': Gregory Campbell, DUP, barred from speaking for day.' 'Curry my yoghurt': Gregory Campbell, DUP, barred from speaking for day – BBC News.

BBCNI. 2017a. 'Irish Language Bursary Funding "Found" Says Paul Givan.' Irish language bursary funding 'found' says Paul Givan – BBC News.

BBCNI. 2017b. 'DUP Will Never Agree to Irish Language Act, says Foster.' DUP will never agree to Irish language act, says Foster – BBC News.

BBCNI. 2017c. 'Irish Language Youth Clubs "Forced to Close" Over Funding.' Irish language youth clubs 'forced to close' over funding – BBC News.

BBCNI. 2017d. 'Gerry Adams: "No Assembly Without Irish Language Act".' Gerry Adams: 'No assembly without Irish language act' – BBC News.

BBCNI. 2018. 'Power-sharing Talks Collapse at Stormont.' Power-sharing talks collapse at Stormont – BBC News.

BBCNI. 2019. 'A Timeline on Renewable Heat Scandal.' Timeline: Renewable Heat Incentive scandal – BBC News.

BBCNI. 2021. 'Irish Language Proposals 'Not Comprehensive Enough.' Irish language proposals 'not comprehensive enough' – BBC News.

Beaumont, P. 2011. 'The Truth About Twitter, Facebook and the Uprisings in the Arab World.' *The Guardian*.

Belfast Telegragh. 2017. 'Sinn Fein Won't Go into Government Unless There Is Agreement on Irish Language Act, Says MLA Pat Sheehan.' *The Belfast Telegraph*.

Beresford, T. 1987. *Ten Men Dead: The Story of the 1981 Irish Hunger Strike*. London.

Black, R. 2016. 'Row Erupts After DUP Minister Changes Name of Boat from Irish to English.' *The Belfast Telegraph*.

Bourdieu, P. 1991. *Language and Symbolic Power*. Cambridge.

Buntman, F. L. 2003. *Robben Island and Prisoner Resistance to Apartheid*. London.

Canny, N. P. 1973. 'The Ideology of English Colonization from Ireland to America.' *William and Mary Quarterly* 30: 575–598.

Caute, D. 1970. *Fanon*. London.

Comerford, R. V. 2003. *Inventing the Nation: Ireland*. London.

Cox, L., and Nilsen, A. G. 2014. *We Make Our Own History: Marxism and Social Movements in the Twilight of Neoliberalism*. London.

Crowley, T. 1996. *Language in History: Theories and Texts*. London & New York.

_____. 2000. *The Politics of Language in Ireland, 1366–1922: A Sourcebook*. London & New York.

Curtis, L. 1984. *Nothing but the Same Old Story: The Roots of anti-Irish Racism*. London.

Curtis, M. 2003. *Web of Deceit: Britain's Real Role in the World*. London.

De Baroid, C. 2000. *Ballymurphy and the Irish War*. London.

De Brún, F., ed. 2006. *Belfast and the Irish language*, Dublin. 'Díomá agus Frustrachas ar Chonradh na Gaeilge faoin Tarraingt Siar ar chuid de Ghealltanais Réamh-thoghcháin.' ráiteas oifigiúil *Conradh na Gaeilge*, https://cnag.ie/ga/nuacht/830-d%C3%ADom%C3%A1-agus-frustrachas-ar-chonradh-na-gaeilge-faoin-tarraingt-siar-ar-chuid-de-ghealltanais-r%C3%A9amh-thoghch%C3%A1in-gaelv%C3%B3ta.html.

Donnelly, D. 2020. 'Communities Taking the Lead as Government Dithers – PPR's response to Lockdown.' Analysis | Communities Take the Lead as the Government Dithers. PPR's Response to Lockdown (Part One) | No-one Left Behind (nlb.ie).

Doyle, S. 2014. 'Irish Medium Schools Facing a Daily Walk Through City's Most Violent Interfaces or 31k Travel Bill.' *The Irish News*.

Doyle, S. 2021. 'Pupils in Irish Language Schools Top 7,000 for First Time.' *The Irish News*.

DUP Party sSsh Language Act Consultation. 2007. January, http//www.dcalni.gov.uk.

Eccleshall, R. 1992. 'Introduction: The World of Ideology.' In *Political Ideologies*, edited by R. Eccleshall et al., 7–37. London.

Fanon, F. 1961. *The Wretched of the Earth*. Harmondsworth.

_____. 1970. *Black Skins, White Masks*. Suffolk.

Farrell, M. 1976. *The Orange State*. London.

Feldman, A. 1991. *Formations of Violence: The Narrative of the Body and Political Terror in Northern Ireland*. Chicago.

Fishman, J. 2005. 'The Soft Smile and the Iron Fist.' In Prefatory remarks in *Rebuilding the Celtic Languages- Reversing Language Shift in the Celtic Countries*, edited by D. Ó Néill. Aberystwyth.

Friere, P. 1972a. *Cultural Action for Freedom*. London.

_____. 1972b. *Pedagogy of the Oppressed*. London.

Gibson, N. C. 2012. *Fanonian Practices in South Africa: From Steve Biko to Abahlali baseMjondolo*. Pietermaritzburg.

_____. 2017. 'The Specter of Fanon: The Student Movements and the Rationality of Revolt.' *South Africa, Social Identities* 23 (5): 579–599.

Gill, S. 2003. 'Grand Strategy and World Order.' Lecture delivered at Yale University in ISS's Grand Strategy Series, revised for publication December 10, 2003.

Giroux, H. 2002. 'Rethinking Cultural Politics and Radical Pedagogy in the Work of Antonio Gramsci.' In *Gramsci and Education*, edited by C. Borg, J. Buttiegieg, and P. Mayo, 41–66. New York.

Gledhill, J. 2000. *Power and Its Disguises: Anthropological Perspectives on Politics*. London.

Glór na Móna. 2017. 'Cruinniú Poiblí I gColáiste Feirste'– (7) Facebook Live | Facebook, April 4.

Glór na Móna. 2017a. 'Hundreds Bring Protest to Education Authority Offices in Support of Irish Language Youth Clubs.' Hundreds bring protest to Education

Authority offices in support of Irish language youth clubs. – Glór na Móna (glornamona.com).

Glór na Móna. 2017b. 'Funding for Irish Medium Youth Services Restored.' Funding for Irish Medium Youth Services Restored – Glór na Móna (glornamona.com).

Gramsci, A. 1971. *Selections from the Prison Notebooks*. London.

Harris, J. 2007. 'Bolivia and Venezuela: The Democratic Dialectic in New Revolutionary Movements.' *Race and Class – A Journal on Racism, Empire and Globalisation* 49 (July–September): 1–25.

Hedges, J. 2017. 'Political Earthquake – Unionism Loses Stormont Majority for First Time in History in Huge Sinn Féin Surge.' *An Phoblacht*.

Hill, C. 1970. *God's Englishmen: Oliver Cromwell and the English Revolution*. London.

Hindley, R. 1990. *The Death of the Irish Language: A Qualified Obituary*. London.

Holder, D. 2020. 'Analysis of the Draft Legislation Published with the New Decade, New Approach Document January 2020.' Talk delivered at 'An Comhaontú Nua: Cad é atá i gceist? Culturlann McAdam Ó Fiach' organised by Conradh na Gaeilge.

Hourigan, N. 2006. 'Movement Outcomes and Irish Language Protest.' In *Social Movements and Ireland*, edited by L. Connolly and N. Hourigan, 124–144. Manchester.

Hutchinson, J. 1987. *The Dynamics of Irish Cultural Nationalism: The Gaelic Revival and the Creation of the Irish Free State*. Dublin.

Janet, M. 2010. *Language and Conflict in Northern Ireland and Canada – A Silent War*. Hampshire.

Kearney, J. 2011. 'Article was Factually Inaccurate.' *Andersonstown News*, September24.

Kiberd, D. 1993. *Idir Dhá Chultúr* (BÁC).

_____. 1995. *Inventing Ireland: The Literature of the Modern Nation*. London.

Klein, N. 2007. *The Shock Doctrine – The Rise of Disaster Capitalism*. London.

Krauss, M. 1992. 'The Worlds' Languages in Crisis.' *Language* 68 (1): 4–10.

Lee, J. 1985. *Ireland 1912–1985: Politics and Society*. Cambridge.

Lloyd, D. 2003. 'After History: Historicism and Irish Postcolonial Studies.' *Ireland and Postcolonial Theory*, edited by Claire Carroll and Patricia King, 46–63. Cork.

Lyons, F. S. L. 1973. *Ireland since the Famine*. London.

Mac Bhloscaidh, F. 2021. 'A United Ireland Means Nothing Without a Just Society.' A United Ireland means nothing without a just society. – BLOSC (wordpress.com).

Mac Giolla Bhéin, C. 2017. 'An Lá Dearg: óráid Chiaráin Mhic Giolla Bhéin.' *An tUltach*, https://antultach.com/pobal/an-la-dearg-oraid-chiarain-mhic-giolla-bhein.

_____. 2018. Speech delivered at 'Lessons for Change' seminar in Gaelionad Mhic Goill as part of Féile an Phobail.

Mac Ionnrachtaigh, F. 2011a. 'Bua do chearta daonna.' *Andersonstown News*, November 5.

Mac Ionnrachtaigh, F. 2011b. 'Language doesn't decline in powerful communities.' *Andersonstown News*, September17.

_____. 2013. *Language, Resistance and Revival- Republican Prisoners and the Irish Language in the North of Ireland.* London.

Mac Seáin, S. 2006. 'Century of Irish Language Growth.' *Andersonstown News*.

Mac Síomóin, T. 1994. 'The Colonised Mind – Irish Language and Society.' *Reconsiderations of Irish History and Culture*, edited by Daltún Ó Ceallaigh, 42–71. Dublin.

_____. 2006. *Ó Mhársa go Magla: Straitéis nua don Ghaeilge* (BÁC).

Magaoill, S. 2014. Interview with Dúchas Oral History Archive interview.

Maguire, G. 1990. *Our Own Language: An Irish Initiative.* Clevedon.

Mallie, E. 2017. 'How Arlene Foster Helped Nationalism Find its Teeth.' *The Irish Times.*

Manley, J. 2017. 'O'Neill Says Won't be Drawing Red Lines for Return to Stormont.' *The Irish News.*

_____. 2021. 'The DUP is Lurching Dangerously from One Populist Cause to Another to Cover its Countless Missteps.' *The Irish News.*

May, S. 2002. *Language and Minority Rights – Ethnicity, Nationalism and the Politics of Language.* Essex.

McCluskey, F. 2011. *Fenians and Ribbonmen – The Development of Republican Politics in East Tyrone, 1898–1918.* Manchester.

McCormick, J. 2020. 'Stormont Deal: One Year On, What's changed?' Stormont deal: One year on, what's changed? – BBC News.

McHugh, M. 2016. 'DUP Pledges to Stop 'Squandering Money' on the Irish Schools.' *The Irish News.*

McKearney, T. 2011. *The Provisional IRA – From Insurrection to Parliament.* London.

McKeown, L. 2001. *Out of Time, Irish Republican Prisoners Long Kesh 1972–2000.* Belfast.

McKittrick, Ds, Kelters, S., Feeney, B., and Thornton, C., eds. 1999. *Lost Lives – The Stories of the Men, Women and Children Who Died as a Result of the Northern Ireland Troubles.* Edinburgh.

Memmi, A. 1965. *The Colonizer and the Colonized.* New York: Orion Press.

Meredith, R. 2016. 'Irish Language Schools: Department Finds Funding for Nurture Units.' Irish language schools: Department finds funding for nurture units – BBC News.

_____. 2021. 'Irish Language Group to Challenge NI Executive in Court.' Irish language group to challenge NI Executive in court – BBC News.

Monaghan, J. 2017a. 'Protesters Call for Irish Language Act.' *The Irish News.*

_____. 2017b. 'Protest Over Decision to Axe Irish Language Bursary to be Held at Department HQ.' *The Irish News.*

Naíonra na Fuiseoige. 1988. *Naíonra na Fuiseoige.* Belfast.

Ní Chathail, C. 2014. 'An Lá Dearg was an Expression of Both a Growing Sense of Anger' at *Slugger O'Toole*, April 18, https://sluggerotoole.com/2014/04/18/an-la-dearg-was-an-expression-of-both-a-growing-sense-of-anger/.

Nic Craith, M. 2001. *Culture and Identity Politics in Northern Ireland.* Dublin.

Nig Uidhir, G. 2006. [Maguire] 'The Shaws Road Urban Gaeltacht: Role and Impact.' In *Belfast and the Irish Language*, edited by F. De Brún, 136–147. Dublin.

Nkrumah, K. 1964. *Consciencism – Philosophy and Ideology for Decolonisation and Development with Particular Reference to the African Revolution*, London.

Northern Visions TV Documentary. 2017. 'Ó Líofa go Lá Dearg.' Ó Líofa go Lá Dearg | NVTV.

Ó Caollaí, É. 2014. 'Thousands March for Language Rights.' *The Irish Times*.

Ó Cathasaigh, A. 2002. *Ag Samhlú troda: Máirtín Ó Cadhain 1905–1970* (BÁC).

Ó Croidheáin, C. 2006. *Language from Below: The Irish language, Ideology and Power in 20th century Ireland*. New York.

Ó Fiaich, T. 1969. 'The Language and Political History.' In *A View of the Irish Language*, edited by Brian Ó Cúiv, 101–111. Dublin.

Ó Gadhra, N. 1989. *An Chéad Dáil Éireann (1919–1921) (agus an Ghaeilge)* (BÁC).

Ó hAdhmaill, F. 1985. *Report of a survey carried out on the Irish Language in West Belfast* (Glór na nGael).

Ó hEallaithe, D. 2004. 'From Language Revival to Language Survival.' In *'Who Needs Irish?': Reflections on the Importance of the Irish Language Today*, edited by C. Mac Murchaidh, 159–185. Dublin.

Ó Huallacháin, C. 1994. *The Irish and Irish: A Sociolinguistic Analysis of the Relationship Between a People and their Language*. Dublin.

O'Leary, B. 2019. 'A Treatise on Northern Ireland: Vol. 1, Colonialism,' 360. London.

Ó Liatháin, C. 2017. *'Unionists Should Welcome Irish Language Act with Open Arms'* at *Slugger O'Toole*, September 10, https://sluggerotoole.com/2017/09/10/unionists-should-welcome-irish-language-act-with-open-arms/.

Ó Maolchraoibhe, P. 1985. 'The Importance of Learning Irish.' In *Learning Irish: A Discussion and Information Booklet*, edited by Pádraig Ó Maolchraoibhe, 3–7. Belfast.

_____. 1986. 'The Role of the Language in Ireland's Cultural Revival.' In *The Role of the Language in Ireland's Cultural Revival*, 1–11. Belfast.

Ó Snodaigh, A. 2006. 'An Teanga agus an Réabhlóid.' *An Phoblacht* (16, March): 12.

Ó Tiarnaigh, P. 2017. *'The Gaelic Spring': Social Media, Líofa and the Re-energised campaign for Acht Gaeilge.*' ag Comhdháil CAIS (Canadian Association for Irish Studies), University of Ulster, Magee.

Ó Tuathaigh, G. 2005. 'Language, Ideology and National Identity' in J. Cleary and C. Connolly (eds) *The Cambridge Companion to Modern Irish Culture* (Cambridge University Press): 43–58.

_____. 2011. 'An Stát, an Féiniúlacht Náisiúnta agus an Teanga: Cás na hÉireann.' In B. Mac Cormaic (eag) *Féiniúlacht, Cultúr agus Teanga i Ré an Domhandaithe* (BÁC), 76–113.

O'Hagan, F., ed. 1991. *Éirí na Gealaí: Reflections of the Culture of Resistance in Long Kesh*. Belfast.

Ó'Néill, E. 2008. 'La Nua a victim of 'dispensation of power-sharing.' *Andersonstown News*.

O'Reilly, C. 1999. *The Irish Language in Northern Ireland: The Politics of Culture and Identity*. London.

Parenti, M. 1995. *Against Empire*. USA.

Pearse, P. H. 1970. *The Murder Machine and Other Essays*. Cork.

Philipson, R. 1992. *Linguistic Imperialism*. Oxford.

Phoenix, E. 2017. 'Dr Éamon Phoenix: Unionism Shocked to the Core.' *The Irish News*.

Pilger, J. 2006. *Freedom Next Time*. London.

PPR Supports Tuistí an Tuaiscirt Campaign. 2014. PPR supports Tuistí an Tuaiscirt campaign for school transport – call for Minister to take action by September 2014 | Participation and the Practice of Rights (pprproject.org).

PPR. (September 2014) 'Tuistí an Tuaiscirt – The Power of the People Working Together to Defend and Promote Rights.' Tuistí and Tuaiscirt – the power of people working together to defend and promote rights | Participation and the Practice of Rights (pprproject.org).

Rees, R. 1998. *Ireland 1905-25* (Down).

RTE website. 2020. 'Stormont Proposals: What Have the Parties Agreed to?.' Stormont proposals: What have the parties agreed to? (rte.ie).

Rudé, G. 1980. *Ideology and Popular Protest*. London.

Said, E. W. 1993. *Culture and Imperialism*. London.

Scraton, P. 2007. *Power, Conflict and Criminalisation*. New York.

Sinn Féin website. 2017. 'Axing of Irish Language Youth Club Funding Worse than Líofa Decision – Ó Muilleoir.' Axing of Irish language youth club funding worse than Líofa decision – Ó Muilleoir | Sinn Féin (sinnfein.ie).

Smyth, G. 1999. 'Decolonisation and Criticism: Towards a Theory of Irish Critical Discourse.' In *Ireland and Cultural Theory: The Mechanics of Authenticity*, edited by Colin Graham and Richard Kirkland, 29–49. London.

The Irish News. 2011. 'PSNI Officers Sign Up for Irish Lessons.' *Irish News*, September 6.

The Irish News. 2017. 'An Lá Dearg, Thousands of People Take to the Streets Calling for an Official Irish Language Act.' *The Irish News*, May 20.

Thiong'o, N. 1994. *Decolonising the Mind: The Politics of Language in African Literature*. London.

Tuhiwai Smith, L. 1999. *Decolonizing Methodologies: Research and Indigenous Peoples*. London.

Walsh, J. 2011. *Contests and Contexts – The Irish Language and Ireland's Socio-Economic Development*. Bern.

Whelan, K. 2005. 'The Cultural Effects of Famine.' In *The Cambridge Companion to Modern Irish Culture*, edited by Joe Cleary and Claire Connolly, 137–154. Cambridge.

Williams, C. 2000. 'Development, Dependency and the Democratic Deficit.' In *Developing Minority Languages: The Proceedings of the Fifth International Conference on Minority Languages, July 1993*, edited by W. Thomas and J. Mathias, 14–18. Cardiff.

# GENERALS TO THE DUSTBIN, ALGERIA WILL BE INDEPENDENT: THE NEW ALGERIAN REVOLUTION AS A FANONIAN MOMENT

Hamza Hamouchene

During the upheavals that the North African and West Asian region witnessed a decade ago (2010-2011)—what has been dubbed the 'Arab Spring'—Fanon's thought and praxis proved to be as relevant as ever. Not only relevant, but insightful to the extent that they have helped us to grasp the violence of the Manichean world we live in, and the rationality of revolt against it.

Fanon's writings took place in a period of decolonization of countries in Africa and elsewhere in the global South. Born Martinican, Algerian by choice, he wrote from the vantage point of the Algerian revolution against French colonialism and of his political experiences on the African continent. One might ask, can his analyses transcend the limitations of time? Can they be universal or impregnated with universalist tendencies? Can we learn from him as a committed intellectual and revolutionary thinker? Or should we just reduce him to another anti-colonial figure, largely irrelevant for our 'post-colonial' times?

For me, as a young Algerian activist, Fanon's dynamic and revolutionary thinking, always about creation, movement and becoming, remains utterly prophetic, vivid, inspiring, analytically sharp and morally committed to disalienation and emancipation from all forms of oppression. He strongly and compellingly argued for a path to a future where humanity 'advances a step further' and breaks away from the world of colonialism and European universalism. In another way, he represented the maturing of the anti-colonial consciousness and was a decolonial thinker par excellence. As a true embodiment of *l'intellectuel engagé*, he has transformed the debate on race, colonialism, imperialism, otherness and what it means for one human being to oppress another.

Despite his short life (he died at the age of 36 from leukaemia), Fanon's thought is very rich, and his work was prolific from books and papers to speeches. He wrote his first book *Black Skin, White Masks* (Fanon, 1986) two years before Dien Bien Phu (1954) and his last book, the famous *The Wretched of the Earth* (Fanon, 1967a), a canonical essay about the anti-colonialist and Third-Worldist struggle, one year before Algerian independence (1962), at a moment when African countries were gaining their independence. In his trajectory, we can see the interactions between Black America and Africa, between the intellectual and the militant, between thought/theory and action/practice, between idealism and pragmatism, between individual analysis and collective movement, between the psychological life (he trained as a psychiatrist) and the physical struggle, between nationalism and Pan-Africanism and finally between questions of colonialism and those of neo-colonialism (Bouamama, 2017: 140-159).

Fanon died less than a year before Algeria got its independence on July 5, 1962. He did not live to see his adoptive country become free from French colonial domination, something he believed had become inevitable. This radical intellectual and revolutionary devoted himself, body and soul to the Algerian national liberation. His experience and analysis were the prism through which many revolutionaries abroad understood Algeria and helped to make the country synonymous with Third World revolution. Fanon's ideas were always influenced by practice and transformative. They inspired anti-colonial struggles all over the world; shaped Pan-Africanism and profoundly influenced the Black Panthers in the US.

Fanon wrote: 'Each generation must out of relative obscurity discover its mission, fulfil it, or betray it' (Fanon, 1967a: 166). The challenge is once again being laid down these last few years with an explosion of revolts and uprisings all over the world that includes the second wave of the Arab uprisings from Algeria to Lebanon and from Sudan to Iraq. Six decades after the publication of his masterpiece *The Wretched*, Algeria is witnessing another revolution, this time against the national bourgeoisie that Fanon railed against in his passionate and ferocious chapter 'The Pitfalls of National Consciousness'.

What would he say about the new Algerian revolution? How might he act in the face of current events? What can we as young Algerians learn from his reflections and experiences? This chapter is an attempt to analyze the 2019-2021 Algerian uprising through a Fanonian lens, trying in this way to shine a light on Fanon's genius, the timeliness of his analysis, the lasting value of his critical insights and the centrality of his decolonial thought in the revolutionary endeavors of the wretched of the earth.

Alice Walker once said: 'A people do not throw their geniuses away. And if they are thrown away, it is our duty as artists and as witnesses for the future to collect them again for the sake of our children and if necessary, bone by bone' (Walker, 1983: 92). It is in this spirit that I embark upon this chapter, as Fanon's theoretical insights and radical praxis have been largely absent from Algerian political thought in the last half century for various reasons that I will delve into.

But before getting there, a little historical detour to the colonial period is needed in order to contextualize Fanon's thought and to lay the ground for his critiques of the predatory bourgeoisie against which Algerians revolted in 2019-2021.

## Fanon and Colonial Algeria

*This European opulence is literally scandalous, for it has been founded on slavery, it has been nourished with the blood of slaves and it comes directly from the soil and from the sub-soil of that under-developed world. The well-being and the progress of Europe have been built up with the sweat and the dead bodies of*

*Negroes, Arabs, Indians and the yellow races.*
— Fanon, *The Wretched of the Earth*

*For in a very concrete way, Europe has stuffed herself inordinately with the gold and raw materials of the colonial countries: Latin America, China and Africa. From all these continents, under whose eyes Europe today raises up her tower of opulence, there has flowed out for centuries towards that same Europe diamonds and oil, silk and cotton, wood and exotic products. Europe is literally the creation of the Third World. The wealth which smothers her is that which was stolen from the under-developed peoples.*
— Fanon, *The Wretched of the Earth*

The Algerian independence struggle against the French colonialists was one of the most inspiring anti-imperialist revolutions of the 20th century. It was part of the decolonization wave that had started after the Second World War in India, China, Cuba, Vietnam and many countries in Africa. It inscribed itself in the spirit of the Bandung Conference and the era of the 'awakening of the South', a South that has been subjected for decades (132 years for Algeria) to imperialist and capitalist domination under several forms, from protectorates to settler colonies.

The colonial period can be summarized by expropriations, proletarianization, forced sedentarization, sheer exploitation and brutal violence. Frantz Fanon described thoroughly the mechanisms of violence put in place by colonialism to subjugate the oppressed people. He wrote: 'Colonialism is not a thinking machine, nor a body endowed with reasoning faculties. It is violence in its natural state' (Fanon, 1967a: 48). According to him, the colonial world is a Manichean world, which goes to its logical conclusion and 'dehumanizes the native, or to speak plainly it turns him into an animal' (Fanon, 1967a: 32).

What followed the declaration of war of independence on November 1, 1954, was one of the longest and bloodiest wars of decolonization, which saw a massive involvement of the rural poor and urban popular classes (lumpenproletariat). Official estimates claim that a million and half Algerians were killed in the eight-year war that ended in 1962, a war that has become the foundation of modern Algerian politics.

Arriving at Blida psychiatric hospital in 1953, Fanon realized quickly that colonization, in its essence, was a big producer of madness and hence the necessity of psychiatric hospitals. For him, colonization was a systematic negation of the other and a frantic refusal of any attribute of humanity to them. In contrast to other forms of domination, the violence here is total, diffuse, permanent and global. Treating both torturers and victims, Fanon couldn't escape this total violence, which he analysed. This led him to resign in 1956 and join the national liberation front (FLN). He wrote: 'The Arab, alienated permanently in his country, lives in a state of absolute depersonalisation'. He added that the Algerian war was 'a logical consequence of an abortive attempt to decerebralise a people' (Khalfa and Young, 2018: 434). He has been unfairly and wrongly accused of being the prophet of violence. What he did was only describing and analysing the violence of the colonial system.

Fanon saw the colonial ideology being underpinned by the affirmation of white supremacy and its corollary 'civilising' mission. The result was the development in the *indigènes évolués* (the 'evolved natives') of a desire to be white, a desire which is nothing more than an existential deviation. However, this desire stumbles upon the unequal character of the colonial system which assigns places according to colour.

In his book *Black Skin, White Masks*, Fanon analyzed the cultural alienation of the colonized/racialized and its reflection in behaviors and identity. He argued that it was the result of enduring domination founded on economic exploitation. Sooner or later, this unsustainable situation unleashes a process of disalienation, resistance and emancipation. Throughout his professional work and militant writings, he challenged the dominant culturalist and racist approaches and discourses on the natives, such as the 'North African Syndrome': Arabs are lazy, liars, deceivers, thieves, etc. (Fanon, 1967b: 3-16). He advanced a materialist explanation, situating symptoms, behaviors, self-hatred and inferiority complexes in the life of oppression and the reality of unequal colonial relations. Therefore, the solution to these issues was to act in the direction of radically changing social structures.

Fanon had high hopes and strongly believed in revolutionary Algeria. His illuminating book *A Dying Colonialism* (Fanon, 1965) or as it is known in French *L'An Cinq de la Révolution Algérienne,* attests to that and shows how liberation does not come as a gift. It is seized by the masses with their own hands and by seizing it they are themselves transformed. He strongly argued that, for the masses, the most elevated form of culture – that is to say, of progress – is to resist imperialist domination and penetration. For Fanon, revolution is a transformative process that will create 'new souls'.[1] For this reason Fanon closes his 1959 book with the words: 'The revolution in depth, the true one, precisely because it changes man and renews society, has reached an advanced stage. This oxygen which creates and shapes a new humanity – this, too, is the Algerian revolution' (Fanon, 1965: 181).

## Independence Period: Bankruptcy of the 'Postcolonial' Ruling Elites

Unfortunately, the Algerian revolution and its attempt to break from the imperialist-capitalist system were defeated, both by counter-revolutionary forces and by its own contradictions. The revolution harbored the seeds of its own failure from the start: it was a top-down, authoritarian, and highly bureaucratic project (albeit with some redistributive functions that significantly improved people's

---

1. The phrase 'new souls' was borrowed from Aimé Césaire.

lives). For example, the creative experiences of workers' initiatives and self-management of the 1960s and 1970s were undermined by a paralyzing state bureaucracy that failed to genuinely involve workers in the control of the processes of production. This lack of democracy was concomitant with the ascendancy of a comprador bourgeoisie that was hostile to socialism and staunchly opposed to genuine land reform (Bennoune, 1988). By the 1980s, the global neoliberal counter-revolution was the nail in the coffin and ushered in an age of deindustrialization and pro-market policies in Algeria, at the expense of the popular strata. The dignitaries of the new neoliberal orthodoxy declared that everything was for sale and opened the way for mass privatization.

Fanon's work, written six decades ago still bears a prophetic power as an accurate description of what happened in Algeria and elsewhere. Reading Fanon's words and especially 'The Pitfalls of National Consciousness', one cannot help being absorbed and shaken by their truth and foresight. Fanon foretold the bankruptcy and sterility of national bourgeoisies in Africa and the Middle East today; bourgeoisies that tended to replace the colonial force with a new class-based system replicating the old colonial structures of exploitation and oppression.

By the 1980s, the Algerian national bourgeoisie, like those in other parts of the world, had dispensed with popular legitimacy, turned its back on the realities of poverty and underdevelopment, and was only preoccupied with filling its own pockets and exporting the enormous profits it derived from the exploitation of its people. In Fanon's terms, this parasitic and unproductive bourgeoisie (civilian and military) has had the upper hand in running state affairs and directing economic decisions for its own interests. This elite is the biggest threat to the sovereignty of the nation as it is selling off the economy to foreign capitals and multinationals and cooperating with imperialism in its 'war on terror', another pretext for expanding the domination of the people and the scramble for resources. In Algeria, this national bourgeoisie, closely connected to the ruling party, the FLN, renounced the autonomous development project initiated in the 1960s and 1970s and did not even bargain for concessions from the West, which would have been of value for the country's economy. Instead, it offered one concession after another for blind privatizations and projects that would undermine the country's sovereignty and endanger its population and environment — the exploitation of shale gas and offshore resources being just one example (Hamouchene and Rouabah, 2016).

This is what has become of Algeria today, with oil money used to buy social peace[2] as well as to strengthen the state's repressive apparatus, corresponding to what Fanon feared. That his vision and truth telling were – and remain – unpopular with the ruling class is one reason why he is marginalized today and reduced to just another anti-colonial figure, stripped of his incandescent attack

---

2. This was achieved through the extension of cheap credit to small and medium enterprises (through ANSEJ, the *Agence nationale de soutien à l'emploi des jeunes*), the maintenance of numerous subsidies and salary increases in multiple sectors, especially the ubiquitous security apparatuses ensuring swift containment of any uprising.

on the stupidity and on the intellectual and spiritual poverty of the national bourgeoisies.

As Edward Said argued, the true prophetic genius of *The Wretched of the Earth* is when Fanon senses the divide between the nationalist bourgeoisie and the FLN's liberationist tendencies. He realized that orthodox nationalism followed 'the same track hewn out by imperialism, which while it appeared to concede authority to the nationalist bourgeoisie was really extending its hegemony' (Said, 1994: 328).

Today, Algeria – but also Tunisia, Egypt, Nigeria, Senegal, Ghana, Gabon, Angola and South Africa, among others – follows the dictates of the new instruments of imperialism such as the IMF, the World Bank and negotiates entry into the World Trade Organization. Some African countries are still using the CFA franc (renamed Eco in December 2019), a currency inherited from the times of colonialism and still under the control of the French Treasury. Fanon would have been revolted at this *bêtise* and sheer mindlessness.

He predicted this dire situation and the shocking behavior of the national bourgeoisie when he noted that its mission has nothing to do with transforming the nation but rather consists of being the transmission line between the nation and capitalism, rampant though camouflaged, which today puts on the masque of neo-colonialism' (Fanon, 1967a: 122). This is where we can appreciate the lasting value of employing Fanon's critical insights when he introduces the question of social classes and describes for us the contemporary postcolonial reality, a reality shaped by neo-colonialism and a national bourgeoisie 'unabashedly... antinational', opting he adds, for an abhorrent path of a conventional bourgeoisie, 'a bourgeoisie which is stupidly, contemptibly and cynically bourgeois' (Fanon, 1967a: 121).

Fanon would have been shocked by the ongoing international division of labour, where we Africans 'still export raw materials and continue 'being Europe's small farmers who specialize in unfinished products' (Fanon, 1967a: 122). The ruling classes in Algeria have trapped the country in a predatory extractivist model of development where profits are accumulated in the hands of a foreign-backed minority at the expense of dispossession of the majority of the population (Hamouchene, 2019).

## Rationality of Rebellion: The Hirak and the New Algerian Revolution

The sad contemporary reality that Fanon described and warned against six decades ago gives little doubt that, were he alive today, Fanon would be hugely disappointed at the result of his efforts and those of other revolutionaries. He turned out to be right about the rapacity and divisiveness of national bourgeoisies and the limits of conventional nationalism.

However, Fanon alerts us that the scandalous enrichment of this profiteering caste will be accompanied by 'a decisive awakening on the part of the people and a growing awareness that promised stormy days to come' (Fanon, 1967a: 134).

So, we can see Fanon's idea or concept of the rationality of revolt and rebellion was made clear by the second wave of the Arab uprisings and other mass protests around the world in 2019-2020. The popular masses in all these countries rebelled against the violence of the political regimes that offered them growing pauperization, marginalization and the enrichment of the few at the expense and damnation of the majority.

Algerians shattered the wall of fear and broke away from an alienation process that had infantilized and dazed them for decades. They erupted onto the political scene, discovered their political will and began again to make history. Since Friday February 22, 2019, millions of people, young and old, men and women from different social classes rose in a momentous rebellion. Historic Friday marches, followed by protests in professional sectors, united people in their rejection of the ruling system and their demands of radical democratic change. 'They must all go!' (*Yetnahaw ga*'), 'The country is ours and we'll do what we wish' (*Lablad abladna oundirou rayna*), two emblematic slogans of this so-far peaceful uprising, symbolize the radical evolution of this popular movement (*Al Hirak Acha'bi*). The uprising was triggered by the incumbent president Bouteflika's announcement that he would run for a fifth term despite being impotent, suffering from aphasia and being generally absent from public life.

The people in Algeria revolted not only to demand democracy and freedom but also to demand bread and dignity, against the oppressive socio-economic conditions under which they had lived for decades. They rose to challenge the Manichean geographies of oppressor and oppressed (so well described by Fanon in *The Wretched*), geographies imposed on them by the globalized capitalist-imperialist system and its local lackeys.

The events that took place in Algeria during 2019-2021 are truly historic. This movement (*Hirak*) is unique is its huge scale, peaceful character, national spread – including in the marginalized south, and massive participation from women and young people, who constitute the majority of Algeria's population. This kind of mobilization has not been seen since 1962, when Algerians went to the streets to celebrate their hard-won independence from French colonial rule.

This revolution is like a breath of fresh air. The people have affirmed their role as agents of their own destiny. We can use Fanon's exact words to describe this phenomenon: 'The thesis that men change at the same time that they change the world has never been manifest as it is now in Algeria. This trial of strength not only remodels the consciousness that man has of himself, and of his former dominators or of the world, at last within his reach. The struggle at different levels renews the symbols, the myths, the beliefs, the emotional responsiveness of the people. We witness in Algeria man's reassertion of his capacity to progress' (Fanon, 1965: 30).

Perhaps one of the greatest achievements of the current popular uprising is the change in political consciousness and the determination to fight for radical democratic change. This liberatory process unleashed an unequaled amount of energy, confidence, creativity and subversion.

After decades of curtailed civil society, silenced dissent, and atomized opposition, the fact that the movement grew from strength to strength for more than two years, not retreating or subsiding but pushing forward, is truly remarkable and inspiring. The Hirak succeeded in unraveling the webs of deceit that were deployed by the ruling class and its propaganda machine. Moreover, the evolution of its slogans, chants, and forms of resistance, is demonstrative of processes of politicization and popular education. The re-appropriation of public spaces created a kind of an agora where people discuss, debate, exchange views, talk strategy and perspectives, criticize each other or simply express themselves in many ways including through art and music. This has opened new horizons for resisting and building together.

Cultural production took on another meaning because it was associated with liberation and seen as a form of political action and solidarity. Far from the folkloric and sterile productions under the suffocating patronage of some authoritarian elites, we are seeing instead a culture that speaks to the people and advances their resistance and struggles through poetry, music, theatre, cartoons, and street-art. Again, we see Fanon's insights in his theorization of culture as a form of political action: 'A national culture is not a folklore, nor an abstract populism that believes it can discover the people's true nature. It is not made up of the inert dregs of gratuitous actions, that is to say actions which are less and less attached to the ever-present reality of the people... It is around the people's struggles that African-Negro culture takes on substance and not around songs, poems or folklore' (Fanon, 1967a: 188-189).

## The Struggle of Decolonization Continues

> *Many colonised people have demanded the end of colonialism, but rarely like the Algerian people.*
> — Fanon, *Toward the African Revolution*

Leaving aside largely semantic arguments around whether it is a movement, uprising, revolt or a revolution, one can say for certain that what is taking place in Algeria today is a transformative process, pregnant with emancipatory potential. The evolution of the movement and its demands specifically around 'independence', 'sovereignty' and 'an end to the pillage of the country's resources' is fertile ground for anti-colonial, anti-capitalist, anti-imperialist and even ecological ideas. This can open the way for a progressive struggle by mobilizing the relevant social forces: workers (formal and informal), peasants, unemployed youth, popular masses, etc.

Algerians are making a direct link between their current struggle and the anti-French colonial struggle of the 1950s, seeing their efforts as the continuation of decolonization. When chanting 'Generals to the dustbin and Algeria will be independent', they are laying bare the vacuous official narrative around the glorious revolution and revealing that it has been shamelessly used by anti-national bourgeoisies to scandalously pursue personal enrichment. This is undoubtedly a second Fanonian moment where people expose the neo-colonial situation, they find their country in and emphasize one unique characteristic of their uprising: its rootedness in the anti-colonial struggle against the French.

Algerians are thus recovering their revolutionary credentials and reaffirming their desire to be the true heirs of the martyrs who sacrificed their lives for the liberation of this country. Slogans and chants have captured this desire and made references to anti-colonial war veterans such as Ali La Pointe, Amirouche, Ben Mhidi and Abane: 'Oh Ali [la pointe] your descendants will never stop until they wrench their freedom!' and 'We are the descendants of Amirouche and we will never go back!'

It becomes clear that the colonialism which Fanon analyzed six decades earlier has not entirely disappeared. Instead, it has metamorphosed, camouflaging itself in sophisticated forms and mechanisms: debt; structural adjustment programmes; 'free trade' treaties; association agreements with the EU; predatory extractivism; land grabs; agribusiness; immigration laws and deadly borders; 'humanitarian' intervention and the responsibility to protect; international cooperation and development; racism and xenophobia; etc. All these constitute forms of domination and control deployed to safeguard the interests of the powerful.

The struggle of decolonization is being given a new lease of life as Algerians lay claim to the popular and economic sovereignty that was denied to them when formal independence was achieved in 1962. Fanon had a premonition about this when he wrote: 'The people who at the beginning of the struggle had adopted the primitive Manichaeism of the settler – Blacks and Whites, Arabs and Christians – realize as they go along that it sometimes happens that you get Blacks who are whiter than the Whites and the hope of an independent nation does not always tempt certain strata of the populations to give up their interests or privileges' (Fanon, 1967a: 115).

## Counter-Revolution: The Reactionary Role of the Army

As with any revolution, counter-revolutionary forces have mobilized to block change. The counter-revolutionary campaign currently underway in Algeria draws support from abroad. Regionally, the UAE, Saudi Arabia and Egypt are using their money and influence to halt potentially contagious waves of revolt in the region. At the global level, France, the US, UK, Canada, Russia and China, along with their major corporations, seeing a potential threat to their economic and geostrategic interests, are all supportive of the Algerian regime.

Times of revolutions and uprisings can also be times of entrenching unpopular economic policies and extending more concessions to foreign investors. The budget law of 2020 and the new multinational-friendly Hydrocarbon Law are illustrative (Rouabah, 2019). We cannot therefore fully appreciate the political situation in Algeria without scrutinizing foreign influences and interferences and apprehending the economic question from the angle of natural resource grabs, energy (neo)colonialism and extractivism (Hamouchene, 2019).

When it comes to the political level, the counter-revolution has been embodied by the military hierarchy. The army has not fired any bullets so far, but it has continued to justify various repressive measures. Since independence in 1962, Algeria has been ruled by a military regime, directly or indirectly. The militarization of society has created a culture of fear and distrust. The brutal repression of past uprisings and the cruelty of the war in the 1990s explain the popular movement's reluctance to directly confront the army.

The military bourgeoisie still proclaims that the 'vocation of their people is to obey, to go on obeying and to be obedient till the end of time' (Fanon, 1967a: 135) and as Fanon castigated it, it's an army that 'pins the people down, immobilizing and terrorizing them' (Fanon, 1967a: 140). However, despite the Military High Command's rejection of every roadmap and appeal for genuine dialogue proposed by the movement, people remain determined to peacefully demilitarize their republic. They have been chanting: 'A republic not a military barrack'. After Bouteflika's overthrow, demonstrations continued in opposition to the military, which has maintained de facto authority over the country.

> In these poor, under-developed countries, where the rule is that the greatest wealth is surrounded by the greatest poverty, the army and the police constitute the pillars of the regime; an army and a police force which are advised by foreign experts. The strength of the police and the power of the army are proportionate to the stagnation in which the rest of the nation is sunk. By dint of yearly loans, concessions are snatched up by foreigners; scandals are numerous, ministers grow rich, their wives doll themselves up, the members of parliament feather their nests and there is not a soul down to the simple policeman or the customs officer who does not join in the great procession of corruption. (Fanon, 1967a: 138)

This raging passage from *The Wretched* is an accurate portrayal of the situation in Algeria and many African countries where repression and suppression of freedoms are the rule – helped of course by foreign expertise – and where greedy elites institutionalize corruption and serve foreign interests. One of the emblematic slogans of the current uprising has been very eloquent in this regard: 'You devoured the country... Oh you thieves!'

Algerians know what the military are capable of and despite the trauma of the 'black decade' (civil war of the 1990s), they are bravely still insisting: 'A civilian state not a military one!'. In this way, the Algerian system is exposed for what it is: a military dictatorship hiding behind a 'democratic' façade.

## Class Struggle, Organizing and Political Education

*In a short time this continent will be liberated. For my part, the deeper I enter into the cultures and the political circles the surer I am that the great danger that threatens Africa is the absence of ideology.*
—Fanon, *Toward the African Revolution*

*All this taking stock of the situation, this enlightening of consciousness and this advance in the knowledge of the history of societies are only possible within the framework of an organization and inside the structure of a people.*
—Fanon, *The Wretched of the Earth*

Despite the odds stacked against it, and the state's efforts to divide, co-opt, and exhaust it, the Hirak has maintained an exemplary unity and peacefulness. This was demonstrated in various slogans such as: 'Algerians are brothers and sisters, the people are united, you traitors'.

The movement is youth-led and relatively loosely organized. There are no clearly identifiable leaders or organized structures propelling it. It is a popular uprising mobilizing mass forces from the middle classes and from the marginalized classes in urban and rural areas. Unlike Sudan, where the Sudanese Professional Association played a leading and organizing role, in Algeria organizing is done horizontally and mainly through social media. The general strike in the first few weeks of the uprising, which was instrumental in forcing Bouteflika to abdicate and shaking up alliances within the ruling class, was organized spontaneously after anonymous calls on social media. Such amorphous, non-structured and leaderless dynamics and movements are extremely vulnerable. While they can generate large inter-class mobilizations and are not an easy target for repression, or for co-option of leaders, they nevertheless manifest fatal weaknesses in the long run.

But what can Fanon teach us when it comes to the class struggle and organising?

Class struggle is central to Fanon's analysis. The Lebanese Marxist, Mahdi Amel, pointing to Fanon's insights on how the revolutionary praxis differentiates and changes its meaning and direction after independence, writes: 'While it [revolutionary violence] was before independence, essentially a national struggle, after independence it becomes a real class struggle' through which the masses discover their true enemy: the national bourgeoisie (Hamdan, 1964a). So, from a strictly national level, the fight moves to a socio-economic level of class struggle. Fanon urges us to move from a national consciousness towards a social and political consciousness when he says, 'If nationalism is not made explicit, if it is not enriched and deepened by a very rapid transformation into a consciousness of social and political needs, in other words into humanism, it leads up a blind alley' (Fanon, 1967a: 165).

However, Fanon invites us to 'stretch Marxism' as a way of understanding the particularities of capitalism in the colonial and postcolonial world. To borrow

Immanuel Wallerstein's words, Fanon 'had rebelled, forcefully, against the ossified Marxism of the communist movements of his era', asserting a revised version of the class struggle breaking with the dogma that the urban, industrial proletariat is the only revolutionary class against the bourgeoisie (Wallerstein, 2009). Fanon thought of the peasantry and the urbanized lumpenproletariat as the strongest candidate for the role of historical revolutionary subject in colonial Algeria. And here, Fanon meets Che Guevara when both point out that in colonized countries, revolution begins in rural areas and moves to the urban towns. It is launched by the peasantry, which embraces the proletariat rather than the other way around as in the case of European capitalist, and even socialist, countries (Hamdan, 1964b).

In a nutshell, class struggle is essential provided we clearly identify the struggling classes. In this spirit, it's crucial to determine the revolutionary classes (and their alliances) in the current uprising. We need to go beyond 'workerism' and embrace a much broader conception of the proletariat in its contemporary expressions, namely the unemployed youth, the urban/rural working people, informal workers, peasants, etc. It is these classes that have nothing to lose but their chains, which makes them potentially revolutionary.

In his chapter 'Spontaneity: its strengths and weaknesses' in *The Wretched*, Fanon expressed concerns that if the lumpen proletariat is left on its own, without organizational structure, it will burn out (Wallerstein, 2009). In order to avoid this and to bar the route against the parasitic bourgeoisie that is still ruling in Algeria, Fanon would probably say: 'The bourgeoisie should not be allowed to find the conditions necessary for its existence and its growth. In other words, the combined effort of the masses led by a party and of intellectuals who are highly conscious and armed with revolutionary principles ought to bar the way to this useless and harmful middle class' (Fanon, 1967a: 140).

Fanon would also repeat to us an important observation he made on some African revolutions, which is that their unifying character sidelines any thinking of a socio-political ideology on how to radically transform society. This is a great weakness that we are witnessing yet again with the new Algerian revolution. 'Nationalism is not a political doctrine, nor a programme', says Fanon (1967a: 163). He insists on the necessity of a revolutionary political party (or perhaps an organized social movement) that can take the demands of the masses forward, a party/structure that will educate the people politically, that will be 'a tool in the hands of the people' and that will be the energetic spokesman and the 'incorruptible defender of the masses'. For Fanon, reaching such a conception of a party necessitates first ridding ourselves of the bourgeois notion of elitism and 'the contemptuous attitude that the masses are incapable of governing themselves' (1967a: 151).

Fanon abhorred the elitist discourse on the immaturity of the masses and asserted that in the struggle, they (the masses) are equal to the problems which confront them. It is therefore important for them to know just where they are going and why. Nigel Gibson eloquently articulated this view in these words: 'for Fanon, the 'we' was always a creative 'we', a 'we' of political action and praxis, thinking and reasoning' (Gibson, 2011). For him, the nation does not exist except in a socio-political and economic program 'worked out by revolutionary leaders and taken up with full understanding and enthusiasm by the masses' (Fanon, 1967a: 164).

Unfortunately, what we see today in Africa is the antithesis of what Fanon strongly argued for. We see the stupidity of the anti-democratic bourgeoisies embodied in their tribal and family dictatorships, banning the people, often with crude force, from participating in their country's development, and fostering a climate of immense hostility between the rulers and the ruled. Fanon, in his conclusion of *The Wretched*, argues that we must work out new concepts through ongoing political education, enriched through mass struggle. Political education for him is not merely about political speeches but rather about 'opening the minds' of the people, 'awakening them, and allowing the birth of their intelligence' (Fanon, 1967a: 159). 'If building a bridge does not enrich the awareness of those who work on it', then according to Fanon, it 'ought not to be built and the citizens can go on swimming across the river or going by boat' (Fanon, 1967a: 162).

This is perhaps one of the greatest legacies of Fanon. His radical and generous vision is so refreshing and rooted in the people's daily struggles, which open spaces for new ideas and imaginings. For him, everything depends on the masses, hence his idea of radical intellectuals engaged in and with people's movements and capable of coming up with new concepts in non-technical and non-professional language. Just as, for Fanon, culture must become a fighting culture, so too must education become about total liberation (Gibson, 2011). This is what we need to bear in mind when we talk about education in schools and universities. Decolonial education in the Fanonian sense is an education that helps create a social and political consciousness. The militant or the intellectual, therefore, must not take shortcuts in the name of getting things done, as this is inhuman and sterile. It is all about coming and thinking together, which is the foundation of the liberated society.

## The Shadow of Fanon: The New Algerian Revolution and Black Lives Matter

> *We are off. Our mission: to open the southern front. To transport arms and munitions from Bamako. Stir up the Saharan population, infiltrate to the Algerian high plateaus. After carrying Algeria to the four corners of Africa, move up with all Africa toward African Algeria, toward the North, toward Algiers, the continental city ... Subdue the desert, deny it, assemble Africa, create the continent.*
> —Fanon, *Toward the African Revolution*

In 2020, a global revolt against white supremacy started in the streets of Minneapolis in the United States following the murder of George Floyd, a 46-year-old Black man by a policeman who knelt with his knee on his neck for almost 8 minutes. Like Eric Garner before him, George Floyd uttered these last words before he died: 'I can't breathe'. The ensuing global rebellion and show of solidarity echo the words of Fanon when he discussed the Vietnamese anti-colonial struggle: 'It is not because the Indo-Chinese has discovered a culture of his own that he is in revolt. It is because 'quite simply' it was, in more than one way, becoming impossible for him to breathe' (Fanon, 1986: 176).

We can no longer breathe in a system that dehumanizes people, a system that enshrines super-exploitation, a system that dominates nature and humanity, a system that generates massive inequality and untold poverty. Luckily, revolts that are fundamentally anti-systemic are taking place on all continents and regions. But for these episodic and largely geographically confined acts of resistance to succeed, they need to go beyond the local to the global; they need to create enduring alliances in face of capitalism, colonialism and patriarchy.

Can these various contemporary struggles, from the Arab uprisings to Black Lives Matter, converge and build strong alliances that overcome their own contradictions and blind spots? Can they usher in a new moment where we question the colonial foundations of our current predicaments and continue on the path of decolonizing our politics, economies, cultures and epistemologies? This is not only possible but necessary as we must envisage such transnational solidarities and alliances because they are crucial in the global struggle of emancipation of the wretched of the earth. Perhaps, we can take inspiration from the past, by looking at the decolonization period, Bandung and Third- Worldism era, the Tri-Continental and other internationalist experiences. I would argue that Fanon (or more accurately his intellectual legacy) could be once again the linkage and the nodal point of these struggles, like he was in the 1960s and 1970s.

Some histories are ignored, others are silenced in order to maintain certain hegemonies and to hide from view an inspiring era of revolutionary connections between struggles for liberation on different continents. We must dig into this past to familiarize ourselves with these histories, learn from them and discern some potential convergences between ongoing struggles.

In the first two decades of its independence, Algeria became, as Samir Meghelli described it, 'a critical node in the constellation of transnational solidarities' being forged among revolutionary movements around the world (Meghelli, 2009). In the heydays of the Civil Rights and Black Power eras, Meghelli shows that 'just as Algeria looked to Black America as 'that part of the Third World situated in the belly of the beast' (Neal, 1966) so, too, did much of Black America look to Algeria as 'the country that fought the enslaver and won' (Joans, 1970).

Algeria became a powerful symbol of revolutionary struggle and served as a model for several liberation fronts across the globe. And given its audacious foreign policy in the 1960s and 1970s, the Algerian capital was to become a Mecca for all revolutionaries. As Amilcar Cabral, the revolutionary leader from Guinea-Bissau announced at a press conference at the margins of the first Pan-African festival in 1969: 'Pick a pen and take note: the Muslims make the pilgrimage to Mecca, the Christians to the Vatican and the national liberation movements to Algiers!'

Thanks to the popular film *The Battle of Algiers* as well as Frantz Fanon's writings, Algeria came to hold an important place in the 'iconography, rhetoric, and ideology of key branches of the African American freedom movement' (Meghelli, 2009), which came to view their struggle for civil rights as connected to the struggles of African nations for independence. Francee Covington, a student in political science at Harlem University in the late 1960s made this point even clearer: 'In the past few years the works of Frantz Fanon have become widely read and quoted by those involved in the 'Revolution' that has begun to take place in the communities of Black America. If *The Wretched of the Earth* is the 'handbook for the Black Revolution', then The Battle of Algiers is its movie counterpart' (Covington, 1970: 245).

The writings of Fanon and his analysis of the Algerian war revealed so many parallels between the experience of colonial domination in Algeria and the racial oppression Blacks had suffered for centuries in America. His book *The Wretched* had become a 'Black bible' to use the words of Eldridge Cleaver. By the end of the 1970s, it had sold some 750,000 copies in the United States. This led Dan Watts, editor of *Liberator* magazine to say: 'Every brother on a rooftop can quote Fanon' (Zolberg and Zolberg, 1970: 198).

In his visit to New York in October 1962, Ahmed Ben Bella, one of the FLN leaders and the first Algerian president, met with Dr Martin Luther King Jr. and made it clear that there is a close relationship between colonialism and segregation (King, 1962). This view advocating for a global perspective on oppression (be it either colonial or racist) was expressed a few years later by Malcolm X. After visiting Algeria in 1964 and the Casbah – the site of the battle of Algiers against French militaries in 1957 – and after responding to the allegations that there existed some sort of 'hate-gang' called the 'Blood Brothers' based in Harlem and calculatedly committing crimes against whites, he declared at the militant Labour Forum: 'The same conditions that prevailed in Algeria that forced the people, the noble people of Algeria, to resort eventually to the terrorist-type tactics that were necessary to get the monkey off their backs, those same conditions prevail today in America in every Black community' (Meghelli, 2009).

It is this global perspective on our struggles that we need to emphasize in order to break away from the many constraints and limitations imposed on our movements in order to embrace a radical internationalism that will actively promote solidarity. Therefore, it becomes essential to rediscover the revolutionary heritage of the Maghreb, Africa, West Asia and the Global South, developed by great minds like Frantz Fanon, Amilcar Cabral and Thomas Sankara, to mention just a few. We need to revive the ambitious projects of the 1960s that sought emancipation from the imperialist-capitalist system. Building on this revolutionary heritage, being inspired by its insurgent hope and applying its internationalist perspective to the current context is of utmost importance to Algeria, to the Black Lives Matter movement and to other emancipatory struggles all over the world.

# In guise of conclusion

The progressive forces in Algeria and beyond have a huge task confronting them: the task of putting the socio-economic issue at the center of the debate around alternatives and injecting a class analysis into the broad movement. It is incumbent upon them, and more specifically upon the radical and revolutionary left, to elaborate new visions that go beyond resistance to the current predatory offensive of capitalism to question the imaginary of development and modernity itself, an imaginary that means we get incorporated into a lifestyle based on overconsumption and inserted into globalization in a subordinate position.

Fanon urged us to invent and make new discoveries and not blindly imitate Europe. The struggle of decolonization, Fanon tells us, must challenge the dominance of European culture and its claims of universalism without being trapped in a romanticized and fixed past. It is these two alienations that colonized people must overcome in their cultural struggle. Decolonizing the mind also means deconstructing Western notions of 'development', 'civilization', 'progress', 'universalism' and 'modernity'.

Such concepts represent what is called a *coloniality of power and knowledge*, which means that ideas of 'modernity' and 'progress' were conceived in Europe and North America and then implanted in our continents (Africa, Asia and Latin America) in a context of coloniality (Mignolo, 2012). These Eurocentric ideas and culture have reinforced the colonial heritage of land confiscations, resource plunder, as well as domination of 'other' peoples in order to 'civilize' them.

These notions ('progress', 'development', 'modernity'...) are imposed notions and are based on a linear conception of the evolution of history that divides the world between 'developed' and 'under-developed'; 'advanced' and 'less advanced'; 'modern' (read Western) and 'backward' (read non-Western). They are concepts that pretend to be universal and issue injunctions to the excluded and dispossessed to follow a pre-determined path in order to enter an imperial and colonial globalization, led by the 'advanced' countries, legitimizing therefore their subordination. Being Eurocentric, these concepts assert their self-claimed superiority by excluding and delegitimizing other forms of knowledge, other ways of life and other civilizations' contributions (Gudynas, 2013).

Fanon did not offer us a clear prescription for making the transition after decolonisation to a new liberating political order. Perhaps, there is no such thing as a detailed plan or solution. Perhaps he viewed it as a protracted process that will be informed by praxis and, above all, by confidence in the masses and in their revolutionary potential to figure out the liberating alternative.

In the conclusion of *The Wretched*, Fanon wrote:

> Come, then, comrades; it would be as well to decide at once to change our ways. We must shake off the heavy darkness in which we were plunged, and leave it behind. The new day which is already at hand must find us firm, prudent and resolute.... Let us waste no time in sterile litanies and nauseating mimicry. Leave this Europe where they are never done talk-

ing of Man, yet murder men everywhere they find them, at the corner of every one of their own streets, in all the corners of the globe... Come, then, comrades, the European game has finally ended; we must find something different. We today can do everything, so long as we do not imitate Europe, so long as we are not obsessed by the desire to catch up with Europe.... For Europe, for ourselves and for humanity, comrades, we must turn over a new leaf, we must work out new concepts, and try to set afoot a new man. (Fanon, 1967a: 251-255)

In this vein, it is paramount to continue the tasks of decolonization in order to restore our denied humanity. Through resistance to colonial and capitalist logics of appropriation and extraction, new imaginaries and counter-hegemonic alternatives will be born.

## Bibliography

Bennoune, M. 1988. *The Making of Contemporary Algeria, 1830–1987: Colonial Upheavals and Post-independence Development*. Cambridge: Cambridge University Press.

Bouamama, S. 2017. *Figures de la révolution africaine: de Kenyatta a Sankara*. Paris: La Découverte.

Covington, F. 1970. 'Are the Revolutionary Techniques Employed in *The Battle of Algiers* Applicable to Harlem?' In *The Black Woman: An Anthology*, edited by T. C. Bambara. New York: Penguin.

Fanon, F. 1965. *A Dying Colonialism*, New York: Grove Press.

_____. 1967a. *The Wretched of the Earth*. London: Penguin Books.

_____. 1967b. *Toward the African Revolution*. New York: Grove Press.

_____. 1986. *Black Skin, White Masks*. London: Pluto Press.

Gibson, N. C. 2011. '50 Years Later: Fanon's Legacy.' *Keynote address at the Caribbean Symposium Series '50 Years Later: Frantz Fanon's Legacy to the Caribbean and the Bahamas,' December 2011*. Accessed July 21, 2020, https://www.pambazuka.org/governance/50-years-later-fanons-legacy.

Eduardo Gudynas, E. 2013. 'Debates on Development and its Alternatives in Latin America. A Brief Heterodox Guide.' In *Beyond Development: Alternative Visions from Latin America*, edited by M. Lang & D. Mokrani. Quito & Amsterdam: Rosa Luxemburg Foundation & Transnational Institute.

Hamdan, H. 1964a. 'La Pensée Révolutionnaire de Frantz Fanon.' *Révolution Africaine*. N72.

_____. 1964b. 'La Pensée Révolutionnaire de Frantz Fanon.' *Révolution Africaine*. N71.

Hamouchene, H. 2019. 'Extractivism and Resistance in North Africa.' *Transnational Institute (TNI)*, November 20. Accessed: 20 July 2020, https://www.tni.org/en/ExtractivismNorthAfrica.

_____. 2020. 'The Algerian Revolution: The Struggle for Decolonization Continues.' *ROAR Magazine*, March 12. Accessed July 20, 2020, https://bit.ly/3eMkqaa.

Hamouchene, H., and Rouabah, B. 2016. 'The Political Economy of Regime Survival: Algeria in the Context of the African and Arab Uprisings.' *Review of African Political Economy* 43 (150): 668–680.

Joans, T. 1970. 'The Pan African Pow Wow.' *Journal of Black Poetry* 1 (13): 4–5.

Khalfa, J., and Young, R. J. C. 2018. *Frantz Fanon: Alienation and Freedom.* London: Bloomsbury.

Meghelli, S. 2009. 'From Harlem to Algiers: Transnational Solidarities between the African American Freedom Movement and Algeria.' 1962–1978. In *Black Routes to Islam,* edited by M, Marable and H, Aidi, 99–119. New York: Palgrave Macmillan.

Neal, L. 1966. 'The Black Writer's Role,' *Liberator* 6 (6): 8.

Rouabah, B. 2019. 'The People's Movement in Algeria, Eight Months On.' *Africa is a country,* October 31. Accessed: July 20, 2020, https://africasacountry.com/2019/10/the-peoples-movement-in-algeria-eight-months-on.

Said, E. 1994. *Culture and Imperialism.* London: Vintage.

Wallerstein, I. 2009. 'Reading Fanon in the 21st Century.' *New Left Review* 57: 117–125.

Walter Mignolo, W. 2012. *Local Histories/Global Designs: Coloniality, Subaltern Knowledges, and Border Thinking.* Princeton: Princeton University Press.

Zolberg, A., and Zolberg, V. 1970. 'The Americanization of Frantz Fanon.' In *Americans From Africa: Old Memories, New Moods,* edited by P. I. Rose. Chicago: Atherton.

# DISCUSSING FANON

Abahlali baseMjondolo and Nigel C. Gibson

*Meeting at*: Abahlali baseMjondolo, 13-16 Diakonia Conference Centre, 20 Diakonia Street, Durban, 4000, March 1, 2020

*Comrades who attended the discussion at the office were*: National Council Members: S'bu Zikode, Mqapheli Bonono, Nomusa Sizani, Zanele Mtshali, Bathabile Makhoba, Joyce Majola, Thuso Mohapi, Mfanufikile Sindane; KZN Provincial Secretary: Nhlanhla Mtshali; Youth Comrades: Busisiwe Diko, Lindokuhle Mnguni, Nhlakaniphi Mdiyastha; Financial Officer: Asiphe Mpumela

**S'bu Zikode:** Nigel is a writer and author of a number of books. One of the books that he has written is *Fanonian Practices in South Africa: From Steve Biko to Abahlali baseMjondolo*. So *Fanonian Practices in South Africa* is also about Abahlali. Some comrades have seen the book. But normally comrades, they borrow the books so they are not here. Imagine Frantz Fanon passed away 60 years ago, but the very practice of Frantz Fanon is still relevant. And what Fanon discovered and said many years ago is sometimes organic and comes from us without us realizing it. That is what Nigel called Fanonian Practices.

This was just an introduction. Nigel, these are Abahlali comrades. Even the one without the uniform is an Abahlali comrade. So, I would ask comrades just to introduce themselves, of course towards my right, and then comrades could tell Nigel which branch you come from, and then what is your task. I do not want to call it a position. We had an induction workshop yesterday with some leaders of three settlements where we've recently been launched. So we were kind of insisting that Abahlali's work is not necessarily positions of power that are fought over but tasks and duties that the movement allocates.

**S'bu Zikode:** I am a former resident of Kennedy Road and currently adopted by the Brighton branch.

Greetings comrades. I am **Nhlakaniphi Mdiyastha**, Youth League of Abahlali baseMjondolo.

Morning. This is **Nhlakanipho Mdiyatsha** from eLindelani branch.

Hi everyone. My name is **Lindokuhle Mnguni** eNkanini branch, Youth structure of AbM.

My name is **Mfanufikile Sindane** from eNkanini branch.

I am **Thuso Mohapi**. I reside in Briardene settlement, just outside Durban North.

**Busisiwe Diko** from Ekukhanyeni branch.

Morning. My name is **Nomusa Sizani** from eNkanini branch.

My name is **Zanele Mtshali** from the eNkanini branch.

I'm **Joyce Majola**, residing in eKuphumeleleni branch. I'm serving as the Deputy Secretary of the organization.

Morning. I'm **Bathabile Makhoba** from Brighton branch next to Durban North, and I'm the national chief whip.

I'm **Asiphe Mpumela** from Briardene branch.

**Mqapheli (George) Bonono:** Comrade Gibson you came at the wrong time. You will see these people, they are introducing themselves, and most of them are Orlando Pirates fans. Now I see while they're introducing themselves like they don't like that you must know who they are. Hi, my name is Thuso Mohapi, no he's angry. You know why? Because the Pirates didn't do a good job for them.

My name is **Mqapheli Bonono George**. I'm a former resident of Foreman Road. Currently now I am adopted by Brighton branch, and I have a duty in Abahlali baseMjondolo to be a national organizer as the elected deputy president.

**Nigel Gibson:** Well, thank you. Now I understand why you were so quiet when you were introducing yourselves.

It's wonderful to be here sitting around the table with you.

As S'bu said, I've been thinking about Abahlali since its birth. It's amazing to think that in that first moment, the first road blockade, that you are still here 15 years later. So the question of time is very important. I'm so happy that the Abahlali youth are here as well.

As S'bu was saying, my book, *Fanonian Practices in South Africa: From Steve Biko to Abahlali baseMjondolo*, came out with S'bu's important foreword which I think is worth reading on its own. If you don't read the book, you should read your president's words in that book because he talks about coming across Fanon, and the inspiration he finds in one of the quotes from Fanon, which is about how each generation has to discover its mission. And so to the youth, they're a new generation. And discovering their mission doesn't mean discovering it out of thin air. It's about reconnecting within a tradition of resistance and struggles for liberation in South Africa and across the world.

Fanon has always been important to my political thinking in relation to South Africa and its struggles for liberation which began with the way Steve Biko had engaged Fanon in the early 1970s. And then in the late 1990s, Fanon again became important to my understanding of what was happening in post-apartheid South Africa. When Abahlali questions democracy, freedom, and humanity it is also a practice; the mandate and task of the membership is to 'humanize the world', as S'bu puts it. For me, this is also a dialogue with Frantz Fanon. In other words, Abahlali's struggle and its living politic was another Fanonian practice in South Africa.

The last book I edited on Fanon was called *Living Fanon* and had a certain resonance with Abahlali, because Abahlali was talking about living, learning, and the relationship between thinking and life – thinking very much to do with doing and with thinking about what to do, grounded in a certain idea of humanism, respect, and dignity. I am meeting with you today as part of a new book project called *Fanon Today, the Reason and Revolt of the Wretched of the Earth*. This book begins with the reason of revolt as a celebration of Fanon, specifically related to international social movements and activists. The focus is about Fanon from the inside of social movements, the work of organic intellectuals. In this sense I'm thinking of you as intellectuals and the reason of revolt being your thinking understood as, and part of, the organization of Abahlali.

S'bu was just telling me about the discussions about the land question. And today I was thinking maybe this discussion of Fanon can be put in conversation with your discussions when you talked about the decommodification of land. I think that the question of decommodification articulates a certain idea about humanity and about human needs and how the human need for land is related to notions of the commons and communities.

But S'bu told me that there have been many discussions about land and about the meaning of land in the communities. These kinds of discussions, and the intellectual work of clarification, are based on including everyone in those discussions. In other words, those who are usually excluded from those kinds of discussions, those who have been thought not to have any thoughts, are recognized as having experiences and knowledge that must be heard. For example, part of the discussion around the xenophobic violence in 2008, and the remarkable statement against that violence that Abahlali put out at that time, is one expression of the reason of revolt – discussions that can hear themselves speak.

I thought I'd begin with a number of quotes from *The Wretched of the Earth*, and give you some kind of context.[1] *The Wretched of the Earth* was written as Fanon lay dying in 1961. It is a book that reflects on his experience in the Algerian revolution, as part of the international movement of African decolonization. One important element of the book is his critical summing up of that moment.

So I'll start backwards, from the conclusion (Fanon, *The Wretched of the Earth* (1968, 313-315). The conclusion is a universal statement that is written for a popular audience of anticolonial fighters. He says, 'So, my brothers [and sisters], how is it that we do not understand that we have better things to do than follow

---

1. The page of quotes from Fanon's *The Wretched of the Earth* was handed out. In the main I used the Farrington translation, occasionally preferring the Philcox translation.

Europe?' That sums up part of the critique he's been making. What happened to those anticolonial movements, and one could say what's happened in post-apartheid South Africa, is that the lure of Europe and its idea of wealth dominated their thinking. The anticolonial movements didn't do much more than follow Europe's model of 'development' and thus emphasized getting hold of the colonial apparatus—its states and institutions—rather than building something new and human from the ground. Fanon considered this a crisis of thought and that is what Fanon is also addressing in *The Wretched of the Earth*.

> That same Europe, where they were never done talking with humanity, never stopped proclaiming that they were only anxious for the welfare of humanity. Today we know with what sufferings humanity has paid for every one of their triumphs of the mind'.

So here is a kind of critical relationship to the ideas of European thought and European humanism. He's not rejecting humanism. He's rejecting the humanism that is being proclaimed in Europe that is based on its hierarchy, colonization, slavery and violence. Human suffering. European humanism dehumanizes. And so 'We must find something different ... But let's be clear, what matters is to stop talking about output, intensification, and the rhythm of work'. Immediately he rejects what is central to European humanism, profit and the reductions of the human to objects understood in terms of productivity, output, and intensification. If you listen to the politicians, they're always talking about output: national output, production, economic growth, and so forth. One could also include here how the rhythm of work is geared to production, getting more output from human beings.

> If we want to turn Africa into a new Europe, and America into a new Europe, then let us leave the destiny of our countries to Europeans. They will know how to do it better than the most gifted among us.

This is kind of ironic. Namely, those leaders who want Africa to become a new Europe, are really second rate leaders. If you want to do that then let the Europeans do it because they know how to do it. This is an essential part of his critique of neocolonialism in *The Wretched of the Earth*. Rather than thinking about a new society, the new ruling elites of the newly independent countries simply see the state as a means to their own accumulation.

Jacob Zuma was a great example. But Zuma was neither unique nor original. Fanon was already seeing a tendency toward kleptocracy and analyzing it before many of the countries were liberated. In other words, he is seeing a contradiction in the liberation movements themselves. Fanon advises: 'But if we want humanity to advance a step further, if we want to bring it up to a different level than that which Europe has shown it, then we must invent and we must make discoveries'. So Fanon is already talking about a new universalism here. He's saying, if we want humanity as a starting point, then we must make new discoveries. What are the new discoveries? Fanon, we should remember, was a philosopher concerned with action and change. The discoveries, in other words, would be made through authentic action, what Abahlali calls living learning. Think, for example, of what you have learned through your actions and thinking and discussing your experiences, and how that also leads you to further reflection and interest in thinkers like Fanon, or Marx, or Biko. That new universalism is internationalist and comes from the bottom up. He says, it's not only for Africa, for us, it's also for everyone: 'For ourselves and for humanity, comrades, we must turn over a new leaf. We must work out new concepts and try to set afoot a new humanity'.

So I started from the last page of the book. We must work out new concepts and set afoot a new humanity. The two are connected. The new concepts emerge from the struggle—and the anticolonial struggle Fanon was involved in was world historic—and needed to be worked out in the context of the struggle. It is worth noting that Fanon had been working out new concepts from the first page of the book.

And that's why he says in the first chapter, 'Decolonization as we know it is a historical process. That is to say that it cannot be understood... it cannot become intelligible nor clear to itself except in the exact measure that we discern the movements which give it historical form and content'. (1968: 35)

So, again, he's talking about history made from below. It's the movements, intentional human action, that give the historical content of decolonization. It's not something that can come from a dictate from above or follows a preconceived form. It has to be produced by people in struggle. That is the historical process, that is making history, that is, making a new history that hadn't been seen before. It is the form and content of those movements in struggle that make history, rather than some group taking over from the colonial powers.

Then in chapter two he says, 'The insurrection proves to itself its rationality'. (1968: 145) This is an absolutely crucial quote for me. You might remember that Abahlali is often spoken of by politicians, and also in the media, as irrational. Around the anti-Slums Bill action Abahlali was tagged as anti-development and irrational. Often the criticism of the Slums bill was translated as a criminal activity and those supporting Abahlali were backward and didn't understand that these decisions should be left to the professional bureaucrats and experts.

Abahlali was pathologized, depicted as other than 'civilized' humans. Abahlali's own history and revolt has constantly faced the accusation that its politics are irrational because it doesn't understand the complexities of 'development'. How could people who were living in shacks think? That was the criticism of some of the provincial ANC and also some of the university researchers. But the actions and Abahlali's own history proves its rationality. Fanon warns that this is sometimes a difficult thing for university trained intellectuals to understand. The movement speaks a different language and Fanon warns these intellectual that when they don't understand, they are actually at the heart of the problem. In other words, they have to listen carefully.

So in this quote he's talking about the rationality of revolt, and so, again, for me, it was thinking about Abahlali's own history that made Fanon's concept so important for me.

The insurrection proves to itself its rationality and demonstrates its maturity every time it uses a specific case to advance the consciousness of the people in spite of those within the movement who sometimes are inclined to think that any nuance constitutes a danger and threatens popular solidarity. (Fanon, 2004: 95; also see 1968: 145)

This new politics is in the hands of ... [those] who use their muscles and their brains to lead the struggle for liberation. (Fanon, 2004: 95-96; also see 1968: 148)

What I like about this is a movement needs people's muscles and brains. There is no division of people here. No division between those who have the muscles and those who have the brains. There are often some in the movements who are inclined to think that people can't really think through problems and grasp their inner contradictions. Rather all they need is a slogan they will follow while the thinking is left up to the leaders. The period after Abahlali were purged from Kennedy Road, for example, and had to go underground was a moment when some demanded that the decentralized and democratic character of the movement needed to be put on hold for security reasons. There are, in other words, always contingent reasons to shut down spaces for discussion and dialogue. This idea mirrors an elite type of organization that says that not all people should be involved in thinking. Because political action requires unity it is argued that to discuss ideas (political, organizational, philosophic) with any nuance (and what he means by nuance is holding on to contradictions or to have an open discussion that leaves contradictions unresolved) threatens popular solidarity and unity.

Part of what Abahlali has been about is thinking things through involving everybody. To come up with a slogan isn't simply about a slogan. It's the thinking that's done and the nuance and discussion around that particular slogan that is important. For example, decommodification of land. There has been enormous discussion around what that means, what it includes and what it means, and all those discussions about what it means aren't excluded from the thinking about it openly and inclusively.

It's like someone might say, 'Well, it means this to me', and someone might say that it means something different to them. That's part of engaging the nuances and how thinking something through and including everyone in discussion is absolutely essential to creating a genuinely democratic organization from the bottom up as well as creating a new society. That work, in other words, doesn't start 'the day after the revolution'.

So Fanon is saying, the rationality of revolt is not only about action but also the discussion and thought that goes into the revolt. He is also thinking of the organic intellectuals in the movements and their work in these discussions thinking through these perhaps contradictory ideas.

He calls it a new politics, because unlike the old politics that is about following and being told what to do, 'this new politics is in the hands of... [those] who use their muscles and their brains to lead the struggle for liberation'.

I like this inclusion of brains and it is reminiscent of Marx in *Capital* when he speaks about the struggle beginning when workers put their 'brains together'. So for Fanon and for Marx, a radical movement is about putting brains together in contrast to thought not emerging from the brains of isolated intellectuals. It is thinking understood socially which recognizes the importance of those social discussions.

The third chapter of *The Wretched of the Earth*, 'The Pitfalls of National Consciousness', is a frank discussion of the betrayal of the popular struggles by the nationalist organizations. 'Instead of being a coordinated crystallization of the people's innermost aspirations', he writes, 'instead of being the most tangible, immediate product of popular mobilization, national consciousness', in other words the idea of a new and free nation, becomes 'nothing but a crude, empty, fragile shell' (2004: 97; also see 1968: 148).

'Such shortcomings and dangers, ,he continues 'derive historically', that is to say it is not about the individual moral integrity of this or that leader, but derives logically from this class, who Fanon calls the national bourgeoisie and their '*incapacity ... to rationalize popular praxis*. In other words, their incapacity to attribute it any reason' (2004: 97-98). Again we are faced with the dialectical interconnection between ideas and action. Here the incapacity to rationalize popular praxis is the class expression of the national bourgeoisie who, to be truly national, Fanon says—and this before Amilcar Cabral spoke similarly—should commit class suicide.

I've italicized the quote, '*the inability of the nationalist leaders to rationalize popular praxis*'. It is expressed in the utter contempt of the masses of people that bring them to power. In fact, Fanon argues, that as soon as they have taken power the leaders order the masses back to the shacks. He says they are sent 'back to their caves' (1968: 183) and told to be silent and be orderly. Like a chorus, they are mobilized now and again to celebrate the leaders. This is one expression of the gulf between the leaders and the popular movements. And at the same time the new government works to co-opt former militants into the patronage system while silencing those it cannot buy off.

**S'bu Zikode:** I don't know how many of you were here during this meeting of the Coalition [of the Poor] who think that Abahlali can be hired to bring the masses, and as if we have no brains and no direction. So they're thinking of protesting. They think Abahlali can bring the numbers. This was just the discussion this week. We're part of the Coalition of different organizations here in Durban. They organize transportation and send leaders with banners but they don't have numbers. They need Abahlali to bring its marchers.

So that's one example of the imbalances of working within a Coalition when one group uses the other just for numbers and not to be directly involved in the thinking.

**Mqapheli Bonono:** I remember something when Abahlali was thinking about having its own 'Unfreedom Day'. I can clearly remember the discussions about Freedom Day, that we must go to a fixed area and sit and listen. When the speaker stops speaking they walk out to have lunch, while we will sit and listen to a good speech and get back to the bus, going back to the same place where we are getting burnt, places where some of us wouldn't eat food that night.

**Nigel Gibson:** I'm so happy you mentioned Unfreedom Day, because for me that is also a great expression of Fanon's critique—namely that in the dawn of freedom, there is no freedom.

Fanon's notion of time is very sensitive to the psychological situation that people find themselves in. He's a psychiatrist concerned with mental health, treating people in the period of a very vicious war against the National Liberation movement in Algeria.

The liberation struggle has created an enormous change in people's consciousness but he is aware that what he calls the awakening of the people as a whole will not be achieved overnight.

In other words, movements take time. There's no instant solution. The awakening is a constant process, and I think, in a certain sense, that also reflects Abahlali's own work.

**S'bu Zikode:** I don't know what comes to comrades' minds when you talk about the awakening because it suggests that people have been sleeping.

So here in Abahlali, we often talk about opening people's eyes. So what that suggests, firstly, is a statement of acknowledgement that our eyes are not widely open and that we acknowledge that somehow we are relating it to waking up. So here he talks about that awakening. It was then suggested that somehow people are not awake and acknowledged that it's going to take time. It is a process. It's not an event. It's not a one day thing.

**Nigel Gibson:** Fanon then expands the idea of time saying, 'The sense of time must no longer be that of the moment or the next harvest, but rather that of the rest of the world'. He's talking about the future of humanity. Humanizing the world means creating a new kind of society, what Abahlali call a 'living communism'. He's talking about the notion of time being the connection to that creation of this new society. It's an incredible project to think like that. It's not about the moment. It's not time measured by the next harvest but a new conception of time. And finally, and this gets back to S'bu's comment, because 'the demoralization buried deep within the mind by colonization is still very much alive'. In other words, a new conception of time is immediately concrete to address the legacies of oppression and the internalization of oppression. So it's almost an awakening from the internalization of oppression. That internalization is often expressed by hopelessness, 'It's pointless doing anything. Nothing will change'. It's no point organizing anything. When's anything good going to come? A kind of demoralization is repeated.

He's talking about the liberation of the mind, but he's connecting it to struggle and action. It's not simply about going to the counselor and your mind is liberated and everything's okay, because, in fact, when you walk out the door, the oppressive reality is just the same as it was before you went into the therapist's office. So new social relationships and new solidarities have to be created in the struggle itself.

And then the last quote, which I've called 'Rethinking Everything'. Don't forget this was written sixty years ago, so you can think about this in different ways and expand it in different ways.

Here he talks about the environment. You could include land and use of land, land expropriation and pollution.

'Perhaps it's necessary to begin everything all over again', which is fascinating to think about. Okay, so we've gone through the struggle against colonization and apartheid and now after all that we have to rethink everything?

So after liberation, he turns around and says the struggle continues, 'Perhaps we need to rethink everything'. In Algeria it was a long struggle for liberation, the same in South Africa and then he turns around and says, 'Perhaps we need to rethink everything'.

So there's a sort of shortfall in that liberation struggle.

> Perhaps it's necessary to begin everything all over again: to change the nature... Now he's getting very practical and he's thinking specifically of that moment, '...to change the nature of the country's exports and not simply their destination, to re-examine the soil and mineral resources, the rivers and—why not?—the sun's productivity. (1968: 100)

So in other words, he's getting back to question what is the nation? What is the land? What are the resources? Can we rethink the way they're being used for human need? Because, talking about human need, the last little quote I had gets back to the question of work, what kind of work should people do, which is implicit to a liberation struggle.

'If conditions of work are not modified...' (1968: 100). In other words, he's talking about forced labor, and that includes forced labor when you're desperately looking for work and you'll do anything that you can. You're forced to labor to survive.

> 'If conditions of work are not modified, centuries will be needed to humanize this world which has been forced down to animal level by imperial powers'.

In other words, he's saying, in this moment of liberation in 1961, that we really need to rethink the economy, not just exports and imports, but rivers and land and sun and what we have and also how we work. If we don't modify the way that we work, if we don't change the ways that we work and think about different kinds of working where work has to do with thought as well, not just manual labor, but thought, then

> 'centuries will be needed to modify the situation that's been imposed on us by the colonial powers'.

This isn't the whole book, but I wanted to introduce some of Fanon's thinking to you and see how he speaks to us through these quotes.

**S'bu Zikode:** I hope again we are following what Nigel has been saying and how some of the things he says resonate with our experiences. The last comment on time and rethinking everything reminded me of the discussion on the land question we had downstairs.

George ended his contribution making the point about how democracy and freedom are terms used to give us hope of real democracy and freedom, when in fact these are just concepts the system hides behind. They are very smart. As soon as you begin thinking about democracy, they are already ahead of you thinking about the ways in which they can still undermine you in the name of democracy and freedom, when in fact in reality it is not democracy and freedom.

**Nhlakaniphi Mdiyastha:** Fanon was a revolutionary. He was not a reformist. As you said, when the colonial powers start to realize that they are losing, they start to negotiate with the liberation movement, they do this to protect their interests. The people who fall into that are reformists. The revolutionaries are those people who want change, who want to change everything. We should change everything.

**Bathabile Makhoba:** I'd like to comment on the quote when he was talking of the awakening of the people as a whole will not be achieved overnight. And the sense of time is no longer of the moment or the next harvest, but the rest of the world. I was reminded of the discussion yesterday at the induction workshop when we used the image of the capitalist system as a pyramid. When Fanon talks about the time that it's going to take to change the system, I am reminded of the challenge that we are facing and the time to slowly but surely change the pyramid upside down, so that the masses comes on the top and those who oppress us are at the bottom of it.

**Mfanufikile Sindane:** Then there was a question that the politicians pull the people out when they are needed, and then send back to their cages [in the discussion Abahlali members heard caves as cages which I think perhaps even better expresses what Fanon was saying] when they have done what they've been called to do. Fanon says that 'the struggle of the people will not be the same'. They are regarded as stupid and they slowly going to realize that they've been betrayed and they have been lied to. It's been eye opening, as the comrades have spoken. People have to be conscientized and mobilized so as to realize that they are being lied to. And so there has to be an alternative strategy in order to realize and see that they need to be awoken. And that is Abahlali because Abahlali was formed by those who were angry, and who realized that we are on our own and that the government was not going to rescue us.

I think we need to challenge, to try and fight so the people are constantly awake. When you mobilize the people who sit tightly in their corners, and only come out when politicians need them, are their eyes open? That's a challenge we face on a daily basis. The people are mobilized by problems, which we try to solve in the struggle. But the clever politicians come back and say, okay, everything's under control … you can go back to your corners.

**Mqapheli Bonono:** You know while you're speaking it reminded me of why we are mobilized for a march. You are there just because they need numbers in the road. That is the first question. The second question is after the march, what's next? Then I started to think, and said to them, look, to go into the road is not the end of this. To march in the road is a form of mobilization which puts people together and we discuss the topic of why we are marching. But these organizers often have some other plan that we don't know. So that is why Abahlali has its own philosophy—a living politic. When we talk about living politic, it is: I don't have water now. I don't have electricity now. The person I'm living with is unhealthy now. We speak about something we really understand, like how it feels when it's raining in your shack. I want to agree with Fanon about how each generation has to fulfill its mission. If some were leading us in 2005 it doesn't mean they are leading us in 2018. This is a social movement, you must know, it will move.

**Nomusa Sizani:** We had a discussion with some of the people who are here for the induction. Everyone was asking, 'Do you really think we can change this world?' Do you really think this can happen? We can change this world. I said, of course we can. Even if we can't change it now, our future generations will.

This world can be changed when those who see what is wrong say something or talk about it. But if we don't say anything, if you know that it is wrong but you don't say anything, you are the one who's wrong. We must go and tell the others, and the others must tell their children and their friend's children. So it becomes the lifestyle.

**S'bu Zikode:** It's not an overnight event. It has to be passed from generation to generation.

**Mqapheli Bonono:** You see how the cities have been planned. When they want to plan a city, they think, how are we going to generate a profit, and how are we going to make a 'smart city'? When they finish working on that smart city, where are the people going to be living? Where are we going to be living? So that is why you find our side saying no to eviction. There are reasons why we are living here. Now they come back and say okay, we recognize you, we'll give you four houses. But they want to expand their share. They forget that we are human beings. At the end of the day we have children who are growing up. They do not get those realities. We explain, 'If you recognize me today, in 2020, and you want to come back in 2031 you must know that my children will already have their own space because they are human beings. Then they say no. We need to put X in this house. It's because their understanding is not really in touch with humanity's, it's only how can we make a profit.

**Manufikile Sindane:** My comment is on the last quote, rethinking everything, 'to change the nature of the country's exports and not simply their destination, to re-examine the soil and mineral resources, the rivers and—why not?—the sun's productivity'. 'If conditions of work are not modified, centuries will be needed to humanize this world which has been forced down to animal level by imperial powers'. Frantz Fanon is trying to make it clear to us that when we're talking economy ... economy is the people, it's collective. Because as people we think when talking of economy we are poor because we don't have money in our hands. So by saying this, essentially, we need to humanize it. We need to change the way we are thinking, and we have to think that when we are talking about economy it is in everything. Even the land issue. We can't talk about the issue without talking about economy and about the conditions of work and life. So this quote tells me that he was thinking that we have to change the way we think about economy in everything. And us, as a new generation, we have to demand something new. When he is saying that the awakening of the people as a whole will not be achieved overnight, we have to wake up. We don't have to fight for money, we have to fight for the power.

So I think our movement must start to do that. They declared that nearby the airport, there are going to be the smart cities. And I was thinking about those people living there that you pass by when you go to the airport. What is going to happen to them? They are not building smart cities in the interest of those people. They are doing this really in the interest of their economy and taking away the resources from the people living there. They are taking away the minerals and soil and the land and they are going to remove the people who are living there and are entitled to the economy. So that's why this book reminded me of those people. It's about our land, our minerals, and our soil.

**Nomusa Sizani:** I like the way the final chapter starts by saying how is it that we do not understand that we have better things to do. I like that question because in terms of everything we said every day in the movement that us as a people or as a working class have a lot of power, but we only understand that we have the power only to follow someone every time. When we need something in our community we have to beg our ward councillor so that the powers are always on us. So I like the way Fanon starts saying that we do not understand that we have better things to do. So to me, in this Africa, on this soil we need a lot of struggling. Sometimes Abahlali is a university. So we need this university of Abahlali to open people's mind, or open people's eyes to understand that we as a people have power, and we as a people have better things to do than follow.

Even in the churches, people, they believe that pastor can clean their sins. When I'm sick, the pastor puts their hands on me, I become better, but all the power is on me. The power is on our side, on ourselves. I do not need others to pray for me, I will pray for myself.

**Busisiwe Diko:** The start of the sentence... 'how is it that we don't understand that we have better things to do than to follow Europe?' You know, this first sentence, it reminds me of what I think. How do we create a new society when we are denied basic needs and land. Without land there is no possible housing, no possible food. There is no possible economy that can be done without land. There's no possible agriculture that can be done without land. And as the president has said that 'Some of this information resonates with our experiences as Abahlali'. I agree with him. And I'm pretty much clear about Fanon. Why? Because I believe that he was a revolutionary, he was a philosopher. But then I have a question for you. Beside the fact that he was a philosopher, what influenced him to become an author and what influences you to keep continuing the work of Fanon?

And lastly, I feel so privileged to be part of this. I don't know if this is a class, is it a class? Why? Because I'm ready enough to take whatever that I have learnt here back home and I think the youth of Abahlali really needs this.

**Joyce Majola:** There's something captured in your talk. The struggle is a school. For me Fanon's prophecy is in terms of decolonization. The struggle is a school. We are claiming our right to have our human dignity, our safety, and in order to pursue the decolonization of quality public education. In other words, to decolonize education. When we look at our country, it's like Fanon's prophecy. He prophesied things that were going on especially to the underprivileged. When we look at education in terms of education, we look at we've got, the national, this NSFAS [National Student Financial Aid Scheme]. It's supposed to be a system for the marginalized poor, but instead it's vice versa. It is a system where the elite use whatever means to apply for this funding.

And when you look at our kids, our youth they've got Matric', others got secondary education, but they cannot have access to this funding to go and further their studies. Why? Because there's that sentence there in that chapter that says that they 'use their muscles and their brains to lead the struggle for liberation'. The youth are being denied this. They are being denied what was supposed to be theirs.

**Busisiwe Diko:** As Mam Majola was speaking on the part about the struggle is a school, I'm linking this last line that states that 'This new politics is in the hands of those who use their muscles and their brains'. I'm just thinking if maybe we can say, 'This new politics is in the hands of Abahlali who use their muscles and brains to lead the struggle of liberation?' As much as we can think of the world, and the societies that we fight for. We're fighting for that liberation, as Baba stated. At first we are in the struggle, we study, but maybe we don't even know who supports us. So it's a privilege, and then we thank a person like Nigel who acknowledges Abahlali knowing that Abahlali are just informal, but also a living politic. So this part is touching me thinking of Abahlali, wondering if they even know that they are the philosophers of their struggle. It's not that Abahlali does not know. Abahlali knows. It is all in our hands as Abahlali to put it in action.

**Mqapheli Bonono:** The ANC rules us. Sometimes we don't give ourselves time to study who the ANC actually is. What was ANC before? What was the mission and vision of the struggle to overthrow apartheid? We were bluffed in 1994. We are given freedom and we are bluffed. I am lucky because I didn't have a right to vote. But I feel so sorry to my grandparents, and my parents who participated. I saw long queues. I took my granny to that election. We were all so happy. When they spoke of Nelson Mandela, we believed something would come to us and that everything is going to be okay. But now you see the ANC killing each other. If you watch [the film] Dear Mandela you can clearly see when Abahlali were attacked in 2009, and then you see Nigel Gumede speaking inside a hall in Kennedy Road saying that Abahlali are criminals. When Abahlali tried making Nigel Gumede accountable for what he said to the people of Kennedy Road, the police were sent in. It's exactly what we see today. Brothers and sisters, why can't we think that we have better things to do? It's because, I think, these people are still in control. They forget about poor people. It's all about themselves. They only want to follow Europe because Europe has those smart cities and those smart bridges on top. They spend billions while poverty is killing the people in informal settlements. So that is why as Abahlali we say poverty is a crime because no one should be going to bed with an empty stomach amidst so much wealth. So now I am just reminded by Mam Majola of the power that we have, but we don't know how to claim it. But we still have a duty you know. We have a duty to go and try to say, 'No comrade'. Some of the people still think everything will come clear when they see Zikode. But that will not solve your problem. You are going to solve your problems.

**Nhlakaniphi Mdiyastha:** So when thinking of 1994 something comes up in my mind. What would Fanon see? This is a new liberated country, independent liberated country. He would expect to see a people with joy, a rich people, a community that is free and liberated from all sorts of oppression. But instead he sees the neoliberal leaders still running the prior system of oppression. We were promised freedom in 1994, but the system is still the same. It is a continuation of the apartheid system. We are still experiencing evictions and lack of amenities in our communities. It's still the system of oppression that was exercised back then, but in a new way and with a new manner of being portrayed to the communities and the people. In the back of their minds people believe that we've got freedom while we've only got the freedom of speech and the rest is in the hands of the elites. If you look at the expropriation of land without compensation we have said that the land should be decommodified but when section 25 of the law was discussed we were not part of that discussion, now things are turning around, they are engaging, or want to look like they are engaging us, bearing in mind they might have an alternative to contradict our one voice.

**Mqapheli Bonono:** Yeah, while you are saying that Nhlaka, I was reminded of what Fikile said. Most poor people do not think about distribution of the land, they think about money. They think about paper money and not about distribution of the land. I was reminded when the Foreman Road community lost baby Jayden [Jayden Khoza, a two week old baby boy died after inhaling teargas thrown into the settlement by the police after a nearby street protest in May 2017]. I remember clearly. I had been in Foreman Road for 18 years. When I came to Foreman Road, there was no water, no electricity, and no toilets. It was 20 cents to buy water and then for limited time only. If you weren't there between 3:00pm and 4:00pm you'd have no water.

The City started saying okay now we have a budget. What is a budget? It's our resources. There is thousands and thousands of people living in Foreman Road. So when the budget comes, what do they say? We have 3 million for speed bumps. No really. People have been burned, people are inside their shack with no water, with nothing. I sat and listened when they were announcing the speed bumps and I raised my hand but I was denied the right to ask a question. I said, 'OK, but can I have the copy of the document?' I took the copy and went back to the community and said, 'All of us should come and analyze this'. Then we went back to them and said, 'We are the ones who are using this road and we have no vehicles. Who are you providing the speed bumps for? We have no food here; we have no shelter'. This is the kind of government we have.

But in this we realized how much power we have. But yes, our power relies on many of us, when we sing, can we sing together? Yes, of course. Foreman Road has electricity now because we said, 'No way'. Up until today there are speed bumps but they are not fixed. If you can follow where the money went, it disappeared. So that's how, when you are saying, we were promised in 1994, we were bluffed. We are given democracy and the freedom to exercise our right to vote. But the reality is we are still suffering. Mam Majola was talking about education. How many students are still outside in universities? They are saying that there is free education in South Africa but how many children are still denied the right to education? And if you go to rural areas, children are still attending class under the trees. This is the same country of rich and poor.

The Marikana massacre was about money. Mining workers were just asking for a little increase in wages. We lost so many lives in a few seconds, killed in broad daylight by the state. How can we still believe that we have a government that is on the side of the poor people? We cannot. So what Fanon thought sixty years ago, Abahlali can say it's really what is actually being done. Today the ANC is speaking about land expropriation without compensation, but to them it's a song not a reality. Go to eKhenana, you will see how Abahlali are expropriating the land. Go to New City, you will see how Abahlali expropriated the land. Abahlali is really doing it.

**Bathabile Makhoba:** It is all of that. It's just like Nhlaka was just saying. It is still the same. They revised it and used some terminology to make it out as if it is still not the same and yet it is. They still operate the way they used to operate. But now Abahlali has seen it. So we are turning the table slowly upside down, but we still need us to be a team and have the power to turn it upside down.

**Joyce Majola:** A team that educates the masses.

**Mfanufikile Sindane:** I agree with you Mam Majola. People, now they know what they have. What is missing is the anger. I remember the youth of 1976 when they were angry about Bantu education. They went to the streets. I remember the women in 1956 were angry about carrying the ID document. They went in the streets. People now know that when they are facing eviction they know they need to go to Abahlali. When they do occupation they go to Abahlali. What is missing is that when you do these induction classes on Abahlali they should also make people to feel anger so that they can act.

**Joyce Majola:** But how do we achieve that if we still have so many churches that insult us? I'm not against any churches, but we have churches that are turning around the history, that instill fear.

**Zanele Mtshali:** Direct fear.

**Mfanufikile Sindane:** It is our duty. I go to church. So it is our duty as Abahlali that we go to church to educate people.

**Joyce Majola:** Away from the church.

**Mfanufikile Sindane:** Even pastors inside the church. Some of the church members even call me Anti-Christ. I say, 'No. I'm not an Anti-Christ'. But we need to educate them. Their eyes will be opened slowly but it won't be like overnight as Frantz Fanon was saying.

**S'bu Zikode:** So comrades, Busi has asked a question of Nigel. If we could allow that. And I just want to remind us that Fanon was writing this book sixty years ago. At the time of the writing it was still the time of apartheid and colonialism. Fanon's thoughts are quite striking. How was it that Fanon knew this? And what is still going to be relevant in the years to come?

He did not just write it because this is how we feel today. But as Wisdom said, this was professed 60 years ago. And part of Busi's question was to ask Nigel what is it that inspires him to continue the work, promote and remind people the work of Fanon and what influenced Fanon even at that time. It was about the question of civilization. Maybe we are lucky today that at least we are reflecting on Fanon. And then there comes the Fees Must Fall and students talking about the decolonization of education. At the time that was the biggest thing that ever happened, the struggle for the decolonization of education by students. But where is the student Fees Must Fall movement today? They touched a very sensitive issue. We are divided today because somehow our minds are still captured. So when one raises the question of decolonization you are really talking to a core issue for African people. You remember how powerful the Fees Must Fall movement was because they were raising decolonization questions not only in terms of education. We call decolonization of land decommodification. It is decommodification because it is anti-African to sell land.

**Nigel Gibson:** It's been a real privilege to listen to your engagements. Fanon argues that one of the most important things to do is to teach the people that the future has to be built by them, that there's no leader or machine from heaven that's going to come down and liberate you, that liberation has to be inclusive and built in the struggle from the bottom up. He mentions how it won't come overnight and the struggle after the colonial forces have left will be measured by the involvement of the dispossessed and exploited in working out the future. As to an earlier question about being outsmarted by the political leaders, who are always strategizing the next move, Fanon has an image about the negotiations between the colonialists and the liberation movement that is suggestive. He says they take place around a green baize table. What is a green baize table? It's one of those green felt card tables. So he's saying that negotiations take place around a card table. And the deck is rigged and the negotiations are also gamed. At the same time, there are ways in which that card game is always being played out, sacrificing our futures. So if it's the land question, then the game is being played but the rules are already decided. They are wondering, what's the cost? How can we talk about the appropriation of land without compensation in a way that's really not about the decommodification of land. So there's always that threat of any words as you suggested, words like democracy and freedom, are taken over and strategies are being played out without being aware of those games being played behind your back. The negotiations of the early 1990s were played excluding masses of people because they are the threat to the dominant players. So the structure of the new society became reduced to the right to vote thus limiting your involvement to a vote every five years. The decisions have been made without you.

As to your question about what inspires me. I was eighteen when the Soweto rebellion happened and could relate to the students' demands. Then Biko was murdered in 1977. And don't forget, the Black Consciousness Movement had a real relationship to the churches, and the churches were about liberation. This is the period of liberation theology and Black liberation theology that was quite different from the present period when churches are linked to personal success measured by making money. Black theology was about liberation, and that's an important part of the kind of history that's perhaps being sidelined in the memory of the anti-apartheid struggle. Bishop Rubin Philip is part of that too, of that generation. In 1980 I met Black Consciousness people in London and became further committed to the idea of South African liberation. I first read Fanon because of Biko's interest in Fanon which I read about in a booklet written by two Black American Marxist-Humanists, John Alan and Lou Turner[2]—and I've continued to read Fanon for 40 years. Fanon, we should not forget, was an internationalist and I suppose that all I can say is that I've remained committed to that. South African liberation remained an important part of my youth activism in the UK and then in the US, and I closely followed all the movements including the UDF, the trade union movements, the general strikes, and mass boycotts. And the names of townships and locations of struggle still have a resonance to me as struggle moments. For example, when I went to the Abahlali celebration

---

2. *Frantz Fanon Soweto and American Black Thought* by John Alan and Lou Turner was first published in 1978.

in 2015 at Curries Fountain, it had meaning for me as the Pro-Frelimo Rally in 1974, but I had no idea it was a football field.

I too was joyous in 1994. But then when I first visited in 1999 I saw that things weren't really happening, and I thought of Fanon's critique. Then when Abahlali was born in 2005 that became important for me in terms of what you've been talking about this afternoon. The struggle for human liberation continues, and that has always been so, despite all the setbacks, a key principle. Let me try to address your question, 'Why did Fanon write?' As an intellectual committed to human liberation, he took it as his responsibility. And for him, it was about changing the world, humanizing the world. Knowing he was dying he wanted to reflect on the decolonization movement of the late 1950s that he was deeply committed to and leave a kind of revolutionary manual for the future. He wrote this book quite quickly though he had been thinking about it for a while. He did not write it for posterity but for that moment. Fanon was both a brilliant and original intellectual, open to engage with the contradictions in the freedom movements and that is partly why he still resonates so long afterwards.

**S'bu Zikode**: So, comrades, some of you have read the handout yesterday about the philosophy of Abahlali. We relate these quotes from Fanon to the Abahlali vision and the kind of society we want to invent. How we also insist on humanizing the workers and building a just and equal society. So Fanon's writing has always been about humanity. And, you know, that has a universal commitment to building the fair human world that doesn't create inequalities or division. So, I'm just wondering if we can relate our vision to Fanon's. When he says, 'so, my brothers and sisters', and maybe not 'comrades' at the time, it shows how those times are really universal and humanistic. So this was a universal message. Of course with the focus to African people. So, for me, that speaks to much of what we do. We must remember, there are times in our city where there is no respect. So Abahlali's struggle is not just about service delivery, it is about the kind of society we want. Where we put humanity first. Nigel, you will also remember the statement we put out around xenophobia in 2008. Our anti-xenophobia work, our anti-violence stance, we remain committed to the idea of peace because at the same time we want to practice the world that we want. So if we talk about the peaceful world, where equality, justice, respect and dignity prevail, then that has to be reflected in our day-to-day work. So I think we are on that path when Fanon was talking about how we could decolonize the world. So the question is whether sixty years later, things have changed significantly to that idea and at the same time the challenge we face is how the imperial system hides the truth and the reality to keep us oppressed. How they can change words. Right now, in South Africa, they talk about radical economic transformation, and you think, 'What a smart word and a radical idea. We must change the economy right now from below without any compromise, and unapologetically'. But is it really happening? And we will upload these new technologies. Yes, radical economic transformation. But what does that mean? The system is so smart to keep on changing methods and technology so that you think that there is a shift when in fact there is no shift. There is a change of words. So we must be able to master that. Which is why many of our Abahlali voices are so important because we are not just inventing ideas but putting them into practice and acting on them. So the new ideas of trying to rethink the world, how our action should reflect that. So our task is to continue to rethink, provide alternative ways for the world to see, and not be caught by terminologies which do not change anything. We must invent ideas, but our praxis must also reflect that.

**Lindokuhle Mnguni:** A revolutionist like Fanon prophesizes this, and here we are, reading it. But this book is something that is probably hidden from the masses. People don't buy it because it would be half your wages and you'd rather buy something to eat for your children. I think at the birth of this movement of Abahlali in 2005, a new politics was at the forefront. They had to rethink politics. Since then this has become even clearer with the Arab Spring, the Yellow Vests in France, the movements in Hong Kong. If politics were not challenged by a new politics, humanity would have failed. People don't realize how much power they have. Of course, if you're put back in cages and then taken out as they need, people won't understand what Fanon's ideas are. So I really appreciate this information. It is information people on the ground really need. For us as a movement, we don't only talk about ideas, we must practice what we talk about. There are many things in these quotes that we could take the whole day talking about. When he says, 'the demoralization buried deep within the mind by colonization is still very much alive'. Well now it's democracy. We say people still have colonized minds while Fees Must Fall was about the decolonization of the education system, but their minds are still not decolonized. So now it's democracy that will save people while actual democrats are criticized when they say that government today is actually playing with people's minds. That if you shake the government of today it will go back to the system of apartheid. And of course, poverty plays a big role in whatever we do because people generally are more concerned whether they have bread and butter on the table. I don't want my children to be living in this same situation as now. So, as much as we have our hands on the present, we must always focus on the future. The politicians want it like this because they know otherwise it would open people's eyes. So I think even if you just read these quotes they are put in such simple terms so that anybody can just understand them, what they say. So we really appreciate this and hopefully we can teach our members so that they can see for themselves. And I'm sure that those who were forming this movement never read Frantz Fanon. It goes to show the level of intellectuals in the informal settlements, and that we can never doubt this level in the informal settlements.

**Nigel Gibson:** You are right the people who created the movement created it out of their own experiences. They weren't told what to do, but from early on through relationships they heard about Fanon and found that Fanon spoke to them. What you said reminded me of 'Biryani politics'. People are concerned about their next meal, that's a material reality, but people do not live by bread alone. So Biryani politics is a crude exchange, a politics of exchanging votes for food. There's a section of Fanon's *The Wretched of the Earth* where he speaks about the leader, and you spoke about how they threaten you saying, 'if you go against us, it'll be a return to apartheid'. Fanon warns that the liberation party leaders don't want discussion, they want you to follow obediently. Fanon talks about how the leader just comes out on certain holidays, struggle days, freedom days, and so forth, to remind people of the struggle and how far they've come. It becomes part of their catechism, to remind people to go to stadiums and listen to speeches that are televised while thousands of people are bussed in and probably given lunch too. The lunch is in exchange to applaud the official memory of the struggle. And then you are told that there is no alternative.

**Mqapheli Bonono:** When Gibson was talking about Biryani politics, I was just looking around at the table, do we understand what he was talking about? When Abahlali was being formed, what was Biryani politics about? That politics is here even now with the government we have. When you live in an informal settlement, we are seen as a bank for votes. Every five years, they remember, oh, we have our bank there. And they say how do we get those people to love and trust only us? That's Biryani politics. Now, in South Africa, how many political parties are there today? There is competition. Which manifesto will come out first? ANC will say something, DA will say something else and so on. Why are we still a bank of votes? There are just a few people who are in charge of electing who is the president and, if they are going to use money, they say, 'how can we use these people that love us only?' and leave all other political parties. Can I go with food parcels? That's Biryani. If I go now in Kennedy Road, with a pot that is well cooked with a nice masala, when I open the pot, the smell is just *mmm* and you'll see how many will come and look at you and then I'll take that advantage before they eat, I must install something on them that they must see me as king. Right?

That's how dirty it is. One of the things about this logo of Abahlali, it is not one-man show or one-woman show. There were a lot of discussions and a lot of meetings about the logo. The youth of this movement sat up and they read and they shared their ideas and discussed. And they came out with something and they said, 'This is what we are proposing'. And then there was a chance for them to ask, 'can you explain to us what this means?' and there was a chance to say, 'This is universality. This is what universality means. This is a roundhouse and this is what a roundhouse means to us. This is what Abahlali means to us. This is what the color black means to us. So you could see the future of this movement. Today, we have lost eighteen comrades. We always say that you can kill us but you cannot kill the idea of this movement. I'm so happy today that we can sit around this table, talking without any disruptions. Not only talking about sticking to the vision of this movement but also talking about 'how do I feel'.

If we agree that Fanon is in line with Abahlali's philosophy, the daily-basis politics of Abahlali lets us take these ideas to go to the churches. When you were right there, you turn things around and you change your platform. No, no, no you can't tell us we should wait for God while we are hungry now. We must go to schools. We must remember something. The apartheid was overthrown not just because the ANC was elected. It was the forces. The ANC was not a political party. There was a social movement. And they never win the war themselves, they had to join the Black Consciousness Movement, the United Democratic Front (UDF). Some of us think, that when we talk about *Umkhonto We Sizwe* (Spear of the Nation), it is the ANC. But what was the role of MK? What role other countries have played to liberate South Africa? Yes, I know it's something that's a little far from us, but if we can think that if we can get into these spaces, into the Churches and into the schools, how can we change people and make them understand this.

You know there's a picture that circulates of an old auntie. She doesn't have shoes; she stands outside the house. And she's been given a T-shirt with a big head of Jacob Zuma on it. The house is falling apart — but they don't mind. They do door to door campaigns and take photos. They come with the banners because they want a photo for someone in Europe, because he's a donor, you want funding. That's nonsense. It has to stop. No, we get distracted that way. You can note, when we say, we want a Coalition what does that mean? I can tell you. Everyone wants to work at Abahlali because Abahlali practices democracy. We are the ones who are still holding onto this mission and saying, 'How can we clear people's minds? How can we open people's eyes?' If we take this and go, we must also know that there will be a gun in the road while we are walking. There will be hitmen. There will be people who frighten you in the road. If you don't notice, they will go and eat with your community. They will start with your people first. And make sure that the people you are with turn against you. So you must be able to brainstorm and get new ideas while you are studying it—we must always be ahead of them, so then we can overthrow them.

**Lindokuhle Mnguni:** Since you touched on the ANC being a movement like us, we are not immune to what happened to the ANC. But if you use these writings, you use this information, could I educate the masses at all times, even if we might not turn out like the ANC?

**S'bu Zikode:** When we were delivering this memorandum [to the City officials] on Monday this guy said to me these people are beautiful, do they really live in the shacks? They cannot expect beauty in the shacks; they cannot expect thinking in the shacks. That is their rationale.

If they cannot expect beauty and thinking in the shacks, surely these people cannot believe that the submission we created collectively comes from the shacks. They think there is a white man behind it or people from overseas are behind it. But under no circumstances could shack dwellers think this way. They still believe this today. When we articulate the issues this way, they simply cannot believe. It is unimaginable for shack dwellers to articulate the issues. Frantz Fanon knew this a long time ago. He has seen always how the masses are something to be used; and once you finish using the masses, you send them back to their cages. It's monkeys that live in cages. So that's how the masses are thought of. Use the masses, and then after the march, let them return to their cages. And only when you need them, then you can bring the masses, because the masses are only there to fill up.

In one of the camps in Abahlali, Nigel, what the comrades are talking about is what I presented that as part of the living politics, Abahlali is a living idea that everyone thinks. Wherever they live, whether in the shacks, in rural villages, in hostels, everyone thinks. I was defending the very idea all the time, to think that people from the shacks think for themselves. So people are amazed by the work of Abahlali today. Even the national parliament. Today they have no choice, they have to engage Abahlali. Even parliament realized that Abahlali can't be a fake for 15 years. So it's slowly a game of liberating the minds, even though those thoughts that people can't think for themselves from the shacks remain. So that's a big politics. A big change. Because when you engage with shack dwellers it is not about anything serious. The thought is, who the hell are these guys, to be listened to, to be considered seriously? That's why, part of the strategy is to frustrate us by ignoring us. That's how they treat us. So when they ignore us, it is actually a strategy based on the idea that if you entertain them, you are actually promoting them. That's how they treat us. So they ignore us and disengage with us in order to frustrate us. But we don't go away. We continue, we persist, we demand attention, we have a voice and we have reached a stage where they can no longer ignore us. So this really speaks to the living politics and to the conclusion of Fanon. So we had to defend the idea that we are not worthless, that we have a brain. So we had to argue this on different platforms. Even if it means we had to lose some of the comrades who supported us. There was a time where we could not compromise on this point. Some would remember a time when we had to refuse to work with the Centre for Civil Society at the University. It's not only the state that thinks Abahlali cannot think for itself. Even the very same intellectuals, academics, NGOs, who say they support us have that mentality. The same comrades that we march with. They think that if Abahlali brings the masses, we will do the thinking. We are a Coalition. When they come to the Coalition meeting, they want to chair the meeting, they know a great deal. What they need is your masses, because they don't recognize that they need the masses as objects who will come to justify their cause, and then they will come with a banner and say, look at how many masses I command.

**Joyce Majola:** To follow what our chair was saying. A journalist did not know or did not believe that Zanele was the chair of the movement who lives in the shacks, because after an interview at her branch she wanted to interview Zanele. So when they went to Zanele's place, they didn't believe her when she said, 'This IS my home!' She said it three times. 'Are you sure this is your house?' the journalist said. Our kids came to the rescue when they came out and called her mommy. Only then did the journalist realize.

**Mqapheli Bonono:** We still have a long way to go, even amongst ourselves. Even in exchange visits amongst our communities. People are shocked when they get to Bonono's house. I said to them no, this is not a toilet, this is someone's house. The comrade was shocked. I am saying this because the movement is growing. When the movement was formed in 2005, there were no measures in place to sustain and control its growth. Because the movement has just grown so much, it's our duty to sit at the tables and relearn leadership, to rethink 'how are we going to sustain this movement'? Some might think that maybe there is a small opportunity that I can become a councillor through Abahlali. Maybe I can become a provincial chairperson, or I can be a president of Abahlali. Then I can be popular. Some of them think, when they see how big Abahlali is, that Abahlali has millions and can help me become a councillor. How are we going to deal with that? That person is inside the movement and you've given them the power. That is why it's important to Abahlali that the power mustn't lie in the leadership. It must be always from the people, so the people can always rule and say, no, no, no. This is something that we don't see clearly.

**Joyce Majola:** Remember our meeting with the mayor — remember what he said? He said, 'Is everyone going to feel comfortable if we speak English? Or should we bring somebody to translate?'

'No, thank you. We understand. .So when they look at us, or they judge us from the way that we live they also think that maybe our brain is also like that. As I said, I think, even in that May march, we must also have our T-shirts and not to wear other people's T-shirts, because they are attracting *their* donors. And many of them are using us.

**S'bu Zikode:** You know when we invite NUMSA [The National Union of Metal Workers of South Africa], we don't invite individual leaders and give them a platform to talk. When we invite them, we invite masses not leaders. They have a membership of 350,000 five times Abahlali membership but they bring people to speak. They just come as leaders and they want a platform. That's not right. They are using us. So we must solve that.

**Nomusa Sizani:** I saw only two people come and NUMSA is a big trade union and these two people wanted to be at the front of the march. I just told them, 'No, you can't be in the front!' This is an Abahlali march.

**Bathabile Makhoba:** Also the guy who was given the platform to speak. Did you hear what he said? It was like he was at a SACTU meeting and there are these banners blocking Abahlali. I got upset when I saw the T-shirts. I said, 'We are not going to wear those T-shirts. It's about time that we stand for ourselves, and not be used by other people, to attract their donors'.

**Mqapheli Bonono** : And the other thing, that we also should be more careful. Let us not forget that we need some of the organizations. Because we can never win this war alone. So if we have a chance, as we have done with the Coalition, let us be honest, and tell comrades, 'if you want to keep this relationship, this is how it should be'. So I'm saying this because, if you read the history of our country, you can never win alone. And then for us, it's for us to give direction. I'm quite happy that this room welcomes everyone. Everyone has a space to meet in Abahlali. As Abahlali, let us use the platform to make it the right platform that it should be. May 1 was Abahlali's march but it was also Workers' Day. So we need to think about, when we go to use a space like that, what is our understanding of why we are there in the first place? The question of how they are using us—these are trade unions, these are social movements—some of them still have this petty relationship with bourgeoisie's mind. Some are still playing around with these organizations. We are stepping back from the Coalition now but we are not leaving. We want to go and reflect as a movement and consider if this space is still relevant. And we want to talk directly to each organization. Because some of them don't understand. They just see us bringing the masses.

**S'bu Zikode**: What we recall from the Coalition is, name your money and how many buses you need so you can fight the wars against the ANC.

**S'bu Zikode**: Thank you comrades. It's after 1:00, we've got the lunch ready. Let's thank Nigel for this opportunity, because it's an opportunity for us, because we often feel, Nigel, we don't have much time to reflect. We get so busy. So next week, it's a pity, if you'll still be in Africa, but we'll have an opportunity to reflect on the march and the discussion and how we take the decommodification of land forward. So it would be good if you would be part of this discussion. But thank you so much. Thank you on behalf of all of us.

**Nigel Gibson**: Can I ask a question?

**S'bu Zikode**: Yes.

**Nigel Gibson**: A final question. I have an idea of what the decommodification of land is but how do you understand it? Can you explain what you mean by decommodification of land?

**S'bu Zikode**: Anyone, want to?

**Lindokuhle Mnguni**: When we say decommodification of land, we say it goes further than section 25 of the Constitution that speaks only of property. When we say 'decommodification' of the land, we say, land must not be a commodity, it must be a right. Land should not be something that is sold. In our vision it must become 'uncommodified'. We want a society where everyone is respected as equal, where the land is distributed equally, to all of us. How we are going to engage in society without decommodification. Today we don't even have jobs.

**Nhlakaniphi Mdiyastha**: There's so much land that's available for everybody in this country. So decommodification means we don't want one person to have so many hectares of land while other people are hungry who need land.

**Mqapheli Bonono**: I think that is why, we will make ourselves clear, that although we agree on appropriation of land without compensation, we are not following what the ANC or the EFF is saying. They understand this to mean take land from the Whites and give it to the Black elite. Abahlali is saying no, it must be given communally, because we are seeing what is happening now with state capture. We cannot trust government anymore.

**Nhlakaniphi Mdiyastha:** Land must not be sold, land must not be put up for rent. Land must be owned by the community. We are clear on who must own the land; it must be owned by the community. It is communal not individual ownership.

**Mqapheli Bonono:** I just wanted to remind you something. There's something I like when we had the discussion around this, and why we think that the land must not be owned by individuals. What we are saying, really, is we are also protecting the land from individuals. Because if you give a person individual ownership of land, tomorrow if that person doesn't have bread and butter, they will take the paper that gives them ownership of the land, and go to the bank? You borrow a million rand, they take the land deed. They can't afford to pay that money back and then the bank owns the land. And when you say Standard Bank, who is Standard Bank?

**S'bu Zikode:** I just want to say that we very appreciate your time. We want to say thanks very much for this. We feel, and we hope, the things that you have said to us will advance our ability to strike, and to strengthen us, the way we articulate, and the way we think. I cannot say it any better, just thanks a lot.

## Bibliography

Fanon, F. 1968. *The Wretched of the Earth*. Translated by Constance Farrington. New York: Grove Press.

_____. 2004. *The Wretched of the Earth*. Translated by Richard Philcox. New York: Grove Press.

# SECTION B:
# FANONIAN PRACTICES IN BRAZIL

"everything went &#9608;&#9608;&#9608; left." &#9608;&#9608;&#9608;

&#9608;&#9608;&#9608; indiffer-
ence &#9608;&#9608;&#9608; is quite normal &#9608;&#9608;&#9608;
&#9608;&#9608;&#9608; in &#9608;&#9608;&#9608; the Western

&#9608;&#9608;&#9608; liberal- &#9608;&#9608;&#9608;
&#9608;&#9608;&#9608; to
&#9608;&#9608;&#9608; them &#9608;&#9608;&#9608; they are being objective. &#9608;&#9608;&#9608; objectivity is always directed
against &#9608;&#9608;&#9608;

&#9608;&#9608;&#9608; the &#9608;&#9608;&#9608;
&#9608;&#9608;&#9608; radical-

&#9608;&#9608;&#9608; the &#9608;&#9608;&#9608;
Third World. &#9608;&#9608;&#9608;
&#9608;&#9608;&#9608; is no
&#9608;&#9608;&#9608; matter &#9608;&#9608;&#9608;

&#9608;&#9608;&#9608; the masses &#9608;&#9608;&#9608;
&#9608;&#9608;&#9608;

&#9608;&#9608;&#9608; rage, &#9608;&#9608;&#9608;
&#9608;&#9608;&#9608; the petrified, motionless world of colonization.
&#9608;&#9608;&#9608; brandishes his &#9608;&#9608;&#9608;
&#9608;&#9608;&#9608; hammers &#9608;&#9608;&#9608;
&#9608;&#9608;&#9608; laughs. &#9608;&#9608;&#9608;

'Blacked-out-poem' by Leah Kindler based on Fanon's *The Wretched of the Earth.*

# THE INFLUENCE OF FRANTZ FANON'S THOUGHT ON BLACK FEMALE INTELLECTUAL PRODUCTION IN BRAZIL

Rosemere Ferreira da Silva

## Introduction

This chapter discusses the entry of Frantz Fanon's thought in Brazil, with emphasis on its importance in Black women's intellectual production as represented in the work of Neusa Santos Souza and Lélia Gonzalez. Fanon's ideas are the basis for discussions about ethnic-racial relations established by these intellectuals. Both Souza and Gonzalez, starting with and including dialogical experiences in the Black Movement in Rio de Janeiro and in academia, raised questions essential to understanding the construction of Black identities, becoming, in the case of the first, a reference in the study of emotional life of the Negro and, in the case of the second, a critical voice on the 'place of the Negro' in Brazilian society. Both intellectual trajectories converge decisively in the interpretation of race, and of gender and class cleavages, as a fundamental condition for Black existence in Brazil.

## Frantz Fanon: A Challenging Read

In 2008, Antonio Sérgio Alfredo Guimarães published an article entitled 'Fanon's Reception in Brazil and Black Identity' ('A Recepção de Fanon no Brasil e a Identidade Negra') in the journal *Novos Estudos*. In it, the author lists three sources of the relative silence about Fanon's thought in Brazil. The first is related to the specificity of the Latin American left bloc in the 1960s. The second is due to how the social and national constitution is interpreted without due consideration of the importance of addressing racial conflicts. The third emphasizes the very small number of professors and researchers declared to be Black and or Afro-Brazilian in Brazilian universities. I would add the still small number of faculty that address the constitution of Black identity based on criticism of the conditions of racially oppressed subjects.

Although the classic, *Black Skin, White Masks*, was published in 1952, Guimarães states that the entry of Fanon's thought in Brazil followed the visit of Jean-Paul Sartre and Simone de Beavoir in 1960. Despite Guimarães affirming that there are no records of Sartre's encounter with Abdias Nascimento, or with any other Black leadership in the previous decade, Fanon in fact appeared as a reference in Nascimento's writings in 1978, in his work entitled *O Genocídio do Negro Brasileiro: processo de uma racismo mascarado.* There Nascimento directly quotes Fanon when classifying the racist as 'a purpose haunted by bad conscience' (Nascimento, 1978: 44-45). In several passages in Nascimento's text, the author's understanding and appreciation of the usefulness of Fanon's ideas for racial discussion in Brazil is clear.

Sartre's presentations in Brazil, according to Guimarães, included discussion about colonialism and struggles for independence of Third World Peoples, but not of race. In that period, understanding race relations was not seen as requiring an independently constituted endeavor. In the Brazilian social imaginary, it was believed that, when ascending economically and socially, Blacks would become increasingly integrated, without race functioning as an impediment. Sociologist Florestan Fernandes vehemently contested this idea in his (1965) book *A integração do negro na sociedade de classes: no limiar de uma nova era*, rejecting the idea that the upward mobility of some Blacks and Mulattos represented evidence of the absence of racial prejudice, discrimination, and racism. He wrote:

> *É preciso que se tenha em mente que a mobilidade social não constitui em si mesma, índice da inexistência de preconceito e de discriminação raciais. Além disso, na situação que nos compete investigar, surpreendemos as condições e os efeitos dos mecanismos sociais de ascensão de uma categoria racial no momento mesmo em que entra em crise final todo um sistema de dominação racial. Portanto, será normal que o lôdo suba à tona. O que antes podia ser dissimulado ou encoberto, precisa vir à luz, para elevar-se à esfera da consciência, da discussão e da crítica.[1]* (Fernandes, 1965: 135)

Another important point in Guimarães' discussion is the contact between Brazilian intellectuals and the writings of Frantz Fanon, which took place in exile. It was in exile that Brazilian intellectuals, such as Abdias Nascimento, Clóvis Moura, Octavio Ianni, and Paulo Freire, encountered how Fanon problematized the alienation of the colonial situation and political responses to colonialist domination. In Guimarães' account, it was only with the return of these and other exiled intellectuals to Brazil and to Brazilian universities in 1980 that Fanon became obligatory reading in higher education classes.

In the foreword to the Brazilian edition of *Black Skin, White Masks*, published in 2008, Lewis R. Gordon mentions the work of Paulo Freire and cites *Pedagogy of the Oppressed*, which Gordon understands as resulting in part from Freire's careful study of Fanon's ideas:

> That was a time when a North American professor lecturing on Frantz Fanon could lead to him or her being fired. In those turbulent years of the

---

1. 'It must be borne in mind that social mobility does not in itself constitute an index of the absence of racial prejudice and discrimination. In addition, in the situation that we have to investigate, we are surprised by the conditions and social mechanisms that give rise to racial animus and hostility as a whole system of racial domination is crumbling. In such circumstances, it will be normal for the sludge to surface. What could previously be concealed or covered up must come to light, rising to the sphere of consciousness, discussion, and criticism'.

1960s and 1970s, the situation was different in South America. In Chile, for example, Fanon's thought was being taught in classrooms, and a close reading of Paulo Freire's *Pedagogy of Oppressed* revels much debt to Fanon. By the 1990s, it was possible to study both Fanon and Freire in such courses as Political Theology, Philosophy of Liberation, and Social and Political Thought, and scholars across the world are gaining an understanding of his relation to other Brazilian intellectuals such as Alberto Guerreiro Ramos and Abdias do Nascimento. (Gordon, 2008: 19)

*Pedagogy of the Oppressed* argues that no one will understand the meaning of the violence of an oppressive society better than the oppressed. However, only with the development of critical conscience will they become open to the pursuit of such truths and freedom. Revolutionary engagement in transforming concrete and objective reality thus emerges through progressive education that cultivates critical study of history that informs ongoing commitment to addressing the unjust social, economic and political order.

An important facet of the article by Guimarães is the affirmation of the publication of *Black Skin, White Masks*, by the publisher Fator, in Salvador, in 1983. This is the year when Florentina da Silva Souza (2005) argued the Unified Black Movement recommended Fanon as one of the authors to read when training its activists and militants. It was the same year when Neusa Santos Souza, an intellectual and activist of the Unified Black Movement, published *Tornar-se negro: as vicissitudes da identidade do negro brasileiro em ascensão social*. Readership of this work, which explored the emotional experience of the socially ascending Black subject and continued contradictions and ambiguities of Black identity, flourished, influencing reading of Fanon in Rio de Janeiro.

Fanon's texts have been circulating, with a pedagogical character, among militants and activists in the Black movement since the mid-1960s, as Guimarães documents. *The Wretched of the Earth*, for example, published in 1968, has been a consistent reference for Black students, especially those interested in discussing the violence of the colonial world, the processes of domination that result from colonization, and the way these processes inform how colonizers and the colonized see themselves. The reader cannot avoid reflecting on the importance of decolonization as an integral questioning of the colonial situation.

Another Black intellectual and member of the Unified Black Movement who was clearly influenced by Fanon's ideas, was Lélia Gonzalez. According to researchers Alex Ratts and Flávia Rios, it was Gonzalez's familiarity with the influence of Fanon's thinking in the Black diaspora that led to her recommending Fanon's books in Brazil:

> *Numa outra linha de pensamento, mas pondo o dedo na ferida da alienação do negro, encontra-se a dramática figura de Frantz Fanon, o jovem psiquiatra que se destacou na guerra da independência da Argélia. Crítico da noção de negritude, escreveu Os condenados da terra e Pele negra, máscaras brancas. Este último é uma das mais acuradas análises dos mecanismos psicológicos que induzem o colonizado e se identificar com o colonizador. Na sua perspectiva, a desalienação do*

*negro está diretamente vinculada à tomada de consciência das relações socioe-conômicas. Sua posição, crítica diante do que considerava como acomodação de seus conterrâneos para com a política assimilacionista francesa, o levou a exigir que após a sua morte fosse enterrado na Argélia. E assim foi feio.²* (Gonzalez in Ratts; Rios, 2010: 142)

One of Guimarães' main arguments about the lack of in-depth studies of Fanon's thinking in the Brazilian academy, revolves around the limited presence of Black people in Brazilian universities. To illustrate this point, Guimarães shows the use of Fanon as a reference by Black movement militants and by Brazilian intellectuals criticizing racism and its implications for colonialism between 1960 and the early 1980s.

Although the argument is well-constructed, including examples of passages by scholars that cite Fanon as their primary focus, it is clear that, since most Brazilian intellectuals are not studying Black identity or combating colonialism, their use of Fanon is relatively limited. By contrast, Black intellectuals, whose work was informed by movements and Black militancy, consistently treated Fanon as mandatory reading. His work was necessary to demystify the claim that, in Brazil, there was no racial problem. Even in this context, the work of the psychiatrist and psychoanalyst Neusa Santos Souza stands out.

Souza was part of a cadre of intellectual Black militants who forged an important bridge between the Black movement and the academy. For Borges Pereira (1981), this phase involved the insertion of discussions that took place within the Black movement of the 1970s in the Brazilian academy. For the first time, Blacks were no longer exclusively the object of social scientific study. They emerged in universities as subjects of their own academic reflection and productions.

Black intellectuals Gonzalez, Beatriz Nascimento, and Souza contributed significantly to introducing racial discussions, followed by discussions of how race intersects with class and gender, to the Brazilian academy. According to Ratts (Ratts in Pereira; Silva 2009), despite the frequent early interruption of their academic careers due to serious illness, murder, or suicide, activists and intellectuals working in the Black movement and in the academy at this stage constituted new senses in making political, social, racial and gender arguments.

Souza's intellectual trajectory was cut short by suicide. On December 20, 2008, at the age of sixty, she threw herself from the top of the building where she lived in Laranjeiras, Rio de Janeiro. As Herkenhoff writes, 'she committed suicide without ever having shown signs of depression or that she could [resort] to the extreme gesture of taking [her] own life... [she] left only a small message, apol-

---

2. 'In another line of thought, but putting his finger on the wound of the alienation of the Negro, there is the dramatic figure of Frantz Fanon, the young psychiatrist who stood out in the Algerian War of Independence. Critical of the notion of Blackness, he wrote *The Damned of the Earth* and *Black Skin, White Masks*. The latter is one of the most accurate analyses of the psychological mechanisms that induce the colonized to identify with the colonizer. In his view, the dis-alienation of Black people is directly linked to the awareness of socioeconomic relations. Critical of what he considered his countrymen's accommodation to French assimilationist politics, his position led him to demand that he be buried in Algeria after his death. And so it was done'.

ogizing to [her] few [dear] friends for [her] radical decision' (Herkenhoff, 2009). Souza was not married, had no children, and collected art objects. Despite the importance of Souza's work, her death was little publicized by the media at the time. There is, however, a brief note regarding it from the Palmares Foundation.[3]

Souza's work can be considered a pioneering contribution to studies of psychiatry, psychoanalysis, and psychology. She used a method of undertaking patient research called social therapy, based on the way Fanon sought to transform the relationship between the doctor and the alienated client. Souza's method, similar to that of Fanon, led the individual to question Black subjectivities through confrontation with the dilemmas involved when upward class mobility occurred. Black individuals discovered that, even when ascending socially, they were not freed from racial problems because:

> A raça, como atributo social e historicamente elaborado, continua a funcionar como um dos critérios mais importantes na distribuição de pessoas na hierarquia social. Em outras palavras, a raça se relaciona fundamentalmente com um dos aspectos da reprodução das classes sociais, isto é, a distribuição dos indivíduos nas posições da estrutura de classes e dimensões distributivas da estratificação social.[4]
> (Gonzalez and Hasenbalg, 1982: 89)

Breaking with racist theories of the nineteenth century, race was now understood as a social construction. In its terms, Whitening, even in the 1980s in Brazil, was framed as the 'solution' for upwardly mobile Blacks to be included in primarily non-Black groups. Souza's work portrays the painful consequences that followed for the Black subject's emotional life when caught between Whitening in order to be socially accepted and assuming a Black identity without denying one's subjectivity.

## I. Neusa Santos Souza: The Emotional Life of Blacks in Brazil

When dealing with racial issues or racism in Brazil, there is a tendency in academic works to leave out the thinking of Black intellectuals. Such research simply passes by female and Black production in its analysis or these works are only cited discursively, but not as relevant or indispensable to the central ideas under debate.

It is in response to this pattern of exclusion and marginalization that I focus on *Tornar-se negro: as vicissitudes da identidade do negro brasileiro em ascensão social*. Written by the psychiatrist and psychoanalyst Souza in the 1980s, it drew from

---

3. Available at :http://www.palmares.gov.br/?p=3166
4. 'Race, as a social and historically elaborated attribute, continues to function as one of the most important criteria in the distribution of people in the social hierarchy. In other words, race is fundamentally related to one aspect of the reproduction of social classes, that is, the distribution of individuals in the positions of the class structure or in the distributive dimensions of social stratification'.

her master's dissertation, which became an important reference for studies of psychoanalysis and psychology with a focus on the Black persona. Before analyzing the text, I would like to introduce some biographical data to situate the writer's intellectual trajectory.

Born in 1948 in the city of Cachoeira in the Recôncavo Baiano, Souza studied medicine at the Faculty of Medicine at the Federal University of Bahia. In the early 1970s, she worked at a mental health clinic in Largo da Lapinha as an assistant to Ana Rocha. Through the experience of working with the patients of this clinic, the researchers organized study groups, such as the Grupo de Estudos Psicanalíticos (NEP or Psychoanalytical Study Group). The group's purpose was to discuss psychoanalysis in Bahia and to engage in intellectual exchange with psychoanalysts from different parts of Brazil. In response to the advice of other psychoanalysts, Souza moved to Rio de Janeiro in order to better develop and expand her studies of psychoanalysis, thereby putting into practice her work experiences that began in Salvador, Bahia.

At the end of the 1970s, Souza was part of a study group of the Instituto Brasileiro de Psicanálise (IBRAPASI or Brazilian Institute of Psychoanalysis), which was founded in 1978. The group included representatives of unions, political parties, and the grassroots community. Souza's intellectual encounters in psychoanalysis therefore came more through contact with psychoanalysts outside the mainstream of the time. She also participated in the Black movements in Rio de Janeiro. Her contact with Black leaders impelled Souza to seek more critical discussions of Africa, the African diaspora, and the positivity of ethnic-racial identity that could contribute to her research.[5]

Her relationship with the Black Movement is important for understanding the place that her theoretical production occupies. It was through the experience of militancy in Black movements that many Black intellectuals developed their research, their political actions, and their projects of intellectual intervention. It was debate on racism in the Black Movement that articulated the relevance of the politicization of race and the modes of operation of the idea of race for the construction of ethnic-racial identities at the individual and collective levels. For researcher Nilma Lino Gomes, this was *the Black Movement educator*, a name used to identify the movement as a 'producer of emancipatory knowledge and a systematizer of knowledge on the racial issue in Brazil' (Gomes, 2017: 14). In response, movement activists brought the urgent interpretation of racism in the Brazilian social context into more scholarly discussions.

As mentioned by Lélia Gonzalez in *Lugar de negro*, where she cites Souza, such study represents 'important work on the drama of being Black in Brazil, [where] mechanisms of concealment and denial are due to the fact that, in psychoanalytic terms, White [is] experienced as an ego ideal' (Gonzalez; Hasenbalg, 1982: 54-55). The way Gonzalez references Souza's work suggests evidence that the two intel-

5. Biographical information about Souza appears in the master's dissertation entitled '*Escrevivências das memórias de Neusa Santos Souza: apagamentos e lembranças negras nas práticas PSIS*' (Penna, 2019).

lectuals were in contact through their shared militancy in the Black Movement in Rio de Janeiro, where both acted as Black female protagonists fundamental to the critical deepening of racial awareness.[6]

## 'Becoming Black': The Effects of Discourse on the Black Subject in a White Society

I approach Souza's *Tornar-se negro: as vicissitudes da identidade do negro brasileiro em ascensão social* here to share knowledge of those who contributed indispensably to discussing race relations in Brazil. Souza, in particular, offered a deeper analysis rooted in exploring the main emotional problems of rising Black subjects.

She asked, to what extent does the violence of racism cause what Frantz Fanon called pathology, as upwardly mobile Black people face converging pressures to conform to a White model premised on total rejection of constructing and affirming a Black identity? Her study could not be more relevant as it illustrates, in its methodology, the experiences lived by Black individuals as they confront their capacity to resist an Ideal of the Ego that is White. The way out, as the author points out, rests on a more politicized attitude about the transformation of History and history.

In 1981, the author defended her master's dissertation in Psychiatry in the Post-Graduation Course of the Institute of Psychiatry of the Federal University of Rio de Janeiro. A work that culminated in the study of becoming Black, according to the foreword by Jurandir Freire Costa, the master's dissertation and later book entitled *Tornar-se negro: as vicissitudes da identidade do negro brasileiro em ascensão social*, was a reflection on violence:

> A violência parece-nos a pedra de toque, o núcleo central do problema abordado. Ser negro é ser violentado de forma constante, contínua e cruel, sem pausa ou repouso, por uma dupla injunção: a de encarnar o corpo e os ideais do Ego do sujeito branco e a de recusar, negar e anular a presença do corpo negro.[7] (Costa in Souza, 1983: 2)

For Costa, the repercussions of the work were muted at the time of first publication because psychoanalysts did not understand the issues of race as relevant to the field of psychoanalysis. They did not understand the problems arising from race relations as an obstacle to the construction of the Black persona. She hoped that they could come to recognize the significance of these obstacles through

---

6. *Lugar de negro* was published in 1982 and *Tornar-se negro: as vicissitudes da identidade do negro brasileiro em ascensão social* in 1983. Gonzalez's quotation from Souza's work reinforces my suggestion about the fruitfulness of looking together at the efforts of these two Black women intellectuals who challenged others to face the psychological, pathologizing effects of racism in Brazil in a most acute moment of silence and repression.

7. 'Violence seems to us to be the touchstone, the central core of the problem to be addressed. To be Black is to be violated in a constant, continuous, and cruel way, without pause or rest, by a double injunction: that of incarnating the body and the Ego-ideal of the White subject and that of refusing, denying, and canceling the presence of the Black body'.

encountering stories characterized not by portrayals of becoming Black as others accepting Black people as a problem, but rather their accepting Black existence and, above all, the ability of Black people to think and produce consequential, even historic, ideas.

Souza brought to the field of psychoanalysis the results of a form of analysis based on knowledge of the reports of Black experiences. She explored these life stories and attempted to understand them based on discourses Black subjects developed about themselves. The main question guiding Souza's methodology was to identify, through case studies[8] and the technique of life histories,[9] the meanings of the experiences of being Black in a White society.

What, she asked, are the effects of speech on such subjects? Her reports put the Black subject in the first person. This Black *persona* concentrated, in their speech, private, and first person reports, on the particularities of their relationships with themselves and with those around them. The language used in these statements translated into a form of pronunciation about facts, which theoretically would pass in the social sphere as unimportant, but which, when narrated by a Black voice, would produce elements of analysis that problematize the existence of racism and the violence of living in a world that actively denies Black experience. This set of voices compose a rich archive from which all of the analyses in the work are constructed. It is these voices, in their discursive materiality, that capture the contradictions and ambiguities of becoming Black.

The book is composed of ten life stories that narrate the social practices of Black subjects in social ascent in a racist and discriminatory society. The analysis of the testimonies collected first highlighted the brutal, uninterrupted violence to which Black bodies are unremittingly subjected and the attempt to deny and even to annihilate the Black body for the sake of an ideal of dominance over the world Ego of the White person. The study reveals the Black person's emotional life, accompanied by their dilemmas, their anguish, and way of reacting to feelings of oppression that directly affect who they are and who they want to be in a society of White hegemony that contradicts the ideology of racial democracy.

During the one-hour sessions, the people, who had been selected according to the criteria of being Black, living in Brazil, and being upwardly mobile, spoke about their lives. They spoke directly about their affections, intimacies, conflicts, and emotions and were only interrupted when something in their narrative was unclear.

The initial telephone contact to schedule the meetings suggested, to the interviewees, that Souza was White. How could a Black person be interested in Black people? Or know how it felt in a social environment that became newly accessi-

---

8. For Souza, the case study is defined as the: 'qualitative method of analysis where any social unit is taken as representative of the analysis'. (Souza, 1983: 69)
9. About the 'life stories', the author explains: 'This technique has a tradition in the social sciences, particularly in Anthropology. More recently, Psychiatry and Psychoanalysis have used autobiographies to study their subject in depth. To cite just one example, invested with greater relevance and significance, we recall that Freud developed the theory of paranoia based on the autobiographical account of Dr. Daniel Paul Schreber - the famous Schreber case' (Souza, 1983: 70-71).

ble through social mobility? Why would the resulting life narratives make sense to use in studying the Black persona? Souza's methodology sought to question whether being born with Black skin and sharing the story of 'uprooting, slavery, and racial discrimination' guaranteed awareness of Black identity.

To possess a Black identity, for Souza, is to become Black through possession of a discourse about oneself. Developing such discourse involves a process that presupposes political awareness, not contradicting the fundamental importance of Black cultures, and facing the systematic presence of racial discrimination and racism in the social sphere.

> Ser negro é, além disso, tomar consciência do processo ideológico que, através de um discurso mítico acerca de si, engendra uma estrutura de desconhecimento que o aprisiona numa imagem alienada, na qual se conhece. Ser negro é tomar posse dessa consciência e criar uma nova consciência que reassegure o respeito às diferenças e que reafirme uma dignidade alheia a qualquer nível de exploração.[10] (Souza, 1983: 77)

Souza is categorical in justifying the importance of her work. She states that there is a precariousness of studies about the emotional life of Blacks in Brazil. In the introductory chapter of the text, she explains that she opted to place in the investigative line of scientism the despised emotion of the Black 'patient' subject. When choosing this mode of scientific investigation, in which discourse about oneself is essential to the emergent knowledge of oneself, she offered the following definition of being a Black woman, psychiatrist, psychoanalyst, and researcher:

> Saber-se negra é viver a experiência de ter sido massacrada em sua identidade, confundida em suas perspectivas, submetida a exigências, compelida a expectativas alienadas. Mas é também, e sobretudo, a experiência de comprometer-se a resgatar sua história e recriar-se em suas potencialidades.[11] (Souza, 1983: 18)

The study's guiding question asks what the emotional cost would be of the subjection, denial, and massacre of the Black existential historical identity? Two paths are possible: one reduces the Black person to a caricatured model of the White, opening a 'narcissistic wound', creating the conditions of 'pathology of the Black'. In the second, the Black person deliberately clashes with the construction of a Black identity, undertaking the eminently political task that arises from contesting the White model to be followed. In both cases, there is an emotional

---

10. 'To be Black is, moreover, to become aware of the ideological process that, through a mythical discourse about you, engenders a structure of ignorance that imprisons you in an alienated image through which you know yourself. To be Black is to take possession of that conscience and create a new conscience that reassures the respect for differences and that reaffirms a dignity alien to any level of exploitation'.
11. To know how to be Black is to live the experience of having been slaughtered in your identity, confused in your perspectives, subjected to demands, compelled by alienating expectations. But it is also, and above all, the experience of committing to rescue Black history and recreating Black identity or Blackness in its potential.

component that introduces difficulties, conflicts, and confrontations. The experience of Black existence that knows itself as Black is to deal with too much.

In the second chapter, Souza traces the historical antecedents of the social ascension of the Brazilian Black, demonstrating that the construction of Black emotionality is rooted in sustaining Black subordination and supposed inferiority in relationship to an identity model based on Whiteness, even after the breakdown of slavery and substitution of it by capitalism. For Souza, race, as an ideological notion, was engendered as a social criterion for distributing unequal structured class positions. In this sense, the social ascension project, the tripod of which corresponded to color, the Whitening ideology, and racial democracy, structured racial relations in Brazil and how it was possible to socially insert Black people, who were considered disciplined, docile, submissive, and useful. It was believed that the social insertion of Blacks in Brazil would transpire, and social ascension be achieved, through the fragmentation/denial of Black identity and in Black assimilation to White patterns of social relations.

In the third chapter, when dealing with the Black myth, the author first defines myth as: 'speech-verbal discourse or visual-form of communication about any object: thing, communication or people' (Souza, 1983: 25). She adds that myth has a social effect; that it can be understood in the convergence of economic, political, ideological, and psychic determinations. Thereafter, Souza explains and discusses how the Black myth is forged to produce the uniqueness of the Black 'problem'.

The Black myth, based on what Souza calls 'three-dimensional singularity', imposes itself as a challenge. It is difficult not to submit to, or to effectively break with, the ideological message that identifies the Black with everything that is irrational, ugly, bad, dirty, sensitive, super powerful, and exotic. In the second chapter, the author draws on a sequence of excerpts taken from the life stories of the research participants for analysis. One, in particular, draws attention. It mentions the way Black subjects should impose themselves, in order to avoid the daily violence to which they are exposed.

But how does one impose oneself? The author refers to Fanon's thought to endorse the assessment that, when living in the world of Whites, the Black ceases to behave as an individual of action. Souza formulates her arguments building from Fanon's text entitled *Escucha, blanco!* She quotes Fanon directly to explain: 'El negro tiene duas dimensiones. Una com su congénere, otra con el branco. Um mismo negro se comporta de modo diferente con um blanco y con otro negro' (Fanon in Souza, 1983: 27).[12] In the author's opinion, when living with White people, the mark of inequality expressed in living with difference is introjected by Black people and, at the same time, reproduced by them in living with their ethnic-racial group. This would explain the fact that, when ascending socially, Blacks would, with Whites, become rational and with Blacks, emotional.

---

12. 'The Black possesses two dimensions: one with fellow Blacks, the other with the Whites. The Black behaves differently with a White than with another Black' (Fanon, 2008: 1, translation modified).

The danger, the author emphasizes, is the reproduction, by the Black, of the White person's speech. In excerpts from the stories told, the reader can see the efficacy of the 'ideological mechanisms' that, at a psychic level, act so that the Black person is a 'subjugate subject'. As the author argues:

> *Passaram por nossos olhos, ouvidos e pele, fragmentos de discursos, colhidos das histórias-de-vida dos nossos entrevistados, onde ouvimos falar o negro enquanto sujeito que introjeta, assimila e reproduz, como sendo seu, o discurso do branco. O discurso e os interesses. Tal façanha– a hegemonia dos interesses dominantes– é valorizada pela eficácia dos mecanismos ideológicos cuja garantia, a nível psíquico, é assegurada por certas articulações estruturais e transações psicodinâmicas que cumpre elucidar. Assim é que se impõe o exame de dois conceitos fundamentais– **Narcisismo e Ideal do Ego**[13] – forças estruturantes do psiquismo que desempenham um papel chave na produção do negro enquanto sujeito – sujeitado, identificado e assimilado ao branco.*[14] (Souza, 1983: 32)

The concept of the Ego-ideal, highlighted by Souza, forms the basis for the fourth chapter. There, the author states that the Ego-ideal guides the self-construction of the individual, based on previous models represented by parents, guardians, and other important elders. The Ego-ideal can be characterized in three ways: perfect ideal, almost perfect ideal, and the ideal interpreted as an instance that structures the psychic subject.

The Black brought into the discussion by Souza is directly related to the one who lives through an ideology imposed by the White as the ideal, whose Ego-ideal is White. At this point in the discussion, Souza's study comes very close to the conception of 'double consciousness' articulated by W.E.B. Du Bois. For Du Bois, double consciousness corresponds to the negrification developed by a process of racialization common to colonial systems. Seen through the eyes of the oppressor, the oppressed perceives himself in two primary ways: in the first, the oppressed retains the ability to see himself with his own eyes, while, in the second, that first look of the oppressed is eliminated, replaced with the way the colonizer sees the colonized. This second look becomes critical because it tends to deracialize the identity of the oppressed subject and to categorize it within another process, that of assimilation (Du Bois, 1903).[15]

---

13. I have added the emphasis in bold. The highlighted concepts are of fundamental importance for understanding the examination, on a psychic level, of what is considered 'Black pathology'.

14. 'Fragments of speech, collected from the life stories of our interviewees, passed through our eyes, ears, and skin. We heard the Black speaks as a subject who introjects, assimilates, and reproduces, as his own, the speech of the White. Discourse and interests. Such a feat - the hegemony of dominant interests—is valued for the effectiveness of ideological mechanisms whose guarantee, at a psychic level, is ensured by certain structural articulations and psychodynamic transactions that must be elucidated. Thus, it is necessary to examine two fundamental concepts - **Narcissism and the Ego-Ideal**—structuring forces of the psyche that play a key role in the production of the Black as a subject – a subject identified and assimilated to White.

15. *Trajetórias de Dois Intelectuais Negros: Abdias Nascimento e Milton Santos.* Thesis (Doctorate in the Multidisciplinary Graduate Program in Ethnic and African Studies), Faculty of Philosophy and Human Sciences, Federal University of Bahia. Salvador, 2010, p. 233.

But the essential question to understand the findings is: how is the Black Ego-ideal constructed? According to the Souza, it is first through the denial and purge of what she calls the 'Black spot'. Denial can provoke the rejection of the physical body itself, followed by acts of violence that manifest themselves quickly and brutally, with the aim of causing the body sometimes irreversible damage.

The family context is identified, by Souza, as the first place where the constituent action of the ego ideal unfolds. Other contexts in the interviewees' lives end up being equally important and are exemplified in the experiences of life on the street, at school, at work, and in spaces of leisure.

The relationship between the ego and Ego-ideal one of constant tension due to the pressure that the Superego exerts on the Ego, in search of an unreachable ideal, an ideal of identity with the ego ideal,. This experience is not the prerogative of Blacks alone. It is an experience that can be undergone by every non-psychotic subject. In the life experiences that guided the highlighted work, it was also observed that between the current ego and the ego ideal there is considerable dissatisfaction with the consequences of the possible achievements of the Black subject. In the search for an affirmation, trying to compensate for the 'defect' of color, being better, in the case of the Black subject, is never enough to guarantee success because 'the Black's Ego-ideal, which is largely built by the dominant ideals, is White. And being White is impossible for him' (Souza, 1983: 40).

Upon realizing the impossibility of achieving the ego ideal, the study shows that Blacks envision two generic alternatives: in the first, the tendency is to succumb to the punishments of the superego, while the second pushes them to search for ways out. When succumbing to the punishments of the superego, melancholy appears as a morbid state characterized by mental and physical depression that can manifest different problems, including the feeling of loss of self-esteem, which, as a psychopathological condition, announces the bankruptcy of the ego. Between the ideal and the possible, various feelings, according to Souza, are triggered by the Black subject, such as 'guilt, inferiority, insecurity, anguish, shyness, withdrawal, phobic anxiety, self-depreciation, conformism, phobic attitude and submission'. Interviewees whose egos fell into 'disgrace' in general felt 'humiliated, intimidated and disappointed' because they could not live up to the expectations of the Ideal in their realization of the ego.

The other alternative is directly related to the struggle to find a way that can substitute for the 'Unrealizable Ideal'. This struggle, as identified in the interviews carried out, is, most frequently associated with the search for a loving object, a means of satisfying **narcissism**, for example, through 'authentic love'. In this, intimacy of the sexual affective relationship with a White partner motivates in the Black subject the identification for the realization of the 'Ideal of the unattainable Ego'. Here, as Souza points out when referring to Fanon, Whiteness is loved and, therefore, she adds:

*O negro que elege o branco como **Ideal do Ego**[16] engendra em si mesmo uma ferida **narcísica,** grave e dilacerante, que, como condição de cura demanda ao negro a construção de um **outro Ideal de Ego.** Um **novo Ideal de Ego** que lhe configure um rosto próprio, que encarne seus valores e interesses, que tenha como referência e perspectiva a História. Um Ideal construído através da militáncia política, lugar privilegiado da construção transformadora da História.[17]* (Souza, 1983: 44)

For Souza, engaging in political practice, in the case of the Black subject, represents a way of recovering self-esteem. It is through political practice, understanding, and the ability to articulate this consciousness in the midst of history, that Black subjects start to affirm their existence and to mark their place as protagonists in the construction of Black identity.

The fifth chapter of Souza's book is devoted to the story of Luísa. It is the only story that appears in its entirety. Through the narrated facts that compose the narrative, Luísa's relationships with her family, with school friends, and with 'loves' are evident and, with them, the feelings, more of rejection, than of identification with being Black. One becomes aware of the difficulties of coping with Black identity and, above all, of doubts, uncertainties, and pains, even in the physical body, that Luísa experiences in her trajectory. Luísa's story is interpreted by the author as follows:

*Luísa logra conquistar uma identidade de mulher negra. Sua identidade, construída de mitos e imagos, estrutura-se como história: é um sistema opaco de desconhecimento e reconhecimento, marcado por todas as ambiguidades provenientes de sua origem imaginária. Identidade feita de contradições, submetida às formações ideológicas dominantes e sobredeterminadas pela história individual e pela História da formação social onde a primeira se inscreve. É com esta identidade que Luísa toma consciência de suas contradições e tenta participar da luta política que busca transformar a História e sua história.[18]* (Souza, 1983: 59)

Luísa's emergence as a protagonist in the conquest of her Black identity comes from a process. As problematized by Fanon, this is the disalienation of her own being. It involves reflection through the course of History on the social situation of Blacks in contexts of domination by White men and of the racism involved in the violence of this relationship. Knowledge of History and of the images rep-

---

16. My emphasis.
17. 'The Black who chooses White as the **Ego-Ideal** engenders in himself a **narcissistic** wound, severe and tearing, which, as a condition of healing, demands from the Black the construction of **another Ego-Ideal**. A new Ego-Ideal that shapes its own face, embodies its own values and interests, that makes History its reference and perspective. An Ideal built through political militancy, a privileged place in the transformative construction of History'.
18. See translation:Luísa succeeds in conquering a Black woman's identity. Built of myths and imagos, the identity is structured like history: it is an opaque system of ignorance and recognition, marked by all the ambiguities arising from its imaginary origin. It is an identity made of contradictions, submitted to the dominant ideological formations, and overdetermined by individual history and by the History of the social formation in which the first one is inscribed. It is with this identity that Luísa becomes aware of her contradictions and tries to participate in a political struggle that seeks to transform History and its history.

resenting the Black subject demand, from the Black subject herself, what Fanon calls 'awareness'.

The awareness proposed by Fanon, and aimed at Blacks, proposes a reading of racial reality that leads to a choice between an 'authentic' or 'inauthentic' situation of Black behavior. With Luísa, it was no different! The ambiguities and contradictions related to the affirmation of Black identity appear glued to the narrative of Luísa's personal history, rubbing against what the author calls 'dominant ideological formations'. How can we see that individual history, in the case of Blacks, is shaped from a collective history of oppression of Black existence?

The answer lies in the proposition formulated by Fanon in *Black Skin, White Masks*. The solution is to transform the Black into a being of action. And for the Black subject to pass consciously through this process of transformation, to emerge as a protagonist with their own capacities. To do so, it is essential that they know their history and that, through it, they find the resources for the affirmation of their racial identity, making it a center of their experience of living with the maturity of responsibility to exercise political practice essential to face the different forms of domination imposed by colonialism.

## II. Frantz Fanon and Becoming Black: Disalienation and Freedom

In addition to the revolutionary thinking it represents, Fanon's work demands a series of interpretations and critical reflection about the senses and meanings of racism that result from colonialism. For Fanon, the violence of the colonial process is responsible for the psychopathology of Black people, as problematized in *Black Skin, White Masks*. Through his capacity for psychiatric analysis, Fanon inaugurates a form of criticism that sheds light on the psychological consequences of colonization. The combination of Fanon's political and intellectual activism, with important consequences for both philosophy and psychiatry, are the basis of his standing as one of the most important intellectuals of anti-colonial and anti-racist struggle in the twentieth century.

As a psychiatrist at Blida-Joinville Psychiatric Hospital in Algeria, an institution now called Frantz Fanon Hospital, the revolutionary intellectual confronted the limitations of classical European psychiatry when working with his patients. His efforts to respond constructively led to his innovative understanding of the psychology of Black people, their delusions, their needs, and their difficulties living in a world of denial of Black existence. The technique of social therapy, which Fanon had practiced with François Tosquelles in France, translated into scientific innovation and lucid epistemology when applied to transforming the doctor's relationship with the alienated patients who were also 'indigenous' and Muslim.

Through the application of this different method of therapy, Fanon sought to understand the dimensions of mental alienation, resulting from a mental illness, for changes in the personality and the reality of patients. The violence of the colonial world alters the becoming of the subject in their individuality and in their collectivity. Alienation, resulting from psychic and traumatic disorders, becomes a state of conflict with a dominant world that constantly interrogates the human status of the dominated.

This state of mental alienation is clearly typified in the examples offered in Souza's book and in the story of Luísa that she chose for analysis. Although recognizing her Black ancestry and, to a certain extent, questioning the White 'model', the 'patient' mainly explores the relationship of Black women with the world around them, reproducing images, starting from a psychoexistential coping complex with the affirmation of Black identity. For Fanon, there is a Black language that defines behavioral characteristics resulting from a colonial ideology. Luísa's grandmother reproduced this language: 'se você vir confusão, saiba que é o negro que está fazendo; se você vir um negro correr, é ladrão. Tem que casar com um branco para limpar o útero' (Souza, 1983: 46). In the life story told by Luíza, there is an attempt to get closer to an ideal of human being. That precludes any possibility of being similar to or reproducing with the Black.

Luísa's life story is also a reflection of loneliness that mixes feelings like anger and shame of being Black, of not resembling a pattern of human being previously established as ideal. She experiences distance from a world that does not speak her language and that does not identify with the language she tries to outline. The girls around Luíza had 'nariz fino e cabelo liso' and she was advised by her mother to put 'pregador de roupa no nariz pra ficar menos chato' (Souza, 1983: 47). The world exemplified in Luíza's narrative is totally disconnected from identity references that could bring her to her reality, to the reality of a Black woman-girl.

Luíza's lived experience of processes of maturation are configured through the love relationship, discussed by Fanon, between the woman of color and the White man. Through it, she faces the feeling of inferiority that enslaves the Black person. Luísa called herself Black-White because she didn't want to be like other Black people. She had contempt for Blacks and admiration for Whites. Her best friends were White Jews. She disliked the poor and Blacks, unless proximity with them enabled her to move closer to the White reference: 'Para mim um homem negro tinha que ser especial. Ser muito melhor que o branco, se destacar, ser como eu. Teria que ser lindo! Muito bonito, muito inteligente. Nunca me apareceu um homem assim...'. (Souza, 1983: 50). With her first White boyfriend, Luiza was never introduced to his family. Although she did not think that race was an obstacle to the relationship, but rather her 'ugliness', the truth was, according to Fanon, how could she know if such feelings of supposed inferiority would ever be overcome?

Souza starts her book, as Fanon would recommend, with a psychological analysis of Luíza's story. For Souza, 'a verdadeira desalienação do negro implica uma súbita tomada de consciência das realidades econômicas e sociais' (Fanon, 2008: 28). What does Fanon propose with de-alienation? Disalienation implies conscience and conscience in freedom. Would the disalienation process free the Black from being interpreted as a problem? Disalienation would remove the Black from the dilemma posed by Fanon: 'to Whiten or disappear'. The modern premise of reason denies Black existence, excluding Black people from humanity.

The Black complex does not come from the Black. It comes from outside and the way the Black is socially interpreted:

> *Se ele se encontra a tal ponto submerso pelo desejo de ser branco, é que vive em uma sociedade que torna possível seu complexo de inferioridade, em uma sociedade cuja consistência depende da manutenção desse complexo, em uma sociedade que afirma superioridade de uma raça; é na medida exata em que esta sociedade lhe causa dificuldades que ele é colocado em uma situação neurótica.*[19] (Fanon, 2008: 95)

Disalienation is the non-bleaching and non-disappearing answer of the Black subject. In other words, it is to appear with an awareness, defined by a new possibility of existing, that frees Black people from this inferiority complex. Fanon draws attention to the unconscious of the Black subject: 'Enquanto psicanalista, devo ajudar meu cliente a *conscientizar* seu inconsciente, a não mais tentar um embranquecimento alucinatório, mas sim a agir no sentido de uma mudança das estruturas sociais' (Fanon, 2008: 95).[20]

The alienated person lives what Fanon calls 'absolute depersonalization', which corresponds to the effects of a domination that directly affects the psychic being of the Black subject. In the political struggle against all forms of oppression, it is important to realize that: 'Lutar contra o racismo é inútil, se não se evidenciam os efeitos da opressão exercida pela cultura dominante, opressão que atinge as comunidades, o político e a cultura, mas também o psíquico' (Cherki[21] in Fanon, 2005: 13). Fanon will address the dominating/dominated relationships and conditions of liberation in *The Wretched of the Earth*. Here, Fanon offers a singular message addressed to the disinherited:

> *Os condenados da terra aos quais Fanon se dirigia eram os deserdados dos países pobres, que queriam realmente terra e pão, ao passo que, na época, a classe operária no mundo ocidental, muitas vezes racista e evidentemente ignorante sobre as populações além-mar, demonstrava uma relativa indiferença pelo destino das colónias de que, indiretamente, se beneficiava.*[22] (Cherki in Fanon, 2005: 12)

---

19. 'If he is overcome to such a degree by a desire to be white, it's because he lives in a society that makes his inferiority complex possible, in a society that draws its strength by maintaining this complex, in a society that proclaims the superiority of one race over another; it is to the extent that society creates difficulties for him that he finds himself positioned in a neurotic situation'. (Fanon 2008: 80)
20. 'As a psychoanalyst I must help my patient to 'consciousnessize' his unconscious, to no longer be tempted by a hallucinatory lactification, but also to act along the lines of a change in social structure' (Fanon, 2008: 80).
21. Alice Cherki, an Algerian psychoanalyst who worked with Fanon in Algeria and Tunisia, signed the preface to *The Wretched of the Earth* for the edition published in 2002 in Brazil. Cherki published *Frantz Fanon: A Portrait*. The book, which is based on memories of the author's interactions with Fanon, informs a biographical reading, which is essential to understanding the trajectory of one of the most important intellectuals of the twentieth century.
22. 'The damned of the earth to whom Fanon addressed were the disinherited from poor countries who really wanted land and bread. At the time, the working classes in the Western world were often racist and evidently ignorant of populations overseas. They showed relative indifference to the fate of the colonies from which they indirectly benefited'.

*The Wretched of the Earth* questions the effects of domination and the consequences of submission for dominated peóples. The text is a plural call for liberation and the 'decolonization of being'. It seems that when dealing with 'de-alienation', one must also deal in 'decolonization'. With this last term, often used in different contexts and without due reference to Fanon, the author combines the perfect ingredients for coping with the violence engendered by and with dominating cultures.

What Souza proposes, at the end of the analysis of Luísa's story, is the transformation of the way that Luiza exists for herself and for the world through the knowledge that involves the engagement of the Black subject in political struggle. The fight is against the violence and dehumanization of colonialism, which works to maintain the consistency of a Black inferiority complex. What is proposed by Fanon and Souza is the dismantling of racial superiority, which frees the Black subject from the hallucinatory and neurotic unconscious of Whitening that is fundamentally maintained by the domination of the colonial world.

For both Fanon and Souza, the violence implied in the rejection of the Black body only thrives when the Black subject does not realize that their body is their perspective on the world (Gordon, 1997). According to Gordon, recalling Sartre (1956), this perspective involves three dimensions: the dimension of seeing, the dimension of being seen, and the dimension of being aware of being seen by others. The combination of these three potential dimensions is essential to the interpretive notion of the Black subject in the world. The Black person's embodied subjectivities can respond to that experience of existence through creating the political conditions to respond to racism and colonialism. It is against the impossibility of being Black in the world that intellectuals like Fanon and Souza fought and made their ideas relevant to discussions on domination and human freedom.

## III. The Black Body of Lélia Gonzalez: The Experience of Becoming Black

Born in Belo Horizonte, Minas Gerais on February 1, 1935, Gonzalez migrated to Rio de Janeiro in 1942, where she would develop her intellectual life. Committed to the city's activism and activism in the Black Movements, she followed an agenda of total attention to racial and gender inequalities in the country. Gonzalez studied History and Philosophy, taught in the public school system, and became dedicated to the study of Anthropology and Popular Brazilian Culture at the Pontifical Catholic University of Rio de Janeiro (PUC-RJ), where she headed the Department of Sociology and Politics. Gonzalez was one of the precursors in introducing the study of Blacks in Brazilian universities, mainly in the form of questioning the representation of Black and indigenous women in Brazilian society. Her work opened multidimensional intellectual space for recognizing the importance of the discussion of Black and Afro-American feminism in the Brazilian context. Among her varied activities, I would highlight her participation in the journal *Mulherio*, founded in the 1980s by researchers from the Carlos

Chagas Foundation who were involved in research on the female condition in Brazil.[23]

The Brazilian Black movements and, specifically, the Black Movement in Rio de Janeiro have harbored the thinking of different Black intellectuals since their founding. Like Souza, Gonzalez, in her remarkable time at Black Movement, was synonymous with great intellectual expression. While her intellectual project began before she joined the movement, MNU was a transformative place for her activity as a philosopher, anthropologist, teacher, writer, militant, and feminist intellectual.

Gonzalez effusively questioned what she called a 'Black place'. It was against this place, to which the post-abolition Brazilian Black was seemingly predestined, that Gonzalez organized her intellectual actions. Her committed teaching and training of students were among the first steps in the development of her project of sustained study of race relations in Brazil. This project centrally considered the ambiguous and contradictory relations between race, class, and gender.

Gonzalez was one of the first Black intellectuals to question the formative conceptions of the feminist movement in Brazil, which defined gender in ways that said little to nothing of the racial and class oppression suffered by Black and poor women. Gonzalez regarded herself as representative of what she called 'silenced minorities'. She worked tirelessly to spread awareness of the existence of Black and indigenous women, who were primarily located on the periphery of favelas and in the country's most needy communities.

Gonzalez's fruitful intellectual trajectory leaves us with no doubt about the dialogue that she had with intellectuals at MNU and with other intellectuals outside the movement. Fanon was one of those intellectuals. The revolutionary spirit of Fanon's ideas appears very appropriately in the ideas leveraged by Gonzalez in her emblematic phrase, 'we are not born Black, we become Black'.[24] (Gonzalez, 1988).[25] For her, being born Black should be understood as the continuation of a colonial project of reproducing the Black individual as inferior, subordinate, and alienated from their own human capacities.

Gonzalez was fundamentally critical of the Brazilian education system. According to her, it did not allow Black subjects freedom to assume their ethnic-racial identity without major consequences for their social existence. When commenting, in an interview for the book *Patrulhas Ideológicas*, on the Whitening process that Black students are pressured to undergo through the school system, Gonzalez affirms, drawing on her own experience as an example: 'I went through that process that I call the cerebral washing given by the pedagogical-

23. The *Mulherio* newspaper is the result of the systematization, by researchers and journalists, of information about the condition of women in Brazil. Specifically, the articles dealt with the problems that involved the condition of women in a serious and, at the same time, humorous way. Further details about the editions are available at: https://www.fcc.org.br/conteudosespeciais/mulherio/historia.html.

24. Available at: https://www.fcc.org.br/conteudosespeciais/mulherio/historia.html.

25. While there is a clear resonance with Simone de Beauvoir's ideas in *The Second Sex* here ('one is not born but becomes a woman'), Gonzalez does not explicitly mention Beauvoir's writing in this text.

Brazilian discourse, because as I deepened my knowledge, I increasingly rejected my condition as Black' (Santiago in Antelo, 1998: 15). It is curious to think that it is through psychoanalysis, as a patient, that Gonzalez found herself Black and achieved greater racial and gender awareness. On this point, Gonzalez reflects as follows:

> *Meu lance na psicanálise foi muito interessante, a psicanálise me chamou atenção para meus próprios mecanismos de racionalização, de esquecimento, de recalcamento etc. Foi inclusive a psicanálise que me ajudou neste processo de descobrimento da minha negritude... Comecei fazendo análise com Carlos Byington, que é jungiano [sic]*[26]. (Ratts; Rios In *Pasquim*, 1986: 10)

Gonzalez's encounter with psychoanalysis leads us to consider two matters: first, the possibility of Gonzalez and Souza meeting in the Unified Black Movement in Rio de Janeiro, since by 1978 the two authors were already known for their intellectual and institutional work. Second, it is also possible that, psychoanalysis or contact with professionals in the field brought their two life trajectories closer together, albeit through initially discrete work. It should also be remembered that, at the time, two phenomena were uncommon. Black patients rarely sought psychoanalytic therapy and there were few or no practicing Black psychoanalysts who were attentive, in their therapy, to the relevance of ethno-racial questions in the construction of racial identity.

Having discovered her Blackness in therapy, Gonzalez categorically testifies that no one is born recognizing him- or herself as a Black subject. This recognition comes, in part, from the subject's confrontations with the social environment, especially when she perceives that environment's rejection of Black existence. Gonzalez tried to mold herself to the policy of social Whitening in Brazil. And for some time she even surrendered to 'double consciousness', looking at herself and her Black body only through and with the colonist's eyes. But as a philosopher, Gonzalez sought answers to two important questions about coping with race relations. The first focused on her marriage with a White man and his suicide. The other demanded a radical turn in her intellectual purposes.

Gonzalez's discovery of herself as Black dialogues directly with the discussion of Lewis R. Gordon in *What Fanon Said: A Philosophical Introduction to His Life and Thought*,[27] when he problematizes the lived experience of the Black body. Gordon considers the expressions 'Black dirty!', which opens chapter five of *Black Skin*,

---

26. 'My bid with psychoanalysis was very interesting, psychoanalysis called my attention to my own mechanisms of rationalization, forgetfulness, repression, etc. It was psychoanalysis that helped me in this process of discovering my Blackness.... I started doing analysis with Carlos Byington, who is a Jungian'.
27. *What Fanon Said- a Philosophical Introduction to His Life and Thought*, written by Lewis R. Gordon, is an objective and clear explanation of ambiguous questions and/or misunderstandings of reading and interpretation about what Fanon proposed for coping with Black existence related to class, gender, sexuality, and the violence of colonialism and racism. Gordon's analysis clarifies not only who Fanon is, but what Fanon said, and how his ideas can be incorporated into contemporary, global debate. The most surprising aspect of the book is that Gordon manages to update Fanon's ideas, expanding the philosophical discussion, and advancing the proposition of 'a new geography of reason', as a critical alternative in the fight against any and all human rationality aligned to oppression. The text represents a deep dive into what Fanon said and continues to say today.

*White Masks*, as one of the most influential passages of the work. Gordon explains the paradoxical construction of the passage, understood through its ironic and autobiographical elements, which Fanon shares with Ralph Ellison. In Gordon's words:

> This passage is perhaps the most influential part of the work. Its impact on post-1950s treatments of oppression is perhaps equaled only by Ralph Ellison's prologue to *Invisible Man*, a text with which it is often discussed in the critical literature. Among the many ironic elements of the passage is its autobiographical status. Its report is paradoxical. Fanon announces the experience of a world that denies his inner life; he examines this supposed absence *from the point of view of his inner life*. The paradox of Black experience is thus raised: Black *experience* should not exist since Blacks should not have a point of view. Nonetheless, Black experience is all that should exist since a Black's subjective life should not be able to transcend itself to the level of the intersubjective or the social. The prejudice is familiar: Blacks live, at best, on the level of the particular, not the universal. *Thus, Black experience suffers from a failure to bridge the gap between subjective life and the world.*[28] It is an experience that is, according to racist logic, not experience. (Gordon, 2015: 48)

The passage analyzed by Gordon concerns the following complete passage in the Portuguese translation of *Black Skin, White Masks*:

> *'Preto sujo!' Ou simplesmente: 'Olhe, um preto!'*
> *Cheguei ao mundo pretendendo descobrir um sentido das coisas, minha alma cheia de desejo de estar na origem do mundo, e eis que me descubro objeto em meio aos outros objetos.*
> *Enclausurado nesta objetividade esmagadora, implorei ao outro. Seu olhar libertador, percorrendo meu corpo subitamente livre de asperezas, me devolveu uma leveza que eu pensava perdida e, extraindo-me do mundo, me entregou ao mundo. Mas, no novo mundo, logo me choquei com a outra vertente, e o outro, através de gestos, atitudes, olhares, fixou-me como se fixa uma solução com um estabilizador. Fiquei furioso, exigi explicações... Não adiantou nada. Explodi. Aqui estão os farelos reunidos por um outro eu.* (Fanon, 2008: 103)

As Gordon uses literature to highlight the impact of the content of the passage of Fanon's text, I add to the philosophical and existential discussion about Black existence and its denial through the writing of 'Emparedado', written by Cruz e Souza. Quickly, but precisely, Cruz e Souza offers an existential point of view: 'As civilizações, as raças, os povos degladiam-se e morrem minados pela fatal degenerescência do sangue, despedaçados, aniquilados no pavoroso túnel da

---

28. My emphasis.

Vida, sentindo o horror sufocante das supremas asfixias' (Souza, 1995: 609-632). And in another excerpt, he states: 'Não! Não! Não! Não transporás os pórticos milenários da vasta edificação do Mundo, porque atrás de ti e adiante de ti não sei quantas gerações foram acumulando, acumulando pedra sobre pedra, pedra sobre pedra, que para aí estás agora o verdadeiro emparedado de uma raça' (Souza, 2008: 609-632). Throughout the text, Cruz e Souza alludes to racial walling and to how suffocating it is for human existence.

## Final Considerations

Gordon states that Black experience collapses when trying to build a bridge between subjective life and the world because, according to the latter's racist logic, the Black experience is not an experience. Fanon attested to the rejection of Black experience in his studies and in the way he defined alienation. But the problem is not with the subjective experience of Black existence. The problem lies in the logic used to deny this experience as experience. And, Cruz e Souza warns, it is this non-logic employed as a logic that binds us.

Both Souza and Gonzalez pursued their intellectual and academic trajectories within a context of non-logic about the importance of what they thought and what they effectively produced as Black intellectuals. They are now considered Black women who were ahead of their time because they realized, drawing on their own Black subjectivities, how becoming Black is not part of a process collapsed in failure. Becoming Black is part of the discovery of a subjective experience, directly linked to the philosophy of human rationality, which affirms and reaffirms us as Black subjects.

The relationship that these intellectuals established with Fanon's ideas, based on their writings and their criticism of colonialism and racism, not only influenced what they systematically produced as knowledge in their areas of activity, but also affected how they came to see themselves in the world. Both plunged into personal and intellectual discovery against the alienation of the psychological state of their human being. Through their intellectual projects, they were able to subvert the surrounding non-logic of the 'Ideal of the Ego' in a productive state of Black experience. Drawing on their female and Black experiences, they undoubtedly took up Fanon's recommendation, making the Black subject a being of action in the Brazilian intellectual context.

## Acknowledgements

I am very grateful for help with the translation of the text from the Portuguese language into the English language by Jane Anna Gordon, Professor, Department of Political Science, University of Connecticut- Storrs-USA.

# Bibliography

Cruz e Souza, J. 1995. *Obras Completas*. Rio de Janeiro: Nova Aguilar.

Du Bois, W. E. B. 1903. *The Sounds of Black Folk*. Chicago: A.C.McCluurg & CO.

Duarte, E. A. (org) 2011. *Literatura e afrodescendéncia no Brasil: antologia crítica*. Belo Horizonte: Editora da UFMG.

Fanon, F. 2005. *Os condenados da terra*, tradução Enilce Albergaria Rocha, Lucy Magalhães. Juiz de Fora: Ed. UFJF.

_____. 1952 [2008]. *Pele negra, máscaras brancas*: tradução de Renato da Silveira. Salvador: Edufba.

Fernandes, F. 1965. *A integração do negro na sociedade de classes*: no limiar de uma nova era, v.II. São Paulo: Dominus Editora.

Freire, P. 1996 [2019]. *Pedagogia da autonomia: saberes necessários à prática educative*. 60ª ed- Rio de Janeiro/São Paulo: Paz e Terra.

Gonzalez, L. and Hasenbalg, C. 1982. *Lugar de negro*. Rio de Janeiro: Marco Zero.

Gomes, N. L. org. 2010. *Um olhar além das fronteiras*: educação e relações raciais. Belo Horizonte: Auténtica.

Gordon, L. R., ed. 1997. *Existence in Black: An Anthology of Black Existenctial Philosophy*. New York: Routledge.

_____. 2008. *An Introduction to Africana Philosophy*. New York: Cambridge University Press.

_____. 2015. *What Fanon Said: A Philosophical Introduction to His Life and Thought*. Fordham University Press: New York.

Herkenhoff, A. 2009. 'Racismo: por que se matou a psicanalista negra que fazia sucesso no Rio?.' Correio do Brasil, a. XII, n. 4444, January 20.

Nascimento, A. 1978. *O Genocídio do negro brasileiro: processo de um racismo mascarado*. Rio de Janeiro: Paz e Terra.

Pereira, A. M., and SILVA, J. (orgs) 2009. *Movimento Negro Brasileiro: escritos sobre os sentidos de democracia e justiça social no Brasil*. Belo Horizonte: Nandyala.

Ratts, A., and Rios, F. 2010. *Lélia Gonzalez*. São Paulo: Selo Negro.

Silva, R. F. 2005. 'Afro-descendéncia.' em *Cadernos Negros e Jornal do MNU*. Belo Horizonte: Auténtica.

_____.2010. *Trajetórias de dois Intelectuais Negros Brasileiros: Abdias Nascimento e Milton Santos*, Tese (Doutorado no Programa Multidisplinar de Pós-Graduação em Estudos Étnicos e Africanos) – Faculdade de Filosofia e Ciências Humanas da Universidade Federal da Bahia. Salvador, p. 233.

_____. 2017. 'Entre o literário e o existencial, a 'escrevivência' de Conceição Evaristo na criação de um protagonismo feminino negro no romance Ponciá Vicêncio.' *Revista EntreLetras* 8 (1): 07.

Souza, N. S. 1983. *Tornar-se negro: as vicissitudes da identidade do negro brasileiro em ascensão social*. Rio de Janeiro: Edições Graal.

# THE WRETCHED BY COVID-19 AND THE COLONIAL FACES OF BLACK GENOCIDE IN BRAZIL

Deivison Faustino

In this chapter I discuss the contributions of Frantz Fanon's *Les damnés de la terre* (*The Wretched of the Earth*) to the comprehension of social and economic relations in societies structured by colonization. I propose a Fanonian analysis of underlying dialectical relations between capitalism, colonialism and racism in the current Brazilian political and sanitary juncture. First, I take the notion of colonial violence from *Les damnés de la terre*, as a reference to problematize Brazilian responses to COVID-19 pandemic. And second, I return to some historic and sociological aspects that elucidate the colonial form of 'entification of capitalism' in Brazil and its influences on the current situation. To conclude, I argue for the contemporary character of Fanonian thought to the unveiling of relations between racism and the current stage of capitalist accumulation in the global periphery.

## Introduction

> The colonial world is a world cut in two. The dividing line, the frontiers are shown by barracks and police stations... In the capitalist countries a multitude of moral teachers, counselors and 'bewilderers' separate the exploited from those in power. In the colonial countries, on the contrary,... the agents of government speak the language of pure force... does not lighten the oppression, nor seek to hide the domination. He shows them up and puts them into practice with the clear conscience of an upholder of the peace... he is the bringer of violence into the home and into the mind of the native....The originality of the colonial context is that economic reality, inequality, and the immense difference of ways of life never come to mask the human realities.
> —Frantz Fanon, *The Wretched of the Earth*

What can explain how Brazil, a country known for having a free and universal health system, arrived in 2021 as one of the countries most affected by the COVID-19 pandemic? Why, among the nearly half a million deaths, is the number of blacks much higher than that of whites? Which social and historical factors can explain the magnitude of such an epidemiological crisis and what does Frantz Fanon's *Les damnés de la terre* have to say to it?

Fanon's *Les damnés de la terre* arrived in Brazil in the 1960s (Faustino, 2020; Guimarães, 2008) and influenced the thinking of important Brazilian thinkers such as Paulo Freire, Florestan Fernandes, Glauber Rocha, Otavio Ianni, Lélia Gonzáles, and Clóvis Moutra (Faustino, 2015a). Nevertheless, the great visibility given to the topic of violence (Faustino, 2020) was at the expense of other themes, such as his reflections on the relation between capitalism and racism, as well as its particularities of class exploitation in countries whose insertion in the capitalist mode of production relied on colonization.

Based on that theoretical frame, I will analyze the context that preceded the arrival of COVID-19 and, above all, the Brazilian Government's stance towards the pandemic in 2020. However, to do this I will re-engage the notion of violence presented by Fanon, to think about its relation to the social order (Faustino, 2018a). I begin by presenting the social conjuncture under which the pandemic spreads, and subsequently take contributions from *Les damnés de la terre* to discuss the functions of racism and the historic and social particularities of capitalism in Brazil.

I recognize, though, that the temporal proximity of the related events, the low availability of academic studies that may serve as theoretical reference and, above all, my positionality and interest in the events, may offer some limits to this sociological analysis. At the time of writing, COVID-19 is ongoing and presents complex and ambiguous dynamics that change every day. On the other hand, the position of the participant observer in the presented set of events offers singular possibilities of collecting and analyzing data. Still, I recognize that some positions taken here deserve further research in order to confirm or refute their validity.

# 1. The Wretched by COVID-19 in Brazil

> *The explosion will not happen today. It is too soon... or too late.*
> —Frantz Fanon, *Black Skin White Masks*

2019 was an appalling year for workers, Blacks, women, Indigenous, and poor people in Brazil. It was the beginning of the militarized government of Jair Messias Bolsonaro:[1] a government made possible by a dismal combination of national and transnational financial interests and the opportunist channeling of diverse popular resentments to the consolidation of an ultra-neoliberal agenda, grounded in anti-leftism, anti-scientificism and fundamentalist neoconservatism. From the start, the government adopted tactics for political sustainability, which seemed to strongly hamper the implementation of the economic agenda agreed upon among Brazilian elites, on the occasion of the illegitimate dismissal of President Dilma Roussef.[2]

---

1. The adjective 'militarized' used here is related not only to the evident support and participation of military sectors in Bolsonaro Government, but also to the warmonger and barely open to criticism tone – marked by the logic of war – that its administration adopted since the beginning.
2. Bolsonaro's election succeeded the deposition of President Dilma Rousseff in 2016. Sometime later, the absence of any juridically justifiable irregularity of her mandate loss was verified.

Constant attacks against 'external enemies', real or imagined, as well as the deliberate attempt to dismantle the government support for leading scientific production and the fundamentalist criminalization of custom[3] presented itself as an obstacle to the legitimation and approval of austerity policies it advocated. To make matters worse, the extreme right and its implicit sectarianism has even threatened Brazil *commodity* exports to some of its greatest commercial partners. As a result, but also in the face of visible uncertainty on the part of some bourgeois sectors, regarding the president's questionable abilities for the post, there followed the fragmentation of the established power bloc and the outbreak of fratricidal disputes around its course.

This set of political and ideological facts was followed, in practice, by the intensification, unopposed to the degradation of labor relations in the country (see Antunes, 2020) and by the scrapping of public services, such as health, education, scientific research, has resulted in a declining standard of life of the population as a whole. In addition, social security and labor reforms threw millions of workers into informality and precarious employment as well as subordinate nano-entrepreneurships, which left them socially and economically unprotected.[4] These intermittent workers, at the mercy of their own fate and to a production rhythm they could not control, no longer had any social protection in case they needed to interrupt their exhaustive work due to force majeure.

It was in this juncture of intensifying effects of the structural crisis of capitalism (see Mészaros, 2002), and political instability, that Brazil registered, on February 27, 2020, the first COVID-19 cases. The first patient was a rich White man from São Paulo, who had traveled to Italy and, after confirming serology, was admitted in Albert Einstein Hospital, one of the most expensive and well-equipped hospitals in the country. From then on, the country began to prepare for the pandemic without wondering about how to cope with the historically unequal conditions of prevention and treatment.[5] Nevertheless, the following events mortally update Fanon's description of implicit violence between the city of the colonized and the city of the settler (Fanon, 2010).

At first, President Jair Messias Bolsonaro broadcasted various speeches underestimating the gravity of the epidemic and counteracting the scientific research that evinced the need of measures to contain population flow. During a trip to the USA (with a great delegation of ministers and federal technicians), Bolsnoaro stated, echoing the U.S. President Donald Trump, that the pandemic

---

3. With special emphasis on the recent achievements of the Black, feminist, LGBTQI and environmental movements.
4. There was plenty of news on companies that fired their employees who had previously had some labor rights, and subsequently rehired their services with no legal liability to their workers' social security.
5. At the time, information on the epidemiological behavior of the SarsCov2 Virus was already available in China, South Korea, Iran and some countries in Europe, and suggested the need to strengthen health systems and epidemiologic surveillance, as well as to adopt government measures to contain human circulation in areas with higher prevalence of the virus. From this standpoint, the question is, how to protect an unequal country as Brazil from the pandemic. See Faustino (2020).

was an overestimated 'fantasy'.[6] It is curious that, weeks after returning – when Brazil already registered its first deaths from Covid-19 – most of the delegation's twenty three members, including some Ministers, were infected with SarsCov2 (Estadão, 2020).

Second, while the pandemic had already become a frightening reality in the country (see Antunes) and, above all, after the announcement that one of the first victims was a Black housekeeper that was infected while caring for their employers,[7] the posture of the Brazilian Federal Government was marked by ambiguity: while the Minister of Health recommended the seclusion of the population in their homes, public suspicions and speculation about the President's eventual infection, was answered by his face-to-face participation in public, criticizing social restraint measures recommended by the World Health Organization (WHO), attacking the Judiciary Branch and supporting the return of dictatorship (see Gomes, Ortiz,*et. al*,. 2020). These political acts were marked by the usual image of the president on the street—in violation of local legislation—hugging his cohorts, wearing no mask.

In this same period, the Federal Government launched an advertising campaign called 'Brazil cannot stop'.[8] The one minute and 30 seconds long video, made available across free access digital platforms, depicted the image of a series of precarious workers, all Black, working in professional activities during the pandemic, while a narrator opines 'for the self-employed workers, itinerants, engineers, street fair workers, architects, masons, lawyers, teachers, neighborhood retailers, salespeople, housekeepers... Brazil cannot stop'.

The campaign aimed at positively responding to the pressure from business people who were against the containment measures and consisted in one of the successive presidential efforts to boycott sanitary measures recommended by WHO. The color of people in the advertising campaign did, however, draw attention. Black people, although composing most of the country's population, have always been invisible in governmental publicity pieces, but now, at the moment when the call to get back to work equated with a call to die, the Black population is, finally, exclusively portrayed. In addition, this campaign took place at the moment when the Ministry of Health had recognized the chances to die from COVID-19, in the richest city of the country, was 62% for Black people (See Junior, 2020).. These were, in other words, the people called upon to risk their lives for the sake of the economy.

In a third moment, when more than 40,000 people, mostly Black and poor, had already lost their lives to COVID-19 and daily death was higher than one thousand, the struggle to maintain the government shifted from the biomedical-

6. Meanwhile, the so-called 'Hatred Office', a cybernetic structure connected to the President and his supporters, started to trigger thousands of instances of fake information associating the virus and epidemiologic scientific research to a Chinese strategy for worldwide communist dominance. About the Hatred Office, see Said (2020).

7. The person victimized by the disease was called... her name was ignored by mainstream media, which referred to her only as a 'housekeeper', observes the philosopher Djamila Ribeiro (2020).

8. The campaign can be accessed through the link: https://www.youtube.com/watch?v=hQQZE7LQIGk

epidemiological field—resulting in the loss of two ministers of Health[9]—to the legal-criminalist field. Important members of the Government and their families started being investigated for an assault against democracy, for spreading fake news and for relationship with militias in Rio de Janeiro (violent paramilitary groups formed by cops and ex-cops)[10]. Since then, amid the very greatest epidemiological crisis in the country's history, the Ministry of Health remains without a Minister, provisionally managed by General Eduardo Pazuello, a man with absolutely no experience with public health.

June 2020 was the most preoccupying of all months. The previous period was marked by a dispute between governors and mayors, on the one hand, seeking to implement measures to contain population circulation and, on the other hand, the Presidency of the Republic, supported by certain economic sectors, seeking to boycott the same measures. Governors and mayors gave in to business pressures and started loosening the very measures, opening commerce, churches, and other non-essential activities, at the moment when the COVID-19 epidemiological curve was still ascending (See Rossi, 2020 and Souza, 2020). As if not enough, the President responded to the law no. 14.019/2020, about the wearing of facial masks in public spaces, softening its efficiency by vetoing their mandatory use in commercial buildings, schools, religious temples and other closed social spaces, leaving the use of masks to individual choice. Bolsonaro also vetoed the obligation of the public power to distribute masks to poor people and people's obligation of wearing masks (See G1, 2020).

The point I intend to emphasize in this account is that such political and economic conjuncture has resulted, first, in the sabotage of real conditions for epidemiological protection for the most vulnerable people in the context of COVID-19 pandemic in Brazil and, second, in the curious convenience of those deaths to the austerity project defended by the government. According to information of the Epidemiological Bulletin of the Ministry of Health, the proportion of Black people dead in Brazil is 40% higher than White people (See Viñas, Duran and Carvalho, 2020). The analysis of age group, gender and social class of the dead suggests the virus may even be democratic, but Brazilian society is not.[11] Historical social conditions of inequality and discrimination have allowed an unequal distribution of opportunities to access prevention, treatment and death.

What draws our attention and deserves further problematization, is the Brazilian State's posture towards the eminent menace to most of its population,

---

9. The fall of the Minister of Health, Luiz Henrique Mandetta (in the post from 1 January 2019 to 16 April 2020) was due to divergences around the sabotage of isolation measures proposed by the Ministry of Health, carried out by the Presidency of the Republic. Minister Nelson Teich fall, one month later, had the same motivation, added by presidential insistences on the use of the medicine Hydroxychloroquine when it had already been considered scientifically inefficient for treating COVID-19.

10. In response to rumors of a possible seizure of the president's cellphone for police investigation, General Heleno, Chief Minister of the Institutional Security Office, threatens the Federal Supreme Court speaking about unpredictable consequences in case the cellphone was in fact seized. Fernando Azevedo e Silva, Minister of Defense and also military, endorsed the General's statement in an official note. See Correio Brasiliense. (2020).

11. Official data from the Ministry of Health reveal the profile of Brazilians dead from the pandemic: man, poor and black. Further than that, the number of dead youngsters (in these groups) is higher than the average of the ones dead in Spain and Italy. Check Soares, M. (2020).

as well as to the convenience of ruling classes in the face of the ongoing genocide. In general, it is expected that the State – even historically subordinate to the needs of capitalist accumulation – seeks to minimally protect its citizens' health in a way the very expanded reproduction of capital is indefinitely possible. What has been seen in Brazil contradicts such expectation and raises questions about what is going on, how and why the Brazilian ruling classes allow and keep supporting a public administration with such characteristics.

What I suggest is that such posture can be understood as a project of neo-colonial segregation and extermination, which is useful to the current interests of capital accumulation in global periphery rather than as a crisis of management from the election of a supposedly incompetent government. More than that, the present posture of the Brazilian government is nothing else than the reflex and continuity of a genocide project based on Brazil's colonial foundation.

## 2. *The Wretched* and COVID-19 in Brazil: How Have We Gotten to this Point?

Consolidation of Brazilian capitalism holds specific and differing economic and social characteristics from the way adopted by the *classic capitalist countries*, such as France and England, or by the so-called *Prussian way* such as Germany, Italy, Portugal and Japan. In France and England the relative universalization of civil, political and social rights was thought, even if abstractly, as a premise for consolidating bourgeois society upon the old estate-based social order. Therefore, as Fanon reminds,

> The European nations achieved their national unity at a time when the national bourgeoisies had concentrated most of the wealth in their own hands. Shopkeepers and merchants, clerks and bankers monopolized finance, commerce, and science within the national framework. The bourgeoisie represented the most dynamic and prosperous class. Its rise to power enabled it to launch into operations of a crucial nature such as industrialization, the development of communications, and, eventually, the quest for overseas outlets. (Fanon, 2004: 52-53)

It is true that the structural inequalities composing capitalism, even in these countries, kept the announced equality and freedoms limited. Yet, as Fanon argues, 'the sweat and corpses of Blacks, Arabs, Indians, and Asians' in territories external to Europe allowed the class exploitation to become hegemonic through control and cohesion strategies, which recognized the relative 'welfare' of the exploited (Fanon, 2004: 53). That is why Fanon unequivocally states that Europe is, 'literally the creation of the Third World. The riches which are choking it are those plundered from the underdeveloped peoples ' (Fanon, 2004: 58).

The path for consolidation of Brazilian capitalism also differs from the experiences of late industrial capitalist development, the so-called *Prussian way*, in which the authoritarian political regime with its ultra-nationalist and chauvinist appeal, systematic restrained individual liberties encouraging theoretical adhesion to irrationalism, led these societies in the period of financial-monopolist competition of imperialism at the beginning of the 20th century.[12] This process of aggressive external competition and internal authoritarianism (including Fascism and Nazism) resulted in capital accumulation that allowed them to contend for political and economic leadership of the capitalist race in Europe or, at least,

---

12. The search for apprehending particularities in the development of capitalism in each country came from Karl Marx. Texts as *Critique of Hegel's Philosophy of Right* (1843-4), *On the Jewish Question* (1843-4), *The German Ideology* (1845-6) and some articles from the *New Gazette Renana* (ends of the 1840s) seek to apprehend the particularities of German capitalism, viewed, by him, as a latecomer in relation to classic cases (Silva, 2020).

reaching a high level of internal development that was not dissolved even after the defeats of World War I and II.

In a distinct way, the particular characteristic of Brazilian social formation is the fact it has been engendered from and in function of colonialism (Chasin, 1980) with social relations of productions based on racial slavery (Moura, 1994). Brazil's insertion in modern capitalist dynamics stems from Portuguese colonization. Because of this, it is subordinate to exogenous interests and, above all, based on production relations, social conformation and internal class struggle dynamics suitable to these ends (Moura, 1994). Notably Fanon's description of the colonized bourgeoisies in *Les damnés* is close to the one diagnosed by Brazilian economists and historians (Fernandes, 1979; Moura, 1994 and Prado, 2000):

> The bourgeoisie of the underdeveloped countries is a bourgeoisie in spirit only. It has neither the economic power, nor the managerial dynamism, nor the scope of ideas to qualify it as a bourgeoisie.... Given time and opportunity by the authorities, it will succeed in amassing a small fortune that will reinforce its domination. But it will still prove incapable of creating a genuine bourgeois society with all the economic and industrial consequences this supposes. (Fanon, 2004: 122)

Expansion of mercantile capital in the Americas engendered Brazilian dependent capitalism. Although Fanon discusses imperialist colonialism in the African Continent,[13] both experiences are similar: dependent economies and fragile democracies, economically, politically and culturally subordinated to central capitalist economies, even after independence.

Eugenics, one branch of the so-called scientific racism, was hegemonic in Brazil up to the 1940s (Góes, 2018). This is not to say that racism is a particularity of peripheral capitalist economies, but to recognize its genesis and peculiar function in a sociability where 'the new always pays a high tribute to the old'.[14] In Brazil the socioeconomic process of the colonial economic matrix was made possible through the existence of anti-Black and anti-indigenous racism,[15] creating a modern society conditioned and fed 'on the preservation of colonial structures and dynamism' (Fernandes, 1977: 13).

---

13. While the first one was carried out, initially, in a moment when capitalism was still not entirely developed (since 16th century) the second one took place from the imperialist expansion of financial-monopolist capital over the African continent, in the end of the 19th century, when American colonies had already carried out their independence processes. Fanon himself recognizes this difference: 'Capitalism, in its expansionist phase, regarded the colonies as a source of raw materials which once processed could be unloaded on the European market. After a phase of capital accumulation, capitalism has now modified its notion of profitability. The colonies have become a market. The colonial population is a consumer market'. (Fanon, 2004: 26).

14. Even recognizing the differences, the statement, formulated by Marx to describe Germany, was retaken by philosopher José Chasin (2019) to describe Brazilian particularities.

15. There is no space here to comment on the consequences of this process on Brazil's indigenous populations. However, it is worth observing that the violence against these populations follows a genocidal logic. This genocide has been taking unprecedented dimensions with the pandemic arrival at indigenous communities and territories. See, in this sense, G1 PA (2020).

The umbilical connection between slavery and internal development of capitalism in Brazil resulted, on one hand, in the engendering of a bourgeoisie after the period of slavery, that was not 'able to effectively draw a perspective of its own economic autonomy or did it too feebly, thus conforming in remaining in conditions of neo-colonial independence or structural subordination to imperialism' (Chasin, 1980: 128). On the other hand, the consequent racial blaming of the 'non-White, oppressed and discriminated segments, and of the Black in particular', by a 'social, economic and cultural inferiority' (Moura, 1988: 65)[16] that this subordinate (colonial) posture resulted. A combination of both factors is still present in Brazilian society: The composition of a fragile ruling class, congenitally dependent on external capital and unresponsive to the real needs of population in general and the promotion of racism as an ideological possibility to transfer the responsibility for the consequences of these choices to the victims themselves.

Explaining the difference between Germanic societal experience in tis search for economic autonomy from the Brazilian congenital dependency, José Chasin argues. The 'colonial way of capitalism entification' (Chasin, 1980: 128-9)is marked – even in cases where the old colonialism had been overcome by the new universalization of the contradiction between capital and labor as the axis of class struggle, after the abolition of slavery—by an 'oscillating and superficial' decolonization (Fernandes, 1977: 13) that is not even capable of absorbing the needs and demands of subordinate classes, nor of positioning itself autonomously in the international economic dispute (Chasin, 1982). In such a way, national evolution and social progress are exclusionary (Chasin, 1989) and the privileged 'do not relinquish a single particle of privileges and wield, for any reason, their White weapons of beheading and their 'sacred' flags that place private property and initiative above their religion, their homeland and their family' (Fernandes, 1986: 74-5).

The bourgeoisie that emerges in this colonial way are anti-democratic, as was the Prussian, but, different from Prussian in that they are incapable, through their own initiative and strength, of breaking with their subordination to imperialism (Rago, 2010). This subservience has always been the mark of ruling classes and Brazilian State has reached unprecedented dimensions of subservience toward international capital seen in the present government posture toward U.S. interests. The shameful incident, in Dallas, Texas, where President Bolsonaro saluted the United States flag[17] was but the prelude to a series of commercial, political and scientific decisions which also risked the interests of some national economic sectors.

Moreover, such political, economic and ideological subservience explains why the Bolsonaro government has opted to follow Donald Trump's rhetoric about

---

16. See, in the same sense, the works of Azevedo, 1987; Seyferthe, 2002; Skidmore, 2012, Mattos, 2016 and Oliveira, 2019.

17. The incident took place in the first month of the President's mandate, in a moment when he received the prize of personality of the year, offered by the Brazilian-American Chamber of Commerce, in Dallas. See Terra Portal (2020).

COVID-19 as nothing more than a Chinese strategy to export communism via the World Health Organization. But the dependency relationship that underlies it (restricted during the Lula period), precedes Bolsonaro and refers to the origin of the Brazilian State. As we have seen, the history of Brazil is marked, from the beginning, by 'concerted transitions' (Fernandes, 2014: 127), that is, conciliations from top to bottom: we were placed in the capitalist economy—and the country itself came into existence as such—from Portuguese colonization via slavery and Indigenous genocide.

Brazil ceased to be a colony and became an independent empire after 1822 with power remaining in the same hands, without any rupture with slavery. Absence of a revolution from the bottom-up, which would have brought an end to slavery, meant abolition without reparation. One year later, after a military coup the republican regime replaced the imperial one. After that, the national bourgeoisie oscillated between the 'various degrees of Bonapartism and institutionalized bourgeois autocracy, evidenced by our entire republican history' (Chasin, 1981: 11).

During these periods, popular demands were always neglected or relegated to secondary by the ruling class and their political representatives. As Fanon (2010) and also Marine (2000) and Mészaros (2002) remind us, democracy and the welfare state in the capitalist centers, were assured through over-exploitation of the peripheral labor force. In Brazil, racism was the great sustainer.

With the advent of the structural crisis of capital at the end of the 20th century (Mészaros, 2002), Brazil's place in the international division of labor was reshaped without major ruptures with its constitutive features. The closing of the colonial way of capitalist entification represented its very consolidation (Sobrinho, 2019).[18] Although with nuances and differences in governments, a consolidation of the subordinate insertion of the country in the structural crisis of capital followed by the internalization of globalization (via expansion of Foreign Direct Investment), specialization of the country in commodity production and liberalization of the financial system. This came from the untouched maintenance of over-exploitation of the labor force, and the anti-Black and anti-Indigenous racism at the ideological and social level. The colonial violence, expressed in *Les damnés de la terre*, continued to express itself through an extremely unequal social order.

Although both administrations of President Lula (2003-2012) had represented an important symbolic exception to the neo-liberal way that stemmed from the late 1990s structural crisis—through offering governmental assistance to welfare and supporting popular demands specifically to the Black movements (Ribeiro,

---

18. One cannot ignore, however, the importance of a series of institutional conquests and absorption of popular demands for the expansion of formal democracy after the official end of the dictatorial period and institution of the National Constituent Assembly, in 1988 (Santos, 2015), as well as, the participation of the Black movement in such process and in the Health Reform and Anti-Asylum movement. Even so, this was the period named 'concerted transition' by Florestan Fernandes since political forces operated in a way that political and economic power remained in the same hands. *Law no. 6.683, e3* of August 28, 1979, which conceded amnesty to military torturers and dictatorship managers, allowed them to remain at their posts with no social sanctions or stigmatization.

2014)—the institutionalization of those demands were followed by the bureaucratization and weakening of Brazilian grassroots social movements.

The juridical-parliamentary coup of President Dilma—Lula's chosen successor—as well as the illegitimate inauguration of Michel Temer (2016-2018), and above all, the weakening of popular movements and the left's inability to oppose it, intensified the austerity agenda and the attacks on previously guaranteed rights. The rise of Bolsonaro to the Presidency, however, has brought these attacks to unprecedented levels. The austerity policies were conducted by Finance Minister Paulo Guedes, a disciple of the so-called Chicago School and an advocate of the economic policies implemented in Chile during the Pinochet dictatorship.

Precariousness, outsourcing, uberization and extensive job cuts imposed by 'the fourth industrial revolution', but also aided by labor and union reforms and the resulting social segregation, have created an environment of growing social vulnerability. Added to this was the gradual aging of Brazilian population and the pressure this changing age pyramid begins to exert on the social security system. Although partially rejected by the Congress in 2019, the initial proposal of reform, presented by Bolsonaro Government, aimed at a complete dismantling of the public social security system and its replacement by a private system of capitalization, in which retirees would receive only 74 dollars a month.[19]

Moreover, the legacy of slavery in Brazil, and the maintenance and updating of racism has had, as one of its outcomes, the marginalization and social vulnerability of the Black population. Due to racism, Black people are not only the ones who are most likely to die from police murder, they are also the most likely to die from diabetes, hypertension, as well as cardiovascular and immunodepressant disorders. They are also the over-represented in the most precarious jobs that are unprotected by labor and social security rights, as well as unemployment insurance.

When the pandemic arrived, Brazil was already a country of intense structural inequality. The pandemic highlighted this and represented a great challenge to the public administration and epidemiologic control of COVID-19. Nevertheless, as I have demonstrated, governmental efforts to control COVID-19 have followed a standard that have sabotaged protection, prevention and treatment measures. Because of this, Brazil ended June2020—a moment when the Ministry of Health provided comparative data of between Blacks and Whites from COVID-19—with almost 70,000 deaths, with Blacks who had not finished school registering a mortality rate three times higher than that of Whites. The country ended January 2021 with 210,000 deaths from Covid-19. In addition, because the Brazilian Government has not given priority to the issue the country is lagging behind in the global race for the vaccine.

---

19. In a country where, due to unemployment, retirees are the main source of family supply and the minimum wage set by law is, currently, 193 dollars, according to an estimate made by the Inter-union Department of Statistics and Socioeconomic Studies. In 2020 they estimated that the necessary minimum wage to sustain a family of four people should be of 808 dollars in 2020 (DIEESE, 2020).

In line with the document 'Rights in Pandemic – Mapping and Analysis of Legal Standards for Response to Covid-19 in Brazil', produced by the Center for Research and Studies on Health Law, the Faculty of Public Health of the University of São Paulo and Conectas Human Rights (CEDEPISA/CONECTAS, 2021), I have suggested that the current scenario was not the result of the Federal Government's incompetence in responding to Pandemic, but of a *deliberate strategy of sabotage to health security measures for the benefit of an ultra-neoliberal economy project*.[20] The thousands of deaths—without mourning—of informal black workers, domestic workers and poor retirees were the result of ultra-neoliberal interests, defended by the government, and minimizing public spending on health and social security. The result is a successful project of contemporary neocolonial genocide that will remain vigorous until it is confronted frontally.

How is this possible? Colonial violence—proper to this capitalism originated by colonization and, for this reason, engenders a ruling class insensible to the popular needs and demands –about which Fanon wrote in *Les damnés de la terre*, is represented in Brazil at present time. Expanding further than the 'barracks and police stations' (Fanon, 2004: 3), it is expressed by the unequal distribution of prevention care, treatment and death by COVID-19.

It is worth remembering, however, that even during the pandemic, the world's deadliest police keep killing Black men and women in Brazil.[21] Any accountability for this unprecedented crime has to begin by dealing with racism that prevents Black people from even being considered human beings. Only then could their death be the object of any commotion and grief. (Faustino, 2020c). It seems that we are far from that recognition.

## 3. Why Fanon, Why Now?

It is not too late to remember, especially this year, sixty years after the publication of *Les damnés de la terre*, that Frantz Fanon's thought remains current and vigorous. His sociological, anthropological, philosophical, political, psychiatric and psychoanalytic contributions have not yet been fully explored by contemporary social and human sciences and offer a powerful theoretical arsenal for the understanding and, above all, the radical transformation of contemporary society (Faustino, 2018b).

Fanon's *Les damnés de la terre* is noteworthy among his various writings. It was his most known work in the 1960s and 1970s, but afterwards disappeared from the international intellectual horizon thanks to its association to the subject of violence. Such reduction of scope, at the moment when the subject of revolutionary violence had lost strength, resulted in the disincentive of the exegetic

---

20. See: Ferreira Liliane, Under attack: Bolsonaro and his govt accused of 'virus propagation strategy', Available at:https://news.cgtn.com/news/2021-01-27/Bolsonaro-and-his-govt-struggle-with-public-inquiry-and-pressure-Xovq11zjpe/index.html Accessed 25/-1/2021.
21. According to the Safety Observatory Network (ROS), a national monitoring body, Rio de Janeiro's police operations increased 27.9 per cent during the pandemic (Ruge, 2020).

investigation about Fanon's thought. His return to Anglophone cultural and post-colonial studies, under the influence of the fall of the Berlin Wall, the concurrent 'success' of global neoliberalism, and the weakening of revolutionary perspectives—from the 1980s and 1990s onwards—kept this invisibility alive electing *Peau noire, masques blancs*, as its bedside book (Faustino, 2015) while *Les damnés de la terre* was considered dated and uninteresting.

Happily, this silence has now been relatively broken and his thought finds an increasing echo in the present. In the Brazilian case, this is due to the inclusive policies for Black students in undergraduate and graduate courses,. who are demanding their teachers include content that represents their experiences. This has helped to qualitatively transform Brazilian intellectual production. Yet, despite this significant achievement, Brazilian social reality is still marked by structural violence, animalization and systematic and naturalized murders of Black and indigenous populations.COVID-19 has only aggravated what was already grave.

This paper was guided by the idea that Fanon's thought can help not only the understanding of our structurally violent reality, but above all, help us think about the possibilities of its radical transformation.

## Bibliography

Azevedo, C. 1987. *Onda Negra, Medo Branco: O Negro no Imaginário das Elites – Século XIX*, Rio de Janeiro: Paz e Terra.

Antunes, R. 2020. *Ricardo Antunes: Pandemia Desnuda Perversidades do Capital Contra Trabalhadores*. Accessed July 2020, https://www.brasildefato.com.br/2020/06/27/ricardo-antunes-pandemia-desnuda-perversidades-do-capital-contra-trabalhadores.

Chasin, J. 1980. *As máquinas param: germina a democracia*. Accessed July 1, 2020, https://www.marxists.org/portugues/chasin/1979/mes/maquinas.htm.

_____. 1982. '¿Hasta Cuando?' *A propósito das eleições de novembro*. Accessed July 1, 2020, https://www.marxists.org/portugues/chasin/1982/10/hasta.pdf.

_____. 1989. 'A sucessão na crise e a crise na esquerda.' Ensaio 17 (18): colocar 1–123.

_____. 2019. 'As vias prussiana e colonial de objetivação do capitalismo e suas expressões teóricas conservadoras: o fascismo e o integralismo. *Verinotio.' Revista on-line de Filosofia e Ciências Humanas* 25 (2): 131–165 [e-journal]. https://www.doi.org/10.36638/1981061X.2019.25.2/131-165.

CONECTAS/CEPEDISA. 'Direitos na Pandemia: mapeamento e análise das normas jurídicas e respostas à COVID-19 NO BRASIL.' Boletin n. 10. São Paulo, Jan 20, 2021. Accessed January 25, 2021, https://www.conectas.org/wp/wp-content/uploads/2021/01/Boletim_Direitos-na-Pandemia_ed_10.pdf.

Correio, B. 2020. 'Ministro da Defesa endossou nota de Heleno sobre celular de Bolsonaro.' *Correio Brasiliense – Política*. Accessed July 1, 2020, https://www.correiobraziliense.com.br/app/noticia/politica/2020/05/23/interna_politica,857743/

ministro-da-defesa-endossou-nota-de-heleno-sobre-celular-de-bol-
sonaro.shtml.

Estadão. 2020. 'A comitiva presidencial infectada pelo Coronavírus. Estadão.'
Política, *Estadão*. Accessed July 1, 2020, https://www.estadao.com.br/infografi-
cos/politica,a-comitiva-presidencial-infectada-pelo-coronavirus,1084402.

Fanon, F. 2004. *The Wretched of the Earth*. Translated by French by R. Philcox.
New York: Grove Press.

Faustino, D. 2015. *'Por que Fanon? Por que agora?': Frantz Fanon e os fanonismos no
Brasil.'* PhD diss. Universidade Federal de São Carlos.

_____. 2018a. *Violência e sociedade: o racismo como estruturante da sociedade e da
subjetividade do povo brasileiro*. São Paulo: Escuta.

_____. 2018b. *Frantz Fanon: um revolucionário, particularmente negro*. São Paulo:
Ed. Ciclo Contínuo.

_____. 2020a. *A disputa em torno de Fanon: a teoria e a política dos fanonismos con-
temporâneos*. São Paulo: Coleção Africamundi.

_____. 2020b. 'O Coronavirus e a quarentena que não chega na periferia: o que
fazer.' Accessed June 20, 2020. *Personal Blog*.

_____. in press. 'Frantz Fanon e a calibanização de Hegel: o colonialismo, a
dialética e a emancipação em questão.' *Revista Sociologias*.

Fernandes, F. 1979. 'Revista Sociologias.' *Circuito Fechado: Quatro ensaios sobre o
poder institucional*. 2a ed. Rio de Janeiro: Hucitec.

_____. 1983. *Marx & Engels: História*. Coleção Grandes Cientistas Sociais, 36. São
Paulo: Ática.

_____. 1986. *Que tipo de República?* São Paulo: Brasiliense.

_____. 2014. *Florestan Fernandes na constituinte: leituras para a reforma política*.
São Paulo: Editora Fundação Perseu Abramo Expressão Popular.

Galvão, L. A. 1997. *Marx & Marx*. São Paulo: Ática.

Gomes, P. H., Ortiz, B., et al. 2020. 'Bolsonaro e pelo menos 11 ministros partici-
pam de ato pró-governo no Palácio do Planalto.' *G1 – Política*. Accessed July 1,
2020.

G1. 2020. 'Bolsonaro veta parte de lei que determina o uso de máscaras em locais
públicos.' *G1 – Jornal Nacional*. Accessed July 3, 2020.

G1 PA. 2020. 'Covid-19 traz riscos de genocídio indígena.' alerta MPF, que quer
que Funai adote medidas urgentes. *G1 – Pará*, April 27, 2020. Accessed July
1, 2020, https://g1.globo.com/pa/para/noticia/2020/04/27/covid-19-traz-riscos-
de-genocidio-indigena-alerta-mpf-que-quer-que-funai-adote-medidas-
urgentes.ghtml.

Góes, W. L. 2018. *Racismo e eugenia no pensamento conservador brasileiro: a proposta
de povo em Renato Kehl*. São Paulo: LiverArs.

Guimaraes, A. S. A. 2008. 'A recepção de Fanon no Brasil e a identidade negra.'
*Novos estudos* 81: 99–114. Accessed July 1, 2020 [e-journal].

Inter-Union Department of Statistics and Socio-Economic Studies (DIEESE).
2020. 'Salário mínimo nominal e necessário.' *Dieese*. Accessed July 1, 2020.

Junior, G. 2020. 'Risco de morte de negros por covid-19 é 62% maior.' diz
Prefeitura de SP.*Estadão – Conteúdo*. Accessed July 1, 2020, https://noti-
cias.uol.com.br/ultimas-noticias/agencia-estado/2020/05/05/risco-de-morte-

de-negros-por-covid-19-e-62-maior-diz-prefeitura-de-sp.htm?cmpid=copiaeco la.

Mattos, A. L. 2016. *Racismo e xenofobia no Brasil: análise dos intrumentos jurídicos de proteção ao imigrante negro*. Monograph, Universidade Federal de Santa Maria. Accessed July 1, 2020, https://repositorio.ufsm.br/handle/1/2796.

Marini. R. M. 1996. *Processo e tendências da globalização capitalista. Dialética da dependência*. Petrópolis: Vozes, colocar o título do site e depois 'website' <colocar o endereço aqui. Accessed July 1, 2020 [e-book].

Mészáros, I. 2002. *Para além do capital*. São Paulo: Boitempo.

Moura, C. 1988. *Sociologia do negro brasileiro*. São Paulo, Editora Ática.

_____. 1994. *Dialética radical do Brasil negro*. São Paulo: Editora Anita Garibaldi.

Oliveira, L. M. 2019. *Imigrantes, xenofobia e racismo: uma análise de conflitos em escolas municipais de São Paulo*, PhD diss. Pontifícia Universidade Católica de São Paulo. Accessed July 1, 2020.

Prado-Jr. C. 1942. *Formação do Brasil Contemporâneo: Colônia*. São Paulo: Companhia das Letras.

Rago, A. 2010. 'A teoria da Via Colonial de objetivação do capital no Brasil: J. Chasin e a crítica ontológica do capital atrófico.' *Verinotio revista on-line de educação e ciências humanas* 11 (6): 71–86. Accessed June 28, 2020, http://www.verinotio.org/conteudo/0.44345918339068.pdf [e-journal].

Ribeiro, D. 2020. 'Doméstica idosa que morreu no Rio cuidava da patroa contagiada pelo coronavírus.' *Folha de São Paulo*. Accessed June 28, 2020.

Ribeiro, M. 2014. *Políticas de promoção da igualdade racial – 1986 a 2010*. Rio de Janeiro: Ed. Garamond.

Rossi, M. 2020. 'Doria afrouxa quarentena e prepara abertura de shoppings mesmo com óbitos por coronavírus em alta.' *El País*. Accessed July 3, 2020, https://brasil.elpais.com/brasil/2020-05-27/doria-afrouxa-quarentena-e-abre-shoppings-mesmo-com-registros-de-morte-por-covid-19-ainda-em-alta.html.

Ruge, E. 2020. 'Violência policial quebra recorde enquanto Rio se torna epicentro da Covid-19.' *Rio on Watch*. Accessed June 28, 2020.

Said, F. 2020. 'Ex-aliados de Bolsonaro mostram como funciona o Gabinete do Ódio.' *Congresso em Foco*. Accessed June 28, 2020, https://congressoemfoco.uol.com.br/governo/ex-aliados-de-bolsonaro-detalham-modus-operandi-do-gabinete-do-odio/.

Santos, S., and da Silva Santos, N. N. 2015. 'Vozes negras no Congresso Nacional: o Movimento Negro e a Assembleia Nacional Constituinte de 1987–1988.' *39º Encontro Anual da ANPOCS. GT32 – 'Relações raciais: desigualdades, identidades e políticas públicas.'* Acessed June 28, 2020.

Seyfert, G. 2002. 'Colonização, imigração e a questão racial no Brasil.' *Revista USP* 53: 117–149, https://doi.org/10.11606/issn.2316-9036.v0i53p117-149 [e-journal].

Silva, V. L. 2020. 'A particularidade da constituição do capitalismo alemão em Marx: algumas passagens dos anos 1840.' *Verinotio – Revista on-line de Filosofia e Ciências Humanas* 25 (2): 40–63. Accessed June 28, 2020, http://verinotio.org/sistema/index.php/verinotio/article/view/524/430 [e-journal].

Skidmore, T. E. 2012. *Preto no branco: raça e nacionalidade no pensamento brasileiro*. Rio de Janeiro: Paz e Terra.

Soares, M. 2020. 'Dados do SUS revelam vítima-padrão de COVID-19 no Brasil: homem, pobre e negro.' *Época* (last updated 8:27 AM on July 3, 2020). Accessed July 3, 2020, https://epoca.globo.com/sociedade/dados-do-sus-revelam-vitima-padrao-de-covid-19-no-brasil-homem-pobre-negro-24513414?utm_source=Facebook&utm_medium=Social&utm_campaign=compartilhar&fbclid=IwAR3k32Tnr5ByldaDzE7ND9xNPVrvgA-H_ns7KjVbPu3xVT8pCDPjIoHBO2Y.

Sobrinho, M. G. J. 2019. 'A inserção subordinada do capitalismo brasileiro na mundialização do capital.' *Verinotio – Revista on-line de Filosofia e Ciências Humanas* 25 (2): 40–63, https://www.doi.org/10.36638/1981061X.2019.25.2/40-63 [e-journal].

Souza, M. 2020. *Doria inicia reabertura em SP no pico da pandemia; Covas mantém quarentena até dia 15*, Brasil de Fato, June 1, 2020. Accessed July 4, 2020, https://www.brasildefato.com.br/2020/06/01/com-avanco-da-pandemia-doria-inicia-reabertura-e-covas-mantem-quarentena-ate-dia-15.

Terra Portal. 2020. *Bolsonaro bate continência à bandeira dos EUA e muda bordão*, Terra Notícias, May 16, 2019. Accessed June 28, 2020.

Viñas, D., Duran, P., and Carvalho, J. 2020. 'Morrem 40% mais negros que brancos por coronavírus no Brasil.' *CNN Brasil – Saúde*, June 5, 2020. Accessed July 1, 2020, https://www.cnnbrasil.com.br/saude/2020/06/05/negros-morrem-40-mais-que-brancos-por-coronavirus-no-brasil.

# TERRITORIALIZING EXISTENCE AS RESISTANCE: A FANONIAN READING ON THE MUNDURUKU AND THE RIVERSIDE PEOPLES COLLECTIVE SELF-DETERMINATION PROCESSES IN AMAZONIA

Léa Tosold

In this paper, I propose a Fanonian reading of the configura(c)tion of the Munduruku and the riverside peoples' remarkable process of resistance to the construction of dams in Tapajós, the last major free flowing river in Amazonia, between 2013 and 2015. I argue that the work of Fanon enables us to precisely apprehend the potential of certain modes of collective self-determination processes in order to strengthen resistance and meaningfully contribute to the establishment of preconditions for structural transformation in contexts ruled by structural violence.

## Framing Existence as Resistance with Fanon

> [T]he black man should no longer be confronted by the dilemma, turn white or disappear; but he should be able to take cognizance of a possibility of existence.
> —Frantz Fanon

There is perhaps no other place in the world where so many forms of expropriation, plunder, and violence are as concentrated as in Amazonia. Since the colonial expeditions, the region accumulates an ongoing history of genocide and exploitation of all sorts—in search of rubber, timber, minerals — as well as the construction of mega enterprises — such as huge dams, bulk ports, railroads, highways, waterways — and their disastrous consequences. More recently, an alarming increase in the burning rates of the forest is also taking place, aimed at the expansion of cattle and soybeans plantations. As the archaeologist Raoni Valle suggests, we are today witnessing 'the re-edition of historical colonization practices' in the region (Castro, 2015).

In such a context, if the Tapajós continues to be the last major free flowing river in Amazonia, this is undoubtedly due to the existence — and resistance

— of the traditional peoples in the region.[1] Drawing on my engagement as an activist,[2] I propose, in what follows, a Fanonian reading of the struggles over the mega project of construction of the São Luiz and Jatobá dams, in the Middle Tapajós region[3] — which, if accomplished, would flood territories inhabited by the Munduruku and the riverside peoples,[4] irreversibly affecting their lives and the environment.[5] As I suggest, Fanon, in particular, opens up the possibility of evidencing modes of existence as resistance that are not primarily nor exclusively referenced to the hegemonic norms, allowing us to move beyond the mere identification of ongoing mechanisms of oppression.

We learned from Fanon that decolonization 'never goes unnoticed' (Fanon, 2004 [1961]: 2): it demands no less than the 'restructuring of the world' (Fanon, 2008 [1952]: 60). Decolonization, then, is no metaphor (Tuck and Yang, 2012) and goes, in a Fanonian perspective, beyond merely reactive modes of action that risk maintaining the white settler colonial norm as standard of reference. If the institution of the colonial system, as Fanon points out, involves the destruction of native 'modalities of existence' (1956: 123), decolonization implies more than a reactive mode of colle(a)ctive action: in a Fanonian perspective, it demands colle(a)ctive action and a contextual (re)creation of communal standards of reference that, by operating in their own terms, not only displace the centrality of the colonial norm, but also denaturalize the violence that is inherent to it. In this sense, colle(a)ctive self-determination processes are regarded as a (pro)positive move that enables to 'tense our muscles and our brains in a new direction' (Fanon, 2004 [1961]: 236), going beyond mere oppositional forms of action that end up (re)producing the very same (neo)colonial *schema* they criticize.

Analysis of resistance processes are usually framed as exclusively reactive to the (neo)colonial *schema*. However, a Fanonian perspective allows us to see that much more is also at stake in such struggles: there are (and should be) modes of existence, with their own standards of reference, orienting resistance processes

---

1. As widely recognized, the areas in Amazonia with the lowest incidence of deforestation and destruction are those where traditional peoples (Indigenous peoples, riverside populations, rubber tree tappers and *quilombolas*, among others) live (Instituto Brasileiro do Meio Ambiente, 2014).
2. I am a member of the Comtapajós (São Paulo's Committee in Support of People's Resistance in the Tapajós River), an autonomous collective that aimed at supporting the resistance struggles of the Munduruku and the riverside peoples against the construction of dams in their territories.
3. This text is based on the 'First Movement' of my PhD thesis entitled 'Self-determination in three movements: the politicization of differences under the perspective of the (de)naturalization of violence' (Tosold, 2018). A detailed version of this argument was also published by the *Journal of Anthropology* (ed. by the University of São Paulo) under the title 'For a life without dams: bodies, territory and the role of self-determination in the denaturalization of violence' (Tosold, 2020). The final version of this text owes much to the exchanges with Álvaro Okura, Marilia M. Pisani, Laura Moutinho, Nayana Fernández and Mariana Ribeiro.
4. The Munduruku people are comprised of approximately 13,000 people distributed in nearly 210 villages over 850 kilometers along the Tapajós river basin in Western Pará, a region traditionally occupied by them over centuries (Fundação Nacional do Índio, 2013). The riverside populations of the Tapajós have been living in the region since 'the rubber time': the localities of Montanha and Mangabal and of Pimental and São Francisco are constituted by about 250 families that, as the Munduruku people, make their living off the river and the land (by hunting, farming, fishing) in a communal way. They have a profound knowledge of the forest and their presence is considered to be the main factor for it to remain 'standing' (Instituto Brasileiro do Meio Ambiente, 2014).
5. In this text, I assume a critical standing regarding the construction of large-scale hydropower plants in the region. For a detailed discussion on 'clean' energy, on the need (or not) for greater energy production, as well as on the links between the construction of dams in the region and various modes of exploitation of the territory, see Tosold (2018).

and the establishment of other possible forms of common living. If, on the one hand, reaction to the (neo)colonial *schema* is imperative — for the colonizer 'only understands the language of force' (Fanon, 2004 [1961]: 42), and shrinks and control all possibility of movement in space — Fanon's *The Wretched of the Earth*—in which he is particularly concerned with the forms decolonial processes could take — shows, on the other hand, that the very possibility of a decolonial (pro)positive movement, one which does not (re)produce nor is exclusively referenced to the (neo)colonial norms, stems from a contextual (re)creation of colle(a)ctive standards of reference. For Fanon, it is 'in the field' that 'a new political orientation which in no way resembles the old' can be forged (Fanon, 2004 [1961]: 95).

To focus on the (re)creation of contextual unique modes of existence, as Fanon proposes, is of special value due to at least three reasons. First, it enables the displacement of binary thinking imposed by the colonial norms, and so is helpful in order to avoid that struggles against such norms end up reproducing their very same *modus operandi* — as, for instance, the simple inversion of the terms of oppression, or the mere fostering of inclusion, in which emancipation projects would coincide with the very expansion of the white settler state. Second, paying attention to the (re)creation of contextual modes of existence gives rise to own standards of reference that enable evidencing and denaturalizing the underlying violence of the (neo)colonial norms. And third, the everyday work on a contextual (re)creation of proper modes of existence that undermines (neo)colonial binary thinking, instead of leading to closure, could enable (un)foreseen connections among different sociopolitical struggles elsewhere (see Fanon, 2004 [1961]: 179-180). In this sense, if '[t]he end of racism begins with this sudden incomprehension' (Fanon, 1956: 131), it is certainly due to fact that decolonization processes are operating with other standards of reference than the one's super*imposed* by the colonizers.

Thus, in my view, Fanon allows us to realize that the force of the Munduruku and the riverside peoples lies, first and foremost, in their existence as resistance, i.e., in their potential for colle(a)ctive and (pro)positive self-organization based on their own terms. In other words, their capacity for resistance does not emanate from a merely reactive position, restricted to the denouncement of the alleged failure of the Brazilian state to comply with laws and international treaties – as, for instance, the Brazilian Constitution or the Convention 169 of the International Labour Organization (ILO). Instead of proposing 'corrections' or 'adjustments' to them — and so run the risk of being held hostage of the *modus operandi* of such norms— these peoples patently expose the limits — or even the bad faith — that are inherent to them. As I argue, this potential to denaturalize the hegemonic norm stems precisely from the primordial and daily commitment of the Munduruku and the riverside peoples with their own modes of social, political and economic organization, which confers them a perspective of their own not only to strategically assess and deal with the norms, discourses, and actions of the government and the private sector, but also to establish a fundamentally distinctive way of acting — one that triggers the possibility of unleashing unpredictable and *co-moving* modes of resistance that are able to reverse the conditions in favor of the traditional peoples of the forest, even under enormous disparity in terms of power balance.

I focus my analysis on the unfolding of significant events in the region between 2013 and 2015,[6] a period marked by the incisive intent, on the part of the state and private initiative, to super*impose* the dam construction project as a *fait accompli*. In what follows, I will concentrate the argument on three key events of the Munduruku and the riverside peoples resistance process in the period: the occupation of the construction site of the Belo Monte dam in the Xingu river; the elaboration of the Munduruku Consultation Protocol; and the process of self-demarcation of the Daje Kapap Eypi (Sawré Muybu) territory.

## The Occupation of the Construction Site of the Belo Monte Dam

In January 2013, an extraordinary assembly of the Munduruku people took place in the Sai Cinza Indigenous village (Alto Tapajós region), attended by about 120 *caciques*, as well as representatives of the Kaiabi, Apiaká, and Kayapó peoples. The moment is one of great tension: the truculent *Operação Eldorado*,[7] coordinated by the Federal Police and the National Security Force, had recently occurred in the Indigenous village of Teles Pires (municipality of Jacareacanga), which culminated in the summary execution of Adenilson Kirixi,[8] as well as countless wounded. Men, women and children were subjected to a series of torture practices (cf. Fernández, 2014). The military operation was taken as a form of intimidation to the resistance process that the Munduruku people had been leading both in relation to the construction of the São Manuel dam on the Teles Pires river,[9] and in relation to the multifaceted forms of harassment aimed at super*imposing* the dams of São Luiz and Jatobá in Médio Tapajós region. On the one hand, researchers hired by contractors interested in the construction of the dams were, at that time, found in the Munduruku and the riverside peoples territory gathering data needed to advance the series of studies for the implementation of the enterprise without any kind of prior notice or consultation.[10] On the other hand, government agents and private initiatives were also attempting to simulate processes of public consultation with the Munduruku and the riverside

---

6. For the analysis, in addition to the public letters and documents written by the Munduruku and the riverside peoples, I also use official documents, reports, and news.
7. A military operation, supposedly created to combat illegal gold mining, which took place on November 7, 2012.
8. On November 7, 2012, Adenilson Kirixi Munduruku, one of the community leaders of the Teles Pires Indigenous village, was murdered by the main officer in charge of *Operação Eldorado* with three shots to the leg and one to the back of the head.
9. The São Manoel dam, the first of a series of hydroelectric power plants planned to be constructed in the Tapajós river basin, was, at that time, already under construction — the São Luiz and the Jatobá dams were the next ones to be carried out.
10. According to the Brazilian law, in order to formally enable the licensing of a hydroelectric power plant it is necessary to conduct what are called Environmental Impact Study (EIA) and Environmental Impact Report (Rima). If several power plants are planned for the same river basin, as in the Tapajós region, also a prior cumulative impact study — the so-called Integrated Environmental Action (AAI) – is needed. For more details, see Fearnside (2015a: 2015b).

peoples in order to fulfill the formal prerogatives related to the dams' licensing process. The threats and the harassment were so intense at that moment that, without even being invited, representatives of government institutions and the private initiatives appeared at the Munduruku assembly at Sai Cinza. They were soon asked to leave (Sena, 2013).

In such a context — which involved, on the one hand, the imminence of conflict escalation that would put their lives at risk, and, on the other hand, the possibility of being 'deceived', as if they had been consulted and consented with the dams in their territory, the Munduruku people decided to write a public letter, addressed to the then president Dilma Rousseff (Munduruku People, 2013a). The letter was an attempt to avoid the worst by formally presenting the situation from their own point of view. The document included 33 claims: among them, the immediate investigation of the murder of Adenilson Kirixi and the formal publication of the so-called Identification and Delimitation Report (RCID) of the Sawré Muybu Territory by the National Indigenous Foundation (Funai), a necessary step to pursue the legal recognition of the Indigenous territory — a historical demand of the Munduruku people, which was underway in the formal instances since 2001.[11]

In spite of an already extreme tension in the region, the so-called *Operação Tapajós* began in March 2013: around 250 military servicemen were ostensibly stationed in Itaituba, Médio Tapajós, with the aim of supposedly providing 'logistical support and security' to 80 researchers conducting environmental licensing studies which had until that point been suspended in court for the lack of prior consultation of the Indigenous peoples potentially affected by the construction of the dams (cf. Cunha, 2013; Conselho Indigenista Missionário, 2013). There were rumors that 60 men would be moved to the Sawré Muybu Indigenous village, where 132 people were currently living (Munduruku People, 2013b). In face of those events, especially the unfortunate *Operação Eldorado* in the Teles Pires Indigenous village, the *Operação Tapajós* generated a climate of terror and apprehension for the Munduruku and the riverside peoples of the Middle Tapajós.

> we communicate that we have being humiliated and threatened by the military operation of the government... the Armed Forces are spread over the Tapajós river, over the Trans-Amazonian highway, and over our territories intimidating and threatening people, preventing us from navigating at our rivers and moving freely in the roads, in the territories, and in Indigenous villages. We can no longer fish, work, swim in the river, hunt, walk freely, and live our lives. (Munduruku People, 2013c)

---

11. With the publication of the RCDI by Funai, the further steps toward the achievement of the legal recognition of an Indigenous territory are: contestation, declaration of limits, physical demarcation, and, finally, official homologation and registration. The publication of the RCDI, at the time, was long overdue: the report had already been concluded in 2008 (Aranha and Mota, 2014). The main factor for the government to avoid publishing it is attributed to its particular policy, characterized by the paralysis of formal recognition of Indigenous and *Quilombola* territories, as well as the so-called 'Conservation Units' (cf. Instituto Socioambiental, 2016).

In addition, the federal government also announced that it had already prepared and presented a model of public consultation with the Indigenous peoples of the Middle and Upper Tapajós 'under the terms of the Convention 169 of the ILO'.[12] (Cunha, 2013). At one and the same time, we see a systematic effort both to super*impose* the continuity of the studies for the construction of the São Luiz and the Jatobá dams — ignoring the need to consult the Munduruku and the riverside peoples who live in the territory — and to super*impose* a process of public consultation in a previously stipulated model, bypassing the construction of a consultation protocol with the active participation of the Munduruku and the riverside peoples.

It was a very difficult moment, amidst the ostensive presence of the Armed Forces in the region: information was conflicting, meetings were constantly scheduled and rescheduled, agendas were unclear or different from those previously agreed upon. All this confusion created enormous uncertainty for the Munduruku people, since they feared that such meetings would be used as evidence of compliance with the consultation in the terms super*imposed* by the government.

> We, the Munduruku people of the Middle and Upper Tapajós, are in the Indigenous village of Sawré Muybu to reaffirm our alliance and to say that the Tapajós river is one as our people is only one... The government... is trying to divide the Munduruku people in order to conquer and destroy the Tapajós river, but the Tapajós river cannot be divided, and the Munduruku people cannot be divided. There is nothing the government can offer that will pay for all the wealth we have. We do not sell our river and territory, our people, our history, or the future of our children. (Munduruku People, 2013c)

In order to demonstrate their purpose in deciding on what terms they would like to be consulted, the Munduruku people scheduled a new assembly for the end of April of that year, in the Indigenous village of Sai Cinza. The discussion of the consultation protocol was on the agenda. The government authorities were invited but did not attend. During the assembly, as a symbolic act, the model of public consultation that the government was attempting to super*impose* was burned.

The situation was perilous and the Munduruku people decided to take a drastic measure in order to draw public attention to the government's plans in the Tapajós region: the occupation of the Belo Monte construction site in Vitória do Xingu.

---

12. The Convention 169 of the ILO — created in 1989 and ratified by the Brazilian government in 2002 — promotes recommendations for state intervention in territories inhabited by 'Indigenous and tribal peoples'. It is currently considered one of the main legal instruments for the guarantee of these peoples rights, even if it does not provide them veto power (International Labour Organization, 1989). In the case of the construction of dams in the Munduruku territory, Convention 169, in principle, determines that, before any territorial intervention, a process of prior, free and informed consultation must take place (cf. Article 6).

> We are the people who live in the rivers where you want to build dams. We are Munduruku, Juruna, Kayapó, Xipaya, Kuruaya, Asurini, Parakanã, Arara, traditional fishers, and riverside populations. We are from the Amazonia and we want to keep the forest standing. We are Brazilians. The river is our supermarket. Our ancestors are older than Jesus Christ.
>
> You are pointing guns at our heads. You are besieging our territories with soldiers and war tanks. You make the fish disappear. You steal the bones of our ancestors buried in our territories.
>
> You do this because you are afraid to listen to us. To hear that we do not want dams. To understand why we do not want dams.
>
> You invent that we are violent and that we want war. Who kills our kin? How many white people died and how many Indigenous people died? You are the ones who kill us, quickly or little by little. We are dying and each dam kills more. And when we try to speak to you, you bring tanks, helicopters, soldiers, machine guns, and stun guns.
>
> What we want is simple: you need to regulate the law of prior consultation with Indigenous peoples. Meanwhile, you need to stop all construction, studies, and military operations over the Xingu, the Tapajós, and the Teles Pires rivers. And then you need to consult us. We want to talk to you, but you are not letting us speak. That is why we occupied your construction site. You need to stop everything and just listen to us. (Munduruku People, 2013d)

The occupation of the construction site of the controversial and violently super*imposed* mega dam of Belo Monte, planned to be the third largest hydroelectric power plant in the world, is of enormous symbolic force. At that moment — May 2013 — the construction of Belo Monte was already at its peak, mobilizing no less than 25,000 workers, 24 hours a day (Almeida et al., 2013).

The occupation of Belo Monte — which lasted a total of 17 days and had the direct participation of 170 Indigenous people, most of them Munduruku — literally *interrupted* the allegedly inexorable movement of progress/development, revealing what it is at its very core: a real 'desert of holes and concrete', as a violent and devastating anti-territorial dystopia in which life becomes impossible.

> We did not want to be back in your desert of holes and concrete. We have no pleasure in leave our homes in our territories and hang hammocks in your buildings. But how could we not come? If we do not come, we will lose our territories. We want the suspension of the studies and the construction of the dams that flood our territories, that cut the forest in the middle, that kill the fish and frighten the animals, that open the river and the land to the devouring mining. That attract more corporations, more logging, more conflicts, more prostitution, more drugs, more diseases, more violence. (Munduruku People, 2013f)

The occupation of Belo Monte reached, day by day, increasingly national and international repercussions. The series of open letters written during the occupation had even been translated and made public in several languages. The government, initially, sought to criminalize the occupiers, refusing to dialogue with the Munduruku people: The General Secretariat of the Presidency of the Republic issued a detailed statement on the case, denying the 'representativeness' of the occupiers, as if they were a mere sectarian group acting on behalf of personal interests (Secretaria-Geral da Presidência da República, 2013).

> The government has lost its mind. Gilberto Carvalho [*then Secretary-General of the Presidency of the Republic*] is lying. The government is completely desperate. It does not know what to do with us. The bandits, the violators, the manipulators, the insincere, and the dishonest are you. And yet we remain calm and peaceful. You do not. You have forbidden journalists and lawyers to enter the occupied construction site, and even deputies of your own party. You sent the National Force in order to say that the government will not dialogue with us. You sent people asking for lists of requests. You militarized the area of the occupation, inspected the people who pass by and our food, took pictures, intimidated and gave orders.
>
> We understand that it is easier to call us bandits, to treat us like bandits. So Gilberto Carvalho's speech may make any sense. But we are not bandits and you will have to deal with it.. It has been six months today since you murdered Adenilson Munduruku. We know very well how you act when you want something.
>
> The bad faith is of Gilberto Carvalho. And, in spite of everything, we want him to come to the construction site to talk with us. We are waiting for you, Gilberto. Stop sending the police with guns in the hands to deliver empty proposals. Stop trying to humiliate us in the press.
>
> We are on your construction site and we will not leave until you leave our territories. (Munduruku People, 2013e)

Despite the government's attempts to criminalize the Belo Monte occupation, national and international pressure in favor of the occupiers continued to grow. Letters and demonstrations of solidarity and support were multiplying, both on the part of Indigenous peoples (Articulação dos Povos Indígenas do Brasil, 2013; Ka'apor People, 2013; Mebêngôkre People, 2013) and on the part of social movements and people in general.[13]

With all this support, the government's attempt to put into question the legitimacy of the occupiers failed — a discursive strategy that aimed at *ignoring* the very possibility of Indigenous self-determination and, consequently, of Indigenous existence as resistance. However, it is interesting to note how the letters of the Belo Monte occupation did not properly seek to *prove* the legitimacy of the occupiers. 'We are who we are and the government will have to deal with it' (Munduruku People, 2013f), they simply respond. The assertion of a 'we', in

---

13. A large part of these demonstrations of support and solidarity are gathered at: <https://ocupacaobelomonte.wordpress.com/category/cartas-de-apoio/>.

the letters, evokes a plurality of voices: 'We are the peoples who live *in the rivers* where you want to build dams' (Munduruku People, 2013d, own emphasis). The very *standpoint* of the occupation becomes an invitation to participate, welcoming multiple rivers and their peoples, as well as the 'forest' and all the 'ancestry'. It is, then, the assertion of a 'we' that gathers multiple forms of existence as resistance, a sort of a meeting of waters in the space and time of the occupation. It is not by coincidence that the solidarity to the occupation continues to grow, for it widens the shared dimension of colle(a)ctive existence as resistance. Like rivers, different modes of existence as resistance cross and grow together in the space and time opened up by the occupation: 'this is a great struggle, it is everybody's struggle' (Munduruku People, 2013g).

> It is not possible that you will keep repeating that we, the Indigenous peoples, were already consulted. Everyone knows that this is not true. From now on the government has to stop telling lies in statements and interviews. And stop treating us like children, naive, under tutelage, irresponsible, and manipulated. We are who we are and the government will have to deal with it. And do not lie to the press that we are quarreling with the Belo Monte's workers: they are sympathetic to our cause! We wrote a letter to them yesterday! Here at the construction site we play football together every day. The other time we left, a worker, to whom we gave many necklaces and bracelets, told us: 'I will miss you'.
>
> We have the support of several kin in this struggle. We have the support of the Indigenous peoples from all over the Xingu river. We have the support of the Kayapó people. We have the support of the Tupinambá people. The Guajajara. The Apinajé, the Xerente, the Krahô, the Tapuia, the Karajá-Xambioá, the Krahô-Kanela, the Avá-Canoero, the Javaé, the Kanela from Tocantins and the Guarani. And the list is growing. We have the support of the whole national and international society and this also bothers you, who are alone with your campaign sponsors and companies interested in craters and money. We occupied again your construction site — and how many times it will be necessary until your own law is kept? (Munduruku People, 2013f)

The letters indicate all the time: we have been speaking for such a long time, and you are refusing to listen, when not actively trying to silence. Would it be possible, then, by interrupting the deafening noise of the construction site of Belo Monte — which, almost as an end in itself, did not seem to be stoppable —, to *open* the ears to the opportunity of making otherwise? 'Even if you are not willing to learn how to listen, we are willing to teach' (Munduruku People, 2013g).

Eventually, the government could no longer ignore the call for dialogue. The occupiers only left the construction site of Belo Monte to fly directly to Brasília for a face-to-face meeting with Gilberto Carvalho.

> We did not come [*to Brasília*] to negotiate with you, because neither territory nor life are negotiable. We are against the construction of dams that

kill the Indigenous territories because they kill the culture when they kill the fish and drown the land. And this kills us without the need of a gun. You continue killing too much. You just kill too much. You have already killed too much, for 513 years. (Munduruku People, 2013g)

From that moment on, the strategy of the government was to invert the equation, suggesting that the occupiers — especially the Munduruku people — were the ones who had been systematically refusing to dialogue. The possibility of dialogue was framed as a mere negotiation of compensations, since prior consultation, in the perspective of the government, would not be deliberative. Any opportunity for dialogue, on these terms, was regarded as *consent*: 'your proposals [*those of the Munduruku people*] shall be incorporated into the *government's* decision-making process regarding the potential usages of water in the region' (Secretaria-Geral da Presidência da República, 2013, own emphasis). Hence, the Munduruku people had to constantly state that dialogue was not the same as negotiating or consenting with the project of dams in their territory, that they were not proposing 'list of requests', but rather reiterating the form through which they wish to be consulted.

> We met the minister Gilberto Carvalho the day we arrived [in *Brasília*]. He called us liars (in other words), refused to sign that he received our documents, and said that we are not the ones who write our letters.
>
> When the meeting ended, Gilberto Carvalho said in national broadcasting: 'We listened at length to what they had to say, their criticisms, but we were absolutely clear with them, saying that the government will not give up its projects'. So we understand the government's message... We understand that the government is saying: 'We will construct the dams in your territory, no matter what you say. And even if you are consulted, we will not consider your opinion'. (Munduruku People, 2013h)

What these considerations reveal is that the Convention 169 — with its prerogative of free, prior, and informed consultation—even though considered the main legal instrument to ensure that Indigenous peoples have control over state interventions in their territories, may also put these peoples in a difficult situation: by not clearly stating veto power for potentially affected peoples, the foreseen consultation processes[14] may end up serving rather to reinforce what Indigenous peoples radically oppose.

---

14. The reportage on the Convention 169 carried out by Renata Bessi (2017) calls attention to the fact that, in the application of the prior consultation in various sites in Latin America, governments systematically refuse to respect results that are not favorable to them. She suggests that the Convention 169, in this sense, could be understood as a 'domination technology'. Since most of the existing 'resources' are located in 'traditionally occupied lands', the consultation prerogative would emerge as 'an attempt to pacify high intensity conflicts generated by the massive influx of development projects throughout the region' (own translation). The report also indicates that the persistence of communities in organizing themselves on their own terms has been fundamental in cases where resistance against mega projects has been successful— as, I believe, has also been the case of the Munduruku and the riverside peoples in the Middle Tapajós.

In such a 'crossfire'—in which to dialogue or not turns out to be the same as consenting to one's own oppression—the Indigenous and riverside peoples could not simply deny engaging in dialogue, nor rely exclusively on the 'law' to claim their demands. In fact, the path found to *co-move* resistance, even under such adverse conditions and power balance, was the option of the Munduruku and the riverside peoples to depart from a (pro)positive perspective, based on their modes of sociopolitical organization: the elaboration of their own protocol of consultation (Munduruku People, 2015).

## The Munduruku Consultation Protocol

By creating a document on their own terms stipulating how they should be consulted, the Munduruku and the riverside peoples ended up conceiving a juridical fact, which not only exposes the coercive logic inherent to the very procedural character of a supposedly participatory consultation mechanism, but also engages, in a (pro)positive manner, in the interpretative dispute over the Convention 169, making it strategically work in their own benefit.

The Munduruku Consultation Protocol (Munduruku People, 2015), fundamentally, ties up together form and content. In other words, the protocol indicates that the *form* the consultation is undertaken is as relevant as the *content* which emanates from it. Thus, a prior consultation only finds validity if it is conducted in the Munduruku and the riverside peoples terms[15] —that is, according to their own territoriality and temporality:

> All meetings shall be in our territory—in the Indigenous village we choose —, and not in the city, not even in Jacareacanga or Itaituba. The meetings cannot be held on dates that hinder community activities (e.g. at the time of sowing, drilling, and planting; at the time of the nut extraction; at the time of the production of flour; during our celebrations; during the Indigenous Peoples Day)... The meetings shall be in Munduruku language and we shall choose who will be the translators. In these meetings, our knowledge must be taken into consideration, on the same level as the knowledge of the *pariwat* (non-Indigenous). For we are the ones who know about the rivers, the forest, the fish, and the land. We shall coordinate the meetings, not the government. (Munduruku People, 2015)

Observations like these implicitly point out that the form in which public authorities sought to super*impose* the consultation process — rapidly, in a 'West-

---

15. The riverside peoples actively participated in the construction of the Munduruku Consultation Protocol. As Convention 169, in principle, applies specifically to Indigenous peoples, the protocol's wording is in accordance with the self-determination of the Munduruku people, but makes also reference to the need of broadening the scope of the Convention so as to also consider the riverside peoples as well: 'We demand that the riverside communities potentially affected by the dams on the Tapajós river (such as Montanha and Mangabal, Pimental and São Luiz) should have their right to consultation guaranteed, in a manner that is proper and specific to their reality. Just like us, the riverside communities also have the right to their own consultation' (Munduruku People, 2015).

ern' fashion, and disregarding the knowledge of the affected peoples — is, from the Munduruku point of view, a violence. In a (pro)positive way, the protocol unmakes any claim of alleged neutrality that could be invoked by the state in the discussion on the procedural terms of a participatory consultation process.

Furthermore, the protocol reinforces that 'the Munduruku people is one', in a way that 'the decisions of the Munduruku people are collective'. Therewith, the protocol aims at preventing that consultation processes be carried out unilaterally, involving single Munduruku associations or 'leaders' in separate (Munduruku People, 2015). In this sense, the mere willingness to *dialogue* cannot be taken as *consent*:

> The Munduruku of all Indigenous villages — in the Upper, Middle, and Lower Tapajós — shall be consulted, including those located on Indigenous territories not yet officially demarcated. We do not want the government to consider us divided: the Munduruku people is only one. The ancient sages, the *pajés*, the seniors who can tell history, the ones who know traditional medicine, that can deal with roots and leaves, those elderly who know the sacred places, they all shall be consulted.
>
> *Caciques* (captains), warriors and leaders shall also be consulted. The *caciques* are the ones who articulate and pass information to all the Indigenous villages. They are the ones who gather everyone to discuss what we are going to do. The warriors help the *caciques*, accompany them, and protect our territory. The leaders are teachers and health workers, they work with the whole community.
>
> Women shall also be consulted to share their experience and information. There are women who are *pajés*, midwives, and artisans. They take care of the farm, give ideas, prepare food, make home remedies and have a lot of traditional knowledge.
>
> University students, Munduruku pedagogues, Ibaorebu students, young people and children shall also be consulted, as they are the generation of the future. Many young people have access to the media, read newspapers, access the internet, speak Portuguese, know the reality, and take an active part in the struggle of our people...
>
> Today, we inhabit about 130 villages, in the Upper, Middle, and Lower Tapajós. But we remember that, because of the social organization of our people, new Indigenous villages may emerge. (Munduruku People, 2015)

The Munduruku Consultation Protocol is a detailed document, which refers to the preconditions — according to the Munduruku unity, territoriality, and temporality — for the consultation process and the form it shall take. Moreover, the protocol requires the official demarcation of the Sawré Muybu Territory as an act of 'good faith' on the part of the government in order to begin the consultation process.[16] And the text also ends by expressly stating: 'We have veto power. *Sawe!*'.

The writing of this document was supported, among others, by the Federal Public Prosecutor's Office (MPF) and was printed in a leaflet format — both in Portuguese and in Munduruku languages (Munduruku People, 2016).[17] The Consultation Protocol, as I indicate below, is intricately linked to the self-demarcation process of Daje Kapap Eypi (Sawré Muybu). Simultaneously, both the Consultation Protocol and the self-demarcation of the Munduruku territory threatened by the dams gained strength and consistency through the persistence of the Munduruku and the riverside peoples in their own self-determination. In this sense, both actions have decisively contributed to alter such an adverse condition — characterized by enormous disparities in terms of power balance — in favor of the traditional peoples of the forest, resulting in the real impediment of the construction of the mega dams of São Luiz and Jatobá in their territory.

## Self-demarcation of Daje Kapap Eypi

After the occupation of the Belo Monte's mega dam construction site, a series of direct actions of the Munduruku and the riverside peoples were intensified, which evidences a twofold character. On the one hand, such (pro)positive movements were in consonance with their own logic of sociopolitical self-determination — which *embodied* existence as resistance, as well as the alliances that were being formed (locally or more broadly) in favor of their struggle against the super*imposition* of the dams. On the other hand, the Munduruku and the riverside peoples also aimed at strategically exhausting, in a direct and (pro)positive way, all the available formal institutional paths related to their struggles, in order to avoid any possibility of delegitimization — or even criminalization — of their own movements of sociopolitical self-determination. In sum, this way of acting, sustained by (pro)positive actions of a double order, opened the way up to the flourishing of the Munduruku and the riverside peoples existence and resistance, as well as to the unveiling of the limits of the norms of the formal institutional sphere.

After the events in Brasília that followed the Belo Monte occupation — which included a series of protests in the country's capital —, at the end of June 2013 the Munduruku people found, within their territory, biologists employed by the Concremat group[18] carrying out studies for the licensing of the São Luiz and

---

16. This requirement denounces the slow pace in the demarcation process of the Sawré Muybu territory, which, as I point out below, is specifically related to the legal obstacles that an official recognition of Sawré Muybu as Indigenous territory would imply for the licensing of the São Luiz dam, which would largely flood it.

17. The Munduruku Consultation Protocol was built through a series of meetings between the Munduruku and the riverside peoples at the end of September 2014 and was approved at the Munduruku General Assembly in December of the same year. In January 2015, the document was formally delivered by the Munduruku and the riverside peoples to the General Secretariat of the Presidency of the Republic in Brasília.

18. Concremat is bonded to the Tapajós Study Group. According to institutional information available at the time, the Tapajós Study Group — formed by companies interested in the construction of the dams (Eletrobras, Eletronorte, GDF Suez, EDF, Neoenergia, Camargo Corrêa, Endesa Brasil, Cemig and Copel) — was created in order to carry out

the Jatobá dams (cf. Santana, 2013b; Sposati, 2013). In total, three biologists were captured and the materials they collected from the Munduruku territory—fauna and flora samples—were taken back: 'We made it very clear to the federal government that we would not let any researchers into our territories' (Munduruku People, 2013i). The biologists were released two days later, after the government commitment to suspend the studies in the area until prior consultation could take place.

Short after these events, the government broke with this agreement. On August 10, 2013, a kind of re-edition of *Operação Tapajós* began in the region, with the ostensible presence of the National Force and 130 researchers in order to execute the studies for the dams (Santana, 2013a). To the climate of tension already experienced in March, during the first incursion of the *Operação Tapajós*, is added, at that moment, the recent escalation of conflicts incited by the local power. At the beginning of September, servicemen and researchers entered the Indigenous village Boca, warning the Munduruku people to not prevent the studies for the licensing of the dams (Santana, 2013c). On this occasion, the militarization of the region by the government ended up attracting even more public attention and several supporters and journalists also joined the struggle.

Based on these double order (pro)positive movements—related to their self-determination and in order to put maximum pressure on state institutions—the Munduruku people revealed the *positioning* of the state in the implementation of its norms, which are managed to the detriment of the Indigenous peoples while supposedly serving to guarantee their rights. In addition, the Munduruku people forged a way to legitimate their own (pro)positive actions of self-determination, undermining the accusations of supposed 'refusal' to dialogue that had been systematically attributed to them until then.

In this sense, the events involving the Munduruku people's decision—in cooperation with the riverside peoples—to self-demarcate their own territory threatened by the dams are especially remarkable. This is a (pro)positive action of self-determination, which, besides reinforcing the Munduruku and the riverside peoples existence and resistance, also contributes to reveal, thoroughly, the 'bad faith' inherent to the *modus operandi* of the state laws by exposing its *positioning*.

In the second half of 2014, the Munduruku people gained access to the Identification and Delimitation Report (RCID) of the Sawré Muybu territory (Fundação Nacional do Índio, 2013) that the government systematically refused to formally publish — a necessary legal step in order to move the official demarcation process of the Munduruku territory forward. As already seen, the Munduruku people had long sought to press, through direct action in the state institutions, for the publication of this report. This issue has even led to a series of disputes between different instances of the government. Gradually, the Munduruku people exhausted all possible forms of formal action within the

---

'technical and economic feasibility studies' and 'environmental studies' that would facilitate the necessary formal steps to the licensing of the construction of the dams.

government institutions, making it possible to reveal, in the very institutional language, the real intentions of the government in not publishing the report. Thereupon, the Munduruku people's (pro)positive actions of self-determination, in turn, were reaching wider legitimacy and publicity, making it practically impossible to continue ignoring, legally, the existence of Daje Kapap Eypi.[19]

The refusal to publish the report coincided with the moment when the federal government was seeking, by any means possible, to advance the licensing of the construction of the São Luiz dam. A dam which would flood the Sawré Muybu territory that was in the process of legal demarcation. Legislation on state intervention over officially recognized Indigenous territories is much more intricate, since it involves, in the specific case, the need to remove Indigenous people from their own territory. The publication of the report would move forward the Sawré Muybu legal demarcation process, imposing a much greater legal barrier to the licensing of dams in the Middle Tapajós. Thus, although the Sawré Muybu territory, at that time, had already been legally identified—according of the official *language* of the demarcation procedures —, the avoidance in accomplishing the formal steps of official demarcation became a state strategy to formally *ignore* the Indigenous presence in the region, facilitating the licensing of the mega dams.

In September 2014, concomitant with the struggles over the official publication of the RCID, the studies related to the construction of the São Luiz dam were supposedly 'concluded'. There was such an institutional rush to approve these studies that, while there were still processing official opinions on the dam project's viability,[20] the Ministry of Mines and Energy (MME) tried to authorize bidding on the dam.[21]

On October 17th, Maria Augusta Assirati, then Funai's interim president, had an emblematic meeting with the Munduruku people. When questioned about the non-publication of the RCID, to which she had expressly committed herself, she ended up verbally revealing that she would not sign nor publish it because of government interests in the construction of the dams that would impact the Sawré Muybu territory. This event was filmed by the Munduruku people (Munduruku people, 2014a) and received great public attention. Nine days later, Assirati resigned from Funai without, however, publishing the report.[22] Following this event, the Munduruku and the riverside peoples, who had access to the

---

19. Daje Kapap Eypi, also known as Sawré Muybu, is the territory historically inhabited by the Munduruku people in the Middle Tapajós region, which, at the time, was in the process of being legally recognized by the Brazilian state.

20. On August 15, 2014, the Funai opposed the studies related to the construction of the São Luiz dam precisely because the so-called 'Indigenous component' was lacking—that is, the studies showed no evidence of having consulted or heard the inhabitants of the potentially affected Indigenous villages. On September 12, a new study was presented, in which the 'Indigenous component' had been added, with the single recommendation of removal of the inhabitants of affected Indigenous villages. On September 25, a Funai's internal opinion declared the 'Indigenous component' insufficient due to lack of field work, among other points presented.

21. This is the *Ordinance N° 485* of 12 September, 2014, which set the date for the auction on 15th December of the same year. With the wide negative repercussion generated by the publication of this ordinance, and by a lawsuit of the Federal Public Prosecutor's Office, it was revoked on September 17. However, the Ministry of Mines and Energy (MME) publicly declared that the auction of the dams in Middle Tapajós would take place in the first half of 2015.

22. The RCID of the Sawré Muybu Territory was only officially published on 19 April, 2016 — precisely during the institutional 'breach' opened by the impeachment against the then president Dilma Rousseff, which took place only a few days later.

Sawré Muybu's unpublished report, decided to no longer wait for the government and began the process of *self-demarcation* of their territory by themselves.

> Securing our territory alive is what gives us strength and courage. Without the land we cannot survive. It is our mother, whom we respect. We know the government is coming against us with its huge projects to destroy our river, our forest, our life...
>
> We have waited decades for the government to demarcate our territory and it has never done so. Because of that our territory is dying, our forest is crying, we found chopped trees left by loggers in a pathway to be sold illegally in the sawmills and in this regard the Ibama [*Brazilian Institute of Environment and Renewable Natural Resources*] should but does not intervene. In a single field, the equivalent of 30 trucks loaded with logs, century-old trees, like the *ipé*, were cut down, and huge areas of *açaizais* were felled to extract palm hearts. Our heart is sad.
>
> In these 30 days of self-demarcation, we have already walked about 7 km and made 2.5 km of trails. We found 11 loggers, 3 trucks, 4 motorbikes, 1 tractor, and countless logs of hardwood on the banks of pathways in our territory, and in the morning of the 15th we were surprised in our camp by a group of 4 loggers, *grileiros* led by Vilmar, who claims to own 6 parcels of land within our territory, he also said that he will not allow the loss of land to us and that next Monday he would be taking the case to the court.
>
> Now we decree that we will no longer wait for the government. Now that we have decided to do the self-demarcation, we want the government to respect our work, to respect our ancestors, to respect our culture, to respect our life. We will only stop when we have finished our work. *SAWE, SAWE, SAWE.* (Munduruku People, 2014b)

Self-demarcation is a (pro)positive action of self-determination that (in)directly denounces the very illegitimacy of the state norms. These state norms were revealed to be not only *positioned*, favouring above all interests contrary to those of the Munduruku people, but also a sign of institutional bad faith. Indeed, the self-demarcation, as an action *co-moved* by their own standards of reference, reinstated the terms of the debate concerning what territory means. Furthermore, the process of self-demarcation gave the Munduruku and the riverside peoples struggle broad public attention. This helped consolidate the recognition of the legitimacy of the Indigenous territory, including all the living beings that inhabit it, and interact with its surroundings, as a fact that could no longer be formally ignored by the government. As an act of spatialization of territorialized bodies, self-demarcation, above all, ended up strengthening the Munduruku and the riverside peoples existence and resistance.

Where there are dams, the whole environment is affected, leveraging the destruction already underway. The notion of territory that the self-demarcation presents, therefore, is fundamentally different from the one super*imposed* by the state, going far beyond the mere delimitation of border marks. While the disputes over the publication of the RCID between Funai and other government bodies were exclusively restricted to a quarrel over whether or not to exceed certain territorial limits — as if the territory was a mere material substratum, subject to the logic of division and appropriation —, the self-demarcation of Daje Kapap Eypi, carried out by the Munduruku and the riverside peoples, showed that the existing *relation* between body and territory is life that, as such, knows no borders: it involves the river, the forest, and everything that *co-moves* in them. Always plural, never static or fixed to presumed limits, life emerges in interaction with the whole environment. There are no bodies without the forest and no forest without bodies: it is in this interweaving that life finds *space* to flourish in its own ways. Conducted on the basis of the Munduruku and the riverside peoples' own referents, self-demarcation, therefore, set the debate in other terms, which are not subsumable to the logic of progress/development that reduces the territory and all that it entails to mere 'resources' to be exploited.

In the first part of the Daje Kapap Eypi's self-demarcation, which took from October 2014 to the end of February 2015, about 20 Munduruku warriors and inhabitants of Montanha and Mangabal, as well as few supporters and journalists, participated in a total of four expeditions. Equipped with a GPS device, each incursion was strategic: self-demarcating the territory according to the so-called 'points' —the physical boundaries of Daje Kapap Eypi, as indicated in the RCID—with help of boards and open trails, in the middle of the forest.

Throughout its course, the self-demarcation became increasingly relevant to the sociopolitical self-determination of the Munduruku and the riverside peoples. In face of the numerous conflicts, both the Consultation Protocol and, in particular, the self-demarcation of Daje Kapap Eypi, as forms of colle(a)ctive (pro)positive movements, strengthened its existence and resistance locally and on its own terms. This was crucial in order to avoid relying on a merely reactive position in face of all the harassment they were passing through. The self-demarcation letters, written during this period, achieved increasing publicization (Munduruku People, 2014b; 2014c; 2014d). As a result, the terms of the debate over the meanings attributed to the territory and its implications were widely politicized.

The second part of the self-demarcation, undertaken in July 2015, involved 3 major incursions and the participation of more than 60 people: at least 40 warriors from Alto Tapajós, coming from at least 10 different Indigenous villages, went to the Médio Tapajós region to participate in the self-demarcation process with local Munduruku warriors and riverside peoples. Once again, supporters and journalists also engaged in the events.

Along the self-demarcation, innumerable pathways opened by illegal loggers were found in the Munduruku territory. They also found *açaizais* exploited by palm tree gatherers, as well as active and abandoned gold mining camps. In addition, they found strong signs of forest destruction in the heart of the Munduruku territory. The warriors gave a warning to gold prospectors and woodcutters: this territory is not yours. This also created a critical situation, increasing local threats to the Munduruku and the riverside peoples.

Self-demarcation is an event involving unquestionably huge risks: with no legal protection, the Munduruku and the riverside peoples found themselves in a situation of high exposure to aggression, retaliation and murder, in a context of constant tension and already characterized by so many conflicts and open wounds. Nevertheless, as one of the self-demarcation letters states, 'without crying or turning tears into courage' (Munduruku People, 2014d), the Munduruku and the riverside peoples also reached, with the self-demarcation, an expanded dimension not only of the destruction of the forest in their territory, but also of the power and relevance of their colle(a)ctive process of existence as resistance, crucial for their and the forest survival and flourishing. In this respect, the passage through Daje Kapap, a sacred place for the Munduruku people, was also included in the self-demarcation route.

> Today, for the first time during the self-demarcation, we arrived at the sacred place Daje Kapap Eypi... We felt something very powerful that involved our body.
>
> Another deep emotion we experienced today was to see our territory being devastated by the gold digging very close to where the boars passed through. Our sacred sanctuary is being violated, destroyed by 50 excavators on land and 5 river dredgers. For each excavator, 5 poor men, in an almost slave condition, working for four foreign owners, explored from morning till night. (Munduruku People, 2014d)

The self-demarcation goes far beyond a mere denunciation of the federal government's failure to comply with its own laws. Within the norms super*imposed* by the state, no matter how (pro)positively one acts, one is inevitably held hostage to a restricted understanding of territory as a material substratum, which underlies the core of the hegemonic norm—a prerequisite for the exercise of the power to define borders, as if it were possible to *divide* the forest, to 'cut the forest in half' (Munduruku People, 2013f).

Instead of reproducing this *schema*, the Munduruku and the riverside peoples, through the self-demarcation of Daje Kapap Eypi, intervened in the debate in their own terms. In other words, in addition to denouncing, with the self-demarcation letters, the destruction in course in Daje Kapap Eypi — and so assuming its existence in spite of no official demarcation—they also take the terms of the debate to a different level, widening the notion of territoriality on the basis of their own self-determination: the talk is not about mere territorial limits, but about a substantive way of life in which body, forest, and river are mutually imbricated, *co-moving*.

The forest, the river, and its living beings— among them, the Munduruku and the riverside peoples—are a plural one. The forest, which knows no borders, makes life flow and bloom though its own and unique mystery. That is essentially what self-demarcation is about. To the extent that, at the end of the second part of the self-demarcation, after all the 'points' had been covered, the *cacique* of the Sawré Muybu Indigenous village (which is in Daje Kapap Eypi) asserted that the self-demarcation, far from over, had just begun: it was only one step that had been accomplished. With a substantive understanding of territory as a colle(a)ctive and mutual making, the self-demarcation of Daje Kapap Eypi opens the possibility of unimaginable movements of existence as resistance that are capable of *co-moving* life despite everything.

## Imag(en)ing

Destruction follows at a stride. Life, though, is urgent, and remains open as the forest itself.

## Bibliography

Almeida, L., Amora, D., Kachani, M., Leite, M., and Machado, R. 2013. 'Tudo sobre a batalha de Belo Monte.' *Folha de S.Paulo*, December 16. Accessed May 20, 2014, http://arte.folha.uol.com.br/especiais/2013/12/16/belo-monte/.

Aranha, A., and Mota, J. 2014. 'Exclusivo: relatório da Funai determina que terra é dos Munduruku.' *A Pública: Agência de Jornalismo Investigativo*. Accessed January 20, 2017. http://apublica.org/2014/12/relatorio-funai-determina-que-terra-e-dos-munduruku/.

Articulação dos Povos Indígenas do Brasil (Apib). 2013. 'Manifesto contra o preconceito institucionalizado do governo Dilma aos povos indígenas.' *Blog Ocupação Belo Monte*, May 7. Accessed June 20, 2013, https://ocupacao-belomonte.wordpress.com/2013/05/08/apib-manifesto-contra-o-preconceito-institucionalizado-do-governo-dilma-aos-povos-indigenas/.

Bessi, R. 2017. 'Consulta indígena legaliza despojo de los pueblos: Convenio 169 de la OIT.' *Avispa Midia*, June 12. Accessed July 20, 2017, https://avispa.org/consulta_indigena/index.html.

2015. *Mundurukánia: na beira da história*, directed by Miguel V. Castro [documentary].

Conselho Indigenista Missionário. 2013. 'Munduruku protestam contra parlamentares que defendem construção de hidrelétricas.' *Portal Cimi*, June 24. Accessed August 10, 2013, https://www.cimi.org.br/2013/06/34982/.

Cunha, C. N. 2013. 'Operação Tapajós: Governo Federal entra em contradição sobre o envio de tropas e intenções de pesquisa.' *Língua Ferina*, March 31. Accessed January 20, 2017, http://candidoneto.blogspot.com.br/2013/03/operacao-tapajos-governo-federal-entra_31.html.

Fanon, F. 2008 [1952]. *Black Skin, White Masks*. London: Pluto Press.

⸻. 1956. 'Racism and Culture.' *Presence Africaine: Cultural Journal of the Negro World* 8–10: 122–131.

⸻. 2004 [1961]. *The Wretched of the Earth*. New York: Grove Press.

Fearnside, P. M. 2015a. *Hidrelétricas na Amazônia: impactos ambientais e sociais na tomada de decisões sobre grandes obras*. Manaus: Ed. do Inpa.

⸻. 2015b. 'Impactos nas comunidades indígenas e tradicionais.' In *Barragens do rio Tapajós: uma avaliação crítica do Estudo e Relatório de Impacto Ambiental (EIA/Rima) do Aproveitamento Hidrelétrico São Luiz do Tapajós*, edited by Nitta, R., and Naka, L., 19–29. São Paulo: Greenpeace Brazil.

Fundação Nacional do Índio (Funai). 2013. *Relatório Circunstanciado de Identificação e Delimitação da Terra Indígena Sawré Muybu (Pimental)/PA*, Brasília, September (Mimeo).

2014. *Índios Munduruku: tecendo a resistência*, directed by Nayana Fernández [documentary]

Instituto Brasileiro do Meio Ambiente (Ibama). 2014. 'Terras indígenas apresentam o menor índice de desmatamento na Amazônia Legal.' *Funai*, July 23. Accessed July 20, 2015, http://www.funai.gov.br/index.php/comunicacao/noticias/2914-terras-indigenas-apresentam-o-menor-indice-de-desmatamento-na-amazonia-legal.

Instituto Socioambiental. 2016. 'O que o governo Dilma fez (e não fez) para garantir o direito à terra e áreas para conservação?' *Portal Instituto Socioambiental*, June. Accessed July 10, 2016, https://www.socioambiental.org/pt-br/noticias-socioambientais/o-que-o-governo-dilma-fez-e-nao-fez-para-garantir-o-direito-a-terra-e-areas-para-conservacao.

International Labour Organization (Ilo). 1989. 'Convention 169: Indigenous and Tribal Peoples Convention.' *OIT*, June 7. Accessed May 18, 2016, https://www.ilo.org/dyn/normlex/en/f?p=NORMLEX-PUB:12100:0::NO::P12100_INSTRUMENT_ID:312314.

Ka'apor People. 2013. 'Povo Ka'apor, do Maranhão, se solidariza à luta do povo munduruku e outros povos indígenas, contra Belo Monte.' *Blog Ocupação Belo Monte*, May 30. Accessed July 20, 2013, https://ocupacaobelomonte.wordpress.com/2013/05/30/povo-kaapor-do-maranhao-se-solidariza-a-luta-do-povo-munduruku-e-outros-povos-indigenas-contra-belo-monte/.

Mebêngôkre People. 2013. 'Carta de apoio à luta contra as barragens.' *Blog Ocupação Belo Monte*, May 10. Accessed July 20, 2013, https://ocupacaobelomonte.wordpress.com/2013/05/15/mebengokre-kayapo-carta-de-apoio-a-luta-contra-as-barragens/.

Munduruku People. 2013a. 'Carta da assembleia extraordinária do povo Munduruku para a presidenta da República [referente à Operação Eldorado na aldeia Teles Pires].' February 1. Accessed February 10, 2013, https://cimi.org.br/2013/02/34410/.

_____. 2013b. 'Carta do povo Munduruku [referente à Operação Tapajós].' March 27. Accessed March 30, 2013, http://xingu-vivo.blogspot.com.

_____. 2013c. 'Carta do povo munduruku para a Justiça, para o Governo e para a Sociedade Mundial e os Povos Indígenas sobre a Operação Tapajós no território Munduruku.' March 29. Accessed April 4, 2013, https://acervo.racismoambiental.net.br.

_____. 2013d. 'Carta I da ocupação de Belo Monte.' May 2. Accessed November 20, 2014, https://ocupacaobelomonte.wordpress.com.

_____. 2013e. 'Carta IV da ocupação Belo Monte: o governo perdeu o juízo.' May 7. Accessed November 20, 2014, https://ocupacaobelomonte.wordpress.com.

_____. 2013f. 'Carta VII da ocupação Belo Monte: governo federal, nós voltamos.' May 27. Accessed November 20, 2014, https://ocupacaobelomonte.wordpress.com.

_____. 2013g. 'Carta IX da ocupação Belo Monte: tragédias e barragens (a luta não acaba nem lá nem aqui).' June 4. Accessed November 15, 2014, https://ocupacaobelomonte.wordpress.com.

_____. 2013h. 'Carta X da ocupação Belo Monte: o governo não quer nos ouvir.' June, 11. Accessed November 15, 2014, https://ocupacaobelomonte.wordpress.com.

_____. 2013i. 'Declaração Munduruku: pesquisadores, não entrem nas nossas terras.' June 22. Accessed May 25, 2016, https://cimi.org.br.

_____. 2014a. 'Funai admite: interesse hidrelétrico compromete demarcação de Território Indígena' [meeting with Maria Augusta Assirati], *Vimeo*, October 17. Accessed December 10, 2015, https://vimeo.com/111974175.

_____. 2014b. 'Carta I da Autodemarcação do Território Daje Kapap Eypi.' November 17. Accessed November 15, 2014, https://autodemarcacaonotapajos.wordpress.com.

_____. 2014c. 'Carta II da Autodemarcação.' November 24. Accessed November 15, 2014, https://autodemarcacaonotapajos.wordpress.com.

_____. 2014d. 'Carta III da Autodemarcação.' November 28. Accessed November 15, 2014, https://autodemarcacaonotapajos.wordpress.com.

_____. 2015. 'Protocolo de Consulta Munduruku.' July 15. Accessed May 20, 2018, https://reporterbrasil.org.br/wp-content/uploads/2016/07/Protocolo-de-consulta-Munduruku.pdf.

_____. 2016. *Autodemarcação Daje Kapap Eipi*, Cartilha (Mimeo).

Santana, R. 2013a. 'Governo federal quebra acordo com povo munduruku e operação militar se movimenta em Jacareacanga.' *Portal Cimi*, August 12. Accessed July 2, 2018, www.cimi.org.br.

_____. 2013b. 'Aldeia Munduruku é invadida por Força Nacional no sul do Pará.' *Brasil de Fato*, September 6. Accessed May 6, 2017, https://www.brasildefato.com.br/node/25813/.

_____. 2013c. 'Aldeia Munduruku é invadida por Força Nacional e cacique geral convoca assembleia.' *Portal Cimi*, September 6. Accessed May 10, 2015, https://www.cimi.org.br/2013/09/35260/.

Secretaria-Geral da Presidência da República. 2013. 'Esclarecimentos sobre a consulta aos Munduruku e a invasão de Belo Monte.' *Portal Secretaria Geral da Presidência da República*, May 6. Accessed May 3, 2017, www.secretariageral.gov.br/noticias/ultimas_noticias/2013/05/06-05-2013-esclarecimentos-sobre-a-consulta-aos-munduruku-e-a-invasao-de-belo-monte1/4.

Sena, E. 2013. 'Tapajós: vendo o dilúvio chegar.' *Instituto Humanitas Unisinos/Adital*, February 15. Accessed June 10, 2017, http://www.ihu.unisinos.br/noticias/517594-mais-uma-materia-de-um-noe-vendo-o-diluvio-chegar-e-o-povo-dancando-carnaval-artigo-de-edilberto-sena.

Sposati, R. 2013. 'Munduruku expulsam pesquisadores de terra indígena.' *Portal Cimi*, June 22. Accessed January 20, 2017, http://www.cimi.org.br/site/pt-br/?system=news&conteudo_id=6990&action=read.

Tosold, L. 2018. 'Autodeterminação em três movimentos: a politização de diferenças sob a perspectiva da (des)naturalização da violência.' PhD thesis, University of São Paulo, São Paulo.

————. 2020. 'Por uma vida sem barragens: corpos, território e o papel da autodeterminação na desnaturalização da violência.' *Revista de Antropologia* 63 (3): 1–33.

Tuck, E., and Yang, K. W. 2012. 'Decolonization Is Not a Metaphor.' *Decolonization: Indigeneity, Education & Society* 1 (1): 1–40.

# ABOUT THE CONTRIBUTORS

**Abahlali baseMjondolo** is a shack dwellers' movement in South Africa which campaigns both against evictions and for public housing. The movement grew out of a road blockade organised from the Kennedy Road shack settlement in the city of Durban, and has grown into a national organization comprising a membership of 100,000.

**Elizabeth Berger** is a child psychiatrist living in New York and a founding/ steering committee member of the USA-Palestine Mental Health Network (https://usapalmhn.com/). She has been involved in teaching and program planning with colleagues in Palestine for many years. She writes for academic and general audiences on mental health and well-being in Palestine from the perspective of public health and liberation psychology, often with co-author and fellow psychiatrist Samah Jabr MD. Dr. Berger is on the clinical faculty of George Washington University School of Medicine and Health Sciences.

**Rosemere Ferreira da Silva** is Titular Professor at the State University of Bahia (Universidade do Estado da Bahia / UNEB), where she has taught since 2012. She is a specialist in Brazilian Literature, Afro-Brazilian Literature, Comparative Literature and Ethnic and African Studies. Her research focuses on Afro-Brazilian and Caribbean Literature. She is the coordinator of Literatura and Afrodescendência research group at UNEB. She is currently writing a book about black intellectuals. Dr. Da Silva is also a Research Scholar in the Philosophy Department at UCONN-Storrs and part of the editorial team of *Black Issues in Philosophy*.

**Alejandro de Oto** is a researcher at the National Scientific and Technical Council (CONICET-Argentina), and a professor of philosophical research methodology and epistemology at the National University of San Juan, Argentina. He holds a doctorate from the Center of Asian and African Studies at the Colegio de Mexico, has been a Research Fellow at Brown University and has participated in the University of Cape Town African Series Seminar. He is a member of different academic associations and he has authored several books including *Frantz Fanon: Política y poética del sujeto poscolonial* (México) (*Frantz Fanon: The Politics and Poetics of the Postcolonial Subject*) (Rowman & Littlefield), which was awarded the "Frantz Fanon Prize for Outstanding Book in Caribbean Thought" from the Caribbean Philosophical Association in 2005.

**Miraj U. Desai** is a writer, psychologist, activist, dancer, artist, and author of *Travel and Movement in Clinical Psychology: The World Outside the Clinic*. He is on the faculty of the Yale Program for Recovery and Community Health, an organization committed to advancing social and health justice. A series of experiences—most notably of the vicious post-9/11 racism that continues to thrive globally—significantly influenced his intellectual and sociopolitical engagements against oppression. His overall work is deeply informed by an anti-racist/decolonial ethos, including via community-engaged, psychopolitical, and participatory action projects against structural racism, in collaboration with communities of color.

**Deivison Faustino** is an anti-racist researcher and disseminator of Frantz Fanon's thought in Brazil. He started his political activities through the hip-hop movement and is currently Professor of the Graduate Program in Social Work at UNIFESP (Brazil). He has experience with the themes of African history, anti-racist thinking and Fanon studies. He is the author of the books *Frantz Fanon: um revolucionário, particularmente negro* ("Frantz Fanon: A Particularly Black Revolutionary") and *A disputa em torno de Frantz Fanon: a teoria e a política dos fanonismos contemporaneous* ("The Dispute Over Frantz Fanon: The Theory of Contemporary Fanonisms") as well as dozens of articles on Frantz Fanon's thinking and his contemporary reception.

**Levi Gahman** works at the University of Liverpool and is an affiliate with the University of the West Indies. His focus includes anti-colonial praxis, environmental defence, community wellbeing, and engaged research with political activists, rural land workers, and Indigenous movements. Prior to Liverpool, Levi lived in the circum-Caribbean for half a decade where he taught *The Wretched of the Earth*. Before that, he was an organizer with *Food Not Bombs* and *Radical Action with Migrants in Agriculture* in Canada and a solidarity brigade member in Mexico. Levi is also author of *Land, God, and Guns: Settler Colonialism and Masculinity* (Zed).

**Razan Ghazzawi** (she/they) is an exiled Palestinian-Syrian scholar-activist and an award winning human rights defender and blogger since 2005. They are currently finishing their doctoral thesis, an ethnographic exploration of sexuality politics in Syria in the context of the 'war on terror' and the 'refugee crisis' in Syria and Lebanon by looking at everyday violence facing Syrian and Palestinian LGBTQ persons on checkpoints and during pre-trial detentions. Razan was detained twice by the Syrian state and was exiled by Al Qayda and ISIS groups in Northern Syria. They are the founder of the Feminist ArQives since 2014 and a co-founder of Karama Bus project in Idlib, Northern Syria, since 2013. They currently reside between Brighton and Chicago and tweets under @razaniyyat.

**Nigel C. Gibson** is an activist and scholar specializing in the work of the Algerian revolutionary Frantz Fanon. Gibson is author of *Fanon: The Postcolonial Imagination* (Polity Press, 2003), which won the 2009 Caribbean Philosophy Frantz Fanon Outstanding Book Award and was translated into Arabic in 2013, and *Fanonian Practices in South Africa: From Steve Biko to Abahlali baseMjondolo* (University of Kwa Zulu-Natal Press and Palgrave MacMillan, 2011) and the co-author with Roberto Beneduce of *Fanon: Psychiatry and Politics* (Rowman and Littlefield and University of Witwatersrand Press, 2017). Along with this edited collection on Fanon, he has edited *Rethinking Fanon: The Continuing Dialogue* (1999) and *Living Fanon* (2011). He teaches at Emerson College, Boston USA and is Honorary Professor in the Humanities Unit at the university currently known as Rhodes University, South Africa.

**Hamza Hamouchene** is a London-based Algerian researcher-activist, commentator and a founding member of Algeria Solidarity Campaign (ASC), Environmental Justice North Africa (EJNA) and the North African Food Sovereignty Network (NAFSN). He is currently the North Africa Programme Coordinator at the Transnational Institute (TNI). His work is focused on issues of extractivism, resources, land and food sovereignty as well as climate, environmental, and trade justice in North Africa. He is the author/editor of two books: *The Struggle for Energy Democracy in the Maghreb* (2017) and *The Coming Revolution to North Africa: The Struggle for Climate Justice* (2015). As well as contributing chapters to various books his other writings have appeared in *Africa Is A Country*, the *Guardian*, *Middle East Eye*, *Counterpunch*, *New Internationalist*, *Jadaliyya*, *openDemocracy*, *ROAR* magazine, *Pambazuka News*, *Nawaat*, *El Watan* and the *Huffington Post*.

**Samah Jabr** is a psychiatrist and psychotherapist living in East Jerusalem, serving as the Head of the Mental Health Unit within the Palestinian Ministry of Health. She is well-known internationally as an advocate and activist for Palestinian human rights and a prolific author and speaker in both scholarly and popular media. She is featured in the documentary film *Beyond the Front Lines* (https://beyondthefrontlines.com/). Dr. Jabr is a founding/ steering committee member of the Palestine-Global Mental Health Network (https://www.pgmhn.org/) and a member of the clinical faculty of George Washington University School of Medicine and Health Sciences.

**Kurtis Kelley** is an artist, organizer, and graduate student at the University of Illinois. As a scholar, Kurtis is researching the history of anti-colonial Black social movements within the United States to better understand the actions of Black students and the transformations for Black people brought about by ideological, cultural, and technological societal shifts.

**Wangui Kimari** is the participatory action research coordinator for the Mathare Social Justice Centre (MSJC) in Nairobi, Kenya. MSJC is a community space in the informalized settlement of Mathare, which seeks to promote social justice through engaged community and social movement platforms.

**Leah Kindler** is a Bachelor of Fine Arts in Media Arts Production Creative Writing student at Emerson College minoring in postcolonial studies. Her senior Honors Thesis concerns Black feminist writers and the radical imagination.

**Toussaint Losier** is an Assistant Professor in the W.E.B. Du Bois Department of Afro-American Studies at the University of Massachusetts-Amherst. He holds a PhD. in History from the University of Chicago and is co-author of *Rethinking the American Prison Movement* (Routledge, 2017). He is a former organizer with the Chicago Anti-Eviction Campaign and Southside Together Organizing for Power (STOP). Currently, he is an active member of the Black Alliance for Peace (BAP), a people-centered human rights project against war, repression, and imperialism.

**Feargal Mac Ionnrachtaigh** is a first generation Irish speaker and a product of the Irish Medium Education system in Belfast. He studied at Queens University Belfast and his doctoral thesis (2009) was published as a book, *Language, Resistance and Revival: Republican Prisoners and the Irish Language in the North* *of Ireland* (Pluto). He is also the author of *Féile Voices at 30'-Memoirs of West Belfast Community Festival Féile an Phobail* (Orpen Press). He works full-time in the Irish language revival movement as Director of Irish Language youth and community organisation, Glór na Móna (www.glornamona.com) and is a prominent member of the An Dream Dearg Irish language rights grassroots campaigning network.

**Ayyaz Mallick** is a political worker of the Awami Workers' Party from Karachi, Pakistan, a left-wing party focussed on organising workers, peasants, students, and women. He recently completed his PhD from York University, Toronto, and is currently a Lecturer in Human Geography at the University of Liverpool. His research interests are in Marxist and postcolonial theory with a focus on labour, urban politics, and social movements.

**David Pavón-Cuéllar** describes himself as a communist and participates in radical Left collectives in Mexico. He has been committed for many years to the Zapatista movement. His academic work develops at the intersection of Lacanian psychoanalysis, Marxist theory, and critical psychology. He is a professor in the faculties of psychology and philosophy at the Universidad Michoacana de San Nicolás de Hidalgo, in the city of Morelia, state of Michoacán, Mexico. His recent books include *Zapatism and Subjectivity: Beyond Psychology* (*Zapatismo y subjetividad: más allá de la psicología*, Bogotá, Cátedra Libre, 2020), and *Marxism and Psychoanalysis: In or Against Psychology?* (London, Routledge, 2017).

**Gene Reid:** As a Black worker I came into this world in 1955 the year of the Montgomery bus boycott in Alabama, which is my birth state. Living under the trauma of southern "state rights" of segregation up until Alabama was forced to integrate in 1968. I was sitting side by side with White students. A new experience but not my first experience as being an "object of curiosity" around racial identity as a Black child under White rule. That experience set in motion a desire to answer the question "Who am I?" At 18 years old I left home for Los Angeles searching for "wealth and fortune" to go west young man ... a fallacy. But I found Fanon in my search, which opened my eyes to Black Identity as a self-movement for social change. I was able to become actively involved in the Black Marxist Movement within L.A. The high point of my activity would have to be the 1992 L.A. rebellion which gave us, Black masses, some breathing space in which I witnessed the short lived gang truce in Watts. I also was active in the South Africa anti-apartheid movement and in the ongoing protests against police shootings in the L.A. area. For about 25 years I was a member of a Marxist Humanist group, News and Letters, and wrote articles for the newspaper around my activities on the Black and labor struggles (including police violence) within our community.

**Johannah-Rae Reyes** is an intersectional feminist activist with a degree in Geography from the University of the West Indies. She currently works with Trinidad based organization WOMANTRA. Her praxis centers on race, class, gender and disability. She intentionally writes on political issues faced by marginalized communities across the Caribbean.

**Annette Rimmer** is a radio producer and Doctor of Education. Her activism, research and publications involve working together with excluded groups, particularly women, to broadcast their unheard voices and intersectional identities. In her past work in youth and community development, social work and lecturing, together with 'service-users,' she established participatory research and teaching projects with those in receipt of services. Her voluntary radio work involves broadcasting the life stories, philosophies and music of diverse and exciting 'ordinary' people. Her current radio project is with Chinese people voicing their feelings about life in Britain.

**Ato Sekyi-Otu** is Professor Emeritus in the Department of Social Science and the Graduate Program in Social and Political Thought at York University, Toronto, Canada. He is the author of *Fanon's Dialectic of Experience* and *Left Universalism: Africacentric Essays*, which was awarded the Frantz Fanon Outstanding Book Prize by the Caribbean Philosophical Association in 2019.

**Léa Tosold** is a researcher and activist. She is a member of the Anti-Racist and Anti-Colonial Studies Intervention Collective (Gira), and a member of the São Paulo's Solidarity Committee to the Resistance Struggles in the Tapajós Region (Comtapajós), among others. She holds a PhD in the University of São Paulo (USP) and was a postdoctoral junior fellow at the Maria Sybilla Merian Center Conviviality-Inequality in Latin America (Mecila). Departing from feminist anti-racist epistemologies, her work focuses on collective forms of existence as resistance in contexts in which violence is naturalized and ongoing.

**Lou Turner** is Clinical Assistant Professor, Department of Urban and Regional Planning, University of Illinois Urbana-Champaign (UIUC), and former Academic Advisor for the Department of African American Studies, 2008-2017. Lou Turner was Research and Public Policy Director for Chicago South Side community organization Developing Communities Project (2000-2014). He is a board member of the African American Leadership & Policy Institute. Turner is the Principal Investigator for Hal Baron Digital Archival, Research, and Publication Project at UIUC. A colleague of the late Hegelian-Marxist philosopher Raya Dunayevskaya, he has written extensively on Fanonian, Marxian and Hegelian dialectics. With Dr. Helen Neville, Turner co-edited *Frantz Fanon's Psychotherapeutic Approaches to Clinical Work: Practicing Internationally with Marginalized Communities* (2020). Lou Turner is coauthor of *Frantz Fanon, Soweto and American Black Thought* (1978; 1986), which circulated in the anti-apartheid underground of the Black Consciousness Movement in South Africa.

**S'bu Zikode** is the founding President of Abahlali baseMjondolo Movement SA. Under his leadership, the movement's audited membership has grown significantly and reached 100,000. S'bu has strongly campaigned for the Right to Housing in the United States National Tour under the theme 'Housing is a Human Right'. His calling includes safe and dignified housing for all in our cities. Under his leadership the movement has won a historic constitutional court case victory on what was an attack on the poor and popular democracy. This piece of Legislation became known as the "Slums Act", which the South

African government thought it was the answer to the Millennium Development Goal (MDG). Again this victory was seen by many South Africans as the victory for all the impoverished and marginalized in South Africa. Abahlali baseMjondolo continues to celebrate their hard-won effort to humanize the world. S'bu believes that real progress on urban issues can be made when there is an agreement that the social value of land must come before its commercial value. He believes that practical steps that can be taken include ensuring that all new housing developments are in well located areas. He believes that all shack settlements should be provided with services and support while they wait for housing.

**Flavio Zenun Almada,** known as *LBC Soldjah*, is a Hip Hop-MC, an antiracist militant artist and researcher, member of Plataforma Gueto (PG) an antiracist, anti-imperialist, anticolonial, anticapitalist and anti-Zionist Black social movement, based in Lisbon, Portugal. He has experience in organizing popular education, national and international antiracist campaigns, African history, Amilcar Cabral studies, Black Panther Party studies and Fanon studies. His two rap works are, *Third World Children– Blood of Tears* (2009) and *Third World – Our Victory is Certain* (2012). He has a degree in Translation and Creative Writing and Masters in International Studies.

www.ingramcontent.com/pod-product-compliance
Lightning Source LLC
Chambersburg PA
CBHW050328270326
41926CB00016B/3358